POLICY FORMULATION
AND ADMINISTRATION

POLICY FORMULATION AND ADMINISTRATION

A casebook of
senior management problems
in business

C. Roland Christensen, A.B., D.C.S.
Robert Walmsley University Professor

Norman A. Berg, S.B., D.B.A.
Professor of Business Administration

Malcolm S. Salter, A.B., D.B.A.
Professor of Business Administration

Howard H. Stevenson, B.S., D.B.A.
Sarofim-Rock Professor of Business Administration

All of the
Harvard University
Graduate School of Business Administration

 Ninth edition   1985

RICHARD D. IRWIN, INC.   Homewood, Illinois 60430

ISBN 0-256-03012-X

Library of Congress Catalog Card No. 84–81121

Printed in the United States of America

1 2 3 4 5 6 7 8 9 0 K 2 1 0 9 8 7 6 5

To
GEORGE ALBERT SMITH, JR. (1905–1969)
Friend
Colleague
Teacher to all

Acknowledgments

As has been our tradition, we wish to acknowledge our thanks to the many individuals who have helped make possible this ninth edition of *Policy Formulation and Administration*. We are indebted to our colleagues here at the Harvard Business School, to our colleagues in other management schools, and to the directors of management development activities in private and public organizations in this country and throughout the world. They have been generous in sharing their wisdom and experience with us.

We are especially appreciative of the constructive comments and suggestions made by the users of this casebook. Many of the changes made in the ninth edition follow from their recommendations; for example, they urged the inclusion of the sections dealing with the management of entrepreneurship and corporate governance. We will continue our dialogue with these colleagues in the months ahead.

Case research and writing is a demanding discipline—a blend of rigorous research method and artistry of presentation. We are especially indebted to the men and women who researched and developed these case studies. Some of these cases are the products of individual efforts; others grew out of collective efforts. Some of them we have written or supervised ourselves; others have been written by our associates here and at other schools of business. We congratulate them for work well done and extend to them our gratitude for their cooperation in making this book possible.

Specifically, we thank the following colleagues for their contribution of the indicated cases: Christopher Bartlett—Questionable Payments Abroad: Gulf in Italy, and for his collaboration with the late Richard Harrigan and Michael Yoshino for Ideal Standard France: Pat Paterson; William Boulton—The Leisure Group, Inc.; Robert Bruner—The Real Paper, Inc. (A); Richard Ellsworth—Baker International Corporation; Linda Elmer—The Dr Pepper Company; Norman Fast—The Lincoln Electric

Company and Environmental Pressures (A); Christopher Gale—IMEDE and the University of Virginia—Nestlé and the Infant Food Controversy (A) (revised); Philippe Haspeslagh—Imperial Corporation (A); Richard King—Hewlett-Packard: Challenging the Entrepreneurial Culture; E. P. Learned—The Rose Company; Leslie Levy—Note on the Soft Drink Industry in the United States; John Matthews—Peter Olson; Hassell McClellan—Sturm, Ruger & Company, Inc.; Glenn Merry—Polaroid-Kodak; Robert Pitts—CML Group, Inc.; Cheryl Suchors—The Seven-Up Company (A); Elizabeth Lyman Rachal—BIC Pen Corporation (A) and BIC Pen Corporation (B); Thomas Raymond in collaboration with Thomas Ashley Graves III—Voltamp Electrical Corporation; Dean John Rosenblum of the University of Virginia and Charles Weigle—Prelude Corporation; Leonard Schlesinger in collaboration with Dr. Debra Whitestone—People Express; James Snider and Michael Roberts—Electrodec; Charles Summer—IMEDE and the University of Washington—BCI Ltd.; Richard von Werssowetz—Michael Bregman; George Yip—Data Resources, Inc.; and Michael Yoshino—Showa-Packard, Ltd. (A).

The text sections of this edition have been written with the objective of helping the student of policy formulation and administration to deal effectively with this book's complicated, real-life case studies. We believe both students and instructors will find Professor Berg's text helpful in their study and discussion of these policy problems. What he has achieved is to combine the senior manager's analytic task of formulating strategies for accomplishment with the critical policy process tasks of implementing that strategy and providing the vital leadership ingredient.

While each student will have her or his individual preferences, we would urge that the section text material be read in its entirety at the beginning and end of each of the major subdivisions of this book. This will provide a useful preview, a guide to analyze and discuss each case, and a way to review and summarize the section upon completion.

In this ninth edition we welcome as a fellow author Howard H. Stevenson, the Sarofim-Rock Professor of Business Administration at the Harvard Business School. His wealth of academic and business experience will help us in the continuing development of this casebook. Professor Stevenson has written the text, and designed the case outline, for a new section of this casebook, Policy Formulation and Administration in the Entrepreneurial Firm.

We also wish to thank the officers and faculty of IMEDE (l'Institut pour l'Etude des Méthodes de Direction de l'Entreprise), of Lausanne, Switzerland. IMEDE is a vital leader in the field of education for international management. We appreciate Dean Derek Abell's willingness to let us include the BCI Ltd. and the Nestlé and the Infant Food Controversy cases in this edition.

We are grateful to the administrative officers of the Harvard Graduate School of Business Administration for their continuing encouragement of this effort. Dean John McArthur and Professor Raymond Corey, Director of the Division of Research, have been most supportive. We also appreciate the contribution of Assistant Dean Joanne Segal and Ms. Audrey Barrett of the Division of Research, and the counsel of Associate Dean for Administration and Policy Planning, Dean Currie. Dyanne Holdman, Meredith Carder, and Eve Bamford have been most helpful in administrative and editorial contributions.

We wish again to acknowledge the great debt which those of us in business policy at Harvard and at our sister institutions throughout the world owe to the late George Albert Smith, Jr., who passed away October 12, 1969. Professor Smith was "The Pioneer" in the development of business policy as an area of academic study. He was a friend and colleague of each member of this authorship group. His influence continues in the work of his students in the field of business, through the active and continuing contributions of the teachers he developed over many decades, and via the concepts and ideas expressed and used in this edition. We hope to honor his memory by the continuing development of those ideas and by this book.

C. Roland Christensen
Norman A. Berg
Malcolm S. Salter
Howard H. Stevenson

Contents

Introduction

The purposes of this ninth edition of *Policy Formulation and Administration* are essentially the same as those of the previous editions. The book provides both text and a selection of cases that can assist men and women preparing for a career in business administration to become acquainted with the opportunities and challenges confronting the senior manager of a firm. This material also provides significant opportunities for learning for middle managers and senior managers enrolled in university or corporate management development programs.

The educational objectives of this edition are the same as for earlier editions. Its orientation is managerial. It seeks to encourage the development of leadership skills. Men and women who can "take charge" of organizations are a scarce resource. The hope of the authors is that the study of the situations presented here may encourage interest in general management skills and may provide an opportunity for the academic practice of skills needed for this organizational position via discussion of selected case problems.

Specifically, the study and discussion of these cases and the accompanying text offer opportunities:

1. To learn about the functions, roles, and skills of senior management: the perspective of the general manager.
2. To develop skill in envisaging goals; to delineate the functions and activities that must be performed to achieve the goals; and to determine what functional strategies are needed for goal achievement.
3. To become familiar with "risk" and its place in general management thinking.
4. To learn to identify, and to attract to a business, personnel with

the requisite technical and emotional abilities to build it into a think-ing, living, organization.

5. To develop the ability to divide the work of a firm into logical and understandable assignments, with limitations of authority and, at the same time, provisions for individual decision-making powers and op-portunities for cooperation.

6. To learn to set standards for measuring performance.

7. To understand how to provide motivation for the members of the management group so that they will apply their skills to meeting the needs of the organization while still satisfying their own needs.

8. To gain insight, self-confidence, and imagination in order to furnish leadership to the organization. Coupled with leadership is the willing-ness to take ultimate responsibility not only for the results of one's own decisions but also for the results of the decisions and actions of all to whom the leader has delegated authority.

9. To anticipate and accept the responsibilities of the leader and those of the organization to the various sectors of society affected by the organization's actions: the investor, the worker, the supplier, the com-munity, and the country.

This casebook provides the opportunity for both instructor and stu-dent to participate in the process of policy formulation and administration. This process, as will become apparent from class discussion, depends upon a melding of intellectual and administrative skills. For example, identifying problems that affect the long-term position of the firm calls for the ability to select and relate disparate bits of information so that an inclusive statement of key problems can be made. Making such a statement requires, however, more than the intellectual skill of analyzing environmental trends and data on internal corporate operations. It also requires the ability to articulate problems in a way that suggests actionable alternatives that can be submitted to careful evaluation. This ability re-flects what we can call an administrative sense. Similarly, setting objectives and formulating a plan of action require both a sense of what is needed and what will work.

The cases presented in this book are not meant to stand alone. They are not traditional research documents which describe important aspects of policy formulation and administration. Nor are they studies which suggest how policy should be formulated and administered by top corpo-rate executives. Instead, the cases have been designed to provide the raw material for students to work out for themselves, under the guidance of a trained instructor, what policies are appropriate for particular firms. We believe that a course based upon these cases will help the student develop an analytical approach to broad business policy problems.

Each case in this book describes an actual situation. To preserve confidentiality, fictitious names have been used in some instances, and sometimes the geographical locations have been changed. Only on rare occasions has the industry been changed or the size of the company materially altered. Almost always the case contains information about the industry and its competitive conditions; some historical background about the company and its principal products; financial data; information about production and marketing methods and facilities; the organization plan; and background on the executive personnel. These cases are the raw materials that facilitate replication in the classroom of the actual discussions carried on informally among managers and in board and committee rooms.

In the tradition of earlier editions, this volume contains a selection of "seasoned" cases used in previous editions as well as a selection of new cases not heretofore published. We have included cases from a wide variety of corporate organizations, ranging in size from the small, new enterprise to the large and very complex conglomerate organization. In addition to cases covering problems of the overall enterprise, we have included, in this edition, one new section focusing on entrepreneurship and another on issues of corporate responsibility.

It has been our experience and the experience of many other instructors that, by using cases such as these, teacher and students together can create "ways of thinking," "ways of feeling," and "ways of doing" that accelerate tremendously both intellectual growth and emotional development.

THE QUESTIONS OR PROBLEMS IN THE CASES AND THEIR SOLUTIONS

At the top level, an executive does not have any "all-wise" adviser to identify what problem or problems he or she should be watching or working on at a particular time—that must be decided personally. And there is no reference book to look into, no infallible aid to give *the* solution. The executive must, nevertheless, find *some* solution, some *workable* solution. This is arrived at through experience and the exercise of judgment, usually after discussion and consultation with others. And neither before a decision is made, nor after, can the executive be absolutely sure what action is *right* or *best*.

The administrator must be willing and able to work in a climate of uncertainty, which is often uncomfortable. He or she must accept the responsibility for reaching decisions under time pressure, on the basis of limited facts, and in the face of many unknowns. Imperfect himself, the administrator must work with people who also are imperfect. Almost always, some associates or other parties involved will disagree, and their disagreement and their views should be taken into account. The administrator is in the usually lonesome situation of being the possessor of ultimate responsibility. He or she inevitably will make some mistakes. If experienced and mature, the administrator will expect this and will allow for it, but will hope to reach wise decisions most of the time. The administrator who succeeds in doing that is a successful business leader.

This clearly suggests that the cases do not include any "official" or "demonstrably correct" answers. We do not have either "official" questions or "approved" solutions. It is part of the student's task, as it is part of an executive's task, to discover questions and to distinguish the important from the unimportant. In some instances, we ourselves do not agree as to exactly what the most fundamental problems or opportunities are; and in still more instances we do not agree on the best possible course of action. If we did, we would question the reality of our cases and perhaps also the quality and integrity of our own views. The cases presented here are complicated business situations taken out of business life. Since we are all different people, with our own special backgrounds and experiences and skills, we will attach to these problems somewhat different interpretations and envision somewhat differing or substantially differing solutions or courses of action.

We do have our own ideas about each of the cases we are offering; so do our colleagues who use them. In some instances we hold our views with strong conviction. In others, we are much less sure of what we think. And we change our views from time to time. So we certainly do not feel that we *know* what should be done in each of the situations presented. The value of the cases in the classroom lies in their discussion, not in the giving or finding of an "authoritative" answer.

ORGANIZATION OF THE BOOK

This edition contains the basic organizational features of the earlier editions, with some modifications. We have divided this ninth edition into five major parts:

   I. Policy Formulation
  II. Policy Administration
 III. Policy Formulation and Administration in Diversified Firms
 IV. Policy Formulation and Administration in the Entrepreneurial Firm
  V. The General Manager and Corporate Responsibility

This plan, with its selected distribution of cases, can give you a sense of the atmosphere in which top-level executives work and can make real to you the individuals in top management, with their range of human frailties and strengths. It also will make clear to you that managers must work through and depend on other people; that they must engage in much routine work; that virtually all they can be sure of is change and the unexpected. You will learn also that policy formulation is not always a formal process; that much policy making is done (and should be done) at fairly low levels in organizations; and that effective authority or leadership is not conferred from above but is earned and rewarded from below.

As you progress in your study of the cases, many other important things will become clear. For example, you will certainly abandon the belief that the executive discovers and solves one problem at a time. On the contrary, he or she deals with many problems concurrently, each at a different stage of development. Furthermore, the focus of attention from size-up of the situation through planning, organizing, putting plans into action, measuring of performance, and reappraisal seldom follows a neat sequential pattern. The route is much more varied, perhaps more like skipping around to different parts of a circle. Even in dealing with one problem, the administrator goes around the circle many times and, as we have said, is simultaneously busy with many circles.

PREPARING A CASE FOR CLASS

The question of how students should prepare a case for class has been put to us many times by our own students, and also by people studying and teaching these cases elsewhere. Actually, the question is often phrased: "What is the *best* way to prepare a case?" That one we cannot answer, for we do not think there is any *best* way. There are, no doubt, many good and useful ways. Each of us must develop the methods that serve us best. Moreover, we all must change our approach somewhat to deal with each new situation. And each case is a new situation. So there is no formula, no basic pattern that we can pass on. We can, at most, make a few overall observations and then try to detail some specific suggestions.

We suggest that you first read through a case to get a general impression of what it is about, how it seems to come out, and what kinds of information it contains. We think there is a real advantage in doing this first reading a day or two before you must do your thorough and final preparation. There is value in having the general situation in mind in time to mull it over, both consciously and subconsciously, for a while. This is true of any important problem one has to deal with—in school, in business, anywhere.

For the second reading, we suggest you take the time to proceed slowly and carefully, studying the tables and exhibits and making notes as you go. Perhaps some headings will occur to you under which you want to summarize especially pertinent factors. Perhaps, however, when you feel you are about at the end of your preparation, it would be well to ask yourself: "Have I worked this thing through to the point where, if I really had a chance to talk to the persons responsible for this company, I could: (1) talk intelligently with them about their company and their job in managing it? (2) show them why the main issues I have selected as a result of my analysis are really of first importance? and (3) give them a coordinated program of action that would be practical and would have a reasonable chance to succeed?"

We urge you to discuss the cases with one another, if possible, while preparing them. Managers in business discuss their problems with other key people. But be sure you do your own independent work and independent thinking. Do not be too stubborn to recognize that an idea may be better than your own, but be sure you really understand and believe in it before you adopt it.

Not infrequently students express the wish for more information than is in a case; they feel they cannot make a decision without more facts. Do not hide behind that excuse. For one thing, business leaders never have all the facts they would like to have. As far as the cases are concerned, each case will contain enough information to enable you to learn from attempting to deal with the issues raised in it. If you do feel that information essential to your analysis is lacking, it may be useful to make the necessary assumptions and to state them explicitly. Before doing this, however, be sure to use all the information you do have.

Beware the temptation to seek the latest bit of information about the companies you are studying. What happened after the date of the case may often be interesting, but learning comes from dealing with the issues as of the time of the case. Just as we can learn much about warfare from studying the Battle of Waterloo in 1815 or the Battle of Midway in 1942, we can learn from studying a case which presents the situation of a company at one point in time without becoming overly concerned about subsequent events.

Finally, do not contact the companies directly to attempt to obtain their views on the issues of the case or information subsequent to the date of the case. This is unnecessary to the learning process for which cases are designed and, more important, it will be a burden to companies that have cooperated in the development of the cases.

THE DIMENSIONS OF GENERAL MANAGEMENT

The focus of this volume is on the functions, roles, and skills of the general manager. One of our authors, M. S. Salter, concludes that there are five basic dimensions to the job of the general manager:

1. Supervising current operations.
2. Planning for future operations.

3. Designing and administering decision-making structures.
4. Developing human resources and capabilities.
5. Representing and holding an organization responsible to its various constituencies.

The most immediate concern of the general manager, he argues, is supervising current operations. This normally involves setting goals and targets for various functional departments and product divisions and periodically reviewing performance against preestablished goals. Sometimes operating goals and policies need to be modified by the general manager (and his/her* associates) as changes in the environment suggest courses of action different from those currently being followed by various parts of the organization. Both the review of current performance and the reassessment of current operating goals and policies require a flow of relevant, reliable, and timely information. Overseeing this activity is an important aspect of the general manager's operating concerns.

Perhaps the most critical aspect of supervising current operations is the occasional need to intervene in disputes over operating problems where those closest to the situation cannot reach agreement on appropriate courses of action. Here the task of the general manager is to identify or extract the relevant policy issues and suggest action that reflects his view of appropriate policy. This intervention must be done selectively and in ways which do not permanently upset established methods for resolving problems at lower levels of management. If every crisis were to be brought to the general manager's desk for resolution, most of his time would be taken up with managing a myriad of small crises which would detract from careful attention to other important general management tasks, such as planning for future operations.

Planning for future operations is paid lip service more often than practiced. In part, this is because many general managers perceive the payoff of comprehensive forward planning as being quite low. For those who are guiding companies that have dominant positions in relatively stable, low growth markets, there is a tendency to accept projections of past experience as solid bases for estimating future resource needs. General managers of relatively weak companies occupying subordinate roles in either growing or stable markets also tend to invest lightly in future-oriented planning; they frequently tend to "wait for the breaks" and scramble as fast as possible when opportunities present themselves. The greatest incentive to invest heavily in comprehensive forward planning is for general managers of companies with dominant positions in dynamic growth markets. Here the costs of losing that position of dominance can be very high. However, it is companies without dominant market positions which can often profit the most from comprehensive forward planning

---

* In this text, for simplicity of presentation, masculine pronouns will sometimes be used instead of the more accurate dual form.

since it is the principal means of organizing the development of competitive strength over time. A large majority of companies fall into this category.

Planning for future operations involves making informed judgments about what opportunities and risks will face the company in the future and identifying alternate means of either exploiting these opportunities or accommodating these risks.

In addition to supervising current operations and planning future strategies, every general manager inevitably becomes preoccupied with forging an organizational structure that fits the company's needs and unique characteristics. In its most basic sense, this structure is primarily a decision-making apparatus. Differences among organization structures result from different ways of allocating decision-making authority and responsibility to administrative subunits and to individuals within these subunits. An organization structure thus defines the locus of decision-making responsibilities and identifies who will make what decisions under normal conditions. At operating levels of management, departmental or product-oriented structures typically provide the basic models for each company's organizational format. At the top policy levels of management, collectives of executives from key operating posts are often asked to review recommendations and approve decisions made at the departmental or product division levels.

General managers must determine which decision-making structure best suits their current and future needs. They must also reinforce its effectiveness by communicating clearly and directly what is expected from each decision maker. Performance measurement and reward systems typically have an important role to play in this effort. Designing and administering these systems is thus another important aspect of the general manager's job.

An additional responsibility of general management is the development of human capabilities and resources appropriate to the organization's present and future needs. The general manager must analyze both current operations and future plans in order to judge how many persons with what kinds of experience and skills are required. Once these needs are identified, the general manager must ensure that realistic plans are implemented to provide adequate human resources at all organizational levels when they are needed.

As straightforward as this sounds, there is perhaps no aspect of general management that is left so much to chance as manpower planning. Recruitment, staffing, job rotation, and training are often handled on an ad hoc basis rather than studied in advance. A common result of this practice is an unsystematic scramble for people, on the one hand, and career blockages, on the other, as companies experience shifting manpower needs. For general managers who proclaim that their organizations' past successes are due to the high quality of personnel, there can be no greater irony than finding that their organizations are equipped with inadequate personnel resources for the future or staffed with persons who face few opportunities for increased growth and development.

Apart from the administrative aspects of manpower planning, the development of an organization's human capabilities rests in large measure on the commitment of individuals to stretch themselves beyond their known limits. The reinforcement of this commitment and the building of high morale within the organization are two of the most elusive tasks of general management. While each successful general manager develops his own approach, a common characteristic shared by many organization leaders is the ability to institutionalize those values and articulate those objectives critical to the organization's success. Few groups of individuals, either inside or outside the business world, have been able to maintain their effectiveness without the leadership of those who can both represent and guide the development of the group's goals and values. This requirement is virtually universal; fulfilling this requirement is unquestionably the general manager's most difficult responsibility.

A final responsibility of general managers is representing their organizations to the world at large. One way of describing the external environment of companies and other purposive organizations is in terms of evolving coalitions of interests and power. These coalitions can be semipermanent alliances, as in the case of joint ventures between companies. They can also be extremely fluid coalitions which have coherence around certain issues and little coherence around other issues. A company's relations with labor unions and industry associations are cases in point. In these coalitions there are elements of both cooperation and controversy, and relations between parties are typically fluid and sometimes volatile. Relations between companies and various levels of government can have these characteristics as well. In this context the general manager has a dual responsibility. First, he must defend the integrity of his organization in these shifting coalitions and lobby for its interests. Second, where contracts, government regulation, and other aspects of law are involved, he must be cognizant of the rules of law and take personal responsibility for ensuring compliance with these rules.

The basic dilemma of the general manager concerns what emphasis to give these tasks and responsibilities at any one time. A primary objective of this book is to provide the student of policy with case and text material whereby he or she can practice and develop the necessary attitudes and skills to deal with that challenge.

OUTSIDE READING

While the text and cases in this book make up the subject matter of a complete course, an instructor may wish to assign outside readings which reinforce the concepts brought out in class discussion. We have not included reading suggestions at the end of each chapter as few readings directly address the concerns of single chapters. There are many books, however, that are relevant to a number of basic issues of general management raised in the cases presented in this book, and a few of these are listed below:

Andrews, Kenneth R. *The Concept of Corporate Strategy*. Rev. ed. Homewood, Ill.: Dow Jones-Irwin, 1980.

Ansoff, H. Igor. *Corporate Strategy: An Analytic Approach to Business Policy for Growth and Expansion*. New York: McGraw-Hill, 1965.

Barnard, Chester I. *The Functions of the Executive*. 30th Anniversary Ed. Cambridge, Mass.: Harvard University Press, 1968.

Chandler, Alfred D., Jr. *Strategy and Structure: Chapters in the History of Industrial Enterprise*. Cambridge, Mass.: MIT Press, 1962. Also available in paperback.

Drucker, Peter F. *The Practice of Management*. New York: Harper & Row, 1954. HBR Reprint Series. Boston: *Harvard Business Review*, various dates.

Porter, Michael E. *Competitive Strategy*. New York: Free Press, 1980.

Salter, Malcolm S., and Wolf A. Weinhold. *Diversification through Acquisition*. New York: Free Press, 1979.

Sloan, Alfred P., Jr. *My Years with General Motors*. Edited by John McDonald and Catherine Stevens. Garden City, N.Y.: Doubleday Publishing, 1964.

Zaleznik, Abraham. *Human Dilemma of Leaderships*. New York: Harper & Row, 1966.

The work by Andrews provides a good overview of the range of policy problems which will be addressed in all the parts of this casebook. Barnard's book is a classic in the field of management literature, but it is not easy reading. *The Practice of Management*, one of Drucker's earliest and most readable books, covers a wide range of management issues. Even though it focuses on the development of General Motors, Sloan's work also touches upon a wide range of these issues.

The books by Ansoff and Porter are primarily relevant to Part I of this book, the formulation of strategy; Zaleznik presents a useful look at the leader as a person, a topic important in Part II. Chandler's book is a classic in the field of the history of diversification; Salter and Weinhold concentrate on the history and logics of diversification via acquisition, topics important to the multibusiness company discussed in Part III.

The above is not a "recommended reading list" in the sense that anyone should read all of the books on the list. However, all could benefit from at least skimming a number of the books, if only to get an impression of how the viewpoints and opinions of those who have studied certain aspects of management can be of help.

Each instructor, of course, will be able to add to this list. In doing so, the relevant criteria for selection should be whether a given work sharpens the focus of policy problems or helps students of administration broaden their perspective in analyzing the cases presented for study.

We will not attempt to list any articles in addition to the collections of articles on related subjects published in the HBR Reprint Series. At present there are 29 books of articles on General Management alone. With regard to periodicals, *The Wall Street Journal* is by far the best source of current business and financial news, and is very widely read by practitioners. *Business Week*, *Fortune*, and *Forbes* are other widely read magazines that provide both useful news and background articles about specific companies as well as business in general. Some sampling of all of these sources is useful to the student of business.

Quite apart from course-specific readings, there is a world of literature from other fields relevant to the study of policy formulation and administration. Biographies and autobiographies offer a rich account of policy formulation and decision making. Similarly, history and political science offer innumerable opportunities to study the evolution of policy and organization. Accounts as diverse as those on the administrative organization set up in France by Napoleon in the 18th century, the development of the railroads in the 19th century, and the path of the social revolutions in the 20th century all offer clues about how organizational leaders manage their affairs.

PART I

POLICY FORMULATION

CHAPTER 1

Policy Formulation: An Overview

The general manager of a company, or of a major subunit of a company is the person primarily responsible for the performance of the human, physical, and monetary assets entrusted to his/her care. These responsibilities are broad and numerous, the tasks often difficult, and the skills required varied indeed. It is a role in which few students of business administration have had direct experience, one to which many aspire, and one which often takes many years to reach. Though the responsibilities are great and the hours seldom short, it is a job that can be highly rewarding to the individual, both in economic terms and in the personal satisfaction that comes from running your own show and from successfully meeting both the intellectual and administrative challenges of the job.

Although some of the readers of this book may not aspire to become general managers, and others may assume that role only after years of gaining experience in a functional field or a staff capacity, we believe that all those who plan to work in any purposive organization can benefit greatly from an exposure to the problems and responsibilities of the general manager, distant though they may be. The knowledge, skills, and attitudes required of the successful general manager are not gained overnight, and early exposure to the nature of the job is beneficial in enabling you to seek and interpret experience that will improve your abilities as a general manager. In addition, a better understanding of the job of the general manager is useful to those subordinates who seek to help managers with their jobs.

We shall not burden you with any detailed checklists of the content of a general manager's job; instead, we hope that you will find more useful an observation by one of our authors, C. R. Christensen, that the good general manager needs the rare ability "to lead effectively organizations whose complexities he can never fully understand, where his capacity to control directly the human and physical forces comprising that organization is severely limited, and where he must make or review and assume ultimate responsibility for present decisions which commit concretely major resources for a fluid and unknown future."

In Part I of this book we invite you to join with us in exploring one major aspect of the general manager's job, that of the formulation of corporate policy or strategy. Since the purpose of the book is to help you enlarge the background of knowledge, improve the skills, and develop the attitudes that will make you a better manager (*and* subordinate), we ask you to attempt to understand and adopt the position of the involved general manager in each of the cases. At times you will be asked to assume that *you* are the "person on the spot"; at times you will be asked to *advise* the manager—either as a subordinate or as a consultant. In any event, it is essential for you to establish the habit of asking yourself "What strategic actions would I take or advise in *this* situation?" and then deal with the uncertainties, conflicts, constraints, unknowns, and ambiguities as best you can—just as the practicing general manager must do. The cases in Part I of this book have been selected and designed to enable you to focus primarily on this strategy formulation aspect of the general manager's job.

Your primary emphasis should be on the identification and solution of the specific problems as you find them in the cases, not on expository writings about various aspects of the general manager's task in general. For this reason, beyond the background readings given in the Introduction, we will make little reference in this text to the abundance of literature on the general manager's job. You will have read much before undertaking this course; and the principal task before you is to draw upon the background readings your instructor may suggest, as well as materials and techniques with which you are already familiar, to assist you in the solution of the problems found in these specific cases. Your objective should be to develop an understanding of an approach to the analysis and solution of the problems of the general manager via the study of a series of specific cases, not to learn what various authors may say about general classes of problems.

We should also note that in Part I of this book, which focuses on the formulation of corporate strategy, we will be concentrating largely on the single-business company or the business (division) level of the diversified company. We will be concerned with developing your ability to identify, evaluate, and recommend a strategy which is primarily for a single principal product and identifiable industry. In Part III of this book, dealing with the diversified company, we will deal turn to the far more complex task of strategy formulation and implementation at the corporate level of the multibusiness company. We do this not because most companies are single-business companies—about 85 percent of the *Fortune* 500 companies are decidedly multibusiness in nature—but because the task of strategy formulation can best be learned by looking at the single-business situation first.

WHAT DO WE MEAN BY "STRATEGY"?

If we are to ask you to read hundreds of pages and spend many hours trying to improve your skills as a strategist, it is surely not unreasonable for you to be concerned at this point with defining "strategy." We all know that it is generally useful to define our terms, and indeed it is important to attempt to do so with regard to the concept of strategy. Many aspects of a statement of strategy can and should be expressed in quantitative terms, as, for example, earnings or growth goals, but it is no more possible to assign a number to a strategy than it is to the health of an individual. That a definition precise enough to enable quantitative measurement—a key step in many of the advances in the physical sciences—neither exists nor seems likely to occur should neither discourage nor detain us.

It is more useful to focus instead on what a statement of corporate strategy should encompass, proceeding in large part from a consideration of the purposes the development and explicit statement of a strategy can serve for an organization:

1. To improve the ability of the firm to select appropriate basic, long-term objectives for itself, and

2. To develop the means by which these objectives can be achieved.

It then becomes possible to suggest the elements that should commonly be included in a statement of strategy in order to accomplish the above purposes.

Selection of Objectives

One major component of the statement of strategy is the selection of the longer term basic objectives of the total enterprise or major business unit. These might include such items as desirable levels of growth, profits, and risk; broad definitions of the industries or products the company intends to engage in; and, if possible, something which captures the somewhat intangible "character" of the enterprise. You will find all of these quite apparent in the case of The Leisure Group, Inc., described later in this book, where the objectives for growth and the means by which it could be achieved were indeed explicit, and captured the imagination of many.

The important point to emphasize is that the general manager has both the responsibility for and some ability to influence the longer term basic objectives of the firm. These are seldom fixed either by law, practice, or edict. We think it will be more fruitful for you to attempt to discover in the specific companies described in the cases what these objectives seem to be, and what they might be, rather than attempt to define exactly what the term *objectives* should include in all cases.

Our definition of strategy, though common to business, is unlike that used by most military writers. The military definition most often accepts an objective or a goal as fixed and often imposed by a higher authority, and views a strategy as a means of achieving that objective. The general manager has the additional task of selecting appropriate objectives for the firm. The manager must be concerned not only with how to achieve an objective but also with what the objective should be.

As you will discover in a number of the cases that follow, the determination of these longer term objectives can be both important and difficult. Objectives that turn out to be too high in terms of growth, profits, or market share can have severely damaging effects on an otherwise healthy business because of the pressures they create to change the basic nature of the business or to take excessive risks. On the other hand, objectives that are too low in view of the opportunities open to the firm and its own resources will be less challenging to the members of the firm, and will likely result in reduced economic performance. More important for the longer run, they may also cause an unnecessary loss of market position and competitive strength. Few firms would admit publicly to objectives as modest as simply "keeping up with" the industry, or with the overall growth in GNP, but this does not automatically make the substitution of higher growth or profit objectives either wise or attainable.

We should note at this point that objectives such as "grow as fast as possible" or "maximize the earnings per share" or "maximize the long-run value of the common shareholder's interest," useful though they may be to the economist or social scientist seeking to perfect models of the firm or of the economy, are seldom a solution to the above difficulties. Without considerable elaboration, they do little more than point a direction. They communicate little about the acceptable level of risk or the character of the business, for example, and provide even less help in the task of translating a strategy into terms that will have meaning to the managers and employees of the business as they go about their work.

Achievement of Objectives

A second major purpose of a strategy is to develop and make explicit the means by which the firm can achieve the objectives it has selected. An examination of those objectives will lead to an identification of the factors that are likely to play a role in their achievement, and therefore those factors that should receive explicit attention. Since there is almost invariably a strong economic element in the objectives firms establish for themselves, a statement of strategy should include some attention to those items that are likely to affect, in a major way, the economic performance of the company.

A statement of strategy should also include something about the nature of the products, not only in the literal terms of what the product is called and is made of, but of what service it provides to the consumer. What, if anything, is distinctive about the product or service? Is it high or low quality, relatively high or low volume, designed for a broad market or a selected portion of the market, and is it rapidly changing or relatively stable? Are we emphasizing function or fashion? Do we offer a limited line or a full line? How important is advertising and promotion to the product or service provided? How, if at all, can our product be distinguished from present and potential competing products or services? The particular dimensions selected for describing the product will vary with the product. It is important, however, that you find a way to move beyond the label of "autos" or "handguns" or "ball-point pens" to a more detailed product description. The value of a simple and durable product strategy should be apparent in the Lincoln Electric Company case, and the difficulty of devising a product strategy valid at the corporate level of the diversified company should be equally apparent in cases on multiproduct companies such as Voltamp Electric Company and Imperial Corporation cases.

The means of financing the enterprise is important, not only with respect to the present, but even more so with regard to the way in which future requirements will be met. Growth requires increased assets, which can only come from internal sources (primarily retained earnings) or external sources. In qualitative terms, what degree of risk is acceptable? More specifically, what maximum proportion of debt can we get and will we tolerate in the capital structure, what level of dividends do we want to pay, and with what certainty, and how willing are we to risk having to sell stock at depressed prices, sell a portion of the assets, or even be forced to merge with another company if things do not work out as planned? In simple terms, balancing growth and profit objectives with financial requirements and the concomitant risks of reduction of control or, in extreme cases, loss of job, forces one to think about the relative importance one attaches to sleeping well as opposed to eating well.

In addition to establishing the nature of the product or service and the means by which we will finance the business, it is important to know specifically how the product or service will be provided. Are we a manufacturer, or primarily an assembler of purchased parts? To what extent have we integrated backwards to provide for our own sources of supply or raw materials, as in the case of Ford Motor Company manufacturing its own steel at the River Rouge complex and steel producers owning coal and iron ore mines? Have we chosen to use our resources to integrate forward from the traditional manufacturing function in order to control or even own our channels of distribution, as in the case of Massey-Ferguson owning some of its own farm equipment dealers? To what extent do we seek and need to take advantage of economies of scale in manufacturing via standard products, high volume, long production runs, and few locations, such as you will see in the BIC Pen Company case? Or are we a more specialized, lower volume, and higher cost manufacturer?

A statement of corporate strategy should also direct attention to the policies to be followed in the major functional departments of the company to the extent that these have not been covered elsewhere. In view of our objectives and the basis we have chosen for achieving them, do we give balanced attention to the various functional areas, or do we favor some over others? What, if anything, is distinctive or unusual about our research and development department, our manufacturing operations, our financial controls, our marketing department, or our personnel policies? There is no one best way to operate any of these functions, and the challenge for the general manager is to establish policies for the major functional areas so that they are consistent with each other and contribute to the achievement of the overall objectives of the company.

As you examine the operations of the Prelude Corporation (lobster fishing) or Sturm, Ruger & Company, Inc. (manufacture of handguns) or The Hudepohl Brewing Company, for example, what is the relative emphasis placed on the marketing, manufacturing, or research and development functions in each of these companies? Given the nature of their products and the manner in which they have chosen to compete, what should the relative emphasis on these functions be in each case? And just as important, what can the companies afford? If you want to devote more resources to one area, where will they come from?

STATEMENT OF STRATEGY

A complete statement of strategy, then, should convey both what a company is trying to achieve and how it hopes to achieve it. The plan for achievement should include attention to the important factors influencing that achievement, as mentioned, and it should specify what major steps are to be taken, in what rough time frame, by whom, what resources will be required, and how the resources will be obtained. It should communicate, in as tangible a way as possible, just how this particular company has chosen to compete in the marketplace. Frequently, this means attention and thought to the issue of how to compete against larger competitors with greater resources and greater potential for economies of scale in research and development, manufacturing, marketing, or management.

We tend to think of the elements of strategy as they apply to the more familiar and visible established manufacturing companies, often with large fixed assets committed to the manufacturing function. It is equally important, however, to think through what the strategy should be for a service company. As you examine the operations of People Express (a new passenger airline) or Data Resources, Inc. (econometric information and consulting) later in the book, it will be apparent that all companies can benefit from dealing explicitly with their strategic problems. This is true, above all, for the entrepreneurial enterprises described in Part IV, where the margin of error is so much less than for an established firm.

We have thus far focused primarily on the purpose and content of a statement of corporate strategy, and have said very little about how one might move from simply identifying the strategy of a company to evaluating it and making recommendations for changes. Developing and explaining an approach which you can apply to case situations is the principal purpose of the next several chapters. Before turning to this main task, however, there are several other items which warrant our attention at this point.

THE GENERAL MANAGER AND STRATEGY FORMULATION

Does strategy make a difference? Of course it does. We are completely convinced, on the basis of our own experience as well as our broader exposure to a great many practicing business executives, that the choice of the products and markets in which to compete, and the basis for competing in them, is of crucial importance to a company. This proposition may be difficult to prove because of the myriad of variables that affect company performance, including the catchall "luck." It is certainly easier to support, however, than the opposite position—that the choice of markets and ways of competing in them is of no consequence to a company.

We would therefore strongly encourage you, as you study the cases in this book, to do for yourself what an experienced and highly successful group vice president of a major diversified industrial company has told us is the first thing he does when he takes over the responsibilities for a new division, often in a business in which he has had no previous experience. He develops, along with the division management, an explicit, brief statement of what the current strategy of the division is before making any attempts to evaluate or change that strategy.

It does not follow from the above, of course, that the task of leading the organization in the implementation of that strategy, to which we shall turn in Part II, is of any less importance. Clearly, skill and success at both is helpful to the overall success of the firm. Music comes from both the violin and the violinist, and if either is poor the results suffer.

Responsibility for and participation in the strategy formulation process are therefore central to the job of the general manager. Participation is essential not only because the outcome is important to the company, but also because the general manager brings a perspective and a level of authority to the task that are likely to result in a better strategy as well as better acceptance of the strategy within the organization.

Of course, this does not mean that the general manager has to do all of the work; for anything but the smallest or simplest business, that would result in a superficial analysis. What it does mean, in our judgment, is that the general manager of any company, no matter how large, must clearly understand the key problems and opportunities facing the company, enlist the help of line managers and staff and perhaps outsiders in collecting and analyzing the information needed and in developing possible courses of action, and then visibly support the choices made.

Staff and subordinate assistance is helpful and often essential, but without the involvement and commitment of the general manager to the results, the staff work is likely to be ineffective. The single greatest hazard facing both the professional corporate planner and the company whose chief executive turns too much of the task of developing the corporate strategy over to the long-range planning department is that the resulting 200-page five-year plan, which may by all objective standards be an excellent plan, will gather dust rather than precipitate action.

In the next several chapters, then, we will turn to the task facing the general manager in the development of strategy for the firm.

CHAPTER 2

An Approach to Strategy Formulation

The strategy of the firm at any particular time is the product of a wide range of factors, including history, happenstance, oversight, external forces, and the conscious efforts of management to influence that strategy. It is our experience that practicing general managers as well as their advisors and those aspiring to those roles can make their efforts to influence corporate strategy more effective by the conscious use of a conceptual scheme or framework of analysis to assist them in the task.

The problems of formulating strategy for a firm can be complex in the extreme in terms of the number of variables which should be taken into account, the difficulty of obtaining reliable estimates for many of those variables, and the judgment required to predict how the variables will interact with and influence each other as well as the overall performance of the firm. The variables can include technical, economic, political, and social factors, and in uncertain environments may often require judgments to be made about some of these matters many years in advance. Even in the case of a relatively small and simple business like that of the Prelude Corporation, the difficulty of predicting a number of variables sure to be important to the company will be readily apparent.

Some may be willing to deal with such complex issues in an unstructured way and venture firm opinions on short notice about the strategy International Harvester should have adopted in order to avoid their financial debacle of 1983, for example, or how electric utility companies should respond to environmental regulations, high capital costs, rapidly rising fuel and plant costs, and increasing consumer opposition to rate increases so as to generate enough profits to ensure that the capital they will need in the next decades will somehow be forthcoming. In attempting to develop answers to such problems, however, all but the few true geniuses among us will find some sort of general framework or approach useful, if not essential.

We would like to suggest to you an approach to analysis of such problems which is simple to state, and widely applicable, but which does require thoughtfulness, practice, and hard work. It has evolved over several decades as a result of the research, teaching, and consulting activities of the authors as well as from discussions with a large number of our colleagues in the Business Policy course at the Harvard Business School. Professor Kenneth Andrews has been the most articulate of those involved in this development, and the authors all acknowledge the great contributions made by him in bringing order and common sense to a still-evolving framework of analysis.[1]

The approach we suggest is designed to help you simplify a complex task so that you can deal with it more effectively. It is not a model that would meet the standards of our academic colleagues in the natural sciences or those with strong interests in quantitative methods, as neither the individual elements of the model nor the relationships among them can be usefully quantified. We would welcome such an advance, but to our knowledge, no such comprehensive "strategy formulation model" useful to general managers exists. What we do propose is an approach that will encourage disciplined attention to several major areas of importance by the practicing general manager faced with the real-life task of formulating and evaluating the corporate strategy of the firm.

The approach we have found general enough to be applicable in a wide number of situations as well as specific enough to be useful in individual and unique situations consists of considering the strategy of a company to be influenced by the interaction of the four main areas shown in Exhibit 2-1. The process of analysis consists of an assessment of the relevant facts and trends occurring within each of these major areas, a judgment of the ways in which these areas will or can be made to influence each other, and the creative development of a strategy suited to the unique situation of the particular company. We cannot emphasize strongly enough the importance in this process of the notion of *fit*, or the need for the strategy to build on what is unique to the particular situation with regard to all of the important factors and the ways in which these factors should complement each other.

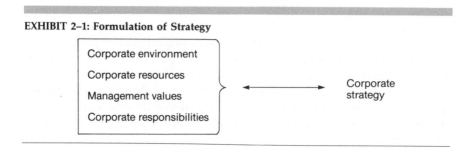

EXHIBIT 2–1: Formulation of Strategy

A strategy should allow for the trends in the company's environment, including the actions of competitors; take advantage of the strengths and minimize the weaknesses of the company; take into consideration the personal values of those managers who are in a position to influence the company; and make provision for what the company either wants to do or should do beyond pursuing purely economic goals in view of what may be expected of it by the broader society of which it is a part.

As you proceed to identify, evaluate, and recommend changes in the strategies of the companies described in the following pages, it will be useful to keep in mind three deceptively simple questions you should try to answer with regard to each unique situation that you study:

1. Where are we now?
2. Where do we want to go?
3. How do we get there?

The approach described above will help you arrive at reasoned answers to the above questions, but not in a mechanical or deterministic way; it provides neither checklists nor "yes-no" questions. It is our experience that such seeming expedients make it less rather than more likely that the creative job that needs to be done will take place.

Neither does the approach ensure that you will arrive at a demonstrably "right" answer, but this is a reflection of the difficulties of formulating strategy in real life as opposed to competing in a computer simulation model or a chess game. No approach of which we are aware does guarantee the "right" answer; experienced and intelligent executives will often disagree in difficult strategic situations. If systematically and carefully followed, however, the approach will result in the logic and assumptions underlying strategic recommendations becoming more explicit and clearer to all. This in turn, has several significant benefits:

1. It permits a more detailed and reasoned examination or "dissection" of the basis for differing strategic recommendations for the same situation. The quality of the assumptions, the logic, and the choices being made with regard to levels of risk, profits, growth, and so on, can more readily be isolated and discussed. To say that an approach does not guarantee a single, "right" answer is not to say that some strategic recommendations will not, upon examination, be judged by most to be of higher quality than others.

2. Because the entire process of strategy formulation is made more explicit, improving one's skills at that process becomes easier. Intuitive approaches by experienced and skillful business people may result in brilliant strategies, but such intuitive abilities are not easy to acquire, either by birth or practice. Although some of the most difficult and important decisions business people must make involve a substantial combination of intuition, creativity, inspiration, artistry, and judgment, students

as well as executives benefit from expanding rather than reducing the explicit and analytical portion of the strategy formulation process and improving their skills at that portion through practice. Because strategic decisions by their very nature are not made frequently, are seldom made by aspiring executives early in their careers, and often require the passage of many years or even decades before their wisdom and quality can be evaluated, practice and skill in making strategic decisions are not easy to come by. Breaking down the process of making those decisions and participating, when possible, in that process as junior members of management facilitate the development of the skills and experience crucial to the successful performance of that key aspect of the job of the general manager.

3. An evaluation of the strategy itself as well as the progress of the organization in carrying out that strategy is made easier if the strategy formulation process and the underlying logic and assumptions are made explicit. Conditions change, unforeseen obstacles as well as opportunities arise, and progress inevitably exceeds hopes and plans in some respects and falls short in others. Periodic reevaluation of progress as well as of the strategy itself is essential, not only to provide guidance to the manager in leading the organization in the implementation of strategy, but also in making whatever changes seem necessary in the strategy itself.

In discussing the steps to be followed in formulating a corporate strategy, isolated from other aspects of the general manager's job, we run two risks that should be addressed at the outset. First, strategic problems in practice seldom appear, nor are they addressed, separately from the problems associated with implementing that strategy within the organization, a topic pursued more fully in Part III. Policy formulation and administration are intertwined in real life, and the effective manager must constantly move back and forth between the tasks of the ongoing administration of the existing strategy and the continual reassessment of that strategy.

We deliberately begin this book with cases that permit concentration on the formulation of strategy rather than the ongoing administration of that strategy for two reasons. First, developing skills in the formulation of strategy can best take place by means of focusing on that portion of the general manager's job. Second, even the most experienced general manager can best make progress by concentrating first on one and then on another aspect of the job. Even though many of one's problems are interrelated, one cannot work effectively on everything at once.

Neither can we present everything at once in a text or series of cases. Although we have chosen to concentrate on problems of strategy formulation in Part I of this book, we hope you will not forget that policy formulation and administration, although separable mental activities, are clearly interrelated in practice. Even though you may concentrate on the strategy of People Express as you study that case, for example, the importance of their approach to organization in the achievement of that strategy will be apparent. Similar interrelationships are a common occurrence.

The cases in Part II include more information pertaining to the administration or implementation of strategy in the company, and many of those cases will provide you with ample opportunity to develop your skills in both the formulation and implementation of strategy in relation to each other. At a minimum, the need to tailor the approach to administration to the requirements created by the strategy of the company will become clear. The cases in Part III, all of which deal with managing the diversified firm, will from the outset require balanced attention to both strategy formulation and implementation, as will the cases in Part IV, where the focus is on the entrepreneurial firm.

The second risk we incur in discussing the strategy formulation process separately is in giving the impression that it is a sequential, "one-time through" procedure in which one can in turn analyze the environment, assess the strengths and weaknesses of the company, ascertain the values and aspirations of the management, allow for the expectations of society, and produce strategic recommendations that will be good for some substantial period of time. Such a procedure does not correspond with practice, or at least with good practice, in two respects: each major factor must be investigated in relation to the others, and the process is a never-ending one.

The basic nature of the strategy will hopefully remain constant over substantial periods of time, but changing industry conditions, company performance, and competitive moves make continual examination and readjustment of the competitive posture essential. In most companies the major strategic evaluations and adjustments take place during the annual planning cycle, which hopefully consists of a thoughtful review rather than a mechanical updating and extrapolation of trend lines. In the better companies attention is also paid to the need to make adjustments between the annual planning periods as conditions change.

Although we discuss the formulation of strategy before devoting much attention to its implementation and discuss discrete elements of the formulation process in sequential fashion, we nevertheless hope you will not lose sight of the fact that strategy formulation in reality can better be described as a continuous process, separable from but not independent of the ongoing administrative problems and characteristics of the company. It is a process of continual examination and adjustment of interrelated elements, not a series of discrete puzzles to be solved in sequence independently of each other.

We will turn in the next chapters to more detailed suggestions as to how you might begin trying to apply the approach just described to the specific case situations that follow.

CHAPTER 3

Strategy Formulation and Corporate Environment

The importance of looking at the competitive environment of a company should not require much elaboration. The issue is not whether to look, but what to look at, how to predict what is likely to happen, or can be made to happen, and what effect these happenings might have on our business. We have listed *environment* first in our approach to strategy formulation, but this is really a matter of personal choice. You might prefer to first make a thorough examination of the strengths and weaknesses of the company. However we have found that in most cases it is better to proceed from a broad investigation of the industry in which a firm competes to a more detailed examination of the firm itself.

WHAT IS "OUR INDUSTRY"?

By the *environment* we generally mean all those factors external to the company which do, or could, have an important influence on the performance of the company. Our first problem is to determine how to define what we will look at so that the task can be accomplished by ordinary mortals in the course of all the other demands on their time and thoughts. It is true but of little help to observe that the world is continuing to become one large interrelated system in which happenings anywhere may impact upon any business. It is also true that events and developments not apparent in the everyday course of business may nevertheless have a significant impact on us.

The environment consists of a spectrum of events, some immediately observable and obviously important, and some with such low probability of impact on us that we can safely ignore them in order to deal more effectively with what we can perceive and comprehend. It is essential to recognize that limits must be drawn, and that the limits must be defined in terms of the specific company and its strategy and products, not just a general notion of the industry. You will have to strike a balance between attempting to include everything; the first carries with it unseen threats and risks of lost opportunities, the second may result in intellectual paralysis.

The principal reason for defining an industry in operational terms for each specific company situation you encounter is the need to identify present and potential competitive products and services and the important factors affecting the demand for the products and services of that industry. You will also need to assess as carefully as you can the apparent strategies of your principal competitors. These questions arise in the first cases in Part I and become more difficult as you proceed, for example, to the cases on the soft-drink industry, Dr Pepper and Seven-Up; the mechanical writing industry and BIC Pen; and Polaroid-Kodak.

In the Polaroid-Kodak case, for example, you will want to think about what difference it makes to the presidents of Polaroid and Kodak as to how they define their industries and when they began to consider each other as competitors. When a young and small Polaroid was offering an instant print of lower quality and at a higher price than conventional prints by the huge and well-established Kodak, were the companies really competitors? When did instant photography and conventional photography begin to compete for the same consumer dollar, as is clearly the case by 1976, when Kodak introduced an instant camera? Similar questions could be raised with regard to BIC Pen and their larger competitors at the time BIC introduced their low-priced, branded stick pen. How one defines an industry has a major influence on the size and growth of the market, who the competitors are, what trends and developments will become relevant, and the possible opportunities for a company.

The problem of identifying the relevant competition has become even more difficult because of the increased globalization of business in the past few decades. The Japanese were not viewed as a serious threat to the American automakers or consumer electronics manufacturers in the early 70s; today the United States has no significant consumer electronics manufacturing capability and has had to resort to import quotas for protection against Japanese autos. We tended first of all to look only at our domestic competition, then we turned to our more familiar European trading partners, and only recently has our attention focused on Japan. While we are making these adjustments in our thinking, Japan is becoming increasingly concerned about competition from newer Pacific Basin countries such as Korea, Singapore, and Hong Kong. For products traded in world commerce, the relevant competitor of tomorrow may be very different than the one of today.

INDUSTRY ECONOMIC PERFORMANCE

After you have defined an industry sufficiently to identify competitive products and services and the companies that provide them, you will want to investigate the economic performance of the industry. What is the approximate size of the market, at what rate has it been growing, what is the average level of profitability of the industry, and how much do these vary from year to year?

The general level of profitability within an industry is obviously of interest, and these levels vary greatly among industries as well as over time within an industry. Measures of profitability of course also vary among companies within an industry. Companies often seek to improve their overall profitability by diversifying into industries with historically higher rates of profitability, a strategy which will be examined more in Part III.

One reason the size of the market is important is that the volume of business reasonably obtainable clearly has implications for the investment that can be undertaken to enter or compete in that market. A small market cannot justify high research, advertising, or capital expenditures, no matter how successful the efforts are; conversely, a large market potential may justify large investments. Indeed, large markets often attract large investments and therefore large companies—a fact of which most small companies are well aware.

Another reason for concern with size is that many companies prefer not to bother with ventures which, even if successful, are unlikely to grow large enough to have a significant effect on the overall operations of the company. Small companies often justify seeking specialized market niches for this very reason—in the hope that larger companies will not find it worthwhile to do battle over small markets. Whether such arguments are valid in the case of the brewing industry, for example, is something you will need to consider as you study the Hudepohl case in Part IV. The question is especially pertinent in view of the consolidation in the brewing industry from 750 breweries at one time to about 50 at present.

The growth of the market is important for a number of reasons. Foremost, of course, is that a growing market may provide sufficient opportunity for all of the competitors to achieve satisfactory rates of growth from the expanding market rather than from each other. Company growth secured from an expanding market rather than at the expense of an embattled competitor is likely to be both more profitable and more pleasant. Many industries, and most recently many branches of the electronics industry, have gone through this phase.

High industry growth does not necessarily indicate high industry profits or opportunity for any individual company, however. More important is the balance between the capacity of the industry and the demand for its products. High-growth industries where capacity exceeds demand, and particularly where strong competitors are determined to increase market share, can be thoroughly unattractive in terms of current profits. Sometimes the slumps last only a few years, as in the case of semiconductors or pocket calculators; sometimes the reduced levels can last for many years, as in the case of the basic chemical industry and the fertilizer industry. Few would seek out low-growth industries except for very special reasons, but high growth is no guarantee of high profits.

In many cases, as with the American automobile industry, the detailed and complete industry figures abound. In the automobile industry, production and sales by manufacturer, by model, and by state are readily available and frequently reported, sometimes by weekly periods. In smaller and less mature industries or product lines, the statistics may be very difficult to come by. Sometimes production and sales figures are more readily available than profit figures; sometimes the opposite is true. In some industries you will be fairly suffocated by statistics; in others you may find the lack of reliable data on market size, growth, and profitability frustrating.

General managers share your difficulties and frustrations, and have learned to do the best they can with the data available. We encourage you to do the same with the data in the cases. You should not flee to the library in search of more statistics, but neither should you avoid making reasoned judgments based on the data available.

The key question, of course, is what is likely to happen in the future, not what occurred in the past. Knowledge of what has happened to date, however, provides the essential base for looking ahead. You will find it useful to try to identify the major factors that affect the growth and profitability of the industry, what trends are occurring, and which of these factors are susceptible to some control.

Some of these factors will be common to many industries—consumer disposable income or the level of capital goods expenditures, for example—but many will be unique to a given industry. They will encompass consumer tastes as well as finances; technical development, both within and outside the industry and country; economic trends; political developments; and social trends or pressures. They will be of varying importance, depending on the industry.

High interest rates generally have an adverse effect on new car sales, for example, but this in turn tends to increase the demand for automobile replacement parts, since people then commonly spend more to repair their cars. For a mortgage banker or anyone associated with or affected by the home construction industry, however, high interest (and therefore mortgage) rates are likely to have a highly adverse effect. The unprecedentedly high interest rates that prevailed in the early 1980s were commonly regarded as the primary cause of the lowest level of housing starts in decades.

Your task will be to predict what such changes may mean for a specific company, when either the threats or opportunities are likely to become significant, and even more important, what the company can do to benefit by, rather than be harmed by, the changes that are coming. National and industry economic statistics are but a starting point for the rest of the analysis. An investigation of the characteristics of the industry such as we suggest in the next section will also help you understand and predict the performance trends of industries, and may also help you in forming judgments as to possible competitive strategies for companies within the industry.

INDUSTRY CHARACTERISTICS

The field of industrial organization, a specialty within the economics profession, developed in the 1930s as a means of providing analytical support for the regulation of industry size and structure in ways thought to be conducive to more competitive corporate behavior. Proceeding from a strong early bias against large firm size and concentrated industry structures, it has come to be more concerned with explaining the behavior and economic performance of an industry in terms of the structural characteristics of the industry, including the suppliers and the customers of the industry. A recent book by Porter is an example of a highly structured approach to the analysis of industries based on the concepts and findings from the field of industrial organization.[1]

We would like to suggest some questions that you might want to ask yourself about various industries for the purpose of understanding "how the industry works." We will be less interested in whether high industry profit ratios are associated with high industry concentration ratios, for example, than in the implications of industry dominance by a few large companies for the remaining companies in the industry.

As you attempt to gain an understanding of the characteristics of the industries in which the companies you will be studying compete, you will find it useful to seek data on the following broad categories:

1. What is the distribution of size of firms (or divisions of firms) with which we compete, and where do we rank? Are there many firms of somewhat equal size, or is the industry characterized by a few very large companies, with consequent large market shares, and then a large number of smaller ones? What are the strategies of firms large enough and strong enough to affect the smaller firms in the industry? Is there a single market leader that tolerates the existence of smaller firms as long as they do not try to expand too aggressively, or are there two giants battling each other for market share, using price as a competitive weapon? Endless combinations are possible, each with different implications for

other firms in the industry. Issues such as these are important to most of the firms you will study in Part I.

2.   What economies of scale are available to firms in the industry? The concept of economy of scale has played a large role in both the development of theory and the empirical research of economists interested in the firm. By economy of scale we mean simply a reduction in the costs of a unit of output that is made possible by an increase in the scale of operations and the accompanying investment.

Economies of scale are thought of as occurring most commonly in production facilities, but they can be achieved in many areas. Large companies can generally obtain both debt and equity funds more cheaply from the capital markets than can small companies; large research and development facilities for some purposes may be much more efficient than smaller ones; national advertising campaigns are cheaper in terms of unit costs than local campaigns; expenditures for management salaries and corporate overhead generally need not increase at the same rate as sales, and so on.

Industries vary widely in the areas in which significant economies of scale, and therefore possible competitive advantage, can be achieved. It is essential for a company to select its own strategy accordingly, as BIC Pen did. What are the advantages of large size, and how can we capitalize on them if we are large and minimize their effects on us if we are small?

3.   Are there significant barriers to entry which either protect us or adversely affect our ability to move in other directions? A barrier to entry may be considered as the minimum ante required to enter the game, or the minimum investment required to compete in the mainstream of the industry. Some industries are characterized by low barriers to entry— tool and die shops serving the automotive industry, plastic injection molding manufacturers, garment manufacturers, and so on. Some—basic steel, the major oil companies, pharmaceutical companies, and so on—have high barriers to entry, for a variety of reasons. The barriers may consist of the minimum investment required in productive facilities, in the distribution system, in research and development and patents, in advertising expenditures and consumer brand identification, among other things. Industries with low barriers to entry tend to be characterized by many small firms and relatively high turnover of firms; the opposite tends to be true for industries with high barriers to entry.

4.   What is important about the financial and operating characteristics of the industry, and how are these likely to influence competitive decisions and strategies? In some industries the combination of high capital and, therefore, fixed costs in relation to variable costs, a production process which either must or can easily be continuous, and a largely undifferentiated product result in pressures to operate at full capacity regardless of demand, with consequent wide swings in prices and profits. The manufac-

ture of paper, basic chemicals, and steel would be in this category, whereas the manufacture of handguns by Sturm, Ruger & Company, Inc. would not.

What operating financial ratios are typical of the industry—items such as amount of increased working capital and fixed assets required to support increased sales, the contribution of each incremental sales dollar to these needs, and so on? What are the implications in relation to the financial condition, profitability, and growth goals of the individual company? To what extent does it seem desirable or necessary to invest in either forward or backward integration, with the consequent increase in assets required to support the same end sales to the consumer? Many items such as these will have implications on the strategic alternatives available to a company and the strategic responses it is likely to receive from competitors.

PIMS AND THE EXPERIENCE CURVE

Two major analytical techniques that seek to provide guidance for the manager with regard to a number of the factors just discussed merit mention at this time. The first of these is the PIMS study, and the second is the notion of the experience curve.

One goal of many business practitioners as well as researchers has been to "quantify the variables that affect the profitability" of a business. This objective sounds disarmingly simple, but it has eluded the efforts of most who have attempted it. The most ambitious attempt was undertaken by the General Electric Company in the early 1960s as a proprietary strategic planning technique. The effort was later transferred to the Marketing Science Institute, an independent research organization, and expanded considerably in its scope. Known as PIMS (for *P*rofit *I*mpact on *M*arket *S*trategy), the project has collected data from 800 businesses supplied by 100 companies. Working with a very large number of variables such as market share, degree of capital intensity, R&D and marketing expenditures as a percent of sales, and so on, the researchers have concluded that 37 variables can explain 80 percent of the observed variation in the profitability of the many businesses studied. Of all the variables, market share is most strongly correlated with profitability.

The application of these findings requires both considerable data and great caution, especially with regard to the definition of the product, relevant costs, and the market. In addition, there is the very considerable difficulty in moving from correlations to cause and effect, and then to "cause" the desired "effect." To put the question perhaps a bit too simply, even if high market share is significantly correlated with high profits and furthermore thought to be a cause of rather than a result of high profits and other factors, how does a company with low market share obtain a high market share?

The PIMS approach has a number of strong critics, and the application of the research findings requires care; nevertheless, these findings generate many interesting questions for the strategist. Two articles which outline the promise of the PIMS approach are included in the Notes.[2]

Another approach that has gained considerable publicity within the last decade or so is that of the reduction in costs which arises as a consequence of the effects of the experience curve, as developed and popularized by the Boston Consulting Group. Simply put, it is the observation that in many cases the unit costs of production are a function of the *accumulated* production of that item, not the present scale of operations, and that these costs will decline (adjusted for inflation and changes in the cost of purchased goods and services) as the total amount of production of that item increases.

The notion of the cost reduction arising from accumulated experience, then, is in some ways a bridge between the economist's concept of economy of scale based on current absolute size and the effects of the learning curve, a phenomenon studied by every industrial engineer and since, World War II, applied to the production scheduling of complex job assembly products such as airplanes and ships.

The proponents of the experience curve claim that it is a much more important and pervasive phenomenon than simply the reduction in direct labor-hours that can be predicted by learning curve theory as a result of production workers becoming familiar with repetitive operations, and that the maximum advantage will be retained only by good managements which use their experience to continue improving their operations and to stay ahead of their competitors with less accumulated experience.

A strategy built upon the need to have the greatest accumulated production experience so as to have the lowest costs in the industry would result in having the highest market share, and would be consistent with one of the findings of the PIMS project. In addition, proponents of the experience curve argue that it is essential to obtain this high market share early in order to have the greatest accumulated experience and therefore the lowest costs in the industry. Thus market share leadership should be obtained at almost any cost, since it will ensure eventual high cash flow and profitability.

Just as with the PIMS approach, considerable care needs to be taken with regard to the application of experience curve concepts to the specific situation. Examples can be found where aggressive pricing strategies based on the desire to take market leadership early and on the assumption that costs will eventually decline to an acceptable proportion of prices have been successful. The pricing and production policies of Texas Instruments in semiconductors and pocket calculators is one of the best-known examples. It should be apparent, though, that if two strong companies decide to follow this basic strategy, a long and very costly battle for market share can make the battle not worth winning.

In addition, the issue of the economies of scale of the single plant is not addressed directly by the proponents of the experience curve; neither is the issue of the impact of new equipment or manufacturing technology in the hands of a competitor, regardless of the scale of the plant; nor is the importance of competitive strategies other than low-cost production such as special marketing expertise, product innovation, and so on.

Even if it seems that the logic of experience curve analysis leads you to recommend becoming the company with the greatest accumulated experience in whatever product the company happens to make, you will need to go on to specify a strategy that will enable the company in question to achieve that position. The more you believe in the applicability of the experience curve, the more important it will be to achieve this position, but the more difficult it will also be to achieve if there is already someone in the industry with greater accumulated experience.

Just as with the PIMS approach, experience curve analysis can suggest many interesting questions for the strategist. Three writings which present both the basic approach and some of the limitations of that approach are given in the Notes.[3]

Both the PIMS data and experience curve analysis lead to a number of important hypotheses concerning the allocation of funds by the corporate level of a diversified company to the various business units comprising the company. We will examine these so-called portfolio planning models in Part III of this book.

SUMMARY

An industry can be thought of as much like the forest pond so frequently described by the naturalist—full of all sorts of animals and plants, many competing for the same limited supplies of sunlight and food, some mutually supportive, some feeding on others, some gaining in prominence or power at times, and some disappearing from the scene. In spite of the activity, there is a reasonable stability and balance until some new animal comes along, or some other change in the environment occurs. A company in an industry is subject to similar forces—a variety of competitors, many larger and stronger, some with different strategies for capturing "our" sources of revenue; unexpected disturbances in the form of new technical developments, government regulations, economic slumps, credit restraints, or raw material shortages—the list is endless.

The questions you can ask and the data you can seek to help you understand the working of an industry are limited only by your own ingenuity and energy. The objective is to create a basis for forming judgments about what opportunities and threats are likely to exist in the years ahead for the specific company with which you are concerned, and to use this for developing some strategic alternatives.

It will be useful to determine which individual companies have done well in the industry and which ones have done poorly. What is more important, how do you explain their performance— both good and bad— and what can you learn and perhaps adopt from their experiences? Five or 10 years from now, what do you think the most successful companies in the industry will look like? What will be the cause of the downfall of the least successful? How can we develop a strategy that will serve our longer term objectives? Before we can go further with developing specific recommendations, it is necessary to undertake a more detailed analysis of the company itself, a task to which we turn in the next chapter.

CHAPTER 4

Strategy Formulation and Corporate Resources

One of the most difficult but important tasks a general manager faces is the determination of just what the distinctive strengths (*and* weaknesses) of the organization are. This is both an intellectual and emotional challenge, and disseminating and acting upon that determination are likely to be significant administrative challenges as well. One of our students stated the problem quite perceptively when he compared it to trying to "be in a parade and on the reviewing stand at the same time." You will no doubt find the task easier from the more detached viewpoint of a student than the involved role of the practicing general manager, but it is a task worth your serious attention.

A corporate strategy has to be designed to fit the needs and capabilities of a specific company, not a typical company. Your strategic recommendations will need to be based upon the problems, opportunities, resources, and aspirations of a given company, not just your analysis of the industry. The challenge is to develop a clear understanding of what the unique or distinctive competencies of the company are, or can be, that will enable it to capitalize on the opportunities and minimize the threats in its competitive environment.

In this chapter we would like to give you some suggestions that may help you to identify the present position of the company, evaluate that position in view of the conditions and trends in the industry, and develop some strategic recommendations that you feel are appropriate to the situation. We have not yet discussed the values and aspirations of the management or the expectations of society as they affect the determination of strategy, and you need to consider these before proposing changes in strategy for the company. We will discuss these areas in more detail in the next chapters. At this point we will turn our attention away from the task of understanding the external world as it affects the company to the task of understanding the internal world of the company itself.

COMPANY STRENGTHS AND WEAKNESSES

In each company you study, the creation of a strategy that matches the distinctive strengths of the company with opportunities in the environment should be your objective. In addition to building on these existing or obtainable strengths, of course, the strategy should also minimize the adverse effects of whatever competitive weaknesses exist. This may result in a strategy that is quite different from simply trying to duplicate the strengths of your competitors so that you may do battle with them on the same basis. David attacked Goliath with a slingshot, not with brute force.

For example, it may very well be that strong dealer relations constitute a significant advantage in some industries, as with Kodak in the consumer photographic market. It may also be, however, that it is more sensible to compete with Kodak in other ways than by trying to duplicate their dealer strengths. Your evaluation of Polaroid's strategy will surely include an examination of this issue. You need to assess your strengths and weaknesses relative to your competitors', and then develop a strategy which will enable the company to turn relative strengths into true competitive advantages.

PRESENT POSITION

Your first task is to gain an understanding of what the company is, how it works, what its strategy is, and what may be major problems or opportunities. We cannot emphasize too strongly the need for constant attention to facts before conclusions at this point, in spite of the desirability of forming some tentative conclusions early in your analysis in order to direct your attention to data and issues that may be important. The ability to make this evaluation of a company is a key skill of the successful general manager, consultant, or company financial advisor. It is not unlike the diagnostic skills of the experienced medical doctor, who must first determine what ails the patient before prescribing a cure. In our experience, it is something at which experienced executives often show an uncanny skill and speed, an ability more akin to intuition or a sixth sense.

You can achieve similar results, although not as quickly, through thoughtful analysis of selected portions of the data present in the cases. The least useful approach, in our view, is the mechanical manipulation of all of the available data, devoting equal attention to all areas.

In each of the cases you study, you should attempt to make educated guesses as soon as possible as to the areas most worthy of investigation, and then pursue them. They will not all turn out to be fruitful, but we believe it will be more useful and educational for you to focus your attention on a series of areas in this manner rather than to routinely complete a checklist.

As much as we would like to discourage you from the mechanical use of a checklist, however, we would like to suggest that there are a number of major areas you will invariably want to at least skim, if the information is available, to see if there appear to be grounds for more detailed investigation.

FINANCIAL ANALYSIS

Early in any strategic evaluation of a company you will surely want to investigate the financial information available to you for whatever leads it may provide with regard to present or potential problem areas or constraints. Many of your strategic recommendations are likely to require the expenditure of money, and recommendations arrived at without attention to the problem of financing them are likely to be of little value. Even more important, you will not find it easy to justify recommendations which do not take account of a current financial crisis, no matter how admirable those recommendations might be for the longer term.

You will want to examine the profit and loss statements for clues to what is happening to the business. What is the level of, and trend in, dollar profits, earnings per share, return on equity, costs, and margins? How do they compare with industry figures, if they are available?

A similar investigation of the balance sheet is appropriate and, together with the information you have gleaned from the profit and loss statements, this may lead you to areas of possible problems. You will particularly want to check the level of and trends in the current ratio, working capital, and debt/capitalization ratios to see if the firm appears to be in, or headed for, short-term financial difficulties. It is essential to have some estimate of the cash flow available from either additional borrowing or the sale of equity, in case the need should arise.

The possible number of items and ratios to look at is large, but the experienced manager has generally developed an ability to skim a large number of items efficiently, focusing on those which may, in combination with other bits of information, signal problems. Some of the most important and perceptive analyses consist of simple arithmetic and the combination of data from various sources, and not the sophisticated manipulation of data which often seems so deceptively appealing to perform. You do not need a computer terminal or even an electronic calculator to draw the important conclusions obtainable from the financial statements of the Prelude Corporation or Sturm, Ruger & Company, Inc. Without those conclusions, however, you will find yourself on shaky ground when it comes to defending whatever strategic recommendations you put forth on those companies.

The overriding concern of any management is likely to be not to run out of plain old cash. The management of cash is likely to be even more critical in the smaller and more entrepreneurially oriented companies, as you will discover as you examine the operations of the Prelude Corporation and the companies in Part IV of this book. There has been much argument by the academic world that investors as well as managers should focus primarily on cash flow rather than reported earnings, but there is little evidence to date that the majority of investors are in fact doing so.

There are many sources of information that can be of help with regard to the techniques of corporate financial analysis; a book by Helfert[1] provides a particularly useful overview.

PRODUCTS AND PEOPLE

You should investigate, to the extent the data are available, the principal products, the technology, and the skills and capabilities of all of the functional areas within the company. You should assess, as best you can, the position and reputation of the products in the marketplace, and the state of the research and development efforts supporting them. It is important to examine the physical facilities of the company with regard to age and efficiency as well as capacity to serve the projected demands to be placed upon them. Quantitative data may be available and useful for some of these items, but qualitative assessments will have to suffice for many.

The quality of the management and the work force is of course an essential factor to consider, and one which is difficult both to assess and, for a manager, to act upon. There is ample evidence from the history of organizations, however, that the skills, interests, and motivation of the people who make up the organization are key factors in the performance of that organization.

It will also be useful to consider whether there are any crises or major efforts occurring in any areas of significance to the company. Is the company undergoing simultaneous transitions in several of these areas which together may cause competitive difficulties? Occasionally small but successful companies find themselves faced with the need to move from entrepreneurial to more professional management at the same time that significant sources of new financing must be found to support a new generation of products which in turn will require new or greatly expanded plant facilities. Each of these transitions can alone pose a significant but surmountable challenge; occurring together, they may provide too much of a challenge for most managements.

You should do your best to determine where the assets of the company are invested, what the profits are in relation to assets of product lines, and what may be expected by product line in terms of sales, profits, and requirements of assets and people. Almost every company can break down its products or services into categories with different production requirements or performance characteristics. Before making recommendations to the company you will want to ascertain, as best you can, what their important sources of profits are, and just where the company has committed, or plans to commit, its assets.

As you progress through your analysis, you should begin to feel confident enough to propose some tentative strategic recommendations that will take into account your investigation of the industry, your evaluation of the present position and problems of the company, and the distinctive strengths on which the company may build. No company can be best at everything, and remedying competitive weaknesses or relative disadvantages takes time, money, and effort. The challenge is to devise a strategy which builds upon the present or readily achievable strengths and minimizes the effects of the areas in which competitive disadvantages exist.

SUMMARY

A strategy which is not based on an awareness of the strengths and weaknesses of a company relative to those of its competitors can very easily lead to difficulties. It may be difficult for a manager to identify accurately those aspects in which a company does have or can achieve a distinct advantage over its competitors. It is difficult and perhaps unpleasant to identify those areas in which the company is at a distinct disadvantage, especially if the areas concern people currently a part of the organization. It is even more difficult for a subordinate to suggest some of these areas of weakness. In altogether too many organizations such statements are interpreted as indicating disloyalty, lack of team spirit, or lack of understanding and true appreciation of the "fine qualities that made this company great." Such judgments need to be made, however, and actions taken as a result of such judgments.

Competitive success comes from the ability to outperform your competition in one or more tasks or combination of tasks that contribute to success—lower manufacturing costs, more effective advertising, better R&D, a stronger distribution system, better overall coordination, superior product strategy, or whatever. The fact is, however, that every company in an industry does *not* offer the best quality or the highest value, is *not* the leader in product development, does *not* have the lowest cost manufacturing facilities, and so on. Strategies which ignore these realities are not likely to be productive. Neither are strategies which blindly attack competitors on their strong points. Strategies which recognize the weaknesses as well as the distinctive strengths of the company, and seek to find a creative match of these strengths with the characteristics of competitors and opportunities in the environment, are much more likely to be successful.

CHAPTER 5

Strategy Formulation and Management Values

We have thus far discussed strategy formulation as a matching of the opportunities and threats in the environment and the strengths and weaknesses of the company itself to achieve economic goals. A strategy based on such factors may be called an economic strategy, even though it takes into account far more than just the economic aspects of the environment of the company. It is economic in the sense that it presumes the objectives of the management are overwhelmingly economic in nature. The process is commonly thought of as one which should be objective and rational, with ample room for different conclusions based on different judgments about critical factors affecting the strategy. The process is complex, but nonetheless the product of reasoned analysis by managers who are assumed not to let their own values interfere with their professional analysis any more than medical doctors would let their personal values influence diagnosis or treatment of a patient. Although strategies may differ, the goal is presumed to be long-term profit maximization within the law, largely uninfluenced by the personal preferences of the managers involved.

It is of course useful to simplify reality, both for purposes of teaching and research. We cannot talk about everything at once, and it makes little sense to talk about the impact of the values, aspirations, or assumptions of management on the strategy the company until we have discussed the economic factors within and outside of the company that strongly influence that strategy. In addition, there are considerable advantages in making the simplifying assumption that firms are—or at least should be—primarily economic units, all seeking the common goal of maximizing the long-run value of the common stockholders' equity in a rational and analytical manner. This has greatly facilitated the development of economic models of firms that purport to explain and predict their behavior and their role in the wider national economy.

INFLUENCE OF VALUES

The everyday observations of all of us, however, should be sufficient reminder that the personal values and the assumptions about what is desirable and possible held by those with power within the organization have an influence on the longer term objectives, the strategies, and the everyday working environment of the organization. In order to understand the strategy of a company, why the company has evolved as it has, why it operates as it does, as well as what kinds of recommendations might be acceptable to the management, it is essential to think about the values of the managers involved. What kinds of people are they? How have the beliefs and assumptions they hold influenced the company? How much would your possible strategic recommendations run counter to their beliefs, and how strong would your case have to be to convince them to change to accommodate your suggestions? And why, if it is the influence of personal values that is critical, are your values better than those of someone else?

The distinction between the effect of personal values on management decisions and actions taken under the general heading of corporate responsibility, discussed in Chapter 6, is not precise. Happily, it need not be. Some managers have a strong desire to use corporate resources to help society, or segments of it, to achieve goals which can only remotely be justified as being in the economic interests of their companies' shareholders in the foreseeable future. We will discuss these issues subsequently. In this chapter we will focus more on the impact of a variety of other personal values on the strategy and everyday operation of the corporation.

A WIDESPREAD PHENOMENON

Evidence of the impact of personal values on the character of a business can be found in many places, including many of the cases in this book. For example, in The Leisure Group, Inc., you will find a company quite different from most in terms of attitudes toward growth, acceptable levels of company and personal risk, and belief in their own ability to restructure companies. In this case two young entrepreneurs with impressive educational and work backgrounds were able to borrow, on the basis of only an $8,000 investment of their own, another $550,000 to enable them to start buying companies in the "leisure industry." In only seven years they increased the sales to $58 million by an aggressive acquisition program and extensive restructuring of the companies they bought, all the while operating with a highly leveraged financial position.

Unfortunately they also lost $30 million, as well as the friendship of a number of their investors, in that seventh year. Their enthusiasm for growth continued undiminished, however. That the character of a company can be strongly influenced by the values and aspirations brought to the situation by its managers seems indisputable, as does the conclusion that the values of managers vary widely.

The values of management affect far more than just decisions concerning the more traditional goals of levels of growth and risk and preferences for lines of business. In the Midway Foods Corporation, for example, a widely studied case dealing with the job of the general manager, the influence of the owner-president on the criteria to be applied in a promotion decision involving a middle-level manager in a small, privately held company is both clear and controversial.

The manager being considered for promotion is a prosegregationist; the president is a liberal and a long-time antisegregationist. The issue is not competence to do the job or management potential, but the person's views, which are fundamentally different from some strongly held personal views of the president. Should we encourage the president to ignore such extraneous factors? Should we accept his reservations and perhaps opposition as regrettable but understandable? Or should we encourage him to stand firm in his opposition on the grounds that any executive team has to be close working and cohesive in order to be effective, and to make promotions which may make that team less effective is simply poor management? From a purely economic standpoint, can a large organization be built and managed within the constraints the president seeks to impose in this case?

We should beware the temptation to believe that the values of the managers are influential only in smaller companies. It is widely recognized that the founders and managers have put their personal imprint on well-known large companies such as Polaroid, IBM, ITT, Xerox, Hewlett-Packard, and Texas Instruments, to name but a few. You will also see ample evidence of the impact of managers on their companies in many of the cases in this book. Indeed, at least a part of the success of many of our outstanding companies can be attributed to the strong personal values of their founders concerning products and ways of doing business, a thesis strongly advanced in the recent best-seller *In Search of Excellence*.[1]

It is also important to note that the relationship between the personal values of the manager and the strategy and operations of the company can have a significant impact on the manager as well as the company. This is clearly demonstrated, for example, by the resignation of the president of Holiday Inns, Inc., a company with revenues of $1.3 billion, in 1977. It was reported that when the company approved its first venture into casino gambling, a proposal to build and operate a $55 million hotel-casino in Atlantic City, New Jersey, Mr. Clymer, the president, chose to take early retirement. A company executive stated that the board felt it was simply a prudent business decision, and that hotel-casinos were a logical extension of their current business. Mr. Clymer, who had long opposed casino gambling in the company's hotels, said that personal and religious reasons prompted him to ask for early retirement. "This is a personal conviction not involving the financial or business aspects of the industry," he stated. "The great concern in my heart is that some may erroneously read into this action a silent judgment of those who have reached a different conclusion. . . . This most certainly isn't the case."[2]

WHAT ARE THE DESIRABLE LIMITS?

The fact that the personal values of the management can have a significant impact on the strategy and the everyday operations of the firm raises the issue of the type and degree of influence by the manager that is appropriate from the standpoint of those affected by the decisions, our own sense of values, and the values of the broader society. Consider, for example, the following quote from an outstanding classic on management, *The Functions of the Executive* by Chester Barnard, who at the time of writing (1938) had long experience as president of the New Jersey Bell Telephone Company:

> **"Fitness"**
> In all the good organizations I have observed the most careful attention is paid to it [the informal executive organization]. . . . The general method of maintaining an informal executive organization is to operate and to select and promote executives so that a general condition of compatibility of personnel is maintained. Perhaps often and certainly occasionally men cannot be promoted or selected, or even must be relieved, because they cannot function, because they "do not fit," where there is no question of formal competence. This question of "fitness" involves such matters as education, experience, age, sex, personal distinctions, prestige, race, nationality, faith, politics, sectional antecedents; and such very specific personal traits as manners, speech, personal appearance, etc. It goes by few if any rules. . . . It represents in its best sense the political aspects of personal relationships in formal organizations. . . it is certainly of major importance in all organizations.[3]

Do these observations seem reasonable to you in terms of today's practices and beliefs? If you attempt to make the very important distinction between the "what is" and the "what should be" in the world, to what extent do these observations still describe the reality, if not your ideal? You will want to explore what degree of influence would be appropriate, and on what kinds of issues, and whether the size of the company or the form of ownership—public or private—is important.

We should also note that the personal values of those in a position of influence can be important in all types of organized activity—law firms, the government, the military, labor, and religious organizations. An interesting recent legal case involved the prestigious New York law firm of Cravath, Swaine & Moore. The plaintiff charged Cravath with violating Title VII of the Civil Rights Act of 1964 for allegedly denying him partnership in the firm because he was a Catholic and of Italian heritage. He also introduced a survey of the 20 largest law firms in New York City, which indicated that of the 912 partners listed, only 15 had Italian surnames and only 62 had graduated from Catholic law schools.

Cravath denied the charges, but also argued that the law did not apply to partnership selections, and that interference in the partnership selection process would violate the firm's First Amendment right of association. As part of the case for the plaintiff, it was argued that law firms, even though partnerships, certainly are a business and provide employment to their members.

That some of the factors mentioned by Barnard exist in contemporary organizations seems apparent. The degree to which they should influence managerial decisions, the remedy to be applied in cases where you think the influence inappropriate, and the way in which you will let your own personal values influence your decisions when you are in a position of responsibility are issues to be explored.

SUMMARY

We raise the issue of the impact of the personal values and the aspirations of the management on organizations because our concern is with the administration of real enterprises involving real people, with all of the complications that entails. The values of the managers on a variety of dimensions— standards of behavior, ways of doing business, technology, products, acceptable growth and profit goals, acceptable levels of risk, criteria for promotion, and so on—exert an influence in all organizations. These influences may enhance or hinder the attainment of purely economic goals, and they may also have an effect on all those who have some dealings with the company.

In taking these personal values into account, you should attempt to:

1. Recognize, as best you can, the extent to which certain practices or decisions are, or have been, influenced by the personal values of someone in a position of power and responsibility.

2. Assess how important these practices or decisions are with regard to the economic well-being of the company.

3. Come to some judgment about the appropriateness of the values them-

selves and the degree to which the manager has let personal values, quite apart from economic considerations, affect professional decisions.

4. Structure and present your recommendations so that a person in power, who may have quite different values than you do, will nevertheless be moved to action along the lines you recommend.

Management, of course, does not "own" the corporation. The law is clear on the responsibilities of the management to manage the company in the interests of the shareholders, which has uniformly been interpreted as the pursuit of primarily economic objectives. Management does, however, have very considerable leeway in practice with regard to how they shall achieve these economic objectives. To assist you in developing some standards by which you might judge the actions both of others and of yourself when you are in a position to influence an organization, we would like to suggest the following questions:

1. Have you allowed for a reasonable input from others in the organization, and from the groups or individuals that might be affected by your decision?

2. Would you be willing to acknowledge publicly your beliefs and the extent to which they have influenced your decision?

3. Do you honestly feel that your decisions or actions are fair to the groups involved, according to reasonably accepted standards of fairness? Would you object to being treated in that way yourself?

We can only judge the values of others in relation to our own standards or those of a broader society, and the question of what is appropriate or better is an unavoidable one. We shall deal more in the next chapter with the issues of what society, or vocal segments of society, expect of businesses in addition to the traditional role of providing employment, goods and services, and a return to the suppliers of capital.

CHAPTER 6

Strategy Formulation and Corporate Responsibility

The fourth major influence on the formulation of corporate strategy that you should take into account is that of corporate responsibility. Although this factor is relevant in a number of the cases throughout the book, several cases concentrating on selected issues of corporate responsibility are presented in Part V.

The concept of corporate responsibility is not well defined, either in theory or practice. The terms *social responsibility* or *public expectations* are sometimes used as well, and we will take these all to signify an important area of concern for the manager interested both in the economic well-being of his company and the role that it plays in the broader society.

It is of course a prime responsibility of the leader of an organization to see to it that the organization obeys the law. However, the concept of corporate responsibility is most often and most usefully applied to actions not specifically covered by law, actions where the issue is not legality but the choices available within the law. Illegal behavior is irresponsible, but not all legal behavior is responsible in the usual sense of the term.

It is apparent that business firms are increasingly being held responsible for far more than the direct economic consequences for their shareholders of the decisions they make and the activities they undertake. Because of the overwhelming importance in the non-Socialist countries of the role of private enterprise in the furnishing of employment and the utilization of productive assets to provide goods and services, society has a legitimate interest in the manner in which these activities are carried out.

It may be useful to think of the many types of claims on and criticism of the corporation that come under the broad heading of corporate responsibility as falling into five rough categories:

1. Those items which are largely a consequence of the manufacturing process itself. Many of our most serious pollution problems are in this category, as are worker health and safety conditions related to the job.

2. Those items related to the sale and use of the product, which can also include pollution and safety aspects, as in the case of automobiles, as well as questionable marketing practices and adverse effects of the product, as with liquor and cigarettes.

3. Vacation, medical, insurance, and retirement benefits and practices which affect primarily the existing employees, but which increasingly are being viewed as proper for external regulation.

4. Actions which a company can take that would affect individuals largely outside of the company and independent of the nature of the product or its manufacture: building or expanding plants in the inner cities or ghetto areas; the hiring, training, and promotion of the disadvantaged (although this can clearly affect existing employees as well); contributions of money and/or time to charitable or educational activities; and participation in urban rehabilitation programs.

5. Actions in which the ethical practices, and not necessarily the results of the practices, are the primary concern: policies on expense accounts and entertainment, bribes and illegal contributions, deceptive marketing practices, investment in undesirable activities or areas, and so on.

The above is of course only a partial list; you may wish to add items that you think should be on it, or items that it is apparent others feel are a responsibility of the corporation.

Neither are the categories mutually exclusive; many items can be placed in several categories. The categories do tend to present different kinds of problems and opportunities from the viewpoint of the manager, however. We will look later at some specific examples of issues that have been much in the news in the last several years.

We will use the term *corporate responsibility*, then, to cover the activities of the corporation that are seen by others as having a sufficient economic or social impact on the broader society, or segments of it, to justify the use of outside (in the sense of nonmanagement) influence, or ultimately law or regulation, to affect these decisions. The influence may come via the traditional legal attempts to place resolutions on the proxy statements for vote at annual stockholders meetings, or via the myriad ways of persuasion, publicity, and pressure open in a free society to individuals and groups with a cause. Ultimately, change may be compelled via law and regulation if those espousing the cause can muster the arguments and the power to achieve their goals through legislative channels, as Ralph Nader, for example, has been so successful in doing.

Responsibility for the resolution of matters affecting the public interest ultimately falls upon the general manager. The issue of corporate responsibility actually breaks down into two basic questions: the *legitimacy* of the power held by corporate executives and the *proper exercise* of that power. Questions concerning the legitimacy of the power derive from the fact that executives are neither selected by nor accountable to the broader community, even though their actions affect that community significantly. We will turn to this issue later in the chapter.

The proper exercise of the power held, totally apart from the means by which that power is achieved, is perhaps the more common concern of those seeking to influence the corporation. If one is dissatisfied with the exercise of the power, it is, however, natural to attack the legitimacy of that power as well, and the issues do become thoroughly intertwined in practice. The broad question you will have to answer remains: *To whom am I responsible, and for what?* Corporate executives have very substantial power over the allocation of resources in the pursuit of economic as well as other goals. The exercise of the power cannot be avoided; decisions have to be made on issues such as product quality and characteristics, plant location, hiring and promotion policies, and so on, some of which affect a large number of people. There have been attempts to categorize the groups affected by the corporation's decisions as "stakeholders" (in addition to the traditional shareholders): employees, the local community, minorities, suppliers, customers, and so on. The purpose of such a classification is to facilitate identifying the impact of the corporation's decisions on various stakeholders as well as to explore means by which the various groups affected by the corporation's actions can gain a voice in the decisions.

EXERCISE OF POWER

We will turn next to the question of what is a "proper exercise" of the power you will have as a general manager. Unfortunately, there is little in the way of theory to provide you with guidance for the above question. Both legal and economic theory in essence state that "The Social Responsibility of Business Is to Increase Its Profits," as Milton Friedman has argued so well in an article with the above title.[1] Even though the increase of profits might benefit the individual firm in the short run, most of us, indeed almost all segments of society, would regard it as falling short of what we would like to see companies do, and less even than would be in the best interests of the broader corporate community, even though it might benefit the individual firm in the short run. It is also less than might be wise for the company to undertake on its own, long before the public brings pressure to bear, in order to minimize the chances of legislation and regulation which could have been avoided by means of foresight on the part of management.

The dilemma, of course, is that the possible claims are endless, the resources and skills are limited, and neither the theory for what should be undertaken nor the mechanism by which conflicts can be resolved is clear. To complicate the matter further, managers do have a responsibility for the health and survival of the firm in purely economic terms, and pursuing these goals in most companies can fully occupy the manager's time and abilities. Indeed, in the economist's ideal world of perfect competition, no manager or company would have the excess resources or time to pursue anything other than profit maximization under the law. It is apparent, however, that the more business is perceived as pursuing that classic goal, the more it is subject to criticism from those who expect it to do more for society.

The range of issues for which business has been criticized, either for not doing enough or for doing the wrong thing, is long. Not all claims and complaints can be heeded, but neither, for reasons of both wisdom and morality, can they all be ignored. A strident criticism of hiring policies is akin to a genteel request for contributions to the local symphony in that they both represent an expectation, or at least hope, of what the corporation will do that it may not be required to do, and which it might find difficult to justify purely in terms of its own short-term economic interests. Improving opportunities for the disadvantaged or raising the cultural level of the community may benefit the company in the long run, but these goals can also be argued to be the proper concern of the broader community, not individual segments of it. For the manager, the issue is to decide what could, and should, be done about such claims. What constitutes the proper exercise of power in the specific case?

CURRENT PROBLEMS

To help you develop guidelines and an approach where so little theory or accepted rationale exists, it might be useful to consider some typical issues that have been much in the news in recent years.

You will discover as you study the Sturm, Ruger & Company, Inc., case that the founder, principal owner, and manager of the company is intensely proud of his accomplishments. In giving his views on the company, William Ruger states:

> I think it's a perfect picture of a model company. It has made money honestly, provided for its employees, advanced the technology of the industry, and continued to grow and be profitable. . . . I like my job and am proud of what I'm doing. I'm proud of this company.

It will not require much additional study to discover also that the principal business of Sturm, Ruger is the design, manufacture, and distribution of high-quality handguns, and that the company is an acknowledged leader in its field. In view of the problems caused by the widespread ownership of handguns in the United States, is there justification for considering this company to be irresponsible because of the occasional tragic consequences of the possession of handguns or similar products supplied by other manufacturers?

Ownership of handguns in the United States on both an absolute and per capita basis far exceeds that of any other country. The number of handguns in circulation has been estimated at around 50 million, and the number is alleged by critics to be growing at an increasing rate. Our rate of homicide by means of guns is also the highest in the world. Public opinion polls generally support more restrictions on handguns, often by a wide margin, especially in and around the larger urban centers of the country. Law enforcement officials are generally much in favor of stricter controls.

Opposition to increased controls has been very effectively voiced by various groups, however, including the National Rifle Association; most veterans' groups; hunters; the general public in the less-populated midwestern and western states, where urban crime is not as much of a problem; and many who resist further incursion by the government into what they consider their private affairs, and particularly their "right to bear arms." The outcome has been few increased restrictions since the 1968 assassination of Robert Kennedy gave rise to much of the concern.

Is Mr. Ruger a model business executive operating a very successful company completely within the law and in an ethical manner, or is his company to be criticized for not living up to its responsibilities? If you do wish to criticize him, what other manufacturers of legal products would you also criticize, and why? The case on Nestlé and the Infant Food Controversy in Part V will introduce you to similar but more complex issues that generated demonstrations, investigations, boycotts, and adverse publicity for the company for years.

Pollution of the environment, both in the manufacturing process and by the product in use, is a widespread problem, and has received much attention in the last decade or so. Companies have been criticized for not taking the initiative in addressing such problems and often opposing remedial legislation. In their defense, companies have pointed to the substantial costs that are involved in remedying many pollution problems, and have argued that no company in a competitive economy can afford to spend much more money than its competitors, either on capital costs or operating costs, without suffering a disadvantage.

And the costs are in fact substantial. During the mid-70s it was estimated, for example, that the paper industry would have to devote about 21 percent of its total capital spending to meet pollution standards, and that the petroleum, iron and steel, and nonferrous metal industries would have to devote about 15 percent to 18 percent of their capital budgets for the same purpose. In the Environmental Pressures case, which deals with the dumping of taconite tailings from an ore-processing plant on Lake Superior, you will have a chance to examine some of the issues involved in the longest and most complex pollution case to date.

Executives have also been quick to point out that in spite of, or perhaps due to, the great increase in regulations and federal agencies, they have often had to plan under such uncertainty as to the applicable standards and available technologies that the only prudent choice would be to delay capital commitments as long as possible. That their claims with regard to the growth of regulations and regulators may have merit is evidenced by the fact that as early as 1970, when the first Earth Day was celebrated, there were 26 quasi-governmental bodies, 14 interagency committees, and 90 separate federal programs dealing with the environment.

By the end of the 1970s, evidence was widespread that the complexity and uncertainty as well as the substance of regulation related to the protection of the environment were causing significant delays in new projects. Planning cycles seemed to be stretching beyond 10 years for major projects such as pipelines and power plants. Because of the lead times and uncertainties that existed concerning nuclear plants, some experts were predicting that no more would be planned. A major oil terminal and pipeline to the Southwest, widely acknowledged as being essential to make efficient use of the oil arriving from Alaska, was finally abandoned by its sponsors in 1979 after many years of seeking the necessary permits from the many governmental units involved. At that point the administration, caught in the midst of the worst oil shortage since the 1973 Arab oil embargo, announced plans to create a new federal agency that would "cut through the red tape" for such essential energy projects as the pipeline.

Few would argue that our method of dealing with our environmental problems has been ideal, but there is little common agreement on better solutions. Many regard the laws and regulations as a necessary way to counter the "irresponsibility" of corporations. That practices which we do not now condone existed, and would likely have continued to exist if laws had not been passed, is clear. It is also important to note that the standards of what is acceptable have changed considerably, partly because of the much greater knowledge that we now have about the harmful effects on the environment of a variety of industrial substances and wastes, and partly because we have set higher health and aesthetic standards for our society in recent years. The regulations arose because individual companies did not, and individually perhaps could not, meet the expectations of society with regard to environmental protection. Were the regulations inevitable, or could more responsible leadership on the part of businesses or business executives have made a difference?

It is not necessary to provide detailed examples of each of the many types of issues that may arise under the umbrella of corporate responsibilities. There is much discussion of these issues in the press, and much that is unique to the specific situation. Public concern with the ethical level of business practice for its own sake, however, has increased greatly in recent years and warrants some further exploration. Two interesting examples that have received much attention in recent years would be corporate investment in South Africa and "Improper Corporate Payments Abroad," now covered by the Foreign Corrupt Practices Act of 1977.

INVESTMENTS IN SOUTH AFRICA

Because of the apartheid policies of the South African government, there has been in recent years a considerable criticism of American companies with investments in South Africa. Strong external pressures have been brought to bear on companies to divest themselves of these holdings on the grounds that such investments help to perpetuate a morally corrupt regime. The nature of the investments is generally not an issue, nor is the question of whether the employment practices of the American subsidiary are better than South African law or custom would dictate. Neither are the arguments that the employment and training made possible by that investment are important in the short run for South Africa's blacks, and that they may contribute to the long-run improvement of the society, seen as persuasive. Although the critics hope that the withdrawal would impose a hardship on the South African regime, the essential element of much of the criticism seems to be that the investment is simply morally wrong. To withdraw and to let someone else—South Africa or third country interests—own and operate those facilities is seen as preferable to permitting American investments to remain within the country.

Some managers, as a result of conscience as well as pressure, spent a great deal of time dealing with this question. Managements may have traditionally considered that their investment decisions in foreign countries should be determined largely by their own business judgment and the applicable national laws or guidelines, but it has become apparent that significant and vocal segments of the public consider it their legitimate concern as well. Polaroid, which devoted significant top executive time to deal with this question, found themselves deeply involved in spite of the fact that it was commonly acknowledged that the company would rank high on any list of "socially responsible" corporations based on their operations in this country, and that their South African investments were minimal in terms of their overall business.

Other companies with more substantial investments in fixed assets, or with a more important share of their revenues in South Africa, were both more vulnerable to criticism and in a more difficult position in the event they did decide to withdraw. Even university investment committees became involved as a result of widespread attempts to persuade universities to eliminate from their investment portfolios the securities of any companies doing business in South Africa.

Policies on investments in South Africa, as well as on the broader question of whether to invest in companies that came under criticism for the level of their corporate responsibility on any matter, were developed and widely debated. The most widely adopted set of principles with regard to South Africa were developed by Rev. Leon Sullivan of Philadelphia. By early 1982, over 130 American companies, operating subsidiaries, or affiliates in South Africa had subscribed to principles calling for:

- Nonsegregation of the races in all eating, comfort, and work facilities
- Equal and fair employment policies for all workers
- Equal pay for equal work
- Initiation of training programs to bring blacks into supervisory, administrative, clerical, and technical employment
- Recruitment and training of minorities for management and supervisory positions and
- Improving the quality of life for minorities outside the work environment in areas such as housing, health, transportation, schooling and recreation.

Over a hundred American companies doing business in South Africa refused to commit themselves to the Sullivan Principles however. Their reasons included a disagreement with some of the principles, an objection to being pressured into subscribing to any set of principles at all, an unwillingness to meet the reporting requirements, or a reluctance to go beyond the laws or practices of the host country. As of 1983, the issue was far from resolved.

FOREIGN CORRUPT PRACTICES ACT

The enactment of the Foreign Corrupt Practices Act in December of 1977 seems also to have stemmed in good part from a concern with the morality of the practices proscribed, and not just from the direct consequences of the practices on American consumers or citizens.

In the course of the investigations of the Watergate scandal during the Nixon administration, it was discovered that substantial amounts of money—in the millions of dollars for many companies—had been paid by American companies to foreign government officials over the years in efforts to secure business. Many of these payments could be called bribes in our sense of the word. They were justified by the companies which had paid them as being necessary to obtain the business because of the demands of the local government officials and the existence of foreign competitors ready to pay the bribes, as well as by the undisputed fact that the practice of bribing officials had been widespread for centuries in many of the countries involved. The payments were denounced by those concerned with the morality of the practice as well as by those concerned by the poor example this set for the rest of the world by the world's leading proponent of the free enterprise system. In the Questionable Payments Abroad: Gulf in Italy case, you will be exposed to some of the complexities of these issues.

A strict law establishing severe criminal penalties for individuals convicted of violating the law, as well as substantial fines for both individuals and companies, was the result. Included in the law was a section charging management with the responsibility for establishing internal controls to prevent violations of the law. Both management and the outside auditors have become responsible under the law for seeing to it that the internal controls are satisfactory, and it appears that management, the auditors, and the directors (and especially the audit committee of the board of directors) may incur individual liability if transgressions occur and the control systems are considered, on subsequent investigation, to have been insufficient. This liability can occur, it should be noted, totally apart from the direct involvement of the manager, auditor, or director in the particular violation.

The supporters of this controversial law see it as essential to improving the image of capitalism, and particularly American capitalism, in the rest of the world. They also point to the basic immorality of paying bribes to secure favors, totally apart from the issue of what others may think of the practice. In addition, they make the irrefutable argument that the citizens in a country in which officials in power have the opportunity to enrich themselves by means of bribes incorporated into the price of the products the government buys are hardly being well served by their rulers.

The critics of the bill, on the other hand, consider it unduly restrictive with regard to its definition of payments that are illegal, as well as an impractical and unjustified attempt to impose the American standard of morality on cultures where seeking and accepting bribes has been a practice for centuries, and is likely to continue regardless of what we desire or legislate. In addition, they point out that the products and services we are selling are generally available from countries such as England, France, Germany, and Japan, among others, and that these countries have shown a remarkable lack of enthusiasm for developing international standards or for enforcing provisions such as ours on their own companies. As a result, it is argued, we are losing a significant amount of business at a time when we can ill afford it in terms of the serious balance of payments deficits the country is incurring.

The principal reason for looking briefly at the Foreign Corrupt Practices Act is not to enable you to debate the merits of the act but to point out how rapidly practices which the business community once thought were not a major concern of the broader society can become the subject of public scrutiny, disapproval, and legislation. Some companies managed to avoid most of the practices proscribed by the act long before its enactment on the grounds that for either moral or economic reasons (or both) they simply did not want to engage in the kind of business that required the payment of bribes, domestically or abroad. Companies that were not as strict in their standards helped bring about the considerable public criticism of business that developed at this time, and no doubt furthered a political climate that resulted in the passage of the act.

In addition, many of these companies also found it necessary to spend considerable amounts of money and time conducting internal investigations and negotiating with the Securities and Exchange Commission (SEC) concerning the amount of disclosure that would be required in public filings concerning their reliance on "improper corporate payments abroad," as the practice was delicately called, to secure business. Several years before the passage of the act, the SEC held that such practices constituted a material fact for an investor with regard to his evaluation of the integrity of the management and therefore the merits of the company as an investment, and would have to be disclosed. If the payments by the company had been entered as tax-deductible business expenses, however, disclosure of payments that would be considered bribes then created the possibility of prosecution for tax fraud—a criminal violation—by the Internal Revenue Service on the grounds that bribes are not deductible for tax purposes. This problem arose, it might be noted, even though foreign bribes—or even domestic, for that matter—were not generally against the law at the time.

Just as with the question of the procedures by which our society has handled the problem of protection of the environment, one could raise the question of whether there is not a better way to improve certain business practices that no one ever defended as being desirable and that many felt were distasteful, if not immoral, although perhaps a necessary evil. The practices brought considerable discredit on business in general and caused expense and embarrassment for individual managers in a remarkably short time.

COSTS OF CORPORATE ACTIONS

You should beware of arguments seeking to avoid the dilemma caused by the fact that actions taken in the name of corporate responsibilities to help the broader society often cost money, and perhaps require the time and talents of busy executives. Some things you may want to do, and perhaps you feel you should do, may be difficult to justify in terms of the demonstrable economic interests of any *individual* company. Although an individual may benefit greatly from the contributions others have made to private universities or The American Cancer Society or the local Salvation Army, YMCA, or symphony orchestra, it does not follow, regrettably, that it is in the best economic interest of any single individual to contribute. So it is for some of the choices companies must make. What charitable and educational contributions should a company make, and why?

Problems such as the ones described above are likely to be incidental to the mainstream activities of the business and limited in their impact on the economic performance of the business. Other problems, such as basic investment decisions, may entail much greater economic consequences.

How much responsibility does a company have to train workers and establish plants in depressed urban areas, as Control Data has frequently done, if it is riskier and more complicated than expanding in existing facilities or familiar surroundings? Do the automobile companies have an obligation to continue to invest in facilities and therefore employment in the depressed Michigan area, or should the management place new investment in more favorable areas in the United States regardless of union and community pressure? Or overseas, as Ford and General Motors have both recently done, thereby making U.S. unemployment and balance of payments deficits even greater in the short run, but hopefully improving the competitive strength and economic performance of the corporation? Or would it be more "socially responsible" to remain in the industrial Midwest, continue with an industry wage structure 50 percent or more above that of most other industrial workers in the United States, and lobby for protective tariffs, quotas, or local content laws in order to stem the flow of imports?

The pollution problem caused by automobile exhaust emissions represents another issue of concern to society for which the solution was expensive. In this case the desired improvements required expenditures in the hundreds of millions of dollars for the necessary research and development work and manufacturing facilities. Unfortunately, they also resulted in automobiles which were more expensive to buy, more expensive to operate, both for fuel and maintenance, and had poorer performance than earlier models. The entire package was neither a financial nor a marketing department's dream, and it is easy to see why individual companies did not take the lead in reducing harmful exhaust emissions.

It is not unreasonable to point out, however, that if anyone was in a position to anticipate the clearly unpleasant and harmful consequences of uncontrolled emissions in large urban areas such as Los Angeles and New York City, it was the larger automobile companies. Perhaps if they had assumed responsibility for calling attention to a problem that was bound to occur, they could have contributed to some form of industry solution earlier instead of being seen much later as obstacles to a solution imposed via a stringent law and a consequent adversarial relationship with still another government agency.

Another example of the problem of incurring significant short-run costs for the individual company would be with regard to the safety characteristics of automobiles. Most safety features such as collapsible steering columns, seat belts, air bags, safety glass, or improved crash protection add more to the price of the car than most consumers would prefer to pay. In addition, many of these advances have required considerable investment in tooling and machinery, and are feasible only if built into the models offered, and not as individual options.

If the manufacturer chooses to add to the cost of his product by building in features that increase the cost above that of his competitors, but the extra features are not perceived as being worth the extra cost by the customer, the manufacturer who chooses to be "socially responsible" is likely to suffer in the marketplace.

POLICING CORPORATE BEHAVIOR

A greatly complicating factor for business in comparison with professions such as law and medicine is that the broader business community has virtually no control over the behavior of the individual company and/or management that chooses to act in a grossly irresponsible manner, even though within the letter of the law. Indeed, it can be observed that unscrupulous practices on the part of one competitor not only go unpunished by the business community but sometimes result in pressure on others to reduce their standards as well.

The more established professions such as law and medicine have an advantage over business with regard to policing both the ethics and competence of their members. Standards for admission to the practice of the professions as well as standards of conduct for members have been developed by the professions themselves and are legally enforceable. Because of the much broader nature of the practice of business, there are no comparable standards that may be applied by business organizations to the conduct of businessmen.

At the level of policing distinctly harmful behavior on the part of those few who might follow that path in the pursuit of their own interests, it is often argued that the only effective course is industry or governmental regulation. The passage of the Securities and Exchange Act 50 years ago probably did more to eliminate certain abuses in the securities industry than 50 years of preaching by the more responsible moral members of the community would have accomplished. Few of us, however, would like to see regulation as the only means by which corporations can be influenced to use their broader powers responsibly.

INDIVIDUAL BEHAVIOR

The question remains of just how education can increase our awareness of the ethical issues and choices that you and others will face as managers, as well as hopefully provide you with a framework and a set of values which will result in behavior most people would regard as responsible.

Based on our experience, simply reading about ethical choices in the abstract, divorced from specific situations, is unlikely to change behavior. Neither, unfortunately, is preaching. What a person considers ethical behavior is influenced strongly by church, schools, family, and peers during childhood and early adolescence. If children have found that highly aggressive behavior, perhaps accompanied by minor chiseling or outright deception, has been a fruitful strategy, it is unlikely that the preachings of a professor will change their norms of behavior much when they get out in the real world.

We believe it will be most useful for you to put yourself in the position of the manager, with all of its competing demands and pressures and constraints, and to develop and defend your position before your peers. What degree of freedom do you have to do what you feel is right and desirable, and how can you create opportunities and new strategies or policies that will enable you to best meet all these competing demands? How can you be more foresighted than some managers have been and anticipate what needs to be and should be done before it becomes a crisis? We have found that it is most useful for you to state and defend your position to peers who think you are not being responsible enough as well as those who think you are doing more than either wisdom or morality would require. Values and sensitivity to ethical issues develop and change slowly, but they seem to us to be influenced more by the need to articulate and defend them than by being told what they should be.

SOCIETY AND CORPORATE RESPONSIBILITY

It is important to remember that private enterprise exists only by the consent of society, and that the "rights" business has with regard to making decisions in its own interest can be abridged or modified by means of our democratic process. If enough people become convinced that a company should not be allowed to reduce employment in a given area without extensive consultation with local authorities and the payment of very substantial termination costs, as is the case in many European countries, such laws will be enacted. If enough people become convinced that business would serve society's interests better under a plan of federal, rather than state, chartering of corporations, with perhaps labor and government representatives on the boards of directors of larger companies, that too will happen.

The difficult decisions for the manager are not with respect to behavior covered by law or regulation, even though they may have been matters that once were at the discretion of business. By far the more difficult questions involve those things a manager wants to do because they seem right—in a moral, personal, and ethical sense. The problem is to perceive what usefully can be done that is not required to be done to contribute to the broader goals of society, and to undertake early and in good faith those things that society may later feel business was remiss in not undertaking. And while doing all of this, you will have to remember that your primary responsibility as a general manager is to maintain the economic health of the corporation. Actions undertaken for reasons of corporate responsibility that severely affect the economic capacity of the enterprise to furnish employment and provide goods and services are not likely to be a net benefit to the society, let alone the shareholders.

Two trends seem evident. First, the public is coming to expect more of business enterprises than the traditional economic role that they have played in the past. Even though business may not be the cause of many of the shortcomings of our society, their resources are increasingly being viewed as available to help solve problems such as those of the disadvantaged minorities, the decaying cities, and the protection of the environment.

Second, it is clear that matters that once could be decided by managements based largely on their own personal values and sense of fairness have in many cases become regarded by the public as a responsibility of the corporation, and these in turn have become the subject of law or regulation in instances where it has been felt that corporations were not living up to their responsibilities. In a sense, many of our laws and regulations can be considered the result of someone not living up to the responsibilities society thinks appropriate.

LEGITIMACY OF POWER

In the preceding pages we have been concerned primarily with the proper exercise of corporate power, as interpreted by the broader public or significant segments of it, as opposed to the legitimacy of that power. No solution has as yet been found to the basic dilemma argued by Carl Kaysen that corporate power is irresponsible, not necessarily because of the exercise of that power in any specific decisions or the motives of management but because those affected greatly by those decisions—employees, the community, and even the stockholders—very often have little or no real voice in the making of those decisions.[2] There have been many efforts to remedy this situation, with attempts to influence management via the media, university investment policies, shareholders' meetings, and so on being perhaps the most common and most visible. That most of these are in Kaysen's sense still irresponsible should be evident; the problem of legitimacy remains.

A more fundamental approach to the problem of corporate governance and therefore the legitimacy of the power that corporations have has been underway for some time by the SEC and others with their attempts to change the composition of boards of directors to include more members "independent of management." Some plans include provision for the election or appointment of directors to represent special interests such as "the community" or "the public" or "the employees," but these proposals have incurred considerable opposition on legal, philosophical, and practical grounds. The SEC has been aggressively expanding the responsibilities and personal liabilities of the directors for corporate misdeeds, however, and this trend will surely continue.

TO WHOM AM I RESPONSIBLE, AND FOR WHAT?

The manager cannot avoid facing the basic question "To whom am I responsible, and for what?" If you decide no one other than stockholders in terms of economic performance, even though within the requirements of the law, you will be doing less than most of us personally would like to do, and less than could be expected of any healthy corporation. If you listen to and follow all who would put a claim on the company's resources and skills, the result is sure to be disastrous for the economic well-being of the company.

For the present, and even for the foreseeable future, there is no theory that will help you make decisions with regard to corporate responsibilities that would satisfy both those who cling to traditional legal and economic doctrines and those who view the corporation as an instrument of society available to help society achieve much more than the traditional economic goals. To help you achieve a proper balance in these matters is one of the goals of a professional education. We believe a strategy which does not make any allowance for the pressures that exist and that will be brought to bear in the broad field of corporate responsibility, as it pertains to that particular company, industry, or community, runs the risk of being deficient by purely economic standards.

More important, we feel it may not take advantage of the opportunities private enterprise does have to make a contribution to the quality of life beyond what is required by current law, practice, or the threat of proposed legislation. If management is to have any valid claim to being a profession, its members need to develop a set of personal standards and attitudes regarded as worthy by the broader society. Knowledge and skills and techniques directed at achieving economic goals—which are so much easier to teach and to learn—will not alone equip you to make the decisions in the area of corporate responsibilities that you will ultimately have to decide for yourself. To attempt to do good while also doing well is neither an illegal nor unattainable goal.

The Job of General Manager: Perspective, Function, Role, and Skills

CASE 1

Sturm, Ruger & Company, Inc.*

Founded in 1949, Sturm, Ruger & Company, Inc., had sales of $19.5 million in 1973 and was an acknowledged leader in the design and manufacture of quality target shooting and hunting firearms. At its headquarters in Southport, Connecticut, and a manufacturing facility in Newport, New Hampshire, the company produced both handguns and long-guns for consumers in the United States, Canada, and some foreign countries. Over the period 1968–73, sales and earnings had increased at compound rates of 16.6 percent and 13.8 percent, respectively, and net profit margins had averaged 14.7 percent for the same period. (For additional financial information, see Exhibits 1, 2, and 3.)

In September 1974, as he assessed the future for his company, William Ruger, president and chairman of the board, reflected on the performance of Sturm, Ruger & Company:

> I think of this company as a composite whole, or picture, which includes design, customers, employees, engineering, and manufacturing. It is a picture that I have painted, and I think it's a perfect picture of a model company. It has made money honestly, provided for its employees, advanced the technology of the industry, and continued to grow and be profitable. If anything, these are the standards by which a company should be judged. The most important of all these criteria is that we have been profitable, and that's been a plus for everyone involved. But deep down inside, it also makes me feel very good to know that we've designed some damn beautiful firearms.

Even as Mr. Ruger reflected on the past performance of Sturm, Ruger,

---

* This case was made possible by the cooperation of Sturm, Ruger & Company, Inc. Copyright © 1974 by the President and Fellows of Harvard College. Harvard Business School case 9–375–114. Reproduced by permission.

69

EXHIBIT 1: Profit and loss data for the years 1949–1973

Year	Net Sales Amount	%	Cost of Goods Sold Amount	%	Gross Profit Amount	%	Selling Amount	General and Administrative Amount	Total Amount	%	Other Inc. (exp.)	Profit before Taxes Amount	%	Taxes Amount	%	Net Profit Amount	%
1949	$ 29	100	$ 35	—	$ (6)	—	$ 7	$ 9	$ 16	—	(1)	$ (22)	—	$ —	—	$ (23)	—
1950	206	100	125	60.7	81	39.3	13	23	36	17.5	(1)	44	21.4	6	3.0	38	18.4
1951	368	100	214	58.2	154	41.8	33	39	72	19.5	(3)	79	21.5	42	11.4	37	10.1
1952	427	100	240	56.3	187	43.7	45	42	87	20.4	1	101	23.6	59	13.8	41	9.8
1953	535	100	303	56.6	232	43.4	51	44	95	17.9	—	137	25.5	87	16.3	49	9.2
1954	802	100	460	57.4	342	42.6	60	46	106	13.2	—	236	29.4	122	15.2	114	14.2
1955	1,297	100	786	60.6	511	39.4	83	73	156	12.0	(2)	353	27.2	188	14.5	165	12.7
1956	1,849	100	960	51.9	889	48.1	107	79	186	10.1	(2)	701	37.9	374	20.1	327	17.7
1957	2,509	100	1,293	51.5	1,216	48.5	144	92	236	9.4	5	985	39.2	525	20.9	460	18.3
1958	2,562	100	1,341	52.3	1,221	47.7	167	101	268	10.4	4	957	37.4	509	19.9	448	17.5
1959	2,938	100	1,493	50.8	1,445	49.2	182	141	323	11.0	8	1,130	38.4	602	20.5	527	17.9
1960	2,742	100	1,536	56.0	1,206	44.0	215	162	377	13.8	10	839	30.6	446	16.3	393	14.3
1961	2,581	100	1,491	57.8	1,090	42.2	298	97	395	15.3	(33)	662	25.6	357	13.8	305	11.8
1962	3,474	100	2,098	60.4	1,376	39.6	286	87	373	10.7	(29)	974	28.0	526	15.1	448	12.9
1963	3,713	100	2,176	58.6	1,536	41.4	312	112	424	11.4	(12)	1,100	29.7	591	15.9	509	13.7
1964	4,121	100	2,478	60.1	1,643	39.9	343	107	450	10.9	(54)	1,139	27.6	587	14.2	551	13.4
1965	5,797	100	3,319	57.2	2,478	42.8	354	183	534	9.2	(36)	1,980	34.2	980	16.9	1,001	17.3
1966	6,023	100	3,490	57.9	2,533	41.1	370	196	566	9.4	63	2,030	33.7	997	16.5	1,003	17.2
1967	7,595	100	4,359	57.4	3,236	42.6	447	228	675	8.9	69	2,630	34.6	1,268	16.7	1,362	17.9
1968	9,068	100	5,364	59.1	3,704	40.9	515	283	798	8.8	63	2,969	32.7	1,568	17.3	1,401	15.4
1969	11,090	100	5,968	53.8	5,122	46.2	631	315	946	8.5	30	4,206	37.9	2,246	20.2	1,960	17.7
1970	12,789	100	6,956	54.4	5,833	45.6	886	296	1,182	9.2	27	4,678	36.6	2,452	19.2	2,226	17.4
1971	13,318	100	9,064	68.1	4,254	31.9	1,050	347	1,397	10.4	45	2,902	21.8	1,440	10.8	1,462	11.0
1972	16,183	100	10,510	65.0	5,673	35.0	1,151	407	1,558	9.6	107	4,222	26.1	2,093	12.9	2,129	13.2
1973	19,542	100	12,643	64.7	6,899	35.3	1,325	490	1,815	9.3	343	5,426	27.8	2,752	14.1	2,674	13.7

Source: Company reports.

EXHIBIT 2

STURM, RUGER & COMPANY, INC.
Consolidated Balance Sheets

	December 31	
	1973	**1972**
Assets		
Current assets:		
Cash and certificates of deposit		
(1973—$4,300,000; 1972—$4,025,000).	$ 6,315,337	$5,565,565
Trade receivables, less allowance		
(1973—$25,000; 1972—$5,000)	1,050,576	1,228,826
Inventories:		
Finished products	709,981	435,105
Materials, supplies, and products in process	5,314,740	4,548,979
Total inventories	6,024,721	4,984,084
Prepaid expenses	110,294	56,340
Total current assets	13,500,928	11,834,815
Property, plant, and equipment:		
Land and improvements	405,298	319,583
Buildings	2,479,145	2,092,641
Machinery and equipment	3,413,030	2,806,755
Dies and tools	1,689,500	1,403,350
	7,986,973	6,622,329
Less: Allowances for depreciation.	3,595,523	2,996,907
Total property, plant, and equipment	4,391,450	3,625,422
Other assets:		
Deferred federal income taxes.		216,600
Cash value of life insurance.	115,175	108,359
Miscellaneous accounts	158,045	136,161
Total other assets.	273,220	461,120
Total assets	$18,165,598	$15,921,357
Liabilities and Stockholders' Equity		
Current liabilities:		
Trade accounts payable	$ 390,506	$ 252,463
Employee compensation.	276,883	220,674
Taxes, other than income taxes	100,134	99,433
Pension plan.	92,400	93,900
Federal and state income taxes	971,603	983,357
Total current liabilities	1,831,526	1,649,827
Deferred federal income taxes.	48,700	—
Stockholders' equity:		
Common stock, par value $1 a share:		
Authorized—3,500,000 shares.		
Issued and outstanding—1,651,320 shares.	1,651,320	1,651,320
Retained earnings	14,634,052	12,620,210
Total stockholders' equity	16,285,372	14,271,530
Total liabilities and stockholders' equity	$18,165,598	$15,921,357

Source: Company annual reports.

EXHIBIT 3: Financial and Statistical Highlights

Highlights	1950	1955	1960	1965	1970	1973
Net sales ($000)	$ 206	$ 1,297	$ 2,742	$ 5,797	$ 12,789	$ 19,542
Net income after taxes ($000)	38	165	393	1,001	2,226	2,674
Net income as percent of sales	18.4%	12.7%	14.3%	17.3%	17.4%	13.7%
Return on total assets	53.5%	39.4%	19.3%	23.2%	19.6%	14.7%
Number of units sold	9,147	42,589	71,111	157,827	271,040	391,863
Average sales price per unit	22.52	30.45	38.56	36.73	47.18	49.87
Average profit per unit	4.15	3.87	5.53	6.34	8.21	6.82
Total number of employees	27	62	104	153	380	694
Square feet of manufacturing space	2,220	6,844	23,192	58,129	96,714	134,000

Supplemental Data

Growth rates:	Sales	Gross Profit	Total Selling, General and Administrative	Profit before Taxes	Net Profit
1959–69	13.8%	13.5%	11.4%	13.8%	13.8%
1969–73	15.2	7.7	13.9	6.6	8.1
1972–73	20.8	21.6	16.5	28.5	25.6

Per Share Data

	Earnings	Dividends	Price Range
1969	$1.19	$0.18	$15½–$10½
1970	1.35	0.20	15 – 8¾
1971	0.89	0.20	23¼– 10
1972	1.29	0.225	18¼– 10¼
1973	1.62	0.30	12 – 6½

Source: Company reports.

he was concerned with developing and implementing the appropriate strategy to ensure the continued viability of his company in the face of potentially adverse legislation and economic circumstances. As the company's product mix was approximately two-thirds handguns, Mr. Ruger believed enactment of handgun control legislation could have a significant impact on the company's future. Although he had not completely rejected the possibility of diversifying outside of the gun industry, he had tentatively decided to prepare the company for the impact of potential handgun control laws by adding police handguns and army rifles to his product line, and shifting the product mix toward long-guns.[1]

As Mr. Ruger pondered the appropriateness of this strategy, he was also concerned with questions of greater utilization of the company's overall skills and resources, its organizational strengths and needs, and his future role in the company.

THE GUN INDUSTRY

Structure and Competition

The firearms industry was one of the oldest industries in the United States, dating back to 1798. The industry consisted of four major segments: handguns, long-arms, ammunition, and accessories. Firearms were usually divided into three categories: handguns, rifles, and shotguns.

Until fairly recently, public data on the U.S. gun industry were extremely scarce as there was no central reporting agency and many of the producing companies were privately owned.

Approximate figures for firearms sales in millions in 1973, however, were reported by the Bureau of Alcohol, Tobacco, and Firearms as shown in Exhibit 4.

In the handgun segment of the industry, the Colt Firearms Division of Colt Industries, Smith and Wesson (a division of Bangor Punta) and Sturm, Ruger & Company were the acknowledged leaders in sales. In long-guns, Remington Arms and the Winchester-Western Division of Olin Corporation were generally acknowledged as the industry leaders, followed by Savage Arms and Marlin Firearms; Winchester-Western and Remington were believed to each have approximately 24 percent of the total market share.[2]

In ammunition sales an estimated 90 percent of the market was

---

[1] Handguns, rifles, and shotguns were the three common types of civilian small arms. Handguns included both revolvers (cartridge chambers in a rotating cylinder separate from the barrel) and pistols (single chamber contiguous with the barrel) designed to be fired with one hand. Rifles and shotguns were classified as long-guns because of their longer barrels.

[2] Source: Industry data and Sporting Arms and Ammunition Manufacturers' Institute.

EXHIBIT 4: Wholesale Shipments of Firearms and Ammunition

	1973		1972	
	Millions	**Percent of Total**	**Millions**	**Percent of Total**
Pistols and revolvers	$ 86.6	21.5	$ 75.8	21
Rifles and shotguns	142.4	35.4	122.6	33.9
Ammunition	173.5	43.1	162.8	45.1
Total	$402.5	100	$361.2	100

Source: Tax records of U.S. Treasury Department—Bureau of Alcohol, Tobacco, and Firearms.

thought to be controlled by Winchester, Remington, and Federal Cartridge Company, a privately held company.[3]

Markets and Uses

The primary uses for sporting firearms were for hunting and target shooting. However, many recent sales were believed to have been motivated by fear, generally of possible burglaries, assaults, and other people with guns.

Some industry observers estimated the number of firearms in civilian hands in the United States to be in excess of 90 million.[4] Studies done for the National Commission on Violence in the late 1960s also indicated that nearly 50 percent of the approximately 60 million U.S. households owned one or more firearms (see Exhibits 5 and 6). Production by domestic manufacturers for private sale in the United States had shown a growth trend which reflected the rising demand for guns (see Exhibit 7). For fiscal year 1973, domestic and foreign gun makers produced approximately 5.7 million firearms for nonmilitary U.S. consumption; of this amount roughly 38 percent were handguns (see Exhibit 8).

EXHIBIT 5: Firearms Introduced into the U.S. Civilian Market (1899–1968) (in millions for every 10-year period)

Period	Rifles	Shotguns	Handguns	Total
1899–1948 (average)	4.7	3.2	2.7	10.6
1949–1958	6.4	9.4	4.2	20.0
1959–1968	9.6	9.4	10.2	29.2
Accumulated total	39.5	34.9	27.9	102.3

Source: Staff report to National Commission on Causes and Prevention of Violence.

---

[3] Source: Sporting Arms and Ammunition Manufacturers' Institute.

[4] Source: Staff report to National Commission on Causes and Prevention of Violence, 1969.

EXHIBIT 6

A. Percentage of U.S. Households with Firearms by City Size

	Rural	Towns	Suburbs	Large Cities
Handguns	19	22	16	21
Rifles	42	29	25	21
Shotguns	53	36	26	18

B. Percentage of U.S. Households Owning Firearms by Region

	East	South	Midwest	West	Total U.S.
Handguns	15	18	20	29	20
Rifles	22	35	26	36	29
Shotguns	18	42	40	29	33
Any firearms*	33	59	51	49	49

* Any firearm = households having any firearm at all.

Source: 1968 Harris Poll.

EXHIBIT 7: Annual Growth of Domestic Firearms Production

	Handguns (percent)	Rifles (percent)	Shotguns (percent)	Total All Firearms (percent)
1960–65	7	11.0	9.8	9.3
1965–68	23	11.8	8.7	14.3
1960–68	13	11.2	9.4	11.2

Source: Staff report to National Commission on Causes and Prevention of Violence.

EXHIBIT 8: Firearms Available for U.S. Domestic Consumption in 1973 (in thousands of units)*

	Total Domestic Production	− Exports	+ Imports	= Total Available for U.S. Consumption
Pistols and revolvers	1,734	95	559	2,198
Rifles	1,830	124	195	1,901
Shotguns	1,280	60	420	1,640
Total	4,844	279	1,174	5,739

* Based on fiscal year July 1, 1972–June 30, 1973.

Source. U.S. Treasury Department—Bureau of Alcohol, Tobacco, and Firearms.

In addition to hunting and target shooting, law enforcement officers and collectors constituted a significant market for guns.

Despite its growth, many observers believed the industry faced an extremely paradoxical and potentially restrictive set of environmental conditions. As described by David Gumpert of *The Wall Street Journal:*

On the one hand, there's growing pressure to limit or outlaw entirely the private ownership of firearms. And even without legal restrictions, gun makers fear that a growing public aversion to hunting—derisively attributed by some in the industry as a "Bambi complex"—is undermining a major source of their business. At the same time, population pressures are reducing the amount of hunting land available, discouraging hunters.[5]

Gun Control Legislation

The question of gun control was one which evoked considerable emotional debate from both opponents and proponents of gun control laws. It involved such prominent individuals and organizations as Senator Edward Kennedy and Mayor Richard Daley of Chicago, on one side, and the National Rifle Association and the National Shooting Sports Foundation on the side opposing gun controls.

Although some proposed legislation was aimed at controlling all firearms, the majority was geared to curtailing the sale and dissemination of so-called Saturday Night Specials, small, concealable handguns costing $10 to $25. Many established gun manufacturers felt that these cheap handguns should be controlled as they gave the industry a bad name and were thought to be of no use for other than killing or wounding a human being. William Ruger noted:

> Often the handguns made abroad are contemptible contraptions and are unreliable and dangerous. It's the importation and assembly of these guns that has caused such adverse public reaction and led to enactment of some of the existing gun control laws.

Opponents of gun control laws stressed the constitutional right of individuals to own firearms for hunting and sporting purposes. Led by the National Rifle Association, with about one million members, opponents of gun controls consisted of a vocal and well-disciplined group of gun manufacturers, sellers, and sportsmen who used their weapons for hunting and target shooting, not for killing people.

Still, the relationship of guns and violence in the United States had provided considerable fuel for the actions of those who pushed for strong federal and state control of firearms. Many of the most outspoken proponents of gun control laws attempted to substantiate their views with data which cited the role of firearms in criminal activity (see Exhibit 9).

In spite of the controversy over gun control legislation, gun sales were expected to continue to grow. These expectations, combined with the profitability of the industry, led some public officials to make statements that many in the industry felt were rather radical and emotional. For example, Representative John M. Murphy of New York was quoted as saying:

---

[5] *The Wall Street Journal,* May 1, 1972.

Manufacturers and sellers who consider only profit divorce themselves completely from the final results of their activity. There's just no conscience on the part of these people.[6]

EXHIBIT 9: Crime and Firearms Data

Type of Crime	Number of Crimes	Percent Involving Firearms
Murder	19,510	67*
Armed robbery.	252,570	63
Aggravated assault	416,270	26

* The data also indicated that approximately 6,928 murders, or 35.5 percent of the total murders, involved handguns.

Source: 1973 Uniform Crime Reports—FBI, September 6, 1974; Crime Index Totals—Year of 1973.

HISTORY OF STURM, RUGER & COMPANY, INC.

Beginnings

Founded in 1949, Sturm, Ruger & Company, Inc., owed its existence principally to the gun designs, engineering skills, and interests of William B. Ruger, Sr. In his early childhood, Mr. Ruger had developed an interest in guns which led to the eventual founding of Sturm, Ruger. As described by Mr. Ruger.

My interest in firearms actually began when my father taught me to hold a rifle to my shoulder when I was eight or nine years old. He had a duck hunters' lodge out on Long Island, and many times he would take me out and let me shoot. These experiences stimulated my initial interest in guns. For my 11th birthday, I received a .22 rifle of my own. Mechanically, the rifle was particularly appealing to me; the fact that it could fire a bullet so fast, and hit a target so far off, was fascinating.

Also, one of the reasons I eventually went into the firearms business was because I liked the life-style the gun seemed to symbolize: the rugged, early western frontier and the outdoor sportsman. In combination with that was a driving interest in machinery and design.

As a boy, I used to go to the library and look at a book on steamboat designs and dream of making one myself. I hung around gun stores and I gained an insight into the design, mechanisms, and engineering of guns. This led me to try to design one of my own. This was a tremendous challenge for me. In view of all the limitations, finding a way of making things you want is perhaps the greatest of challenges.

You know, there are two kinds of boys: those that like baseball and those that like guns; I liked guns. When I was about 14 years old, I saw

---

[6] *The Wall Street Journal,* May 19, 1972.

an article in a magazine about a machine gun and I was awed by the simplicity of the technology, although the machine gun was really a leap forward in technology. A machine gun design played a very important role in my later life.

Although his childhood experience laid the foundation, Mr. Ruger did not become actively involved in the gun industry until 1937. After attending the University of North Carolina for two years, Mr. Ruger took a job with the War Department as a draftsman in the Springfield Armory. Although he had developed several gun designs, Mr. Ruger had had no formal training as a draftsman. He explained:

> At the time, I was 22 and really wasn't a very good draftsman. In fact, until the War Department job, I had never been inside a real drafting room. I worked there for a while but didn't stay long. When the War Department made an invitation for drawings for a new machine gun. I submitted one I had done. On the strength of that design, I got a job with the Auto Ordnance Corporation, for whom I worked all during the war. Auto Ordnance, now McGuire Industries, was famous for the Thompson submachine gun. While working for Auto Ordnance, I was one of the youngest people working and developing a real perspective on gun design.

Mr. Ruger went on to describe the events leading to the founding of Sturm, Ruger & Company, Inc.:

> I left Auto Ordnance Corporation in 1945 and was still interested in a company of my own. For about three years, I tried to make a go of a little machine shop making small parts. It began losing money and finally went into receivership in 1948. Later that same year, Alexander Sturm came to me and offered to finance me in a new company to manufacture an automatic target pistol I had designed. This .22 pistol looked something like a German Luger. The design of the gun led to low production costs, which enabled us to have a cost advantage of about 20 percent less than the then competitive models of Colt and High Standard. With the $50,000 provided by Alex Sturm, we went into production. Although this gun had some technical improvements, we would not have survived if we had not had a price advantage, since we didn't have the reputation that Colt and other gun makers had.
>
> Another important factor was timing. People had suddenly begun to become involved in hobbies and specialty interests. The war was over, the depression was over, and it was an entirely new atmosphere. In effect, the company's start couldn't have occurred at a more opportune time economically.

Priced at $37.50 (retail), this target pistol proved to be a tremendous success. In 1950 the company had net sales of $206,000 and net profits of $38,000 for a net return on sales of 18.4 percent. The company sold approximately 9,147 guns in 1950.

1950–1960

With the death of Alexander Sturm in 1951, complete responsibility for the business fell on Mr. Ruger. Over the next ten years, Mr. Ruger continued to add new handguns to his product mix. By 1961 the Sturm, Ruger product line consisted of the following small arms: the original automatic pistol, still at $37.50; a single-action .22 Western style six-gun at $54.50 to $75.50; a Blackhawk line single-action revolver, introduced in 1955 for big caliber cartridges, at $87.50 to $116; and the Bearcat .22 single-action revolver at $49.50. By 1960 sales had risen to $2.7 million and net income totaled $393,000, Mr. Ruger commented:

> After the first target pistol, our next product was a single-action Western style six-gun. This gun was the kind that the shooter had to cock the hammer after each shot. For some reason, Colt had abandoned this product, although there was a demand for it. They saw their primary market as the police and law enforcement. I thought they were out of touch with the market. I was a gun and shooting enthusiast, however, and was completely familiar with the market. I knew this gun would sell.

Mr. Ruger's calibration of the market potential proved accurate, and the company sold thousands of the handguns. According to the vice president of marketing, Edward P. Nolan, "Some were even bought by people who buckled on a six-gun to watch television Westerns."

Growth and Product Line Expansion

In 1961, with sales of its handguns approximately $2.6 million, Mr. Ruger broadened the company's product line by introducing a hunting rifle called the Deerstalker. Mr. Ruger described the development of this rifle:

> We had developed the Blackhawk revolver for the .44 magnum cartridge, which is the most powerful handgun cartridge made. As a result of the revolver, we had acquired a reputation for having the best revolver for the .44 magnum. As a hunter, I thought the .44 cartridge would make an excellent deer rifle and would appeal to hunters. There was no market research, just a gut feel that it would sell and that selling only handguns would limit the company's growth.

Enjoying considerable success with this long-gun, Sturm, Ruger added additional rifles to its product line. By 1971 the company manufactured four rifles, priced from $56.50 to $265, and six handguns, priced from $47.50 to $125.[7] Most of the company's success during this period was attributed to the intuitive approach and design skills of Mr. Ruger. One writer in *Outdoor Life,* a leading magazine for hunters and fishermen, wrote:

---

[7] Retail price.

Bill Ruger, the president of the Sturm, Ruger Company which manu-factures the Ruger firearms, has a number of things going for him. Among them he is a gun nut of the first order, a guy with a sentimental love of guns for their own sake. He is also a firearms designer who can look at a blueprint of a gun mechanism, visualize the gun, see how it works, and know how it should be manufactured.

He is attuned to the same wave-length as a considerable part of the gun-loving, gun-buying public, and he has always felt that if he was inter-ested in and liked a certain design that enough gun buyers would feel the same way to make the manufacture profitable. He is also fortunate in that he is for all practical purposes the Sturm, Ruger Company and he has no board of directors on his neck to second-guess him.

Ruger's initial success, the one that put him in business and financed other ventures in the field, was the .22 automatic pistol, which was shrewdly designed for reliable functioning, simple manufacture, and eye appeal. His next success was a single-action .22 rimfire caliber revolver. In outward appearance it was the spitting image of the old Colt Frontier revolver.

At the time Ruger began manufacture of his single action it was generally believed in the trade that the single-action revolver was dead beyond recall. When Ruger showed me the prototype of his .22 single action and asked me how I thought it would go I told him I thought it would sell like mad. Some straws were then in the wind. One was that a single-action Colt in good condition was bringing from four to six times the price it had brought new before the war.

Another was that movies and the infant TV were leaning heavily on horse operas and that in such exciting dramas the single-action revolver is a prop of prime importance.

Like many a gun nut Ruger had always admired the appearance of the . . . single action. I'm quite sure that Ruger made no consumer surveys, didn't consult his dealers and failed to test the market. If Ruger had a genius with a Ph.D. from the Harvard School of Business Administration doing market research and chained to a desk in a back room somewhere, I am sure the guy fainted when Ruger told him what he had in mind.[8]

Diversification Effort

Again reflecting Mr. Ruger's interests and skills as an engineer, the company in 1965 initiated an attempt to diversify into the automobile business. At Mr. Ruger's direction, the company undertook to design and build a working prototype of a luxury sportscar similar to the British-made 1929, 4.5 liter Bentley. The intent was to sell these cars on a limited basis, at a price of approximately $12,000–$13,000 per car.

The Ruger Tourer was designed to be a sports-touring car with a soft top and body styling of the 1929 vintage Bentley, but with a modern power plant and structural mechanics. The car was to be equipped with

[8] Jack O'Connor, *Outdoor Life*, 1967.

EXHIBIT 10

"... when cars and car makers seem to be tumbling off assembly-lines with a desperate dreary sameness, a kind of cookie-cutter uniformity, a little outrageous automotive non-conformity may be just what the doctor ordered."

It was a Bentley Vanden Plas that provided the inspiration for the Ruger Tourer. The body is double-walled fiberglass reinforced at stress and attachment points with bonded-in steel pieces. The floor, battery box are molded in as well.

Source: Reprinted from December 1970 *Motor Trends.*

a 427 V–8 Ford racer motor, sophisticated Monroe shocks, Bendix brakes, and a double-walled fiberglass body (see Exhibit 10).

In interviews with the casewriter, Mr. Ruger and Mr. Nolan, vice president, marketing, described the rationale and events leading to the company's efforts in this area. Mr. Ruger explained:

I've always been interested in cars and motorcycles since I was young. I've tinkered around with a number of cars, including Jaguars, Rolls Royces, and Ferraris. In the process, I noticed that there was a lot of overlap between guns and cars among purchasers. I felt that a well-known reputation for quality and engineering design in guns would be useful in selling a particular type of car; hopefully, the name Ruger would correlate the two. I also felt I had some insight into what people would like to have in cars. I thought we could come up with a beautifully engineered car that we could sell at a profit.

Mr. Nolan indicated the automotive project was in line with Mr. Ruger's skills and interests in engineering and design which had made the company successful in guns.

Bill had a love for engineering and design in everything, particularly cars. When we used to go to lunch and I would stop for gas, Bill would get out and look underneath the cars on the racks. After he bought one Bentley, I remembered he set up a guy in a garage to work on it. We would go to lunch and then stop by the garage afterwards; Cal always kept a second slide board, and before you knew it, Bill had his coat off and was banging around underneath the car and talking about it for hours with Cal. I started taking work with me to lunch because I knew we would wind up at the garage.

Two prototypes of the Ruger Tourer were built at a cost of approximately $400,000 for design and development. Those prototypes were displayed at various auto shows, including the New York Automobile Show, and received the attention of several widely read car magazines. In the December 1970 issue of *Motor Trend*, a feature article discussed the Ruger car and the man behind it:

Bill Ruger won't fit on anybody's bar-chart, nor will his car jibe with any bean-counter's forecast of what's happening in the world of personal transportation. He's made a fortune designing and building firearms that combine the elements of nostalgia, classical good taste and faultless function with reasonable price—and he's flown in the face of doubting "experts" and conventional wisdom at every stage of his upward climb. Therefore, it's no surprise that he's decided to build and sell a car that combines these same principles, despite the doubts and chuckling disapproval of entrenched automotive nay-sayers.

Bill Ruger, then, is not of the common herd. He is the product of another time, a different environment. He is more like the merchant-princes of the Italian Renaissance or the go-getter nobility of Victoria's reign than today's interchangeable captains of industry. His collections of art and antique arms are remarkable, and he has steeped himself in history and the classical lore of the gentle folk.

It's been remarked that nothing of redeeming social value has ever been devised in committee, and Ruger's success would seem to bear this out. His firm, Sturm, Ruger & Company, recently went public and now has a proper board of directors and all the other trappings of a modern manufacturing concern. What's more, there are a number of Ruger heirs and relations scattered through the company's hierarchy. Yet one cannot visit either of his two factories—one in Southport, Connecticut, and the other in Newport, New Hampshire—without the feeling that the company and all its products are cast exclusively in the image of William B. Ruger himself. Ayn Rand would have loved him.

In this sense, one is reminded forcefully of other, similar business enterprises headed by the likes of Ettore Bugatti and Enzo Ferrari. Ruger resembles Bugatti in the way his products are so profoundly influenced by his personal tastes and enthusiasms, and he's like Ferrari in that he's been able to make it pay handsomely.

He has owned a fair fleet of exotic automobiles over the years, and though his automotive buying habits have been quite catholic—spanning the distance from a Pontiac GTO or a Plymouth Hemi to classic Bentley and Rolls-Royces, salted liberally with Jaguars and MGs and God knows what else—his true loves are more sharply defined. For instance, right now he owns three Ferraris, a Land Rover, a Mercedes-Benz 6.3 sedan (for his wife) and a 4.5 liter Bentley Vanden Plas tourer built in 1929.

Over the eight-year period from 1965–73, the company attempted to assess the realistic potential for the Ruger car. These efforts included the preparation of an extremely comprehensive and detailed production and financial plan by Ernst and Ernst.[9] However, in 1974 the following statement appeared in the company's 1973 annual report:

> In previous reports, I have mentioned the company's automotive project with great pride and enthusiasm. During the past year we have been reassessing our position in connection with this project. After weighing all the alternatives, in view particularly of the current stringent requirements for antipollution devices and the marked trend for compact, high mileage per gallon automobiles, it was reluctantly decided to abandon this project. This is a substantial disappointment in view of the time and money expended, but our decision is undoubtedly correct.

Mr. Ruger commented to the casewriter:

> I really felt this car would sell, but unfortunately we got a very ambiguous market reception. Then there was also a mechanical problem in the steering which caused the car to drift. This blasted some confidence in the car. We finally decided to abandon the program in 1973.

STURM, RUGER & COMPANY, INC., IN 1974

Product Policy

In 1974, Sturm, Ruger manufactured several basic models of pistols, revolvers, and rifles for a variety of sporting purposes. In addition to its sporting guns, police revolvers were added to the company's product

---

[9] This plan projected required sales of approximately 180 cars per year for the company to show a profit on automobile business.

line in 1969. A program was also underway to develop and manufacture shotguns and a carbine for law enforcement and military use.

The keynotes of Mr. Ruger's product policy were design quality and purchaser utility. Mr. Ruger emphasized that his guns "appealed primarily to hunters and sportsmen who demanded exceptional performance." In the 1973 annual report to stockholders, Mr. Ruger elaborated on this subject:

> The demand for our entire range of firearms continues to be highly gratifying. These products which have achieved market leadership continue to grow in popularity, while our newer products appear to be rapidly gaining the recognition we hoped for.
>
> Our products are engineered and produced to the highest possible standards of quality and performance. It is, therefore, not surprising that we have a growing share of the market for firearms, and that we have enthusiastic supporters among all categories of users. Our identification with quality manufacturing and unique engineering capability is the result of 20 years of constant effort.

All of the company's guns were sold under the name "Ruger," and while they were not subject to annual design change, the company's policy was to strive for product improvements. Many of the guns were available in varying models for different cartridge calibers, ranging from .22 caliber to .44 magnum and .458 magnum. Some were also manufactured in such special finishes as stainless steel to appeal to particular market segments or geographic areas, for example, gun collectors, performers, and/or to individuals in areas where heat and humidity were a problem.

Handguns.   Pistols and revolvers accounted for approximately 62 percent of the company's sales in 1973 (see Exhibit 11). In total, 248,337 units were sold for an average manufacturer's price of $48.85 in 1973. Distributor pricing ranged from $34.80 to $84.95. The basic retail prices ranged from $61.75 for a standard target pistol to $152.50 for a Security-Six Stainless Steel Magnum.

Rifles.   Rifles and carbines accounted for roughly 34 percent of the company's 1973 sales. The company sold 143,526 of the four basic models in 1973. Prices to distributors ranged from $40.93 to $148.02. The basic retail price ranged from $66 for a .22 rifle to $265 for a Number One Single Shot Rifle (see Exhibit 12).

In addition to guns, Sturm, Ruger also sold component parts and accessories for and with its guns. These included extra revolver cylinders, magazines for selected rifles and pistols, telescope mounting rings, and panels for handguns. Sales of these accessories and related services accounted for approximately 4 percent of total revenues and amounted to $791,128 in 1973.

EXHIBIT 11

Product Breakdown

	1969 (in thousands of dollars)	1970 (in thousands of dollars)	1971 (in thousands of dollars)	1972 (in thousands of dollars)	1973 (in thousands of dollars)
Handguns:					
Sales	$7,768	$9,375	$8,813	$10,621	$12,132
Percent total sales	70%	73%	66%	66%	62%
Income before taxes	$3,464	$4,002	$3,283	$ 3,501	$ 3,995
Percent total income before taxes	82%	86%	113%	83%	74%
Rifles:					
Sales	$3,062	$3,074	$3,896	$ 4,913	$ 6,618
Percent total sales	28%	24%	29%	30%	34%
Income before taxes	$ 611	$ 527	$ (538)	$ 431	$ 1,058
Percent total income before taxes	15%	11%	(19%)	10%	19%
Parts and service:					
Sales	$ 260	$ 340	$ 609	$ 649	$ 791
Percent total sales	2%	3%	5%	4%	4%
Income before taxes	$ 132	$ 149	$ 158	$ 290	$ 382
Percent total income before taxes	3%	3%	6%	7%	7%

STURM, RUGER & COMPANY, INC.
Pine Tree Castings Division
Profit and Loss Statement

	Six Months Ended June 30, 1973	Six Months Ended June 30, 1974
Net sales	$2,101,459	$2,304,409
Cost of goods sold	930,513	1,104,264
Operating profit	1,170,946	1,200,145
Expenses:		
Selling	$ 10,938	16,611
General and administrative	11,460	13,542
Total expenses	22,398	30,153
Income (loss) before taxes	$1,148,548	$1,169,992

Marketing

Sturm, Ruger competed, through one or more of its various models, with the active domestic and foreign arms industry. Most of its competitors, such as Colt, Remington, Savage, and Winchester, were older, larger, and better known, but Mr. Ruger stressed that his company sought to compete by concentrating on limited lines of high-quality products and building unique qualities into his guns. Although Mr. Ruger believed

EXHIBIT 12: Models and Prices of Ruger Firearms*

	Suggested Retail Price List	Dealer Price (tax inc.)	Net Distributor Price	Distributor Price (fed. tax inc.)

Pistols:

1. Standard model: This was the company's original product and was designed for target shooting and small game hunting.

	Suggested Retail Price List	Dealer Price (tax inc.)	Net Distributor Price	Distributor Price (fed. tax inc.)
Lowest priced model . .	$61.75	$46.93	$34.80	$38.28
Highest priced model . .	66.90	50.84	37.70	41.47

2. Mark 1 target model: A refined version of the standard model and was intended for formal, competitive target shooting.

Lowest priced model . .	$78.50	$59.66	$44.24	$48.66
Highest priced model . .	83.45	63.42	47.03	51.73

Revolvers:

3. New model super Single-Six: Designed in 1952, it was modeled after the .45 caliber Colt Army model of 1873 and was intended to capture the flavor of the Old West. Intended for use as an informal target or hunting gun, the Single-Six was the most expensive single-action .22 on the market. When sold with an extra cylinder for the use of .22 magnum cartridge, it was called the Single-Six Convertible.

Lowest priced model . .	$ 92.25	$ 71.30	$53.34	$58.55
Highest priced model . .	143.85	111.20	83.00	91.30

4. New model Blackhawk: Blackhawk revolvers were essentially enlarged Single-Six revolvers and were made for the most powerful handgun cartridge available, such as the .357 magnum, the .44 magnum, .41 magnum, and the .30 caliber cartridge. These guns were intended for informal target shooting and hunting.

Lowest priced model . .	$119.75	$ 91.01	$67.49	$74.24
Highest priced model . .	148.50	112.86	83.69	92.06

5. Security-Six—Double Action: These weapons were designed for police and law enforcement use.

Lowest priced model . .	$102.00	$ 77.52	$57.49	$63.24
Highest priced model . .	152.50	115.90	85.95	94.55

6. Speed-Six—Double Action: A smaller, lighter revolver, the Speed-Six was intended for use in police work.

Lowest priced model . .	$102.00	$ 77.52	$57.49	$63.24
Highest priced model . .	120.00	91.20	67.63	74.39

7. Old Army (Cap & Ball): This firearm was intended for target shooting and hunting.

Lowest priced model . .	$125.00	$ 95.00	$70.45	$77.50
Highest priced model . .	140.00	106.40	78.90	86.79

Rifles:

8. Model 10/22: Purported to be one of the most popular .22 rifles on the market, the 10/22 was intended for use in informal target shooting and small game hunting.

Lowest priced model . .	$66.00	$ 49.50	$36.87	$40.93
Highest priced model . .	77.50	56.58	42.18	46.82

9. Model .44 carbine: A short, light self-loading firearm, the .44 magnum carbine was designed particularly for deer hunting in heavily wooded areas.

Lowest priced model . .	$131.56	$ 99.94	$73.44	$81.52
Highest priced model . .	134.50	102.22	75.12	83.38

* Prices shown are for highest priced and lowest priced guns of each model. Other models with variations such as longer barrels, walnut panels, or stainless steel were available at prices within the two price limits.

EXHIBIT 12 *(concluded)*

	Suggested Retail Price List	Dealer Price (tax inc.)	Net Distributor Price	Distributor Price (fed. tax inc.)
10. M77 bolt action: The M77 was designed primarily for large game hunting.				
Lowest priced model . .	$193.00	$144.75	$107.79	$119.65
Highest priced model . .	278.30	208.73	155.43	172.53
11. Single-shot rifle: Conceived as a luxury product, the single shot was a high-powered rifle meeting a wide range of requirements including hunting and target shooting.				
Lowest priced model . .	$165.00	$123.75	$ 92.16	$102.30
Highest priced model . .	265.00	198.75	148.02	164.30

Source: Company's distributor price list.

that pricing was often competitive, he indicated that price was not a major factor for many of his guns:

> Some of our models are price competitive, but many have unique qualities which enable us to get a premium price. For example, in our single-shot rifle, we have no major competitors, so competitive pricing is not a prime factor and we peg the price up considerably more than we do with a high volume product like our 10/22.

The company sold its products throughout the United States, Canada, and several other countries. Management, however, estimated that foreign sales represented less than 10 percent of the company's business. According to Mr. Ruger, foreign sales had considerable potential in spite of the company's relatively small share of foreign sales. As he explained:

> In foreign markets, we are almost unknown, although foreign governments and law enforcement groups prefer American revolvers. To my knowledge, there is no quality revolver made in Europe, so there is little foreign competition. Primary competition in foreign markets would come from Smith and Wesson, which is selling a lot of revolvers abroad and is quite well known.

Sales of the company's product were promoted by advertising in national magazines and assorted firearms specialty magazines, for example, *Outdoor Life,* the *Rifleman,* and *Field and Stream.* Mr. Nolan, vice president, marketing, indicated that approximately $250,000 was spent on advertising in 1973 to keep the ultimate consumer familiar with Ruger guns.

Because the company's firearms were used primarily for hunting and target shooting, sales records indicated that sales tended to be highest in nonurban areas and in the Southeast and Southwest. Rifle sales were greatest in the period from July to November in anticipation of the fall hunting seasons, while handgun sales were fairly constant throughout the year. A one-year warranty against defective materials and workmanship was extended to retail purchasers of all its products. Through 1973,

Sturm, Ruger had not been required to expend material amounts of money as a result of warranty claims. Mr. Nolan commented:

> We emphasize service and quality, and there is a place in this industry for a company with good service. We also make a better product, and at a better price than the competition.

Mr. Nolan, who had joined the company in 1956 when the company's sales approximated $1.8 million, went on to state:

> Year in and year out, the market for guns is pretty static. I would estimate that the total market for guns is about 15 million people. If we are to grow in this static market, we have to win some market share away from competition.
>
> Because of this static market, I think our future is definitely in long-guns. In fact, our sales ratio has begun to change slightly; for the first six months of 1974 ending in June, our sales mix was roughly 54 percent handguns versus 46 percent for rifles, compared to a ratio of about 64 percent for handguns the previous year. That's a major shift. Keep in mind our total sales were up.

Distribution and Sales

Distribution of the company's products was accomplished through a group of approximately 160 wholesale distributors in 43 states. These distributors varied in size from an organization with one salesperson in the field to an organization with over 300 salespersons calling on retailers. Approximately 48 percent of the distributors were hardware specialists, 26 percent were sporting goods distributors, and the remaining 26 percent were composed of firearms specialty distributors and chain stores. These distributors supplied several thousand retailers. The company did not sell directly to retailers nor to the ultimate user, directly or by mail order. No salespersons or field representatives were employed by the company. Contact with the distributors was maintained by correspondence, telephone, and personal visits by company executives.

At the beginning of each year, Sturm, Ruger requested "firm" annual orders from its distributors, although the company usually allowed them to reasonably adjust their orders throughout the year. At the end of the year, Sturm, Ruger canceled all outstanding unfilled orders and asked the distributors to place new orders. The company's outstanding unfilled orders from dealers/distributors on March 1, 1974, were $37,651,000 as compared to approximately $21,599,000 on March 1, 1973. Management indicated that the company would be able to produce and ship a large part of these orders during 1974, but not all. It was also management's belief that 10 percent to 15 percent of these orders were inflated as customers wanted to ensure receiving an adequate supply of Ruger guns.

New Markets

Mr. Ruger had decided to develop several new products for new markets in light of several environmental and market trends. In 1969 the company had introduced a revolver designed for law enforcement use (Exhibit 13). Development and marketing of a shotgun and a police/military firearm were also underway, with the latter two products scheduled for introduction in 1974. The shotgun was expected to retail at about $400 with roughly 60 percent going to Sturm, Ruger. John Kingsley, executive vice president, indicated that the company had high hopes for its shotgun and that as many as 50,000 units might be sold over a two- to three-year period after initial introduction. Mr. Ruger indicated that the marketing of the police revolver posed some new problems for the company. He stated:

> We put out our first police revolver in the late 1960s. Ed Nolan had come to me and said "Let's put out one." We did so, but it's just starting to become a significant contributor to our sales. The cost of the product is high so that the product is less profitable. The police revolver line presently constitutes less than 10 percent of our business.
>
> We have to approach the law enforcement market and government market differently than we do the consumer market. With consumers, you are involved with many buyers, with many different tastes, often looking for unique and new products. In the law enforcement and government market, we have to deal with purchasing agents who want items they are familiar with. They are not interested in new and innovative products. These markets, however, can produce large sales. Our strategy will have to be to seek an opportunity to see technical purchasers and attempt to familiarize them with our guns before bids are given out. Then when we submit a bid, our products won't be new to the purchasing agent.

Development of these products had also been influenced by some concern with the possible threat of gun control legislation. Mr. Ruger discussed his concerns:

> There is a lot of talk about gun controls, but the real question is whether laws will make it more difficult for individuals to own firearms. Unfortunately, the trend is for people to be more and more supervised by government, which is a personal abbreviation of personal liberties. There's an old saying that "a country that would pass a law like Prohibition can't be trusted." Democracy, I'm afraid, is an unpredictable beast. All of this has given rise to a slight fear on my part that we might be legislated out of business. Enactment of laws like those *requiring* people to fasten seat belts before they can drive their cars suggests that a bureaucratic process might develop a restriction on firearms.
>
> I still regard firearms legislation as remote. People do want the right to defend themselves, and they have a right, a God-given right, to do so. Still, we have begun to diversify our product line so that the focus of gun control will not completely dominate our sales. We have moved rather

EXHIBIT 13

RUGER®
SECURITY-SIX®
DOUBLE ACTION REVOLVER

CROSS SECTION VIEW

FIELD-STRIPPED VIEW

STURM, RUGER & CO., INC.
Southport, Connecticut, U.S.A.

© 1972 STURM, RUGER & CO., INC.

quickly but carefully to develop the shotgun and the Mini 14, which is a Ruger version of the Army M14 rifle. What we want to do is have our long-guns successful but have our handguns continue to grow. Therefore, if our handgun business were lost, it would cause some problem to shrink this company, but we would still have a strong position in long-guns.

Mr. Nolan also commented on this issue:

Legislation would have definite impact on our industry, but as long as we continue to make a quality product, the world will still want our guns.

Overall, I am very optimistic and realistic about our future growth and rate of growth. We are still young and unknown by millions of people who buy guns. We're young and ambitious, and we make decisions our large and lethargic competitors can't make because of committees. They also don't innovate or have a Bill Ruger.

We can march into areas that companies already make guns for, because if Bill Ruger makes it, everyone knows it will be good. We're presently making a film about Bill because when Bill has finished designing, he will have contributed more to the state of the art and exceeded the productivity of John Browning or any other gun designer.

Mr. Ruger also stated:

We have done nothing to frustrate gun control laws other than to testify against some which purported to control guns but also abbreviated the right of citizens to own guns. Unfortunately, most of these proposals don't have an effective screening mechanism to differentiate between the criminal and the responsible citizen. As a shooter, I also oppose proposals that would give local police chiefs discretionary authority on the issuance of firearm permits; they are simply not trained to do this and end up denying permits to everyone.

Research and Development

During fiscal 1973, Sturm, Ruger spent approximately $146,664 on material research activities relating to the development of new products and the improvements of existing products. Approximately four employees engaged in research and development activities, but it was generally acknowledged that Mr. Ruger was an integral part of the company's design, engineering, and research activities. All work was conducted under his personal supervision. Research expenditures were charged to expense in the year incurred. Mr. Kingsley, executive vice president, indicated "that R&D had generally been less than 2 percent of sales."

Primarily through Mr. Ruger's efforts, the company owned approximately 20 patents and trademarks. Management indicated that none of these patents were considered basic to any important product or manufacturing process of the company.

Production and Manufacturing

Manufacturing of the company's guns took place in its plant facilities in Southport, Connecticut, and Newport, New Hampshire. The Southport plant contained approximately 33,000 square feet on the ground floor, of which approximately 26,000 square feet was devoted to manufacturing operations and the balance was used for office, shipping, and warehousing facilities. The plant was located on a 2⅓-acre site near the Connecticut Turnpike. During 1970 a second story was added, giving approximately 2,200 square feet of office and design space.

In a tour of the Southport headquarters and plant, the casewriter observed that the plant appeared to be fully utilized. Many offices looked out onto the shop floor, which was clean, well organized, and crowded. There appeared to be little room for expansion unless the employee parking lot was eliminated.

The Newport plant, located on 8½ acres of land, contained approximately 114,000 square feet, of which approximately 6,000 square feet was office, shipping, and warehouse space. Approximately 40,000 square feet of the building was occupied by the company's Pine Tree Castings Division which manufactured steel investment castings. Approximately 4 acres of land had been acquired in the rear of the plant for expansion, and an additional 60,000 square foot manufacturing plant was scheduled for completion by the end of 1974 to handle expected demand for the shotgun and other new products.

Many of the parts used in the company's products were readily available from several outside suppliers. The company purchased a great majority of its rifle barrels, but equipment to produce a portion of this requirement had been installed at the Newport plant, and some barrels were produced there. The company produced its own walnut and other wood stocks in its woodshop in the New Hampshire plant. The wood used was purchased from several domestic suppliers.

Mr. Ruger indicated that the company's production methods and facilities were probably the equal of any in the industry. He was supported in this assertion by an article in *The Wall Street Journal* which described Sturm, Ruger's manufacturing operation:

> Production methods have also changed relatively little over the years, remaining highly dependent on hand labor with little automation. The gun industry "has tended to be a little slower than other industries to change," says William Ruger, president of Sturm, Ruger.
>
> Indeed, there isn't even a moving assembly line in Ruger's Southport plant. In one area, machinists and other technicians turn out gun frames and other parts. Elsewhere, men seated at tables spread out batches of parts and assemble them into complete revolvers. In a small room off to one side, the weapons are test-fired on a miniature target range by two men wearing soundproof earmuffs.[10]

---

[10] *The Wall Street Journal,* May 31, 1972.

The Pine Tree Castings Division, formerly a subsidiary, produced high-quality steel investment castings for use in the firm's guns. Although 90 percent of the division's output was consumed by Sturm, Ruger, management felt that Pine Tree had the capability to develop substantial outside business. One view was expressed by Mr. Kingsley:

> Our Pine Tree operation is an excellent opportunity for diversification. This operation makes plumbing valves, firearms components, and metal pieces of all sizes and shapes. Although only 10 percent of Pine Tree's output presently goes to the outside, I would like to see Pine Tree do 50 percent of its sales with outside customers.
>
> Although coordination and integration is somewhat of a current problem, I don't think a major management restructuring will be required to expand Pine Tree's operation. However, our management structure is pretty thin now. Bill's philosophy has always been to have as low overhead as possible and try to put as much personnel as possible on the production side.

Mr. Ruger also commented:

> Our Pine Tree Castings Division offers a range of diversification possibilities. It can manufacture plumbing valves, high-strength metal parts, bits for bridles, and hardware for saddles. Boats, for example, also have created a demand for equipment made of stainless steel and investment castings.
>
> The big question with our Pine Tree situation is the need to develop a strong marketing and sales organization. We currently use sales reps, and our outside orders are rather informal. In fact, it's basically a New England market. In the long run we are going to have to develop a national sales force if we are going to build a substantial outside market for Pine Tree. We might even have local sales offices or even go the route of having multiple plants.

Finance

The initial financing of Sturm, Ruger & Company, Inc., had been $50,000 provided by Alexander Sturm. By year-end fiscal 1973, retained earnings accumulated throughout the years had built the net worth to $16,285,372.

In September 1974, Sturm, Ruger had approximately 900 stockholders as a result of a public offering in 1969. This public offering resulted in the sale of a total of 330,264 shares to the public at a price of $14 per share, with net proceeds to the selling stockholders of $13.05 per share. Mr. Ruger sold 264,000 shares, and the daughter of his deceased partner sold 66,264 shares. As explained by Mr. Ruger, the decision to make a public offering in 1969 was influenced by other alternatives.

> In 1968 I was approached by a major conglomerate who offered me $28 million for the company. At that time I owned 1,320,000 shares, or about 80 percent of the outstanding shares; the other 20 percent was owned by Joanna Sturm. I considered this offer, which was basically a stock deal,

and would have been based on bottom line and volumes performance for a specified period, but the alternative was to go public. I chose the latter alternative since it enabled me personally to diversify my assets. After the public offering, I didn't have all my own eggs in one basket and I was still free to operate the company with my own philosophy.

As of September 18, 1974, the company's stock was traded in the over-the-counter (OTC) market at a selling price of 6¾ bid, 7¾ asked.[11] Mr. Ruger owned approximately 906,000 shares out of a total of 1,651,320 shares outstanding; an additional 50,000 shares were owned by William Ruger, Jr.

Commenting on the company's financial posture, Mr. Kingsley noted:

> We've been fortunate to not have to use any outside financing, and in the future we plan to finance our expansion internally. A key to this will be our ability to manage our inventories more judiciously. I think, however, we can grow and still maintain our net profit margins at about 15 percent of sales.

Personnel

In 1973 the company employed approximately 250 persons in its Southport plant, 356 in the Newport plant, and 88 in its Pine Tree Castings Division. Approximately six of the individuals at the Southport headquarters and three at the Newport facility were listed as "executive."

None of the employees of the company or of Pine Tree were represented by a labor union, although a union drive had been attempted during the summer of 1974. The scheduled elections were never held. Mr. Ruger commented on the company's labor relations policies:

> On three occasions, unions have tried to organize our shop, I must admit, I've always felt that if a union came in, I would take it personally, as it would mean I had been a little foolish and had done something wrong. I've always felt that men should work hard and be paid well without the need for a union.
>
> We just had a union drive, but the union backed down before the election. Our campaign against the union was not really a campaign; it was sort of a review of our labor relations in the past. We basically argued that we have a proven record.

Management and Organization

Although no organization chart existed, the casewriter learned that the key managers and executives at the Southport headquarters reported directly to Mr. Ruger; these included the executive vice president, the

---

[11] *The Wall Street Journal,* September 19, 1974.

vice president of marketing, and the vice president of manufacturing of the Southport operation. Also reporting directly to Mr. Ruger were the vice presidents of sales for the Pine Tree Castings Division and of manufacturing at the Newport plant. Mr. Ruger and other members of management indicated that he deeply involved himself in all aspects of the company's operations.

The executive vice president, John Kingsley, had joined the company in 1971 after serving as a consultant to Mr. Ruger. Mr. Ruger indicated that Mr. Kingsley, a Harvard MBA, and former investment banker and a CPA, was brought in to help bolster the company's management structure, particularly in finance and planning. He added:

> John came in at a particular necessary time as Walter Berger, our secretary and controller, was retiring. However, we were also a public company by then, and we needed to do things a little more openly and improve our reporting to the public. In addition to his title of executive vice president, John is primarily responsible for financial matters.

Other members of management included Edward Nolan, vice president of marketing, who had joined the company in 1956. Prior to coming to Sturm, Ruger, Mr. Nolan had been a district sales manager with Winchester. William B. Ruger, Jr., was also employed in the firm. He had formerly been the vice president of manufacturing at the Southport plant, and was now involved in other areas of the company. Mr. Ruger commented:

> Bill, Jr., now has more of a planning function in the company. This gives him an overview which he should have as he may eventually be president. My son-in-law, Steve Vogel, is also with us, and is responsible for developing government sales.

Mr. Kingsley, 42 years old, and William Ruger, Jr., 34, were both directors of the company. Other directors included William B. Ruger, Sr.; Townsend Hornor, first vice president of White, Weld and Co., Inc.; Frank L. McCann, president of Mohawk Aluminum Corporation; Norman K. Parsells, a senior partner of Marsh, Day & Calhoun; Richard Kilcullen, member of Bathe, Fowler, Lidstone, Jaffin, Pierie & Kheel; Lester A. Casler, partner of Little & Casler; and Hale Seagraves, former partner of Pennie, Edmonds, Morton, Taylor & Adams.

A VIEW TOWARD THE FUTURE

As Mr. Ruger articulated the future opportunities and potential problems for his company in 1974, he commented on the start of the company and his philosophy. When the casewriter asked what had contributed to the success of his company, Mr. Ruger replied as follows:

I think my being extremely familiar and identifying with gun enthusiasts, hunters, and sportsmen has been one very important factor. This was our market, and I have been fortunate to design guns that appealed to their technical and esthetic needs. But I've often thought about another very important factor over the years. At the time I started this company, my confidence was shaken. Everything I had tried had failed. I wasn't sure I had the qualities to be an entrepreneur. As I look back, I was perfectly qualified. I had a mix of interest, experience, and health. In my first business, I think I failed because I didn't think everything through. I had focused on the creative side of the business and not enough on the management side; both have to be of interest if you want to succeed.

You've also got to love money to be an entrepreneur. My uncle, who was on the wealthy side of my family, used to say: "The way you keep score is by how much money you make. When you see a successful company, making money, it means they are making something that people want."

Mr. Ruger indicated, however, that environmental and market circumstances posed entirely new and different problems than had been encountered by the company in the past. The most immediate threat to the company's principal business appeared to be the various pending gun laws. Mr. Ruger voiced his views and concerns as follows:

Unfortunately, politicians and newspapers who are talking about this issue don't have any knowledge of what they are talking about. Of course I think there should be some controls of maniacs and irresponsible people getting guns, but as I told the governor of New Hampshire, people should be licensed, not guns. Unfortunately, you have people like some of the editors on the *Boston Globe* who have personal biases, but their views are not universal beliefs. I and quite a few other people believe that there is some truth in those bumper stickers that say, "If guns are outlawed, only outlaws will have guns." Besides, if people didn't have guns, they would use sticks, stones, or some other instrument to injure others.

In light of these concerns, Mr. Ruger felt that broadening the company's base of products and achieving some measure of diversification was in order. Diversification, however, as seen by both Mr. Ruger and Mr. Kingsley, required some relationship to the company's skills and resources. Mr. Kingsley commented:

We have looked at a few acquisitions; for example, we recently looked at an instrument company with sales of a little over $1 million and net profits at about 10 percent. We decided not to follow through, however. If we eventually do purchase another company, it will have to have a sound and strong management team. I don't rule out some potential acquisitions, but I don't see us becoming a mini conglomerate.

Still, diversification is an issue for us. Bill considers the new Mini 14 and shotguns to be a part of our diversification. I think he's right, but I don't think the marketplace will ever change the multiple on our stock because we develop a new gun. I would basically like to see us with an earnings tripod: (1) guns; (2) castings from Pine Tree; and (3) some other type of operations, preferably metal manufacturing. I don't, for example, see us in fast foods.

Mr. Ruger also discussed the issue of acquisitions:

We have taken a concentrated look at a few companies but have never seen one that would be perfect for us. Our drive to diversify has been compromised by our need to exploit the businesses that we are in. It dawned on me during the car project that we needed to spend more time on the gun industry.

In looking at the company's future organizational needs, Mr. Kingsley made the following observations:

A key question is whether this company can be transformed from an extension of a man to a professionally managed company. Bill has been 100 percent responsible for the success of the company, and whether the company will ever reach the point where Bill Ruger is not the most important factor is an open question. With our new guns, Bill thinks that our sales will exceed $40 million in the near future. The biggest problem thus will be to take a step up the growth curve, and do so profitably.

Mr. Ruger, in speaking of the future, expressed the following thoughts:

Although we've done extremely well in guns, the gun industry won't grow dramatically. Hunting never was a mass sport. One man needs a lot of land to wander over and that land is getting pretty scarce. Technology won't influence the industry much, either, as technical innovations in this industry are few. Our own growth in guns will have to result from continually seeking increased market share, but that becomes more difficult as you get larger.

Over the long run, however, I would like to bring the company up to a point where it's well established in all areas of the gun business, including government business. I would also like to see Pine Tree with an established outside market and a good management structure. If we get much bigger, I would also like to see a little more vertical integration.

Overall, I would like to remain essentially the same company, but with twice our present sales. There might be a unique event, such as a merger with a big company, but I like my job and am proud of what I'm doing. I'm proud of this company. I think a job or a career should always have a tie-in with your interests. I could never understand how anyone could make a career of working for Procter & Gamble selling soap. With this company, I feel like an artist or writer; just because you've painted a good picture or written a good book you don't stop. It's the interest that counts. However (pointing to a picture on the wall behind him that showed barrels overflowing with dollar bills), when I get too involved in my work, that picture is there to remind me of what I'm here for.

CASE 2

Prelude Corporation

In June 1972 Prelude Corporation could look back on 12 years of pioneering in the newly developed offshore segment of the Northern lobster fishing industry (see Appendix). Having accounted for 16 percent of the offshore poundage landed in 1971, this Massachusetts company ranked as the largest single lobster producer in North America. Joseph S. Gaziano, president since 1969, looked forward to a still more dominant position and, in the long run, to further vertical integration beyond what he had already introduced:

> Basically, we're trying to revolutionize the lobster industry by applying management and technology to what has been an 18th-century cottage industry heretofore. Other companies have become giants by restructuring such commodity businesses as crab, tuna, avocados, celery, and chicken; we want to become the Procter & Gamble of the lobster business. Until we opened up the offshore resource there was no way to bring about this revolution, but now the chance is there. Furthermore, the technology and money required to fish offshore are so great that the little guy can't make out; the risks are too great. The fishing industry now is just like the automobile industry was 60 years ago; 100 companies are going to come and go, but we'll be the General Motors.
>
> We have toyed with the idea of establishing a restaurant chain featuring the Prelude lobster, similar to Black Angus or Red Coach (local chains which offer only a small selection of beef as their fare), but have never really gotten serious about it. We find we have enough to manage now. The Deep Deep and Wickford distribution systems, which we purchased in the past fiscal year, have given us some vertical integration.

As Mr. Gaziano voiced these expectations, Prelude hopefully saw

EXHIBIT 1: Average Monthly Company Landings per Trip (as Percentage of Fiscal 1971 Average)

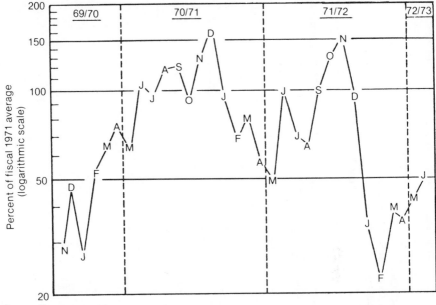

Source: Company records.

itself as starting to recover from a recent precipitous and unexplained decline in its per-trip catch (Exhibit 1). This decline had plunged the company back into the red for the fiscal year ending in April (Exhibit 2) and had raised the specter of depletion of the offshore lobster population by pollution or overfishing. Mr. Gaziano viewed these possibilities as bleak, but discounted them:

> The vessels we have are especially designed and constructed for our lobster gear and couldn't be used for any other purpose without costly refitting. I suppose we could go south into the Caribbean for crawfish or go after finfish that are amenable to the longline techniques. We could even use the vessels for research, laying cables, or as oil-survey ships. Practically speaking, if someone said tomorrow that we couldn't sell lobsters due to mercury content or some other reason, I guess we would be forced to close the doors. However, I foresee this risk as minimal. Certainly it is possible, but there are no studies or indications that this is at all a likely occurrence.[1]

---

[1] In support of his belief that depletion of the resource was unlikely, Mr. Gaziano employed a widely used argument—namely, that the average weight of offshore lobsters caught was holding steady at about 2½ pounds (with a range of 1–11 pounds or more), a fact taken to indicate that the more mature lobsters were not being fished at a rate higher than their natural replacement.

EXHIBIT 2

PRELUDE CORPORATION
Statement of Operations and Accumulated Deficit, 1967–1972
(in thousands of dollars)

Year Ended April 30

	1967	1968	1969	1970	1971	1972 (consolidated)*
Net sales	$ 128	$ 176	$ 152	$ 371	$1,511	$ 3,064
Costs and expenses:						
Vessel operations	108	161	225	445	832	1,175
Purchased seafood						1,062
Depreciation	22	23	21	68	135	253
Selling, general, and administrative†	53	90	193	249	271	265
Total costs and expenses	183	274	439	762	1,238	3,055
Income (loss) from operations	(55)	(98)	(287)	(391)	273	9
Other income (expenses)		(1)	(69)	(21)	(107)	(157)
Income (loss) before income taxes and extraordinary items	(55)	(99)	(356)	(412)	166	(148)
Provision for income taxes					84	
Income (loss) before extraordinary items	(55)	(99)	(356)	(412)	82	(148)
Extraordinary items:						
Write-down of vessels				(133)		
Credit arising from carry-forward of operating losses					72	
Net income (loss)	(55)	(99)	(356)	(545)	154	(148)
Accumulated deficit at beginning of year		(55)	(154)	(510)	1,055	(901)
Accumulated deficit at end of year	(55)	(154)	(510)	(1,055)	(901)	(1,049)
Income (loss) per share of common stock assuming full dilution	$(0.23)	(0.41)	$(1.25)	$ (1.15)	$ 0.28	$ (0.27)
Shares assumed outstanding	240	240	285	474	550	550

* Includes the results of subsidiary operations from November 1, 1971, on.
† Includes all operating costs incurred after landing, such as vehicle operations, salaries of delivery and restaurant personnel, and tank maintenance, as well as executive salaries and general overhead.

Source: Company records.

HISTORY

Prelude's predecessor company had been organized in 1960 to develop techniques for deep-sea lobster fishing. Its founder was an ordained minister, the Rev. William D. Whipple, and its name reflected Mrs. Whipple's profession—music. In the course of raising money for a company that was never in the black until 1971, Rev. Whipple had incorporated in 1966 and had arranged a private placement of 140,000 shares (58 percent of the total). This brought in $350,000, which was supplemented by debt. Late in 1968, when Rev. Whipple felt ready to start commercial operations, prospects for growth plus creditor pressure led to additional financing, some of it completed before the end of the go-go market in 1969:

Date	Financing	Amount
February 1969	250,000 common shares at $8.50	$2,125,000 gross
September 1969*	10 percent senior (John Hancock Insurance Co.) . . .	500,000
September 1969	40,000 rights at $6.75 (John Hancock)	270,000
June 1970	50,000 common shares at $3 (private placement) . .	150,000

* This financing became necessary when an expected government subsidy for fishing fleets failed to materialize.

Also during 1969, Rev. Whipple agreed to bring in Mr. Gaziano as president, and to have him put together a professional management team. The purchase of two 101-foot trawlers for $1,585,000 completed Prelude's makeready, and the year ending April 30, 1971 brought operating earnings of $273,000 from a lobster catch of 1.1 million pounds.

Spurred by this success, Prelude purchased two more ships of 96 feet and 125 feet for $1,118,000 and acquired two nearby subsidiaries in the lobster distribution business. The latter were the Wickford Shellfish Company and the distribution segment of Deep Deep Ocean Products. These would, it was hoped, reduce price fluctuations and raise margins by reducing Prelude's dependence on independent wholesalers. In the three fiscal years prior to their purchase, Wickford had had two nominal profits and one nominal loss. Deep Deep had suffered significant losses, but these were laid by management chiefly to Deep Deep's operation of three ships which Prelude did not buy—although it agreed to market their catch.[2] Prelude saw both firms as competently managed but beset by inability to raise enough capital to finance their rapidly expanding sales which were as follows:

	(thousands of dollars)			
	1969	1970	1971	1972
Wickford (years ending February 28).	—	$ 870	$1,000	$1,600
Deep Deep (years ending December 31)	$950	1,623	1,414	—

---

[2] By June 1972 one of these ships had been sold.

Both Prelude's new ships (which began fishing in July 1971 and January 1972) and its acquisitions (effected in December and January) led to additional financing:

Date	Financing	Amount
April 1971	Two ships mortgages consolidated at 1 percent above prime	$1,200,000
December 1971	Paid 17,500 common shares, valued at $7*	122,000
	for Wickford, plus cash	170,000
January 1972	Paid 22,845 common shares valued at $7 for Deep Deep distribution, plus assumption of certain liabilities	—

* According to the terms of sale, if the former owner should sell his or her stock at less than $6.50 a share, the company would pay the difference.

Still another episode in Prelude's history deserves mention because of the worldwide attention it received. In the spring of 1971, Prelude became the focus of a well-publicized international incident involving the United States and Russia. Early in the year, ships of the Russian commercial fishing fleet had caused the loss of more than $70,000 of Prelude's gear by dragging fishing nets over the bottom on which Prelude's traps were resting, clearly marked by buoys and radar reflectors. Such fixed gear had legal right-of-way, so Mr. Gaziano not only sued the Russian government for $177,000 in actual damages plus $266,000 in punitive damages but also caused a Soviet merchant ship to be attached in San Francisco. The actual out-of-court settlement was for only $89,000, but it was hailed as a precedent in commercial relations between the two countries. (See Exhibit 3 for Prelude's balance sheets for years 1971 and 1972.)

PRELUDE IN 1972

In mid-1972, Prelude was organized primarily along functional lines, with departments for operations, engineering, research, and finance and administration. Distribution functions were divided among the Deep Deep and Wickford subsidiaries (see Exhibits 4 and 5).

Operations

Fishing. Fishing operations and the logistics involved in landing and distributing the lobster catch were under the direction of Robert E. (Gene) White, age 33, vice president, operations. Prelude's four ships operated year-round on a two-week cycle, ten days fishing and four days in port for unloading and resupply. Each ship carried a crew of ten: captain, mate, engineer, cook, and six deckhands. After a 12-hour steam to the

EXHIBIT 3

PRELUDE CORPORATION
Balance Sheet
(in thousands of dollars)

	April 30	
	1971	**1972 (consolidated)**
Assets		
Current assets:		
Cash and marketable securities	$ 460	$ 253
Accounts receivable	22	243
Lobster and seafood inventories	13	62
Trapping supplies	158	323
Prepaid expenses	55	108
Total current assets	708	989
Fixed assets	2,743	3,471
Less: Accumulated depreciation	189	420
Total fixed assets	2,554	3,051
Goodwill	—	315
Total assets	$3,262	$4,355
Liabilities and Stockholders' Equity		
Current liabilities:		
Notes payable	$ —	$ 350
Current portion of long-term debt.	79	270
Accounts payable	107	257
Accrued taxes and expenses	46	75
Total current liabilities	232	952
Long-term debt.	1,616	1,857
Stockholders' equity:		
Common stock:		
Authorized—1,100,000 shares		
Issued and outstanding—569,985		
shares in 1972, 530,000 shares in 1971	265	285
Additional paid-in capital	2,065	2,325
Accumulated deficit.	(901)	(1,049)
	1,429	1,561
Less 6,200 treasury shares	15	15
Total stockholders' equity	1,414	1,546
Total liabilities and stockholders' equity	$3,262	$4,355

Source: Company records.

offshore lobster grounds, the crew would begin hauling pots 12 hours a day (see Appendix). When the lobsters were brought up and removed from the pots, their claws would be pegged with a red plastic peg which displayed the Prelude brand, and then they would be stored in the hold. The empty trap would be rebaited and stacked until the line was ready to be played out again for three days of fishing.

EXHIBIT 4: Organization Chart

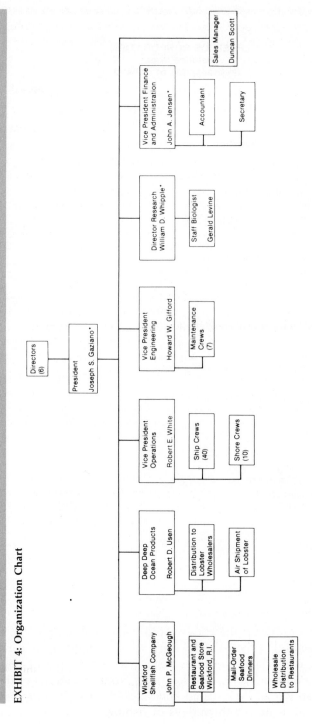

* Indicates director of corporation.
() Indicates number of personnel involved.

Source: Company records.

Whether the trawl was relaid where it had been, or in another location, was a decision made by the captain, depending very much on how the catch was running. In any event, the captain was charged with bringing in as many pounds of lobster as possible on each trip, an amount which could vary tremendously. Although Prelude's ships averaged about 20,000 pounds per trip, the results of a single trip could range from 4,000 to 40,000 pounds. (An indication of the variation in the size of the catch can be obtained from Exhibit 1.) In Mr. Gaziano's words:

> The biggest problem in the production process is the variability in the size of the catch. It is not like a manufacturing business. The size of the catch is uncertain. There is no proven way of forecasting where the lobsters will be on a given day. Mating habits, weather, and so on, are some of the many variables which determine the size of the catch. Black magic is used by the captains to find lobsters. Presently, it is an art, not a science. Actually, it is on a trial-and-error basis. If one canyon is not producing, the skipper moves to another location.

Work Force. Along with dispatching and supplying the vessels, Mr. White was responsible for staffing both the ships and Prelude's truck fleet and storage facility. These operations used 50 people who were engaged in manning the ships or moving lobster. Because Prelude was located in Westport Point, these workers were nonunion. In nearby New Bedford, where the larger portion of the fishing industry was located, unions were a predominant force. Unlike most others in the fishing industry, who were required by the union to pay their crews a straight percentage of the catch, Prelude paid a base salary plus a sum of 20 cents a pound on everything over 25,000 pounds, to be divided among the crew on a pro rata basis. Mr. White commented on some of the problems with people:

> The fisherman is an independent worker. He is always in demand and has a job waiting at his beck and call. His reputation stays with him, although references are not easy to evaluate. Since there is "always a ship leaving," he does not hesitate to tell his boss to "get screwed" if he is unhappy about something. How do you get a reference on somebody who has told his last three bosses to "get screwed"? So we end up hiring them and taking a chance based on their informal reputation, which I get from my sources in the industry. We spin our wheels on quite a few. We attempt to hire experienced fishermen, but 20 percent of our crews are bank tellers and "potato farmers" who want to try something more exciting and more financially rewarding. We start the experienced fishermen at $225 per week and the layman at $150. If the latter pans out after two or three trips, he goes to $225, also.
>
> The cook is one of the most important men on the ship. If I get a bad cook, morale goes to hell. Most ship cooks are drunks—it is just a question of whether they are good drunks or bad drunks. I try to have at least one crewman on each ship with welding expertise. This avoids having

EXHIBIT 5: Personal Data on Officers and Management Personnel

	Joseph S. Gaziano	John A. Jensen	W. D. Whipple
Title(s).	Director, president, CEO	Director, VP finance and administration	Director, director of research
Age	36	33	41
Education	MIT, BSEE, 1956 AMP programs: Harbridge House Sloan School	Babson Institute: BS/BA, 1962 MBA, 1963	Princeton, BA, 1953; Boston University School of Theology, STB *cum laude,* 1958
Previous experience	Raytheon Co., 1962–67, rising to manager, Major Space Systems Allied Research Associates, Engineering and Systems Division, 1967–69, VP and GM	U.S. Army, September 1963–February 1964 Price, Waterhouse & Co., 1964–June 1968	Owner of charter yacht business, 1954–58 Inventor and innovator in the area of fishing equipment, especially for deep-water lobster fishing, 1958–59
Date of entry . . .	January 1969, executive VP	June 1968	Founded predecessor company, 1960
Office(s) held . . .	President	VP, June 1970; director, September 1971	President, 1960–69

Note: The three outside directors were Chester A. Barrett, chairman, Merchants National Bank of New Bedford; Joshua M. Berman, partner Goodwin, Proctor and Hoar; Robert F. Goldhamer, vice president and vice chairman of the executive committee, Kidder, Peabody and Co.

Source: Company data.

to return to shore to make minor repairs. Engineers are hard to get—their education allows them to earn good money on shore and avoid the hard sea duty. Lobstering is a hard and demanding job. Guys over 40 break up after several trips.

Logistics. Since the inlet leading to Prelude's headquarters in Westport Point was not deep enough for the draft of the four ships, the company rented 225 feet of pier space at the State Pier in Fall River, about 15 miles away. Here the vessels tied up for unloading, maintenance, and resupply. The company owned and maintained a fleet of refrigerated trucks with which to transport the catch. After a returning ship had docked, the mesh baskets of pegged lobsters were lifted out of the hold

Howard W. Gifford	Robert E. White	John P. McGeough	Robert D. Usen
Vice president engineering	Vice president operations	President, Wickford Shellfish Co., Inc.	President, Deep Deep Ocean Products, Inc.
37	33	31	42
New Bedford Institute of Technology, BS	U.S. Navy Nuclear Sub School	Providence College, BS, 1962	Tufts University, BA
Electric Boat Division of General Dynamics, rising to supervisor in mechanical engineering department	U.S. Navy, 1960–69, rising to 1/C Engineman; held technical assignments, including mechanical inspection, systems, and machinery testing	Former professional football player; increased sales of Wickford almost tenfold in the five years prior to its acquisition	Over 15 years' experience in several family-owned seafood businesses, including Tabby Cat Food Company; as president had expanded this to $25 million sales volume prior to its sale Founded Deep Deep in 1968
May 1969	March 1969	December 1971	January 1972
VP, September 1971	Vice president	President of subsidiary	President of subsidiary

and into these trucks. If the catch had already been sold, the truck, driven by a member of the shore crew, began its delivery rounds immediately.

If there was an excess, however, or if it was desired to hold the catch for better prices, then the truck would make the 20-minute run to Westport Point, where the lobsters would be transferred to the Prelude holding tank. This tank, built during 1968 and 1969 at a cost of $250,000, was capable of holding 125,000 pounds of lobster in seawater cooled to 42°F. The tank was designed around an experimental system aimed at reducing handling costs by keeping the lobster in mesh baskets aboard ship and stacking these baskets in the storage tank. The system had not worked out well in practice, however, since one dead lobster could cause the loss of 10 percent to 15 percent of its tankmates within a 24-hour period. As a result, the baskets had to be hauled out and culled regularly. Prelude management felt that it they did expand their holding capacity it would be with conventional three-tier tanks which, even though they required more space and lobster handling, could be culled more efficiently and could be built for only $1 per pound of storage capacity. Security measures, both at the holding tank and on the trucks, were important since lobster was a readily marketable commodity at any roadside stand.

Engineering

Engineering activities at Prelude were under the direction of Howard W. Gifford, age 37, vice president, engineering. These activities included the maintenance and procurement of vessels and equipment, as well as the development of gear, and so on.

Maintenance. With each ship representing an investment of over $500,000 and subject to continual stress at sea, maintenance was an important and continual activity. This work was carried out by a seven-person maintenance department located at the pier in Fall River. Available there were complete facilities for the welding and machinery necessary to overhaul and repair a ship's engines, life-support equipment, and trap-handling gear. Additionally, this crew performed periodic preventative maintenance on the holding tank at Westport Point. This life-support system was particularly important since its failure, if the tank was full, would result in the loss of 125,000 pounds of lobster. Mr. Gifford was responsible for the hiring and firing of the maintenance personnel. Also, even though the ships' engineers were under the operational command of Mr. White, Mr. Gifford was responsible for their technical direction.

Purchase of Ships and Gear. Mr. Gifford was responsible for evaluating potential vessels for use as fishing platforms; writing the specifications for their conversion; and initiating, supervising, and approving their fitting out. In all these activities Mr. Gifford worked closely with Rev. Whipple in improving designs. Mr. Gifford also spent considerable time working with manufacturers' representatives on developing improved refrigeration technology for the life-support systems. The corrosive nature of the seawater, coupled with the lobster's sensitivity to trace amounts of certain metals which were traditionally used for refrigeration systems, made this a difficult area.

Research

Rev. Whipple, age 41, held the title of director of research. Since 1958 he had devoted a major portion of his time to commercial fishing and to developing a number of improvements and innovations in its equipment. Among these were a hydraulic power block and various rigging and hauling devices related to high-speed handling of deep-water lobster trapping systems.[3] Rev. Whipple was constantly evaluating the operational design of the ships' fishing gear and experimenting with ways to improve it. A qualified captain himself, Rev. Whipple would often take a ship out when a captain was sick or missing for some reason. In any case, he was generally aboard the vessel whenever there was a new idea to be tried out, a frequent occurrence.

In an effort to enhance their knowledge about the habits of the lobster, Prelude's management had recently hired a marine biologist. Mr. Gaziano remarked as follows regarding research on the "product":

> We knew a lot about management and lobster fishing when we started, but we didn't know a damn thing about the lobster. We hired Jerry (a marine biologist) to give us some expertise in this area. He started with the task of accumulating all the data he could find on the lobster. It turned out nobody really knows a heck of a lot about them. He has three current projects. One is to set up a lobster-rearing facility downstairs (corporate headquarters) and see what we can learn from that. The second project is to help us figure out what to do with the crabs we catch in our traps along with the lobsters. They are highly perishable and only bring 25 cents per pound. There is not much market for them, but since we haul them in from the sea in quantities equal to or greater than the lobsters, we would like to exploit the resource. And last, we've chartered a little research sub. Jerry's going to spend five days on the bottom seeing what really goes on down there. It's going to cost us $25,000, but we will have information that no one else has.

Marketing

Prior to the acquisition of Wickford and Deep Deep late in fiscal 1971, Prelude sold most of its catch directly to wholesale lobster dealers in large lots, usually an entire shipload. As a result, the number of transactions was limited, and Mr. Gaziano was able to handle the telephone negotiations himself. He commented on the bargaining process as follows:

> The distributor knows when you have a large catch. He may say, "You have 30,000 pounds—well, we don't really want any today," and thereby drive down the price. Even with our large holding capacity we have been caught in this situation. There are no long-term, fixed-price contracts. It is cutthroat haggling to a great degree. We are really in the commodity trading business—buy and then sell at a profit; there is very little value added.

With the acquisition of Wickford and Deep Deep, each of which owned a variety of trucks and sorting tanks of 50,000 pounds capacity,

---

[3] Although the company held design patents on certain of these mechanisms, management stated that the patents were no protection against competitors using similar but not identical equipment.

marketing arrangements had changed. The original plan was for the two acquisitions combined to handle some three fourths of Prelude's catch, although, in line with the intent to treat all three entities as profit centers, each could sell or buy where it got the best price. In any event, the Wickford and Deep Deep acquisitions happened to coincide with the precipitous drop in lobster catches, so all of Prelude's lobsters were sold "inside" during the first half of 1972.

Wickford, located in North Kingston, Rhode Island, had brought Prelude a business in live lobsters (about 70 percent of sales) and in other types of seafood, including other shellfish and frozen-fish products. It distributed these products in various ways. It had a combined retail seafood store and restaurant located in its hometown, which accounted for 30 percent of its sales; it had a mail-order business in prepackaged clam and lobster dinners; and it operated a wholesale business in a market area that extended along the Eastern seaboard south to Pennsylvania. Customers were restaurants and small dealers, whom it reached by making four delivery runs a week, locally, and to Pennsylvania, Connecticut, New York, and New Jersey.

Deep Deep, located in Boston, Massachusetts, brought Prelude a business that consisted of distributing lobsters to dealers and restaurants in New England, New York, the Midwest, West, and South, the latter three markets being served by air shipments. Deep Deep's major accounts, however, were wholesalers serving restaurants in New York City. Shipments to these accounts had to be made by common carrier, since Prelude's nonunion drivers could not gain safe access to the city's highly organized Fulton Fish Market.

Critical to selling all accounts of both companies was knowing who wanted to buy what, where, when, and at what offered price. Contacts were a marketer's paramount asset in the lobster trade. Prelude's management believed that John P. McGeough, former owner of Wickford, and Robert D. Usen, founder and ex-president of Deep Deep, were highly qualified in this regard, basing this opinion partly on a three-week cross-country trip that the financial vice president had made with Mr. Usen prior to the Deep Deep acquisition.

Both Messrs. Usen and McGeough had agreed to follow their companies into Prelude, where they continued to serve as presidents of the two subsidiaries. Here the compensation of each would be based primarily on the total profit of his unit. Although the decline in the lobster catch had prevented a full-scale testing of the two companies' performance, Prelude management indicated that their expectations had been largely fulfilled to date.

Besides bringing in Mr. Usen and Mr. McGeough, Mr. Gaziano had staffed marketing with a new sales manager, hired in November 1971. This was Duncan Scott, who had been on the road since his arrival, "cold calling" potential new distributor and restaurant accounts, and visiting old ones. Any business Mr. Scott turned up was referred to either Wickford or Deep Deep.

In still another marketing move in the spring of 1971, $15,000 had been invested in advertising on two Boston radio stations, WBZ and WHDH. This advertising was aimed at raising the ultimate consumer's awareness of Prelude's offshore lobster. Mr. Gaziano outlined the rationale behind this program:

> We are trying to establish brand identification for the Prelude lobster. We want people to ask for Prelude lobster—not just lobster—similar to the Chiquita banana strategy. Toward this end we have used radio advertising and promotional devices in the form of handouts and red plastic lobster pegs with the Prelude name etched on them. The handouts are put in our lobster shipping boxes, and Scott leaves them wherever he goes. We plan to start direct mailings. But our radio advertising was ill timed in that we didn't follow up soon enough with sales calls, and our catches were not large enough to satisfy the demand we created.

Finance and Administration

John A. Jensen, age 33, was in charge of the financial affairs of the company. In the past he had been responsible for shepherding the financial transactions required to raise needed capital. Mr. Jensen kept close tabs on the day-to-day state of affairs, maintaining an eight-week cash flow projection which he revised weekly, monitoring the daily transactions of the subsidiaries, and monitoring accounts receivable. (Restaurants and their suppliers were notoriously slow payers.)

His most current concern was centered around providing the funds needed to finance the two new ships which were planned for 1973. Exhibit 6 shows the projected income statement assuming the two new ships were added. The cost of the two vessels was estimated at $1.3 million, of which all but $300,000 could be mortgaged. Additionally, Mr. Jensen and Mr. Gaziano were concerned about the impact of interest charges on net income, interest being the main component of the fairly substantial figure carried in the operating statement as "other" income and expense (Exhibits 2 and 6). They felt that they needed a reduction in short-term debt of between $200,000 and $450,000 to clean up their balance sheet and reduce interest charges.

The company's underwriter had prepared a prospectus proposing a private placement of 100,000 to 150,000 shares of stock at $5 per share in order to secure the needed funds. Unfortunately, the release of the prospectus in March 1972 coincided with drop in the catch and the issue had had to be withdrawn.

EXHIBIT 6

PRELUDE CORPORATION
Projected Statement of Operations
(in thousands of dollars)

For Years Ending April 30

	Actual 1972	Projected 1973	Projected 1974
Sales:*			
Prelude	n.a.	$2,656	$3,990
Wickford†	n.a.	1,250	1,360
Deep Deep†.	n.a.	850	840
Total sales	$3,064	4,756	6,190
Costs and expenses:			
Vessel operations.	1,175	1,464	2,146
Purchased seafood	1,062	1,420	1,316
Depreciation.	253	312	362
Selling, general, and administrative.	565	780	1,014
Total costs and expenses.	3,005	3,976	5,108
Income (loss) from operations	9	780	1,082
Other income (expense)‡	(157)	(123)	(180)
Income (loss) before income taxes.	(148)	657	902
Provision for income taxes	—	338	464
Income (loss) before extraordinary items.	(148)	319	438
Extraordinary credit from operating loss carry-forward	—	272	347
Net income.	$ (148)	$ (591)	$ 785

Sources and Uses of Funds

	For Years Ending April 30	
	1973	1974
Uses of funds:		
Increase in fixed assets (new vessels).	$ 300	$ —
Increase in current assets (32% of sales).	531	460
Reduction in note payable	350	—
Reduction in long-term debt	370	270
Total uses of funds	1,451	730
Sources of funds:		
Increase in accounts payable (11% of sales)	191	157
Net operating income	319	438
Anticipated operating loss carry-forward	272	347
Depreciation.	312	362
Total sources of funds	1,094	1,304
Funds needed (surplus)	$ 357	$ (574)

n.a. = not available.
* Assumes that fishing conditions parallel those of May 1970–January 1972; that two new ships for a total of six begin fishing in fiscal 1974; that sales of the subsidiaries continue at mid-1972 levels; and that Prelude receives a price per pound of $1.33, with 25 percent of its sales to outsiders.
† Assumes that the subsidiaries will handle 75 percent of sales reported by the parent.
‡ Primarily interest expense.

Source: Company records.

OUTLOOK FOR THE FUTURE

By the summer of 1972, Prelude had weathered the downturn of fishing catches which had so far occurred that year. The company's boats had been able to bring in enough lobster to meet its $198,000 per month cash flow break-even (including the subsidiaries).

Break-even costs were divided as follows:

Vessel operations. . . .	$120,000	S,G&A	$23,000
Selling	42,000	Taxes, interest	13,000

In terms of break-even per trip, this monthly $198,000 (which excluded depreciation of about $25,000) worked out to about $22,000. The break-even catch in pounds varied, of course, with the price attainable in the market. In the spring of 1972 it ran about 8,000 pounds a trip, since the wholesale price of select lobster had risen to more than $3 per pound during some of this period.

Although the lobster catch had recently risen (Exhibit 1), no one knew when or whether it would return to normal. On the one hand, industry optimists argued that the scare condition was only a transient event and that there were still "plenty of lobsters out there for everybody." On the other hand, industry pessimists, championed by federal fishery officials, raised doubts about the long-term viability of the resource and were calling for some form of management to sustain the yields.

Competition

Even under managed conditions, Prelude's leaders expected the company to survive if not to prosper—barring total disappearance of the offshore lobster. They felt that they had the staying power to outlast the one-boat competitors who had come in on a shoestring, and, further, that they had an edge of experience and success which would enable them to outdistance the newer and better capitalized multiboat competitors. Chief among these had been Deep Deep; Mr. Usen had had three new boats fishing out of Boston since 1968 but had not been able to make them pay. He was presently operating two of these boats under a separate company but selling his catch at market price to Prelude and attempting to dispose of the fleet. A second established competitor, MATCO, which fished five boats off the Virginia coast, was also reported to be in financial trouble, having been dragged under by its allegedly overextended parent, Marine International Corporation. Although three other firms were putting three to five boats each out to sea, Mr. Gaziano was not particularly worried about the threat they presented. He summed up his feelings as follows:

> This is going to be one hell of an interesting summer [1972]. We're going to have some new boats out there, each backed by some rich Johnny

who is fascinated by the sex appeal of lobstering. They're going to find out the hard way how much it really costs to pot fish offshore. We have got a real shakeout coming.

In management's eyes a more real threat was that Prelude itself would be taken over by a larger company. Although there were no blocks of stock large enough to make for an easy takeover, the depressed state of Prelude's stock made a tender bid not unlikely.[4] For example, Mr. Jensen had heard a speech in which a spokesman for a West Coast seafood firm with 1971 sales of $25 million had stated:

> We are, then, a seafood company. And we want to remain a seafood company. The potential in utilizing the rich harvest of the sea is enough to keep any company of our size busy for as long into the future as we care to look.
>
> Already we are expanding from a solid base in the Pacific salmon industry into a much broader segment of the total spectrum of Alaskan and Northwestern fisheries. But we do not see ourselves as confined to Alaska and the Pacific Northwest. Rather we are interested in fisheries virtually anywhere on the globe if we can find a way to enter them in a sound and profitable manner. And, yes, we are constantly looking for acquisitions which could expand and complement our activities in the seafood industry.[5]

Expansion and Diversification

With the acquisition of Wickford and Deep Deep, Prelude had achieved integration all the way through to the consumer, and management was considering expanding this chain in several ways. One way would be to develop more restaurant/lobster stores similar to the one in North Kingston. Another way would be to enlarge on the branding program already underway. One California firm, Foster Farms, Inc., had been very successful with branding its fresh chickens and placing them in supermarkets.

A third alternative entailed broadening the product base by marketing other types of seafood that could be purchased outside and then resold through the company's distribution system. Flounder, trout, clams, and oysters were among the types of gourmet seafood products bought by restaurants in much the same way as lobster was.

---

[4] In June 1972 the bid price of Prelude's stock was in the range of $2¼–$3. Five brokers made an over-the-counter market in the 530,000 shares outstanding. Of these, Rev. Whipple held 92,400; a prominent Boston family, 70,000; Mr. Usen, 22,845; and Mr. McGeough, 17,500. The balance of the holdings were widely fragmented, with no individual or institution owning more than 15,000 shares. No other officer or employee held more than a few thousand shares, although this group as a whole held qualified options granted at prices of $6.50 to $9.00 on 53,500 shares.

[5] Larry M. Kaner, vice president, Whitney-Fidalgo Seafoods, Inc. Speech to Boston Security Analysts, February 9, 1971.

Processing and marketing crab meat was another possibility, but somewhat remote. Canning crab meat required a multimillion-dollar investment in centrifuging equipment and a continuous supply of crab meat. Although Prelude did catch a lot of crabs, they could not be stored together with lobsters, and furthermore, the catch was sporadic. There was, however, a minority small business company in New Bedford which was using government funds to develop a crab processing plant, and Prelude was watching this development with interest.

Nor were Mr. Gaziano's interests entirely confined to seafood. Previously, the company had looked at the possibility of acquiring a manufacturer of small boats, but had been beaten out by the CML Group, Inc. In any event, Mr. Gaziano did feel that any future expansion or acquisition efforts should be seaward oriented, once the present difficulties were resolved.

APPENDIX

Appendix on the Lobster Industry

Having graced the Pilgrims' first Thanksgiving, the northern lobster remained a U.S. gourmet delicacy, demand for which was growing abroad. Supply had not kept pace, however, even though the U.S. market drew 80 percent to 90 percent of the Canada-landed catch, thereby roughly doubling poundage available for domestic consumption and export.

From a 1960 peak of 73.2 million pounds liveweight, supply had dropped to 56.5 million pounds in 1967 but rose again thereafter, partly owing to the success of new techniques of offshore fishing (Exhibit 7).

EXHIBIT 7: Total U.S. Supplies of Northern Lobster (Liveweight in Millions of Pounds)

	1968	1969	1970	1971
U.S. landed	32.6	33.8	34.2	33.3
Imports*	31.3	31.6	30.2	34.5
Total	63.9	65.4	64.3	67.9

* Converted to liveweight equivalent.

Source: National Marine Fisheries Service.

Shortage had sent prices rising even faster than general inflation, and in 1971 the 33.3-million-pound, U.S.-landed catch brought fishermen $35.1 million in sales, making lobsters the second most valuable single species (after Gulf shrimp) in the $643 million fishing industry.

THE RESOURCE

The northern lobster inhabited the chilly waters of the North Atlantic from Newfoundland to North Carolina. Two populations had been observed, one in the shallow water from Canada's Maritimes south to New Jersey, the other further out, usually in the deep, cold canyons of the continental shelf from Massachusetts to the Carolinas. During the spring and fall the latter population migrated, and could thus sometimes be found crawling across the flats of the shelf. Estimated weights and numbers for "legal-sized" (legally fishable) lobsters in the two populations were as follows:

Population	Total Weight (millions of lbs.)	Annual Replenishment (millions of lbs.)	Number (millions)	Average Weight (lbs.)
Inshore	25–31	15–20 est.	20–25	1¼
Offshore	100–120	25 est.	25–30	4

Besides fluctuating from year to year, lobster catch rates were seasonal, being lowest in the winter when lobsters and fishermen were least active, and highest in October and May. Since demand was highest in midsummer (shore-dinner time), prices rose then, giving dealers a motive to buy and hold lobsters in enclosed tidal pools until values increased.

HARVESTING THE RESOURCE

Inshore Fishing.   Inshore and offshore lobster fishing differed in technique, the inshore method being much the same in the 1970s as in the 1840s. A 30-foot boat, manned by its owner and a relative, could manage 300–800 lath traps or pots, sinking each at depths of less than 30 fathoms, and hauling it up with a power winch to empty, bait, and toss overboard again.

By 1971 some 8,000 individuals were engaged in inshore lobster fishing, and a million pots were being used. Fishing was so intensive that government sources estimated that 90 percent of the legal-sized inshore lobster population was caught every year. Of this total, some 70 percent was delivered to ports in Maine. Optimum investment for entering this trade was estimated at $8,000–$10,000, but anyone could enter who had a few used traps, an outboard motorboat, and a license.

Offshore Fishing.   Only after World War II were feasible methods devised for fishing the offshore lobster population, and only in the late 1950s did the industry start significant growth. By 1968 two techniques were being used: trawling and potting on long lines.

Trawling involved scooping up migrating lobsters from the offshore flats by dragging weighted nets along the bottom. With the government pointing the way on methods, catches rose quickly, fluctuating around

5.5 million pounds a year in 1965–71, but ranging between 3.9 million in 1966 and 7.1 million in 1970.

Attractive features of offshore trawling included the absence of competition from Canada and Maine (where it was illegal to land the catch), relatively modest manning requirements compared with other types of fishing, and the low investment needed to equip a boat for switching back and forth from ground fish to lobsters. Increasingly, unattractive features included overcrowding, loss of expensive gear when nets were dragged across the rising number of offshore pots, and injuries to the catch which might render 50–70 percent of it unsalable. Thus, government sources believed that this industry segment would level off at 100–130 boats.

Offshore lobster potting started with experiments to develop gear for trapping lobsters in the deep canyons of the continental shelf, where government researchers reported a year-round abundance. Prominent among the first experimenters was Prelude's Rev. Whipple, who finally settled on a method that entailed a mile-long line, buoyed and anchored at each end, to which 50–75 weighted traps were attached by four-foot wires. Keys to his system were gears strong enough to haul the heavy line, and also a special clip to permit the automatic attachment and detachment of the traps as the ship steamed along.

In 1970 this technique proved its worth when Prelude landed nearly all of the 1.5 million pounds attributed to offshore potting in the first statistics to segregate this figure. In 1971 the offshore potting catch rose to 2.3 million pounds, but this was shared by a growing number of competitors, lured in part by Prelude's success. By mid-1972, 92 vessels were fishing 50,000 offshore pots, nearly half of which had come into service during the previous six months.

Such an influx brought technical problems. These included loss of gear when one's boat line was laid across another's, or when the lines were cut by boats pursuing finfish. Crowding, too, was a problem in the canyons, with the result that some pot lines had been set upon the flats, where they ruined the offshore trawlers' nets and motivated trawlers to retaliate.

Costs varied widely for putting a vessel into offshore lobster potting, some vessels having been converted from dragging to potting for as little as $50,000, whereas Prelude's fourth ship came to almost $600,000, including both cost of the hull and conversion.

REGULATION

Lobstering was a regulated trade, the regulations being set by the states, the federal government, and international conventions. Thus, to protect the resource, all states except North Carolina and Virginia set a minimum size for a landable lobster, and most states forbade the harvesting of egg-bearing females. To protect the consumer, the federal government required all lobsters to be alive when sold, and forbade U.S. ships to process them at sea. To govern fishing rights, nations had agreed not to fish within 12 miles of one another's coasts, and most had signed an international convention establishing a court-enforced code of conduct for vessels.

One clause in this code, of special interest to lobstermen, gave right-of-way to fixed equipment, such as pot lines. This requirement tended, however, to be ignored by ships in hot pursuit of finfish, particularly, lobstermen believed, by foreign ships. In any event, losses were frequent and significant. One incident alone could damage or destroy several trap lines costing about $7,000 each and thereby put a one-boat operation out of business. Lobstermen vociferously complained, but the U.S. Coast Guard lacked enough patrol boats for adequate policing. New England members of Congress, however, had been persuaded to sponsor a bill in the amount of $500,000 to reimburse fishermen for cumulative gear losses.

In other future plans, the federal government was pressing the states to enact uniform and more stringent laws for resource protection within the three-mile limit, which was the area of state jurisdiction. To protect the resource farther out, the federal government might take several steps, from imposing a federal license requirement to extending the 12-mile limit to a highly controversial 200 miles. What fishermen favored was bringing foreign as well as domestic deep-sea lobstermen under federal control, an objective that could be accomplished by officially declaring lobsters to be "creatures of the shelf" as opposed to "free-swimming" fish.

How urgent it might be to take protective action on the offshore resource was not clear. Reported removal of 14 million pounds[6] by all takers was well below the 25 million pounds a year that government biologists estimated could be removed without depleting the resource, but no one knew how many pounds were being taken out unreported or how many were maimed and killed through fishing operations. One highly placed official admitted, "it would not be at all unreasonable to speculate that as much as 25 million pounds might be being removed."

HANDLING AND TRANSPORT

Unlike inshore lobstermen, offshore lobstermen making ten-day runs required refrigerated tanks to hold their catch, not just barrels and some seaweed for moisture. Once delivered to the dock, most lobsters again went into holding: perhaps for a few days in a dockside car or floating tank, then for a few months in a pound or tidal pool, and then for a

---

[6] In 1972 U.S. offshore trawling and potting reported 5.7 million and 2.3 million pounds, respectively; foreign lobstermen about 5 million; and U.S. ground fish fishermen about 1 million.

few more days in a dealer's sorting and culling tank. In total, cars, pounds, and dealers' tanks in the Northeast could accommodate an estimated 7 million pounds.

With the advent of refrigeration and lightweight packing containers, shipments by rail or truck posed no problem, and shipment by air could carry northern lobsters to far-distant points.

Over the years, consumers had come to expect their lobsters live. Weak and dying lobsters could be culled and cooked, then canned and frozen, but despite high prices these operations barely recovered their costs, so dealers pressed suppliers for a high-quality catch.

AQUACULTURE

Although worked on for some time, techniques to supplement lobster fishing by farming remained undeveloped in 1972. Progress had been made, however, especially on the biological side. Lobsters had been developed to breed in captivity, and experiments had been started to breed selectively for fast growth, bright color, two crusher claws, and high meat content. Already, lobsters had been grown to one-pound size in

EXHIBIT 8

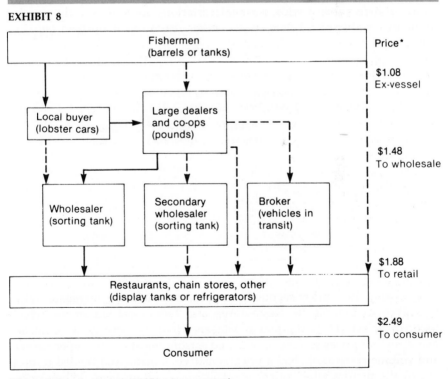

* Casewriter's estimate, typical 1971 price per pound.

two years, compared with six years in the wild. And lobsters had been grown to half-pound size in six to seven months, with tails bigger than any commercially available shrimp.

The big problem lay with engineering the life-support system. Depending on investment in development and plant, the start of commercial operations was put at two to five years away by the best-known authority in lobster hatchery.

MARKETING THE RESOURCE

Channels.   As indicated by solid lines on Exhibit 8, lobsters typically moved from the fishermen's barrel or tank to a local buyer with a lobster car or so, who then sold to a larger dealer operating a lobster pound. From there, the lobsters passed to a primary wholesaler, who sold to a retail outlet—most likely to a restaurant, since about 80 percent of all lobsters reached the consumer that way. Lobsters could pass to the retailer in several alternate ways, however, as indicated by dotted lines on Exhibit 8. These could either add or eliminate a step.

Price.   As indicated by the price data on Exhibit 8, prices more than doubled between the fisherman and the consumer, with retailers (largely restaurants) accounting for the biggest rise. The estimated price figures shown conceal wide seasonal variations, as well as variations for different weights of lobsters, and a steep year-to-year uptrend (see Exhibit 9).

EXHIBIT 9: Liveweight Wholesale Prices per Pound, Fulton Fish Market, New York City

	"Chix" (1⅛ lbs.)	"Quarter" (1¼ lbs.)	"Duces" (2 lbs.)
1970:			
High	$1.85	$1.88	$1.89
Low	1.24	1.34	1.36
1971:			
High	2.06	2.14	2.66
Low	1.45	1.46	1.47

Source: National Marine Fisheries Service, *Shellfish Situation and Outlook, Annual Review, 1971.*

Two major market segments combined to yield the aggregate statistics given in Exhibit 10. Restaurants and fancy seafood stores, which favored "select" (1½–2½-pound lobsters), had a relatively constant demand, so that prices sometimes reached astronomical levels. Supermarkets and volume restaurants had a price-sensitive demand and tended to drop out of the picture when prices went above a certain level. When prices

EXHIBIT 10: Weighted-Average Annual Price per Pound Paid to Maine Fishermen

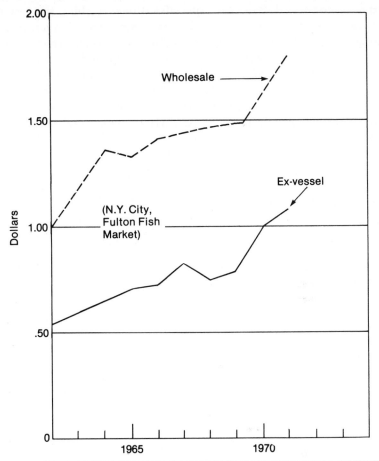

were low, however, chains tended to buy for promotions, thus helping to stabilize the market.

Competition among Distributors. Companies of varying types and sizes were engaged in lobster distribution, and they competed fiercely to handle the limited supply on a price basis favorable to themselves.

Two of the largest entities in the business were J. Hook and Bay State, both of Boston, who together handled an estimated 30 million pounds a year. Despite their size, they might find themslves outbid by "small lotters," who were able to sell crate lots in Europe for twice what their large competitors were getting from a high-volume restaurant account.

Hook and Bay State operated quite differently, thus illustrating the wide variety of ways that entities in lobster distribution could be linked together or combined. Bay State specialized in furnishing the restaurant trade with sorted lobster at a stable year-round price, which might be above or below the current market. While it had preferred to confine itself to a wholesale function, it had recently been forced to enter the dealer function of running a pound in order to secure its sources of supply. In contrast, Hook maintained only a skeleton staff year-round, but geared up when the market was good to provide tremendous quantities of case lots of unsorted lobsters to secondary wholesalers. Hook also brokered a large volume to chains.

CASE 3

Baker International Corporation

*Operating a company based on historical trends is like
driving a car looking in the rear view mirror.*

E. H. Clark, Jr.
President and CEO,
Baker International Corporation

For the decade ending in 1978, the performance of Baker International Corporation, a supplier of tools and services used in the drilling and maintenance of oil and gas wells, was among the best in American industry. During this period, the appreciation of Baker's common stock plus dividends provided the highest return to shareholders of all *Fortune* 500 companies, and the company was selected by *Fortune* as one of the 10 "business triumphs of the Seventies." In addition, based on results through 1978, Baker's 10-year compounded growth rate in earnings per share of 24 percent ranked 24th among the *Fortune* 500.

Since 1965, Baker's strategy had been formulated and directed by E. H. ("Hubie") Clark, Jr., a 54-year-old, disciplined yet entrepreneurially spirited engineer who was Baker's chief executive officer. Shortly after the close of fiscal 1979,[1] Clark had to ponder several dilemmas posed by the extraordinary historical performance and the promising potential of Baker's existing businesses through the 1980s. How could Baker sustain its performance record through the 1990s and into the 21st century? What

---

[1] Baker's fiscal year ended on September 30. Copyright © 1981 by the President and Fellows of Harvard College. Harvard Business School case 9–381–179. Reproduced by permission.

123

changes in Baker's way of managing would be required by the increased size and complexity brought on by continued rapid growth? What would Clark's future role in the company be?

During the 1970s, the company rode the crest of the worldwide boom in oil and gas exploration that followed the 1973 oil embargo. In 1979, Baker management was predicting that the increasing value of oil, coupled with the geopolitical considerations arising out of instability in the Middle East and the Iranian revolution, would increase both exploration for new oil and workover and the stimulation of old wells to unprecedented levels. As a result, the company was predicting that the demand for its products during the first half of the 1980s would rival its postembargo compounded annual sales growth of 28 percent. If this growth materialized as expected, it would tax Baker's existing financial and managerial resources. Moreover, the industry's increased demand for talented, proven managers posed the threat that members of Baker's top management would be pirated away by other companies.

The rapid growth in demand for oil-field equipment and services, however, was not expected to continue indefinitely. The bulk of Baker's business was tied to oil—a diminishing resource. As a result of the anticipated decline in the demand for Baker's present products, Clark was becoming increasingly concerned with how to continue the company's exceptional performance beyond the 1980s.

Before we address the dilemmas facing Clark in 1979, let us examine Baker's history, the nature of the oil-field equipment industry, Baker's strategy, and its way of managing.

HISTORY

Baker International was initially incorporated in 1913 as Baker Casing Shoe Company. By 1965, when Hubie Clark became president and chief executive officer, sales had risen to $45 million.[2] However, the company remained primarily a producer of high-quality packers, cement retainers and hydraulic, oil well bottom-hole pumps. The company had no significant product diversification and had no financial leverage.

Clark held two convictions that began to tranform the company when he assumed the additional position of chairman of the board in 1968. First, Clark believed "leverage was no different than any other working tool that a company had." Second, he felt future worldwide supply and demand considerations for oil provided a unique opportunity for diversification. Clark reflected:

---

[2] Clark joined Baker in 1947 after receiving a master's degree in mechanical engineering from California Institute of Technology and serving three years in the United States Navy.

I had a firm belief that the U.S. was going to lose its grasp on the price of crude. The industrialized nations were holding the price down with surplus supply in the United States and we were losing that surplus supply. While the U.S. had been producing at about 40 percent of capacity, it was up to 50 percent in 1955 and by 1968, we were producing at 68–69 percent of capacity. I couldn't see any breaks in this trend. I couldn't see the U.S. restoring its reserves or capability to produce. I said to myself, "When we lose that excess capacity, we are going to see the price of crude go up. When the price of crude goes up, it is going to change the ball game, particularly in the U.S. There are a lot of [oil-field service] companies that right now are flat on their backs and dirt cheap. We ought to be acquiring companies and expanding." So we staked our careers on the price of crude going up in the 1970s. If it hadn't, we'd have been dead ducks.

He believed that four factors would contribute to a significant increase in exploratory and development drilling: (1) the Western world's increasing consumption of energy; (2) a significant slowing in the technological advance of recovery techniques; (3) the failure of nonpetroleum sources of energy such as nuclear power to supply their expected share of the total energy requirements of the 1970s; and (4) the threat to the United States' national security and balance of payments posed by the growing import of oil from countries with which it was not politically allied.

When Clark made these predictions, the industry was in the midst of a prolonged period of declining drilling activity. (Exhibit 1 indicates the level of the United States drilling activity from 1950 to 1978.) This decline, which began in 1955 and continued through 1971, was primarily the result of two factors: (1) post–World War II expansion in exploration and production had led to a surplus in production capacity, and (2) new reservoir management technology had added significant reserves without requiring investments in new wells.

In 1968, when many others in the industry considered drilling to be a stagnant business, Clark began to act on his positive prognosis. Baker's management identified market segments that promised "growth with minimal risk." To enter new markets and to augment its position in the targeted markets in which it was already present, Baker began an active acquisition program. By the end of 1979, this program had resulted in 20 acquisitions, summarized in Exhibit 2.

The company also began to reinvest heavily in product development with an emphasis on quality and a goal of achieving a "technological edge on competition." This groundwork in market positioning and technology provided Baker with significant competitive advantages when drilling activity turned upward in 1972.

By 1979, Baker's revenues had reached $1,169 million, of which approximately 79 percent was in the United States and Canada (up from

EXHIBIT 1 Oil Drilling Activity in the United States

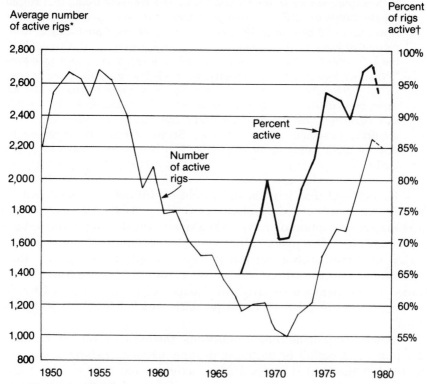

Average number
of active rigs*

Percent
of rigs
active†

* Source: Hughes Tool Company.
† Source: Baker International Corporation. Census taken in August of each year. Data for years prior to 1967 are not available on a comparable basis.

58 percent in 1974). The 1979 geographic allocation of revenues was as indicated in the table below.

In 1979, Baker's principal operations were divided into three management groups: the Drilling Group, Baker Oil Tools Group, and the Mining Group. Each group was managed by a group president. (A more detailed

Geographical Allocation of 1979 Revenues (percent)*

	U.S. and Canada	Latin America	Western Europe	Middle East, North Africa, and Other
Sales	56.6	4.0	5.3	5.4
Services and rentals . . .	22.3	1.0	2.2	3.2
Total revenues	78.9	5.0	7.5	8.6

* Before transfers between geographic areas.

EXHIBIT 2

BAKER INTERNATIONAL CORPORATION
Summary of Acquisitions

Year	Company Acquired	Group of Which a Division	Estimated Acquisition Price ($ millions)	Form of Payment*	Accounting Method	Baker's P/E Ratio at Time of Acquisition†
1968	Technical Oil Tool Corp.	Drilling equipment	$ 2.0	Common stock (420,000 shares)	Pooling	16X
1969	Galigher Corp.	Mining equipment	6.5	Cash ($3.6) and long-term notes ($2.9)	Purchase	16X
1970	Lynes, Inc.	Drilling equipment	7.5	Common stock (1,490,496 shares)	Pooling	13X
1970	Dixie Oil Tools, Inc.	Oil tools		Cash	Purchase	13X
1971	K. E. Hallikainen Instruments	Drilling equipment (TOTCO)‡	2.0	Cash	Purchase	18X
1971	Mud Separators, Inc.	Drilling equipment (Milchem)‡		Cash	Purchase	23X
1971	Milchem, Inc.	Drilling equipment	12.2	Common stock (1,603,000 shares)	Purchase	22X
1971	Harold Brown Co.	Oil tools			Pooling	22x
1972	Automation Engineering Service, Inc.	Oil tools	2.7	Common stock (279,864 shares)	Pooling	23X
1972	Exploration Logging, Inc.	Drilling equipment	21.2	Common stock (736,000 shares)	Pooling	27X
1972	Tri-State Oil Tools Industries	Drilling equipment	23.6	Common stock (697,096 shares)	Pooling	32X
1973	Compressors Automation Controls Inc.	Oil tools	2.2	Common stock (174,036 shares)	Pooling	23X
1974	Hydraulic Workover, Inc.	Oil tools	3.4	Common stock (272,794 shares)	Pooling	18X
1974	Ramsey Engineering Co.	Mining equipment	9.0	Cash	Purchase	19X
1975	Virg's Testers, Inc.	Drilling equipment	N/A	Common stock	Pooling	19X

EXHIBIT 2 *(concluded)*

Year	Company Acquired	Group of Which a Division	Estimated Acquisition Price ($ millions)	Form of Payment*	Accounting Method	Baker's P/E Ratio at Time of Acquisition†
1975 . .	Reed Tool Co.	Drilling equipment & mining equipment	103.4	Common stock (4,649,354 shares)	Pooling	14X
1977 . .	Magna Corp.§	Oil tools	9.4	Common stock (415,728 shares)	Purchase	14X
1977 . .	Chas. S. Lewis & Co.	Mining equipment	13.6	Cash	Purchase	14X
1978 . .	Energy Services, Inc.	Oil tools	42.0	Cash	Purchase	10X
1978 . .	West Virginia Armature Co.	Mining equipment	8.0	Common stock (242,000 shares)	Pooling	12X

* Number of shares adjusted for stock splits.
† Based on stock price in month of acquisition and prior four quarters of reported earnings per share.
‡ Not maintained as a separate division, but became a part of another operating division parenthetically indicated.
§ Remaining 80 percent not previously held.

description of each group's business and a summary of their operating performance are shown in Exhibits 3 and 4, respectively.)

EXHIBIT 3
BAKER INTERNATIONAL CORPORATION
Summary of Business Areas by Group

Drilling Group: This group provided a broad line of products and services used in the drilling of oil and gas wells and was one of the four leading suppliers of both drilling fluids (muds) and rock bits in the industry. Muds were used to clean the bottom of a hole by removing cuttings, to cool and lubricate the bit and drill string, to control pressures, and to seal porous formations. Baker also manufactured equipment used to remove sand, shale, and silt from drilling fluids; provided technical services in the formulation and use of drilling fluids; manufactured tool joints and supplied drill pipe; provided equipment and services to detect the presence of hydrocarbons, to identify formations, and to monitor the drilling process; and provided fishing tool services to retrieve damaged pipe, tools, or other objects from the hole. A system with substantial market potential that would allow downhole logging while drilling was under development in 1979.

Baker Oil Tools Group: This group manufactured and sold products and services used after the well was drilled to achieve safety and long-term productivity and to protect against pressure and corrosion damage. The first step was to line the hole with casing. Baker manufactured centralizers and cementing shoes and collars used in installing and cementing the casing and the hole. After the casing was cemented, tubing was generally run inside the casing to serve as a flow tube for the gas or oil. Packers were used to seal off the space between the tubing and the casing to protect the casing from reservoir pressures and corrosive fluids or gases and also to maintain the separation of productive zones. Baker's packers were considered the industry standard and commanded the largest share of the worldwide market. The group also manufactured and serviced hydraulic and electrical downhole pumping systems, products that controlled well production rates, and offered other completion and production products and services. Other Baker products, such as retrievable cementers and bridge plugs, were used when chemical or mechanical stimulation was required to achieve or increase commercial production of oil or gas, and to repair casing. The company also furnished hydraulic workover equipment and services which permitted a well to be worked on while still under pressure.

Mining Group: This group manufactured a wide range of equipment for the mining and mineral-processing industries (primarily coal, copper and iron ore) such as high-performance rock bits and tubular products for rotary blast hole drilling employed in surface mining activities; products for tunneling, shaft sinking and raise boring; truck- and tractor-mounted rotary drilling equipment and underground mine equipment for transporting personnel and material. Baker also produced ore beneficiation and mineral-processing equipment including flotation cells, equipment for handling corrosive and highly abrasive slurries, and process control equipment.

EXHIBIT 4

BAKER INTERNATIONAL CORPORATION
Financial Performance by Operating Group*
($ million)

Year Ended September 30

	1974	1975	1976	1977	1978	1979
Drilling Group:						
Revenues	$191.8	$258.6	$282.1	$340.3	$428.4	$559.2
Net income . . .	17.2	31.7	32.1	39.2	49.8	64.0
Net capital employed	96.9	138.6	161.2	207.7	316.1	426.2
RONCE†	17.7%	22.9%	19.9%	18.9%	15.8%	15.0%
Oil Tools Group:						
Revenues	157.0	209.5	245.5	296.3	379.9	478.3
Net income . . .	11.5	22.4	25.4	28.8	37.3	53.6
Net capital employed	94.8	134.6	156.5	196.5	250.4	321.8
RONCE†	12.1%	16.6%	16.2%	14.7%	14.9%	16.7%
Mining Group:						
Revenues	66.5	95.2	96.0	108.6	111.0	127.9
Net income . . .	3.4	7.3	4.7	5.9	5.6	9.8
Net capital employed	37.7	47.9	59.0	59.0	61.6	66.7
RONCE†	9.0%	15.3%	8.0%	10.0%	9.2%	14.7%

* Data have been restated to reflect the operating units comprising each group as of December 31, 1979, and to include historical financial data for periods prior to the date of acquisition. Purchase accounting adjustments relating to the revaluation of assets and liabilities are excluded from the data.
† Return on net capital employed.

The Drilling Group consisted of eight operating divisions that sold equipment and services used in the initial drilling of oil and gas wells. Its principal products included drilling fluids ("muds") and rock bits.

The Baker Oil Tools Group, comprised of 10 operating divisions, provided products and services used at the conclusion of drilling a commercial well and when chemical or mechanical stimulation was needed to restore or increase an existing well's production. The group's principal products included packers, casing, and cementers.

In 1969, Baker entered the mining equipment industry with the acquisition of Galigher Corporation. By 1979, the Mining Group had grown to five operating divisions that manufactured a wide range of equipment for the mining and mineral processing industries. Although the Mining Group represented only 7.5 percent of Baker's 1979 sales, the performance of this business had met management's expectations for growth and return on investment. Three favorable trends were expected to affect the outlook for the mining equipment business: (1) increasing population and per capita consumption, (2) increasing efforts to develop alternate energy sources that had to be mined, such as coal, oil shale, and tar sands, and (3) the diminishing availability of prolific, high-grade ore deposits, a condition that would require greater quantities of mined materials to be handled per ton of useable ore. Considering these forces, Baker management expected the Mining Group's markets to grow 5–9 percent annually for an "indefinite period."

THE OIL-FIELD EQUIPMENT AND SERVICE INDUSTRY

The OPEC price increases and the political instability of the Middle East in the 70s stimulated a worldwide search for more secure sources of oil. Price increases also made the production from many marginal reservoirs economically feasible. The management of production from these fields generally required a larger number of wells drilled much closer together, and these wells required more frequent maintenance and workover. Because of the resulting growth, the oil-field equipment industry had been generally capacity-constrained since 1973, which led to firm prices and the maintenance of high margins.

Later in the 1980s, natural gas and energy from tar sands and oil shale were expected to become increasingly important markets. Since gas had not been sought extensively prior to the 1950s, the geological prospects for gas were thought to be brighter than for oil. Also, gas was generally found at deeper levels than oil and thus required more tools and services per well. (The increased difficulty of drilling for new oil and gas in the United States is indicated in Exhibit 5 by the increase in average well depth since 1955 and by the 2.7-fold increase in the average cost per foot experienced between 1971 and 1978.)

To bring more marginal deposits into production in order to reduce the West's dependence on the prolific oil fields of the OPEC countries, more wells would increasingly be required per barrel of displaced OPEC oil. For example, Exhibit 6 indicates the comparative reservoir quality of the world's four largest oil-producing countries in 1978. Baker management believed that as the world moved away from the Middle East reservoirs and produced oil elsewhere, from 10 to 300 times as many Baker products would be required per barrel of oil relative to the Middle East.

In the 1980s, as formations grew older, more wells were expected to be needed to manage a reservoir effectively. The number of wells affected both the rate of recovery and the percentage of the reservoir recovered. The potential for expanding the recovery of reserves through improved methods of stimulation was substantial. For example, as indicated in Exhibit 7, through 1978, it was estimated that 453 billion barrels of oil had been discovered in the U.S., of which 335 billion barrels were still in the ground. Higher prices for crude oil and technological advances in well stimulation methods such as steam injection, fire flooding, and carbon dioxide displacement were expected to increase the potential recovery of the remaining reserves threefold (from 28 billion barrels to 88

EXHIBIT 5: Footage Drilled, Well Depth and Cost per Foot in United States (1953–1978)*

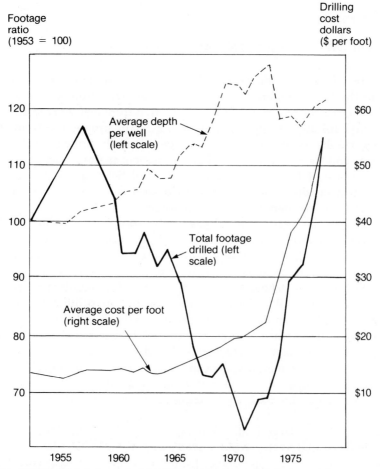

* Representative absolute figures for total drilled and average well depth are as follows:

	1953	1968	1978
Total footage drilled (MM)	198.8	143.1	230.6
Average depth per well (ft)	4,035	4,839	4,943

Source: "Joint Association Survey of the U.S. Oil and Gas Producing Industry," Annual, American Petroleum Institute, Independent Petroleum Association of America, Mid-Continent Oil and Gas Association, Table 10a, April 1980.

EXHIBIT 6: World's Four Largest Producers (comparison of reservoir quality)

Country	Number of Wells Required to Produce 1 Million Bbls/Day in 1978
Saudi Arabia.	61
Iran	79
Soviet Union	6,000 est.
United States	58,630

Source: Baker International Corporation.

EXHIBIT 7: 1978 U.S. Oil Reserves (recovery potential)

	Billions of Barrels
Found but unrecovered oil:	
Recoverable at 1979 levels of prices and technology.	28
Potential for additional recovery through enhanced techniques.	60
Projected unrecoverable	247
Total unrecovered reserves.	335
Oil already recovered	118
Total discovered U.S. oil	453

Source: Baker International Corporation.

billion barrels).[3] Thus, substantial market potential existed in the additional drilling and stimulation equipment and services required to increase the recovery of the known U.S. reserves.

The trends towards more wells per reservoir and deeper wells were expected to increase the proportion of the cost of producing a barrel of crude represented by drilling and well completion. Thus, products which allowed companies to drill faster, such as logging-while-drilling systems and more efficient bits and muds, were expected to become increasingly important to the competitive posture of oil-field equipment companies.

As a result of these trends, Baker management expected average active domestic rig count to increase 11.6 percent annually from 1979 to 1984 and 6.8 percent annually from 1984 to 1988. Management also predicted that the footage per rig per year would increase over this period, which would result in total footage drilled increasing somewhat faster than the growth in active rigs.[4] (Management's projections of rigs and

[3] By comparison, the U.S. Geological Survey's mean estimate for the nation's undiscovered oil was 82 billion barrels.

[4] Baker's projections were more optimistic than those commonly quoted in the trade press in 1979, which forecast a 5–6 percent annual increase in the sale of oil-field equipment from 1979–1990.

EXHIBIT 8

BAKER INTERNATIONAL CORPORATION
Domestic Rig and Footage Projections

	Actual		Projected									
	1977	1978	1979	1980	1981	1982	1983	1984	1985	1986	1987	1988
Rig projections:												
New rig additions in U.S.*	240	342	337	372	411	449	479	493	508	524	539	555
Remade rigs, transfers, etc.	128	78	16	0	0	0	0	0	0	0	0	0
% attritions.	1.0	1.0	3.0	1.5	2.0	2.0	2.0	2.5	2.5	3.0	3.0	3.0
Year-end existing rigs	2652	3051	3313	3635	3974	4343	4736	5111	5491	5850	6214	6583
Average existing rigs	2482	2852	3182	3474	3804	4159	4540	4923	5301	5671	6032	6398
% workable	96.6	97.7	90.3	93.0	93.0	93.0	93.0	93.0	93.0	93.0	93.0	93.0
Average workable rigs	2398	2786	2873	3231	3538	3867	4222	4579	4930	5274	5610	5950
Utilizations %.	83	81	76	82	82	82	82	82	82	82	82	82
Average active rigs.	1990	2259	2169	2649	2901	3171	3462	3754	4043	4324	4600	4879
Footage projections:												
Footage per rig per year (mm ft/rig/yr)	107	101	107	104	105	105	107	109	111	113	115	115
Total footage (mm ft)	212.9	228.2	232.1	275.5	304.6	333.0	370.4	409.2	448.7	488.7	529.0	561.1

* "New Rig Additions" are based on a forecast of growth in manufacturing capability due to capacity expansion and increased efficiency net of the percentage of United States production shipped overseas.
Source: Baker International Corporation.

footage drilled are shown in Exhibit 8.) Activity growth combined with inflation and increasing market share was expected to offer the potential for the company's revenues to increase 25–27 percent per year from 1979–1985. In the 1990s, the growth rate of the oil-field equipment market was projected to decline to 2–3 percent per year and eventually reach a point of negative growth because of the diminishing availability of oil.

Competitive Factors

The principal competitive factors in the industry were the quality of product, the technical proficiencies of a company's personnel, and the availability of products and services in the field.

The high costs associated with product failure made a company's reputation for quality important. For example, although a drilling bit cost approximately $3,000, on an offshore well it could cost $10,000 in equipment and manpower time just to get the bit to the bottom of the well and back. Similarly, if the mud system became unbalanced, causing the drill string to freeze in the casing, it could cost $200,000 to $300,000 to correct the problem. Because of the high cost of downtime on drilling rigs (an offshore rig cost approximately $4,000 per hour in 1979) and the potential physical problems (such as the collapse of the hole) that could develop in the hole if the drilling equipment was removed for an extended period of time, the ready availability of equipment and services was of extreme importance to the customer. As a result, most companies in the industry maintained large inventories and idle manpower in the field.

The high cost of failure, the importance of product and service availability and the small portion of the total cost of a well represented by most oil-field products and services (see Exhibit 9 for an estimate of the cost components of completing a well), reduced customers' sensitivity to price. Thus, the industry enjoyed one of the highest net margins of any U.S. manufacturing industry. The high margins were also facilitated by two other factors: (1) a successful find tended to decrease a customer's concern with "pinching pennies," and (2) the petroleum industry was characterized by a rather closely-knit network of personal friendships that generated loyalty to people and, therefore, to their companies. This latter factor, combined with the importance of a company's reputation for quality, created a significant barrier to the entry of new firms into the industry other than by acquisition.

One industry observer believed that the lack of price sensitivity was in part due to the nature of the customers. The bureaucratic characteristics of state-owned oil companies, and to a lesser degree, major U.S. oil companies, motivated the individuals making the buying decision to

EXHIBIT 9: Estimated Percentage Cost Breakdown of Drilling and Equipping U.S. Wells

Payments to drilling contractors		36.6%
Purchased items:		
Casing, tubing, and casing hardware*	18.2	
Site preparation, transportation, and fuel	9.1	
Drilling mud and additives	6.9	
Cement and cementing services	3.7	
Logs and wireline services	3.2	
Special tool rentals.	3.1	
Formation treating	3.0	
Well site monitoring systems and tests	1.9	
Wellhead equipment	1.8	
Drill bits and reamers	1.6	
Other equipent, services, and overhead.	10.9	
Total cost of purchased items		63.4
		100.0%

* Primarily supplied by steel companies.
Source: Compiled from *World Oil*, February 15, 1980, p. 121.

minimize risk. Thus, they preferred to buy from the companies with a reputation for reliability. Name overrode price.

While the pace of technological change was expected to increase in the 1980s, many of the important forces of the 80s were anticipated to require more wells rather than significant advances in technology.

Baker's principal competitors were the six companies indicated in Exhibit 10. (Comparative financial data on these companies are shown in Exhibit 11.)

CORPORATE STRATEGY

Goals

Baker's two basic objectives were identified as the achievement of "(1) an above-average rate of return whether measured in terms of revenues of capital; and (2) an above-average rate of growth in the revenue or investment base on which that return was earned."

Although management indicated that these objectives translated into an earnings per share growth objective of 15 percent to 25 percent per year, Clark emphasized that growth was clearly secondary to return on investment:

The number one god at Baker, financially is "RONCE." We would sacrifice growth always for return on net capital employed [RONCE].[5] Size

EXHIBIT 10: Business Areas of Principal Competitors

Company	Bits	Other Down-Hole Tools	Muds	Well Completion Equipment/ Packers	Rig Outfitting Products	Cementing, Stimulating, or Remedial Services
Baker International*	x	x	x	⊠	x	x
Dresser Ind.	x		⊠	x	x	x
Halliburton			x	⊗		⊠
Hughes Tool	⊠	x	x	x		x
NL Industries	x	x	⊗		x	x
Schlumberger				x	x	x
Smith International	⊗	⊠			x	x

⊠ = Leading market share.
⊗ = Second place market share.
*Baker's market share ranked fourth in drill bits, and third or fourth in muds, and the company was the major producer of portable hydraulic workover equipment among the stimulation and remedial products.

EXHIBIT 11: Comparative Company Performance Oil-Field Equipment and Services Industry ($ millions)

	Compound Annual Growth (1974–1979)			1968 Total Sales	1979 Sales		1979 Net Income	1979 Net Income as a Percent of		1979 Debt to Total Capital
	Sales	Net Income	E.P.S.		Total	Oil Field		Sales	Average Stockholders' Equity	
Baker Int'l.	34.8%	41.8%	31.1%	$ 58	$1,168	$ 984	$ 99	8.5%	19.9%	30.8%
Dresser Ind.	19.9	29.3	20.6	624	3,457	978	228	6.6	17.2	19.6
Halliburton	20.2	11.2	10.8	805	7,766	2,046	377	4.8	17.8	10.8
Hughes Tool	30.8	30.0	24.2	82	804	804	84	10.5	17.9	27.0
NL Industries	2.5	1.9	(5.1)	858	1,810	921	86	4.8	14.8	29.2
Schlumberger	18.0	27.8	34.2	409	3,641	2,038	502	19.2	30.6	16.9
Smith Int'l.	22.3	29.3	23.4	60	545	460	55	10.0	17.7	27.0

targets really haven't been a compelling motivation for me or anyone else. The critical question is: "Are you doing the right thing?" Size becomes an effect of doing the right thing.

Clark believed that the return on the incremental investment necessary to achieve growth in excess of 25 percent was small ("maybe only 5 percent") due to the difficulty of managing such rapid growth, particularly the management of inventories and the expansion of plant.

Baker's RONCE objective ranged from 15 percent to 18 percent. It fluctuated with inflation by an amount calculated to provide the company with a constant asset replacement capablity in real terms.

RONCE, as an objective and as a measure of performance, permeated Baker's management system. It was the principal measure used for control and was a key determinant of incentive compensation. Approximately one-fourth of a divisional president's incentive compensation, and substantially more for corporate management, was determined by performance against RONCE targets.

Diversification Strategy and Product Policy

Baker's initial diversification objective, established in the late 1960s, was to obtain a balanced market position in oil-field drilling. To a large extent, this was accomplished by acquisitions during a period of weakness in the drilling industry. In fact, in the early 1970s, others in the industry were openly critical of Clark, judgmentally asking him, "What are you doing acquiring those doggy drilling companies?" The competition was slow in following Baker's lead. Those competitors that eventually did undertake acquisition programs, such as Hughes Tool and NL Industries, did not do so until the 1974–1978 period. Others such as Dresser and Halliburton never became acquisitive in the oil-field equipment and service segments of their businesses.

Baker considered "energy" mining, equipment and services, particularly related to coal, as its second major area of diversification. The increasing emphasis on mining acquisitions occurred at a time when (1) Baker's oil-field product lines had been considerably broadened and (2) the high price/earnings ratios of oil-service companies were making it difficult to find acquisitions that would meet Baker's return criteria. In contrast to oil-field service companies, management felt that the stock prices of

---

[5] Baker calculated RONCE as follows:

$$\frac{\text{Profits}}{\text{Sales}} \div \frac{\text{Net Capital}}{\text{Sales}} = \frac{\text{Profits}}{\text{Net Capital}}$$

where Profits were after taxes but before interest charges and Net Capital was defined as total assets less interest-free liabilities.

many companies serving the mining industry were depressed relative to the companies' future earnings potential. Based on their belief that, of geopolitical necessity, coal would be called upon to supply a substantial proportion of the United States' future energy needs, management hoped that Baker would be able to emulate its petroleum industry performance in the mining industry.

Baker's criteria for entering into new businesses reflected its general operating strategy and was composed of four basic elements: (1) expansion had to be in markets that Baker knew and understood, and the business had to interface with two or more of Baker's areas of expertise (technology, manufacturing, domestic marketing, or international marketing in the areas of petroleum, natural gas, and minerals recovery); (2) capital goods had to represent less than half of the revenue mix with the emphasis being placed on expendable products, replacement parts, or service/maintenance activities (in 1979 approximately 80 percent of Baker's sales were derived from expendable products and services); (3) the products or services had to have a high technological content; and (4) the market had to be sensitive to quality and reliability, with a high cost associated with product failure. The objective of the second element, above, was to reduce the volatility of the company's revenues, and the third and fourth elements were intended to remove the company from strong price competition and to assure high margins. Financially, acquisitions were expected within five years to achieve Baker's internal return on investment and growth objectives. Clark's enforcement of the acquisition criteria tended to be rigid; he vetoed any proposed acquisition that did not fit from a product standpoint.

The acquisitions were financed primarily by the exchange of common stock. To avoid dilution of earnings per share, Baker's rule of thumb was to acquire only companies whose price resulted in an effective P/E ratio that was one-half to three-quarters of Baker's P/E. Exceptions were companies with earnings that were unusually depressed because of unique circumstances. Clark explained Baker's early acquisition strategy:

> Our strategy was to use acquisition funny money [the difference between Baker's and the acquired company's P/E ratios] to give us some short-term pops in our earnings. Our objective was to double our indigenous, ongoing growth rate in EPS through our acquisition work, and we did just that. When the oil-field market turned and the horse race began, we planned to have bought all of the right horses cheaply and to be ready to run with the upturn. Then we planned to stop acquisitions and to ride our indigenous growth.

Baker derived three principal benefits from the fuller product line achieved through acquisitions: improved R&D, more effective well planning for its customers, and a transfer of Baker's reputation for quality to acquired companies with names of lesser recognition. Since bits, muds, and instruments were an interlocking system, the performance of the bit depended not only on the nature of the formation, but also on the mud and on the weight and torque on the bit. Instruments provided information on and/or control of these variables. Thus, the exchange of technical knowledge between, for example, Milchem's mud engineers and Reed's bit engineers improved the design of both products. In-house technical knowledge of each major segment of the drilling and production systems also allowed Baker's divisions to more effectively advise their customers on the complement of equipment and mud that would optimize their drilling or production activities. Since Baker's divisions operated under a high degree of autonomy, self-interest—rather than corporate mandate—was the motivating force that caused divisions to share information. Clark indicated that such cooperation was standard within the industry:

> The idea of forming a coalition with another company in order to provide a value [to the customer] that neither of you could provide independently is a concept that has been in existence in this industry as long as I can remember. The fact that it's a sister company, it's the same difference. However, if it comes to forcing coordination and that forcing impinges on entrepreneurial, independent decision making, I would give up forcing *every* time.

Research and Development

In 1979, Baker employed 283 people in research and development activities. Although the R&D emphasis was on the improvement of existing products and services, efforts were also expended on the development of new products. R&D expenditures in 1978 and 1979 approximated 1.4 percent of sales. All R&D took place in the operating divisions.

To encourage divisional management to undertake new product development, each division could request that up to 100 percent of the cost of a development program be financed at the corporate level. Since the costs associated with a project would then be carried on the corporate books, not the division's, the division's RONCE performance would not be penalized. However, upon successful completion of a project, the division was required to repay corporate's investment in the ratio of $2 for each $1 invested. If a project failed, the corporate level would absorb the development costs.

Marketing

A great emphasis was placed on understanding market trends. According to Clark, "Having a feel for the market is one of the most important things a person running one of our divisions can do."

Although many of Baker's operating divisions sold to a common customer (the drilling contractor, rig operator, oil company, etc.), each division was responsible for its own marketing. Baker management believed that their customers' entrepreneurial nature and loyalty to specific manufacturers for certain products reinforced the need to market their products through separate sales forces and under separate names (Reed, Milchem, Baker Packers, etc.). Customers were thought to prefer the freedom to select different components from different companies and to maintain personal relationships with multiple suppliers. In fact, customers had rejected previous attempts of oil-field service companies to sell integrated packages of products. Clark, in disagreement with the predictions of several other Baker managers, expected the relationship of the oil-field service company to its customer to change in the future:

> Since the bits, muds and instruments form an interlocking system, eventually those with the best system design are going to win. In the early days, the operator bought the components and was the system integrator. My prediction is that by the year 2000, the vendor will be the system integrator. We will recommend not just a bit for a formation, but a package of instruments, muds, and bits.

Manufacturing Policy

Quality assurance and the investment in adequate capacity to meet projected demand were cornerstones of Baker's manufacturing policy. Where appropriate, Baker would move quickly to improve the quality control of newly acquired companies.

Based on Clark's forecast of increased domestic exploration and production, substantial investments were made in additional capacity to meet the expected future boom. Even though some of these investments initially operated at only moderate levels of capacity, they were expected to allow Baker to increase its market share as competitors became capacity-constrained. This willingness to expand capacity in excess of near-term market requirements was evident in late 1978, as Clark explained:

> In our judgment, the Iranian revolution was going to have a more profound impact on the actions of people throughout the world than the embargo did in 1973. Everyone knew that the embargo was an economic move, that there was a huge amount of oil, and that the embargo would not last. With the Iranian crisis, the world came face-to-face with a true shortage and the fact that, depending on what happened in certain countries, we actually might not have enough oil to survive without rioting and chaos in the streets. We shot craps on the fact that this would have a more profound effect than the embargo and that activity would move to a level 50 percent higher than it was in the five years following the embargo. That told us that, if we believed our own press, we should build capacity. We said, "Roll the dice."

The resulting capital expenditures in 1978 and 1979 totalled $318 million, which was 142 percent of the book value of year-end 1977's net property, plant, and equipment. The impact of the expenditures on the competitive position of some of Baker's businesses was dramatic. For example, in response to a present and projected industrywide shortage of drill pipe, Reed Tubular Products doubled its tool joint capacity in 1978. As a result, Baker's tool joint sales increased 50 percent per year during 1978 and 1979, and market share approximately doubled during this period. Similarly, beginning shortly after its acquisition in 1978, Energy Services International's (ESI) capacity for the plastic coating of pipe was tripled by building two plants back-to-back. By the end of fiscal 1979, the first plant had been in operation for approximately 14 months and sales had increased approximately 57 percent during that period. Again, ESI's market share increased significantly relative to its principal competitor.

Financial Policy

Baker's rapid growth produced a substantial demand for capital. From 1975 to 1979, net assets tripled. This level of expenditure placed heavy demands on Baker's ability to generate external capital. To accommodate this growth, in 1977 and 1978 Baker's debt increased $172 million, $40 million of which represented a convertible debenture issue. In early 1979, the company issued an additional $61 million in common stock.

Clark believed that (1) for companies and managements in which the financial community had confidence and which had produced a satisfactory record of performance, capital was unlimited, and (2) as long as the stock market felt that the company was going to be "reasonably financed" in the long run, the debt ratio at any point in time did not have any impact on stock price. To Clark, the critical element was generating opportunities that provided an adequate return. If these returns were realized, he believed they would guarantee capital availability. The company's financial objective was merely to enable itself to undertake the right investments and to finance them in such a way as "not to foul up the company financially." (Baker's financial statements for 1974 through 1979 are summarized in Exhibit 12.)

Based on these beliefs, Clark established clear financial policies comprised of three principal components: (1) the maintenance of a debt/equity ratio of 50 percent (plus or minus 10 percent) over the longer term; (2) the issuance of equity when necessary to maintain the desired debt/equity ratio, and (3) the retention of 80 percent to 85 percent of the firm's earnings for reinvestment. Clark explained the selection of the target debt/equity ratio:

EXHIBIT 12

BAKER INTERNATIONAL CORPORATION
Condensed Comparative Consolidated Financial Information
(in thousands of dollars except per share amounts)

	1979	1978	1977	1976	1975	1974
Summary of operations:						
Total revenues	$1,168,811	$919,022	$708,696	$552,582	$509,777	$372,989
Costs and expenses:						
Cost of sales, services, and rental	612,804	486,643	371,840	291,482	275,766	210,386
Marketing and field service expense	266,241	208,387	166,159	130,835	108,912	83,978
General and administrative expense	88,869	69,770	54,016	35,637	33,818	28,729
Interest expense—net	33,607	19,174	10,598	10,696	10,144	6,168
Other	—	—	—	—	—	2,408
	1,001,521	783,974	602,613	468,650	428,640	331,669
Income from continuing operations before income taxes	167,290	135,048	106,083	83,932	81,137	41,320
Income taxes	167,861	57,878	45,669	35,085	35,730	19,102
Income from continuing operations	99,429	77,170	60,414	48,847	45,407	22,218
Discontinued operations	—	—	—	—	—	269
Net income	$ 99,429	$ 77,170	$ 60,414	$ 48,847	$ 45,407	$ 22,487
Net income per share:†						
Primary	$3.25	$2.67	$2.12	$1.76	$1.71	$.90*
Fully diluted	3.10	—	—	—	—	—
Dividends:						
Per share†	$.52	$.38	$.27	$.22	$.20	$.19
Aggregate	15,909	$ 10,984	$ 7,818	$ 5,835	$ 4,376	$ 3,834

Financial position:						
Current assets	609,356	$495,458	$390,673	$302,555	$278,055	$211,795
Property—net	458,491	335,362	223,654	174,859	144,426	104,902
Other assets	55,137	57,383	26,091	16,700	15,768	14,590
	$1,122,984	$889,193	$640,418	$494,114	$438,249	$331,287
Current liabilities	232,783	196,935	138,146	92,491	105,810	78,678
Long-term debt	272,685	242,519	132,795	106,134	94,847	86,751
Deferred income taxes	51,036	37,208	26,808	18,451	10,515	4,745
Accrued pension liabilities	3,978	5,667	7,830	10,445	11,616	11,389
Minority interests in subsidiary companies	2,716	1,705	2,596	2,526	2,001	1,367
Shareholders' equity	559,786	405,159	332,243	264,067	213,460	148,357
	$1,122,984	$889,193	$640,418	$494,114	$438,249	$331,287
Book value per share of common stock†	17.72	13.91	11.54	9.44	7.77	5.73
Current ratio	2.62	2.52	2.83	3.27	2.63	2.69
Return on equity based on year-end shareholders' equity	17.8%	19.0%	18.2%	18.5%	21.3%	15.0%

* Consists of $.89 from continuing operations and $.01 from discontinued operations.
† Adjusted to reflect 2-for-1 stock splits in May 1978.
Source: Baker International Corporation 1979 Annual Report.

If I was a boy genius, I might try to seek out an optimum debt/equity ratio. But since I am not, I don't try to. Instead, I look at the rating agencies' criteria for companies with acceptable risk levels [A-rated companies]. Since they have had a lot of historical experience with financial risk, why should I, as an engineer, try to outguess these standards? They represent historically proven levels of risk. In addition, this debt/equity ratio provides a comfort zone in my mind. I can gamble on certain investments within this ratio and still be comfortable. If the company should drop $40 million in one area, Baker would still be financially sound. In essence, this is my comfort blanket.

Baker management's willingness to issue equity acted as a safety valve to relieve the pressures on expenditures that otherwise could result from a well-defined and maintained capital structure policy. The policy on equity financing had led to three common stock issues and one convertible debenture issue from 1974 through fiscal 1979. These issues totalled $140 million, which represented approximately 25 percent of year-end 1979 shareholders' equity (adjusted for the conversion of the convertible debentures.)[6]

From 1968 through fiscal 1979, Baker's long-term debt, including the convertible debentures, rose from $1.0 million to $272.7 million. Thus, Baker, a company that had only $56.8 million in assets in 1968, had used $371.7 million in external financing to fuel its growth over a ten-year period.

WAY OF MANAGING

Outsider observers disagreed as to the degree to which Baker's performance was the result of the company's domination by one man—Hubie Clark—and of a strategy personally formulated by him with "prophetic" insight and conducted through a highly personal management style. For example, one leading industry analyst expressed the opinion that Clark's "greatest legacy" might be "his having made himself dispensable through an excellent planning and control system and a reasonable degree of decentralization." More often, however, Baker's success was viewed in terms of a "one man show." In discussing Clark, whom *Business Week* described as being "held in near-awe on Wall Street," a security analyst remarked, "If Clark's plane crashed, so would Baker's multiple."[7] Was this position well founded, or had a management system been infused in the organization that could maintain the company's performance with-

---

[6] The effective price/earnings ratio of these four equity offerings ranged from 12.1 to 25.4 times Baker's EPS for the 12 months preceding the offering. However, based on earnings for the 12 months following the offering, their P/E was 10.1 to 11.5 times.

[7] Security analysts commonly defined Clark's value to Baker in terms of price/earnings multiples (for example, "Clark is worth 2 to 3 P/E points").

out Clark? To assist us in addressing this question, this section outlines Baker's management style.

Encompassing the planning process and the control, measurement, and reward systems, Baker developed a way of managing that placed a heavy emphasis on divisional autonomy, on each general manager possessing a personal feel for the market, and on teamwork and communication within the divisional management groups. Managers were constantly charged with the responsibility to look further into the future. Clark observed:

> The general manager's (whether divisional or corporate) prime obligation is to "feel" his business—to have a sensitivity to the market trends and geopolitical forces that will impact his market. If you don't sense where the market is going, then all else can be lost. This sense needs to be a very personal one and is difficult to achieve working through a staff.

In discussing his tendency, when problems arose in the divisions, to opt to protect the concept of autonomy rather than to intercede directly in decision making, Clark explained:

> When you start to get involved in divisional decision making, it is certain death. You cannot ever extract yourself. When a management problem arises, we try—as long as we feel safe—to encourage, train, and enhance the people that are there. We never remove their decision-making authority.
>
> If we really think a manager is heading for the rocks and our attempts to consult, cajole, and convince fail, rather than pull the steering wheel away from him and steer the ship away, we'll fire him before he hits the rocks.

Clark felt that, for general managers who could not be motivated to refocus their attention on understanding the critical market trends, or for whom there was clear evidence that the division had outgrown their managerial abilities, the "salvage operation" involved in retaining them was "very high risk for everyone including the individual."

Organization

Baker operated with a small corporate management group of approximately 35 people including group-level management, secretaries, and accounting personnel. There was no corporate planning staff or centralized marketing, manufacturing, purchasing, or R&D functions. Each operating division possessed self-contained management resources in all functional areas and had a president who reported to one of Baker's three group presidents.

Management's objectives for its decentralized organization structure were (1) to facilitate "a more coherent market perception" in part by locating decision making close to the "fighting ground"; (2) to increase the motivation for personal progress; and (3) to encourage operating level efficiencies by heading off the proliferation of bureaucratic structures. In line with these objectives, corporate management defined its primary role to be threefold:

1. As the testing ground for divisional activities and ideas, assisting the divisions in developing acceptable plans and objectives and actively monitoring and evaluating actual performance.
2. As a banker, providing the capital to be used in divisional operations.
3. To invest "opportunity" money in areas outside the perspective of existing divisional activities.

Acquired companies were normally left intact under their own management rather than being consolidated into other divisions.[8] Clark considered the maintenance of divisional autonomy to be one of the most important strategic moves that he made during the 1970s. Retaining the separate identity of the acquired companies allowed the "entrepreneurial spirit" present in many of these companies to be maintained and did not interrupt the buying-habit patterns that customers had developed around these companies' products.

As described by an executive of one of Baker's largest divisions, the divisions considered autonomy an obligation of the parent company:

> From the divisional standpoint, we view the relationship between the division and Baker as a "written" contract. It is our obligation to do what we said we were going to do and, as long as we perform accordingly, corporate will stay out and supply the necessary capital. In return, we agree to use the capital in a certain fashion and within certain limits.

Planning and the Management of the Autonomous Divisions

All of the planning for existing operations was done by the operating divisions. Corporate management's approval of a division's operating plan provided division management with spending authority as long as performance was in accordance with this plan. Since 1968, a capital budget had never been taken to the board of directors for approval and there were no formal spending authority limits within the company. If a division president forecasted an acceptable RONCE over a five-year period and performed well against that goal, corporate management did not restrict his expenditures.

Planning provided the vehicle to assure the focus on "living in the future" which Clark so highly valued and which was considered the most important goal-setting process in the company. Through this plan-

---

[8] Each company was given a clearly defined "market charter" that prevented it from encroaching on the businesses of other Baker companies. In addition, acquired companies were not required to change their chart of accounts. Clark, however, developed a financial reporting system that consisted of approximately 20 key line items for each division.

ning process, joint commitments were obtained across levels of management as to the critical trends affecting the business and the action that should be undertaken in response to those trends. Management described the planning and control system as being predicated on two "fundamental beliefs":

1. That an operating business plan should not reflect simply what management believes the future to hold, but rather what management is committed to achieving; and,

2. That to achieve a plan once it is established, the only truly effective form of control is self-control.

Clark expanded on his view of the planning system:

> The greatest purpose of a plan is not to create the plan but to tell the manager what he should be doing with his time. The plan is not important. *What is important is that the people who make the plan know what they must do.* Every time we make a plan, each divisional chief executive must report to the group president the five most important things he must do to make the plan happen. It's most important that a person and his boss are together on what they should be doing. A boss has the obligation to use his experience to help. If someone is about to put his foot in a bucket and the boss doesn't see it, then they are making a "co-mistake." When it comes time to lay the lash, the boss is going to be more tolerant and fair.

In an attempt to assure accurate forecasting, management gathered market data at both the divisional and the corporate level. During the 1970s, Hubie Clark developed an extensive network of personal contacts, including heads of state, the heads of major oil companies and rig manufacturers, and bankers. Based on the data from these sources, Baker's executives (usually Clark himself) developed a long-term forecast of drilling activity by geographic regions of the world that placed a heavy emphasis on geopolitical considerations. Corporate management felt that their ability to forecast enabled them more thoroughly to question divisional assumptions about the marketplace and as a result, the divisions were motivated to do a better job of keeping abreast of the market themselves. In addition, the corporate forecasts provided background information for use with outsiders (such as security analysts) to display management's knowledge of the market.

At the divisional level, data on drilling activity were gathered on a regional basis from operating personnel in oil companies and were aggregated to determine current rig activity levels and short-term trends.

The result of these activities was a planning system that won accolades from the financial press. *Dun's Review* stated that Baker had "one of the most accurate forecasting and planning systems in the entire petroleum industry" and *Fortune* proclaimed Clark to have "a prophetic view of the whole energy business."

FUTURE DIVERSIFICATION

Shortly after the close of fiscal 1979, Hubie Clark faced a decision of significant strategic, organizational, and personal proportions: should he substantially reduce his involvement in the management of Baker's existing businesses in order to execute a major diversification in a new industry ("NEWCO")? This issue represented the convergence of several problems that Clark had been wrestling with for some time. Consideration of NEWCO began in 1978 at a time when Baker was projecting cash flows and debt capacity for the early 1980s considerably in excess of the reinvestment opportunities in existing businesses. (The need for substantial investments to meet the surge in demand following the Iranian revolution subsequently postponed this outlook until the mid-1980s.) Organizational concerns also motivated Clark to consider reducing his participation in the management of Baker's established businesses. Baker's increasing complexity during the 1970s had reduced Clark's ability to manage the company with the same degree of personal involvement in divisional strategy as in the past. In addition, the more control he exercised over the group presidents, the greater the likelihood that they might leave the company and the slower and more uncertain would be the process of providing for management succession. Yet he was troubled by the prospect of removing himself from the day-to-day operations of the company.[9]

In preparing to make a decision on these issues, Clark spent considerable time with his four top corporate managers discussing the implications of the alternative actions: the top managers' potential new roles, the probability that Clark could successfully back away from existing operations, and their predictions of what Clark would do relative to NEWCO. Through these discussions, Clark felt that he gained "additional insights" into his own motivations and capabilities and the impact of the alternatives on the organization. Although the management team confirmed many of Clark's beliefs, they took issue with some. For example, if Clark were to remove himself from active involvement in Baker's businesses, he felt he should delegate the strategic forecasting function. Other corporate officers questioned whether this function, which had been critical to Baker's past success, could be split between the three proposed companies and retain its effectiveness.

Strategic Concerns

Clark was motivated to seek diversification into a third industry in part to reduce Baker's substantial reliance on the oil-field services indus-

---

[9] To test his self-discipline to abstain from such direct involvement and his ability to gain personal satisfaction from a more distant relationship, Clark had begun to sit as a director on the boards of several non-Baker companies.

try. The decline in the industry's growth expected in the 1990s would require that Baker enter into a new industry of considerable potential in order to maintain the company's superb growth record.

Clark described the process of diversification as matching Baker's strengths and "personality" with major social, technological, or demographic changes that would generate business opportunities. As Clark began to think of the problem, he identified six principal strengths of the company upon which diversification might build: (1) the ability to gain an in-depth understanding of an industry through long-range planning and to manage through the planning process, (2) knowledge of the supply side of the energy industry, (3) experience in international operations (Baker operated in over 100 countries), (4) a management system that enabled the company to maintain high margins and a high return on investment while managing a 15 percent to 30 percent growth rate in revenues, (5) a reputation for making acquisitions at a reasonable cost that fit into an overall image acceptable to the financial community, and (6) the ability to maintain the entrepreneurial characteristics of the acquired companies while improving their performance.

Clark wanted Baker to avoid industries characterized as (1) cyclical ("I don't want to be in a business where kids don't know whether they're going to be able to go to college next year because the old man may get laid off"), (2) dependent on nonrenewable resources or having life cycles of less than 50 years, (3) dominated by large companies such as IBM, Xerox, and General Motors ("we've watched people take on the giants . . . there have got to be better things to do than to punch King Kong in the nose"), (4) having more than seven competitors, and (5) being the type that portfolio managers, security analysts, and investors would have difficulty analyzing and as a result, would not have the confidence to put Baker common stock on their buy lists. Emphasizing the latter characteristic, Clark said: "In the final analysis, getting the Baker we put together on a buy list is the only way our shareholders can take something out. If I keep earnings and sales growing at 35 percent per year and the stock price grows at 2 percent a year, what have I done? I've botched the whole damn thing."

Clark characterized the criteria for businesses the company would consider entering as in keeping with its historical acquisition criteria: (1) high-technology products with a high service content and with a high cost of failure to the customer, (2) businesses with gross margins in excess of 40 percent, (3) companies with a 10 percent or greater share of an uncluttered market (that is, not price-sensitive markets), (4) growth potential at least equal to three times the growth of GNP, and (5) in an industrial sector with the potential of becoming 2–4 percent of the GNP by the turn of the century.

Clark had broached the NEWCO issue with the financial community, particularly security analysts, and generally had received a negative response. Clark summarized this feedback as follows:

Security analysts have asked me, "Why diversify now?" in a very critical sense. They say, "It's going to divert resources from the best industry in the world. Whatever you choose it's going to be second best to what you're in. Hubie, you know this industry well enough that anything you do outside of it is a waste of your time compared to enhancing this business."

They are right that there's a very good probability that our industry has the best outlook for the next ten years of any business in the entire world. When you are riding the top of the heap, there is no diversification that is not a step down. I try to tell them that there's nothing happening out there that I could *make* happen. I have people who are doing it as well, if not better, than I can. But there's some problem in getting people to believe that. There is still some tendency to say, "You're the guiding genius," and all that malarkey.

Clark identified another problem posed by diversification—the dilution of earnings per share over the next decade.

I don't have to do anything in order to have good growth rates during the 1980s. Almost anything I do is likely to cut my growth rate of earnings per share. But you have to believe you're doing the right thing for the 25-year period. If I do the right thing, the rest will take care of itself. There's nothing I can do to have an impact on the next ten years except maybe negatively. The best thing I can do for the next ten years is sit on my hands! Right?

Organizational Concerns

Clark was also considering removing himself from the bulk of the general management responsibilities for the company's three operating groups. He envisioned the group presidents becoming chief executives of their own businesses with the accompanying authority, each with his own "annual report" complete with president's letter, and with his own board of directors dominated by outsiders who would also sit on the parent company's board. To reduce the temptation for Clark to remain actively involved in the business of the individual companies and to accentuate the autonomy of the company presidents, Clark planned not to sit on the board of any of the subsidiaries. His formal involvement would be restricted to quarterly reviews of the operations of the three companies by Baker's board and the allocation of capital among the companies. However, Clark would reserve the right to intercede in a company's affairs if he saw it "heading for the rocks."

Clark saw three advantages of such an organizational move: (1) it would free his time for the intensive search required to identify NEWCO; (2) it would help maintain the company's dedication to decentralization; and (3) it would provide the group presidents the sense of satisfaction that would come from running their own show, thus reducing their motivation to leave the company. Clark felt that in a rapid growth industry the most valuable resource was highly competent executives and that any of the company's group presidents could get a job as a chief executive officer with little difficulty. If one left Baker, Clark believed it would not be for money (Baker's compensation package was highly competitive), but in order "to do his own thing." He wanted to provide the vehicle for them to do that within Baker. Clark explained, "I need to get out of their way so that they can say, 'Those tracks in the sand are mine, not Hubie Clark's.' "

Warren Kane,[10] president of the Drilling Group, in reflecting on the possible organization change, considered it in part a reflection of Baker's increasing size:

> The size of the corporation brings on change, whether you like it or not. The bigger Baker gets, the more structure we must impose to manage the company. This pushes Hubie further away from the operating side of the business day by day.
>
> Security analysts get enamored with an individual as the true leader of the company and lose sight of the day that even the best of leaders lose control because they can no longer communicate with the operators.

Personal Concerns

As Clark pondered the decision, he wrestled with substantial personal questions. Could he discipline himself to stay out of the management of the company he had created? Even if he could, would he find sufficient satisfaction in his new role? Should he risk destroying the substantial reputation that he enjoyed? Were the critics in the financial community right that it would be an unnecessary diversion of Baker's critical managerial and financial resources? He recognized that there was not a compelling strategic reason for him to make such a move now—it could be done later during the 1980s. So should he move now?

Clark reflected on his role in the company and the personal aspects of the decision:

> To some extent, I feel that I've either got to do it or get out. A very personal pressure says, "You don't have a choice. You have to go this way or retire." Another pressure is that I know it's right. This company's business is based on an asset that someday is going to be gone. I know that it's right for our shareholders that I do this and the sooner I do it the better off we're going to be. Waiting until the last minute is probably the worst thing we could do.
>
> When I reflect on my contribution to this company, I think it is

---

[10] Motivated in part by the desire to obtain greater operating autonomy, Warren Kane, a director of Baker since 1971, left his position as senior vice president of a major international engineering and construction company to join Baker in 1976 as president of the Mining Group. He became president of the Drilling Group in 1979.

probably anticipation. I'm not sure my contribution is in the execution and realization of that anticipation, although I think I can do it. Thus, I take the position that I would lose nothing if I devoted my efforts to the pursuit of NEWCO because of the people we've got and the fact that the market is predestined. The market is going to happen no matter whether I stay, leave, or die. The indicators are now clear and much more stabilized. It's no longer a kaleidoscope. We have enough history now that what must happen and why it must happen is predictable. If I say to myself, "Clark, you have an ability to walk in the future," then I should be spending it where other people aren't looking, instead of where 50 to 100 people can walk in that track as accurately as I can. So, I say to myself, "First of all, I'm not needed over there; I'm not needed for looking down the road because what's going to happen is clear. We've already posted road signs. I need to be out where there's trees and no roads and you've got to figure out where the road should go. That's my greatest contribution." I totally disagree with the security analysts who say that my leaving would be a diversion of resources. I do not think it would be. I think it would clear the way for other resources to flower.

The critics in the financial community also talk about diversion of financial resources and I say, "Baloney, I can get all the money I need." There is no competition for financial resources. I can sell common stock. I've got a 16 P/E. If I tell you that I need money, you know that I know enough about the business to have identified good investment opportunities. If I give you a shot at buying some of my stock, you're going to jump at it. So when you talk to me about competition for resources, you're not facing reality.

Yet from my perspective, there's a psychological problem I have to wrestle with. I could sit here and ride through to retirement and look damn good. I'm 54 now, and I've probably got more net worth than I can drink up or eat up . . . so I could ride the crest of this wave and never be there when it crashes on the beach. So I say to myself, "Why should I gamble? I've got a good reputation as a soothsayer. What if I walk out in the dark forest and say, 'You all come down this road,' and I take all the troops over a cliff?" I'm going into an uncharted area that I don't know. The last time I did this, I had grown up in the industry, I had a desire, I knew those wells from top to bottom, I knew drilling, I knew production, I knew everything. Now I've got to go out in a world I don't know and conquer it. You build up a good reputation; you're a reported soothsayer and all that sort of stuff. Why should I gamble my reputation to go into an area I don't know?

Section B

Establishing Objectives and Formulating Strategies for Accomplishment

CASE 4

Note on the Soft Drink Industry in the United States

"The soft drink is one of the greatest of American traditions," commented a reporter, "really far more American than apple pie (which originated in France) or hot dogs (which are of German extraction). The soft drink was born and raised in the U.S. of A., and most of us were born and raised with soft drinks—or soda pop for those of western heritage."

Some might well object to this nationalistic interpretation since naturally carbonated water was used as medicine by the ancient Greeks and soft drinks had been commercially available in Europe for years. Yet clearly the American consumer has had a long love affair with "soda pop." In 1974 total soft drink sales were over $7.8 billion at wholesale and per person consumption was over 429 eight-ounce containers per year. And the romance has been of long duration; buoyed by population and real income growth, per capita consumption doubled from 1962 to 1973. Soft drink case sales rose from 1,668 million to 3,772 million during that period moving from 16 percent of total beverage consumption in 1960 to almost 25 percent in 1973. This sales growth brought prosperous days to concentrate makers, bottlers, and retail organizations.

In 1974 and 1975 industry growth patterns changed, with case sales and per capita consumption remaining approximately level. Had the bloom disappeared from the rose—or should we ask, had the "fizzle disappeared and the soda pop gone flat"? Industry analysts seemed to agree that the 7 to 8 percent annual unit growth rates of the past were probably no longer possible. But what next? One analyst noted, "The industry is in a period when sales will basically plateau." Maxwell Associates, a consulting firm, predicted 3 to 4 percent sales growth in 1976. But these modestly enthusiastic future predictions by analysts did not seem to deter the competitive ambitions of the industry's leading firms. Each of the top five companies, according to Standard & Poor's *1976 Beverage Industry Reports,* had clear-cut expansion goals. "Dr Pepper expects to continue to grow at two to three times the industry rate and is confident of being number three in national sales in the not too distant future. Pepsi hopes to extend its string of 52 consecutive months of market share gain, and, nevertheless, Coke expects to continue to gain market share on a total product basis." The president of the Seven-Up Company, on another occasion, announced, "We really believe and we're seriously dedicated to the point of view that 7UP can and should be the number one selling soft drink in the United States."

In addition to this development, the industry was confronted with pressure from private environmental groups and increasing interest on the part of regulatory agencies in its operations. Private environmental groups and federal and state agencies were attempting to find ways of limiting the use of nonreturnable containers. Governmental concerns about health forced the industry to drop cyclamates as a substitute for sugar in diet drinks, and government antitrust concerns had resulted in legal action against the franchise system—regarded by many company executives as important to the industry's success.

Commenting on the overall scene, one corporate officer queried, "Where is this industry going? I'm not sure! Competition is getting worse. Nothing seems to stay pinned down—franchising, distribution, ingredients, and packaging are all 'up for grabs.' One competitive development has already started. Billboard advertising has always had a 'product message,' but now they are being directed to a 'cents per ounce' price theme. Food stores will become a battlefield." This note explores the soft drink segment of the U.S. beverage industry; as such it gives but limited attention to the international market and to other beverages such as coffee, tea, chocolate, milk, bottled waters, juices, and alcoholic drinks. In sequence, the note will cover 6 areas: the product—past success and current situation; industry structure and participants; key industry functional strategies; new competitors—the intruders; the industry's critics; and future market directions—a cloudy crystal ball.

In studying this note, the reader should keep in mind the complexity of the territory being described and the simplicity of this map. He or she will note that some of these data are not comparable, that experts sometimes derive diametrically opposite conclusions from common data, and that some very useful data were simply not available. Any judgments made, by necessity, must be tentative.

PRODUCT

Soft drinks, or nonalcoholic carbonated beverages, consist of a flavoring base such as cola, a sweetener, water, and carbonation. Most soft drinks are consumed cold, and the product has a seasonal sales pattern, peaking in hot summer months.

Originating in a Philadelphia apothecary shop, soft drinks were first sold primarily through drugstore soda fountains where flavors and carbonated water would be mixed for immediate sale to an on-premise customer. This early association with apothecaries and drugstores gave soft drinks a medicinal association which still prevailed, to some degree, in the 70s. The executive vice president of Seven-Up commented, "There was a group for whom our green bottle had almost medicinal or therapeutic overtones, the thing to take when you had the flu and the doctor told you to take a lot of liquid."[1]

The development of manually operated filling and bottling machines in the mid-1800s encouraged the establishment of thousands of local bottling works. Each of these supplied carbonated beverages to its nearby market under a variety of brand names, which the researcher found fascinating: Cardinal Necter, Queer, Marrowfood, Creme Puncho, Peach Bounce, Muscadine Thrill, Wami, and Egg Soda—the latter coming in an egg-shaped bottle.

In 1884 Hires Root Beer advertised in *Harper's Magazine*. The trade name Dr Pepper was copyrighted in 1885, followed by Coca-Cola in 1886. Brad's Drink, which became Pepsi-Cola, appeared in 1886. The predecessor company of Seven-Up was formed in 1906 (7UP was introduced in 1920), and the predecessor company of Royal Crown appeared in 1924 and introduced Royal Crown Cola in 1935.

In 1976 regular soft drinks came in a variety of flavors with cola accounting for 58 percent of the market. Most of these used sugar or sugar plus high fructose corn syrup as a sweetener; diet drinks (15 percent of the market) used a noncolor artificial sweetener, in 1976, usually saccharin. Diet drinks in most cases carried related brand names, for example, Diet Pepsi, Sugar Free Dr Pepper; but in some cases they were promoted under different brands, for example, Tab (Coca-Cola) and Diet-Rite Cola (Royal Crown). National brands accounted for approximately 67 percent of the U.S. market in 1975 (see Exhibits 1 and 2).

The Industry's Past Success

The soft drink industry had enjoyed consistent and substantial growth over a period of several decades; per capita consumption had

---

[1] "Can Uncola Make Cola Cry Uncle?" *The Grocery Manufacturer,* June 1972, p. 82.

EXHIBIT 1: Market Share by Flavor

Flavors	1971	1972	1973	1974	1975	1976*
Regular cola	52.0%	51.5%	51.0%	51.0%	50.0%	50.5%
Diet cola.	5.6	6.0	6.2	6.6	7.3	7.8
Total cola	57.6	57.5	57.2	57.6	58.0	58.3
Regular lemon-lime	11.4	11.3	11.4	11.3	11.0	10.9
Sugar free lemon-lime	0.6	0.7	0.8	1.2	1.7	2.0
Total lemon-lime.	12.0	12.0	12.2	12.5	12.7	12.9
Regular orange	4.8	4.7	4.6	4.4	3.9	3.6
Regular root beer.	4.4	4.4	4.0	3.9	4.1	4.2
Dr Pepper and Mr. PiBB	3.9	4.3	5.0	5.2	5.7	6.0
Diet Dr Pepper and Mr. PiBB.	0.2	0.4	0.5	0.7	0.9	1.2
Total Pepper	4.1	4.7	5.5	5.9	6.6	7.2
Ginger ale, tonic, carbonated water, and soda	4.4	4.6	4.7	4.8	4.9	5.0
All other (regular grape, Mountain Dew, chocolate, black cherry, etc.).	9.6	9.0	8.3	7.4	6.0	4.8
All other diet, diet orange, and root beer	2.9	3.0	3.4	3.6	3.8	4.0
Total regular drinks	90.6	89.8	89.0	87.9	86.2	85.0
Total diet drinks.	9.4	10.2	11.0	12.1	13.8	15.0
Total	100.0%	100.0%	100.0%	100.0%	100.0%	100.0%

* Estimated.
Source: J. C. Frazzano, Oppenheimer & Co., *Beverage World*, February 1977, p. 8.

EXHIBIT 2: Top Ten Soft Drink Brands 1966–1975

1966		1970		1975	
Brand	**Percent Share of Market**	**Brand**	**Percent Share of Market**	**Brand**	**Percent Share of Market**
Coke	27.6	Coke	34.8	Coke	26.2
Pepsi	16.1	Pepsi	14.2	Pepsi	17.4
7UP	6.4	7UP	5.8	7UP	6.6
Royal Crown Cola	3.8	Royal Crown	3.5	Dr Pepper	4.9
Dr Pepper	2.4	Dr Pepper	3.4	Royal Crown	3.4
Diet Pepsi	1.9	Sprite (Coke)	2.3	Sprite (Coke)	2.6
Diet-Rite Cola (Royal Crown)	1.6	Diet-Rite Cola (Royal Crown)	1.8	Tab (Coke)	2.6
Sprite	1.5	Fresca (Coke)	1.4	Diet Pepsi	1.7
Tab	1.4	Canada Dry Ginger Ale	1.1	Mountain Dew (Pepsi)	1.3
Mountain Dew (Pepsi)	1.4	Diet Pepsi	0.9	Canada Dry	1.2
	64.1	Tab (Coke)	0.9		66.7
			70.0		

Source: Maxwell *Consumer Service Reports on the Soft Drink Industry,* February 23, 1976; used with the permission of the Dr Pepper Company.

EXHIBIT 3: Historic per Capita Soft Drink Consumption
and Wholesale Sales Levels, Selected Years

Year	Wholesale Sales ($ millions)	Cases (192 ounces) (millions)	Per Capita (8-ounce containers)
1859	$ 1.4	2.8	2.2
1929	214	272	53.1
1950	877	1.002	158.0
1960	1,698	1,477	192.0
1970	4,800	3,097	362.8
1972	5,684	3,541	406.4
1973	6,223	3,772	429.6
1974	7,827	3,798	429.4

Source: Adapted from data furnished by the National Soft Drink Association,
1975; used with permission of the Dr Pepper Company.

increased from 17.5 gallons in 1960 to 31.6 gallons in 1974, an increase
of 65 percent. Soft drinks, a Boston physician decried, are "cradle to
grave. We wean babies to Coke and serve 7UP to the geriatrics ward."
A casualty in the gallonage race was water.

Four primary factors, the researchers believed, had contributed significantly to this success: the growth in disposable income, marketing
innovations, packaging developments, and the industry's competitive culture (see Exhibits 3, 4, and 5).

In commenting on the first factor, Emanuel Goldman of Sanford
Bernstein and Company noted:

> The work that I've done clearly indicates that the industry is most
> sensitive to real disposable personal income . . . when real DPI was pumping
> along at about 3.5 to 4.0 percent growth rate in real terms, soft drink gal-
> lonage was growing at some faster rate. . . . Similarly, during recessionary
> periods, 1954 and 1958, for example, the recession of '60 to '61, and the
> recession of mid-'74 to mid-'75, there was a definite softness, with a decline
> in soft drink volume in the mid-year to mid-year periods.[2]

Second, corporate executives stressed the importance of marketing
to the industry's past accomplishments. W. W. Clements, chairman of
the Dr Pepper Company, noted:

> This industry has several characteristics that place it somewhere in
> between true service industries and purely manufacturing industries. It,
> in addition, does not qualify as an industry relying to any great extent
> on engineering development or research. The sophisticated part of the soft
> drink industry is the marketing area.[3]

[2] "The Beverage Industry," *The Wall Street Transcript,* May 24, 1976, pp. 43, 766.

[3] Unpublished speech to Thunderbird School of International Management, June 8,
1972.

EXHIBIT 4: U.S. Beverage Consumption, 1960–1974

	1960 Gallons per Capita	1964 Gallons per Capita	1970 Gallons per Capita	1974 Gallons per Capita	Percent Increase (decrease) 1964–74	1975 Gallons per Capita
Coffee.	40.2	39.2	35.5	32.8	(15)	31.6
Soft drinks	17.5	19.1	27.0	31.6	65	31.4
Milk.	28.0	25.9	25.0	25.9	(7)	24.5
Beer	15.4	16.0	18.5	21.3	33	21.6
Tea.	6.0	6.2	6.9	7.6	23	7.4
Juices	4.0	3.2	4.8	5.7	78	6.1
Distilled spirits . . .	1.3	1.4	1.8	2.0	43	2.0
Wine	n.a.	1.0	6.3	1.7	70	1.7
Total	112.4	112.4	125.8	126.9		126.3

Imputed water consumption: 1966, 67.3 gallons per capita; 1975, 56.7 gallons per capita.

n.a. = not available.
Sources: Maxwell *Consumer Services for 1960–1974*, used with permission of Dr Pepper Co. The 1975 data from *Advertising Age*.

Since the 1930s, industry operations had been substantially influenced by the competitive struggle between Coke and Pepsi. Pepsi, during that era, began to challenge the industry giant with a series of marketing innovations. In 1939 Pepsi used the first singing radio commercial: "Pepsi-Cola hits the spot. Twelve full ounces that's a lot. Twice as much for a nickel too. Pepsi-Cola is the drink for you." In 1942 reporter Robert Scheer noted that a survey showed this jingle to be the best-known tune in the United States—ahead of the Star-Spangled Banner. In 1976 most soft drink companies were heavy investors in all kinds of worldwide consumer advertising. To his dismay, Scheer found a soft drink sign greeting visitors as they climbed the steps to the apadana to view the magnificent ruins of Persepolis in Iran.

EXHIBIT 5: Disposable Income and Soft Drink Industry Growth

Year	Disposable Personal Income ($ billions)	Percent Increase	Constant $ D.P.I. ($ billions)	Percent Increase	Soft Drink Industry Percent Increase
1972	$795.1	6.9	$579.0	4.3	5.6
1971	744.3	8.0	544.7	4.1	8.3
1970	689.5	8.8	533.2	3.9	6.3
1969	634.0	7.3	513.6	2.9	4.9
1968	591.0	8.2	499.0	4.6	12.1
1965	473.2	8.0	435.0	6.6	8.0
1963	404.6	5.1	381.3	3.9	7.0
1961	364.4	4.1	350.7	3.1	3.2
1959	337.3	5.8	330.0	4.4	0.0

Source: Based on Bureau of the Census data, 1973.

Pepsi also began to systematically survey changing life styles and relate its marketing program to that moving target.

> Pepsi being a modern corporation takes its cultural contributions seriously and all of the execs . . . are quite aware that they have never been in the business of simply selling a product but rather a way of life. Throughout the years of Pepsi-Coke rivalry, the arena has always been in the packaging and sales effort and not the concentrate, which has stayed the same while the companies' fortunes have gone up and down. It was, therefore, not the taste that mattered but rather how the public was taught to perceive it. The same stuff could be "light," "sociable," a healthful tonic—it could make you "stay young and fair and debonair" and gets you into The Pepsi Generation. This magic is worked for a concentrate that is basically the same for all of the colas and the much-guarded secrets can be obtained from a flavor chemist's handbook.[4]

---

[4] "The Doctrine of Multinational Sell," Robert Scheer, *Esquire,* April 1975, pp. 163–65.

Industry innovations in packaging were also credited with increasing soft drink consumption. Developments occurred on many fronts: the introduction of soft drinks in cans and nonreturnable bottles, which encouraged increased out-of-the-home consumption; the introduction of new types of carrying containers, for example, the six-pack beverage package; and an increase in number of sizes of bottles and cans (see Exhibit 6). Between 1960 and 1975, available package sizes had increased from 2 to 10 sizes ranging from 6½ to 64 ounces, plus 1- and 2-liter sizes. One executive estimated that 24 ounces and larger packages accounted for over 30 percent of all soft drinks sold for home consumption in 1975.

EXHIBIT 6: Soft Drink Package Types, 1960–1975

	1960	1965	1970	1975
Returnable bottles	94%	83%	46%	34%
Nonreturnable bottles. . .	2	5	25	31
Cans	4	12	29	35

Sources: *Soft Drink Annual Manual*, 1971–1972, *Beverage Industry*, 3/19/76, and NSDA Sales Survey, 1960.

A final factor impacting industry growth was the corporate "climate" of the leading soft drink firms. As described by business jounalists, it seemed to be a mixture of general management leadership style, a concept of business competition as a "war game" and a set of corporate values which emphasized belief in your product, volume growth, market share improvement, and by all means "beat the competition and sell that drink." The latter goal was neatly summarized by a vice president who, speaking at the prospect of the Bamboo Curtain coming down, said, "There are 800 million gullets in China and I want to see a_____in every one of them."

Long dominated by "Mother Coke," the soft drink industry's recent competitive posture had been substantially influenced by two men—Donald Kendall, president of Pepsi-Cola, and W. W. Clements, president of Dr Pepper. Robert Scheer characterized Mr. Kendall and Pepsi's corporate "ambience" as follows:

> In ten years' time Don Kendall was to kick, pull, and make a bumbling, small one-product company into a modern multinational conglomerate giant. One of his first acts was to begin plans for the new world headquarters. The Purchase, New York, world headquarters of PepsiCo is on one hundred forty-one acres of choice Westchester property, sullied by not a single Pepsi-Cola sign. An "elegant modern" seven-building complex designed by Edward Durrell Stone is focused on an imported-cobblestone courtyard. Five thousand new trees (thirty-eight varieties), it is said, remind Kendall of his native Washington State and, as a somewhat personal touch, there is

jet d'eau in the lake which shoots up eighty feet whenever Kendall pushes a button on his desk.

I asked Kendall for his opinion of John Kenneth Galbraith's theory that corporations, being large planning units, could simply plan to have lower levels of growth. I might just as well have advocated bisexual love. "No growth! What?" It was the same disbelief that I found when I put the question to the other execs—like telling a missionary that the number of converts doesn't matter.[5]

W. W. Clement's aggressive leadership of Dr Pepper illustrated the "war game" characteristic of the industry. President of a company with profits amounting to but one-twentieth of Coke's, Mr. Clements's campaign to expand Dr Pepper's sales was described in part by Dudley Lynch:

One crisp November morning in 1969 Woodrow Wilson "Foots" Clements and his team of executives stepped into a cab outside New York's Waldorf-Astoria Hotel. Mission: To pull off what some would call the biggest coup in soft drink history. Clements and his Dr Pepper executives, representing an easy-going beverage which had stayed home in Texas and minded its own business for 85 years, headed over to the 34th Street offices of Coca-Cola Bottling Company of New York, the world's largest distributor of soft drink's Goliath: Coca-Cola. Objective: to convince Coca-Cola of New York to bottle Dr Pepper. Seven months later the arrangements were completed.

Dr Pepper's invasion of Coke's independent bottlers didn't go unnoticed at Coke's parent company headquarters, 310 North Avenue, Atlanta. Amidst Dr Pepper's campaign to sign up Coke bottlers came the New York coup, followed two years later by Dr Pepper's signing, in Mother Coke's backyard, of Coke's independent Atlanta bottler. Now the Coca-Cola parent company would take guests through the Atlanta bottling works and find themselves walking along halls bedecked with Dr Pepper signs. That was too much. "What Dr Pepper doesn't understand," suggests an Atlanta observer, "is the insult involved. What Dr Pepper did to Coke is something you just don't do to Coca-Cola—at least that's the way Coke views things. . . ."

Adding to the insult was Dr Pepper's foray two years ago into Japan, a market that in 1973 produced 19 percent of Coke's worldwide profits. Dr Pepper signed a joint venture, with yes, you guessed it, Tokyo Coca-Cola Bottling Company, to introduce Dr Pepper to Japan. . . . Jumping into Japan was like waving a red flag, says Richard McStay, formerly research director at Atlanta's Irby & Co. "To Coke, Japan is motherhood, virginity, apple pie or anything you want to call it."[6]

An additional industry characteristic should be noted: market characteristics for soft drinks varied substantially by region. The highest per capita consumption according to industry analysts was in the South and

---

[5] "The Doctrine of Multinationals," *Esquire,* April 1975, p. 126.

[6] "Dr Pepper Takes on Coke," *D Magazine (Dallas/Ft. Worth),* September 1975, p. 61.

Southwest. The popularity of diet drinks, flavor, packaging, and retail outlet preferences also varied by region (see Exhibit 7). Historically, soft drink companies had originated in the South, and in 1976 four out of the top five firms had their headquarters in the South and Southwest.

The Early 70s Market

In the early 70s soft drink sales plateaued: Per capita consumption was 31.9 gallons in 1973, 31.6 in 1974, and 31.4 gallons in 1975. Among industry analysts interviewed, there seemed to be general agreement that two critical factors at least partially explained this development: the 1974–75 decline in real disposable income and the approximately 50 percent retail price increase created by cost increases—primarily sugar (see Exhibit 8).

One analyst, commenting on the 1975 situation, said:

> From what I can tell, based on quarter-to-quarter changes in real income, generally soft drink consumption varies around those changes, but more dramatically. For example, in a bottlers survey that I completed, in the February–March period a year ago, when real income was down close to 5 percent, soft drink consumption was off 7 or 8 percent. Generally, when real income is growing on an annual basis at 4 to 5 percent, similar to the 10 years ending in December of '73, soft drink consumption was growing at a rate of about 7.8 percent compounded.[7]

The implications of price trends and consumer routines were viewed somewhat differently by another investigator:

> Sometime late in 1974, Andy Pearson (President of PepsiCo) made the statement that before PepsiCo's soft drink unit volume declined, soft drink bottling prices advanced by 54 percent. By that time, which was at the end of 1974, we did have real income starting to decline, and we had prices up 50 or 55 percent or whatever. So you did have the worst of two worlds, and I think this was one of the most important things that could happen to the soft drink industry because they realized that they had an enormous amount of pricing flexibility, and that volume was not impacted to any significant degree.[8]

INDUSTRY STRUCTURE AND PARTICIPANTS

There were four major participants involved in the soft drink industry: concentrate producers; soft drink bottling and distribution companies; retailers—primarily food stores, restaurants, and vending machine opera-

---

[7] *The Wall Street Transcript,* May 24, 1976, Mr. J. C. Frazzano, pp. 43, 766.

[8] Ibid., pp. 43, 767.

EXHIBIT 7: Regional Variations in the Soft Drink Market

	North-east	East Central	West Central	South	South-west	Western	Pacific
Diet	13%	8%		9%	11%	13%	14%
Flavors:							
Cola	30	47		55	42	53	41
Lemon-lime . . .	16	17		19	10	18	20
Package sizes:							
10 and 12 ounce . .	37	60		58	56	51	54
Over 24 ounces . .	40	16		18	16	22	20
Package type:*							
Returnable bottles. .	20	50		41	53	46	48
Nonreturnable bottles	38	9		25	13	10	18
Cans	33	22		24	27	30	24
Fountain	9	10		10	7	15	11
Outlets:*							
Food stores	70	54		72	60	54	73
Restaurants, bars . .	10	13		6	6	21	8
Service stations . .	5	12		10	12	10	8

* Percent of packaged volume.
Source: Company records based on data supplied by National Soft Drink Association.

EXHIBIT 8: Cola Carbonated Drink Consumer Price Indexes (1967 = 100)

Date	CPI	Change from Previous Year
January 1973	129.7	1.5
January 1974	136.5	5.2
July 1974	165.6	25.9
January 1975	203.3	48.9
July 1975	197.6	19.4
January 1976 (est.)	193.2	−4.9

Source: U.S. Bureau of Labor Statistics.

tors; and packaging and raw material suppliers. This industry classification system was imprecise with some firms operating in more than one category. Exhibit 9 gives the researcher's overview of the industry, with estimates, where available, as to the dollar amounts of 1974 intersector transactions.

Concentrate Producers

In 1975 there were approximately 56 concentrate producing and marketing firms in the United States. Major firms sold flavoring concentrate or syrup (concentrate plus sugar) to independent, franchised bottlers. Large concentrate firms might have from 300 to 800 separate franchise operations.

EXHIBIT 9

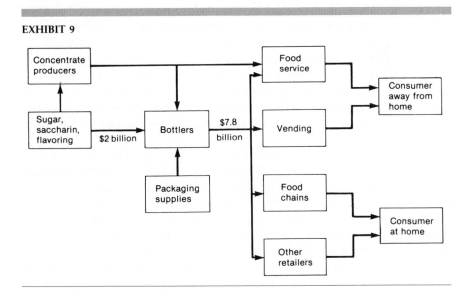

The concentrate sector was dominated by the "Big Six": Coca-Cola, PepsiCo, Seven-Up, Dr Pepper, Royal Crown, and Canada Dry (see Exhibit 10). Each of these firms served the U.S. markets and, in some instances, sold in international markets. Each had created a valuable consumer franchise by substantial and continuous brand, promotional, advertising, and marketing programs. Three members of the Big Six had achieved substantial diversification from their original product lines: Coca-Cola into noncola beverages and PepsiCo and Royal Crown into nonbeverage lines. Canada Dry (division of Norton-Simon), Seven-Up and Dr Pepper had remained primarily soft drink specialists.

EXHIBIT 10: Big Six Sales Net Profit and Product Breakdown, 1975 (in thousands of dollars)

	Sales	Net Profits	Major Product Lines
Coca-Cola . .	$2,872,000	$239,304	Beverages
PepsiCo . . .	2,300,000	104,600	Beverages, $1,035,000; food, $805,000; sporting goods, $230,000; transportation, $207,000
Royal Crown. .	257,451	13,294	Beverages, $159,000; citrus products, $43,000; home furnishings, $55,000
Seven-Up. . .	213,623	20,341	Beverages and flavors
Canada Dry*. .	180,032	13,861	Ginger ale, mixers, and standard flavor line
Dr Pepper . .	138,250	11,904	Beverages

* Division of Norton-Simon; 1975 overall sales of $2,443,027.
Source: Company records.

The second group of concentrate producers (see Exhibit 11) included smaller, independent national firms such as Dad's Root Beer (1.2 percent of 1975 market) and Squirt (0.8 percent of the market) as well as product divisions of larger companies, such as A&W Root Beer, a division of United Brands. These firms had geographically scattered representation often with smaller, less competitive bottlers. In addition, regional firms, such as Faygo in Michigan, produced a wide variety of regular and diet drinks in what the industry called flavor lines, for example, orange, strawberry, and grape. A decreasing share of market was controlled by small, local bottlers.

Two other competitive factors were the private label brands of local and national food chains and the products of the Shasta Beverage Division of the Consolidated Foods Corporation. Private labels had been on the competitive scene for many years. One trade source estimated that national brands sold in 1975 for about 2 cents per ounce (12-ounce can) while private labels sold for 1 to 1.2 cents per ounce. *Beverage Industry* in commenting about the current position of "Store Brands" noted "chain executives surveyed noted a significant decline in gross margins in private label soft drinks, currently about 21–22 percent. It was as high as 27 percent before current price increases. When warehouse costs (5–7 percent) are deducted from gross, the net profit is below that earned on national brands."[9] Typically, private brands were produced by nearby bottlers or contract canning companies.

EXHIBIT 11: Industry Participants' Percentage of Market

	1966	1972	1975
The Big Six:			
Coke.	33.4	34.7	35.3
PepsiCo	20.4	19.8	21.1
Seven-Up	6.9	7.2	7.6
Dr Pepper	2.7	3.8	5.5
Royal Crown	6.9	6.0	5.4
Canada Dry	4.2	3.6	3.4
Total	74.5	75.1	78.3
Small nationals and regionals:*			
Total	7.5	11.5	11.9
Supermarket private labels:			
Total	0.2	2.4	1.1
Shasta	0.9	1.9	2.5
All others (small, local firms)	16.9	9.1	6.2
Total cases (millions)	2,910	3,675	4,460

* Includes operations such as Hires, Orange Crush, Cott's, Dad's Root Beer, Squirt, Schweppes, Moxie-Monarch, Nugrape, A&W Root Beer, No-Cal, Faygo, White Rock.
Source: Data compiled from trade sources by the Dr Pepper Company.

Shasta, a subsidiary of Consolidated Foods (1976 sales of $2,754 billion—net income $89,453 million; soft drink and food division $239.3 million—pretax income of $17.2 million) produced standard flavors with diet drinks making up approximately 50 percent of overall sales. Sales were made to large purchasers, such as food stores, airlines, and government departments, with the bulk of the product being delivered directly to customer warehouses.

The Coca-Cola Company of Atlanta, Georgia, was number one among concentrate producers in terms of marketing franchise, sales, profit, share of market, and financial strength. Coke's 1975 balance sheet listed cash and marketable securities of $148 million, long-term debt of $9 million, and deferred taxes, capital stock, and surplus of $1.25 billion. Analysts estimated that Coke's international sales were growing more rapidly than domestic; the company had been the pioneer in international soft drink operations. Originally, and for decades, a specialist in cola drinks, Coke introduced a line of flavor drinks—Fanta orange and grape; Sprite, a lemon-lime drink; Mr. PiBB, a cherry cola drink; and diet drinks—

---

[9] *Beverage Industry 1975–76 Annual Manual,* p. 38.

Tab and Fresca. In the 1960s Coke added Minute Maid orange juice, instant tea and coffee, and bottled spring water.

PepsiCo of Purchase, New York, was the second largest company in the industry with 1975 sales approximating 80 percent of Coca-Cola's and its net profit 44 percent of Coke's. PepsiCo was involved in four major domestic product areas plus international operations. Its principal soft drinks were regular and diet Pepsi-Cola, Mountain Dew, and a new product, Pepsi Light (a semidiet, combination cola and lemon-lime drink). PepsiCo's food division was the leading snack food, for example, potato and corn-based products, producer in the United States with its own route delivery system. Two smaller divisions were involved in sporting goods and intercity truck transportation.

The 7UP brand was the third largest selling soft drink in the world; its product specialty was a lemon-lime drink sold in both regular and diet formula. Seven-Up, located in St. Louis, Missouri, dominated that flavor with an estimated 60 percent share of market, outselling the next product—Sprite—by three to one. Since 1968 the brand had grown about 7 percent annually versus an average 5½ percent for the industry. In 1970 the company began a modest acquisition program.

Dr Pepper, of Dallas, Texas, the fourth largest selling brand, shared with Seven-Up the record of having the industry's highest earnings growth rate from 1968 to 1975—18 percent. Its share of market had moved from 2.7 percent in 1966 to 5.5 percent in 1975. Company operations were concentrated in the North American market with Dr Pepper, in regular and diet formulas, comprising 99 percent of company sales. Dr Pepper, a unique fruit-based flavor, had only one direct competitor—Mr. PiBB. Company gallonage growth rates had been historically targeted by management at 15 percent, but industry analysts did not believe that objective had been reached in 1974 and in 1975 were estimating future gallonage growth of 10 percent.

Royal Crown Cola of Atlanta, Georgia, was the fifth largest selling brand (1975 market share—4.2 percent for regular and diet Royal Crown Cola plus 1.2 percent market share for associated flavor lines). Royal Crown had been a leader in the introduction of diet cola drinks, and its market share in that product segment originally equaled or exceeded Coca-Cola's. Originally a soft drink specialist, Royal Crown began to diversify in 1969 and 1970 into home furnishings and into the processing of citrus fruits and juices. In 1976 the company announced the acquisitions of Arby's, a roast beef sandwich, fast-food chain, headquartered in Youngstown, Ohio.

Soft Drink Bottling and Distribution Companies

Franchise owners were granted, without cost, in perpetuity, the exclusive right to bottle and distribute a concentrate company's line of branded soft drinks as long as conditions of the franchise agreement were met. Key elements in the franchise involved maintaining product quality standards, bottling facilities, distribution and marketing programs within a franchise territory, not selling product to organizations that might transship to another franchised territory, and a willingness not to handle a directly competitive brand, for example, a bottler could not bottle both Coca-Cola and Royal Crown Cola.

A Pepsi-Cola franchise owner could, however, handle a noncompetitive brand such as Dr Pepper—a product type not produced by PepsiCo.[10] Also, a franchise owner might elect not to handle one of PepsiCo's secondary brands, for example, Teem, a lemon-lime drink, and instead bottle and distribute 7UP, the leading lemon-lime brand. A franchisee might also take on a minor line such as Dad's Root Beer or Squirt, a citrus-flavored drink. In addition, if the territory were too small to support both a bottling and canning line, the franchisee could purchase canned products from other sources.

The franchise system was originally developed to achieve local delivery economics and to enable concentrate companies to obtain intensive market coverage at minimum capital investment. In 1975 the sector was still dominated, numerically, by family owned and operated firms despite a 42 percent decline since 1960 in the number of plants operating. Approximately 60 percent of these bottlers (1971) were located in cities with a population of 50,000 or less. An industry observer commented, "Local bottlers and the concentrate manufacturers are in a family relationship. It sounds corny, but it's true. Coke is the best example; they really try to watch out for the small bottlers. Some of them are run by the third generation of a family." (See Exhibit 12.)

EXHIBIT 12: U.S. Bottling Plant Distribution by Sales Category, 1972

Annual Sales per Plant	Number of Plants	Change in Number of Plants since 1971	Percent of Total Bottler Sales
Over $10 million. . . .	124	48%	26.6
$5–10 million.	129	50	19.4
$3–5 million	226	13	19.2
$2–3 million	360	56	12.2
$500,000–$1 million . .	539	−4	9.1
$300,000–$500,000 . .	393	−21	3.3
$100,000–$300,000 . .	582	−24	2.9
Under $100,000. . . .	321	−19	0.6
Unclassified	51		
Total.	2,725	−4.9%	

Source: Bureau of Census data.

---

[10] A court decision in 1962 interpreted franchise bottler agreements to allow a bottler to sell noncompeting brands.

The bottler segment of the industry could be divided into four major sectors. First were privately owned, usually small, bottlers such as Coca-Cola Bottling Company of Annapolis; it serviced 1,335 accounts and had sales of $1.1 million. Some of the larger of these franchisees, located in small metropolitan districts, had achieved substantial growth by buying up franchise operators in contiguous areas and by an aggressive policy of taking on secondary brands such as Dr Pepper or 7UP. The average sales of a bottling plant in 1973 were just over $2 million.

The second sector included large, publicly owned, multibrand firms, based in major metropolitan districts. Coca-Cola Bottling of New York, for example, bottled and distributed Coke, Dr Pepper, and minor soft drink brands and other beverages in a five-state area from multiplant sites. The company had also expanded operations into wine and the manufacture of coolers (see Exhibit 13). One analyst estimated that the pretax return on assets for three large publicly owned bottlers (1968–72) was 19.2 percent versus 30.3 percent for Coke, 16.4 percent for PepsiCo, and 46.8 percent for Dr Pepper.

EXHIBIT 13: Comparative Sales of Six Largest Publicly Owned Bottlers, 1974

Bottlers	Sales ($ millions)	Bottlers	Sales ($ millions)
Coca-Cola Bottling, Los Angeles	$702	ME-1	$220
Coca-Cola Bottling, New York	645	Pep-Com	168
Associated Coca-Cola Bottlers	558	General Cinema Bottling Division	157

Bottling operations of conglomerate companies such as Beatrice Foods and Borden comprised the third sector. These firms not only owned large bottling operations but in some cases minor concentrate manufacturers. Industry experts predicted that both the publicly held bottlers and the conglomerates would continue to grow in part via the acquisition of other franchise operations.

Seven of the eight largest concentrate companies owned some bottling operations. Coca-Cola owned and operated bottling facilities in Chicago, San Francisco, Seattle, Oakland, San Jose, Baltimore, and Boston. PepsiCo packaged approximately 20 percent of its domestic gallonage in company-owned plants. Senior management spokespersons for the concentrate companies unanimously supported the existing franchise system, and the presidents of Coca-Cola and Dr Pepper had taken public positions that their firms did not want to own any more bottling operations.

In surveying developments in the franchise bottling field, an industry spokesman states:

The overall effects of the market developments since 1945 can be identified as these: (1) The increased power of retail chains strengthened the popularity of franchising through the emphasis on national brands. (2) Availability of the one-way container enabled the easy market entry of store-owned brands as well as national and regionally shipped brands, and further strengthened the retail market position of chains as soft drink outlets. (3) Larger market spheres for many bottlers were brought about by the growth of urban centers, necessitating greater capital requirements and redefinition of territories. These needs were met by a high degree of mergers, sales and other interindustry ownership transactions. (4) High growth rate of product volume began to attract "outside" money for the first time in the industry's history and companies not previously identified with soft drinks began entry into the industry. Availability of this new capital assisted the industry in its accommodation of newly dimensioned markets. (5) The one-way container brought substantial influence on the price of the product in the market. In 1950 the retail price was the same as it was in 1887, approximately a nickel a glass, but as a growing share of product moved to single use packages, the cost of soft drinks has inevitably reflected the higher cost of packaging.[11]

Federal Trade commission officials, however, took a critical view of these developments asserting they had resulted in high industry concentration levels and in the companies' ability to raise prices substantially:

Because such large firms engage in soft drink bottling, high concentration levels exist in this industry. The 24 largest Coca-Cola bottlers serve nearly 61 percent of the United States population and account for approximately 24 percent of the total soft drink sales. The 10 largest Pepsi bottlers serve 48 percent of the population and account for almost 8 percent of total soft drink sales. The 12 largest Seven-Up franchisees, two of which are also two of the top Pepsi franchisees, serve 41 percent of the population. Approximately 40 bottlers account for more than one-third of total soft drink sales.

However, the relevant measure for concentration in the soft drink industry is the concentration in local markets. Local markets, not national markets, are the locus of competition in soft drink bottling as territorial restrictions confine bottlers to competing in local markets. To put it simply, bottlers compete on the local level, not on the national level, and concentration of sales among local bottlers is quite high. According to the Bureau of Census, in 1963, the four largest bottlers in nine large metropolitan areas had, on the average, 68 percent of the market. This high concentration level among bottlers at the local level parallels the high concentration level of the four largest syrup manufacturers who share about 70 percent of the national market. Thus, a similar concentration level would naturally exist at the local level since bottlers' sales reflect, to a great extent, the market share of the brands they sell.

---

[11] Statement of president of the National Soft Drink Association before the Subcommittee on Antitrust and Monopoly Legislation, August 8, 1972.

One reason for the high level concentration among bottlers is the extent to which bottlers produce products of several syrup manufacturers. For example, in New York City, both Coca-Cola and Dr Pepper products are marketed by Coca-Cola Bottling Co. of New York. Certainly, there can be no real competition between these brands bottled by a common bottler as a firm is not going to engage in price competition with itself. In 1970, of the 1,654 bottlers of products of the eight largest syrup manufacturers, 738 bottled products of more than one such manufacturer. Because of the large number of bottlers who bottle more than one brand, effective competition between different brands does not exist.

The high concentration among bottlers in local markets is reflected by the ease at which they have been able to increase prices in recent years. In this regard, it should be noted that for the period 1959–70, Bureau of Labor Statistics data indicate the wholesale price of cola soft drinks, which account for about 60 percent of the soft drink industry, has increased by 65 percent. Similarly, the Consumer Price Index records a 64 percent price increase in cola soft drink prices. This 64 percent rise in cola soft drink prices on the Consumer Price Index is a much faster price rise than the 33 percent price rise for all food prices during the period 1959–1970.[12]

Retailers

Industry analysts typically assigned soft drinks to three retail market segments: packaged goods sold via food stores; vending machines; and the fountain trade, the latter subdivided into two areas—restaurants and fast-food chains. A fourth category—the institutional market (e.g., hospitals and industrial plants)—was assigned in some cases to the vending section, in other statistical surveys to the fountain trade. Because of this, market share estimates varied substantially from one to another analyst's survey.

In 1975 Oppenheimer & Co. Inc., estimated food stores sales at approximately 55–60 percent, vending at 10 percent and fountain at 30–35 percent. Another analyst estimated, respectively, 50 percent, 20 percent, and 30 percent. But all agreed that food stores were still the dominant market. In 1900, 70 percent of soft drinks were consumed on the premises of the vendors and 30 percent at home. In the 50s and 60s the amount of products sold via food stores increased to 70 percent of the total market. The food store market was dominated by Pepsi-Cola and Coca-Cola with Pepsi having a modest share-of-the-market advantage. Some analysts believed Pepsi had a significant long-run strategic advantage over Coke, however, because of its major position in the snack food field.

Food stores sold $2.6 billion worth of soft drinks in 1975, making them the single largest retail outlet for soft drinks and accounting for

---

[12] Statement of Mr. Alan Ward, Director of Bureau of Competition, Federal Trade Commission. Hearings before the Subcommittee on Antitrust and Monopoly, 92d Congress, part 1, pp. 223–24.

approximately 55 percent of the cases sold that year. Case sales had increased steadily between 1960 and 1973 when industry marketing efforts had been concentrated on the take-home market segment. Food stores' share of total soft drink sales, however, had declined from 70 percent in 1960 to 60 percent in 1970, and were expected to decline further to 50 percent by 1980. Supermarkets had been the site of most national brand, soft drink competitive battles during the early 1970s.

Food retailers' sales of $131 billion in 1974 ranked them as one of the nation's largest businesses; supermarket chains played an important role in the industry, accounting for only 10 percent of stores but 45 percent of total sales. The three largest supermarket chains and their respective 1974 sales were Safeway, $8.19 billion; A&P, $7.03 billion; and Kroger, $4.78 billion. Many independent supermarkets were members of large cooperative buying groups or voluntary wholesaler groups which provided distribution economies of scale and staff services.

Soft drinks were of major interest to supermarkets since their 22 percent gross margin was one of the highest for any grocery items and the category achieved high turnover. In 1974 the average supermarket carried over 100 different brands and sizes of soft drinks which generated $2.3 billion in total sales and $503 million in gross margin. Product shelf space allocations by chain store management directly correlated with market share. In 1975 canned soft drinks maintained their position among the top ten grocery product volume leaders.

The 1960s had been a period of rapid growth and prosperity for supermarkets, but the future looked less promising for the 70s and early 80s. Predictions of things to come by supermarket executives included little growth in real per capita food expenditures and little population growth. They anticipated increasing price competition, a rapid decline in the number of supermarkets operated, and increasing pressure for operating efficiencies, including more automated warehouses and full truckload delivery systems.

Another development in food retailing was the rapid growth of convenience stores (1967 estimated sales of $6.2 billion with estimated $1.6 billion of beverage sales). These stores were relatively small, had limited stock, long operating hours patterns, and serviced a local community area. Many soft drink bottlers viewed these expanding outlets as a prime sales opportunity. An executive of the Dr Pepper Company noted that selling to convenience stores was very different from supermarket selling. He noted, "The loss-leader approach commonly used in supermarkets was unworkable, whereas tie-in and theme promotions did seem effective. Convenience stores show a noticeable trend in selling sandwiches and other prepared-on-the-premise food items and therefore offer beverage tie-in possibilities."[13]

---

[13] *Beverage World,* January 1977, p. 36.

Vending machines, manufactured to serve a variety of containers from cans to bottles to paper cups, were employed to service the single-drink market. Costing the bottler between $800 to $1,000, these machines blanketed locations such as service stations, small stores, and sports arenas. An estimated 1.7 million machines were in operation in 1975, and some corporate executives believe this to be a mature or even potentially declining market sector. Coke was experimenting with the installation of small REFRESH office units. These units vended drinks at 10 cents a cup in private and public offices. Coke hoped to have 20,000 units in place by 1976.

Some bottlers, whose distributor salespeople originally serviced only soft drink machines, were expanding into the full-line vending business—including foods, candy, and cigarettes. Such firms could then contract to serve a factory or a public institution where a bank of vending machines had replaced the traditional cafeteria arrangement.

The fountain trade subdivided into two segments: the traditional restaurant, specialty restaurant, and coffee shops market; and fast-food operations. Americans seemed to be in the midst of a major shift toward "eating out," and the primary beneficiary seemed to have been chain operations. An observer noted, "Many independent full-service/atmosphere restaurants have been forced to close in recent years. . . . In contrast, chain operations in the coffee shop, specialty, and fast-food areas have expanded rapidly with the greatest growth coming from multisite operations in the fast-food segment. According to the U.S. Department of Commerce and A. D. Little, total personal consumption for food and beverages spent in fast-food outlets grew from about $400 million in 1960 to over $13 billion in 1976."

Fast-food chains operated with corporate owned (one fourth) and through franchise arrangements (three fourths) with the percentage of franchises gradually declining as franchisers purchased their own large franchise operation. Analysts noted further that "the top seven firms, McDonald's, Kentucky Fried Chicken, A&W Root Beer, International Dairy Queen, Tastee Freeze, Burger King, and Pizza Hut accounted for 47 percent of all fast-food units and 46 percent of sales. While fast-food chains dominate the fast-food segment they do not dominate the entire restaurant industry; the top 35 chains still accounted for only one quarter of total domestic eating and drinking industry sales. McDonald's, the largest independent, accounted for 3 percent of total food service sales (1975 sales of $2.616 billion). Burger Chef (General Foods) and Kentucky Fried Chicken (Heublein) were divisions of larger firms."

Suppliers

In 1975 the soft drink industry purchased approximately $4 billion of raw material ingredients and packaging supplies. This included approximately $1.7 billion for sugar, $200 million for high fructose corn syrup, $5 million for saccharin, $408 million for flavorings, $1 billion for cans, over $750 million for glass containers, and $127 million for closures and cartons. The soft drink industry accounted for 23 percent of the sugar consumed in the United States, 70 percent of the saccharin, and was one of the largest customers for companies such as Continental Can, and Crown Cork and Seal.

Sugar prices were vulnerable to major short-term price fluctuations in response to small changes in demand, since 96–97 percent of world production was sold under long-term contracts. In 1974 and 1975, increasing world demand and poor crop yields pushed prices as high as 75 cents per pound, compared to 2 cents to 9 cents per pound between 1950 and 1973. Recent sugar price increases prompted the use of high fructose corn syrup (HFCS) which at 20 cents per pound was 10–15 percent less expensive than sugar for equivalent sweetening power. By 1975 most major concentrate producers, except Coca-Cola and PepsiCo, had authorized their bottlers to use a 50/50 or 75/25 sugar/HFCS mixture, but

EXHIBIT 14: Soft Drink Bottlers Operating Income and Expense Ratios as Percent of Net Sales, 1973

	Top 10 Percent in Net Operating Income	All Units	Under $1,000	$1,000 to $3,000	$3,001 to $6,000	$6,001 to $10,000
Cost of sales:						
Materials	13.11	17.32	15.63	16.72	16.76	14.83
Packaging expense	10.61	12.55	4.30	9.93	17.69	15.36
Plant labor	4.14	4.83	5.89	4.85	4.87	4.36
Indirect	3.44	4.07	3.90	3.90	3.99	4.12
Total	31.30	38.77	29.72	35.40	43.31	38.67
Contract purchase (finished beverages)	26.70	24.52	32.92	28.23	19.48	25.46
Total cost of sales	58.00	63.29	62.64	63.63	62.79	64.13
Gross profit	42.00	36.71	37.36	36.37	37.21	35.87
Total other operating income	3.36	2.15	2.26	2.53	1.98	1.67
Gross operating income	45.36	38.86	39.62	38.90	39.19	37.54
Operating expenses:						
Warehousing	1.69	2.81	1.93	3.22	1.95	1.77
Selling	19.70	21.12	20.76	20.67	21.56	22.43
Administrative	5.89	7.97	12.03	7.84	7.52	7.72
Total operating expenses	27.28	31.90	34.72	31.73	31.03	31.92
Net operating income	18.08	6.96	4.90	7.17	8.16	5.62

Source: National Soft Drinks Association 1973 financial survey.

actual usage was modest due to limited high fructose production capacity. Capacity was not expected to be adequate to meet demand until 1980. Saccharin was the primary artificial sweetener used in diet soft drinks, with approximately 2 million pounds purchased in 1974 at $2.40 per pound from one domestic producer.

Glass containers accounted for a substantial percentage of all soft drink packages used in 1974. Sales to the soft drink industry accounted for approximately 23 percent of the $5 billion glass container market in 1976. There were two dominant glass container manufacturers: Libbey-Owens (1975 packaging material sales, $1,400 million) and Anchor Hocking (1975 sales, $411 million).

Five can companies accounted for 98 percent of the cans sold to the soft drink industry with American Can Company (1974 sales, $2.7 billion) and Continental Can Company (1974 sales, over $3 billion) accounting for over 50 percent of the market. Crown Cork and Seal, National Can Company, and Reynolds Aluminum were the other major participants.

Packaging manufacturers, while typically dominant in one packaging technology, often engaged in the manufacture and sale of multiple types of packaging, for example, both glass and plastic. These manufacturers carried on most of the packaging research and development for the soft drink industry. A recent improvement in the popular, large-size glass containers (all one-way packages) was a clear or semiclear plastic coating which reduced breakage and required less glass, therefore reducing package weight and distribution costs. In 1976 Owens-Illinois "Plastic-Shield" coated 33 percent of the 28- and 32-ounce bottles and 50 percent of the 48- and 64-ounce bottles which it produced.

KEY INDUSTRY FUNCTIONAL STRATEGIES

Marketing

"In this industry the key strategic function has been marketing—that includes advertising, promotion, packaging, and distribution," an analyst commented. "Finance, so far, hasn't been limiting; and with one exception, the concentrate people are in very conservative positions. Production hasn't been that critical, but changing logistics and possible changes in product technology make it increasingly important. And don't forget there are three teams playing in this game—concentrate producers, bottlers, and the government. Their interests are different, and it makes the game complicated."

Soft drinks were inexpensive, frequently purchased products often consumed on impulse by a broad spectrum of the population. According to Standard & Poor's, in 1975, 90 percent of U.S. teenagers consumed at least seven soft drinks per week, 74 percent of young adults consumed that many, and 43 percent of the population over 50 drank one soft drink a day. Efforts to increase consumer awareness, achieve extensive availability, and appeal to consumer desires for product variety and user convenience involved the joint participation of both concentrate producers and bottlers.

Large, national concentrate producers did overall market research and planning, determined advertising and promotion themes, introduced new container sizes and materials, and developed and tested products. They financed national advertising, staff and development services, and paid part of the cost of local advertising and promotion of new packages and products.

Bottlers worked with national concentrate representatives to determine the advertising media, promotion themes, product mix, package mix, and price points to most effectively meet the particular consumer preferences, distribution channels, and competitive situations of their local market area. The bottlers were responsible for day-to-day implementation of the marketing plan. They usually paid about 50 percent of the cost of local advertising and promotion, and most of the costs of new packing and vending and dispensing equipment. Local cooperative advertising and promotion budgets were usually based on both concentrate producers and bottlers contributing a fixed amount per gallon of product sold in the territory.

Marketing strategies for local and regional companies and minor national brands generally followed a pattern of sales through food stores; few had vending machine exposure and few received much media advertising support. Local and regional firms usually concentrated on flavor lines and competed on a price basis. Minor national brands "piggybacked" on the franchise bottlers of the top six concentrate manufacturers. Schweppes and Canada Dry competed primarily as premium priced "mixers" for use with alcoholic drinks.

An industry marketing executive commented that the seven critical ingredients for industry success were advertising, availability, promotion, packaging, pricing, personal selling, and new product introduction.

Advertising.   Consumer advertising was a critical element in selling soft drinks and accounted for a large proportion of concentrate producers' annual marketing budgets. Exhibit 15 indicates amounts spent on national media alone by the largest advertisers between 1960 and 1975. Most national brand advertising was directed toward achieving or maintaining consumer "top of mind" awareness. The emergence of 7UP as an aggressively advertised soft drink brand with its "Uncola" theme was considered to be an industry advertising success story. The initial Uncola campaign relied heavily on 60-second spots on network television. Later billboards, newspapers, radio commercials, and prime-time television spots were

EXHIBIT 15: Soft Drink Advertising Expenditures for Selected Brands ($ millions)

	1960	1968	1970	1971	1972	1973	1974	1975
Coca-Cola:	$4,423							
Coke	3,837	$19,092	$20,243	$18,664	$17,965	$24,108	$22,122	$20,261
Fresca		—	3,861	4,317	2,862	2,590	2,545	2,381
Sprite		2,500	1,063	1,198	1,835	1,738	2,463	2,601
Tab		6,162	3,443	4,248	3,814	5,435	5,278	6,496
Fanta		800	470	396		392	147	74
Dr Pepper:	27							
Regular		2,950	4,098	4,945	4,082	5,363	5,402	4,872
Diet		244	24	285	687	1,208	1,759	1,548
PepsiCo:	3,148							
Pepsi		16,512	15,939	17,797	15,268	13,520	14,856	14,995
Diet Pepsi		1,465	4,034	4,593	4,254	4,321	4,139	3,673
Teem		41	22	10	—	—	—	61
Mountain Dew		796	263	148	162	350	635	2,577
Pepsi Light								918
Seven-Up	2,229							
Regular		8,993	11,496	13,169	12,835	10,438	10,437	10,180
Diet		2,242	576	1,481	1,725	2,398	1,967	3,255
Norton-Simon:	313							
Canada Dry		5,790	6,659	8,528	6,139	5,503	4,859	5,213
Barrelhead Root Beer						239	561	1,314
R. C. Cola:	1,003							
Regular		2,980	3,082	4,779	4,230	4,885	5,695	10,509
Diet Rite		4,961	2,303	3,095	2,472	2,351	2,131	3,497
Shasta							2,324	2,828

Sources: Abstracted from *Advertising Age* and company reports.

used. Between 1966 and 1976, 7UP case sales increased from 200 million to 340 million.

Industry executives anticipated increasing competition in the advertising arena in 1976. According to *Beverage Industry:*

> With another no-growth year just ended, the major thrust in advertising is coming from those companies who have seen their individual market shares increase at the expense of both the best known brands and the regional or private label soft drinks. Because of this, the key word for this year is product identity, and ad agencies across the country are turning out television and radio spots designed to leave the consumer with an indelible memory of their clients' product.

Availability. An ornithologist does not need a laboratory full of measuring instruments to prove that geese are migrating; rare will be the reader who has not, in the previous week, had several soft drinks, consumed in a variety of places. A researcher walking down a city street provided ample evidence of the industry's merchandising impact: soft drinks were available at 12 locations (including a funeral parlor for an undesignated clientele); men and women, young and old, black and white were observed consuming their favorite beverage; several hundred cans provided typical big city litter; and 64 soft drink advertisements "decorated" one four-block street section.

Soft drink availability accomplished three objectives for soft drink marketers. It provided a safe, cold, palatable drink almost anywhere people became thirsty. Second, point-of-sale advertising in hundreds of thousands of locations contributed to brand awareness. Finally, extensive availability was an important sampling device which helped to create and maintain consumer flavor preferences. Several industry sources stated that Coca-Cola dominated the cold, single-drink market. In some regions of the country, however, other brands had achieved substantial single-drink availability; Pepsi in the Midwest, for example, and Dr Pepper in the Southwest and parts of the Southeast.

In food stores and supermarkets the major national brands vied with local and regional brands and the stores' own private label soft drinks to best appeal to the consumer's varying degree of thirst (6 ounces to 64 ounces), the size of the consumer's family (single bottles, 6-ounce cartons, 8-can packs), budget, weight consciousness, desire for convenience, and ecological concern (returnable, resealable bottles, cans, nonreturnable glass containers).

Sales Promotion. Recent point-of-sale promotional activity focused primarily on increasing packaged product sales through food stores. Consequently, most of the interaction took place between the bottlers, food retailers, and the consumers. Executives noted that usually the larger the size of display and shelf-space allocations and the greater the frequency of appearances in weekly food store newspaper advertising, the faster a particular soft drink brand sold. Thus, a wide variety of programs fell under the general category of promotions in the competition for consumers' and retailers' attention. They included installing point-of-sale signs, obtaining special end-of-aisle or high-visibility display areas, providing special permanent display racks and in-store refrigerated coolers. One industry source estimated that bottlers spent as much or more money on promotions as on advertising. Another industry participant estimated that bottlers annually spent the equivalent of 2–3 percent of sales on advertising and promotion efforts, or $100–$150 million in 1975.

Packaging. "The proliferation of packaging has led to wider availability, particularly in vendors, to greater consumer convenience, and to increased consumption," an industry analyst commented. "The explosion in larger size packages has also increased gallonage sales. The grocery store consumer usually buys the same number of bottles or cartons of soft drinks each week. The more ounces each of those bottles or cartons hold, the more ounces go home with the consumer each trip. That's why the new plastic bottles are going to give such a boost to gallonage sales. The bottles themselves are smaller and lighter, so more containers can be put in a carton at the same weight. But the big ones create shelf shortage problems too! Look at the soft drink aisles in your supermarket; they have cases of gallon bottles stacked all over the place."

In addition to increasing total consumption of soft drinks by getting more product in the consumer's refrigerator, each new container size or material provided the opportunity to increase a brand's supermarket shelf "facings." Packaging variety also gave price choices within and among brands. Generally, soft drinks in larger size containers cost the consumer less per glass because packaging accounted for a lower proportion of total raw materials cost. The consumer also paid a lower price per ounce for beverages in returnable containers since the container cost was amortized over 10 or more fillings.

The most frequently purchased container sizes in the early 70s were 10- and 12-ounce containers with 58 percent of unit sales; followed by 16-ounce containers, 20 percent; 24 ounces and larger, 16 percent; and 6–9 ounces, 6 percent. The 10- and 12-ounce *cans* accounted for 38 percent of unit sales, one-way *bottles* accounted for 28 percent, and returnable *bottles* for 34 percent. According to one analyst:

> Packaging innovations are usually led by the companies who have the most money. This is a me-too industry—once one company brings out something new, the others aren't far behind. Coke was the first with the plastic bottle, but Pepsi was first with the 64-ounce size and 7UP with the liter bottle. Royal Crown was the first company to come out with cans, but it took Coke and Pepsi to really put that package on the map.

In 1976 one new packaging innovation was already in the market testing stage—plastic bottles. The introduction by Coca-Cola of 32-ounce plastic bottles in the Providence, Rhode Island, market had been described as "successful," capturing over 50 percent of that particular Coke bottler's entire product mix. Over the years plastics may be adding 1 percent a year to industry growth, one analyst concluded.

Plastic pouches and plastic "bags" encased in a corrugated paper box were being used in the wine and fruit juice industry. Mirolite, a plastic pouch wrapped in a paper sleeve, was manufactured by ICI in England. When European soft drink producers first adopted the package they had to reformulate some of their high carbonation drinks to retain their original flavor and lower carbonation level.

Can manufacturers were developing lighter, two-piece tin and aluminum cans, and nonreturnable bottle manufacturers were marketing lighter and stronger bottles. "Weight's important in this game—you are shipping water and metal around. You can't do much with the water but you sure try to cut down container weight. With the trend toward bigger bottles (64-ounce) you get difficult-to-handle products."

Pricing.   Retail prices for soft drinks varied substantially by geographic region of the country, by container type, by channel of distribution, and a host of other factors such as local manufacturing costs, retailer markups, and degree of competition. For example, food retailers rarely achieved more than a 25 percent margin, while fountain retailers often achieved 65 percent to 75 percent gross margin of soft drinks. Exhibit 16 shows the range of average retail soft drink prices by regions for 1964–72, and their steady increase over the period.

Some industry analysts believed that the market for soft drinks was relatively price inelastic. They also believed that even greater pricing flexibility existed at the concentrate producer's level because concentrate cost accounted for such a low proportion of finished product cost, 4 percent in the case of Coca-Cola, and comparable amounts for other producers' soft drinks. Seven-Up was the only concentrate producer yet to put the

EXHIBIT 16: Retail Pricing Trends of Fruit-Flavored Soft Drinks by Region, 1964–1972 (per 72-ounce carton)

Region	1964	1965	1966	1967	1968	1969	1970	1971	1972
Northeast . . .	56.8¢	54.7¢	55.2¢	59.0¢	63.5¢	64.7¢	69.8¢	75.4¢	75.4¢
South	n.a.	n.a.	n.a.	n.a.	55.0	58.7	59.7	63.1	64.4
Midwest . . .	54.7	57.6	59.5	60.4	62.8	70.2	74.9	77.2	75.6
West	63.0	64.2	63.9	64.2	69.5	72.3	81.4	83.3	84.4
All regions . .	53.4	53.6	54.8	57.0	60.5	63.1	69.1	72.6	72.7

n.a. = not available.
Sources: Bureau of Labor Statistics, and *Beverage Industry*, July 28, 1972. The 1972 figures as of March of that year.

theory to a major test. According to one analyst. Seven-Up increased its concentrate prices 11 percent in October 1974 and 25 percent the following June. The company apparently quelled bottler resistance to the second price hike by promising to spend more money on advertising and local promotion.

Personal Selling.   Concentrate producers employed two types of selling organizations: bottler-oriented sales personnel and fountain salespersons. Concentrate producers' bottler sales personnel worked with franchised bottler management to tailor national brand plans to the individual requirements of the local market area. Franchised bottlers were independent business people so the persuasiveness of the concentrate producers' salesperson as marketing consultant was important. However, the salesperson did not have to rely completely on charm or intimidation: incentives such as cooperative advertising and promotion funds were available.

Some concentrate producers, including Coca-Cola, Seven-Up, and Dr Pepper, maintained their own sales organizations to sell fountain syrup directly to retailers. Pepsi-Cola and other producers relied primarily on their franchised bottlers and independent jobbers to sell to fountain outlets. Most fountain retailers carried a maximum of four different brands because standard dispensers were equipped to handle but four flavor lines. Thus, the main task of concentrate producers' fountain sales personnel was first convincing the franchise chain's home office to approve the inclusion of their brand on the list of products which the local franchisee might use. Later they might help bottlers or jobbers sell individual retailers on carrying company products. Fountain sales personnel were also responsible for placing point-of-sale advertising and implementing cooperative advertising and promotion programs. The syrup producer or supplier also provided the retailer dispenser maintenance and repair services, usually free of charge.

New Product Introduction.   New product introductions had played a relatively minor role in the marketing of soft drinks. Companies infrequently did introduce new brands, usually for a variation in the formulation of an old standard flavor, for example, Pepsi's introduction of Teem—a lemon-lime drink. Exactly what constituted a "new" soft drink product was difficult for industry executives to define. One type of product innovation involved introduction of a new flavor, such as Cott's diet mint; another, a new combination such as cherry-flavored chocolate drinks. One firm had recently introduced a chocolate-flavored, high-protein health drink into several foreign markets. However, 7UP, first marketed in 1920, and Dr Pepper, first sold in 1885, were the only flavors outside of cola which had achieved major national brand status.

Most industry observers did agree that diet beverages were a new product category. First introduced in the early 1960s, diet drinks had achieved a 15 percent market share in 1969. When the Food and Drug Administration banned cyclamates as an artificial sweetener, sales dropped precipitously to 6.7 percent of the market in 1970. By 1976, diet beverages again accounted for 15 percent of industry sales and were the fastest growing product category. One bottler characterized Coke's introduction of Fresca, its citrus-flavored diet drink, as the most successful new product introduction in which he had ever participated. "I gave Fresca away to every one of my outlets in quantities amounting to 20 percent of each outlet's monthly 12-ounce Coke sales. When Coke wants to move in— they *move in.''*

Pepsi Light, Pepsi-Cola's reduced-sugar, cola-plus-lemon was, in the view of some analysts, the major new product of the 70s. The drink used some artificial sweeteners while still containing only half the sugar (and half the calories) of regular cola. At the end of 1975, Pepsi Light was in selected markets covering about 50 percent of the U.S. population; national advertising expenditures had already reached close to a million dollars.

The Pepsi Challenge.   One example of the increasing competitiveness among major national brand soft drink producers was the major advertising campaign begun by Pepsi-Cola in April 1974, in Dallas, which declared, "Nationwide, more Coca-Cola drinkers prefer Pepsi than the taste of Coca-Cola." *The New York Times* described the genius of the campaign in an article on July 5, 1976.

> . . . research had indicated that more than half the Coke drinkers who participated in a blind test of Pepsi and Coke preferred the taste of Pepsi. . . . So Pepsi decided to launch a "challenge" campaign in a marketing area where it had been weak: Dallas and Fort Worth.

In Dallas, over nine months of heavy advertising and price promotions by both cola producers resulted in a small increase in market share for Coke, approximately 30 percent at the end of the period, and almost a doubling in market share for Pepsi, from 7 percent to 14 percent. Retail soft drink prices had fallen to almost half their prechallenge prices, and the two colas had increased their combined market shares from 36 percent to over 44 percent at the expense of the smaller competing brands, especially Dr Pepper. The challenge, and the competitive reaction, had spread to other cities by the summer of 1976, including San Antonio, Corpus Christi, New York City, and Los Angeles.

Distribution

The soft drink industry had achieved both extensive distribution of major national brands and a substantial degree of control over the

EXHIBIT 17: Consumption of Soft Drinks (selected years)

	1966		1970		1971	
	Million Cases	Percent of Market	Million Cases	Percent of Market	Million Cases	Percent of Market
Coca-Cola Co.:						
Coca-Cola	806.0	27.7	1,045.0	28.4	1,040.0	27.1
Sprite	43.0	1.5	65.0	1.8	71.0	1.8
Tab	42.0	1.4	49.0	1.3	66.0	1.7
Mr. PiBB	—	—	—	—	—	—
Fresca	33.0	1.1	46.0	1.3	52.0	1.3
Others	48.0	1.7	71.0	1.9	85.0	2.1
Total	972.0	33.4	1,276.0	34.7	1,344.0	34.0
PepsiCo, Inc.:						
Pepsi-Cola	470.0	16.1	625.0	17.0	687.0	17.4
Diet Pepsi.	55.0	1.9	40.0	1.1	52.0	1.3
Mountain Dew	40.0	1.4	34.0	0.9	35.7	0.9
Teem	15.0	0.5	14.0	0.4	14.0	0.4
Pepsi Light	—	—	—	—	—	—
Others	15.0	0.5	15.0	0.4	15.0	0.4
Total	595.0	20.4	728.0	19.8	803.7	20.4
Seven-Up Co.:						
7UP	185.0	6.4	257.6	7.0	271.4	6.9
Sugar Free 7UP	13.0	0.4	6.5	0.1	8.4	0.2
Howdy flavors	2.0	0.1	3.0	0.1	2.3	—
Total	200.0	6.9	267.1	7.2	282.1	7.1
Royal Crown Cola Co.:						
Royal Crown.	110.0	3.8	142.0	3.8	153.0	3.9
Diet-Rite Cola	48.0	1.6	36.0	1.0	42.0	1.0
Nehi and others	43.0	1.5	45.0	1.2	46.0	1.2
Total	201.0	6.9	223.0	6.0	241.0	6.1
Dr. Pepper: Regular Dr Pepper	79.0	2.4	135.2	3.7	147.7	3.7
Sugar Free Dr Pepper	8.0	0.2	5.0	0.1	7.2	0.2
Total	87.0	2.6	140.2	3.8	154.9	3.9

Source: *Beverage World,* April 2, 1976, p. 28; based on data supplied by John R. Maxwell, Jr., Wheat First Securities, Inc.

distribution process itself, compared to other nonperishable food products. Exhibit 14 gives some information on distribution costs; they are included in the category—selling. A key element in the distribution process, especially for food stores and vending machines, was the franchised bottler's sales force.

The franchised bottler's sales force comprised driver salespeople who combined both delivery and sales functions. Each morning route salespeople left the plant with trucks full of the soft drink assortment they expected customers to buy that day. The route salespeople stocked the customers' shelves directly from their mobile inventory, often handling billing and collections on the spot. They were usually compensated with

| 1972 | | 1973 | | 1974 | | 1975 | | 1974–75 |
Million Cases	Percent of Market	Million Cases	Percent of Market	Million Cases	Percent of Market	Million Cases	Percent of Market	Percent Change
1,125.0	26.8	1,190.0	26.7	1,180.0	26.5	1,170.0	26.2	−0.8
81.0	1.9	95.0	2.1	105.0	2.4	115.3	2.6	+9.8
85.0	2.0	97.0	2.2	100.0	2.2	115.0	2.6	+15.0
5.0	0.1	15.0	0.3	23.0	0.5	37.5	0.8	+63.0
48.0	1.2	44.0	1.0	38.0	0.9	35.0	0.8	−7.9
95.0	2.3	100.0	2.3	100.0	2.2	100.0	2.3	—
1,439.0	34.3	1,541.0	34.6	1,546.0	34.7	1,572.8	35.3	+1.7
735.0	17.5	777.4	17.4	780.0	17.5	778.0	17.4	−0.3
58.0	1.4	60.3	1.4	68.0	1.5	75.0	1.7	+10.3
35.0	0.8	42.0	0.9	47.0	1.0	56.0	1.3	+19.1
14.0	0.3	14.8	0.3	14.0	0.3	13.5	0.3	−3.6
—	—	—	—	—	—	2.0	0.1	—
15.0	0.4	16.0	0.4	15.8	0.4	15.0	0.3	−5.1
857.0	20.4	910.0	20.4	924.8	20.7	939.5	21.1	+1.6
289.6	6.9	317.7	7.1	311.3	7.0	295.5	6.6	−5.1
10.1	0.2	12.7	0.3	27.3	0.6	43.6	1.0	+59.7
1.8	0.1	1.4	—	1.5	—	1.4	—	−6.6
301.5	7.2	331.8	7.4	340.1	7.6	340.5	7.6	+0.1
165.0	3.9	165.0	3.9	150.0	3.4	153.0	3.4	+2.0
44.0	1.0	42.0	0.9	34.0	0.8	36.0	0.8	+5.9
49.0	1.2	53.0	1.2	56.0	1.2	51.0	1.2	−8.9
258.0	6.1	268.0	6.0	240.0	5.4	240.0	5.4	—
180.0	4.3	208.7	4.7	216.0	4.8	217.0	4.9	+.005
11.0	0.3	14.8	0.3	18.0	0.4	28.0	0.6	+55.0
101.0	4.6	223.5	5.0	234.0	5.2	245.0	5.5	+4.7

a percentage of sales commission, and their check sometimes came directly from the concentrate producer rather than the bottler.

In recent years, however, some bottlers had begun to use "presold, bulk delivery" techniques with large supermarket accounts. An advance salesperson called on the store and took orders and the product was delivered the next day, via large vans holding up to 2,000 cases. Large carts, each holding up to 40 to 70 cases, were wheeled into the store's warehouse area. The next day the bottler's merchandising staff arrived and personally stocked the store's shelves. Supermarket owners approved of the system because it improved the store's receiving and stocking efficiency; bottlers estimated they saved about 10 cents per case delivery cost.

In-store merchandising, whether carried out by a route salesperson or a separate merchandising force, was considered crucial to maintaining high sales levels. An executive of the New York Coca-Cola Bottling Company explained:

> Unlike other businesses where the product comes through a warehouse and is at the mercy of whatever the supplier may want to do with it, or even comes through a food broker who does not have the kind of service dedication that exists in the soft drink business, the soft drink business is service dependent. So the man who goes in there (a) rotates the stock, (b) is in a constant battle for shelf space, both in terms of quality and quantity; he is trying to get it on the shelf in the best possible place, (c) in terms of helping the dealer, (d) in terms of pricing, we believe even if our price is on the high side, it is important to have it marked, clearly marked, (e) in terms of promotion or special display that needs to be built, to be sure that it is properly in place.[14]

The efficient management of this route delivery system was a major determinant of bottler profitability and required efficient routing and skill in matching inventory load to customer demand. Five to 10 percent of a bottler's accounts represented 20 percent to 45 percent of their total volume. Many of the smaller accounts, particularly those under five cases per stop, were marginally profitable at best and were serviced as a form of advertising through product availability and as an aid in keeping total plant volume above the break-even level. To support this extensive route delivery system, the industry supported the nation's largest private trucking fleet, second only to the U.S. Post Office.

Changing Marketing and Distribution Patterns

The researchers noted several industry trends which they believed would influence concentrate company-bottler relationships and which would impact local bottler marketing and distribution patterns.

First, new cooperative relationships would be needed to handle sales to the expanding fast-food market. Food stores' share of market had been decreasing while sales to fast-food chains had increased from 20 percent (1960) to 25 percent (1970) to 30–35 percent (1975). Of the restaurant and food service market, sales to the fountain/fast-foods market, in contrast to food stores, required different sales and promotional techniques and organizational arrangements.

Second, local bottlers increasingly were dealing with chains which served market areas larger than an individual bottler's territory. A chain promotional campaign might necessitate the coordination of several fran-

---

[14] Kuhn, Loeb summary of *Federal Trade Commission Hearings in the matter of Coca-Cola et al.*, May 19–23, 1975, p. 50.

chise bottlers, a concentrate company's advertising manager, and the chain buying staff.

Third, during the 1950s, bottlers typically handled only one concentrate company's product line. Beginning in the early 60s and spurred by Dr Pepper's aggressive campaign to sign up Coke and Pepsi bottlers, bottlers were increasingly managing multibrand operations. A Pepsi bottler might, for example, handle 7UP and Dr Pepper.

Finally, there appeared to be basic changes evolving in local bottler profit economics. Bottling executives testified that profit margins had been declining as a consequence of packaging proliferation and increased ingredient and operating costs and that their business was becoming more capital intensive as larger plants, larger sales volume, and larger market areas were needed to achieve cost economies. Smaller bottlers often lacked the capital to buy a bottling line ($250,000) or lacked a market large enough to break even on a canning-type operation ($2 million in sales). Some bottlers, to deal with this situation, had developed cooperative canning and distribution facilities with nearby bottlers holding similar franchises. A Dr Pepper executive commented that Coca-Cola and PepsiCo had been urging their franchised bottlers to cooperate among themselves for the last 8 to 10 years, while this was a relatively new policy at Dr Pepper. The most extreme illustration of this trend so far had occurred in Charlotte, North Carolina, where a dozen Coke bottlers had closed down their separate production facilities and opened a central plant ringed by a number of distribution centers. Warehousing and order filling took place at the distribution center from which bottlers served their traditional territories.

Production

Production operations in the soft drink industry were divided between concentrate producers and bottlers. Quality control was one area where branded concentrate producers exercised influence over bottlers' and canners' production activities. Quality control required meeting plant, equipment, and process sanitation standards, as well as standards for product composition. Product composition standards covered the proportion of flavoring, sugar, and water in drink, degree of carbonation, taste, and appearance. Quality control violations were one of the few grounds on which concentrate companies could revoke a bottler's franchise rights.

Concentrate and syrup production were simple processes involving little investment in plant or equipment and a low labor component. One analyst estimated that the Coca-Cola Company could double its syrup-producing capacity with a $200,000 capital investment. The concentrate process itself involved mixing fruit extracts and other liquefied natural and artificial flavorings with water and sugar in large vats. The resulting concentrate was shipped to bottlers and canners. Concentrate contained only a small proportion of the sugar needed in the finished drink and was more economical to ship; consequently, one or two concentrate factories might efficiently serve bottlers all over the United States.

Franchise companies which produced concentrate shifted the bulk of sugar purchasing requirements onto their franchised bottlers. Coke was the only major company to produce and ship syrup rather than concentrates. Coke maintained 22 regional syrup production centers to minimize the high costs of shipping. It partially handled the problem of sugar purchasing risks by charging its bottlers a syrup price which fluctuated depending on average quarterly sugar prices.

Soft drink bottling was also a simple, nonlabor-intensive, manufacturing process, although it was more capital intensive than concentrate production. One source estimated that bottlers' total investment in plant, equipment, supplies, and distribution vehicles was close to $2 billion in 1975. The researcher estimated that approximately 30 percent of that $2 billion represented investment in plant (manufacturing and warehousing space) and 10 percent was in machinery and equipment.

Depending on its age, filling equipment currently in use in the industry ranged in capacity from 100 to 1,000 bottles per minute. Bottle washing, filling, and packing equipment had limited flexibility in terms of the range of container sizes and materials it could handle. Consequently, a bottler producing the full-size range of 6 to 64 ounces might require two or three lines.

Much of the industry's canned product was produced by large bottlers, by contract canners, and by concentrate company-owned canning lines because of the scale of capital investment required. Cans were lighter and easier to handle than bottles of comparable capacity, so canning production could be more easily centralized than bottling. The Coca-Cola Company was, in terms of capital investment, the most forward-integrated producer. Its canning operations were carried out by a wholly owned subsidiary called Canner for Coca-Cola Bottlers, Inc. (CCCB). CCCB put the bottling companies' syrup in cans for a fee at six different locations. The company's depreciated investment in canning plant was $21 million in 1975. CCCB accounted for approximately 1 percent of Coke's pretax profits in 1974, and 42 percent of its output went to company-owned bottling plants serving 14 percent of the U.S. population, and 38 percent went to independent franchised bottlers.[15]

NEW COMPETITORS—THE INTRUDERS

"Concentrate production is a license to steal," an industry analyst remarked. "The industry is bound to attract competitive interest." While

---

[15] Mr. Ogden, Coca-Cola Company, quoted in summary of and excerpts from the *Hearing before the Federal Trade Commission.* Kuhn, Loeb summary, May 5–9, 1975, p. 1E.

other industry observers did not agree with the "extremity" of this judgment, they did agree that the industry was most profitable. They noted that compound earnings growth among the industry leaders ranged from 10.5 percent to 16.8 percent and ROI capital ranged from 12.3 percent to 25.4 percent for the five-year period ending in 1974.

In 1976 old players were experimenting with new games and new players were joining the battle. Cash-and-carry chains were making their appearance in the United States and Canada. Shasta Beverages, with a different concept of distribution, was moving from a regional to a national basis; beverage powders were expanding in sales volume; and rumors of significant new technological developments were "bubbling," in trade circles.

Cash-and-Carry Franchise Outlets

The original cash-and-carry concept combined soft drink bottling and retailing functions in a single company. Independent bottlers, whose proprietary brands were being pushed out of supermarkets by national brands, sold their beverages at reduced markups from their own plant or at a separate retail store. While data were difficult to obtain, some industry observers estimated that cash-and-carry sales accounted for between 2 percent and 10 percent of packaged soft drink sales, depending on the region in the United States, and a higher percentage in Canada.

In the early 1970s, local bottlers' interest in cash-and-carry operations accelerated as two firms—Towne Club and Pop Shoppes—developed a franchise system of operations for that market. Towne Club, formerly an independent bottler, owned and operated 40 sales outlets in the metropolitan Detroit area, supplying these operations from a central bottling facility. In addition, Towne Club had franchises in six other metropolitan areas in five states with over 100 outlets.

Pop Shoppes, a Canadian operation, opened its first state-side operation in Phoenix, Arizona, in 1972. In 1976 the company had 24 factory plants in the United States and 25 in Canada supplying approximately 400 retail outlets. Both firms planned major further expansion; and in 1975, Pop Shoppes' major Canadian competitor, Pick-A-Pop, sold a 50 percent interest to Moxie Industries, an Atlanta-based concentrate producer. That firm immediately began franchising operations in the western United States.

Pop Shoppes, for example, provided a franchised store owner with site selection tips, marketing plans, advertising and co-op promotion plans, and training programs. Typically, the independent bottler would open a sales outlet at the bottling plant and expand to other retail sites later. Sales strategy was based on low prices (approximately 50 percent of supermarket prices), only returnable bottles, limited numbers of bottle sizes, a complete flavor range (25–32) from colas to fruit flavors, and fast, quick service. All sales were in case lots, and one of the two persons operating the shop managed the cash register while the other stocked floor displays and helped customers load their cars.

Shasta Beverages

Shasta soft drinks were produced and distributed by the Shasta Beverage Division of Consolidated Foods, located in Chicago, Illinois. Consolidated operated in a number of food-related areas: sugar refining, meat packing, convenience food stores, institutional and volume feeding operations, and restaurants; some of its well-known brand names included Sara Lee frozen foods and Popsicles.

Shasta's competitive posture differed substantially from other industry participants. Its soft drinks were not sold via franchised bottlers but were sold directly by the company to buyers who operated their own warehouse facilities. Shasta produced 20 standard flavors, in both diet and conventional formulations, primarily in steel cans (80 percent), but also in 28-ounce and 64-ounce nonreturnable bottles. Product was manufactured in 21 plants, each of which also had warehouse distribution facilities; and in some cases was distributed in Shasta's own trucks, in truckload lots, to large-volume customers.

A 250–300 persons sales force worked with large chain store personnel assisting them with product display, pricing, and promotion. The company gave discounts off list price to chains with the view that the chains would pass that lowered price on to the consumer. More than 80 percent of Shasta's business was to food stores; the company did not attempt to sell the single-service market. Shasta did not impose a geographic limit on its wholesale purchasers. They could resell Shasta products in whatever area they liked. Retail prices were established locally; Shasta beverages were generally sold at higher prices than private labels, but lower than national brand prices.

Since 1960 Shasta (sales $6 million) had gone from regional to national distribution and had achieved a 2.5 percent share of the U.S. market with estimated 1976 sales of over $200 million. The company's 1976 annual report reported that Shasta had initiated price reductions and had increased promotional expenditure. Pretax income increased 13 percent in fiscal 1976.

"POWDERS—A $600 Million Stir in the Soft Drink Market"

So headlined the lead article in *Beverage World*, reporting that "mix-it-yourself" drinks were enjoying extraordinary sales success with a 50 percent sales gain in 1974, another 50 percent sales gain in 1975, and predictions for 1976 being similarly optimistic.

> Beverage powders, for years dismissed as "kid stuff" and virtually ignored by most beverage manufacturers, are fast making their presence felt in the market. There are no specific figures indicating that powdered beverages are cutting drastically into carbonated soft drink volume, but their tremendous sales growth, sparked by consumer resistance to higher-priced carbonated drinks . . . clearly shows that powder manufacturers are capturing a share of the carbonated soft drink market.[16]

In 1976 finished beverage powder gallonage was estimated to be 1.2 billion, about 20 percent of the approximately 6.3 billion gallons of soft drinks expected to be purchased that year.

Beverage syrups and powders had been on the market for almost 50 years. Originally sold as fruit drinks, they offered the homemaker the advantages of low price and carrying convenience. And, in addition, they provided the fountain and institutional market a colorful visual advertising display—a large, glass container with a jet spray of constantly moving, brightly colored juice. In recent years, bottle syrups for home use had declined in sales importance and, therefore, in amount of supermarket shelf space. Beverage mixes came in five basic flavors, and trade sources estimated consumer preferences as (1) lemonade, (2) grape, (3) orange, (4) strawberry, and (5) cherry. Mixes came with sugar, without sugar, and in Pillsbury's new entry "Squoze" a sugar-plus-artificial-sweetener formula that contained half the regular calories, and they were packaged in compact containers with lower per ounce prices for the consumer. Mixes were also available in envelopes or packets (60 percent of market), ranging from 1 to 3 ounces to 12 ounces (retail price 99 cents) and the kitchen-type canisters (40 percent of the market) from 24 to 45 ounces ($3.19 retail).

A random series of interviews with housewives in Boston supermarkets could be summarized by the following:

> I've quit buying the bottled stuff. These mixes are cheaper, they allow me to regulate the amount of sugar the kids get, they don't break my back carrying them to the kitchen from the car, and it cuts down the trip to the dump. My daughter says they are ecologically superior.

Three major food marketing companies dominated the grocery trade mix business in 1976: General Foods' Kool-Aid (40 percent of the market), Borden's Wyler's (40 percent), and Pillsbury's Funny Face and Squoze (10 percent). Each of these firms had substantial marketing skill and distributive capacity. Most employed broad-scale couponing, free premiums, special price offers, and display assistance to the supermarket. All of the companies allocated significant advertising dollar support to these products; Kool-Aid spent $7.6 million in 1974, while Wyler's allocated $1.9 million. One industry source noted that the companies spent $17

---

[16] John D. Stacey, *Beverage World,* March 1976, p. 30.

million in 1974 and estimated they would spend $30 million in 1975 on beverage powder advertising.

In April 1976, RJR Foods (a division of the former Reynolds Tobacco Company) announced its entry into the field with a powdered mix version of its single-strength, canned, Hawaiian Punch drink. The company allocated $6 million in advertising funds for the first-year introduction. "The consumer shifted away from single-strength fruit juices for economy reasons," a company spokesperson said. "What kept them from totally switching back again as sugar prices came back down was that they discovered manufacturers had vastly improved the quality since they had last tried it as kids."[17]

By 1976 other companies were testing the mix market. A&P and Kroger were leaders in introducing their own private label mixes. This decision had been spurred by the major success of "canister" packaging which gave the retailer a bigger "ticket-price" item to promote. Coca-Cola Foods Division had been test marketing fruit-flavored powders under its Hi-C (a canned single-strength juice line) for almost a year in Florida and Michigan.

There seemed to be some consensus in the trade that the boom in powders had been permanently influenced by what sales executives referred to as "product repositioning." Promotion had moved from selling "kids'" to a "family"drink. Advertising was changed to highlight *soft drink* mixes as opposed to fruit drink syrup and powders and shifted from a seasonal to a year-round promotional program. Attractive new display racks were installed next to, or near, the soft drink shelf space in food stores. Natural flavors were substituted for artificial flavors, and powder packages were supplied to the consumers in an increased number of sizes. In predicting the future, an industry expert noted:

> Beverages powders by their nature probably will accelerate the thrust toward fruit and citrus flavors and possibly affect carbonated soft drink flavor favorites. In view of the popularity of fruit flavors with young consumers, it poses the question of how much this might change future adult soft drink flavor preferences.[18]

In addition to a $400 million, 1976 consumer market, the trade sold an estimated $250 million to the food service and institutional feeding market. Of the over 100 companies operating in this field, General Foods led with 15 percent of the volume, followed by Nestlé (11 percent), Wyler's (10 percent), and Standard Brands (7 percent).

> This market is both huge and unseen. . . . While public eating places offer opportunities for promoting beverage brands, the institutional market (plants, hospitals, etc.) is often controlled by dieticians. Many such institu-

---

[17] "The Mix-It-Yourself Boom," *Business Week,* May 17, 1976, p. 56.
[18] John D. Stacey, *Beverage World,* March 1976, p. 35.

tions do not serve carbonated beverages, preferring to serve beverages made from powders or syrups. In these outlets, powders compete with syrups . . . buyers frequently switch to the cheapest one.[19]

Product Technology

In the course of interviews with industry executives, the researchers heard infrequent references to possible, upcoming technological changes. It was difficult, however, to obtain any definitive information about the specifics of these possible developments or their future impact on the industry. In some overseas markets, an old product—the siphon bottle—was again being pushed as a way of manufacturing carbonated drinks in the home. Another source noted that one firm was experimenting with the sale of packages of carbonated ice cubes and syrup.

A number of references were made to the possible entrance of General Foods and Procter & Gamble into the field. The alleged P&G entry basis would be a self-carbonating product—probably a coating on the bottom of a cup—which would effervesce with the addition of water and syrup. Some observers believed P&G already had patents on such a product. Procter & Gamble's interest, they stated further, was the fact that soft drinks commanded an average of 120 linear feet of chain store shelf space versus 100 for detergents and 45 for coffee; also that soft drink sales per square foot of shelf space were almost twice that of coffee or detergents.

THE INDUSTRY'S CRITICS

"We are under attack on a number of fronts," an industry executive stated, "but our critical concerns are health issues, the bottle and can disposal problems, and antitrust action to break up the franchise system. In some ways the first area is the most difficult with which to deal. Our critics range from government agencies to consumer, health-oriented, private pressure groups, to individual technical critics with strong interest in the safety of specific drugs or the nutritional value of certain ingredients. And the impact of government edict can be disastrous. Do you recall the 1969 cyclamate ban; it almost liquidated Royal Crown—they had specialized in diet drinks with sugar substitutes."

Questions as to the public health record of the industry centered on two key-related issues: first, the more general question as to the nutritional contribution—or danger—of soft drinks on American eating patterns; and, second, on the safety or hazards posed by product ingredients, for example, sugar, caffeine, and chemical additives.

---

[19] Ibid., p. 35.

A dietician in a veteran's hospital commented:

> World War I vets are strictly meat and potatoes men. World War II and Korean vets like a more balanced, varied diet. But Vietnam veterans don't eat meals at all. They don't eat breakfast . . . and in the morning they start getting hungry and begin munching hamburgers, hot dogs, French fries, and soft drinks. They'd probably eat every meal at McDonald's if they could.[20]

Nutritional experts engage in lengthy public debates about the dietary wisdom of these "fast-food" eating habits and of possible dangers in the consumption of large quantities of soft drinks.

With per capita soft drink consumption substantially over 400 eight-ounce containers, some nutrition experts questioned the wisdom of ingesting high quantities of sugar into the human body. Dr. Jean Mayer, president of Tufts University, was a strong proponent of this point of view. In a June 20, 1976, *New York Times Magazine* article entitled "The Bitter Truth about Sugar," he stated that "purveyors of health foods and natural foods are unanimous in their statements that white sugar is toxic and . . . there is a strong suspicion that a large sugar intake may be causally related to diabetes." An equally well-respected expert, Dr. Frederick J. Stare, chairman of the Department of Nutrition at Harvard University, took a diametrically opposite position: "There are hazards in foods but they don't come from sugar or additives; they come from eating (and drinking) too much and lack of elementary principles of sanitation."[21]

The Food and Drug Administration in 1969 had banned the use of cyclamates as a sugar substitute in diet soft drinks, alleging that research evidence indicated that it would cause bladder cancer in rats. In 1976 the FDA again ruled against the use of cyclamates, noting that there were "unresolved questions about the product's potential for causing cancer, its effects on growth and reproduction, and the possibility that it might damage chromosomes, the basic genetic apparatus."

In October 1976 Senator Gaylord Nelson, a consistent critic of the Food and Drug Administration, charged that a report by the General Accounting Office "shows that the FDA actually violated the law by allowing continued use of saccharin without making final determination of safety."[22] The FDA allowed the use of saccharin for more than four years on a "temporary basis." Saccharin was believed to be the industry's only practical alternative to cyclamates. The most serious circumstance would be if both sweeteners were banned. Drink reformulation would be possible if an approved, noncaloric sweetener could be developed. The risk was that the consumer might or might not like the new taste.

---

[20] *Prevention Magazine,* November 1971, p. 30.

[21] *New York Times Magazine,* Letters section, July 18, 1976.

[22] The *New York Times,* Wednesday, October 26, 1976, p. 40.

The introduction and major success of Diet Dr Pepper and Diet 7UP had occurred during the time saccharin took the place of cyclamates.

In 1976, as a part of its review of several hundred food additives—the so-called GRAS list (Generally Recognized as Safe)—the FDA was reviewing the safety status of caffeine. A "split" report, released by the department, indicated that some members believed it was "prudent to assume" there might be a potential health hazard, particularly for children because cola drinks might expose them to daily caffeine in their period of brain growth and development. A 12-ounce cola drink contains two thirds the caffeine found in a cup of coffee.

The 1970s had witnessed a steady acceleration in criticism of the industry for its part in "trash pollution." Senators Hatfield, Javits, Mc-Govern, Packwood, and Stafford introduced a bill in February of 1975 "to prohibit the introduction into interstate commerce of nonreturnable beverage containers." While this bill failed to pass, beginning in September 1975, "throwaways" were banned from federal installations and national parks by administrative order.

On the state level, a ban on throwaways was in force in Vermont and Oregon where proponents stated it had reduced can and bottle litter along the roads by 75 percent. Industry spokespersons disagreed with this finding. In the November 1976 elections, four states—Colorado, Massachusetts, Maine and Michigan—had proposals for mandatory deposits on bottles and cans for voter consideration. The Maine plan called for a 5-cent deposit on bottles used by several firms, a 10-cent deposit on bottles used by one firm only; deposits were also required on beverage cans. In addition, efforts were being made to ban the use of pull-top lids for beverage cans. The editor of the industry's leading trade magazine commented:

> The beverage industries and the United States of America still survive this kind of misdirected, simplistic, well-intentioned, but really dumb legislation. It is not what mandatory deposit bills will do to individual bottlers that matters so much as the potentially disruptive effect they could have on the over-all market picture. Such legislation, for example, might go a long way toward helping the food processing industry in its current effort to position various packs and sizes of powders, concentrates, fruit juices, and fruit flavored drinks as *soft drinks* in both the consumer's mind and in the supermarket. This will have a lot more impact than the development of franchise cash and carry soft drink chains, which are in place and ready to reap the benefits of mandatory deposit legislation in many key states.
>
> Most soft drink bottlers are in no position to either fight or join such a shift in products, packaging, sales, and marketing. And there is no evidence so far that the parent companies are going to respond directly to the threat. Everyone knows that a 4-oz. pouch is no match for a 64-oz. bottle. Right?[23]

---

[23] "The Editor's Notebook," *Beverage World,* July 1976, p. 8.

Industry executives generally believed that the major costs of a non-returnable ban, if such legislation were to be widely enacted, would fall on the franchised bottler. One New England–area Dr Pepper bottler commented:

> Excluding the construction of new plant and warehouse space, I would need over $1 million to convert back to returnable bottles. I would need new filling and handling equipment, more delivery trucks and route people to handle the double volume, and money to convert vending machines. The working capital invested in bottle float alone would be tremendous: each 6½ ounce bottle costs 12 cents, and I sell 3 million 24-bottle cases per year.

As an alternative to forced deposit systems and nonreturnable bans, the industry supported a group called the National Center for Resource Recovery, Inc. The group was a cooperative effort involving the federal government and packaging manufacturers whose objective would be to fund profit-making ventures to reclaim all of a municipality's solid waste, 6 percent of which would be reclaimable as energy. Pilot projects were already under way in St. Louis, New Orleans, and Macon, Georgia. Should the project expand to the national level, its initial funding might come from a tax on packaging manufacturers.

A third major regulatory uncertainty concerned Federal Trade Commission action to substantially modify the industry's franchise bottler system. In 1971 the FTC cited the eight major concentrate producers, charging their exclusive territorial agreements were anticompetitive. In what some observers described as a "counterattack," the beverage industry pressed Congress for legislative approval of the exclusive territorial franchise system. The industry's bill came close to passing in 1972, but failed. Industry efforts to gain congressional support of their position continued in 1976. In 1975 FTC Administrative Law Judge J. P. Dufresne ruled that territorial provisions in franchise agreements did not unreasonably restrain trade but resulted in greater rather than lessened competition. The FTC appealed this decision and hearings continued into 1976.

The franchise controversy was covered in the business press, was a popular topic area in industry and company publications, and was investigated by the Senate Subcommittee on Antitrust and Monopoly in the summer and fall of 1972. Thousands of pages of data resulted. The researcher has attempted to summarize the critical arguments for both government and industry; chances for error or omission, however, are substantial.

The franchise system, pioneered by Coca-Cola, authorizes a bottler to manufacture, distribute, price, and sell a soft drink only in a designated territory. In summary, the FTC alleged that this exclusive franchise territory system kept soft drink prices artificially high and prevented intrabrand price competition. The specific charge stated:

Respondent's contracts, agreements, acts, practices, and method of competition aforesaid have had, and may continue to have, the effect of lessening competition in the advertising, merchandising, offering for sale, and sale of premix and postmix syrups and soft drink products, deprive, and may continue to deprive, the public of the benefits of competition . . . in methods of competition and unfair acts or practices, in commerce, in violation of Section 5 of the Federal Trade Commission Act.

The complaint ordered franchise companies to "cease and desist" from entering into agreements which prevented bottlers from selling products to any type of customer in any location, from restricting the location of the bottler's place of business, and from refusing to sell concentrate to or otherwise penalizing a bottler for selling outside his territory or selling to central warehousing customers. In the words of one industry executive, "The FTC was gung-ho to sink us, and it was frightening."

In a more philosophical vein, the counsel to the Senate subcommittee stated that committee's interest in the question:

Isn't it inevitable that in this industry there is going to be change from the status quo in order to accommodate modern technology and modes of distribution trends, and if there is, shouldn't the shift in business be determined by the marketplace without having erected artificial restraints which in large part permits the parent company to determine who is going to stay in business and who is not going to stay in business?

At the hearings, a number of witnesses, many of whom operated small bottling operations, testified in opposition to the FTC complaint. They argued that breaking down the franchise system would (1) drive many small bottlers, particularly those near large metropolitan areas, out of business; (2) would reduce product availability because large bottlers wouldn't want to service small customers; (3) would reduce local advertising and promotion funds; (4) would increase the power of chain stores to push their own private labels; (5) the era of returnable bottles would end since chain stores would not want to handle them and door-to-door delivery and pickup would diminish; and (6) soft drink prices would not drop.

Ms. Alice Brady, of Kuhn, Loeb & Co., summarized the FTC charges and the industry's rebuttal as follows:

The marketing structure of the soft-drink industry, as described by the Coca-Cola bottlers who have testified to date, has remained practically unchanged for almost 70 years. This structure has depended on substantial capital investment by individual entrepreneurs, whose willingness to invest in the industry was closely tied to the contractual promise of territorial exclusivity. Under the umbrella thus provided, the individual bottling organizations have been encouraged to develop their markets to the fullest extent possible, serving all potential customers in each area at a uniform price, regardless of account size . . . territorial protection has enabled (in fact, forced) the small bottler to place his products in virtually every conceivable outlet, thereby achieving a total fluid volume that would be otherwise unattainable . . . removal of the territorial umbrella would probably cause industry-wide contraction in the number of bottling companies, package and brand varieties, and accounts served. In addition, a multi-tiered pricing structure would be the likely result, with the probability of higher average unit price. Ineluctably tied to the foregoing would be a decline in total consumption of soft-drink gallonage.[24]

The Federal Trade Commission views were summarized by Alan S. Ward, director of the Bureau of Competition, before the Senate committee.[25] He stressed three points:

In summary, territorial restrictions in the soft drink industry have actually contributed to the decline in the number of bottlers. Small bottlers have been denied the opportunity of expanding their sales and growing to efficient size, and, thereby, to continue to do business in this industry. Consequently, they have been induced to leave the industry. If the territorial restrictions are removed, small bottlers will be given an opportunity to expand their operations to the point at which they can support an efficient plant.

Ending territorial restrictions will neither cause the end of service to small customers nor force them to pay higher taxes. Many small soft drink buyers currently purchase other food products from wholesalers who operate warehouses. Such wholesalers will provide soft drinks to small stores along with other food products. Indeed, it may be cheaper for these small stores to depend on one source for all their food product needs rather than having to split their business as currently must be done.

The end of territorial restrictions will not have the drastic effect on ecology predicted by some bottlers. First, more and more consumers are demanding nonreusable containers and this trend would be expected to continue regardless of whether territorial restrictions are eliminated or maintained. Second, chain grocers handle the products demanded by consumers and handle returnables if consumers wish these products.

An industry analyst agreed with some of Mr. Ward's conclusions, stating:

Warehouse distribution is coming. A "drop" to a vending outlet or Mom or Pop store costs 45 cents. The average delivery cost per case is 35 cents, but the cost for the warehouse delivery is but 15 cents. Major concentrate producers and the consumer would benefit from warehouse deliveries via a reduction in national brand prices. The current franchised bottler system is the main deterrent to warehouse delivery, and this is because of the relatively small size of a franchise territory. Franchise territories were originally defined when there was a single 6½-ounce returnable package,

---

[24] Summary of and excerpts from the *Hearing before the Federal Trade Commission in the matter of Coca-Cola Company et al.,* May 19–23, 1975, pp. 1792–2468.

[25] *Hearings before the Subcommittee on Antitrust and Monopoly,* 92d Congress, part I, p. 225.

and small territories were very efficient for handling this type of distribution. Now, with package and flavor proliferation and the big increase in one-way bottles, traditional franchise territories are inefficient. Smaller territories were also advantageous to the concentrate companies because they could increase consumption with total availability and pushed their bottlers to service vending machines and small outlets. Now, with the increase in transportation costs, bottlers realize they're losing money on those small stops, but they need them for volume.

Not all franchise owners were in sympathy with the "industry" position taken at the subcommittee hearings. A critical view of the franchise system was outlined by Mr. John M. Alden, president of the Royal Crown Bottling Corporation of Denver, Colorado, in ten pages of committee testimony. Excerpts from his testimony follow:

> What protections do territorial restrictions provide, then, if there is not sufficient business in a franchise area to support a costly, modern and efficient plant? The concentrate houses know this. They have had game plans and programs, which they are implementing . . . they definitely plan to concentrate the industry with major production centers and major distribution centers.
>
> This concept in itself, put to work, eliminates a lot of small bottlers. At best, it permits that little bottler to become a distributor, and just a distributor. What does that have to do with territorial restrictions?
>
> We think it is only a matter of time before supermarket purchases of soft drinks will have to be totally serviced, at the central warehouse. We are also convinced that every major concentrate house, in the confines of their own offices, agrees. The strategy question is, what the hell do we do about it?
>
> At the moment concentrate houses are frozen with a lot of franchise agreements. If all the franchise contracts could be washed out tomorrow, I believe the major concentrate companies would happily go ahead and operate unburdened, free of small bottlers. But, at this hour, the courts are honoring the validity of the bottlers' trademark licensing agreements.
>
> They may say, "This man has paid for this franchise. You just can't throw him out the window. He has some equity in it." And if you add it up, and laminated all these sums of money, this involves sums of money too big for even the largest concentrate houses in the country to pay off on. Therefore, another strategy and alternate must be developed.
>
> Every major concentrate house has already set targets and time schedules for the consolidation of production and distribution of their major brands concentrated in major trading areas where the food-store warehouses are located. The clue is in the hurried efforts during the past year to structure production centers and distribution enclaves in major marketing areas, and the emphasis there is on the warehouse profile rather than the old geographical county lines on which franchise areas were crudely structured. In other words, the concentrate houses are "getting on the ball" so territorial restrictions can be ignored if they are still in effect. To me, it looks like an adaptation of the cartel system used by European corporate giants to divide the

world market among themselves. I think we now have in this country a version of the cartel method of allocating markets areas, which will end up being shared by not more than 100 or 200 major bottler-canner companies, at most, and any remaining bottlers, still alive, will be doing yeoman's work as distributors for the key bottler and canning operations in the hands of a few giants.

As one of the few voices in the soft drink industry to speak up for elimination of territorial restrictions, I do so fully aware of continued harassment, and possible additional reprisal actions and economic sanctions that may be initiated against my operation by concentrate house interests.[26]

Senior officers of the concentrate firms unanimously and strongly publicly backed the franchise system. W. W. Clements, president of the Dr Pepper Company, testified to the same committee about the dangers in the government's suit, noting:

The small independent bottler would be a thing of the past. Dr Pepper would be forced into owning and operating a great number of bottling plants throughout the United States. . . . This would happen in varying degrees to other brands. However, the larger companies with greater resources would have a tremendous advantage. The industry would end up with a very few large bottling companies, and they would all be owned by large companies, such as franchise companies, public-owned companies, and food chains.

Predictions of the future varied by market segment. With regard to diet drinks an analyst stated:

There is real potential to create new markets and increase consumption in diet beverages. Company advertising and promotional activities are very effective in increasing soft drink consumption, but advertising expenditures for diet drinks have been disproportionately low. Most companies are one product companies, even Coke. They never needed diet drink sales or secondary flavors before, and were never very successful with them. Coke grew at 6.5 percent per year on sales of regular Coke alone. No company except Seven-Up has been very aggressive with their diet brands, especially the colas. They've been scared stiff to heavily promote diet brands because they thought they would lose brand loyalty and brand identity for their main products. Now the major companies can't meet their growth objectives with their flagship brands.

A number of analysts were optimistic about the fountain market; one made the following comments:

Fountain, or on-premise sales in food service outlets, is the only growth area left in the domestic soft drink industry, and it belongs to Coke. The growth of fast-food chains has been responsible for the rapid growth of sales in this area, and the chains' continued rapid growth will continue at 6–8 percent per year for the next five to seven years.

---

[26] Ibid., pp. 370–80.

The fountain business is very different. The retailer buys syrup from an independent jobber or directly from the concentrate manufacturer. Most bottlers did not sell fountain syrup. The syrup is mixed with carbonated water by a dispenser at the point of purchase. There are 5–6,000 independent jobbers who have no territorial limitations on their sales areas. For most jobbers, soft drinks are loss leaders, for example, Martin Brauer distributes Coke syrup to McDonald's at only pennies per gallon.

Coke dominates the fountain market. Seventeen percent of its total domestic gallonage is sold through fast-food chains, and an additional 16 percent is sold through other types of food service outlets, such as restaurants and ice cream shops. Pepsi was late in entering the fountain sales part of the business and has a very convoluted distribution structure. Franchised Pepsi bottlers formulate syrup or purchase it from the company, then sell it to jobbers who, in turn, sell to retail outlets. Consequently, only 15 percent of Pepsi's total gallonage is from on-premise sales, and the proportion will probably diminish in the future. The only major chain to carry Pepsi is Burger King.

Another analyst commenting on Coke's competitive position stated:

Intensified brand and price competition in the 1977–80 period would be unlikely to dent Coca-Cola's dominant position in the fountain or vending markets. About one-half of Coke's domestic fountain installations are owned by the Coca-Cola Co., and major restaurant chains are unlikely to switch allegiance. A longer term concern, albeit premature, is the possibility of backward integration into soft drinks by a restaurant chain to develop an additional and significant profit center. McDonald's Corp. currently accounts for an estimated 10 percent of Coca-Cola's fountain volume or 3 percent of Coke's domestic syrup gallonage, has a captive and expanding customer base, and has become increasingly new-product oriented.[27]

Other analysts estimated Coke's share of the fountain market as close to 80 percent, but they expected competition to increase as Dr Pepper and Seven-Up made increased fountain sales a major objective of growth strategies. "The picture spells competition, challenge, and, bluntly, we must also gain share from the competition to meet our new sales objectives," a Seven-Up executive remarked to a *Beverage World* editor in April 1976.

Two analysts commented on the future of the vending machine market:

In the past, the percent of sales through vending was higher, but the energy shortage hit vending hard. Also, prices in vendors only change in fixed increments, for example, 5 cents or 10 cents and price changes are slow to catch up with rising distribution costs. In the last year or so, vending has become more profitable due to price increases, and all the concentrate companies are trying to increase their participation in the vending market.

[27] Paine, Webber, Jackson, and Curtis, "Soft Drink and Beer—Midyear, 1976 Review."

Bottle, can, and cup vending account for approximately 20 percent of soft drink sales in the United States today, but it's a declining area. For independent soft drink bottlers, the vending part of their business just keeps the public aware of their products. But now, distribution costs are rising so fast that I see zero or a net decrease of 1.5 percent in industry sales through vending outlets.

A prediction as to the future of the third major market segment— food stores—was made by another analyst:

In the last few years, the total number of food stores has been declining, and there has been a net contraction of shelf space for soft drinks. Sales growth through the industry's most important outlet will be at most 1 or 2 percent per year.

FUTURE MARKET DIRECTIONS—A CLOUDY CRYSTAL BALL

Where is this industry going in the next decade? I wish I knew the answer. Just skim the trade press and you get a feel for the jet pace of this game. Coke is test marketing a health drink called Samson! Implications? Washington is in on every issue. If franchising breaks down, this industry may go the way beer has—just a dozen major firms. Two more good-sized franchise operations have just been purchased by conglomerates.

Did you see that West German health officials have removed cyclamates and saccharin from the cancer-producing agents list, and they are both available for use in soft drinks? Our FDA won't release cyclamates! And the international market's fascinating: Schweppes is moving into the USSR and Shasta into Canada. We are even getting new products—Nestlé and Lipton are pushing canned tea. They are big internationally, too, and already are in fruit drinks abroad.

OK, Professor, what's *your* answer? What's coming up, when, and what does it mean for me?

CASE 5

The Dr Pepper Company

The Dr Pepper Company of Dallas, Texas, manufactured, distributed, and marketed concentrate for a unique fruit-flavored soft drink called Dr Pepper. "It's a corporate Horatio Alger story," an industry observer noted. "And a lot of the credit goes to the marketing abilities of its president; he is one of the best in the United States."

Since 1962 the company had been growing at two to three times the industry rate while it maintained a net return on investment of approximately 24 percent. During the past decade Dr Pepper had displaced Canada Dry Ginger Ale and Royal Crown Cola to move from the sixth to the fourth largest selling soft drink in the United States (see Exhibits 1 and 2).

Senior management attributed much of the company's success to two key factors: the strength of the Dr Pepper bottler network and the "uniqueness" and "goodness" of their soft drink. In the past decade the company had established a national network of franchised bottlers spreading the distribution of Dr Pepper from its regional southwestern base to the entire United States. "If there's one secret to the success we've had, it's the strength of our bottling organization," an executive stated. Senior management devoted much of their time to cultivating effective bottler-company relations. For despite the successful franchising of 100 percent of the U.S. market, product availability in 1976 was only 70 percent; some bottlers did not fully service their franchise territory. Management noted, too, that one of their continuing challenges was to get the multibrand bottler (who might also bottle Coke, Pepsi-Cola, or 7UP) to allocate the necessary amount of time, money, and effort to effectively distribute Dr Pepper.

EXHIBIT 1

THE DR PEPPER COMPANY
Consolidated Statements of Earnings and Retained Earnings, 1970–1975

	1970	1971	1972	1973	1974	1975
Net sales	$57,449,749	$63,622,653	$77,396,257	$98,918,466	$128,299,707	$138,250,075
Cost of sales	27,428,675	29,787,613	37,310,346	50,791,111	74,659,678	77,831,275
Gross profit	30,021,074	33,835,040	40,085,911	48,127,355	53,640,029	60,418,800
Administrative, marketing, and general expenses	19,835,343	21,991,585	25,402,094	31,262,480	36,297,111	37,702,958
Operating profit	10,185,731	11,843,455	14,683,817	16,864,875	17,342,918	22,715,842
Other income	899,051	894,811	842,982	1,502,848	1,121,634	414,588
Earnings before income taxes	11,084,782	12,738,266	15,526,799	18,367,723	18,464,552	23,130,430
Federal and state income taxes	5,455,761	5,966,125	7,424,580	8,632,223	8,562,853	11,226,295
Net earnings	5,629,021	6,772,141	8,102,219	9,735,500	9,901,694	11,904,135
Retained earnings at beginning of year	15,518,210	18,239,639	21,398,131	26,016,511	31,452,612	36,006,705
Dividends paid	2,907,592	3,613,649	3,878,553	4,299,399	5,347,606	6,018,782
	21,147,231	25,011,780	29,500,350	35,752,011	41,354,311	47,910,840
Retained earnings at end of year	$18,239,639	$21,398,131	$25,621,797	$31,452,612	$ 36,006,705	$ 41,892,058
Earnings per share	0.61	0.73	0.43*	0.51	0.52	0.62
Dividends per share	0.31½	0.39	0.20⅘*	0.22¾	0.28	0.31½

* 1972, 2-for-1 stock split.

EXHIBIT 2

THE DR PEPPER COMPANY
Consolidated Balance Sheets, 1970–1975

Assets	1970	1971	1972	1973	1974	1975
Current assets:						
Cash	$10,760,891	$11,818,371	$15,778,158	$ 872,776	$ 364,141	$ 145,276
Marketable securities	—	—	—	18,147,335	4,790,445	21,676,451
Receivables:						
Trade accounts	2,907,310	3,746,097	4,106,580	5,369,462	7,509,935	7,137,317
Other notes and accounts	972,108	930,663	1,162,725	1,310,362	1,605,048	452,976
Inventories (FIFO):	1,906,624	2,155,307	—	—	—	—
Finished products	—	—	1,267,301	1,469,919	2,046,557	2,152,623
Raw materials and supplies	—	—	1,162,371	1,584,520	3,682,058	2,209,723
Prepaid expenses	1,046,045	1,844,082	2,235,984	3,314,330	3,548,258	1,990,119
Total current assets	17,592,983	20,494,520	25,713,119	32,068,704	23,546,442	35,764,485
Marketable securities held for investment	470,656	1,153,352	1,519,251	1,779,325	8,156,618	5,573,586
Notes receivable and other investments					1,260,829	738,243
Property, plant, and equipment:						
Land	4,027,325	4,546,716	4,615,832	5,753,104	1,951,050	1,951,050
Buildings and improvements					6,102,342	6,385,146
Machinery, equipment, and furniture	8,237,902	8,922,629	10,531,118	14,446,416	16,478,513	18,126,276
	12,265,227	13,469,345	15,146,950	20,199,520	24,531,905	26,462,472
Less: Accumulated depreciation	5,249,478	5,594,253	6,535,564	8,902,926	9,171,248	10,421,632
Net property, plant, and equipment	7,015,749	7,875,092	8,611,386	11,296,594	15,360,657	16,040,840
Formulas, trademarks, and goodwill	272,910	272,910	272,910	272,910	270,910	270,910
Total assets	$25,352,298	$29,795,874	$36,116,666	$45,417,533	$48,595,456	$58,388,064

EXHBIT 2 *(concluded)*

Liabilities and Stockholders' Equity	1970	1971	1972	1973	1974	1975
Current liabilities:						
Accounts payable and accrued expenses.	$ 2,859,195	$ 3,537,896	$ 3,412,671	$ 6,006,509	$ 4,884,550	$ 6,321,455
Federal and state income taxes . . .	715,455	996,987	1,551,370	1,240,930	73,469	2,505,819
Total current liabilities	3,574,650	4,534,883	4,964,041	7,247,439	4,958,019	8,827,274
Stockholders' equity:						
Common stock without par value . .	3,538,009	3,862,860	5,530,828	6,717,482	7,630,732	7,668,732
Retained earnings.	18,239,639	21,398,131	25,621,797	31,452,612	36,006,705	41,892,058
Total stockholders' equity. . .	21,777,648	25,260,991	31,152,625	38,170,094	43,637,437	49,560,790
Total liabilities and stockholders' equity . .	$25,352,298	$29,795,874	$36,116,666	$45,417,533	$48,595,456	$58,388,064

Heralded in company promotional efforts as either a "misunderstood drink" or as the "most original soft drink ever," the uniqueness of Dr Pepper's flavor was cited as a second major corporate strength by company managers. The difficult to describe flavor had what management described as consumer "staying power"; once a customer sampled and liked Dr Pepper, s/he became a constant user and could consume many bottles each day. Dr Pepper was the only noncola product ever to achieve per capita consumption of 100 or more bottles per year in many key markets.

Dr Pepper's success, however, had not gone unappreciated—executives of major bottling firms spoke in extremely complimentary terms of the firm's record—or unchallenged by competitors. In 1972 Coca-Cola introduced Mr. PiBB, a new soft drink which, to many, tasted remarkably like Dr Pepper. This was not Coke's first competitive entry into this flavor field; they had previously test marketed two drinks, Texas Stepper and Chime, but neither succeeded commercially. A common industry interpretation was that Coke introduced Mr. PiBB to provide its bottlers with a product which they could sell to the Dr Pepper taste market. Dudley Lynch, a business journalist, commented:

> Predictably, Coke discouraged any thoughts that Mr. PiBB was aimed at Dr Pepper. "I haven't tasted Dr Pepper myself," said a Coke spokesman blandly, "so I wouldn't know how similar Mr. PiBB is to it. I don't think it was meant to compete with Dr Pepper—as far as I know Coke just felt there was a market for this kind of soft drink." Curiously enough Coke decided to test its new soft drink in Waco, birthplace of Dr Pepper, where more Dr Peppers are consumed than any other drink.[1]

The completion of Dr Pepper's national franchising program and its resultant almost 5.5 percent share of the 1975 soft drink market, some industry executives believed, had given the company both new status as well as a new competitive position. "They are playing in a different ball game now—against the big boys. And that game is getting rough, with an increasingly rough competitive battle between Coke and Pepsi-Cola. They are like two bull elephants locked in combat; it's dangerous to be in the same ring."

There did not seem to be much doubt that the U.S. soft drink industry was becoming increasingly complex and competitive (see Note on the Soft Drink Industry in the United States). The immediate, visible manifestation of this increased competitive circumstance in 1976 was an outbreak of retail price cutting in certain southwestern markets—Dallas and Ft. Worth—as well as a national, stepped-up, aggressive Coke versus Pepsi-Cola advertising program in which competitors' advertising claims were attacked in sometimes "savage" ways.

---

[1] Dudley Lynch, "Dr Pepper Takes on Coke," *D Magazine (Dallas/Ft. Worth)*, September 1975, p. 60.

Labeled by *Time* magazine as a "likeable Lilliputian," Dr Pepper's total sales were only two thirds of Coca-Cola's 1975 net profits. But competing with billion-dollar giants did not seem to concern Dr Pepper senior management. The company announced an objective of making Dr Pepper America's number one soft drink with projected nationwide market shares of 10 percent in 1980 and 15 percent in 1985. Projected sales and earnings growth were targeted at 15 to 20 percent a year.

COMPANY HISTORY

Dr Pepper's historical background would provide any novelist with all of the ingredients of an exciting corporate drama. Formulated by an unknown fountain clerk, named after his girl friend's physician father to help "gain her hand," the drink came to the attention of R. L. Lazenby, a chemist. First dispensed at the Old Corner Drug Store in Waco, Texas, in 1885, it came on this local market approximately at the same time Coca-Cola was being introduced in the state of Georgia.

The early history of the company was characterized by family management, modest growth into contiguous territories, and a product reputation which combined a refreshment and a medicinal product mission. From the early 1920s well into the 1950s, the company was under the leadership of Mr. J. B. O'Hara, who was responsible for the transfer of company headquarters from Waco to Dallas and for the introduction of a bottlers' franchise program in 1926. Prior to that time Dr Pepper had been shipped to surrounding towns by Wells-Fargo Express. The company's advertising featured, as a trademark, an iron anvil, bordered by braided grain with the headline—DR PEPPER'S PHOSFERRATES— Wheat and Iron.

While family management and influence continued (in 1975 Mrs. O'Hara was the company's second largest shareholder) two critical developments occurred in the late 1950s. In 1956 Mr. W. R. Parker, a former General Foods Corporation executive, joined Dr Pepper and brought to the company a variety of modern marketing and advertising promotion techniques. He was assisted in this effort by Mr. W. W. Clements, who was named vice president of marketing in 1957. Their task was a formidable one. Dr Pepper's growth during the 30s and 40s had been modest; company marketing and management practices were conservative, and company bottlers tended to serve moderate-sized towns and rural areas, primarily in the southern areas of the United States.

The second critical development was legal in character. In 1962 the Pepsi-Cola Company sued Dr Pepper for alleged trademark infringement over Dr Pepper's use of the word "pep." Pepsi-Cola won the suit; however, Dr Pepper countersued, and the result was the ruling that Dr Pepper was not a cola drink but a unique and separate flavor. This judgment, later reaffirmed by the Food and Drug Administration, marked a turning point in the company's history. Coke and Pepsi-Cola franchised bottlers, the most powerful in the industry, could now also bottle Dr Pepper without violating their cola franchise. A company officer summarized the development as follows:

> Traditionally, up until about this time period, bottling companies produced under one basic franchise agreement. For example, there was a bottling company producing Coca-Cola and its flavor line—Fanta; another bottling company producing Pepsi-Cola and the Pepsi-Cola flavor line; and a Seven-Up bottling company producing that product. Included among the bottling companies would perhaps be a Dr Pepper company. These Dr Pepper bottlers inherently would be the ones least financially able and equipped to make a major effort at market penetration in competition with the entrenched and well-established and financed cola companies. With the court decision ruling that Dr Pepper was not a cola, the Dr Pepper Company legally was in a position to solicit franchise agreements with the strongest of the cola-producing bottling companies in any geographical area.

By 1962 the company had entered a phase of rapid growth which brought company sales from $17 million to $138 million in 1975 and an even more rapid profit expansion. This expansion program was climaxed by Dr Pepper's introduction to the New York City area market in 1970.

> One crisp November morning in 1969 Woodrow Wilson "Foots" Clements and his team of executives stepped into a cab outside New York's Waldorf-Astoria Hotel. Mission: To pull off what some would call the biggest coup in soft drink history. Clements and his Dr Pepper executives, representing an easy-going beverage which had stayed home in Texas and minded its own business for 85 years, headed over to the 34th Street offices of Coca-Cola Bottling Company of New York, the world's largest distributor of soft drink's Goliath—Coca-Cola. Objective: To convince Coca-Cola of New York to bottle Dr Pepper, load it on Coke trucks, and sell America's "most misunderstood" soft drink to 20 million New Yorkers.
>
> Seven months later Millard[2] and Clements shook hands. New York Coke would bottle Dr Pepper. After 85 years Dr Pepper hit the big time, beginning a fascinating David and Goliath battle that in five years has brought Dr Pepper headlines and stirred the ire of Coca-Cola, whose dominance of the soft drink market is even greater than General Motors' dominance of the auto industry.[3]

By 1973 domestic franchising was virtually 100 percent complete and Dr Pepper made its first major move into the international market. It introduced Dr Pepper in Japan via a franchise agreement with the Tokyo Coca-Cola Bottling Company, Ltd.

---

[2] Coca-Cola of New York's president.

[3] "Dr Pepper Takes on Coke," pp. 59–60.

Central to this period of growth and profit was the leadership of W. W. Clements, who became executive vice president in 1967, president and chief executive officer in 1970, and chairman of the board, president, and chief executive officer in March 1974. In 1976 Mr. Clements noted enthusiastically, "We have just started. The potential is tremendous." Some evidence of that potential was detailed in a *Fortune* magazine article:

> Consumption of Dr Pepper remains heavily concentrated in the areas where the drink traditionally has been popular. Five southwestern states with 10 percent of the nation's population account for 37 percent of the company's gallonage, while at the other extreme, nine northeastern states with 24 percent of the population account for a mere 6 percent.
>
> The strongest market of all, appropriately enough, is Waco, the old home town, where Dr Pepper outsells Coca-Cola and Pepsi-Cola combined. The 95,326 citizens of Waco drink more Dr Pepper than the 1,512,893 citizens of Detroit. If the rest of the country were to rise to even half of Waco's per capita consumption of over 250 bottles a year, Dr Pepper's domestic revenues would approach $1.5 billion. That kind of formulation may seem starry-eyed to outsiders, but it is taken quite seriously at Dr Pepper headquarters.[4]

PRODUCT

Dr Pepper was a carbonated, soft drink made of 23 flavorings, plus some phosphoric acid, caffeine, and caramel color. Its exact formulation was a closely guarded company secret. Dr Pepper was unique among soft drinks on two dimensions: its palatibility when served hot or cold and its basic flavor. The unique Dr Pepper flavor was summarized in the following company advertising message:

> Dr Pepper is different from any brand of soft drink. It is not a cola, nor a root beer, nor any single flavor, but a blend of 23 flavors. As most customers say . . . THERE IS NOTHING LIKE DR PEPPER!!! IT'S DISTINCTIVELY DIFFERENT.

The drink's uniqueness, however, created promotional challenges for the company. Dr Pepper's unusual flavor was an acquired taste for many people and required repeated trial before acceptance. One bottler estimated that it required eight bottles of the beverage in two weeks to turn a potential customer into a regular Dr Pepper drinker.

Moreover, numerous consumer misconceptions about Dr Pepper inhibited its acceptance, especially outside of the South and Southwest. Its caramel coloring led some to expect a cola, others thought it made of prune juice or pepper sauce, while its name led others to believe it was a medicinal drink.

---

[4] A. M. Lewis, "What Happened When Dr Pepper Began Thinking Big," *Fortune*, December 1973, p. 128.

A diet Dr Pepper was introduced in 1962. Sales increased steadily until 1969, when sales stopped because of the ban on the use of cyclamates as artificial sweeteners. Reformulated to use saccharin as the sweetener, sales of Sugar Free Dr Pepper increased from 7.2 million cases in 1971 (0.2 percent of the market) to 18 million cases in 1974 (0.4 percent of the market) and 28 million cases in 1975 (0.6 percent of the total market). The increase in sales from 1974 to 1975 was 55.6 percent, outpacing the total diet drink market which increased by only 16.8 percent. Company executives attributed Sugar Free's spectacular competitive performance to its ability to mask saccharin's bitter aftertaste better than cola drinks and to the first Sugar Free advertising campaign initiated in 1974.

In the mid-1960s Dr Pepper had attempted to broaden its product line with a sophisticated ginger-flavored soft drink from Sweden called Pomac. Initial market introductions were not successful due to improper "positioning" and inadequate advertising and promotion support, according to Mr. Clements, and the product was withdrawn by 1967.

Regular Dr Pepper remained the company's leading product in 1976, accounting for 85 percent of unit sales in 1975. Regular Dr Pepper sales had grown steadily over the past decade with market share doubling from 2.4 percent in 1966 to 4.9 percent in 1975. Sugar Free accounted for 14 percent of sales, while the company's flavor lines Salute, Waco, and Hustle together accounted for 1 percent. Salute and Waco were six standard soft drink flavors manufactured only as a service to Dr Pepper bottlers who needed a wider range of product to service multiflavor vending machines and soda fountain dispensers. No sales, advertising, or promotion efforts were expended on them. Hustle was a skim-milk based, high protein, vitamin and mineral fortified, controlled calorie drink distributed primarily to athletic teams.

A FIRST VISIT WITH PRESIDENT WOODROW WILSON CLEMENTS

"Sure, I can take you there. It's 5523 Mockingbird Lane, and they have a beautiful building and I'll bet at least nine acres of beautiful park land. They're a Dallas company, you know, and we are proud of them. My kids drink Dr Pepper by the case. You folks have it up North?"

At corporate headquarters the researchers were introduced to a ritual which was later repeated in every office visited. "Welcome! We are pleased to have you here. Would you like a Dr Pepper? It's a great drink." While consuming their hot Dr Pepper, the Yankee guests were given a tour, starting with a visit to a replica of the Old Corner Drug Store of Waco, Texas, a quick look at the concentrate production facilities, and a walk through various offices. The atmosphere was informal, and the researchers sensed an atmosphere of warmth and good spirits.

"Let's go to Foots's office now; he asked about you. Everybody calls him Foots, by the way; there's a great story behind that nickname and he ought to tell you about it."

Mr. Clements's office was large, deeply carpeted, and with the help of green decorative plants seemed to subdivide into three areas: a large conference table section, a conversation-oriented cluster of modern Knoll chairs with throw rugs accenting the soft wall and chair colors and Mr. Clements's desk area. Mr. Clements's desk, backed by a massive office chair, was flanked by two large lamps and a super-polished brass spittoon. Two telephones, pictures of grandchildren, and a tray of marbles were evident on the desk top. The adjacent walls were covered with personal memorabilia, organizational memberships, and the Distinguished Salesman Award given by the Sales Executive Club. An antique clock and abstract painting completed the decor.

Lighting up an ever-present cigar, Mr. Clements welcomed the researchers, ordered them another Dr Pepper, and expressed his full support for the case research. Sipping a Dr Pepper, he observed:

> This is a wonderful company, and I have been with them since I started as a route salesman in Tuscaloosa, Alabama, in 1935. You will meet some fine people.
>
> As to my nickname, well, I'll be glad to tell you. There's about 49 different versions of it—but the *real* facts are my feet just grew up before I did and I had rather small legs and I played football rather young and my feet in those days were turned that way. So when I was playing football with the football pants just reaching my knees and those big feet, and not too graceful, why that's where I picked up the nickname. I was not sensitive about my given name but just felt like it was, you know, a name that everybody says, "Well, you're named after the President—Woodrow Wilson—you're a Democrat." My mom wanted me to be President, by the way. So since my schooldays I've always used my nickname. I send my Christmas card out in footprint form, and everybody calls me Foots. When I became president, an executive suggested that I might want to go to using my real name—it was a little more sophisticated. I said no—I *got* here using the nickname Foots and I'm going to continue to use the nickname Foots. Now of course I sign my checks differently—but everything else is Foots.
>
> Let me try to give you a first start at understanding Dr Pepper. We have a small number of company-owned bottling plants and a can operation. The latter is located in Dallas and produces canned Dr Pepper for the markets that can be economically served from that location—about 150 miles. It services bottlers who do not have canning abilities. We also have a fountain operation which sells syrup to theaters, fast-food chains, or to vendors at major sports facilities. Finally and most important is our franchise bottler operation. It is responsible for the sale of concentrate and syrup to franchise bottlers.
>
> We have a different philosophy than Coke and Pepsi-Cola. We consider ourselves as in the franchise business and not in the bottling business.

Now we do own Waco, Dallas, Ft. Worth, and San Antonio. We took over a plant in San Angelo but sold it later. We bought Ft. Worth three years ago because we felt Ft. Worth and Dallas are really one market. We feel that operating a plant does give us a chance to learn a great deal, to try out programs and experiment. We then take these programs to our franchise bottler, and he makes the final decision.

We've been successful. But we still have only about 6 percent market share. In this part of the country we may have as high as 30 or 40 percent; in New York City, we will have 1 percent; in Boston, 1/10 of 1 percent. Our problem there is to get the right bottler and enthuse him and train his people in marketing fundamentals.

I was frustrated during part of 1974 when things began to waver a bit. I knew the bottlers needed some stimulation and needed some inspiration and I had seven echelons between me and the bottler. So I came back and restated the basic fundamentals to my own people and to my bottlers. I had less than 25 people out of my top 200 that had been in their present position more than five years. I never make a speech now that I don't hammer at those fundamental marketing precepts.

You might be interested in these excerpts from my opening speech to the 1975 Dr Pepper Bottler Meeting:

> We have been working hard in getting our own people fully aware of the correct way to market Dr Pepper. The difference is in building a business on an original flavor with a distinctive taste, and a name that is a misnomer, from doing business with a flavor that is well known and a name that identifies that flavor.
>
> Now, what is our program? There isn't any one answer, but there is one absolute and rigid criterion for every market. Every program for every market must be built around and with the complete utilization of the basic fundamentals—not just one—but all five. J. C. Penney once said they don't rewrite the Bible every Sunday; the same applies to these basic fundamentals.
>
> **Perfect product:** We are selling taste and building a business on an original flavor with a unique taste. The products must taste right when they're consumed.
>
> **Distribution and availability:** Even though Dr Pepper now has theoretical national distribution, as all the United States is under franchise, we have poor distribution in far too many markets—and much room for improvement in every market. We are weak in the most important segment of the market—single-drink accounts. There isn't any way you can build a high per capita on Dr Pepper in any market without concentrating on the single-drink outlets. We must never forget we are building a business on a unique drink—and it is much easier to get them to try one drink than a 6-pack—or 8-pack—or a 32-, 48-, or 64-ounce bottle.
>
> **Sampling:** The need for sampling is obvious. And **point-of-sale advertising** still performs the same important function in the basic fundamentals it always has.
>
> **Media advertising:** I am not going to dwell on this—not because I don't think it is important, because I recognize the important and productive part it plays in building a consumer franchise and a profitable Dr Pepper volume—and if there is anything all of us are oversold on, it is media advertising.

Following Foots's suggestions, the researchers decided just to study the marketing aspects of Dr Pepper, then examine in sequence manufacturing, research and development, finance, the impact of federal regulations on company operations, international operations, and finally review briefly the formal organization structure of the company.

COMPETITION

"Basically," a senior executive said, "we compete for space in the consumer's stomach, for space on the retailers' shelves, and for the time and attention for our multibrand bottlers. Competition is the name of the game, and marketing is the key player." All company officers seemed marketing oriented, all had almost a "messianic belief" in the goodness of their product, and all "believed" in the Dr Pepper Company and its potential. Marketing seemed to be as much a state of mind at Dr Pepper as basic techniques.

In its "tummy" competition, Dr Pepper obviously competed with all liquid refreshments, but its primary competitors were other soft drinks—particularly cola products. Company executives believed that a balanced package of advertising, point-of-sale promotion, extensive distribution, competitive packaging, and pricing tailored to specific franchise market areas was the key to success.

Recent competitive action by PepsiCo provided dramatic evidence of the intensity of competition between Dr Pepper and the major colas. Labeled the "Pepsi Challenge," the Pepsi-Cola Company introduced a major share of market campaign in Dallas in mid-April 1974. At that time industry observers estimated Dr Pepper's share of market was 25 percent, Coke's was 28.6 percent, and Pepsi's was 7.6 percent. After 10 months of vigorous advertising effort and extensive price-off promotions (cola prices were slashed to one third their normal level), Pepsi had increased its market share to 14 percent, Coke had increased to 30.5 percent, and Dr Pepper had declined to 20 percent. Responding to Coke and Pepsi "would have been degrading to our product," said vice president Bruce Conner.

Dr Pepper was the dominant factor in its flavor type as was 7UP in the lemon-lime category. Dr Pepper's only direct flavor competitor was Coca-Cola's Mr. PiBB. First introduced in 1972, just after Dr Pepper had successfully franchised many Coca-Cola bottlers, Mr. PiBB simulated the taste of Dr Pepper and had received extensive marketing support in areas where Dr Pepper was popular. Sales of Mr. PiBB had grown from 5 million cases in the year of its introduction to 37.5 million cases in 1975, representing an 0.8 percent share of market. Coca-Cola, it appeared, attempted to market Mr. PiBB in any area where Dr Pepper achieved a 5 percent market share, and especially in the areas of the Southwest and South where the flavor was most widely accepted. One analyst believed that Coca-Cola considered Mr. PiBB only a regional flavor and had no intention of marketing the drink nationwide. If a Coke bottler was bottling Mr. PiBB, his franchise agreement would legally prevent him from bottling Dr Pepper.

Fortune magazine, commenting on Mr. PiBB, states:

> Clements maintains that he isn't terribly concerned about Mr. PiBB. He doesn't expect to lose bottlers who are doing well with Dr Pepper, he says. "Any bottler who has only had us for a short time, and whose Dr Pepper volume is so low that it's only a small percentage of his profits—those are the bottlers vulnerable to switching. There may be 20 of them all together, and if we lost them all, it wouldn't even mean $100,000 in gross volume." Clements adds, with some glee, that more than 50 Coca-Cola bottlers signed on with Dr Pepper even *after* Mr. PiBB was introduced.[5]

Mr. Clements reviewed the competitive situation in 1976 as follows:

> Coke's promotions on Mr. PiBB have broadened our market because it calls attention to the flavor, and we had no help in all those years. We were doing it by ourselves. Basically it stimulates our people to do a better job, and our market share and sales volume usually improve when Mr. PiBB comes into the market. Our main emphasis now to combat Mr. PiBB is to make sure that we are doing the right kind of fundamental job on Dr Pepper.
>
> Coke has tried to introduce Mr. PiBB in some international markets, and it has failed worse than it has here. I've said lots of times, half in jest, that if Coke had known how hard Dr Pepper was to sell, they would never have tried to imitate it. Coke and PepsiCo will be back pushing Coke and Pepsi-Cola, if they're smart, rather than these less important brands. Their problem is dilution—not at the national advertising level—they have plenty of dollars—but dilution at bottler "level of effort."

At the retailer level, Dr Pepper competed for shelf-space allocations, display opportunities, and cooperation on promotional events. In larger supermarkets Dr Pepper was judged by store managers on the basis of product sales performance in terms of gross margins and turnover and frequency and efficiency of delivery. Some retailers demanded price-off promotions, all of which were not passed on to the consumer. In fountain and cup vending outlets, Dr Pepper competed primarily against Coke and 7UP for one of the four lines which a typical dispensing machine could handle.

At the bottler level, Dr Pepper competed for the best available bottlers, and once the franchise had been signed, competed for his or her time and enthusiasm.

---

[5] A. M. Lewis, *Fortune,* December 1973, p. 124.

TARGET CONSUMERS

Sugar Free and regular Dr Pepper were targeted at two different consumer groups. Sugar Free's target was women 18–49 years of age who were the largest consumers of diet soft drinks. Sugar Free, formulated with a saccharine sweetener, was the second fastest growing diet soft drink in the country. "Aggressive marketing has enabled many of our bottlers to capture over 20 percent of the diet business in their market and in some cases the share of market for Sugar Free is approaching 50 percent of the total diet market. In Seattle the Dr Pepper Company with the Portland bottler had developed and conducted a separate test marketing program for Sugar Free Dr Pepper with superior results."

Young people 8–18, Mr. Clements explained, were the primary target group for regular Dr Pepper, with secondary emphasis on the 19–34-year-old group.

> We feel the teens is the time to really concentrate on making the lifelong Dr Pepper drinker. When people get older, they're very hard to change, but the teens are looking for something unique to discover and make their own drink. After all, they are the biggest per capita consumers of soft drinks. Market studies now indicate the preference of this age group for Dr Pepper; and once a consumer acquires a taste for Dr Pepper, the loyalty for our product remains extremely strong.

In 1975 Dr Pepper gallonage was divided along product lines—85 percent regular and 14 percent Sugar Free; by channel, 59 percent bottler, 20 percent fountain, and 21 percent cans.

Advertising and Promotion

Advertising was a key, direct link between Dr Pepper and its bottler and consumer markets. "One of our major challenges is to build consumer taste habits for a unique and indescribable drink. Milk tastes like milk, coffee like coffee, and Dr Pepper like Dr Pepper. You don't know what it is like until you taste it," Mr. Clements stated. "One of the first things I did as executive vice president was to bring in a new advertising agency." *Fortune* magazine described that event:

> Clements says he is delighted with Young and Rubicam. "They were quick to grasp the potential we had," he remarks. "They took our market research, and came up with a concept that they were able to translate into a clever sales message." As anyone who has watched television, listened to the radio, or glimpsed a billboard in recent years undoubtedly knows, Y&R produced the slogan "America's Most Misunderstood Soft Drink." Young and Rubicam felt that the notion of a "misunderstood" soft drink would appeal to young people—traditionally the biggest consumers of soft

drinks—who like to think *they* are misunderstood. But the slogan also had some basis in fact; Dr Pepper, it appeared, *was* misunderstood.[6]

Dr Pepper engaged in three types of advertising and promotion: national and local media advertising, including television, radio, magazine, and outdoor advertising; sales promotion materials and campaigns; and a bottler equipment assistance program. Ten percent of advertising and promotion funds were used to help reduce the cost to the bottler of purchasing vending and dispensing equipment for the single-drink market. Dr Pepper management say increased advertising and promotional funds are crucial to achieving growth goals. These expenditures were programmed for a 20 percent annual increase for the next five years, and a special "ready-markets" program had been developed to invest extra advertising and promotional efforts in key market areas.

In 1975 one industry analyst estimated, Dr Pepper spent approximately $6.5 million for television and magazine programs, or an estimated 30 percent of its advertising and promotion budget. Another approximately $4.5 million, the analyst estimated, was matched by bottler funds in cooperative programs to buy local television and radio spots, outdoor and newspaper advertising. Although Dr Pepper advertising funds were higher per ounce than per ounce expenditures of the two leading cola companies, they were meager compared to the dollars Coke and PepsiCo spent on national advertising. Mr. Clements commented on this circumstance:

> We are providing more money for marketing support for Dr Pepper than at any time in our history, but it is small compared to some of our competition, inadequate to the objectives we would like to achieve, and too little compared to our needs and opportunities. We will provide some national advertising, still far too little and too thin to give us any significant impact, but it will help in creating and keeping alive awareness of Dr Pepper with the consumer.

The content of Dr Pepper media advertising was the same whether the commercials were used in a national, cooperative, or "ready-market" program. Dr Pepper followed a strategy different from the traditional patterns of the two major cola producers. Most Coke and Pepsi-Cola advertising featured upbeat music, music or jingles that frequently repeated the brand name and associated it with an attractive scene of young people enjoying themselves in a sports activity or a pleasant family situation. It was designed to keep a high level of "top of mind awareness" consistent with a soft drink's position as an impulse purchase item. Dr Pepper advertising, on the other hand, was designed to build both awareness of the brand and to position Dr Pepper as a unique and original

---

[6] Ibid., p. 121.

flavor that was not a cola. Dr Pepper's current campaign focused on the theme of "the most original soft drink ever."

The placement of Dr Pepper television advertisements also deviated from Coke and PepsiCo's; the latter companies used a "scatter approach" which meant the regular placement of frequent 30- and 60-second "spots" on a variety of programs. Dr Pepper, with the objective of maximizing the impact of its budget, sponsored entire programs. In 1975 the program began with a New Year's Eve special over ABC starring Chicago, the Doobie Brothers, Olivia Newton-John, and the Beach Boys. Other programs included the "Grammy Awards" in March, the "Emmy Awards" in May, and the "Miss Teenage America Pageant" in November.

Company marketing staff also prepared tailor-made complete advertising programs for all franchise bottlers. In addition, Mr. Clements in 1976 reintroduced his ready-markets concept. In this program, additional funds were allocated to supplement cooperative advertising expenditures in key market areas where Dr Pepper's medium-term growth potential was high. It focused on already developed markets where current penetration was relatively high and areas with relatively high per capita soft drink consumption, such as the Southeast. Mr. Clements said the program resulted in more predictable growth for the company because it put resources against potential. It also rapidly increased sales volume which, in turn, provided funds for development of other markets.

Although only four bottlers, serving populations of 500,000 to 2 million each, were the ready-markets program in 1976, and little money was being spent, close to 5 percent of 1977's advertising budget would go to ready-markets development. Mr. Clements said the company was phasing back into the program after having drifted away from it in 1974–75. The full program would eventually involve 18 markets on a rotating basis, with three markets added and three dropped each year.

In addition to media advertising, corporate funds sponsored "special marketing programs." F. F. Avery, executive vice president, reviewed these:

> For the past several years we have had prize-winning floats in the Orange Bowl parade, in the Annual Tournament of Roses parade in Pasadena, California, and in the Cotton Bowl parade in Dallas. Second, approximately two years ago the Dr Pepper Company purchased Miss Teenage America, and it is now operated as a separate division. Third, we have signed an exclusive sponsorship agreement with the North American Soccer League. Finally, I would like to make you aware of the fact that Dr Pepper has had for some time the marketing rights to a product called Hustle.

Dr Pepper sales promotion activities were designed to motivate the consumer at the point of purchase. Sales promotion expenditures included the costs of retail point-of-sale materials for packaged goods such as display racks, seasonal end-of-aisle display promotions, price-off deals to both the consumer and the retailer, coupons, giveaways, posters, and Dr Pepper–identified route sales force uniforms and delivery vehicles. In fountain outlets sales promotion funds were spent on signs, Dr Pepper–identified menu-boards, and decorative paper cups.

All Dr Pepper sales promotion funds (approximately 40 percent of the company's advertising and promotion budget) were spent in conjunction with the cooperative advertising program. Industry analysts estimated Dr Pepper's contribution was approximately $8 million in 1975 and was allocated to bottlers on the basis of concentrate purchases. This resulted in the better developed market receiving the most sales promotion dollars.

Sugar Free employed a related advertising campaign using the theme "It Tastes Too Good to Be True." In 1975 Sugar Free received about one fifth of company advertising funds—the first time significant resources had been allocated to the product. Some bottlers allocated as much as 50 percent of their cooperative advertising and promotion funds to Sugar Free, believing that it was a superior product and that diet drinkers had a propensity to experiment with new flavors.

THE FRANCHISE BOTTLER SYSTEM

Major company objectives between 1967 and 1973 had been to build a strong franchise bottler network and to achieve national distribution of Dr Pepper by upgrading the network in territories already served and franchising strong bottlers in areas where Dr Pepper was not yet available. In 1976 company management believed both of these objectives had been achieved, giving Dr Pepper a major advantage over its next largest competitor—7UP. National distribution had been achieved substantially through associations with Coke and PepsiCo bottlers (see Exhibit 3).

EXHIBIT 3: Dr Pepper Franchises by National Brands Produced

Brand Configuration	Number of Plants
Dr Pepper only	45
Dr Pepper and Coke*	192
Dr Pepper and Pepsi†	164
Dr Pepper and minor brand(s)	96
Total	497

* Dr Pepper and Coke were the primary brands, but the bottler might also bottle secondary brands.
† Dr Pepper and Pepsi were the primary brands, but the bottler might also bottle secondary brands.
Source: Researcher's estimate on the basis of very limited and perhaps inaccurate data.

In 1976 Mr. Clements announced a new corporate target—"deeper market penetration." One aspect of deeper market penetration involved increased attention to expanding the single-drink business—a task assigned to the Fountain Division. The company ranked third nationwide in fountain syrup sales. In recent years fountain sales had been the fastest growing part of Dr Pepper's business and accounted for over 20 percent of concentrate volume in 1975.

Mr. Clements stated:

> And we want to continue to upgrade our existing franchise network. What we bring a prospective, strong bottler is an opportunity to increase total sales by broadening his market base. It brings new soft drink consumers to him, and we offer higher growth rates than the rest of the industry; Coke and PepsiCo have as high a share of market as they are going to get in cola products. These are easily substantiated claims in areas where Dr Pepper has some consumer franchise. Where an established franchise is switched to a different bottler, it's an immediate sales addition that's really golden because it is on top of an already profitable operation.

Historically, Mr. Clements's decision to obtain the best and strongest bottler for Dr Pepper was a major shift in company policy. Prior to 1967 the company emphasized the importance of Dr Pepper being the bottler's only, or at least primary, product. Management felt Dr Pepper would be neglected if the bottler held another brand franchise, especially a cola. Franchised bottlers were members of the Dr Pepper "family."

The national franchising program not only increased the number of franchisees but it impacted the personal approach and feeling of family which were an important part of Dr Pepper's bottler relationships. A number of new multibrand franchisees were substantial organizations run by professional managers who operated multiple-plant firms. J. K. Hughes, executive vice president, remarked:

> We try harder to build and maintain a close, personal relationship with each of our bottlers because this is important to the character of our operation; we do a superior job at it. But it does get increasingly difficult as we get larger and our bottlers get larger.

The 497 bottlers who made up the Dr Pepper network varied substantially by type of market area serviced, degree of market penetration, distribution methods, and management and financial capabilities. The franchisees' independent status and Dr Pepper's position as a secondary brand meant that the company did not have full accessibility to data on the franchisee's total sales, profits, and capital investment. Management was in agreement that a strong bottler had an aggressive route sales force that achieved substantial shelf space in supermarkets and extensive distribution in other outlets, ran frequent promotions, had good production facilities, was profitable and had a good capital base. The strongest bottler usually had the highest local market share—typically this was Coke or

EXHIBIT 4: Per Capita Standing by Franchise for Representative States and Franchises in Representative States for Period Ending December 31, 1975*

Arkansas: 11

California:
1. Bakersfield
2. Brawley
3. Fullertown
4. Fresno
5. West Sacramento
6. Oxnard
7. San Diego
8. Chico
9. San Bernardino
10. Ukiah
11. Sunnyvale
12. Gardena
13. Eureka
14. Daly City
15. Mt. Shasta

Colorado: 7

Connecticut:
1. Meriden

Maryland: 4

Massachusetts:
1. Sagamore
2. Springfield
3. Newburyport
4. Needham

Michigan: 10

New Mexico: 7

New York:
1. Jamestown
2. Olean
3. Rochester
4. Batavia
5. Plattsburg

6. N. Tonawanda
7. New York Metro
8. Endicott
9. Buffalo
10. Syracuse
11. Glens Falls
12. Massena

North Carolina: 21

Pennsylvania: 18

Rhode Island: 1

South Carolina:
1. Spartanburg
2. Abbeville
3. Greenwood
4. Columbia
5. Rock Hill
6. Florence

South Dakota:
1. Rapid City
2. Huron
3. Sioux Falls
4. Pierre
5. Aberdeen

Tennessee: 17

Texas: 55

Utah: 6

Vermont: 1

* Arranged with number 1 being highest per capita sales in state.
Source: Company records.

PepsiCo. Dr Pepper used per capita sales and percentage sales growth as the main measures of performance by a franchisee (see Exhibits 4 and 5).

All but 45 franchisees also bottled other brands; 53 did not actually produce Dr Pepper at all. One hundred six franchises were held by 25 companies who operated multiple bottling plants and who sometimes engaged in other lines of business. The company referred to these firms as "conglomerates." One of the larger firms was General Cinema Corporation of Boston, with total soft drink sales of just under $200 million; it

EXHIBIT 5: Per Capita Leader Cities in Consumption of Dr Pepper

1. Waco, Texas
2. Forth Worth, Texas
3. San Marcos, Texas
4. Lufkin, Texas
5. Nacogdoches, Texas
6. Dallas, Texas
7. Elk City, Oklahoma
8. Longview, Texas
9. Amarillo, Texas
10. Mt. Pleasant, Texas
11. Sherman, Texas
12. Mangum, Oklahoma
13. Paragould, Arkansas
14. Paris, Texas
15. Childress, Texas
16. Sulphur Springs, Texas
17. Lubbock, Texas
18. Dublin, Texas
19. Palestine, Texas
20. Plainview, Texas

Source: Company records. Cities arranged in order of consumption: Waco highest, Plainview lowest of the 20.

operated 16 Dr Pepper franchises. Other major firms holding multiple Dr Pepper franchises were RKO General, Universal Foods Corporation, Wometco, and M.E.I. Approximately 50 percent of the 25 conglomerate companies were independently owned Coke or Pepsi-Cola bottlers; for example, Coca-Cola Bottling–Los Angeles and Coca-Cola Bottling Company of Memphis. The latter firm, operating six Dr Pepper franchises, had joined the Dr Pepper Company in 1975 and immediately and substantially improved Dr Pepper's competitive position in this trading area.

The variety of bottler and territorial circumstances meant Dr Pepper had to design a wide number of marketing programs for its bottlers. Mr. Clements elaborated:

> You'll have one franchise that is almost totally rural with one town with 5,000 people where the soft drink business hasn't changed in three generations. Then you'll have a territory like New York City that's totally urban and very volatile. Franchisees vary, too, in their sophistication.

A New England bottler talked about his business and his new Dr Pepper franchise:

> I hold three of the four top national brands in this area, Coke, 7UP, and Dr Pepper. I also bottle Squirt and my own label flavor line. I took on Dr Pepper because it is a flavor leader. Coke offers Mr. PiBB, but PepsiCo has no entry in that flavor market. If I take on the Dr Pepper franchise, my Pepsi-Cola competitors can't have either Mr. PiBB or Dr Pepper. Introducing a new flavor is difficult. I'm not making any money on Dr Pepper right now, but I have it for its long-term growth potential over the next 10 or 15 years.

Bottler Sales and Relations

Industry trade sources gave Dr Pepper high marks for its bottler philosophy and organization. Mr. Clements outlined this philosophy:

> We don't go take orders for concentrate to make Dr Pepper. We sell ideas and marketing programs. In the franchise system the bottler is *independent*. He can live up to the franchise contract and still not do a maximum job in developing the market. Our job is one of persuasion. Right now our toughest challenge is to get the multibrand bottlers to do a good job on Dr Pepper.

The task of persuading 497 franchised bottlers to work harder for Dr Pepper fell to the 34 zone managers, 7 divisional managers, and 2 area managers who made up Dr Pepper's bottler field sales force. Zone managers called directly on the franchisees within their territory, working with the bottler to set sales and distribution goals and administering cooperative advertising funds and other bottler-oriented incentives. Zone managers also initiated Central Trading Area meetings involving several bottlers with contiguous territories. These meetings developed and coordinated special promotions with chains whose trading areas covered common territories.

Zone managers prided themselves on their capacity to build close Dr Pepper–bottler relationships. One commented:

> Dr Pepper has an enviable reputation. To bottlers Dr Pepper reps are "good old boys, one of us." They think Coke reps are pompous and stuffy, 7UP distant and cool, and PepsiCo a corporate machine. At the same time, Dr Pepper reps have the most professional approach to market planning and budgeting. Our annual specific marketing plans include monthly case sales forecasts by package type with coordinated advertising, promotion, distribution, and sales force incentive programs. Few of the small family-run bottling businesses would do any planning on their own. Nobody else offers anything like our special marketing plans.

A primary assignment, and one zone managers regarded as critical to the motivation of bottlers, was the management of cooperative advertising and promotion funds. In support of the local bottlers' Dr Pepper marketing program, the zone manager planned local television, radio, newspaper, and billboard advertising, as well as retail point-of-sale materials. The costs of coupon campaigns, merchandise, and price-off promotions also came out of these funds.

The base budget for Dr Pepper cooperative advertising was 25 cents per gallon of forecasted sales, with Dr Pepper and the bottler each contributing 12½ cents per gallon. Supplementary cooperative funds were available to newly franchised bottlers, ready-market areas, and special markets like New York City. Instead of the 50/50 contribution system in the base budget, Dr Pepper contributed 65 percent of supplementary funds while the bottler contributed 35 percent.

Dr Pepper zone managers could offer additional programs to bottlers in the form of packaging and equipment assistance. In the packaging program Dr Pepper made cash payments to the bottler to reduce the package costs outlay when introducing new package sizes. The equipment assistance program helped reduce the bottler's capital investment.

The company also used a variety of other incentives to motivate franchisees and their sales forces. On the national level there was the annual Dr Pepper Bottler Meeting, a three-day resort extravaganza where Dr Pepper executives introduced the coming year's marketing and distribution strategies to bottler top management and their spouses, amid swimming, golfing, dining, and sightseeing. An annual travel incentive contest for Dr Pepper bottlers with significant sales increases was also popular.

The Dr Pepper zone manager also worked with bottler management to set up periodic cooperative sales incentive programs for the bottlers' sales force, who could win prizes and premiums from a special catalog. The zone manager could also ask for help from the parent company staff: a consumer relations specialist would run sampling programs or appear on local television and radio interview shows, a promotion expert would consult on sales motivation programs, and a national chain store account contact person would help in calling on large accounts.

The Franchise

The basic definition of the relationship between the company and its bottlers was the Dr Pepper bottler's license agreement, or franchise contract, and all such contracts were secured in a vault in Dr Pepper's Dallas headquarters. It granted the franchisee, without cost, the exclusive right to produce and distribute Dr Pepper soft drinks in a defined geographic area as long as the franchisee met the terms of the agreement. It required the Dr Pepper Company to provide adequate amounts of concentrate of good quality.

The franchisee had the right to terminate the contract on 90 days' notice, but as long as s/he was party to the contract the list of obligations and restrictions was substantial. Most important were maintaining high sanitary and product quality standards and not selling the product outside his or her territory, nor knowingly selling to a third party who subsequently resold outside the territory. Prior to a 1970 court ruling in a dispute between the Coca-Cola Company and one of its franchisees, franchise rights could be revoked relatively easily if a bottler failed to sell the product. Since that decision, however, franchise cancellation had required a three- to four-year-long process during which the franchise company built evidence of cause and gave the franchisee opportunities to correct the offenses or sell his or her franchise. The franchisee was free to sell the territory to whomever he or she chose, if the buyer met the company's qualifications.

The selection of appropriate franchise candidates, negotiation of a sale, and the enforcing of franchise agreements were the responsibility of the franchise department, directed by Don Antle. "My role in a franchise sale is to save taxes for both parties," said Mr. Antle. Due to industry overcapacity, Dr Pepper franchise sales were made to already established bottlers. Mr. Antle explained, "An outsider would have difficulty investing in the soft drink business today because of the low ROI. A franchise is only salable to a buyer for whom it is incremental volume." In 1976 franchises sold for between $1.50 and $2.00 per case of Dr Pepper business per year.

Packaging

Dr Pepper was packaged in 16 different sizes and types of containers in 1976, as shown in Exhibit 6, although not all packages were available in every market. Container sizes and materials were selected by individual franchised bottler, depending on their equipment capability, their desire to invest working capital in packaging materials, packaging offered by competitors in their territory, and consumer preferences. Many bottlers did not own their own canning lines, so approximately 50 percent of the Dr Pepper sold in cans was produced at corporate-owned canning lines in Dallas or by various contract canners around the country for resale to Dr Pepper who resold it to franchise bottlers.

EXHIBIT 6: Dr Pepper Package Assortment, 1976

	Ounces							
	6.5	**10**	**12**	**16**	**24**	**32**	**48**	**64**
Returnable bottles	x	x	x	x	x	x		x
Nonreturnable bottles	x	x	x	x	x	x	x	x
Cans			x					

Maintaining a competitive packaging position was a particular problem for Dr Pepper. Dr Pepper was not widely available in the large 16-, 32- and 64-ounce sizes until 1975, and industry analysis attributed the plateauing of regular Dr Pepper growth in 1973, 1974, and 1975, in part, to lack of larger package availability during a period when consumers were especially price conscious. Maintaining a competitive packaging position was complicated by Dr Pepper's being only one of several brands competing for a franchisee's attention. No one company was dominant in introducing new packages; successful introductions were usually accompanied by heavy advertising and promotion expenditures by the concentrate producing company and required substantial bottler working capital investment in packaging materials, advertising, and promotion.

Experimentation in all phases of packaging was a characteristic of the industry in 1976. Supplier firms were developing new forms of old containers—"thinner" cans and more effective plastic shielded bottles; new sizes of present packages—a gallon glass bottle; and new types of containers—a plastic bottle.

Pricing

The only prices directly controlled by Dr Pepper were the prices charged franchised bottlers for bottling concentrate and food service retailers for fountain syrup. Wholesale prices for the finished product were set by individual bottlers and varied from territory to territory depending on bottler costs and market conditions. Each retailer also set his own price.

Dr Pepper price policy attempted to maintain a fixed contribution rate, as a percentage of sales, while at the same time keeping concentrate prices competitive. Contribution averaged between 50 percent and 40 percent of sales after deducting ingredient, packaging, and advertising costs. Dr Pepper increased syrup and concentrate prices only to recover increases in ingredient costs and believed similar policies were followed by Coca-Cola and PepsiCo. Although Dr Pepper concentrate prices were slightly higher than the other four major concentrate producers, it required less sugar so that finished product costs were competitive. Exhibit 7 presents estimated comparative cost data for the five major concentrate companies.

EXHIBIT 7: Estimated Cost Information

Product	Bottler Cost per Unit/Gallon Concentrate	Bottler Cost per 16-oz. Case @ $20 Sugar	Product	Bottler Cost per 16-oz. Case @ $20 Sugar
Dr Pepper.	$218.28	$0.9884	Pepsi-Cola	$0.9242
Sugar Free Dr Pepper	400.17	0.8630	Sugar Free Pepsi.	0.8878
Coca-Cola			Mountain Dew.	0.9900
(finished syrup)	2.08	0.9600	Teem.	0.7900
Mr. PiBB	67.84	0.9049	Royal Crown (2 gals)	0.8611
Sprite	76.10	0.9435	Sugar Free RC/Diet.	0.7917
Tab.	194.00	0.8954	7UP	0.9915
Fresca.	161.79	0.9190	Sugar Free 7UP	0.7197

Source: Company records.

Dr Pepper attempted to price bottler concentrate so that bottlers could sell finished product at prices competitive with Coke and Pepsi-Cola, before special price promotions, although concentrate represented only a small portion of finished product cost. For example, a case of a dozen, 32-ounce bottles of Dr Pepper wholesaling at $3 contained less than 47 cents worth of concentrate. Consequently, Dr Pepper's cooperative advertising expenditures, allowances for special price promotions, and cash contributions for equipment and packaging materials were more important than concentrate prices in influencing bottlers. Special retail price promotions played a small role in Dr Pepper's pricing policies as the company hoped to build a customer base loyal to the drink's unique flavor rather than attract less loyal, price-conscious consumers. Larger package sizes, however, such as 32, 48, and 64 ounces, were used to appeal to value-conscious consumers as packaging represented a smaller proportion of total costs than for smaller packages, thus reducing consumer costs per ounce of soft drink.

Analysts noted that the sale of fountain syrup was a price-competitive business; Dr Pepper usually met Coke's, the dominant factor in this market segment, fountain syrup prices. Retailer deposits on the steel tanks containing fountain syrup and point-of-sale promotion materials were also competitively priced. Like bottler concentrate, fountain syrup cost was only a small proportion of the price the consumer paid for the finished drink. Finished drinks from a $15 tank of syrup would yield $140 or more in finished drinks.

Fountain Division

The Dr Pepper Fountain Division accounted for 21 percent of company dollar sales in 1976. Mr. Rautenberg, Fountain sales manager, defined the division's mission as selling the "idea" of Dr Pepper to a retail outlet, and then arranging for Dr Pepper's Manufacturing Division or for a franchised bottler to supply the syrup. Fountain or postmix syrup was different from bottling concentrate in that it was already partially mixed with water and contained 100 percent of the sugar necessary to make the finished drink. At the point of sale, dispensers, most of which could handle only four different flavors, mixed the syrup with carbonated water. Fountain syrup was sold in 5-gallon reusable steel tanks or in 1-gallon disposable plastic cartons.

Dr Pepper's Fountain Division was organized into six regional sales territories covering the Northeast, north central states, Midwest, Southwest, Southeast, and the West. Mr. Rautenberg commented that his division's organization was very much like Coca-Cola's Fountain Sales Division. Exhibit 8 presents an estimate of fountain personnel and annual gallonage for the five major concentrate producers.

Dr Pepper Fountain Division served eight different types of accounts: fast-food chains, vendors, theaters, schools, concessionaries, bottlers, military installations, and jobbers. The 7,100 direct sale accounts purchased 84 percent of the division's total gallonage and had 8,000 delivery points serving 48,000–50,000 individual retail outlets. Indirect sales, through independent jobbers, who were free to set their own prices to retailers, accounted for 16 percent of total fountain syrup gallonage.

EXHIBIT 8: Comparative Fountain Division Personnel and Sales Estimates, 1975

	Coca-Cola	PepsiCo	Seven-Up	Royal Crown	Dr Pepper
Personnel.	490	12	7	n.a.	94
Percent of company gallonage	30	16–17	<5	<2	21
Annual sales, millions of syrup gallons . . .	110%	<20%	2%	n.a.	10–20%

n.a. = not available.
Source: Researcher estimate.

Mr. Rautenberg noted that Fountain Division profitability was sensitive to small increases in sales volume, as most operating costs were fixed and only direct product costs increased with gallonage increases. He was proud that the division had the company's lowest operating costs, on a percentage of sales basis, and believed their costs to be lower than Coke's and PepsiCo's.

The division's goal was to double gallonage in the next five years and to double again by 1985. This was to be accomplished through wider availability, particularly through adding more fast-food chain accounts. Mr. Rautenberg remarked that, "one good McDonald's with $70,000 a year in sales will sell as much Dr Pepper in four months as a supermarket does in a year. This is because they sell a lot of drinks in large-size containers, frequently 14–20 ounces at a time."

In 1976 Dr Pepper was sold in 1,100 of the 3,400 McDonald's outlets in the United States, up from 50 stores in 1972 and 25 stores in 1971. In most fast-food installations, management believed Dr Pepper was the second most popular brand, selling between 12–35 percent of the outlet's soft drink sales. The average McDonald's sold 1,000 gallons of Dr Pepper syrup per year. Prior to the introduction of Dr Pepper, cola flavors might account for 85 percent of soft drink sales in a typical outlet, with the three other flavors accounting for the remaining 15 percent. Mr. Rautenberg commented that Seven-Up was aggressively pursuing fast-food accounts. He believed that they had not been as successful as Dr Pepper due to installation problems, as fountain dispensers in each store had to be carefully adjusted to mix the correct amount of syrup and carbonated water for each specific flavor. Dr Pepper management believed that their quick and efficient installation service gave them a competitive advantage.

MANUFACTURING

Dr Pepper engaged in three manufacturing activities: concentrate production, the production of finished product in cans, and the operation of five wholly owned subsidiary bottling and distribution businesses. The production of concentrate (the basic flavor-coloring liquid) for franchise bottlers and syrup (concentrate plus sugar) for the company's Fountain Division was Dr Pepper's central and most profitable business. The researcher estimated that it provided approximately 44 percent of company dollar sales, 64 percent of total gallonage, and 79 percent of company profits. The five Texas bottling and distribution subsidiaries accounted for 28 percent of company dollar sales and most of the remaining company profits. The canning of finished product, the researcher estimated, accounted for 23 percent of company dollar sales and approximately 21 percent of total gallonage.

Concentrate Production

Concentrate was produced in a section of Dr Pepper's headquarters building in Dallas and in Birmingham, Alabama. The process required few employees and simple equipment, and output could be doubled from current facilities with minimum capital investment. Producing concentrate began with piping the flavoring ingredients from large stainless steel tanks to three sealed mixing vats in an adjacent room. From there the concentrate was piped to a filling line to be packaged in 1-gallon moulded plastic jugs for shipment.

Canning

The company operated a canning facility in Dallas. With a capacity of 6 to 7 million cases a year, this operation supplied the company's own subsidiaries as well as regional franchise bottlers. The remainder of needed canning capacity was obtained via a network of 52 canners located throughout the United States. Of that number, 34 were Dr Pepper bottlers who operated as contract canners as well as producing their own requirements; 18 were independent companies who did contract canning for a number of soft drink companies.

Under the contract system, Dr Pepper determined the production schedule, purchased all raw materials and packaging required, paid the canner a fee for mixing and packaging the drinks, and then sold the finished products to franchisees at a break-even price of 15 cents to 20 cents per case over cost. This system involved major working capital requirements for Dr Pepper and a higher per case cost for the franchisee than for franchises with their own canning line. But management stated that it did make canned Dr Pepper available to all territories and did minimize the company's capital investment in canning equipment.

Bottling and Distribution Subsidiaries

Dr Pepper's four subsidiary bottling plants in Dallas, Ft. Worth, Waco, and San Antonio, plus the company-owned Southwest Fountain Supply Company, accounted for most of the company's capital investment and most of its labor force. Dr Pepper was in the bottling business, management said, in order to better control operations of its important home-market areas, to build a base of operating experience from whence to advise franchisees, and to experiment with new production and distribution techniques. Dick O'Connor, vice president, corporate bottling plants, in charge of these operations, considered Dr Pepper Bottling to be an industry leader in devising new distribution methods in response to cost pressures and changing retailer needs.

The four plants produced regular and Sugar Free Dr Pepper and

Salute flavors, in multiple-sized, returnable and nonreturnable bottles; canned product was obtained from the Dallas canning plant. All four plants usually achieved a 20 percent or better share of market; selling prices, production costs, and profitability varied according to competitive market conditions and plant efficiency. Management considered its newer Dallas facility to be about average in performance compared to other plants of its scale. An industry analyst commented, "They have a fine operation. As far as I know, Dr Pepper is the only major concentrate producer whose bottling operations are profitable. They must do as well as an average local bottler who probably takes down 10 percent, after-tax ROI."

The four plants employed approximately 700 production and delivery personnel, most of whom were unskilled. Dr Pepper plants were not unionized, but the Teamsters Union had conducted a vigorous and almost successful campaign in 1973.

Southwest Fountain's objectives were similar to those of the bottling plants. Its rate of sales growth was higher than for bottling operations, but profits tended to be minimal. Southwest sold Coca-Cola and other fountain syrups as well as Dr Pepper.

Mr. O'Connor identified increasing capital requirements, increasing distribution and production costs, and changing distribution methods as the three major trends affecting operations of bottling companies in recent years. New production equipment with greater efficiency, capacity, and better quality control capabilities, along with larger vans needed to carry the greater number of products and package sizes, had led to a minimum capacity of 5 million cases per year for an efficient bottling plant. This factor, as well as current capacity constraints, had led the company to embark on the construction of a single large bottling facility to serve Dallas, Ft. Worth, and Waco. It was to be completed by 1978. Projected cost of the facility, an industry analyst estimated, was approximately $15 million. It was to be completely financed from internal sources of funds.

Dr Pepper's experimentation with new distribution methods came about as a result of rapidly rising labor and transportation costs, combined with substantial retailer pressure for increased price flexibility and improved services. Currently Dr Pepper corporate bottling plants employed four distribution methods: direct sales of premix (ready to be dispensed) and postmix syrup (soda fountain adds carbonated water) sales to fountain outlets (12 percent of total volume), traditional route sales of packaged goods to small outlets (50 percent), chain store delivery tandems (18 percent), and presold bulk delivery (20 percent).

Route sales were the traditional method of soft drink distribution; a driver/salesperson visited each account on a weekly schedule selling off the truck. Currently 50 percent of the soft drinks sold through the route system were made through vending machines or in coolers in small stores. Many high-volume, chain store accounts had been diverted from route selling to tandem or presold methods. The chain store delivery system used two route salespersons with two delivery trucks working side by side to provide adequate volume and selection for service to major chain store outlets.

Presold bulk delivery, the most efficient distribution method, was only a few years old; and Mr. O'Connor expected it would soon expand to 50 percent sales of total sales volume. In 1976 only two bottlers in Texas, in addition to Dr Pepper, were successfully using presold bulk delivery. This method required advance salespersons who called on chain headquarters and store management to sell weekly orders for later delivery in specific quantities on a specific schedule. At the appointed time, large vans delivered the palletized and containerized soft drinks. Later the same day, Dr Pepper merchandisers stocked the shelves and arranged displays and point-of-sale advertising. Retailers liked this system because palletizing decreased receiving and handling costs in the store. Mr. O'Connor explained the system's benefits for Dr Pepper:

> Presold bulk delivery is cheaper by 10 cents per case, but that's only the tip of the iceberg. The real benefits come when we get top salespeople and top merchandisers on our staff into the large chain stores. We'll get better availability and better shelf space allocations and create a better relationship between store management and ourselves.

PURCHASING

Raw materials were the largest single expenditure category at Dr Pepper. Although the department dealt with over 1,000 suppliers of bottles, cans, crowns, cartons, chemicals, and flavors, two items—containers and sugar—accounted for the bulk of purchases.

Sugar presented special purchasing problems according to Mr. Hughes, executive vice president:

> While our franchise bottlers purchased their own sugar requirements to make Dr Pepper syrup from our concentrate, we buy considerable quantities of sugar for our own use for fountain syrup in our canning operations and in company-owned bottling plants. The average price of raw sugar duty-paid at New York was $9.14 in February 1973. By November 1974 it had reached $57.30, increasing more than six times within 22 months. The prices remained in the upper $20 to $40 during the first four months of 1975, but showed constant declines through the end of the year with raws averaging $14.80 in December.

Large sugar purchases near the 1975 high had adversely impacted the company's 1975 earnings. Dr Pepper did not employ "hedging" practices in its sugar operations.

Dr Pepper bought containers from large national packaging companies at competitive prices. It did not purchase supplies for its franchise bottlers, but it did help them with advice concerning equipment. Mr. Hughes commented:

> Having Dr Pepper in cans, available to all of our bottlers, is a high priority. We are now in the midst of a program to assist our canners to convert their can lines to two-piece aluminum cans as rapidly as possible. We want their lines to have the capabilities of producing two-piece steel cans as well.

RESEARCH AND QUALITY CONTROL

Frank Phillips, head of the research and quality control department, stated his group's primary task was "to keep quality Dr Pepper in the marketplace." Most research activity was centered on keeping abreast of new products, production processes, packages, and raw materials being developed by competitors and suppliers. Tests done on finished beverages ensured that Dr Pepper products met standards of appearance, were adequately filled and capped, and contained the proper levels of carbonation, acidity, concentrate, sugar, and coloring. Eight field quality control technicians visited each of the franchised bottling plants and contract canning facilities four times a year to collect samples and inspect production facilities and procedures.

Already developed, but not yet marketed, Dr Pepper products included individual servings of powdered hot Dr Pepper in an aluminum foil packet, as well as individual servings of cold Dr Pepper in plastic syrup packs to which the consumer would add carbonated water. In production process technology, attention was directed at spray and freeze-dry powdered Dr Pepper mixes and high-protein powdered beverage mixes.

Plastic bottles were being given considerable departmental attention. Industry proponents believed they would be safer and lighter weight than glass, when perfected, reducing consumer safety problems and cutting distribution costs. Critics pointed out that there were still technical problems; for example, bottles swelling under pressure and leaking carbonation and that high-speed equipment necessary for full utilization was not yet available. Until early in 1975, Du Pont and Monsanto led in the plastic bottle field, but Du Pont dropped out of the business, "selling its technology and patent processes to willing parties." Monsanto, in close cooperation with Coke, recently announced plans for two new production sites. Mr. Phillips estimated that industry costs to produce plastic bottles, on a scale large enough to compete with glass, would involve more than an $80 million to $100 million investment. He estimated that conversion to plastic bottles would be expensive for bottlers, too, requiring an investment of $50–$100,000 to modify each bottling line for the new container.

FINANCE

"This has always been a great company, and I enjoy working here! I've been drinking Dr Pepper since I was a kid," enthused Alvin Lane, Jr., vice president of finance. "And it's a great industry to be in. Until recently raw material and supply prices have been remarkably stable. And when costs, particularly sugar, went up so dramatically in 1974, we were able to pass along most of these increases fairly rapidly. We can change our concentrate price to bottlers when required; Coke changes its price only once every three months."

Reviewing the statements (see Exhibits 1 and 2), "You will note that net profit margins increased to 8.6 percent in 1975 as compared to 7.7 percent in 1974. This improvement was due primarily to a combination of strong sales growth and good control of expenses. Let me admit that the lowering of sugar prices which began in the spring of 1975 was very important to our results. Looking ahead, we do not see sugar prices rising during 1976. Beyond 1976 the crystal ball becomes clouded, but we feel that the availability of corn and synthetic sweeteners together with an improved supply/demand relationship for sugar portends well for consumers. As you know we have approved for use in Dr Pepper high-fructose corn sweeteners on a 50 percent sucrose (sugar) replacement level and are testing even higher levels.

"An important key to the bottom line though is advertising and promotion (see Exhibit 9). It typically has run around 20 percent, but a 1 percent swing there can have a dramatic impact on results.

"Almost 50 percent of our total assets are invested in cash equivalents. Our receivables are almost all current—only 7 percent over 30 days

EXHIBIT 9: Distribution of Revenues as a Percent of Sales

	1970	1971	1972	1973	1974	1975
Retained in business.	4¾	5	5½	5½	3½	4½
Dividends.	5	5¾	5	4½	4½	4½
Other operating expenses.	1¼	1½	1½	1½	1¾	2½
Depreciation and maintenance.	3	2¾	2¾	3	2½	2½
Taxes on income.	9½	9½	9¾	8¾	6¾	8¼
Payrolls	11	11	10	10¾	9½	9
Promotion, advertising, and expansion	21½	21½	21	19¼	17½	16½
Raw materials and packaging.	44	43	44½	47	54¼	52¾

Source: Company records.

and virtually nothing over 60 days—turnover every 19 days and our inventories turn over about every 20 days. Most of our fixed assets support our bottling business."

Dr Pepper had paid quarterly dividends for 184 consecutive quarters and had increased dividends every year for the past 14 years. It was company policy to pay out approximately 60 percent of its prior year earnings in dividends to its shareholders. It was also company policy not to incur long-term debt.

Dr Pepper had initiated three stock splits since 1967 with the objective of gaining wider share distributions; no public offering of common stock had been made in recent years. Increases in the number of shares outstanding were due to the issuance of new stock for an executive stock option plan and the issue of 146,000 shares in 1973 in a "pooling of interest" acquisition of Dr Pepper Bottling Company of Ft. Worth and three related companies. Officers and directors owned less than 5 percent of Dr Pepper's common stock, and no ownership group owned 10 percent or more of the stock. Dr Pepper's common stock, listed on the New York Stock Exchange, had ranged in price as follows: 1972, $23 to $27½; 1973, $18¾ to $30; 1974, $6½ to $22⅞; and 1975, from $7 to $15⅛.

GOVERNMENTAL INTERVENTION

Dr Pepper, along with other soft drink manufacturers, was subject to federal regulation by the Food and Drug Administration, the Consumer Product Safety Commission, and the Federal Trade Commission. The Food and Drug Administration established product purity requirements and labeling requirements for soft drinks. Dr Pepper's franchised and corporate-owned production facilities passed sanitation inspections conducted by the FDA. The company was also required to assure the FDA that the ingredients used in the secret Dr Pepper flavoring formula were FDA "permitted ingredients."

The Consumer Product Safety Commission monitored injuries caused by broken or exploding soft drink bottles through its representative hospital reporting system. Management was also concerned over the possibility of citizens' consumer groups making an issue of bottle safety. Changing packages to 100 percent canned product would be particularly time consuming and costly to the Dr Pepper Company. One executive explained:

> It would take years to rebuild capacity. There are only two line manufacturers in the United States, each producing 25 can lines per year. Many smaller bottling companies would go out of business because the plant and working capital expenditures would be prohibitive. We will just have to sweat this out. Packaging legislation and franchise illegality would hurt the industry, but it would hurt us more than the big guys. Now, a small

bottler can break even on a $500,000 minimum investment in a bottling line on 500,000 cases per year. With a $2 million minimum investment in a can line, he or she would need to sell 2 million or more cases per year to break even. We don't have the resources to buy canning lines for our bottlers, and our multibrand bottlers would look to their bigger selling products first if there is a capacity shortage.

The still unresolved Federal Trade Commission challenge to the legality of exclusive franchise territories was a matter of substantial concern to the Dr Pepper management. They believed that the elimination of the exclusive franchise system would pose a greater problem for Dr Pepper than for its two larger competitors. Both Coke and PepsiCo owned more bottling franchises, including a number in very large metropolitan areas, than did Dr Pepper. Dr Pepper still had a substantial proportion of its total volume moving through smaller, nonurban, independent franchised bottlers.

Consequently, they supported the National Soft Drink Association and the Dr Pepper Bottlers Association in supporting general legislation "to declare legal the current system of exclusive franchised soft drink territories." At the hearings in support of that legislation, Mr. Clements stressed that the system was particularly important to a small growing firm such as Dr Pepper, first because it best supported a route delivery service operation which supplied hundreds of thousands of small outlets, and second because the franchise system enabled the company to conduct better sampling programs essential where a distinctive flavor/new product was being introduced. The legislation was still "in process" in the fall of 1976, with hearings scheduled for September. The Federal Trade Commission had announced its opposition to the legislation.

ORGANIZATION

Dr Pepper was organized along functional lines (see Exhibit 10). Mr. Clements (62) was chairman, president, and chief executive officer. He was assisted by two executive vice presidents—Mr. Hughes (49) and Mr. Avery (46), and a staff of eight vice presidents heading up major subunits. Since 1971 the company had undergone several reorganizations with the objective of obtaining effective functional groupings, to make the best use of existing managerial resources, and to facilitate the attraction and introduction of new management talent.

Mr. Clements discussed some of the reasons for these organizational changes with the researcher.

> People are the key to carrying out our strategy of being number one; limited management resources can hold us back. I'm proud of our people. But lack of management depth is a challenge.

When we hit that flat period in 1974–75, operations didn't turn around as quickly as I wanted them to. Some of the policies and procedures I felt were important had eroded, and we'd kind of drifted away from our strategy and the importance of the bottler. Money wasn't being spent on prime-ready markets as it should have been.

We had kind of drifted away from our strategy, and I think strategy is something you don't change unless there is a major, basic need. You don't try to win every battle, you just try to win the war. If we changed our strategy to combat Mr. PiBB and abandoned our strategy of being number one—why we would have just weakened our position! We've gotten our discipline back.

The market isn't going to wait. We need even more organizational strength. We are going to see a dramatic difference in our future rate of growth. We have so many opportunities. We're not in a position to acquire anything because we don't have the depth of management to spare. But we are building some management strength in our four bottling plants, and we will soon be in a position to pick up some more bottling plants when and if we need them. We don't yet have the knowledge and expertise to do the international job we would like to do. Our computer system is not adequate for some of the things we want to do. We should use it to help exploit our fountain opportunities.

A key need is to build organizational strength into marketing. We are doing just that—we are adding 16 managers now and more down the line. Really we have never had product managers before, and that is the kind of people we are hiring.

INTERNATIONAL

Dr Pepper's major international operation was in Japan; other market areas included Canada, Puerto Rico, Guam, the Bahamas, and overseas U.S. military installations; distribution in these areas amounted to less than 1 percent of company sales. The Japanese venture had not yet shown a profit, and one industry analyst estimated 1975 losses at $2 million. But management remained confident of the soundness of the Japanese move. In March 1976 Mr. Hughes commented:

> During the past summer we conducted a consumer research program in Japan. The results were similar to results we have seen in new Dr Pepper markets in this country: (1) we achieved an above-average level of consumer awareness and consumer trial; (2) we had been most successful in gaining product support with teenagers; (3) our marketing direction needed a shot in the arm of a basic Dr Pepper sales program—sampling and more sampling—particularly among the youth.

Dr Pepper had first become interested in international soft drink markets in the late 1960s. At that time, Japan was the most attractive soft drink market outside the United States, with per capita consumption approaching 100 bottles and growing in a sound economy. In 1972 Dr Pepper entered into a 50/50 joint venture with the world's largest soft drink bottler who held the Coca-Cola franchise for Tokyo and served two other large urban market areas. It offered good production facilities, well-established distribution, and a very favorable pricing structure. However, by the time Dr Pepper came on the market in July 1973, supported by a heavy advertising and promotion campaign, inflation and price increases had triggered a precipitous decline in the Japanese soft drink market. By mid-1976, company management described the Japanese market as improving and Dr Pepper as having "a little niche."

Beverage World's survey of the Japanese soft drink market predicted a rebound in 1976 and longer term growth settling down to about 10 percent a year. Per capita soft drink consumption in 1973 was 45.4 liters as opposed to 120 liters in the United States. Cola, lemon-lime, and grape were the dominant flavors, enjoying 79 percent of the market. Vending machines accounted for 25 percent of all soft drink sales; soft drink sales in supermarkets accounted for less than 10 percent of total soft drink sales.

Mr. Hughes commented about the firm's international position:

> First of all, we don't want to bite off more than we can chew. We only have a two-person international staff. Second, we already have a commitment in Japan that's worth putting a lot of resources behind to ensure success. And, finally we don't want the glamour of international business to divert financial and management resources from achieving our full potential in the United States.

Despite the company's difficult entry into Japan, Dr Pepper management still considered international expansion the company's next challenge after establishing a strong domestic position. The attractive aspects of international expansion were that, generally, soft drink margins were higher overseas, bottlers had to provide fewer package and container types, and per capita consumption was substantially lower than in the United States, presenting room for potential growth. On the negative side, there was a high cost of market entry in terms of "up-front advertising" and promotion expenditures (management estimated in excess of $1 million per year for three to five years in each new market), and the already entrenched market positions of Coke and Pepsi.

Mr. Clements explained his company's international opportunities:

> When you talk about international opportunities, we're like a kid in a candy store with just one thin dime. He has to pick the best from lots of good opportunities. I'd like to move into all of the markets. But one thing I've always held onto was the importance of concentration—capitalizing on the opportunities we have here first. I haven't wanted us to dilute our time and our resources—you don't want to get diverted. This is one reason why we dropped Pomac and Schweppes. Schweppes is an

EXHIBIT 10: The Dr Pepper Organization, 1976

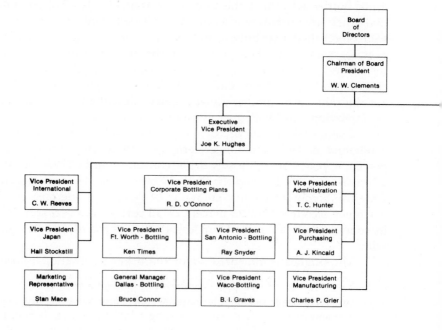

excellent product, and we had the entire Southwest. But I dropped it and Coke of Dallas picked it up.

International markets are profitable once they're established. It was easier and less expensive when Coke and PepsiCo got in. But you don't have to buy connections and influence any more. Prior to the payoff exposures, our guy would just pack his bag when we saw payoffs were needed, even when we were invited to go there. We may look at the Mideast and follow Seven-Up strategy there—that is lower the concentrate price and put all of the advertising and promotion burden on the franchisees plus making specific contracts for type and amount of advertising.

We have had a three-year ban on acquisitions. We were lucky not to get caught up in the conglomerate craze. It's hard to find anything as profitable as concentrate production, and I don't want us to spend a lot of management time on evaluating deals.

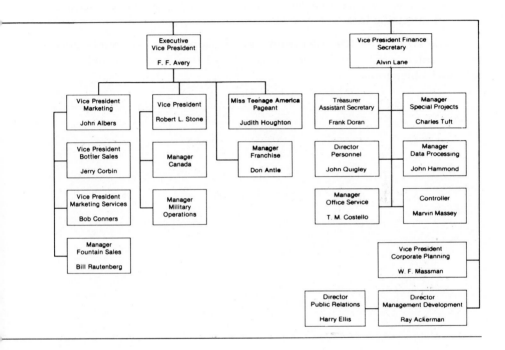

A PERSONAL MANAGERIAL PHILOSOPHY

At the conclusion of a long interview and many Dr Peppers, the researchers asked a question about the box of inscribed marbles on Foots's desk.

They have the Golden Rule on them. I've given thousands of them away to my own people, to my bottlers, and to the sales and marketing groups of which I am member. You can keep one on your desk or carry it in your pocket but what counts is in your heart. Maybe they will remind you to practice the Golden Rule in relationships with other people.

I've had many people ask me, "Can you build a competitive business on the Golden Rule?" I feel you cannot build any business that will last unless you practice the Golden Rule. That rule is our foundation, and we try to watch carefully that our people don't engage in anything that will damage the integrity of this company.

I write my bottlers a letter occasionally, especially during National Bible Week, and suggest a need for all of us to read the Bible, and I never make a speech without referring to my belief in God. I just couldn't do it any other way. A majority of my colleagues share this belief—Harry (Ellis) and Rick (Avery) do. We have that kind of people in our company.

I don't hesitate to profess my beliefs in God and in my business. He gave you whatever talents you have. You can't just take; you have to put something back.

The twinkle in Mr. Clements's eye disappeared; his countenance became solemn. The researcher was convinced that Foots believed—and followed—his words.

CASE 6

The Seven-Up Company (A)

You ought to go out to St. Louis and visit the Seven-Up people; they have a most impressive track record and bright prospects for the future. As the industry's "David," they won't liquidate our two "Goliaths," but they have clearly outperformed Coke and Pepsi in lemon-lime. They have done a first-rate management succession job too with a new top-management team in place. Bill Winter, the new CEO, has already made some very sensible moves, particularly bringing in John Kidwell to strengthen Seven-Up's marketing thrust. And Paul Young is a first-rate, experienced treasurer; Seven-Up doesn't try to manage its income flow reporting—they call it the way it is.

Specializing in a clear, carbonated, lemon-lime flavored soft drink, Seven-Up had approximately 60 percent of this flavor market in the United States, outselling Coke's competitive product Sprite by almost three to one. Pepsi's Teem had approximately 0.3 percent of the overall U.S. soft drink market, Coke's Sprite, 2.6 percent, while Seven-Up enjoyed a 7.6 percent market share. 7UP was sold in the United States, Canada, and 81 other nations.

The company's legal trademark, the Uncola, some industry reporters indicated, was symbolic of the company's efforts to portray 7UP to the consumer as competitive with, yet distinctive from, cola products which dominated the soft drink field. Bottled labels identified the product as 7UP beverage rather than a lemon-lime drink. Company advertisements featured product name rather than the specific flavor category.

The company reported consolidated sales of $213.6 million for 1975 with aftertax profit of $20.3 million. This was the first year that company sales had exceeded $200 million; it had been only six years earlier that Seven-Up had broken the $100 million mark. Since 1967 the company's average annual growth rate in sales and net income had been 12.1 percent and 18 percent, respectively, while recent return on market invested capital averaged 25 percent. In 1970 the company purchased a manufacturer of food colors, flavors, and perfumes; and in 1973 a producer of lemons, lemon concentrate, and oils. But in 1975 soft drink sales were still 80 percent of total sales and 89.5 percent of total profits (see Exhibit 1).

EXHIBIT 1: Net Sales and Income before Taxes in Percentages for Major Product Categories

	1971	1972	1973	1974	1975
Net sales:					
Soft drinks	83.3	82.7	81.8	80.6	80.2
Lemon products.	10.8	10.4	10.7	10.5	12.9
Flavors, colors, and fragrances.	5.9	6.9	7.5	8.9	6.9
Income before taxes:					
Soft drinks	82.4	85.5	86.2	84.5	89.5
Lemon products.	5.5	3.8	2.8	2.0	5.6
Flavors, colors, and fragrances.	12.1	10.7	11.0	13.5	4.9

Source: Company records.

In commenting on Seven-Up's performance, one analyst commented:

> Seven-Up has benefited from two major marketing successes, whose momentum is still continuing. In repositioning itself away from older users toward teenagers, Seven-Up in 1968 bet upon the highly memorable "Uncola" theme. This not only strengthened the brand with all users, but also opened the door to improved distribution in the fountain market, an area the company had previously left to competitors. The second big success was Sugar Free 7UP introduced in 1974, which was far more popular than anticipated.[1]

Another analyst noted privately, "Seven-Up has its challenges, too! Their primary brand—regular 7UP—lost market share in 1974 and 1975; that is always a danger signal. They had a period in 1975 when bottler relationships were bad, although the new senior vice president in marketing has made major improvements there. He has his job cut out for him; competing against Coke—with all of their power—is rough, and Coke seems to be moving more aggressively with Sprite now. In addition, there is the ever-present problem of governmental action re saccharin and the unknown of changes in franchising.

"But I'm optimistic about their future. Their new advertising program 'UNdo it' is brilliant and well timed. Their move into the United Kingdom with Cadbury-Schweppes indicates they may become more aggressive in the international field. There are real opportunities for a lemon-lime drink abroad since that flavor is preferred in many areas to a cola drink. And, trade rumors have it that they intend to move rapidly into the lemonade powder mix game. They could do some interesting things there."

---

[1] Faulkner, Dawkins, and Sullivan, *Industry Review,* March 4, 1976, p. 15.

COMPANY HISTORY

The history of Seven-Up mirrored many of the elements of a traditional Amercian entrepreneurial success story. In a "rags-to-riches drama," the founder C. L. Grigg was born in a log cabin in Prices Branch, Missouri, population 25. Coming to St. Louis to seek his fortune, he worked first in dry goods and later in advertising, without great success. In 1920, joining with a coal merchant, E. G. Ridgway, he formed The Howdy Company to manufacture an orange drink. At a later date this partnership was joined by a lawyer, F. Y. Gladney, after the latter's unsuccessful personal efforts to sell stock in the infant firm. Descendants of these three families were part of the executive group in 1976, and the company still evidenced in it policies and practices the fundamental family values of its founding fathers.

Corporate executives espoused and practiced a leadership philosophy which emphasized the partnership of all parties, for example, company and franchised bottlers and the importance of concern for all individual needs. Management communications stressed accurate presentation of facts and circumstance, and company officers were willing to view corporate accomplishments as a combination of luck and skill. H. C. Grigg, the son of C. L. Grigg, commented on the company's historical record: "We sat on a horse backward, rode him in the wrong direction, and he ended up just where we wanted to go."

Grigg's son was referring to events surrounding the introduction of "Bib Label Lithiated Lemon-Lime Soda," as the new drink was first known. The drink was introduced in October 1929, just before the stock market crash. In 1937, renamed 7UP, the drink had to compete with over 600 other lemon-lime drinks in the marketplace. By 1976, 7UP was the third largest selling soft drink in the world. Because it utilized less sugar than cola drinks, World War II sugar rationing provided opportunities for sales expansion nationally and internationally.

During the mid-60s, however, company sales began to plateau. The owning families installed a new president, Ben H. Wells, son-in-law of founder Gladney, a former preparatory school teacher of English, and for several decades the head of the company's marketing department. Under Mr. Wells's leadership, management made three strategic decisions which still were critical to the company operations in the mid-70s. One of Mr. Wells's early moves was to commission a consulting study of the current market position and product image of 7UP.

During prior years, 7UP had the dual reputation of a medicinal health drink and as a mixer for alcoholic beverages. Basic product quality, a green, medicinal-looking, small bottle plus an advertising campaign with slogans such as "Tunes Tiny Tummies" gave the drink its entry to the children's and adults' health market. Advertising slogans such as the "Cure for Seven Hangovers" were used. 7UP plus Seagrams Seven

Crown Whiskey became a popular midwestern drink. "People were buying 7UP for a mixer or for indigestion," Mr. Wells commented. "Our problem was we weren't a soft drink."

With the decision made to identify with and compete as a soft drink, the company advertising agency developed the "7UP The Uncola" trademark and an advertising program to support this slogan. Trade observers commented that the decision was critical and successful both in concept and execution. "What they did was to, in effect, bet they could dominate the lemon-lime sector, and also take sales away from the cola sector which has traditionally held over 50 percent of the soft drink market. It meant they were going to step up their competition against Coke and Pepsi. They have done it well!"

Second, in 1967 Seven-Up went public with a substantial but non-controlling block of stock being sold to the general public. In 1974 William E. Winter, formerly marketing vice president, was made president and chief operating officer of the firm—the first nonfamily member to hold that position.

Finally, under Mr. Wells's direction the company purchased the Warner-Jenkinson Company in 1970. That firm had been the dominant source for 7UP extract for over 50 years. In 1973 the company acquired Ventura Coastal Corporation which supplied Warner-Jenkinson with some of its lemon oil requirements. In 1974 Ventura purchased the Golden Crown Corporation, a producer of reconstituted lemon, prune, and lime juice, as well as a manufacturer of lemonade powder mix. In 1972 the company purchased the Phoenix, Arizona, 7UP bottler, their only domestic, company-owned franchise territory. Exhibit 2 gives a statistical summary of the Seven-Up Company from 1969 to 1975.

A FIRST VISIT TO THE COMPANY

"That must be it," the taxi driver indicated pointing at an 11-story, boxy brick building with Seven-Up in green script letters over the main entrance. Entering the building, the researcher found a narrow lobby bounded by a curtained glass wall on one side, a bust of what appeared to be a "founding" father at the far end, and a uniformed guard sitting a desk on the other side.

"I'll call public relations for you," he said. "They are on the 10th floor; a secretary will meet you there." Stepping out of the elevator the researchers were reminded that they were, indeed, in the heartland of 7UP. In a scene common to all operational departments, there were clocks with 7UP faces, 7UP wastebaskets, 7UP Uncola murals, and in the center of the room a festive Christmas tree constructed of red and green 7UP beverage cans. Each floor had its own large vending machine filled with

7UP, and the company cafeteria welcomed customers with the sign "Have a 7UP Today."

Later, escorted by the head of public relations, the researchers were taken to W. E. Winters's 11th floor office with its decor of plexiglas, abstract paintings, contrasting Mayan sculpture, and modern floor coverings. At one end was a large executive desk graced with a family picture; shelves, containing business books and AMA publications, provided the background. At the other end of the large office was a beautifully appointed, conversational grouping of chairs in front of a large picture window.

"Welcome to Seven-Up. I'm Bill Winter. We are pleased to have you here, and we want to cooperate with your research in every possible way. Let's sit over here where it is more comfortable and you can check the view."

In the next hour, Mr. Winter covered, in depth, a variety of topics including the history of the company, corporate strategic goals, the current situation and organization of 7UP bottlers, and the competitive situation confronting Seven-Up. At times, in answer to a researcher's question, he referred to tabulated volumes of reports to pin down a specific detail.

There is no status quo in this industry; it's competitive and fast changing. You either go backward or forward—there's no middle ground. We are going to go forward! In terms of our corporate sales and profit objectives we look to an annual 9–11 percent growth in dollar sales and 10–15 percent growth in net income. We believe we are going to have to meet those objectives over an extended period of time; as an average, over a five- to seven-year period. We are going to have to do that to be consistent with industry standards. Now in order to achieve those goals we see growth taking place in three different ways and have developed an ongoing five-year plan for 1976 through 1980.

Our strategy includes basically three things: one is developing increased volume and increased market share through existing businesses. A second is the development of new products in existing businesses, and the third is via the acquisition of new businesses. By the way, we have five criteria for evaluating acquisition prospects. First, the prospect must be in the food, or food-related industry; second, it must have continuing good management; third, it must have demonstrated growth in sales and earnings over the past three years; fourth, in terms of sales, it should be in the $15–$20 million range. Finally, we must be able to arrange a merger transaction that is mutually satisfactory and that will not dilute Seven-Up's earnings.

Obviously to meet objective number one, we need the cooperation and sincere commitment of our *developers*—we don't call them *bottlers*. Personal relationships are so important. We have to compete not only for the housewife's dollar but for developer time and loyalty. Our developer organization is quite different now than it was when I joined the company in 1946. Then 75 percent of them bottled 7UP exclusively; now almost all bottle

EXHIBIT 2: Seven-Year Statistical Summary, 1969–1975

Year Ended December 31

	1975	1974	1973	1972	1971	1970	1969
Net sales	$213,622,918	$190,879,628	$146,748,362	$132,519,867	$124,379,262	$111,648,288	$103,007,833
Cost of products sold	112,421,231	110,046,723	75,783,214	69,722,488	66,247,526	60,047,748	55,044,699
Gross profit	101,201,687	80,832,905	70,965,148	62,797,379	58,131,700	51,600,540	47,963,134
Selling, administrative, and general expense	61,263,716	51,212,637	45,164,104	40,153,791	36,550,453	32,461,502	30,014,561
Operating profit	39,937,971	29,620,268	25,801,044	22,643,588	21,581,247	19,139,038	17,948,573
Net miscellaneous income (deductions)	(93,508)	2,456,835	1,304,302	606,197	661,145	457,011	228,885
Income before income taxes and extraordinary items	39,844,463	32,077,103	27,105,346	23,249,785	22,242,392	19,596,049	18,177,458
Federal, state, and foreign income taxes	19,504,000	15,489,000	13,023,000	11,205,265	10,914,386	9,779,390	9,587,856
Income before extraordinary items	20,340,463	16,588,103	14,082,346	12,044,520	11,328,006	9,816,659	8,589,602
Extraordinary items (net)	—	—	—	—	—	—	(198,159)
Net income	$ 20,340,463	$ 16,588,103	$ 14,082,346	$ 12,044,520	$ 11,328,006	$ 9,816,659	$ 8,391,443
Net income as a percent of sales	9.5	8.7	9.6	9.1	9.1	8.8	8.1
Per share of common stock:							
Net income*	$1.88	1.54	1.30	1.10	1.03	0.89	0.75
Dividends†	0.75	0.61	0.4325	0.416	0.40	0.325	0.24
Book value†	7.93	6.45	5.50	4.62	3.72	3.08	2.50
Market price range (OTC) Common (high-low bid prices)†	36–14¾	30¾–10½	37¼–21¾	50⅛–33⅜	36⅛–26¾	30¾–17¾	22¾–14¼
Depreciation and amortization	2,899,639	2,347,569	1,750,273	1,339,384	1,129,534	1,189,705	1,134,413
Capital expenditures	6,839,430	6,819,836	7,506,958	3,086,443	2,565,297	1,902,143	2,892,668

Working capital:							
Current assets	$ 86,594,829	$ 67,331,096	$ 58,761,951	$ 52,329,788	$ 45,845,959	$ 40,674,266	$ 35,416,921
Current liabilities	34,815,728	24,933,460	20,054,165	17,711,046	15,944,106	15,164,446	14,681,230
Total working capital	51,779,101	42,397,636	38,707,786	34,618,742	29,901,853	25,509,820	20,735,691
Current ratio	2.5 to 1	2.7 to 1	2.9 to 1	3.0 to 1	2.9 to 1	2.7 to 1	2.4 to 1
Other assets:							
Land, buildings, and equipment	32,739,830	29,101,568	24,626,482	19,310,765	17,155,484	15,976,359	14,805,879
Miscellaneous investments	2,454,842	2,953,990	1,800,626	2,298,733	1,930,319	1,926,520	2,655,864
Intangibles	4,205,133	4,295,836	4,388,420	3,539,410	2,499,686	2,522,549	2,494,957
Total other assets	39,399,805	36,351,394	30,815,528	25,148,908	21,585,489	20,425,428	19,956,700
Total	$ 91,178,906	$ 78,749,030	$ 69,523,314	$ 59,767,650	$ 51,487,342	$ 45,935,248	$ 40,692,391
Capitalization and reserves:							
Long-term debt	2,129,352	2,652,860	3,140,984	2,447,818	1,735,063	2,805,964	3,249,580
Other liabilities	596,131	389,399	442,043	379,122	364,788	353,440	660,662
6% cumulative preferred stock	3,588,000	3,588,000	3,588,000	3,588,000	3,588,000	3,588,800	3,588,800
$5.71 convertible class A preferred stock	—	4,615,100	4,860,600	5,079,900	7,307,900	7,390,400	7,408,800
Common shareholders' equity	84,865,423	67,503,671	57,491,687	48,272,810	38,491,591	31,796,644	25,784,549
Total	$ 91,178,906	$ 78,749,030	$ 69,523,314	$ 59,767,650	$ 51,487,342	$ 45,935,248	$ 40,692,391
Return on common equity—at end of year	23.6%	23.9%	23.6%	23.7%	27.8%	28.9%	30.0%
Average shares of common stock outstanding†	10,636,841	10,467,739	10,457,812	10,378,538	10,345,034	10,335,038	10,326,961

* Based on weighted-average number of shares outstanding during each year adjusted to reflect shares issuable upon exercise of stock options and for stock splits in 1969 and 1972.

† Adjusted for 2-for-1 stock splits in 1969 and 1972.

All data have been restated on a pooling of interest basis to include the operations of Warner-Jenkinson Co. acquired in 1970 and Ventura Coastal Corporation acquired in 1973.

Source: Company report.

and distribute other national brands. We have to make our interests and our developers' interests compatible.

Of course we are always on the lookout for new products for our existing organization. We have thought of beverage powder sales sold through our developers . . . particularly in the institutional trade. We have had opportunities to buy fast-food chains, but at least currently we have no interest. If the right kind of snack food opportunity comes along, we might take a good look at that.

We don't have immediate plans for further acquisitions of bottling plants. We were asked by the owners of the Phoenix, Arizona, franchise to buy them out and we own one Canadian bottling operation.

We have made two important acquisitions of new businesses—Warner-Jenkinson in 1970 and Ventura Coastal in 1973. Our annual report details the results [see Exhibit 2]. We are now in three product areas, and all are profitable. In each of these areas, though, competition is intense and we have competitors who have greater sales and financial resources.

Mr. Winter also spoke about the nonsoft drink product areas of The Seven-Up Company. His comments, along with those of other executives, are combined with industry data in the section on nonsoft drink divisions. Following this section comes material on the soft drink division. The information in this section is organized by function. Because of the complexity of the marketplace, the marketing function is expanded by an investigation of Seven-Up's position in the various soft drink market segments.

NONSOFT DRINK DIVISIONS

In 1970 Seven-Up acquired the remaining 80 percent of the shares of Warner-Jenkinson, the company's longtime supplier of 7UP extract. The price paid was 74,095 shares of Seven-Up convertible preferred stock with a stated value of $100 per share and carrying a rate of 5.1 percent. These shares were converted into 316,172 shares of Seven-Up common stock over a five-year period at various prices. As of December 31, 1975, the market value at $32.50 would produce a total value of $10,275,590. Warner-Jenkinson sales (excluding intercompany transactions) and net income dropped from $22,328,000 and $2,554,000 in 1974 to $18,991,000 and $1,176,000 in 1975 because of recession and regulatory circumstances. But, by 1976, sales and earnings had returned to normal patterns and the company's St. Louis manufacturing facilities were being substantially expanded.

Warner-Jenkinson, in addition to producing 7UP extract, was a highly respected technical leader in the manufacture of flavors, colors, and fragrances for food, drug, and cosmetic companies. With the exception of one large and very profitable firm—International Flavors and Fragrances—the majority of companies in these industries were small with sales averaging about $1 million. Typically firms had a proprietary interest in a formula and a customer list. A frequent method of entering the highly fragmented industry was to buy a company for its brand names, formulas, and customers. In 1973 and 1974 Warner-Jenkinson made two cash acquisitions, a flavoring company for $1.2 million and a small manufacturer of fragrances for $100,000.

Warner-Jenkinson competed against several hundred other companies which manufactured over 1,000 different flavors. Some of the nation's best-known producers of food mixes, candies, and cereal were its customers. The subsidiary had been a technical leader in the production and synthesizing of flavors and had recently introduced spray dried flavors and imitation chicken and beef flavors. The subsidiary also manufactured 10 basic food colors and 400 derivative blends. Colors were subject to governmental regulations in the form of certification of each production batch by the Food and Drug Administration. That federal agency's banning of Red Dye #2, used in the United States since 1906, had been in some measure responsible for the 1975 decline in this subsidiary's profit. By 1976 Red Dye #40 was in active production and customer use.

In 1973 Seven-Up acquired Ventura Coastal Corporation for 133,590 shares of common stock; in 1974 Ventura purchased the assets of the Golden Crown Citrus Company of Evanston, Illinois. Seven-Up had purchased about 20 percent of its lemon oil needs from Ventura prior to acquisition; this was approximately 2–3 percent of Ventura's central overall sales volume. Benefiting from the best lemon crop in California's history and from an unusually hot summer throughout the United States, the Ventura subsidiary's 1975 sales were $26,906,000, an increase of 43.2 percent over 1974. Net income was $985,000, significantly higher than the $44,786 earned in 1974. Although 1976 results were not expected to reach these levels because of the January–July California drought, an expansion of fruit processing facilities was underway at Ventura which would double capacity by 1977. Lemon was one of the fastest growing flavors in the food industry, and management was optimistic with regard to its future.

Ventura was in the business of processing and packaging frozen concentrate for lemonade and the growing, processing, and selling of fresh lemons and lemon products. One analyst stated that Ventura was to the frozen lemonade market (1974 market, at retail, over $40 million) what Coca-Cola's Minute Maid was to the frozen orange juice market; it sold between 35 percent and 40 percent of the market. Ventura sold the principal portion of its concentrate production to large grocery chains under 56 brand names; its ten largest customers accounted for approximately 70 percent of its sales. Ventura's dominant competitor was a cooperative—Sunkist Growers, Inc.—which processed over 75 percent of the orange and lemon production in the western United States. Sunkist sold

Warner-Jenkinson about 65 percent of the lemon oil required for 7UP extract production.

Paul Young, executive vice president and treasurer, commented:

> We use California and Arizona lemon oil in our extract, and Ventura had the reputation of producing the highest quality lemon oil in the world. There are an estimated 75,000 acres of land suitable for lemons in those two states. With Ventura we acquired 2,300 acres plus an additional 2,800 under contract. In 1974 we planted 135,000 new lemon trees on some 750 acres of land; they will yield fruit in 1977, The record 1975 lemon crop increased by 30 percent the availability of lemons to Ventura and eliminated the traditional need to purchase lemon juice concentrate from outside sources. And it positions Ventura to meet the growing needs of Golden Crown.

Golden Crown's original products had been reconstituted lemon, lime, and prune juice. In 1975 its product mix was expanded to include diet frozen lemonade, lime, orange, and grape concentrates, all of which were produced for Golden Crown by Ventura. In 1976 it was test marketing a lemonade flavored powdered drink mix. Expanding West Coast juice sales prompted planning for a bottling plant to be built in that area in 1977.

SOFT DRINK OPERATIONS

The product category which dominated all others in its share of corporate sales appeared in the company's annual report as "Soft Drink Extracts and Finished Products; Canned and Bottled Soft Drinks and Fountain Syrup." "Extracts," 37 percent of 1975 sales, were sold to Seven-Up bottlers who produced the final consumer products. Packaged 7UP and fountain 7UP syrup were available to consumers in the take-home and fountain markets, respectively, in regular and sugar-free form.

"Finished Products" accounted for 43.2 percent of corporate sales. These final products constituted the sales results of the company-owned franchised bottling plants (two in the United States and Canada) and of the Seven-Up enterprises division of Seven-Up, U.S.A., Inc. The latter organization was formed to supplement bottler production capacities to ensure that the required mix of 7UP packages was available in each territory. Primarily, the subsidiary produced and delivered 7UP in cans, though it had expanded recently to include production of fountain syrups and of bottled products in the economy sizes of 64 ounces and 2 liters.

Though the packaging of soft drink products had undergone multiple changes over time, the basic ingredients and formula for regular 7UP had not been altered substantially since the product's invention in 1929. However, the company had introduced fountain 7UP essentially as a new product when it entered the fountain segment in 1960. Other variations on the 7UP theme took place in the diet market. These began with a reduced calorie drink called "Like" which was replaced by "Diet 7UP" in 1970. Diet 7UP was taken off the market when the saccharin-sweetened Sugar Free 7UP was perfected and introduced in February 1974. In addition to these products in the 7UP line, the company marketed a line of Howdy flavor drinks which had accounted for about 1.5 percent of sales for the past several years.

Production and Purchasing

Production facilities for the supply of extract sold to Seven-Up developers were concentrated in the Warner-Jenkinson subsidiary. This company manufactured all domestic and some international extract in its St. Louis facility. The production process required fewer than 20 people to produce the volume necessary for the 7UP consumed in the entire United States.

The Seven-Up Company did not purchase cans, sugar, or glass for its bottler network. The company did purchase sugar for its own use in producing finished products in the soft drink and nonsoft drink divisions. Seven-Up had recently begun to buy forward in the futures market in an attempt to deal with price changes in sugar. The supply of another key ingredient, lemon oils, was secured by purchasing roughly 20 percent of the amount from Ventura and contracting for much of the rest.

The Distribution Game

Mr. Winter commented:

The soft drink business, and I don't think I'm being overdramatic about it, as a franchise business is extremely different than most other types of franchise businesses. The kind of personal rapport that is established between the franchiser and the franchised bottler impacts greatly on the performance of both parties. Our developers all see themselves as marketing and advertising professionals. We must convince them that their greatest asset is the 7UP trademark and that we have the marketing know-how to develop not just a national but an international brand. Regardless of where the consumers are, the brand must be presented in one consistent posture; if we didn't do that in the United States, for example, we would wind up with 469 different kinds of advertising and marketing strategy for 7UP.

It's a very emotional, attitudinal kind of thing. We must position the brand . . . yet consider the individual developer's point of view. This is particularly important when you consider, say, a 7UP Coca-Cola bottler. That person has just so much time, effort, and money to put into selling each of those two products, so it's critical to have a developer's commitment. Over-all, it's pretty difficult; it's a real challenge.

The Agreement

At Seven-Up, bottlers were called developers because, as one executive explained, "almost anyone can handle the mechanical procedures involved with bottling a product, but the real test is how to go about developing the territory." The development aspect of a bottler's function was clearly implied in this title, though not specifically spelled out in sales terms in the domestic franchise agreement. Distribution targets were given, and bottlers had to maintain a minimum penetration of 65 percent of the beverage outlets in their territories. Developers were not allowed to sell 7UP outside of their particular territories, sell knowingly to a third party, allow a retailer to warehouse the drink for resale, or promote and distribute an imitative lemon-lime drink.

In exchange, a franchisee received the rights to produce both regular and Sugar Free 7UP in packaged and fountain form. A separate agreement was necessary to can 7UP products, since all plants did not have the volume to justify a canning line. If a developer did not take advantage of the franchise to produce any of the bottle products, the company reserved the right to step in on its own and do so, though such an action was not always practicable. Under all other circumstances, developers held the right to the sale of 7UP within their respective territories and expected The Seven-Up Company to maintain and promote the 7UP trademark nationwide.

The Players: Developers

The smallest Seven-Up developer marketed to a population of roughly 15,000 people and sold an estimated 50,000 to 75,000 cases annually. This was in stark contrast to the largest developers who were located in cities containing several million people with sales of several million cases per year. The researchers estimated that roughly 100 bottling operations accounted for nearly 70–75 percent of Seven-Up's volume. This left the remaining 350+ plants responsible for 25–30 percent of domestic sales.

This was a significant change from earlier days when most developers had been small-scale entrepreneurs. In 1975 some of these family-run, smaller developers remained, yet added to the team were those entrepreneurs who had started small and enlarged their base through acquisition of their neighbors. Moreover, an entirely new breed had entered the game: the corporate conglomerates. The largest developer in this category was the Leisure Division of Westinghouse which owned franchises in southern California, Indiana, and Puerto Rico. According to Mr. Winter, the conglomerates tended to have larger, more successful operations, though when sales were measured in terms of bottles per capita, the smaller developers outperformed them. Mr. Winter felt that there was a growing trend toward conglomerate franchise ownership which had slowed somewhat due to concern over the eventual outcome of the FTC ruling and of the convenience-packaging legislation.

Regardless of the size or success of the franchisee, however, there were no domestic developers who bottled 7UP to the exclusion of all other soft drinks. Within the network there were 13 so-called exclusive bottlers; the word "exclusive" here meant that 7UP was the only major brand of soft drink they distributed. In some cases these developers bottled another drink for private labels, or under their own label; in other cases they produced another franchise drink which was not considered a major brand, such as Hire's Root Beer.

The remainder of the 469 Seven-Up developers held franchises for other major branded products as shown in Exhibit 3.

EXHIBIT 3

	Bottlers
7UP (exclusive).	13
Coke and other.	97
Pepsi and other	153
Dr Pepper and other .	36
Royal Crown Cola and other	104
7UP and other franchises	66

Source: Research estimates.

Several industry analyst believed that the developer network at Seven-Up was hampered competitively by the number of small bottlers it included and that, because of their size, these bottlers were not able to take advantage of the proliferation of large packages as promptly as the competition. In early 1976 one executive at Seven-Up explained, "We are behind Coke and Pepsi. They introduced the 64-ounce and got a big jump on that; now we are catching up. But as we're catching up, we've been losing share, and I think you can look at where they've introduced some of their larger sizes and you can see the impact it's had. The fact is, you have to get the bottler committed to saying, 'I need the big size.'"

Rapport between the developers and the company was given high priority by top management in 1976. Direct contact with developers was maintained through district sales managers. As part of this program, a group called the Association of Seven-Up Developers had been established in 1974. The group's objectives were to solidify company-developer relationships and to formalize developer input into marketing, legal, and public affairs decisions. Senior company officers met with committees of the association both informally and formally several times a year.

Mr. Kidwell noted, "For some of the strategic direction of the campaign
. . . we discuss the programs with the group in advance, share the research,
and get their concurrence before going into finished advertising."

The Players: Seven-Up Bottling Company

The Seven-Up Company itself owned only two bottling plants in
Phoenix, Arizona, and Toronto, Ontario. At Coke, company-owned bottlers were responsible for 10 percent of total volume. Some trade observers
commented that Coke was encouraging bottler consolidation. This led
to speculation regarding the continuation of Coke's policy of independent
versus company-owned bottling operations. The Seven-Up Company
stated that they were not actively encouraging developer consolidation,
but when the opportunity presented itself, they recognized the marketing
economies of scale to be gained from working with a single territory in
place of several. Company management stated that they did not currently
foresee additional company purchases of franchises, and explained that
in the case of the Phoenix plant, the owner had come to the company
and asked to be bought out as he wished to retire. Further, the franchise
was located in a warm-weather, rapid-population-growth area. Management added that buying up franchises was a complicated issue when
the majority of franchisees owned competitor's franchises as well; Seven-
Up was not interested in purchasing a plant which also bottled and promoted a major competitor's beverage.

The Players: Seven-Up Enterprises Division of Seven-Up, U.S.A., Inc.

As a service to developers, Seven-Up Enterprises provided canned
and bottled 7UP products for those developers unable to produce them
within their own facilities. Through the operation of Seven-Up Enterprises, the company stated "All 7UP developers are assured access to
the wide range of 7UP packages required to serve their respective markets."

This division produced finished products in cans, bottles, and fountain syrup containers through nearly three dozen production centers nationwide. These centers were canners contracted on a 30-day basis, cancellable by either party. Since the early 1950s, when the division really
got its start with the introduction of cans into the U.S. market, there
had been relatively little turnover among these producers despite the
30-day terms. Contractors were of two types: independently owned firms
and Seven-Up bottlers or canners. The latter were authorized by The
Seven-Up Company to produce product requirements not only for their
own territory but for other franchise areas as well, and thus bore full
ownership responsibility. The independent contractor, on the other hand,
relied upon The Seven-Up Company to bear all business risks revolving

around inventories, and so forth, as s/he had no title to ingredients or finished product, which belong to Seven-Up.

Production centers were located in 34 cities in 25 states. In geographical terms, a partial breakdown was as follows: three centers in the Far West, four in the East, eight in the Midwest, and ten in the South. Arnold Larson, vice president and general manager of Seven-Up Enterprises, commented, "We can reasonably economically blanket the country with a new package. While we retain our organizational autonomy, we maintain a close relationship with home office marketing because we can really help break in new products. For instance, after the cyclamate scare many of our franchises were gun shy of our reformulated diet product, and we were able to produce the product, demonstrate its appeal, and in this way help the marketing department sell its new product."

Seven-Up Enterprises was also expected to provide strong support to the introduction of the new 2-liter packages in several major markets, and in general to produce the over-32-ounce packages for those developers who could not yet invest in these popular sizes. As stated in the 1975 annual report, "Many 7UP bottlers now have facilities for producing the variety of package types and sizes they need in their local markets; however, many other still do not. For this latter segment, Seven-Up Enterprises provides a practical solution to their packaging needs."

Domestic Marketing

In early 1976 John Kidwell was appointed senior vice president and director of marketing. He had been president of Seven-Up of Canada Limited from 1970 to 1976. An industry commentator noted, "When John took over as director of marketing, he inherited some major strengths as well as several problems, not the least of which was the sustained loss in market share for regular 7UP. He and his predecessor appeared to respond differently not only to this challenge but also to goals for the marketing area. I believe poor developer-company relationships were a major factor in the decline of regular 7UP market share."

"I am much more of a strategist than a marketing and advertising creative man," Kidwell stated. He believed that the steps he had taken thus far reflected the strategic orientation citing his work with the developer network, his reorganization of the marketing department, and recruitment of new personnel as well as the development of the "UNdo it!" campaign. In the following sections, he and his team describe their opportunities and challenges.

Mr. Kidwell commented on developer relationships, "When I returned I met almost immediately with the executive committee of the Association of Seven-Up Developers. I was amazed at the deterioration that had occurred between the company and our developers just in regard to simple human relationships. When you had a bad franchisor-franchisee relationship, you have to understand that it has taken a long time to develop, and for that reason you can't solve the problem overnight. But progress has been made in these last months. Some of the credit should go to our reorganization. We wanted not only to achieve strategic goals but to bring about closer contact and clearer communication with the developers—specially in the development of their individual marketing plans." Later in that year he remarked, "I would say that the developers themselves are pleased with the direction we've taken. But it's true that we still have to live together for a while before the relationship is fully reestablished."

Departmental Reorganization of Domestic Marketing

Mr. Winter, in a trade paper interview, explained some of the rationale behind John Kidwell's marketing restructuring. "Before, our marketing organization was action oriented. We were structured to prepare for action . . . and, quite frankly, there was confusion in our marketing communication. Now we are building on top of that some organized planning and a base for credibility for our marketing actions."

Prefaced by a comprehensive analysis of the marketplace, taking place over a period of months, John Kidwell divided marketing into five subunits: market development, services, research, sales, and fountain syrup sales (see Exhibit 4). Each was given "clearly defined functions and responsibilities and was to be headed by experienced persons."

Michael Baker, formerly director of marketing for Canada, was brought in to head up the new market development group. Reporting to him were market development managers, whose responsibilities were similar to those of brand managers, for each of the three major market segments: packaged 7UP and packaged Sugar Free 7UP, Fountain 7UP, and Sugar Free 7UP. These managers were seen as "conceptualizers" who assisted the sales organization in analyzing and solving the marketing needs of Seven-Up developers.

While these managers had periodic contact with the developers to keep in touch with the marketplace, the day-to-day responsibilities of working with the developers fell to the sales function. This function was divided into two departments, the packaged sales department and a new fountain syrup sales department. Both departments were responsible for the execution of sales programs and the attainment of sales objectives for products in their respective markets. They were to sell home office marketing programs to the developer network and to be the direct communication link with developers for all marketing affairs.

The packaged sales department, by far the larger of the two, was organized geographically into an eastern and a western division. These division sales managers supervised regional and area sales managers. It was the area sales managers who worked most closely with developers

EXHIBIT 4: Organization Chart

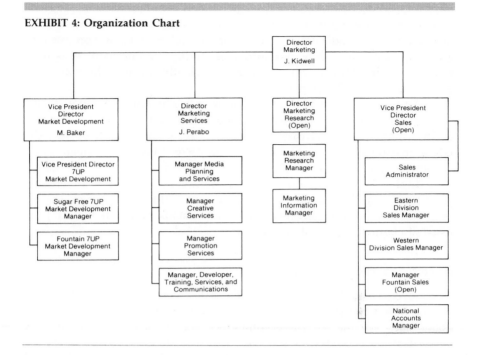

to determine how the allotted marketing dollars could best be combined with the developers' own funds and spent within the developers' territory.

The third function, marketing research, supported the work of the first two functions, development and sales. The research function was divided into two departments, marketing research and marketing services. The former was a new addition to the marketing organization; formerly marketing research had been conducted on a less formal basis or by an outside organization. James Perabo had been hired as the director of marketing services. The work of this department included media planning (with the exception of local advertising which was the responsibility of the market development manager), promotion services, packaging, graphics merchandising racks, vending, and sales and management training—all services provided for developers.

As an example of how the new organization worked, John Kidwell explained the critical process of the development of the company's advertising program.

First, market development recommended to Kidwell a strategy based on supporting documentation provided by marketing research. Upon his approval, the suggestion went back to market development where a document was prepared for presentation to the advertising agency. Then followed a discussion of the campaign with the agency to see if the proposed objectives could be met. Once the agency had come up with its program, that effort was presented to the Creative Review board of the company (Kidwell, Baker, and Perabo). The strategy had next to be approved by Mr. Winter before being put into operation. The company sought to involve the developers in the process, principally through the marketing committee of the Developers Association.

A third critical marketing area, to which John Kidwell devoted substantial attention early in his new assignment, was a review and redirection of the company's advertising thrust. One result of this effort was the UNdo it campaign, launched in October 1976. "From a strategic point of view Seven-Up is where it should be at this point in time," he stated. "We think of UNdo it as a strategic positioning rather than an advertising execution." To understand better the current UNdo it campaign, the researcher reviewed the company's advertising history and talked with John Kidwell about the current situation.

Advertising and Promotion

Seven-Up's 1975 soft drink dollar sales were roughly one third the size of those of Pepsi and one fifth the size of Coca-Cola sales. Total dollar sales volume for these companies was 11 and 13 times that of Seven-Up, respectively. These differences in scale naturally provided the two larger companies with certain advantages. In 1975 Seven-Up paid out approximately 17 percent of sales in marketing expenditures for a total of $36 million (see Exhibit 5). Seven-Up could expect to be outspent

EXHIBIT 5: Comparison of How the Sales Dollar Was Spent

	1970*	1971	1972	1973	1974	1975	1976
Cost of product sold	53.8¢	53.3¢	52.6¢	51.6¢	57.7¢	52.6¢	50.2¢
Marketing services	17.1	17.1	17.3	17.2	14.9	16.8	18.6
Employment costs	12.0	11.1	8.2	8.0	7.3	7.3	7.4
Payroll and fringe benefits							
All other expense (net)			4.4	4.7	3.3	4.7	3.6
Taxes	8.8	8.8	8.4	8.9	8.1	9.1	9.6
Paid to shareholders	3.5	4.2	3.7	3.4	3.6	3.9	5.3
Reinvested in the business	4.8	5.5	5.4	6.2	5.1	5.6	5.3
Total	100¢	100¢	100¢	100¢	100¢	100¢	100¢

* Restated to include Ventura Coastal Corporation.
Source: Company records.

in marketing by the two leading colas alone at the rate of roughly eight or ten to one. In terms of advertising expenditures specifically, one industry analysis estimated that for the years 1972 and 1975 Pepsi's outlays were $34 and $42 million; Coke, $35 and $42 million; Seven-Up, $14 and $14 million; Royal Crown, $8 and $14 million; and Dr Pepper, $4 and $4 million.

The Uncola Campaign

In 1968 Seven-Up initiated an aggressive program to change the 7UP image from a mixer or stomach tonic to a soft drink, going head to head with the colas in the process. This was the birth of the "7UP The Uncola" campaign, developed by the J. Walter Thompson advertising agency. The Uncola strategy focused on 7UP as an alternative drink of equal quality and enjoyment to the colas if not, in fact, their superior in refreshment. Advertising began with a heavy reliance upon television, with particular emphasis on network TV and its 60-second appeals to the targeted youth audience of 16- to 24-year olds. Later in the year, the full array of advertising media came into play with the usage of outdoor billboards, newspaper supplements, radio, and prime-time TV.

Graphics and delivery of the advertisements were progressive and designed to convey an impromptu contemporary feeling, just off-beat enough to appeal to the teens and 20s of the era. The campaign utilized the unique colors and drawings of pop art and "art nouveau" forms which broke sharply from the typical commercial art techniques. Print ads using lots of white space were strikingly simple, dominated by bold headlines proclaiming 7UP as "The Uncola." Advertising copy was littered with puns such as "Don't be left out in the Cola"; "Turn Un"; "Give Un to Others"; and "For Fast Relief from the Common Cola."

The campaign was not launched without reservation, however. For one thing, the slogan seemed to counter the traditional advertising caveat against the use of negatives; for another, the campaign itself was a far cry from the standard soft drink "life-style" advertisements depicting beach and party scenes of energetic young soda drinkers. Another type of resistance came from some Seven-Up developers who also bottled a cola product. However, it was difficult for anyone to maintain opposition in the face of the deluge of requests for Uncola posters, lamps, decals, and buttons that poured in from precisely the youth market Seven-Up intended to engage.

"See the Light" Campaign

In 1975, as unit sales of regular 7UP continued the decline begun in 1974, the company attempted to put a fresh face on The Uncola image with a new theme called "See the Light." This campaign was intended to portray 7UP as a clear, clean "uplifting" beverage highly compatible with food. Colors and design of packages were modified to resemble an illuminated marquee in which the brand name was set off "in lights." The campaign, however, did not achieve desired objectives.

"UNdo It!" Campaign

Seven-Up management saw the new "UNdo it!" campaign as a logical extension of the company's eight-year investment in the Uncola trademark and believed that it reinforced regular 7UP as *the* alternative to colas. The "UNdo it!" slogan carried both a positive and a negative message: don't drink another cola and do drink the Uncola instead. The intent of the campaign was to make the cola drinker aware of her or his cola drinking "habit" and to provide a challenge to that habit with an Uncola. The "UNdo it!" advertising campaign had extension through promotion, display, and packaging contacts with consumers.

John Kidwell explained, "Cola consumption is a habit, but people who consume cola also drink 7UP, and they do see advantages in interrupting their 'cola habit.' If we marketed strictly to the 7UP drinker, there wouldn't be any growth."

Mr. Kidwell, on several occasions talked about the target audience for UNdo it. "Our target group is concentrated among the 16–34 age group." In addition, citing the company's own research, he noted that approximately 55 percent of the 18+ age group are multibrand soft drink consumers and that this group also had high priority. "One thing about this industry is that it's not like the toothpaste, cigarette, or even beer industry where people tend to use one product or product category to the exclusion of another."

7UP consumer statistics, moreover, were unusual in the industry being skewed to the older population. Seven-Up marketers inferred from this fact that "older people" were using 7UP as a mixer. The company maintained certain cooperative programs with some liquor companies, although the overall marketing thrust did not stress the potential of 7UP as a mixer. "Our principal objective is to get . . . cola drinkers to drink more 7UP. At the same time we don't want to sacrifice that part of the market represented by heavy 7UP users."

According to Kidwell, the frequency of advertising exposure was a critical factor in breaking the "cola habit." This was one reason why "UNdo it!" would break with both industry norms and the historical pattern of 7UP by cutting back on both spot and network television while increasing the usage of network radio, print, and outdoor media in its mix. Kidwell commented, "The cost of television has gone up disproportionately high to what the industry can afford. . . . The Seven-Up strategy in the past had depended heavily on TV, but now we are using a balanced media mix and putting almost equal weight on television, radio, and outdoor. We're able to attain much increased frequency this way, and frequency is very important to us this year." A large part of the media purchases were planned during high cola-drinking time periods such as weekends, the summer months, and during high-consumption hours such as lunch and late afternoon. In the past, Seven-Up had established its budgets on a per capita basis, but now the company had set minimum reach levels for all markets with the developers in the more important areas receiving extra media dollars.

The Seven-Up Company, as the franchisor responsible for trademark control, made the final decisions on overall marketing programs but in cooperation with the Developers Association. Their cooperation was important because, for the most part, 7UP local advertising and promotion programs were done on a 50–50 cost basis. The franchisee elected to use or not use these programs, but it would have been highly unusual for a developer not to participate in them. Company marketing personnel helped each developer to tailor a specific promotional program for his territory.

The promotional arm of the "UNdo it!" campaign also stressed flexibility. "Flexibility" referred to the ability of the promotional program to adapt itself to the individual bottler's needs both in terms of timing and frequency. It was hoped that promotions at the local level would be responsive to the fact that while there was a minimum level below which a bottler should not go, some markets were more competitive than others and as a consequence required more promotional support. Frequent special "cents-off" activity was planned to facilitate the habit-changing decision of the consumer, for research had indicated consumers were price-aware.

Thus Seven-Up hoped to bolster frequency of purchase, gain competitive ground, and recover from the effects of the price-cutting activity of competitors in 1975 which Kidwell termed "almost predatory." He commented, "We couldn't keep up with either Coke or Pepsi. I think that price promotion is one of the things which had an impact on our share of market for regular 7UP. It's one of the things we've had to take into consideration in our marketing plans. It is extremely important in determining the particular brand that a person chooses at a particular time."

A National Promotion Fund, a Frequency Promotion Fund, and a National Merchandising Fund had been established to support developers.

The National Promotion Fund provided funds to encourage the participation of all Seven-Up developers at four different time periods when 7UP products would be promoted nationwide. As a promotion ran for two weeks, this encompassed only eight weeks out of the year. The Frequency Promotion Fund was established, therefore, to make available to developers a series of additional monies, up to a fixed amount, upon which they could draw for promotional campaigns other than the four nationally scheduled ones. The National Merchandising Fund supported developers' purchases of point-of-purchase materials, principally illuminated signage.

One analyst estimated that about 70 percent of the Seven-Up 1975 media expenditures in the United States were assigned to spot TV, 10 percent each to national TV and to spot radio, and 8 percent to outdoor billboards with minor amounts to newspapers and magazines.

Another analyst sensed a shift in the Seven-Up marketing budget from a preponderance toward media advertising to an increase by an estimated 50 percent in dollars spent on local promotional programs, for example, "cents-off," display, and packaging programs. He estimated the breakdown of marketing expenditures for 1977 at 40–45 percent of the pie for advertising, another 35–40 percent for promotions, 10–15 percent for packaging, and the remainder for market research.

Packaging

Seven-Up had been an innovator in packaging. In 1971 the company introduced the award-winning Plasti-Shield bottle; glass encased with plastic which kept the beverage cooler longer and decreased breakage. The new containers were lighter, easier to handle, and conserved shelf space as well.

In 1975 Seven-Up was the first soft drink producer to switch to metric packaging. Since the FDA had ordered all alcoholic beverages to be packed in metric sizes by 1979, Seven-Up may have anticipated similar legislation for its industry. They were well received by consumers in the 60 markets in which they were introduced by 1976. One reason cited for this reception was that the packages offered more product for the money; a liter holding 33.8 ounces generally sold for the same price as the conventional 32-ounce bottle. To announce the metric innovations the company had used Seven-Up humor in slogans such as "Follow the Liter" and "A Quart and Liter Bit More."

"We are still behind our major cola competition in the availability of 32- and 64-ounce bottles," Mr. Kidwell noted. "We have many incentive programs for developers to encourage usage of the larger sizes and metric packages." The company was also monitoring plastic bottle developments.

Pricing

Within the take-home market segment, price leadership was often taken by Pepsi. During the summer of 1975, Pepsi preempted Coke to become the leading firm in this market area. Pepsi's success was attributed to an aggressive marketing policy that took advantage of Pepsi's owned bottlers to squeeze margins in key urban markets and thereby underprice Coke. Coke's retaliation had led to increased "cents-off" promotional activity during 1975 and 1976.

By the middle of 1976, however, retail prices for the major soft drinks showed no significant differences from one to another, though Seven-Up obviously felt it had to increase its level of promotional support to bottlers to keep up with the pricing strategies of the leading colas. In October 1974, Seven-Up had increased its extract price to developers by 11 percent. This was the first increase in three years. Prices were again raised by the company in June 1975 by 25 percent; these increases not only offset rising costs of sugar and inflation but were earmarked for added marketing support. Developers initially did not appear pleased with the 1975 concentrate price hike, but since the company had stated its intention to plough back much of its increased revenue into advertising and promotional programs, they seemed more accepting.

The only clear price differential which continued to exist at both the retail and wholesale level was that between Sugar Free 7UP and the diet drinks of the other major producers. The developer ingredient cost per case for Sugar Free 7UP was considerably below the cost of competitive diet brands.

In the fountain market, Coca-Cola was the dominant figure and price leader. As sales to this segment were extremely price sensitive, wholesale margins were significantly lower than in the take-home market; thus by maintaining a low price to jobbers Coke could make it difficult for competition to make any headway in this market. Seven-Up products, generally speaking, were comparable in price to Coke's. At the fountain retail level, prices to the consumer remained consistent for all of the major soft drinks and were rarely discounted.

Two Key Markets

The take-home market (primarily grocery stores) was the largest market segment of the soft drink industry and provided nearly 60 percent of Seven-Up soft drink sales. It was a competitive area in which one of the company's products, Sugar Free 7UP, had enjoyed substantial success and in which regular 7UP had experienced loss of share of market during the last several years. In 1975 the industry in the United States suffered an average decline of 0.2 percent for all brands; regular 7UP sales declined an average 3.6 percent. In the first quarter of 1976, industry average sales increased 13.9 percent and regular 7UP sales increased 8.7 percent.

Senior management stressed the importance of reestablishing the growth pattern of regular 7UP. Mr. Kidwell told the researchers that his immediate goals for regular 7UP were to reverse the decline in market share and to recapture the 7½ percent share of all markets previously held by the regular product; this called for an increase of one percentage point from the Seven-Up estimated 1976 share.

Kidwell believed Seven-Up had already taken important steps towards reaching this goal. The reorganization of the marketing department was expected to help regular 7UP get back to, and stay on, target. He anticipated that the market development function, which had not existed previously, would be of particular importance in this endeavor. In addition, the reorganization divided the fountain syrup and regular sales groups into two individual units so that different strategies could be worked out for each.

A further consequence of the new system was that Sugar Free 7UP was also treated as a separate entity from regular 7UP. Prior to Kidwell's tenure both products had been included in the same "integrated marketing plan." He suggested that this invited cannibalization of the regular sales by Sugar Free 7UP. "We can't prove that conclusively, but the fact is we have been marketing the two products together for the last two and a half years, and this might have contributed to the regular 7UP problems."

An industry analyst noted that one strategic unknown would be Coke's program for Sprite, its lemon-lime drink. "Their primary interest has been in promoting their cola drinks. Sprite right now is only available to about 50 percent of the U.S. consuming public. But, what if this should change?" Mr. Kidwell commented, "We have to be very concerned about Sprite. Coke is powerful, and where it is very strong—in the Southeast and Southwest—Sprite is very strong. But we have strength too. Many of our Coke bottling relationships go back before they had Sprite; I don't think those bottlers would give up 7UP for Sprite. Our reserve power would be to shift the brand to the local Pepsi bottler."

Sugar Free 7UP had been a major success story in both the take-home and fountain markets. Diet drinks comprised approximately 15 percent of soft drink volume, and Sugar Free was acknowledged to be the fastest growing diet drink in this field. It ranked third in market share with Diet Pepsi first and Tab second.

Mr. Kidwell was optimistic about Sugar Free's future and had set a goal of 10 percent of the diet market segment to be achieved by the end of 1977. The product's critical characteristic was that most consumers could not distinguish between the taste of Sugar Free and regular 7UP whereas they noticed differences in taste between the regular and diet colas. On this premise Seven-Up had used "taste tests" to sell accounts in the fountain market. Champagne glasses filled with Tab were compared to those filled with Sugar Free 7UP. In 1975 these "taste tests" led to breakthrough fountain sales with McDonald's.

Company market research indicated that the diet soft drink consumer was, typically, female and somewhat older than the consumer of regular drinks. To reach these consumers, Seven-Up planned to capitalize on the perceived taste advantage of Sugar Free 7UP. "Through independent research studies we have established that we have the best tasting diet soft drink on the market." Sugar Free's 1977 advertising theme would be "Taste More Taste." This approach was innovative in that it emphasized taste as the principal quality of the diet drink; most competitors stressed their diet products' low calorie attributes. Seven-Up expressed the opinion that by virtue of the product's name, consumers already understood this fact and, therefore, it was not necessary to repeat the message in its advertisements. National consumer sampling would play a large role in the campaign, principally through retail outlets.

"Fountain is the other key market to keep your eye on," a seasoned industry executive commented, "not just because it's a high-growth area but because it is so critical strategically. That is why Pepsi, Dr Pepper, and Seven-Up are working so hard at 'cracking' Coca-Cola's dominance. Coca-Cola must have been between 60–90 percent of that business. But, to understand 'fountain,' you have to keep three points in mind: first, it is extremely complex; second, it calls for sophisticated selling policies; and third, it is a rough competitive game."

That the fountain business was complex was readily apparent to the researchers. Part of the complexity resulted from the fact that it was not one but multiple markets—fast-food chains, vending companies, certain military and institutional accounts, and anywhere else that soft drinks could not be bought in a bottle or a can. In one sense, simply defining where a fountain market existed, what its segments, trends, and opportunities for growth were, was a major task. One result of this complexity was a paucity of reliable data on which to base company plans.

The process of selling to the fountain trade was a complicated maneuver. Using McDonald's as an illustration, the first step of the process meant gaining headquarter's approval. Once this was secured, the product could become automatically available in the 800 McDonald's *company-owned* franchise operations. However, like most franchise organizations, McDonald's was not legally allowed to dictate to its *independent* franchises which beverage they should purchase and it was under pressure from the FTC regarding such tie-in arrangements. Therefore, the independents could choose between the soft drink brands headquarters recommended. This meant that Seven-Up, after selling McDonald's, had yet to convince 2,800 franchised outlets across the country. At this stage, salespeople presented their case to the 12 or 13 regional McDonald's representatives, and if successful, were then able to approach individually the 83 cooperative groups of McDonald's franchises. Adding to this uncertainty was the fact that no legal contracts were made in the fountain market, leaving clients free to switch products at any given moment.

Coke, the key player in the fountain trade, determined the competitive ground rules. That company was both a manufacturer and the seller of fountain syrup. Historically, Coke had gotten its start in soft drinks as a fountain operation, and had retained the right to sell its syrup directly to beverage wholesalers without having to involve Coke franchises in the process. In this way Coke benefited not only from the economies of scale in producing the syrup in approximately a dozen centers (as compared to Seven-Up's approximately 400 fountain developers) but also could avoid some of the cost of an intermediary distribution network. Another critical advantage was that since the Coca-Cola Company did sell the product, Coke could control all pricing for the fountain market from its headquarters in Atlanta and could quote one national price to beverage buyers.

Most recently Coke had begun a new development in distribution called "cross-franchising." Regional distribution centers were set up, on a profit/loss basis, from which Coke itself would fill orders for clients within the fountain market of an entire region, without being restricted by any wholesalers or middle persons. Pepsi had just lost the Burger Chef account, and some trade analysts believed Coke's cross-franchising program was hurting Pepsi's position within the fountain market.

Pepsi, as opposed to Coca-Cola, did not manufacture or sell fountain syrup directly to wholesalers, except through its own bottling operations, and, therefore, could not set a single national price in the same way that Coke could. Pepsi, therefore, engaged in a complicated process of buying fountain syrup from its franchisees which PepsiCo then resold to beverage wholesalers. In this manner Pepsi could act as the seller of the product for its franchised bottlers and, in combination with the syrup produced in company-owned facilities, could manage to develop a national pricing policy without violating the legal ramifications of its franchise agreements.

According to Tony Rebello, manager of Seven-Up's fountain market development department, there were two key competitive characteristics in the fountain business. First, all involved parties were highly price sensitive and everybody is squeezed but the final account. Coke has certainly played a major role in keeping prices to wholesalers and accounts low, but the food service companies themselves are a dominant force in maintaining low margins for concentrate producers. Retail margins, on the other hand, did not suffer the same pressure. The average cost of a gallon of syrup to a fast-food chain was $2; after adding the ice, water, and cups, the chains resold the syrup to consumers for an average of $25 per gallon.

Seven-Up did not enter the fountain market until 1960. The company had had to overcome quality control problems with the filtration of city water supplies used at fountains and cup vending machines. By 1970 fountain sales represented a 7 percent share of 7UP unit sales. By 1974 the company could note that fountain sales were growing at a rate double that of overall company sales and had reached 12 percent of unit sales. In 1975 they dipped to 10.6 percent. One industry analyst believed this was due to the tremendous rise in sugar prices which left the bottlers unable to meet "national prices" suggested by Seven-Up for leading nationwide fountain customers.'

In 1975 Seven-Up negotiated the distribution of Sugar Free to McDonald's, the first time a major chain had taken on a diet drink. In 1976 the 1,000-unit Burger King and 2,400-unit A&W Root Beer chains were sold. In some areas of the country such as Atlanta, Sugar Free had gained 0.8 percent of the market versus a 0.5 percent share for Tab. While analysts estimated that marketing and promotional allowances made this a break-even operation, Seven-Up management believed fountain had good long-term possibilities (see Exhibit 6).

EXHIBIT 6: Seven-Up Distribution in the Fast-Food Area

Chain	Market Share (Sales $ percent of fast-food market)	Type of 7UP Sold
McDonald's	20	Sugar Free
Kentucky Fried Chicken	11.7	Regular
International Dairy Queen	6	Regular
Burger King	4.8	Both
Burger Chef	2.8	Sugar Free
A&W International	2.7	Both
Hardy's	2.6	Sugar Free
Denny's	2.6	Regular
Jack-in-the-Box	2.5	Not sold
Pizza Hut	2.5	Regular

The 1976 reorganization of the marketing department had divided fountain sales into two subunits: one aimed at national fast-food accounts, and the second aimed at key developers. Mr. Kidwell's target was an increase of 10 percent in fountain sales by the end of 1977. He commented about the fountain market: "We are taking a very hard look at the whole economics of this business as it affects our bottlers and as it affects our company. We are attempting to determine just where the profitable end of the business is and where the unprofitable end is. There are areas of cost accounting, for instance, in fountain that need clarification. Often in cold drink sales accounting, a developer includes vending, fountain, and cold bottle. Yet all the expenses are lumped against the fountain department only. So, until we get our developers to differentiate their expenses, it's going to be difficult to determine where we stand profitwise with fountain. We think there is the strong possibility for some pretty significant gains, both in profits and volume."

Mr. Kidwell sought guidance on the question of reinstituting a "suggested national pricing program" for large accounts and had hired a consulting firm to deal with this issue. In 1975 the demise of the national pricing policy cost Seven-Up the accounts of several large vending companies.

All concentrate producers considered price to be a major factor of their marketing program; in some cases it seemed that determining a price was the entire marketing program. Rebello, however, spoke of the necessity for Seven-Up to design a fully integrated marketing program which included components other than price alone. New marketing plans for fountain sales included pricing allowances to help developers in their distribution efforts but also involved advertising on menus and signs within accounts and point-of-purchase displays. Special ads were developed showing 7UP being consumed in athletic stadiums, and newspaper advertising was also to be used. Promotional items included Uncola glasses and free-drink coupons given with McDonald's sandwiches to increase both 7UP consumption and traffic through McDonald's outlets. Seven-Up stated it would reimburse developers for every free gallon given away in a promotional effort and would financially assist incentive programs for developers' fountain salespeople.

One industry analyst predicted Seven-Up had yet to face a major challenge to its expansion within the fountain market. "You look at Coke's power in the fountain business," she suggested, "and imagine to yourself what would happen to Seven-Up if Coke decided it wanted to create consumer demand for Sprite. The best place to start would be in the fountain area where Coke rules and sell Sprite to the food service people as a product of the Coca-Cola Company with the Coca-Cola quality guaranteed. To sweeten the deal, Coke could relate the distribution of Sprite to that of Coca-Cola with tie-in programs, that is, 'Buy a certain amount of Coke and get a gallon of Sprite free . . . or buy Coke, Sprite, and Fanta flavors and we'll give you the equipment for it.' Once Sprite was reasonably well established here, Coke could move into the packaged segment with a product that had already been recognized and sampled by millions of Americans."

Canada

The first move of Seven-Up into non-U.S.A. markets began in 1935 when Canadian operations were initiated; in 1975 Seven-Up Canada Ltd. contributed 12 percent of corporate sales. 7UP market penetration exceeded that achieved in the United States; it was second only to Coke in share of market. Sugar Free 7UP, introduced in 1975, had captured 15 percent of the diet market, including sales to McDonald's. In 1976 competition had increased dramatically and the company announced the objective of "containing market share erosion in the face of extreme competitive pressure and legislative uncertainty. Over the long term, however, sales were expected to have a 10–15 percent growth rate."

The company's 1975 annual report noted that Canadian and other international sales amounted to about 20 percent of total consolidated sales with net income at a slightly lower percent to total. The net profit figure was achieved after an unusually high foreign exchange loss, primarily from Argentina and Mexico, which reduced net income by $1,146,574.

International

"Seven-Up has major opportunities in International," an industry observer noted, "just because the market is so large and growing and they are such a tiny factor at present. They have done a superb job in Canada, and they are strong in parts of South America." Mr. Charles Thies, president of Seven-Up International, was also optimistic. "True we miss the days when you could get into the market inexpensively, but our objective is still to color the world with green 7UP bottles—gradually."

In 1975 International was responsible for roughly 8 percent of company sales and coordinated a network of 186 franchised bottlers in 81 nations. Seven-Up International had but a few exclusive bottlers; it was in combination with Coke bottlers in 30–35 international markets and with Pepsi bottlers in a similar number of markets. 7UP was bottled in tandem with Orange Crush in 16 plants and with R.C. Cola in a dozen plants worldwide. The remaining hundred plants bottled 7UP in combination with local brands. Operations ranged in size from Amsterdam, where 9 million cases of 7UP were sold annually, to a small Australian "outback" station with sales of a few thousand cases.

Current goals were to again double sales volume within a five-year span, while continuing to contribute 10 percent of overall company profit. To achieve those goals, International's program was to concentrate increasing advertising and promotion efforts on markets in developed countries in an effort to reduce dependency on Mexico and Argentina. One analyst estimated the geographical breakdown of sales to be 80 percent in Latin America, 8 percent in Europe, and 12 percent in other areas.

Seven-Up International was organized into seven regions each headed by a regional director bearing profit responsibility. While in some cases marketing activities could be performed regionally (as in the case of the Andean or Benelux countries), more often it had to be done on a country-by-country basis. Moreover, it was not possible to transfer marketing themes directly from the domestic to international markets. Aside from language problems, colas were not necessarily the primary soft drink within foreign countries so that the Seven-Up Uncola and "UNdo it!" campaigns were not applicable. A small marketing staff in the United States provided services to the regional directors; this staff was comprised of a vice president of marketing to whom the two coordinators of market planning and of marketing services reported. Chuck Thies commented: "The whole structure is not entirely defined. We hope to grow to the point of having a regular market function within each region. For this reason, the regional director may have quite a bit of marketing autonomy."

Overseas franchise agreements varied from country to country, depending upon what Seven-Up could negotiate. However, they typically included quotas for a minimum percentage of sales growth and spending in support of the brand, a percentage figure regarding distribution penetration, and a time of agreement which ranged from five to 10 years. In general these terms were similar to those employed by the two leading cola companies. Seven-Up International felt that some of the advantages a potential franchisee gained when working with Seven-Up were that the prices charged for extract were more reasonable and that the franchisee was allowed much more autonomy, in developing the local market.

Most industry analysts noted that the key to success in the international markets was a strong and committed local bottler. For this reason Seven-Up recently had been giving increasing attention to signing on very successful bottlers. This represented, however, one of International's greatest challenges. Chuck Thies explained: "In most developed markets, there are fewer and fewer available bottlers, so the opportunity to go with one of them is reduced. If you don't fit with their product portfolio, they are simply not interested. A bottler can't start out with 7UP alone anymore because it simply is not profitable to bottle only one drink and have only one brand riding in your trucks given the relatively small size of most of the markets. In Sao Paulo, for example, trucks carry rum along with 7UP; and in Holland, though this is dying out, 7UP is sold from milk trucks. Furthermore," he added, "Coke has the ability to use economic leverage to preserve fidelity among its bottlers abroad." He cited the case of a South African bottler who had owned franchises for Coke, Schweppes, Canada Dry, Pepsi, and 7UP. Coke bought out the franchise, retained the Coke, Schweppes, and Canada Dry franchises, and eliminated Pepsi and 7UP.

This type of situation sometimes left Seven-Up International in the position of having to deal with less-than-optimal franchisees. In cases where the bottlers were not strongly motivated or did not have the financial strength to properly develop the market, Seven-Up management staff worked with them to develop marketing plans and contributed sometimes as much as 80 percent of initial marketing expenditures. If all else failed the company tried to renegotiate the franchise. In the past Seven-Up had made a policy of not owning any franchises abroad in deference to the nationalism of various countries. In 1976, however, Thies felt they would consider investing in an enterprise in a country with a stable currency.

In 1977 International planned to "attack" seven or eight "threshold" markets similar to the programs unleashed in London and Sydney, Australia, in 1976. "Beachheads" would be established in the city's metropolitan area and then distribution would fan out from this established basis. In the United Kingdom the "beachhead" agreement was with the Schweppes organization in London. Initial efforts were quite successful, aided by a long, dry summer season. There were, however, still some problems to be worked out. Schweppes, being a mixer company, did not have production or "glass" capacity to produce larger bottle sizes and the range of packages consumers desired. Nor did Schweppes bring to the arrangement a particularly strong distribution system within food stores due to the nature of their own line of products.

Even in threshold markets like London, it was difficult for Seven-Up to conscientiously spend as much money as it felt it should for effective market entry. Mr. Thies explained that the amount of money the company spent to develop a market depended upon primarily two elements—reach and availability. "Reach" referred to the cost of reaching people through the media, promotions, and so forth; and "availability" referred to the availability of product or the percentage of outlets which offered 7UP. The reach figures varied dramatically from country to country depending upon general economic conditions. Availability of product most often depended upon the capacity of the bottler. While both favorable reach and availability figures had to coexist for Seven-Up to be able to justify marketing expenditures in an area, most frequently availability proved the critical factor.

Chuck Thies stressed two other key factors impacting international operation: investment considerations and local and international competition. With regard to investment, he was interested in the "break-even" period for the company and Seven-Up's ability to bring home profits. "In countries which are unstable, the break-even period acceptable to us is quite a bit shorter than say in Scandinavia where we are willing to wait three or four years."

Naturally, competition was also critical for 7UP's performance in a given market. Often when 7UP entered a foreign market, rapid expansion was inhibited by the presence of local, less expensive lemon-lime-flavored products. 7UP's primary advantage over these products was its high quality, though this necessitated higher costs as well. In terms of the colas, 7UP was at something of a disadvantage in that its taste was more fragile and could vary greatly according to the quality of the water and of the sugar used in its production. The major international competitors of 7UP were Pepsi and Coke.

PepsiCo International provided technical and marketing assistance to 534 franchised and 21 company-owned facilities in 134 countries around the world. Pepsi's strongest operations were in Central and South America and Eastern Europe. Pepsi was also active in the Middle East where Coca-Cola was under Arab boycott pressure.

It was estimated that 46 percent of Pepsi's 1975 gallonage came from overseas markets, with 22 percent sold in Latin America. Estimates of foreign unit growth approached 6½ percent, as compared with domestic growth rates of 3½ percent. By 1975 Diet Pepsi had been introduced in 28 areas in six different countries. Along with its Pepsi line, the company marketed abroad a Miranda line of flavor beverages as well as a pure juice product. Since 1965 Pepsi-Cola sales had increased 293 percent; this performance was greatly exceeded, however, by the Miranda flavor line which grew 563 percent in the same period.

Coca-Cola, the dominant international firm, sold its product in 134 countries around the world, through 750 bottlers, 16 of whom were company owned. An estimated 44 percent of Coke's sales dollars and 55 percent of its earnings came from international operations. Coke made it evident that the country intended to take a long-range view of market opportunities. Efforts were underway to imprint Coke as a brand name, even in some countries where the drink was not yet available. In 1976, for example, Coke launched a program promoting soccer clinics and games for children in Africa and the Middle East which was expected to cost the company about $5 million over the next few years.

Coca-Cola, it appeared, was trying to break into the Egyptian market. Two of its subsidiaries, some journalists noted, made the company increasingly interesting to Egypt: The Foods Division and Aqua-Chem, Inc., which manufactured water purification equipment. Both divisions could provide technology sought after by the Arab countries. In addition, because Coke was so diversified geographically, some maintained that it would not be so badly hurt as other soft drink companies by currency complications. Coke was the only major producer, for example, to be strong in both Latin America and in the more stable, developed markets of Europe.

Chuck Thies talked with the researcher about a decision which he believed highlighted the complexities of developing overseas markets.

> Should we enter the Cairo market? It has a population of approximately ten million and would be relatively inexpensive in terms of "reach" costs for Seven-Up—perhaps $50,000 the first year. But the Egyptian pound is a "soft" currency, and it is a major problem getting money out because of Egypt's balance of trade problems.
>
> One way to handle this difficulty would be for Seven-Up to plough back its share of whatever money the bottler made the first year into marketing expenditures to develop the brand. By the second year we might expect something in hard currency with more to come the third year—providing the Egyptian economy didn't turn down. The investment problem is exacerbated since initially the franchise would probably have to purchase bottling equipment outside of Egypt for hard currency. One possible device might be for the local investor to manufacture glass for export to bring in hard currency income with which to make the initial capital investment and to buy extract from us.

There is a soft drink vacuum in Cairo. Currently, U.S. soft drinks are being black-marketed, which suggests a strong demand for quality soft drinks. Labor is relatively inexpensive; and, therefore, distribution costs would not be a problem. Coke is presently making every effort to enter the market, while Pepsi which had owned a plant in Egypt has been nationalized. All of these factors spell "opportunity." However, it's a gamble because the real opportunity lies ahead: Anyone reporting to shareholders reports on the basis of what they can see, and in U.S. dollars. To enter Cairo you have to gamble on the Egyptian economy. Coke could afford to make a mistake here, or could even do it wrong the first time and come in and do it right a second time; Seven-Up could not. Should we try?

Finance

Paul H. Young, executive vice president and treasurer, spoke with the researchers about his association with the company and critical company financial policies.

This is a fine company. One of the reasons it has been so successful is that everyone here lives and breathes 7UP; no one here has taken a bath in it, but they are dedicated. And that dedication to 7UP has kept us from going into other distant fields. We are not going to acquire just any type of company.

Since becoming a public company in 1967, Seven-Up had traded on the over-the-counter market. Approximately 55 percent of the equity was still owned by families of the co-founders. With a relatively small float and a trading volume that averaged between 150–250,000 shares per month, Seven-Up stock prices had been relatively volatile. Company objectives for its shareholders were to achieve share price appreciation and provide a fair dividend. A 40 percent dividend payout ratio had been typical at Seven-Up. Expansion had been financed almost entirely through internally generated funds, and Mr. Young noted that one of the company's major short-run concerns was "protection against unsound capital utilization." To guard against such an event, all capital decisions involving $100,000 or more are referred to the board of directors for financial justification. "We have the best rate of return on reinvestment of any company in the industry."

Capital expenditures for property, plant, and equipment, orchards development and acquisition investment amounted to approximately $9 million in 1973, $7 million in 1974, and $7 million in 1975. Approximately 45 percent of the total 1975 expenditures were allocated to the development of nonsoft drink product group facilities. Estimated 1976 capital expenditures were $8.5 million with 80 percent being allocated to soft drink product group facilities, primarily a new bottling and canning facility for the company-owned Phoenix operation.

Technical

Seven-Up maintained strict quality evaluations of all franchised bottling plants. The plants were monitored by the technical field service
group, 11 people who worked directly with the bottlers. Said Dr. B. C.
Cole, vice president and technical director, "It's our goal to see that all
Seven-Up bottling plants are in such sanitary conditions and operate
with such sanitary controls that they need not fear, in fact, they may
even look forward to visits by state and federal inspectors because of
the control programs and plant evaluation program we have which outline
what we consider good manufacturing practices." The company had set
up a rigid system of quality specifications that culminated in an award
for those sites which met the standards, and bottlers competed vigorously
to achieve this symbol of high-quality maintenance. During the past 30
years the company had terminated few franchise agreements.

Pertinent to the subject of diet drinks, Cole explained that saccharin
was approximately 300 times as sweet as sugar; cyclamates 30 times as
sweet; and research was being done presently on the usage of high fructose
sugars which were 140 times as sweet as ordinary table sugar. The high
fructose sugars were produced from any starchy material, such as potatoes,
wheat, barley, or corn. Their advantages lay in the facts that once fully
developed, they would be readily obtainable from materials within this
country, and that they could be used in place of ordinary sugars to lower
the calorie level of soft drinks without lowering the sweetness level.

In light of the dynamic future predicted for another new form of
product, powdered drinks, the researchers asked Dr. Cole about the possible development of a carbonated 7UP soft drink in powdered form. He
responded:

> To the best of my knowledge you'd have to revise the nature of
> the laws of the solubility of gasses (CO_2) in water to do that. Unless you
> put the mixture under pressure, you can't stir in the carbonation, or get
> it in any way other than by packing it in under pressure as we do now.
> Not even adding dry ice pellets, which are pure CO_2, could you get the
> mixture carbonated beyond a level of one volume. 7UP is presently carbon-
> ated at a level of 3.7 volumes.
>
> Now people have been doing things with powdered drinks and they
> have not done them because they had an equal carbonation and an equal
> product, but because there are lots of people who will mix it up readily
> . . . it's a good product. It is not a carbonated soft drink; it is a drink of
> a different character.

The researcher learned from Dr. Cole that 7UP at a carbonation level
of volume one tasted much the same as any soft drink that had lost
most of its carbonation: flat, without sparkle, watered down. Cole added,
"7UP is designed to be carbonated, and if we were going to make it to

be used as a noncarbonated product, we'd have to change its flavor constituents quite a lot."

Another research subject broached with Dr. Cole was that of nutritive drinks such as Hustle (Dr Pepper). His response was:

> It is not the purpose of the carbonated soft drink industry to supply to the consumer a balanced diet. In fact, it is not the purpose of the soft drink industry to supply health foods.
>
> Undoubtedly in the life of each person there should be some happiness and enjoyment. Carbonated beverages fit into this field. They are fun products and were never designed to supplement the diet or to replace foods commonly called "nutritious foods."
>
> Soybean-based beverages constitute an excellent source of protein, but they are not carbonated soft drinks at all; they are now more like beef broth or something. We are now talking about a way to supply nutritious materials to people who are underfed.

Dr. Cole added that in his own personal opinion it would be much less costly to distribute a nutritive product in a dry, concentrated form rather than to package it in bottles which had to be washed, sterilized, and so forth, if one's goal were to provide economical, balanced diets to poverty-level consumers.

CASE 7

BIC Pen Corporation (A)

Described by an economic observer as "one of the classic success stories in American business," the BIC Pen Corporation was widely acknowledged as a leader in the mechanical writing industry in 1973. "The success was dramatic," the observer had said, "because it was achieved from the residue of a deficit-ridden predecessor company, over a short period . . . , in the extremely competitive, low price sector of the industry. 'BIC' had become a generic name for inexpensive ball-point pens."

Robert Adler, president of BIC, was extremely proud of the firm's success, which he attributed to "numerous and good management decisions based 40 percent on science and 60 percent on intuition." BIC had reported its first profit in 1964 based on net sales of $6.2 million. Over the following nine years, net sales increased at a compounded rate of 28.2 percent and the weighted-average aftertax profit as a percentage of net sales was 13.2 percent. (See Exhibits 1 to 3 for a summary of financial data from 1964–73.)

Until 1972 BIC concentrated exclusively on the design, manufacture, and distribution of a complete line of inexpensive ball-point pen products. The most successful pen was the 19-cent Crystal, which accounted for over 40 percent of BIC's unit sales in ball-point pens and about 15 percent of industry unit sales in ball-point pens in 1972. That same year, BIC expanded its writing instrument product line to include a fine-line porous-point pen. In 1973 it added a disposable cigarette lighter.

COMPANY HISTORY

The name "Waterman" meant a writing instrument since Louis Waterman invented the first practical fountain pen in 1875. For many years,

EXHIBIT 1: Financial Highlights 1964–1973

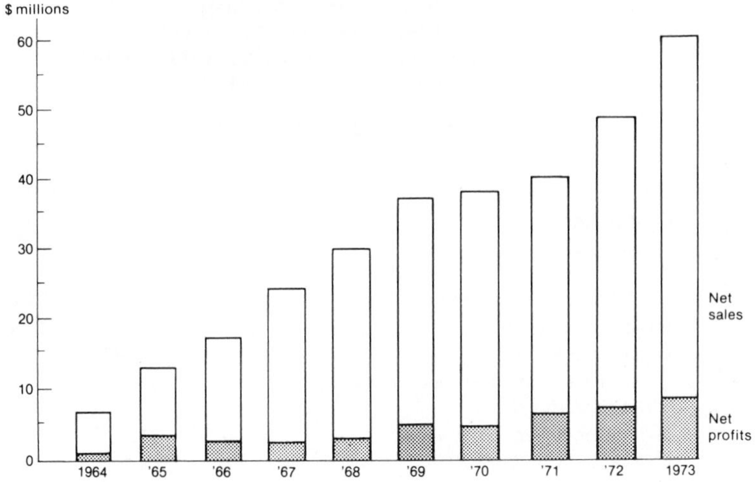

$ millions

	1964	'65	'66	'67	'68	'69	'70	'71	'72	1973
Net sales ($ millions)	6.2	12.8	17.8	24.0	29.6	36.6	37.7	39.5	47.6	58.3
Net profit ($ millions)	0.8	3.4	3.1	2.9	3.2	4.2	4.0	5.5	6.3	7.4
Net profit/Net sales (percent)	12.9	26.6	17.4	12.1	10.4	11.5	10.6	13.9	13.2	12.7

Source: BIC Pen Corporation annual report, 1973.

the Waterman Pen Company led the world in the manufacture of fountain pens. But in the late 1950s, when the shift to ball-point pens swept the United States, the Waterman company continued to concentrate on its fountain pen line, and its performance slipped substantially.

In 1958 Marcel Bich, a French businessman well established as a leading European pen maker, bought the facilities, trademark, and patent rights of the ailing Waterman company, which then became the Waterman–BIC Pen Corporation. Believing strongly that the ball-point pen was the writing instrument of the future, M. Bich established the objective of becoming the leading firm in the low-price disposable ball-point pen industry. To obtain that position, management proposed the use of forceful consumer advertising and mass-distribution policies.

At the time of M. Bich's purchase of Waterman, ball-point pens constituted only 8 percent of Waterman's unit sales. By 1964, however, all fountain pen and ink products had been eliminated, and most sales came from the 19-cent stick-type ball-point pen. The conversion process was costly, as reflected in the five years of deficits (1959–63). BIC reached its turning point in 1964, marked by the national success of its Crystal pen.

EXHIBIT 2

BIC PEN CORPORATION
Consolidated Financial Statements
For the Years Ended December 31, 1973 and 1972
(in thousands of dollars)

Consolidated Statement of Income

	1973	1972
Net sales.	$58,326	$47,571
Cost of goods sold	26,564	19,892
Gross profit.	31,762	27,679
Selling, advertising, and general and administrative expenses.	17,191	15,248
Profit from operations	14,571	12,431
Other income	589	269
Total profit from operations	15,159	12,700
Other deductions	327	196
Income before income taxes	14,787	12,504
Provision for income taxes.	7,357	6,240
Net income	$ 7,430	$ 6,264
Earnings per share	1.15	1.00

Consolidated Statement of Retained Earnings

	1973	1972
Balance—beginning of year	$11,683	$10,262
Net income	7,430	6,264
Total	19,113	16,526
Dividends:		
Cash:		
Common shares.	1,750	1,603
Preferred shares		
Total cash	1,750	1,603
Common shares		3,240
Total dividends	1,750	4,843
Balance—end of year	$17,363	$11,683

Source: BIC Pen Corporation annual report, 1973.

From 1964 through 1973 the company expanded its ball-point pen line to include 12 models of retractable and nonretractable pens offered in varying point sizes, ink colors, and barrel colors at retail prices between 19 cents and $1. A 29-cent fine-line porous-point pen was added in 1972, and a $1.49 disposable butane cigarette lighter in 1973. In addition to product-line expansion, BIC established a 100 percent-owned operation in Canada (1967), joint ventures in Japan (1972) and Mexico (1973), and a distributor arrangement with a firm in Panama (1973).

On May 1, 1971, the company changed its name to the BIC Pen Corporation. The Waterman trademark was subsequently sold to a Zurich

EXHIBIT 3

BIC PEN CORPORATION
Consolidated Financial Statements
December 31, 1973 and 1972
(in thousands of dollars)

Consolidated Balance Sheet

	1973	1972
Assets		
Current assets:		
Cash.	$ 683	$ 919
Certificates of deposit and short-term investments—at cost, which approximates market	8,955	10,000
Receivables—trade and other (net of allowance for doubtful accounts, 1973—$143,000, 1972—$102,000).	9,445	8,042
Inventories.	9,787	6,299
Deposits and prepaid expenses	644	633
Total current assets	29,514	25,893
Property, plant, and equipment—at cost (net of accumulated depreciation, 1973—$9,687,000, 1972—$7,091,000)	15,156	9,687
Investments and other assets	1,790	1,329
Total assets.	$46,460	$36,909
Liabilities and Shareholders' Equity		
Current liabilities:		
Notes payable—banks.	$ 21	—
Construction loan payable (due March 21, 1974)	560	—
Accounts payable—trade.	3,872	$ 1,245
Mortgage payable	62	58
Accrued liabilities:		
Federal and state income taxes.	1,231	815
Pension plan	306	265
Other.	488	402
Total current liabilities	6,540	2,785
Deferred liabilities	361	275
Mortgage payable	459	520
Minority interest*	91	—
Shareholders' equity:		
Common shares.	6,480	6,480
Capital surplus	15,166	15,166
Retained earnings	17,363	11,683
Total shareholders' equity	39,009	33,329
Total liabilities and shareholders' equity.	$46,460	$36,909

* Mexican subsidiary is 80 percent owned.
Source: BIC Pen Corporation annual report, 1973.

firm, and BIC went public with an offering of 655,000 shares of common stock listed at $25 per share on the American Stock Exchange. In 1973 BIC's parent company, Société Bic, S.A., held 62 percent of the BIC stock.

MEN OF INFLUENCE

Marcel Bich

Marcel Bich has been described as having done for ball-point pens what Henry Ford did for cars—produce a cheap but serviceable model.

In 1945, Bich and his friend Edouard Buffard pooled their wealth— all of $1,000—and started making ball point refills in an old factory near Paris. Soon it occurred to Bich that a disposable pen that needed no refills would be more to the point. What his country needed, as Bich saw it, was a good 10¢ pen. Today the cheapest throwaway Bic sells for close to that in France—about 7¢. In the United States the same pen retails for 19¢, and it is the biggest seller on the market. . . .

Marcel Bich is a stubborn, opinionated entrepreneur who inherited his title from his forebears in the predominantly French-speaking Val D'Aoste region of northern Italy. He abhors technocrats, computers, and borrowing money. At 58, he attributes his business successes to his refusal to listen to almost anyone's advice but his own. Bich says that his philosophy has been to "concentrate on one product, used by eveyone every day." Now, however, he is moving toward diversification. A disposable Bic cigarette lighter that gives 3,000 lights is being test marketed in Sweden; if it proves out, Bich plans to sell it for less than 90¢. . . .

In the United States, Bich is best known for his fiasco in the 1970 America's Cup Race: His sloop *France,* which he captained, got lost in the fog off Newport. He speaks in aquatic terms even when describing his company: "We just try to stick close to reality, like a surfer to his board. We don't lean forward or backward too far or too fast. We ride the wave at the right moment."[1]

Société Bic, S.A., was known as a "one-man empire" which in 1972 accounted for a third of the ball-point pen sales worldwide and included full operations in 19 countries. M. Bich's personal holdings were estimated to be worth about $200 million. "The only way he could control his empire," BIC's treasurer Alexander Alexiades had said, "was to have certain rules and guidelines. All Société Bic companies were quite autonomous once they had become consistent with his philosophies."

Bic Pen Corporation had been characterized as the "jewel in M. Bich's crown." In the firm's early years, M. Bich had provided much of the machinery, production techniques, and supplies from the French par-

---

[1] "Going Bananas over BIC," *Time,* December 18, 1972, p. 93.

ent company. By 1973 the only substantial business exchange which still remained between the two firms was in research and development. One of the few visible signs of the American company's European heritage was the Renaissance artwork which M. Bich had hung in BIC's reception and board rooms.

Robert Adler

In 1955, the day after Connecticut's Naugatuck River raged out of control and flooded the countryside, Mr. Adler reported to work at the old Waterman Pen Company as a newly hired junior accountant fresh out of Pennsylvania's Wharton School of Finance. Instead of being shown to his desk and calculating machine, he was handed a shovel and ordered to help clean out the mud which had collected in the plant during the flood. Nine years later, at the age of 31, he became president of the Waterman–BIC Pen Corporation, which under his leadership became the largest ball-point pen manufacturer and distributor in North America.

Mr. Adler was described by a business associate as "a president who liked to be totally familiar with and completely immersed in every area of his company's operations, one who felt that he should never quash his instincts with an overdependency on numbers and facts alone . . . a shirt-sleeved president who made it his personal concern to know intimately every facet of the BIC marketing and manufacturing process, including highly technical matters involving complex moulding equipment, advanced production techniques, merchandising, advertising, and sales . . . a do-it-yourself investigator-president who regularly made the rounds of the plant, keeping himself available at all times."

Mr. Adler had stated that he personally selected his colleagues on the basis that they demonstrated aggressiveness and an unswerving belief and conviction that they were serving a company that produced the world's finest writing instruments—products of exceptional quality and value. "A businessman is born, not made," he said, "and education can only enhance and refine what already exists." He attributed much of BIC's success to the fact that in the firm's early years he had consciously hired persons who were unfamiliar with the industry and who therefore did not question BIC's ability to succeed by selling an inexpensive ball-point pen via extensive advertising. He emphasized the importance of his own role in determining BIC's performance by stating:

> A lot of decisions are easy because there is only way to go. Sometimes you're lucky and sometimes, no matter what, you'll get the same outcome. A president gets paid to make decisions. That's his big job. What's important once a decision is made is to make sure that it comes out right. The decision is not so important; it's the outcome. A president must say to himself: "I will now make my decision successful."

WRITING INSTRUMENT PRODUCT LINE

The BIC Pen Corporation manufactured and sold inexpensive writing instruments in a variety of shapes: stick or pocket pen; ink colors, 1–10; point sizes, medium or fine; and retail prices, 19 cents to $1. All retractable pens were produced in a pocket pen shape; all nonretractables in a stick shape.

The most successful product, the Crystal, accounted for over 40 percent of all ball-point pen units sold in North America. Its sister product, the 25-cent Fine Point Pen, which differed from the Crystal only in point size, accounted for over 15 percent of all ball-point pen units sold.

In 1973 writing instruments accounted for approximately 90 percent of BIC's consolidated net sales. Nonretractable pens accounted for 80 percent of the writing instrument unit sales, retractable pens for 6 percent, fine-line porous-point pens for 12 percent, and refills for 2 percent.

Exhibit 4 presents the 1973 BIC writing instrument product line.

EXHIBIT 4: 1973 Writing Instrument Product Line

Product Name	Ink Colors	Point Sizes	Retail Price
Ball-point pens:			
Nonretractable/nonrefillable:			
Crystal	4	m	$0.19
Fine Point	4	f	0.25
Reproduction	4	m	0.25
Eraser	4	m,f	0.25
Deluxe Eraser	4	m,f	0.29
Deluxe	4	m	0.39
Accountant	4	f	0.49
Retractable/refillable:			
Clic	4	m,f	0.49
Two-color pen	2	m,f	0.69
Four-color pen	4	m,f	0.98
Citation	1	m	1.00
Retractable/nonrefillable:			
Pocket pen	3	m	0.29
Fine-line porous-point pen:			
BIC Banana	10	m,f	0.29

Source: Corporate records.

Nonretractable/Nonrefillable Ball-Point Pens

The Crystal, a nonretractable/nonrefillable ball-point pen, was introduced on the market in 1959 at a retail price of 29 cents. As the first product of the newly formed Waterman–BIC Pen Corporation, the BIC Crystal was intended to become a "brand name replacement for all no-name,[2] disposable pens in a market where no dominant competitor existed." Its retail price was dropped to 19 cents in 1961. In commenting on the success of the Crystal, Jack Paige, vice president of marketing, remarked:

> We built this company on the 19-cent pen. In 1961 it was selling for 19 cents, and in 1973 it is still 19 cents. One third of all retail sales are from the 19-cent stick. It's a highly profitable business. We've found ways to become more efficient and still maintain our profitability.

Between 1961 and 1968, BIC expanded its nonretractable ball-point pen line to include six other models of varying point sizes, ink colors, and usages. Nonretractables were priced from 19 cents to 49 cents.

Retractable/Refillable Ball-Point Pens

In 1968 BIC introduced its first retractable/refillable ball-point pen, the 49-cent Clic.[3] Management felt that the Clic would (1) improve the overall corporate profit margin; (2) enable the company to sell merchandise in multipacks (quantity selling in one package), such as school specials; and (3) increase distribution—as some retail outlets, particularly those not dependent on BIC for their profits, had been reluctant to sell the 19-cent and 25-cent pens.

Following the Clic, four other retractable ball-point pens were added to the BIC product line. Three imported French pens—the 98-cent 4-color pen (1971), the 69-cent 2-color pen (1972), and $1 Citation pen (1973)—were introduced to "upgrade ball-point pen sales." The 29-cent pocket pen, the only nonrefillable pen in the retractable line, was added to "expand primary demand for ball-point pens."[4]

Fine-Line Porous-Point Pens

In April 1972, BIC introduced its first nonball-point pen product, the 29-cent BIC Banana, which was a fine-line porous-point pen produced in a stick shape. Mr. Paige commented on the Banana decision as follows:

> The development of the concept of entering the porous-point pen market was not a sudden decision. Our philosophy was simply that as soon as we had a porous-point pen that would reflect BIC quality and

---

[2] No-name products were those which were not advertised and were marketed at retail prices far below the comparable, inexpensive, national advertised products.

[3] In retractable pens, industry sales volume in dollars was concentrated in the high-priced products and in units in the no-name brands.

[4] Despite a major introductory campaign ($1.5 million spent on advertising), sales in the pocket pen were "disappointing," according to one company spokesperson. He attributed the poor results to styling problems and a lack of room for new products in a market with a declining sales growth rate.

could be mass marketed at a popular price that anybody could afford, we would then move into that business.

For openers, we were faced with a couple of major problems. First we were a late entry and the market was dominated by a 49-cent strong brand name of good quality that had a 50 percent market share. Maybe for some companies that stark statistic would have been enough not to enter. However, at BIC there is an aggressive attitude about marketing. That attitude manifested itself a year and one-half ago when we began plotting our sales course for the introduction of this new product. (BIC spent $3 million on advertising the BIC Banana in 1972.) We took the attitude that we weren't going to be squeezed into that remaining 50 percent share that the leading brand left for the rest of the field. Our plan was to expand the consumer market for this type of writing instrument—to make it grow. In a larger market, we felt we would have the opportunity to build a franchise that would give us a substantial share.

In reviewing the same product decision, Mr. Alexiades said:

In 1966 we saw the product opportunity for the soft-tip pen, but Marcel Bich owned 90 percent of the company, and we had a difficult time convincing him that this was the right approach. He thought that the soft-tip pen was a passing thing and that it was impractical because it wouldn't write through carbon. But we're in a carbon society, and there's no logical explanation for the consumer. However, M. Bich's philosophy changed. Years ago, he only wanted to sell ball-point pens. He's now interested in inexpensive, disposable, mass-produced items. He has the marketing know-how, the distribution, the name.

We saw that the porous-point pen was not a fad so we got in, perhaps a little late, but at least we entered an expanding portion of the market. The growth rate of ball-point pen sales had leveled off. If we didn't enter the porous-point pen market, it would have been difficult to grow since we're so dominant in the industry. We knew that the only way to grow was through product-line diversification or acquisition.

Our objective is to become the largest producer of fine-line porous point pens. We are in ball-point pens. It might be difficult because Gillette's Flair has been there for five years. Papermate brand is not a no-name brand with no resources like those which we initially attacked in the ball-point pen market.

A competitor commented on the market entry of the BIC Banana:

Many people associated BIC with the ball-point pen. BIC had a difficult time because people thought that the Banana was a ball point. It's a stick shape and looks like a ball point. They don't have that problem with the lighter (1973) because it is a different looking product altogether. BIC hasn't done well with the Banana against the Flair. After all, who could enter the stick pen market now and do well against BIC? But at least BIC broke the price point (49 cents) with its 29-cent point which softened the retail and commercial markets. Maybe they'll get smart and get out.

THE MARKETS

Mr. Adler's philosophy had always been "to sell BIC products wherever there was a doorknob." Consistent with that view, marketing efforts had been focused on all writing instrument markets, with special emphasis placed on the "four key sales volume opportunities"—the retail, commercial, ad/specialty, and premium markets, which represented about 90 percent of the dollar sales volume in the writing instrument industry in 1973. The other three markets—government, military, and export—accounted for the remaining 10 percent. In 1973 the Writing Instrument Manufacturers Association estimated total industry sales at $353.3 million.

Retail Market

The retail market, or over-the-counter market, was the largest mechanical writing instrument market, accounting for over 50 percent, or $176.6 million, of the total industry dollar sales in 1973. Of significance in the retail market was the growing trend away from indirect selling through retail distributors to independent stores toward direct selling from the manufacturers to mass-merchandise outlets.

Since the national success of the 19-cent Crystal pen in 1964, BIC had completely dominated the ball-point pen segment of the retail market. By the end of 1973, BIC held a 66 percent share of that segment, followed by Gillette with 15 percent and Lindy with 5 percent. In fine-line porous-point pens, Gillette was the front runner with a 35 percent share followed by BIC with 22 percent, Magic Marker with 8 percent, and Pentel with 5 percent.

Management attributed BIC's successful penetration of the retail market to its aggressive marketing and distribution policies, as well as to the low price and high quality of its products.

Commercial Market

The commercial market, or office supply market, was the second largest mechanical writing instrument market, accounting for about 20 percent, or $70.6 million, of total industry sales in 1973. Selling in the commercial market was primarily handled through commercial distributors, who channeled products from the manufacturers to office supply dealers, who in turn sold to commercial customers. Large office supply dealers bought directly from manufacturers and used distributors to fill in inventory gaps.

At the end of 1973, management estimated that the leading market shareholders in ball-point pens in the commercial market were BIC with 50 percent, followed by Berol with 18 percent, and Gillette with 5 percent. In fine-line porous-point pens, it was estimated that Gillette held a 40 percent share; Berol, 25 percent; Pentel, 10 percent, and BIC, 4.5 percent.

In commenting on BIC's 4.5 percent market share in fine-line porous-point pens, Mr. Adler said:

> We have had difficulty in the commercial market because that market is conditioned to something like the Flair, Pentel, or Berol porous pens which sell for 49 cents and allow good margins to the distributors. The model which BIC manufactures does not compete head on with Flair. Ours is a stick model; theirs is a pocket model. Because of the design of the product, it's difficult to get a certain percentage of the market. The Flair product costs twice as much to manufacture (has a clip, etc.). The 29-cent Write-Brothers also has a clip. For us, we're a long way from being number one. To get into the porous-pen business, we had to use the stick model. Our problem is that the distributors do not want to push the Banana because they have a 49-cent market. Naturally, they make less on a 29-cent model. It will take time.

Ad/Specialty and Premium Markets

The ad/specialty and premium markets together accounted for approximately 20 percent or $70.6 million of the total industry dollar sales volume in 1973.

Ad/specialty sales referred to special orders made through specialized distributors for products imprinted with a slogan or organization name. Competition in the ad/specialty market was based heavily on price which accounted for the strength of the no-name brands in that market. BIC held close to a 5 percent share in the ad/specialty market in 1973.

A "premium" was defined as a free promotional item which was attached to another product in order to promote the sale of that product. Premium sales were made through distributors or direct from the manufacturer to customer. As in the ad/specialty market, competition was based upon price. Unlike that market, it was also based upon brand recognition and included a broader base of product types, not just writing instruments. Although it was a small market, management considered BIC's participation in the premium market as important in "reinforcing the firm's dominant position in the pen business." BIC held close to a 100 percent market share among writing instrument firms in the premium market in 1973.

THE COMPETITION

In 1973 approximately 200 firms were engaged in the manufacture and sale of mechanical writing instruments in the United States. Most firms competed selectively in the industry on the basis of (1) product type—fountain pen, mechanical pencil, ball-point pen, or soft-tip pen; (2) price range—high (>$1), medium (50 cents to $1), and low (<50 cents);

EXHIBIT 5: 1973 Selected Product Lines

| | | | Gillette | | | |
Product Type	BIC	Berol	Paper Mate	Write-Bros.	Lindy	Pentel
Ball-point pens:						
Retractable:						
Refillable	$0.49	$0.29	$0.98	—	$1.00	$2.98
	0.69	0.39	1.50			5.00
	0.98	0.49	1.98			7.00
	1.00	0.59	3.95			8.50
		1.49	5.00			
			5.95			
Nonrefillable . . .	0.29			$0.39		0.79
Nonretractable . . .	0.19	0.19		0.19	0.19–	
	0.25	0.25			0.59	
		0.29				
		0.39				
Fine-line porous-						
point pens.	0.29	0.29	0.49	0.29	0.59	0.29
		0.49	0.98			0.35
			1.95			0.49

Source: Corporate records.

and (3) market—retail, commercial, ad/specialty, premium, military, government, and export. Strong advertising programs and mass-distribution networks were considered critical for national success.

In management's view, BIC had four major writing instrument competitors: Berol, Gillette, Lindy, and Pentel.[5] The five firms competed at price points with similar products (see Exhibit 5).

The Berol, Lindy, and Pentel corporations were well known for product innovation. In 1973 the Berol Corporation, best known for its drafting products, particularly for its Eagle brand pencils, was the second firm to introduce the rolling writer combination pen, a pen which performed like a regular fountain pen, yet could write through carbons. Lindy Pen Corporation had earned its reputation as an early entrant into new markets, yet lacked the advertising strength to back the sale of its new products. Lindy introduced a 39-cent stick pen prior to the introduction of the BIC Crystal in 1959, a fine-line porous-point pen in 1969, and a disposable lighter in 1970. Pentel Corporation had earned the reputation of "revolutionizing the U.S. mechanical writing instrument industry" with the introduction of the soft-tip pen in 1964 and the rolling writer combina-

---

[5] The Magic Marker Corporation was considered a strong competitor in fine-line porous-point pens with four models selling from 19 cents to 49 cents and comprising an estimated 8 percent share of the retail market. However, Magic Marker was best known for its broad-tip markers (10 models, from 39 cents to $1.29). Its ball-point pen products were sold strictly as no-name brands.

tion pen in 1969. Like Lindy, it lacked the resources to support heavy advertising and mass distribution programs.

Gillette

The Gillette Company was considered BIC's major competitor in all writing instrument products. The comparative performance in writing instruments for the two firms from 1968–73 is shown in Exhibit 6.

In 1973 Gillette competed in the high-price market with its Paper Mate products and in the low-price market with its Write-Brothers products. The Paper Mate ball-point pens had been the mainstay of its writing instrument business since the early 1950s. In the late 1960s, management at Gillette "recognized the potential of Pentel's new soft-tip pens." Backed by a large research and development capability, a well-known corporate name, and advertising and distribution strength, Gillette set out to capture that market with a fine-line porous-point pen called "Flair," which retailed in three models from 40 cents to $1.95. In 1972 Gillette created the Write-Brothers products: a 39-cent retractable ball-point pen, a 29-cent fine-line porous-point pen, and a 19-cent nonretractable ball-point pen, in order "to take advantage of growth opportunities in the low-price end of the mechanical writing instrument market." The Write-Brothers name was selected to prevent confusion on the part of consumers who had associated the Paper Mate name with high-priced ball-point pen products and middle- to high-priced Flair products.

Retail market share patterns for BIC and Gillette are shown in Exhibit 7. (The BIC Banana was introduced in May of 1972 and the Write-Brothers products in July of 1972.)

Over the five-year period 1969–73, BIC and Gillette made the advertising expenditures on writing instruments shown in Exhibit 8.

In commenting on advertising programs and the BIC/Gillette competition in general, David Furman, advertising director at BIC, said:

> Our stategy has been to emphasize profit, and therefore look for the mass market. Gillette has said: "Let's make the most money and not worry about the size of the market." Gillette had a nice profitable business with Flair. It kept Paper Mate alive. But they can't stay alive with one-dollar-plus pens. We expanded the market so now their unit sales are up. The philosophy of Gillette has been to spend heavily to develop the product, then let the products decay and spend on new product development. Their unit sales continue to go up but their loss of market share is considerable.

COMPANY POLICIES AND STRUCTURE

Mr. Adler had sometimes described his company as a car with four equally important wheels—sales, manufacturing, finance, and advertis-

EXHIBIT 6: Comparative Performance in Writing Instruments (consolidated statements)

	1968	1969	1970	1971	1972	1973
BIC:						
Net sales ($ millions)	$29.6	$36.6	$37.7	$39.5	$47.6	$52.4
Net income ($ millions)	3.2	4.2	4.0	5.5	6.3	7.3 (est.)
Net income/sales	10.8%	11.7%	10.6%	13.9%	13.2%	14.0% (est.)
Net sales/total assets*	—	—	1.6	1.4	1.3	1.3
Total assets/total equity	—	—	1.3	1.2	1.1	1.2
Gillette (Paper Mate Division):						
Net sales ($ millions)	$33.2	$36.5	$47.0	$51.1	$60.9	$74.5
Net income ($ millions)	2.5	3.3	3.3	2.5	3.0	4.3
Net income/sales	4.5%	9.0%	7.0%	4.9%	4.9%	5.8%
Net sales/total assets*	1.4	1.4	1.3	1.3	1.3	1.3
Total assets/total equity	1.8	1.8	1.8	1.9	2.0	2.1

* Estimated total assets allocated to writing instruments.
Source: Corporate 10-K reports.

EXHIBIT 7: Bimonthly Retail Market Share Patterns (units)

	Jan.-Feb.	Mar.-Apr.	May-June (1972)	July-Aug.	Sept.-Oct.	Nov.-Dec.	Jan.-Feb.	Mar.-Apr.	May-June	July-Aug. (1973)	Sept.-Oct.	Nov.-Dec.
Ball-point pens:												
Total BIC	66%	67%	65%	65%	66%	65%	67%	66%	65%	66%	68%	66%
$0.19 Crystal	36	35	34	33	31	31	32	32	31	31	31	31
0.25 Fine Point	12	14	13	13	11	13	13	12	13	13	11	12
0.29 Pocket pen	—	1	2	2	3	3	3	3	3	2	2	2
0.49 Accountant	8	7	7	8	9	7	8	7	7	8	10	9
0.49 Clic	8	8	7	7	9	8	8	8	8	8	9	7
Other	2	2	2	2	3	3	3	4	3	4	5	5
Total Gillette	8%	8%	9%	13%	13%	13%	13%	15%	15%	14%	14%	15%
$0.19 W-B	—	—	—	3	3	3	4	6	5	5	5	5
0.39 W-B	—	—	1	2	2	2	2	2	4	2	2	2
0.98 Retractable	4	4	4	4	4	4	4	4	4	4	4	4
Other	4	4	4	4	4	4	3	3	4	3	3	4
Lindy	7	7	8	7	6	7	6	6	6	5	5	5
Other	19	18	18	15	15	15	14	13	14	15	13	14
Total	100%	100%	100%	100%	100%	100%	100%	100%	100%	100%	100%	100%
Fine-line porous-point pens:												
BIC	—	—	5%	11%	15%	16%	16%	19%	19%	20%	23%	22%
Total Gillette	49%	46%	45%	43%	43%	40%	39%	37%	36%	37%	35%	35%
$0.49 Flair	45	43	41	36	34	33	32	30	30	30	28	29
0.49 Hotliner	2	2	1	1	1	1	1	1	1	1	1	1
0.29 W-B	—	—	2	5	7	5	5	5	5	5	5	4
Other	2	1	1	1	1	1	1	1	—	1	1	1
Lindy	5	5	4	4	4	4	3	3	2	2	2	2
Magic Marker	—	—	—	—	—	—	6	6	7	8	9	8
Pentel	9	9	9	7	7	7	7	6	6	5	4	5
Other	37	40	37	35	31	33	29	29	30	28	27	28
Total	100%	100%	100%	100%	100%	100%	100%	100%	100%	100%	100%	100%

Source: Corporate records.

EXHIBIT 8: Writing Instrument Advertising
Budget Estimates ($ millions)

	1969	1970	1971	1972	1973
Gillette .	$1.9	$4.0	$6.0	$8.5	$9.0
BIC . .	3.6	4.0	4.3	7.0	6.8

Source: Case researcher's estimates derived from corporate records, interviews with company officials, and journal articles.

ing—all of which had to be synchronized in order for the car to accelerate and sustain itself at high speed. That car, he claimed, had equal responsibility to its stockholders, employees, and customers. It followed, therefore, that management's attention should be focused on achieving a good return on investment, which Mr. Adler felt was derived by improving (1) productivity (unit production per hour), (2) efficiency in production (cost savings methods), and (3) quality control standards and checks.

Finance

In the spring of 1971, BIC Pen effected a recapitalization which resulted in an aggregate number of 3.03 million outstanding common shares, 87 percent of which were owned by Société Bic, S.A., 3 percent by M. Bich, 9 percent by Mr. Adler, and 1 percent by other officers and directors (stock bonuses).[6] On September 15 of that year, 655,000 of those common shares were offered to the public at $25 per share, resulting in a new capital structure of 67 percent of the shares owned by Société Bic, S.A., 3 percent by M. Bich, 7 percent by Mr. Adler, 1 percent by other officers, and 22 percent by the public. Proceeds from the public offering after underwriting discounts and commissions amounted to $15.4 million. On July 27, 1972, M. Bich exercised his warrants for the purchase of 210,000 shares of common stock at $25 per share, totaling $5.25 million, which BIC received in cash. That same day, the company declared a 2-for-1 share split in the form of a 100 percent share dividend of 3.24 million shares, $1 par value, which resulted in the transference of $3.24 million from retained earnings to common stock. At the end of 1972, 6.48 million shares were outstanding of the 10 million shares authorized in June of 1972; none of the 1 million authorized shares of preferred stock had been issued.

Since 1967 the company paid cash dividends as shown in Exhibit 9.

---

[6] Four million common shares were authorized.

EXHIBIT 9: BIC Pen Corporation Dividend Payment History

	1967	1968	1969	1970	1971	1972	1973
Consolidated net income ($ millions) . .	$2.862	$3.231	$4.233	$4.033	$5.546	$6.264	$7.430
Dividends ($ millions)	2.591	—	1.175	1.166	1.319	1.603	1.750
Adjusted net dividend/share* . . .	0.43	—	0.19	0.19	0.22	0.26	0.27
Stock price range* . . .	—	—	—	—	12¼–18	16¼–37	11⅝–32½

* After giving retroactive effect to a 2-for-1 share split in 1972.
Source: BIC Pen Corporation annual report, 1973.

Regarding dividend policy, Mr. Alexiades said:

> When we were a private firm, there was no dividend policy. Dividends were only given when declared by M. Bich. In 1969 when we knew that we would be going public, we tried to establish a policy to find the proper relationship between earnings and dividends. Twenty to twenty-five percent of earnings seemed like a good target policy. Now we're having trouble increasing our dividends, due to government guidelines, although we would like to increase the payout in accordance with our rise in earnings.

The purchase of the original BIC plant from the Norden Company in 1963 was financed with a 5¾ percent mortgage loan from Connecticut General, payable in monthly installments of $7,749 (principal and interest) until January 1, 1981.[7] The three plant expansions—$1 million for 110,000 square feet in 1965, $1.8 million for 100,000 square feet in 1969, and $5–$6 million for 275,000 square feet in 1973—were financed through short-term loans and cash on hand. Regarding the 1973 expansion, Mr. Alexiades said: "We decided to use our own cash so that if something develops in 1974 or 1975, such as an acquisition or new product opportunity, we can always fall back on our credit rating."[8]

In keeping with BIC's informal organizational structure, management used no formalized budgets. "We use goals, not budgets. We just keep surprising ourselves with our performance," said Mr. Alexiades, "although perhaps as we mature, we will need a more structured arrangement."

BIC was known in the New Haven area for its attractive compensation plan. It was Mr. Adler's belief that good people would be attracted by good pay. Plant workers received the highest hourly rates in the area ($4.53 base rate for the average grade level of work). All employees were invited to participate in a stock purchase plan whereby up to 10 percent of their salaries could be used to purchase stock at a 10 percent discount

---

[7] The loan had not been paid off by 1973 because of its low interest rate.

[8] BIC borrowed on a seasonal basis to meet working capital needs, using bank lines of credit ($15.5 million available; maximum borrowed was $10.6 million in 1970).

from the market price, with BIC assuming the brokerage commission cost. Executives participated in a bonus plan which Mr. Adler described as follows:

> We have a unique bonus system which I'm sure the Harvard Business School would think is crazy. Each year I take a percentage of profits before tax and give 40 percent to sales, 40 percent to manufacturing, and 20 percent to the treasurer to be divided up among executives in each area. Each department head keeps some for himself and gives the rest away. We never want bonuses to be thought of as salaries because they would lose their effect. So we change the bonus day each year so that it always comes as a pleasant surprise, something to look forward to.

Manufacturing

Manufacturing had emphasized the development over the years of a totally integrated, highly automated production process capable of mass producing high-quality units at a very low cost. Except for the metal clips, rings, and plungers, all components—even the ink—were produced in the Milford plant. Société Bic had supplied the basic production technology, machinery, and research and development.[9] Some raw materials, particularly the brass, were still imported from France.

The U.S. energy crisis posed a major threat to BIC in 1973. Polystyrene, the key raw material used in making pens, was a petroleum derivative. Mr. Adler commented on the shortage of plastic:

> We've reached a point in our economy where it's become more difficult to produce than sell. I mean I have this big new plant out there [pointing to the new $5–$6 million addition] and I may not be able to produce any products. I have to worry about the overhead. I'm reluctant to substitute materials.
>
> I predict that in 1974 polystyrene will cost more than double what it costs in 1973, which is 15 cents per pound. It represents about 10 percent of the manufacturing cost of the ball-point stick pen.

The production process consisted of three stages: (1) manufacture of parts, (2) assembly of parts, and (3) packaging. Porous pens (4 parts) were the simplest instrument to manufacture followed by ball-point pens (7 parts) and lighters (21 parts). Some parts, such as nonretractable pen barrels, were interchangeable, which built flexibility into the production process. Production rates were steady throughout the year, while inventory buildups were seasonal. In mid-1973 BIC was producing on average about 2.5 million ball-point pen units per day and 0.5 million porous pens per day, which was close to plant capacity.

---

[9] BIC Pen Corporation spent $30,368, $15,254, and $128,553 on R&D in 1971, 1972, and 1973, respectively.

Management felt that production costs were substantially controlled by the strict enforcement of a quality control system. One fourth of the plant's employees participated in quality control checks at each stage of the production process, which was precision oriented, involving tolerances as close as 0.0002±. Charles Matjouranis, director of manufacturing, had stated that it was his job to search for cost-savings programs which would protect profit margins on products. He said:

> We are in the automation business. Because of our large volume, one tenth of one cent in savings turns out to be enormous. Labor and raw materials costs keep increasing, but we buy supplies in volume and manufacture products in volume. One advantage of the high-volume business is that you can get the best equipment and amortize it entirely over a short period of time (four to five months). I'm always looking for new equipment. If I see a cost-saving machine, I can buy it. I'm not constrained by money.

In 1973 there were 700 persons working at BIC in Milford, of which 625 were production personnel represented by the United Rubber Workers Union under a three-year contract. Management considered its relations with employees as excellent and maintained that BIC offered the best hourly rates, fringe benefits, and work environment in the area. Weekly meetings between supervisors and factory workers were held to air grievances. Workers were treated on a first-name basis, and were encouraged to develop pride in their jobs by understanding production technicalities and participating in the quality control program and production shift competition. Most assembly-line workers were women. At least 40 percent of the factory workers had been with BIC for over 10 years, and 60 percent to 65 percent for over five years. Despite increased automation, very few layoffs had occurred because workers were able to be retained for other positions to compensate for the increase in production unit volume. Over 50 percent of the workers had performed more than one job.

Marketing and Sales

In admiring his BIC ring studded with six diamonds, each representing an achieved sales goal, Ron Shaw, national sales manager, remarked:

> It's almost a dream story here. When I started with the company in 1961 as an assistant zone manager, we were selling 8 million units a year. We now sell 2.5 million units a day. Everyone said: one, we couldn't sell 5,000 feet of writing in one unit and succeed; two, we couldn't have the biggest sales force in the writing instrument industry and make money; and three, we couldn't advertise a 19-cent pen on TV and make money. Well, we did and we're number one!

Distribution. The BIC products were sold in the retail and commercial markets by 120 company salespeople who called on approximately 10,000 accounts. Those accounts represented large retailers, such as chains, as well as wholesale distributors. Through those 10,000 accounts, BIC achieved distribution for its products in approximately 200,000 retail outlets, of which 12,000 were commercial supply stores. In addition, the salespeople called on 20,000 independent retail accounts which were considered important in the marketplace. In the case of those accounts, the BIC salespeople merely filled orders for the distributors. A specialized BIC sales force sold ad/specialty orders to ad/specialty distributors and most premium orders directly to corporate customers.

The backbone of BIC's customer business had originally been the mom and pop stores. They had initially resisted selling BIC pens, but were later forced to trade up from the no-name products once BIC had become a popular selling brand. As product distribution patterns moved away from indirect selling towards more direct selling to large chains and discount houses, the mass merchandisers became eager to carry BIC products, which had earned a reputation for fast turnover, heavy advertising support, and brand recognition. In 1973 BIC did 60 percent of its sales volume through distributors and 40 percent through direct sales channels.

Pricing Policy. BIC had never raised the original retail prices of any of its products. Management, therefore, placed a great deal of importance on retail price selection and product cost management. Advertising expenses generally ran 15 percent of the manufacturer's selling price; the combined costs of packaging and distribution approximated 20 percent to 30 percent of the manufacturer's selling price. The distributor's profit margin was 15 percent off the listed retail price; the indirect retail buyer's was 40 percent; and the direct retail buyer's was 55 percent. Regarding pricing policy, Mr. Adler said:

> If I increase my price, I help my competition. The marketplace, not ourselves, dictates the price. We must see what people are willing to pay. You must sell as cheaply as possible to get the volume.

Customary Marketing Tools. In a speech made before the Dallas Athletic Club in September 1972, Mr. Paige remarked: "We're in the *idea* business. Selling is an idea. Many people have products but we have ideas."

BIC used four basic marketing tools to sell its "ideas": (1) advertising, (2) point-of-purchase displays, (3) packaging forms, and (4) trade and consumer promotions. Management felt that the only way to enter a new market was to be innovative either by (a) introducing a new product, (b) creating a new market segment, or (c) using unique merchandising techniques designed specifically for that market. The BIC salespeople were known to be aggressive.[10] Products were always introduced on a regional rollout basis with the entry into each new region attempted only after market saturation had been achieved successfully in the prior region.

Advertising was considered the most important element of the BIC marketing program. Company research had shown that seven out of ten writing instruments sold were impulse purchase items. With that knowledge, management felt that widespread distribution of a generic name product line was essential for success. It was further felt that retailers and commercial stationers preferred to carry nationally advertised brands.

BIC used TV advertising, "the cheapest medium when counting heads," almost exclusively. In 1973 BIC added advertising in *T.V. Guide* and the Sunday supplements "in order to reach more women, the biggest purchasers of writing instruments."

In keeping with the belief that merchandising techniques should be designed differently for each product and market, BIC varied its TV commercials substantially, depending upon the intended product usage, time of entry into the market, and demographic interest. Each advertising message was designed to be simple and to communicate *one* idea at a time. Exhibit 10 presents examples of four different themes: (1) BIC has a lighter (BIC Butane), (2) BIC's products are durable (Crystal), (3) BIC has coloring instruments for children (Ink Crayons),[11] and (4) BIC offers a "new and fun way to write" (BIC Banana).

Another marketing tool was the *point-of-purchase display.* Mr. Paige remarked:

> Merchandise well displayed is half sold, particularly on a low consumer interest item. Displays must be designed to fit every retail requirement because, for example, what's good for Woolworth's may not be good for the corner drugstore.

Packaging was considered another form of advertising. "We want to make the 19-cent pen look like a $1 pen," Mr. Paige had said. BIC was one of the first firms to use the concept of multipacks. Packaging forms were changed as much as six times a year. Regarding packaging and *promotions,* Mr. Alexiades commented:

> We've created a demand for constant innovation, excitement in the marketplace. Many people say that's the reason for BIC's success. We change the manner in which we sell (blister packs,[12] multipacks, gift packages), which makes our merchandise turn and keeps our name in front of the

---

[10] On average, assistant zone managers earned $12,000 and zone managers earned $22,000 a year. Compensation consisted of a base salary plus commission.

[11] Ink Crayons consisted of a multipack of BIC Banana pens in an array of ink colors.

[12] Blister packs were product packages which were designed to be displayed on pegboards.

EXHIBIT 10: Television Advertising Themes

BIC BUTANE	BIC CRYSTAL	BIC INK CRAYONS	BIC BANANA
"For $1.49 and thousands of lights, it's a Pretty Good Lighter. BIC Butane."	"Dear BIC . . . You're probably not going to believe this but...."	"You can't write with blueberries, but you can write with a BIC Banana, the new porous tip pen."	"BIC Banana Ink Crayons. In ten bright colors. The only fruit you can draw with."

Source: BIC Pen Corporation annual report, 1972.

wholesaler and retailer all of the time. The consumer remembers us because we offer a true value. The retailer and dealer remember us because they receive special incentive offers, free merchandise, and promotional monies, plus their merchandise turns.

Organizational Structure

Throughout its 15-year history, the BIC organizational structure had remained small and simple. (See Exhibit 11 for the 1973 organizational

EXHIBIT 11: 1973 Internal Organizational Chart

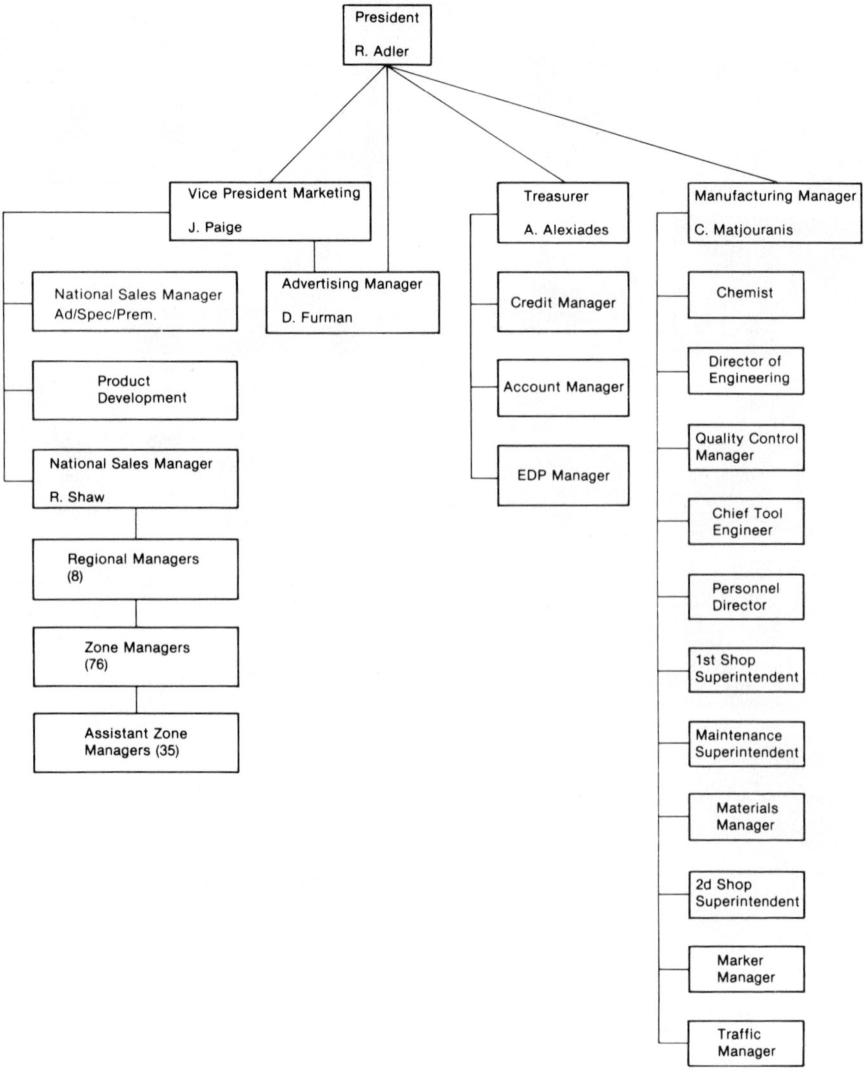

Source: Corporate records.

chart.) In 1973 the average tenure (since 1958) of the six key executive officers was 13 years. At least 40 percent of the factory workers had been at BIC for over 10 years. Several of the managers commented on the BIC environment:

We try to run this company as a family organization. We don't try to run it as a General Motors. We've been very successful with this concept. It's a closely knit management group—very informal. Decisions are made immediately. A young guy comes here. He sees that we [management] exist. We understand him. He gets his decisions immediately. We try to get him to join the family. Inside of two to three years, if he's not in the family, he won't work out.

> Robert Adler
> President

Part of the success of management is our ability to communicate with one another. We're trying to remain the same. It's one of the regrets that growth has to bring in departments and department heads, but we're trying to maintain a minimum.

> Alexander Alexiades
> Treasurer

We have few managers, but the best. One real good one is better than two average.

> Charles Matjouranis
> Manufacturing director

This company does not believe in assistants. Philosophically, we try to stay away from any bureaucracy. There are no politics involved here, no knifing, no backbiting. Part is a function of size. Everybody knows his place and area of responsibility. We don't want to break from that.

> David Furman
> Advertising director

We promote from within. We recognize the abilities of our own people.

> Ron Shaw
> National sales manager

THE BIC BUTANE DISPOSABLE CIGARETTE LIGHTER

The Lighter Decision

In March 1973 BIC Pen Corporation introduced its first nonwriting instrument product, the BIC Butane disposable lighter, at a retail price of $1.49. Management viewed the BIC Butane as a logical extension of its current product line as it was inexpensive, disposable, of high quality, and able to be mass produced and distributed through most writing instrument trade channels, especially retail. It differed from writing instruments in that it required 21 rather than the basic 7 assembly parts, more precise manufacturing, and was subject to strict governmental standards. Mr.

Furman made the following statement regarding BIC's decision to enter the disposable lighter business:

> For years we were in the high-level profitability trap. We had had it as far as that market would go. The Banana was the first break out from the trap and now the lighter. We utilize our strengths, but we're no longer a writing instrument company. We're in the expansion stage where writing instruments are a base from which we are expanding. We're using the skills we've gained and are applying them to any kind of mass-produced product.

Introductory Campaign

The decision to sell a disposable lighter dated back to 1971 when Marcel Bich purchased Flaminaire, a French lighter company, with the objective of marketing a substitute for matches in Europe. Matches had never been free in Europe, and for that reason disposable lighter sales had been very successful there far before they caught on in the United States. The BIC Butane was imported from Flaminaire but was scheduled to be produced at the Milford plant on a highly automated production line by March 1974.

The BIC Butane was introduced first in the Southwest, where management claimed it had captured a 32 percent retail market share by year's end. Management expected its national retail market share of 16 percent to rise to 25 percent when the product reached full national distribution in February of 1974. The regional rollout was backed with a $1 million advertising campaign. A $3 million campaign was planned for 1974. Lighter sales approximated 10 percent of BIC's consolidated net sales in 1973. An industry source estimated their pretax margin at 15–21 percent.

The Cigarette Lighter Industry

Lighters were categorized in three basic product classes: disposables, regular refillables, and electronics. Disposable lighters contained butane gas; electronic lighters contained butane gas or a battery; regular refillable lighters contained either butane gas (90 percent) or liquid fuel (10 percent). There were three basic price categories: <$2 (all disposables), $2–$12 (most regular refillables), and >$12 (all electronics and fancy regular refillables). It was estimated that from 75 percent to 80 percent of all cigarette lighters sold in 1972 were priced below $6.95 at retail.

Cigarette lighter sales in the middle-price range had begun to fall off in the early 1970s. As a replacement for matches, disposable lighters had expanded the primary demand for lighters and represented the major growth opportunity in the U.S. lighter industry (Exhibit 12).

EXHIBIT 12: U.S. Cigarette Lighter Retail Sales (dollars and units in millions)

	1969	1970	1971	1972	1973 (est.)
Total lighters ($)	$94.9	$98.1	$106.9	$115.0	$153.0
Disposables ($).	n.a.	8.5	18.0	36.0	50.0
Units (=)	—	—	13	21	40

n.a. = not available.
Source: Case researcher's estimates based on trade and company interviews and unpublished figures from the *Drug Topics* magazine research group (1972).

Major Competitors

By 1973 many firms, particularly manufacturers of writing instruments, had entered the disposable lighter business. Most firms served as distributors of foreign-made products, many of which were reputed by trade sources to be of questionable quality. As with writing instruments, BIC's management believed that industry success was heavily dependent on the strength of a firm's advertising program and distribution network, although most firms did well initially due to the excessive demand for disposable lighters relative to the available supply.

There were three clear contenders for industry dominance in the disposable lighter business: Gillette, Garrity Industries, and BIC, with Scripto a distant fourth. Gillette's Cricket lighter was the leading market shareholder, accounting for one third of all disposable lighter sales in 1973 (Exhibit 13).

EXHIBIT 13: 1973 Major Competitors in Disposable Lighters

	BIC	Gillette	Garrity	Scripto*
Market entry (year) . .	1973	1972	1967	1972
Product . .	BIC Butane	Cricket	Dispoz-a-lite	Catch 98
Price . . .	$1.49	$1.49	$1.49	$0.98
Product produced in .	France (→1973); U.S. (after)	France (→mid 1973); Puerto Rico (after)	France	Japan
Ad $ strategy (1973).	Consumer	Consumer (¾); trade (¼)	Trade	None
Distribution emphasis*	Mass/chains	Mass/chains	Smoke shops, hotel stands, drugstores	Independent retailers

* In 1974 Scripto planned to raise the price of the Catch 98 to $1.19, add another Japanese disposable lighter at the $1.39 price point, and produce a $1.69 disposable lighter in its Atlanta plant.

Source: Casewriter's interviews with corporate marketing managers.

In speculating on the future of the BIC Butane lighter, Mr. Paige stated:

> We think that the disposable butane will cannibalize every low-priced lighter. BIC, Dispoz-a-lite, and Cricket will do 90 percent of the business in 1973. Cricket advertises extensively. BIC will compete with Cricket at the $1.49 price point. BIC and Cricket will dominate the industry in the future. The cheaper disposables of lesser quality will only sustain themselves.

CASE 8

BIC Pen Corporation (B)

News Release: January 11, 1974

BIC Pen Corporation, which has specialized successfully in mass-marketing consumer products, soon will introduce a new product which it will distribute in the $1.3 billion retail pantyhose market, Robert P. Adler, president, disclosed today.

"The sale of pantyhose is for BIC a further expansion into other mass-produced disposable consumer products," Mr. Adler said. "Because of BIC's strong reputation for value, and our ability to merchandise successfully to the consumer through more than 200,000 retail outlets, we believe our new pantyhose product will be well received in this marketplace."

THE WOMEN'S HOSIERY INDUSTRY

Hosiery had always been the most rapidly consumable apparel item in a woman's wardrobe. For years the women's hosiery industry had been stable in unit sales and repetitive in product offerings. Many low-profile brands were sold in a wide range of sizes and typical colors. The business "kicked up its heels" in the late 60s with the advent of the convenience product pantyhose and miniskirts. Hosiery became a fashion item, costing as much as $10 a pair, depending upon style, texture, color, and brand name. Prosperity did not last, however; and by 1973 the $2 billion women's hosiery business was characterized as "having to run faster to stay in the same place." The market had become plagued by an uncertainty in consumer demand, sagging profits, price battles, distribution changes, and the rising fashion trend of women's pants. Hosiery makers claimed that women had begun to go without hose or to wear ripped stockings under pants (see Exhibit 1).

The Pantyhose Market

As an attempt to interject some life into the stable pantyhose market, the three big hosiery makers—Hanes Corporation, Kayser-Roth Corpora-

EXHIBIT 1: U.S. Women's Hosiery Industry Trends

	1964	1965	1966	1967	1968	1969	1970	1971	1972	1973
Numbers of:										
Companies.	645	609	576	579	574	530	502	471	457	390
Plants	828	782	750	746	741	734	699	665	604	521
Annual per capita consumption:										
Pantyhose	—	—	—	—	2.3	9.0	13.3	11.0	12.7	11.7
Stockings	14.8	15.7	17.3	19.5	18.1	12.7	6.3	4.2	3.1	2.5
Knee-highs, anklets . .	0.1	0.1	0.1	0.1	0.1	0.1	0.1	0.3	0.6	1.2
Total consumption . . .	14.9	15.8	17.4	19.6	20.5	21.8	19.7	15.5	16.4	15.5

Source: National Association of Hosiery Manufacturers.

tion, and Burlington Industries—launched an unprecedented $33 million promotional campaign in 1973. They case aside their established merchandising techniques and began pushing new, low-priced pantyhose in supermarkets. The firms adopted catchy brand names and used dramatic advertising campaigns centering around "trendy" packaging. Their assumption was that women would buy more pantyhose if the products were cheaper, more accessible, and more attractively displayed than before. No longer were branded products available exclusively in department or specialty stores at $3 a pair; rather they could be purchased at every corner market for 99 cents to $1.39. As a result, pantyhose sales in food outlets rose from 5 percent in 1968 to 28 percent of the industry pantyhose sales in 1973, with analysts predicting a 50 percent share by 1975. Despite the surge in supermarket buying, sales of pantyhose declined by 7 percent in 1973.

The private label business represented 50 percent of the hosiery sales in food stores in 1973, with some labels selling as low as 39 cents a pair. The supermarket invasion by known brands—"L'eggs" by Hanes, "Activ" by Burlington, and "No-Nonsense" by Kayser-Roth—resulted in a general upgrading in the quality of the private label brands and an expansion of the branded lines to cover additional market segments, such as pantyhose in large sizes for heavier women and pantyhose for less than $1 for price-conscious women.

In describing pantyhose purchase behavior, one industry source said:

> Generally, all women are interested in quality, price, fit, and availability, but purchasers do tend to fall into three basic categories: (1) women who think that all hosiery is the same and therefore look for the lowest price; (2) women who feel that an extremely low price implies inferior quality; and (3) women who switch off between high and low prices, depending upon their needs.

L'eggs was the largest selling brand name in 1973 with a 9 percent dollar volume share of the total hosiery market. The idea for L'eggs was born out of the recognition that no high-quality name brand dominated the highly fractionated pantyhose market; nor was one available at a reasonable price (<$2) at convenience locations (supermarkets). The L'eggs integrated marketing program centered around the theme "Our L'eggs fit your legs" and the distinctive egg-shaped package. The L'eggs direct selling approach leaned heavily on a platoon of 1,000 young delivery women clad in hot pants and traveling their appointed routes in distinctive white vans. Their task was to restock flashy "L'eggs Boutiques" in super-markets and drug chains. L'eggs retail sales rose from $9 million in 1970 to $110 million in 1973. Hanes spent $20 million on their promotion in 1972 and $13 million in 1973.

Activ and No-Nonsense pantyhose were priced at 99 cents a pair, in contrast with L'eggs at $1.39.[1] Both brands were backed by $10 million promotional campaigns in 1973. The "Activ Girls" competed with the "L'eggs Ladies." Similarly clad and driving red vans, they also sold prod-ucts on consignment. Besides supermarkets, Activ pantyhose appeared in outlets serviced by tobacco distributors, thus supporting Burlington's motto: "Activs are everywhere." Kayser-Roth shunned the distribution system favored by the other two hosiery makers and delivered its No-Nonsense brand-name pantyhose to food brokers at supermarket ware-houses. The No-Nonsense approach—without vans, hot pants, and comely delivery women—allowed the retailers a 45 percent profit margin, compared with the 35 percent return guaranteed by Hanes and Burlington.

THE PANTYHOSE DECISION

David Furman, advertising director, commented on BIC's entry into the pantyhose business:

> The hosiery industry used to be dominated by manufacturing, not marketing, companies. L'eggs was the first attempt to change that. The success of L'eggs and other industry leaders has depended on an extremely expensive direct selling distribution system which is good for large-volume outlets but is not feasible for smaller stores or local advertising. BIC intends to use its usual jobbers and make it profitable for them to act as middlemen and garner the independent stores.
>
> Nearly all companies deal primarily with pantyhose as a fashion item. The market is moving away from the fashion emphasis, which cannot be successful in food stores. BIC will address the fit problem by using the slogan: "It fits there, it fits everywhere"; hence the name—Fannyhose. Ours is a utility story as it was with ball-point pens.

---

[1] Hanes introduced First-to-Last pantyhose at 99 cents a pair to counter the price competition from Activ and No-Nonsense pantyhose.

In introducing Fannyhose to the trade, management used the theme of "taking a simple idea and making it pay off." The quality product was priced at $1.39, came in two sizes and three colors, and was packaged in a compact little can with a see-through top. The advertising program centered around the "better fit" concept, as was illustrated in animated television commercials and Sunday supplements. Product promotions included cents-off coupons and free samples.

In contrast with its major competitors, BIC planned to act as a distributor of pantyhose, rather than as a manufacturer/distributor, and to establish a specialized sales force to sell the product direct or through distributors to its wide variety of writing instrument retail accounts. BIC's supplier was DIM, S.A., one of France's largest hosiery makers ($100 million in sales), which M. Bich bought control of in 1973. Mr. Furman called the BIC plan "a brilliant stroke around L'eggs. Theirs is a fixed system— low profits, no risk, fixed price. We add promotional profits by passing on to the trade the money we've saved by avoiding the need for our own service crews."

BIC's Investors React

An article appearing in the February 4, 1974, edition of *The Wall Street Journal* described the reaction of the investment community to BIC's entry into the pantyhose business. One analyst cited several obstacles which BIC faced in its new venture, namely: (1) the limited pricing flexibility which BIC would have because of import duty costs[2] and (2) the fact that BIC had not been particularly strong in supermarkets. Another analyst took a more positive view, citing the recent market price decline in the BIC stock to "investors' questions over the competitive nature of the pantyhose business without understanding the philosophy of BIC— to produce inexpensive disposable consumer products once there is an established market for them and to use its widespread marketing system to become a powerful force in the industry." A third analyst predicted a bright future for BIC in the pantyhose business because of its "access to materials through Société Bic, its reputation for high-quality products, its well-developed distribution system, and its commitment to marketing, rather than to manufacturing, pantyhose."

---

[2] Duty fees averaged 33 percent per unit. One analyst speculated that the pretax margin on Fannyhose was 15 percent.

CASE 9

The Real Paper, Inc. (A)

The Real Paper (TRP) and its "giveaway" school edition counterpart, the *Free Paper*, were organized in July of 1972 by a group of former staff members of the *Cambridge Phoenix* for the purpose of publishing "metropolitan Boston's weekly journal of news, opinion, and arts."

All of *TRP*'s founders were former members of the Phoenix Employees Union. Their decision to form *The Real Paper* came after a bitter dispute with the ownership of the *Cambridge Phoenix*, which featured strikes, lockouts, picketing, fistfights, and legal action. Central to the organizing group's concept, *The Real Paper*'s operations and ownership were to be on a "community" basis. Staff members owned equal shares of TRP, Inc., and elected its board of directors. Paula Childs, a member of the editorial staff described *The Real Paper* as "a staff-owned, capitalistic enterprise. It's a group of people who came together so that they could have control—complete control—over their own business and at the same time make money doing it."

Starting without facilities, operating funds, or an established circulation organization, *TRP* achieved revenues of $462,000, profit before tax of $53,000, and a circulation of approximately 30,000 paid and 40,000 free in its first eight months of operations. Comparable data for fiscal 1974 were $998,000, $73,000, and approximately 40,000 paid and 50,000 free circulation.

Substantial achievements, however, had not left the staff of *The Real Paper* without uncertainties. Bob Rotner, publisher of *TRP*, commented, "*The Real Paper* is making money, but we're still not out of the woods. We are subject to too many ups and downs." Jeff Albertson, associate publisher, noted, "The personality of this paper is hard to talk about. It has been a problem, and we have had an identity crisis starting from day one. No one knows what 'it' is, and 'it' suffers from this lack of clearly defined purpose." And Paula Childs reflected:

> *The Real Paper* was founded on the theory that most cooperatives are formed on—you know—everyone shares equally and things are fair, just, and good—and all that kind of stuff. But I, and a lot of people who came to the paper since its founding with those same thoughts about it, have since been disillusioned. Within *The Real Paper* there's a definite hierarchy, and there's a definite kind of bureaucracy. It's—it's a real—I mean it's in some ways just like any other business.

The Milieu

Leaving the Harvard Business School with its carefully pruned plantings, manicured lawns, and freshly painted doorways, the researcher walked across the Larz Anderson bridge into Cambridge, past the Georgian-styled undergraduate living halls guarded by their high iron fences, and headed for the Lampoon Castle (home of Harvard's humor magazine). The Castle, itself a parody on Harvard's red brick and ivy style, served as a rough marker dividing University Cambridge from its more egalitarian neighborhood, Central Square.

Walking down Mount Auburn Street, the researcher dodged plastic bags of refuse awaiting collection as he passed a potpourri of small shops featuring services ranging from Chinese Laundry and Tim's Lunch to the Mules Mirage (a boutique) and Bowl and Board (an expensive furniture store). *The Real Paper* offices were located at 10-B Mount Auburn on two floors of a yellow, wood frame building nestled between the Cambridgeport Problem Center ("Free counseling, nonhassling assistance for legal, psychological, social, and family problems") and a row of triple-decker rooming houses. Ten-A housed a hairworks salon ("haircuts for men and women") and a school of dance whose students seemed to continue their lessons as they walked out of the building onto the sidewalk at the end of the class. Across the street other converted triple-deckers housed a number of research and professional offices.

The lamppost in front of *The Real Paper*'s office tolled a counterculture zeitgeist:

> Boycott Grapes: March! East–West Foundation Seminars in Spiritual Development. Meditations: Yin Meditations, Yang Meditations—Meditations of Light, Nectar, Inner Sound, Love, and Inner and Outer Infinity— Declaration of Godhood; Basic Techniques of Palm and Spiritual Healing; Stop Outrages in Psychiatry; Old Cambridge Common Pet Parade; Save the Cambridge Common Concerts; Filmmakers—Workshops; Boycott Lettuce; Our Rights We Will Defend with Our Lives if Need Be!

Mt. Auburn was a busy Cambridge street. Mixed with a heavy flow of commercial traffic were bicyclists, motorcyclists, and hordes of small foreign cars jousting with an infrequent standard size model as traffic inched its way forward to Central Square. Joggers were there, too, but in a minority position. And the pedestrian flow was heavy. Almost universally young, the passersby walked with a bounce that often sent long hair flying in the wind. Legs and faces tended to be unshaven. Clothing was simple: smocks or T-shirts, army surplus rucksacks, colorful headbands or hats of Humphrey Bogart fame, blue jeans and sandals or hiking boots were the order of the day. The researcher was reminded that the metropolitan Boston area was a youth center heavily influenced by large numbers of young people who studied or worked there, or who merely drifted in and out.[1]

A loud exhaust backfire from a blue Porsche—a student with patched jeans of bright and varied hue—provided the last insight to the Mt. Auburn Street scene. "Porsche and Patches" mused the researcher as he turned and entered the door marked *The Real Paper*. Coming into the ground-floor area, his first impression was that the area was too small for the ten desks and numerous people working there. The main room was often a maelstrom of phone calls, shouts, advertising personnel walking back and forth, and a steady stream of visitors coming to place classified advertisements with Ellen Paul, the staff person in charge of that activity.

On one side of the main door a bicycle was stored; on the left wall a bulletin board hosted a series of announcements—a lost cat, flea market sales, advertisements for the City Dance Theater, numerous plays, and The 100 Flowers Bookstore. Ellen's dog, Martha, padded around the room seeking attention, occasionally barking but never committing any grave social errors. To the left was the receptionist Cyndi Robbins, wearing a flannel shirt, blue jeans, and sandals. Social pleasantries completed, she commented, "It is a hassling job with the phone and so many visitors, but I like it here—the people, the experience, and the atmosphere."

Looking to the back of the room, the researcher noticed a man (later identified as the comptroller, Howard Garsh) sweeping the floor and stacking telephone reminder slips in a cabinet. Cyndi's directions to the publisher's office sent the researcher to the back of the main room where the publisher and the advertising sales director shared a small office, furnished in the same spartan manner as the remainder of the office.

---

[1] At a later date, the researcher obtained some population data on two- and four-year colleges, degree-granting technical-trade institutes and universities located in the New England area. There were over 35 of these institutions in metropolitan Boston, with approximately 130,000 students; approximately 120 schools in Massachusetts, with approximately 320,000 students; and 250 in New England, with approximately 600,000 students (of which 2,262 were primarily students of religion). He was intrigued with the academic program for one of the schools: "The Institute of Anatomy, Sanitary Science and Embalming."

In a brief meeting the researcher explained his general interest in the alternative newspaper industry and his specific interest in *The Real Paper*. Both Rob Rotner and the researcher agreed there were opportunities for learning in the development of a case history on *The Real Paper*. Later, after consultation with other staff members, Bob welcomed the researcher to the group and agreed to collaborate on the project (see Exhibits 1, 2, and 3).

EXHIBIT 1

THE REAL PAPER, INC.
Statement of Income for Year
Ended April 26, 1974, and Eight Months
Ended April 27, 1973

	1974	1973
Net sales	$995,793	$462,557
Other income	2,675	269
	998,468	462,826
Costs and expenses:		
Cost of publication	618,802	273,468
Selling, general, and administrative	304,674	135,738
Interest	372	124
Total costs and expenses	923,848	409,330
Net income from operations before provision for federal income tax	74,620	53,496
Provision for federal income tax	1,092	2,100
Net income	73,528	51,396
Retained earnings, beginning of period	51,396	—
Retained earnings, end of period	$124,924	$ 51,396
Net income per common share, based on the weighted-average number of shares outstanding at the end of the year, which was 2,800 shares in 1974 and 3,300 shares in 1973	$26.26	$15.57

HISTORY OF *THE REAL PAPER* AND ITS COMPETITION

Early interviews with staff members highlighted the need to study the intertwined history of *The Real Paper* and its primary local competitor, the *Boston Phoenix*.

The story seemed to begin in September 1965 when *Boston After Dark (BAD)* was born, in a spirit of entrepreneurialism, as a special center-fold supplement to the *Harbus*, the Harvard Business School student paper. *Boston After Dark* was meant to be a student's guide to Greater Boston's arts and entertainment world. As a "freebie" its distribution soon expanded to other Boston campus locations. In 1970 Stephen Mindich, a Boston University graduate and former art critic and advertising salesman

EXHIBIT 2

THE REAL PAPER, INC.
Balance Sheet
April 26, 1974, and April 27, 1973

Assets	1974	1973
Current assets	$161,812	$88,812
Fixed assets	6,220	2,223
Other assets	7,606	1,407
Total assets.	$175,638	$92,442

Liabilities and Stockholders' Equity	1974	1973
Current liabilities	$ 48,507	$37,320
Stockholders' equity.	127,131	55,122
Total liabilities and stockholders' equity	$175,638	$92,442

for *BAD,* purchased the paper. His early and major innovation was to add politically oriented news to *BAD*'s coverage of arts and entertainment.

The second critical historical event was the founding, in October of 1969, of the *Cambridge Phoenix* by a 26-year-old Vietnam veteran as an "alternative" newspaper for the Boston area. The *Phoenix* statement of purpose indicated that it "was conceived with the discovery that Boston, the intellectual, artistic, and economic center of New England, was a journalistic vacuum." Within a year, the undercapitalized *Phoenix* was bought by Richard Missner, a 26-year-old MBA. Throughout 1970 and 1971, brisk competition developed between the *Phoenix* and *BAD.*

Fusion magazine, commenting on the competitive situation noted:

> Local college students had a twin forum in which to see their revolutionary outrage expressed. . . . Horror stories of government murder and graft ran alongside reviews and advertisements for films and rock performances that created for viewers a fantasy world of glamorous sex and violence. . . . Needless to say, both writers and readers were college educated, white and middle class, reveling in selfrighteousness as they defended people they rarely met, attacking the economic system while enjoying some of

EXHIBIT 3: Cost Breakdown (provided by Howard Garsh)

	Cost	Percent
Printing, composition, trucking, and circulation.	$368,515	37
Salaries—editorial, circulation, art, free-lance editorial (including bonus)	217,147	22
Salaries—sales, accounting, and clerical.	125,613	12
Selling, general, and administrative expenses	212,001	21
Net profit before tax (note: bonus totaled 4%)	74,620	8

the most extravagant luxuries it could provide. Boston's weeklies provided access to the many valuable varieties of this lifestyle, as well as the impression that it was profound.

The *Phoenix*, however, soon began to develop major operating and financial problems. Its financial backer withdrew, and the staff of the *Phoenix* became increasingly disgruntled with Missner, his leadership style, and his vision of what the paper should be. Once, holding up a copy of *The Wall Street Journal*, Missner indicated editorial changes he wanted made.

On May 2, 1972, the *Phoenix* staff agreed to form a union in support of a popular, just-fired editor-in-chief, whom Missner had planned to replace with a former advertising executive. A strike, a series of confrontations, and negotiations ensued. By the end of the month, compromises were effected and the union was officially recognized. Chuck Fager, one of the union leaders and a current member of *The Real Paper* staff, made the following comments on the strike and the effect it had:

> It was really a surprise that we unionized. Sort of WHAM! There it was. People in every department had gripes of their own. . . . So we went out. As a result of the strike, we went through a proletarianization. For instance, we noticed the mailman. Well, he saw our picket signs and he refused to cross the line. Management had to go down to the post office to get their mail. We hadn't seen things from this perspective. . . . But once we were out, our jobs were on the line; we stood to lose everything. . . . But it was fun too. We were working together in a way that we had not worked before—making signs, picketing, and cooking food.

TRP was "born" on July 31, 1972. The *Boston Globe* reported this event as follows:

> On July 27, in a 2:00 P.M. memo, he [Missner] informs all Phoenix staffers to get out by 5 o'clock. The paper, it seems, has been sold to none other than B.A.D.'s Stephen Mindich for a figure Mindich claims to be $320,000. Outraged at Missner's move, they met outside their locked offices and decided to publish their own newspaper by working without pay. It hits the streets on July 31, and it is called The Real Paper. On the same day, the new Boston Phoenix, with a second section called Boston After Dark, appears.[2]

Born into a field of competitive entrepreneurs, yet itself a creature of communal militance, *The Real Paper*'s trials were not yet over. For the first four weeks investors were sought, but to no avail. Chuck Fager said, "The most serious was the *New York Magazine,* but they weren't certain as to how willing we would be to respond to management policy. They were quite right to question that."

Walter Harrison[3] recalled some of the sacrifices of that period:

---

[2] *Boston Globe–Globe Supplement,* June 9, 1974, p. 11.

[3] Assistant to the publisher.

We worked virtually 24 hours a day. The financial sacrifices were great. We all started collecting unemployment compensation. People donated phones and office space. We had meetings virtually every night. For the first two weeks with donations and sales we just broke even.

Then, by the fourth week, having found no backers but having established the viability of their new enterprise, Fager said, "A decision was reached. We had a meeting. Everyone wrote down on little cards what they had to have in order to keep going. Rotner presented a financial statement. And we found that we could cover salaries. Suddenly we had the option of independence, and almost everyone was willing to take it. Why have a backer if you don't need one?"

One hundred shares of stock were issued to each employee in lieu of back pay. Corporate and administrative positions were filled by elections. According to Fager, "We had the equivalent of $50,000 to $100,000 of capital in our momentum, that is, free press coverage, willing advertisers, and hawker and reader willingness to buy."

The early months of the new association were rewarding, if not in a financial, certainly in a communal, sense.

The biggest change, some of the staff members say, has been the new atmosphere. Paul Solman, *The Real Paper*'s editor, says: "Having our paper shot out from under us may have been the best thing that ever happened. Coming over here and starting a new paper and running it ourselves, we've set a real precedent. Before this, 'democracy in the newsroom' has always had the clinker that one guy owns the paper, and you can't really tell the people what to do with their own money. But we've gotten rid of the clinker now."

Joe Klein, another writer, says that there is a greater feeling of participation at the paper by all of its staff. "I've never felt as close to the whole process of something I've worked on. I've never been so interested in the business side of the paper. . . . Everybody talks about how much like a family it is here."[4]

In the intervening year and one half, staff attention was turned to consolidating and expanding *TRP*'s position. Advertisers and readers gained confidence in *The Real Paper* as evidenced by its substantial growth in revenues and circulation. And, as would be expected, operational policies and practices were modified and personnel came and left. In 1974 *The Real Paper* was a well-recognized Cambridge phenomenon.

THE ALTERNATIVE NEWSPAPER INDUSTRY

Various members of its staff characterized *The Real Paper* as an alternative newspaper. Local newspaper columnists had, on occasion, described

---

[4] *Nation,* April 23, 1973, p. 531.

The Real Paper and the *Boston Phoenix* as "underground press" or "counterculture" papers. Some news distributors interviewed referred to them as
"radical sheets" or "sex papers for freaks."

With circulation in the tens of thousands and distribution via hundreds of news outlets, the term "underground" seemed inappropriate to
the researcher. If *The Real Paper* and the *Boston Phoenix* were alternative
papers, alternative to what? What were the key, current developments?
A survey of literature available in libraries and observations by industry
members provided some limited information and insight.

Although the alternatively weekly was often referred to as "a paper,"
the genre suited more a magazine than a newspaper model. It assumed
a readership that obtained its basic news from other sources, such as
daily newspapers, radio, or television. The alternative press typically serviced one or two specialized segments of a larger reader market, for example, a politically liberal or youth subcommunity. Most of the large and
thriving alternative papers were located in large cities or near large college
campuses.

In 1972 the Underground Press Syndicate estimated that there were
300 regularly published underground papers in the United States, with
a combined readership of 20 million. The UPS also estimated that one
in three persons in the 15–30 age bracket were regularly exposed to underground publications.

The model for the alternative newspaper was judged by many observers to be the *Los Angeles Free Press*. That paper, founded in 1964, was
described by the Underground Press Syndicate as:

> . . . in basic ways demonstrably different from all predecessors. First,
> the Los Angeles Free Press was specifically designed for a mass, though
> specialized, audience; second, it was in a format inexpensive to produce,
> simple to learn, yet with high readability, creativity, general appeal and
> possibilities for development and refinement; third, it was economically
> self-supporting and self-spreading—it was successful; fourth, it was both
> hip and radical (the same thing, as we now know); and fifth, it was part
> of a people's movement and remained a part because it was, in general,
> operated in a communistic style.

Paul Solman, editor of *TRP*, commenting on the history of the industry and current trends noted:

> The rise of the underground press in the 1960s was concurrent with
> the rise of "The Movement" in this country. They were not so much busi-
> nesses as they were political organizations. The relative inexpensiveness
> of offset printing enabled these organizations to turn to printed media.
> There was little stability and a great deal of manpower turnover within
> these organizations. Then as The Movement began to wane, these enterprises
> waned. The inheritor of these underground publications is the contemporary
> Alternative Press. It features the same format—offset tabloid—and many

of the same people. But there was a dramatic transition in becoming a stable Alternative Press. This involved a commitment to becoming an ongoing business institution. It meant accepting responsibility, getting away from drug cartoons and sex stuff, avoiding the utter tripe we used to get, and making a transition from being purely political—and using language like "pig" and "Amerikka"—to doing something more than just indulging your political biases.

Change and evolution appeared to be very much a part not only of the alternative but also of the wider newspaper industry scene. That industry was the 10th largest American industry in terms of revenues ($5.5 billion in 1972) and the fifth largest employer (380,500 in 1972). Some 75 percent of that revenue came from advertising—local retail, classified, and national; the latter category appeared to be diminishing somewhat in terms of importance.

Economically the industry had to bear the cost of high capital investment characteristic of many manufacturing operations, as well as the relatively high labor cost of many service organizations. Efforts to improve profits, described as marginal by some investment houses, depended on the newspapers' abilities to deal with distribution problems, antiquated production facilities, and a continuing rise in the cost of newsprint. The latter item has habitually made up 25–30 percent of the revenue dollar. Cost of Canadian newsprint had gone up 20 percent in 1973; and further major increases, as well as shortages, were expected to occur in 1974. Some papers had adopted a strategy of diversification into related communication areas as a "solution" to these problems.

THE REAL PAPER AND THE FREE PAPER

The Real Paper "book," as it was referred to by its staff, was an unstapled and folded collection of newsprint pages, typically 50 to 60 in number, in tabloid format. The front page usually featured *TRP*'s logo as well as a multicolored graphic design, which related to one of the feature articles in that issue. Titles or references to other stories were also highlighted on the front page.

In describing the paper's content, *TRP*'s editorial department distinguished between "the front of the book" and "the back of the book." The front of the book section accounted for the first 20 to 25 pages. It typically included several long feature articles, human-interest articles—for example, an attempt by girls to enter the all-male Boston Little League baseball competition—and a number of shorter news or political items. In addition, there were four regular features: Letters to the Editor; "Short Takes," a news column; a political cartoon; and Burt Solomon's "Cambridge Report," a column covering the political and cultural life of Cambridge.

Paul Solman, the editor, indicated that two to three "compelling" front of the book feature articles were the key to his editorial composition of the paper. A random sampling of some of these articles from the spring of 1974 issues follows: "The Great Commuter Race. Bikes Beat Cars and MBTA by a Wheel"; "TV Guide to Impeachment"; "The Behavior Mod Squad. Clockwork Prisons: Brainwashing Saga Continues"; "A Shopper's Guide to Confession. What You Have to Know to Get the Best Deal on Penance"; "Have You Been Swindled? Nuclear Disaster Strikes Plymouth: A Shocking Scenario for the Future"; "The Death and Resurrection of the Black Panthers"; "The Strange CIA Past of Deputy Mayor Robert Kiley"; and "Prostitutes in Boston." It was evident, from a review of the titles listed on the front cover of these same editions, that feature and news articles ranged from local and national to international topics and touched on a variety of cultural and political topics.

Letters to the Editor made interesting reading in their own right and often created a dialogue between readers and staff that gave continuity to the weekly issues of *TRP*. The letters printed were usually only a fraction of those received. A random survey indicated letters from a variety of well-known personalities (Daniel Ellsberg) to unknown readers—from Boston College and MIT professors to AWOL American soldiers living in Sweden. Most of the letters printed appeared to be from students, or the young in age or spirit living in the metropolitan Boston area. Correspondents' addresses, however, indicated readers in each of the New England states.

The second regular front of the book item, "Short Takes," in the words of its compiler Craig Unger, "tries to get six or seven news items which I think are most interesting, amusing, and politically significant that get the least media play. It has very broad limits ranging from local news to international news. About two thirds to three quarters are of a political nature, and the rest are amusing."

The back of the book section accounted for approximately 60 percent of *TRP*'s pages. It featured a number of regular departments, such as commentary and reviews on theater, cinema, music, and art; and "Local Color" by Henry Armetta, a column about the metropolitan Boston's entertainment field; plus a back page calendar for the upcoming week, which listed events of artistic interest in the Cambridge–Boston area. The staff of *TRP* believes that its coverage of arts and entertainment, particularly the music field, was excellent, and customers interviewed by the researchers tended to support that conclusion.

A substantial section of the back of the book was devoted to listings and classified advertisements. The researcher's random sample of approximately 100 purchasers of *TRP* indicated that the Listings and Classified sections were extremely popular. Listings provided an accurate and thorough calendar of well-known artistic events, as well as information on a host of lesser publicized activities, many of which were available at no or minimum cost. The film rating service gave staff evaluations of each film on a scale of worthless to masterpieces.

The classified pages' popularity was readily understandable to the researcher. They seemed to be an open-door communicating device among the many subgroup cultures in the community. This section had its own language system—the researcher was a WM–24–Stu (can you translate?). The advertisements or notices were a potpourri of every known youth interest or need. There were advertisements for jobs, apartments, and where to get advice about drugs, pregnancy, VD, and low-blood-sugar problems; Personals—"Sarah from Newton—why did you walk out on me?"; leads on where to buy a wide range of products, inquiries for pen pals—often from prisoners; and a variety of travel and educational opportunities were presented (see Exhibit 4).

EXHIBIT 4: Representative Classified Advertisements

WARM, sincere attractive WJM. Pisces, 29, dislikes dating bars and phony people, would like to meet warm, sincere, affectionate, cuddly slightly mesugah WJF 18–30, short and pretty, with long hair, for lasting relationship. Write CF, PO Box _____ Framingham, Mass. 01701

WHITE male 25 Walpole Prisoner wants letters and visits from young woman. I'm 6' tall weigh 160 blond hair blue eyes. *The Real Paper*, Box 749

TALL, dark, and sane. Are you still out there? Sorry didn't get in touch. Please

send phone number or suggest meetings. Let's get it together this time. Patricia, Box 750

I'M a young woman planning to bring former hillside farm in Western Mass. to long lost fullness. Educated, intelligent, willful, crazy, occasionally impossible, but often spontaneous, loving, energetic, able, funny, practical. Smoke insanely and visions a joy to me. Physically attractive, but so what? Want to feel the isness of things but that takes time and living. Want to make a home for friends to visit when in need of

love, slowness, wholeness, rest, healing. Box 728

WM 27 grad student, warm, aware, seeks female to enjoy the intoxication of spring with. I like tennis, books, nature, hiking, beautiful sex, politics, playing guitar. Let's get together. *The Real Paper*, Box 752

ONE well-adjusted woman wanted to share sunny spacious, furnished 2-bedroom apartment in North End for summer. $100/month rent. Please call Joan at _____.

And if the reader wanted new relationships, they came offered in group packages from "encounter" to "philosophic" discussion meetings. If one wanted individual companionship it came in a variety of formats: male–female, male–male, and female–female.

Bob Williams, *TRP*'s advertising manager commented on the importance of the listing and classified sections in an interview with a *Nation* writer.

> The real reasons our paper or *BAD* are essential to the lives of the people who read them are the classified ads and the listings, Around here, people move around a lot, a couple of times a year at least. Things change hands all the time—apartments, stereos, TVs, cars, sex. There has to be a way for the things and the people to get together. Let's face it, Boston is one big party, with 350,000 kids looking for something to do. So the film listings, and the listings in general, are a big selling point. These things are the spine of the paper—the writers give it a competitive edge.[5]

The *Free Paper* edition of *TRP* was similar to *TRP* in most respects. In any given week there were some differences in editorial content because of a post office ruling that price preferences given one reader over another must be accompanied by a minimum 20 percent content difference. The post office also required that a certain percentage of a paper's circulation must be paid to obtain second-class mailing privileges. Circulation of the *Free Paper*, since it was distributed to school living and dining halls, varied with the local student population, dropping during vacation periods.

Supplements to *TRP* and the *Free Paper* were added to the regular editions about once each month. Jeff Albertson, newly assigned supplements editor, felt that the frequency of supplements would increase in the fall of 1974. Supplements were similar to the regular book in format and design. However, each was typically organized around one theme, such as buying guides to high-fidelity equipment, camping equipment, and so forth. Articles on the theme were prepared, and advertisers with a particular interest in that field were sought.

The Metropolitan Boston Competitive Situation

In addition to several dozen weekly suburban newspapers covering their local scenes, three standard daily and two major weekly alternative newspapers were published in Boston. The daily newspapers included the *Christian Science Monitor*, whose masthead declared it to be "An International Daily Newspaper," and whose principal circulation was outside of metropolitan Boston.

The second paper, the *Boston Herald–American*, owned by the Hearst Corporation, was a recent merger of the *Herald-Traveler*, which had circulation strength in the suburbs, and the *Record-American* with "blue-collar" readership in Boston. An industry observer described it as an "independent, conservative, Republican paper. It's probably losing a lot of money.

---

[5] *Nation*, April 23, p. 533.

There is a rumor that Mr. Mindich is considering launching a major Boston daily, contingent upon future plans of the *Boston Herald–American.*"

The *Boston Globe* was the largest of the three standard papers in circulation and was financially the most successful (net income of $3 million on $90 million in revenues in 1972). Local journalists conceded the *Globe*'s competitive aggressiveness, citing its use of specialists covering such topics as urban renewal, mental health, affairs of the elderly, and the women's movement. One observer described the *Globe* as a paper "which serves the liberal educational community well and the City of Boston with less enthusiasm. The *Globe* espouses its liberal causes stridently and rarely hesitates to show a bias in its reporting."

In attempting to gain information about the alternative newspaper competitive situation, the researcher visited a dozen newsstands in the Greater Boston area. Clearly the leaders in this race were *TRP* and the *Boston Phoenix*. But the customer had a variety of papers from which to make a selection, depending upon his or her particular mix of reading interests. Larger newsstands typically carried, at a minimum, three other nonlocal alternative papers: the *Village Voice,* the *Free Press,* and *Rolling Stone.* The *Village Voice* (weekly price 35 cents, 125 pages, over 150,000 circulation) was owned by *New York Magazine;* its masthead stated that it was "The Weekly Newspaper of New York." The *Voice* had an East Coast and national distribution pattern. Its content was focused on a wide range of local New York and national political issues and personalities; it had major, in-depth coverage of art, music, and the theater. As a member of the Audit Bureau of Circulation its advertisers included prominent local and national firms.

The *Los Angeles Free Press* (weekly, 35 cents, about 40 pages, circulation 150,000) also had achieved regional and national distribution. Its coverage included politics, the arts, and a 20-page classified "sex" insert—literally a cornucopia of erotica. In contrast to the more academic style of the *Voice* (an interview with three African female jurists and an analysis of Shakespearean theater), the *Freep*'s editorial style seemed to the researcher to be sensational and its word system and headlines were strident in character.

The *Rolling Stone*'s (biweekly, 75 cents, over 100 pages, circulation 300,000) content was heavily built around popular music and the entertainment world, with some political coverage, for example, an interview with Jane Fonda on her latest visit to North Vietnam. While both the *Voice* and *Rolling Stone* carried classified advertisements, these tended to down play sex themes and products.

A Boston newsdealer mentioned the *Texas Monthly* as a prototype of recent entries in the field. *Newsweek* magazine reported that it sold for $1, "has taken provocative looks at the inner workings of the state's highway lobby, banks, law firms and daily newspapers, dismissing the latter as strikingly weak and ineffectual.' The *Texas Monthly* received the prestigious 1974 National Magazine Award for Specialized Journalism."[6] "*Ramparts,* of course," the newsdealer said, "has been around a long time, and there are a batch of others of the same cast."

In metropolitan Boston, *TRP*'s primary competitor was the *Boston Pheonix.* Both papers were similar in format and price, both were published weekly, both used the same distribution methods—although with different emphasis—and both had free school editions.

Differences were also apparent to the researcher. The *Phoenix* was a larger book—often over 80 pages compared with *TRP*'s 50- to 60-page editions. The larger *Phoenix* was divided into two distinct subparts: the *Phoenix* and its insert, *Boston After Dark*—the Arts and Entertainment section. The *Phoenix* enjoyed a larger circulation; industry estimates ranged from 80,000 to 110,000, with approximately 40,000 being the free edition. The *Phoenix* appeared to the researcher to enjoy a wider range of local and national advertisers than did *TRP*. In terms of visual appearance, the *Phoenix* appeared to be more crowded and less willing to use open space to lead the reader's eye around a page than did *TRP*.

The researcher wanted to obtain data on why a customer purchased *TRP* versus the *Phoenix* and what was the market for these two papers. A random survey of purchasers by the researcher obtained limited information. Most could not make explicit their preference for one paper over the other. *TRP* customers often mentioned "better Cambridge coverage," "more liberal," "easier to read," while *Phoenix* purchasers stressed "red hot classifieds" and "*BAD* is the best guide" (see Exhibit 5).

In reviewing this competitive situation between *The Real Paper* and the *Phoenix,* a *Boston Globe* writer commented:

> The two papers continue in the image of advocacy journalism planted firmly left of center and sprinkled with occasional muckraking. But while in days past they overlapped on stories, they almost never do today. In fact, except for arts coverage—particularly music—you can browse through two issues of the same week and not see two pieces about the same thing. What you will find is that the *Phoenix,* reflecting its publisher's little-subdued dream to become a force in the community, concerns itself more with the news of the day, dealing with many of the same subjects and events as the city's dailies. "We've made a shift to respond to news happenings," says Miller. "We want to be topical." *The Real Paper,* on the other hand, seems to be moving more and more towards becoming a weekly magazine, opting for stylized features and columns rather than news reporting. Part of the reason for this is undoubtedly *The Real Paper*'s constituency, which is more Cambridge-oriented than that of the *Phoenix.* . . .[7]

What was the market for the two publications? Bob Williams, advertising manager for *TRP*, gave one specific definition.

---

[6] *Newsweek,* June 17, 1974, p. 29.

[7] *Boston Globe–Sunday Supplement,* June 9, 1974, p. 7.

EXHIBIT 5: Comparison of Article Content of *The Real Paper* versus the *Boston Phoenix*

	The Real Paper		Boston Phoenix	
Category	Number of Articles	Percent	Number of Articles	Percent
International events or politics. . . .	2	1.7	5	2.8
Art, movies, books, TV, dance	32	26.7	59	33.0
Exposés	5	4.2	1	0.5
Rock music, other types of music, album review columns	15	12.5	32	17.9
Local events/politics	21	17.5	34	19.0
Counterculture, e.g., communes, drugs .	1	0.8	2	1.1
National events/politics	9	7.5	20	11.2
Movements, including prison reform, women's, gay	9	7.5	4	2.3
Sports	2	1.7	14	7.8
Miscellaneous, including food, "local color," travel, tax information	24	20.0	8	4.5
Totals	120	100.1	179	100.1

Source: These data were prepared by Kim Panushka of *TRP* staff. She surveyed eight issues of each paper for the months of March and April 1974. The total number of major feature articles for TRP was 120; for the *Boston Phoenix*, 179. Excluded were regular columns from staff writers.

In Boston you have 350,000 young people, under 30, within 2.5 square miles of space. You don't find a concentration like that anywhere in the country except Boston. It's a unique market. These kids spend around $40 million or $50 million a year.[8]

Dennis Hale, staff writer for the *Nation* magazine, gave a more general comment.

So the New Journalism is not so much "new" as it is specific in its choice of audience. For the most part that audience consists of young, white, relatively affluent college students, graduates and dropouts. Like newspaper readers everywhere, these people have a set of opinions, of whose truth they are fairly certain, and they do not enjoy seeing these opinions challenged in print. At least, not too often. And the editors of "underground" and "alternative" papers are as sensitive as editors everywhere to the outer limits of their readers' tolerance.

Over a period of months, the researcher observed *TRP*'s operations and interviewed a substantial number of its staff. Early in his research, he studied the production process, the financial and accounting systems, the circulation department, and the advertising sales activity. As the research progressed he then worked with the editorial area. A summary of this information follows.

---

[8] "Prospects for the Alternative Press," *Nation*, April 23, 1973, p. 533.

Production

Getting the "book" out each week was a central activity at *TRP.* As in any daily or weekly publishing operation, this activity was characterized by speed, deadlines, coordination of a host of detail and people, and the ever-present last-minute changes.

The production of *TRP* basically involved the laying out and printing of five types of copy within the time constraint of weekly publication and the size constraint of how large a paper could be profitably published. This process could be summarized around six stages of production.

First, the various "copy traffic controllers" accumulated the five kinds of copy: editorial, advertising, art, classified, and listings. Each controller determined the space required for his or her copy and relayed that information to the layout editor.

Second, on Thursday, as the accumulation of copy was drawing to a close, the comptroller, managing editor, and advertising sales director met to determine the number of pages in the book. The comptroller would project the week's profit and loss statement under varying assumptions about advertising, density, and number of pages in the book.

Third, the layout editor was informed as to the number of pages to be published as well as about additions or deletions to copy. He then proceeded to allocate sections of each page of the book to various kinds of copy. This involved the use of a "paste-up board," a full-scale representation of a page.

Fourth, the paste-up boards were transferred to the composition shop. Here copy, which had been typed in even columns, was physically pasted onto the paste-up boards, which were photographed and the resulting negatives developed. These negatives, along with the negatives of copy photographs—called "halftones"—were combined by taping them together.

Fifth, the final negatives were taken to the printing plant where printing plates were made and the paper was printed on a web offset press. It took about three hours to print an edition of 50,000 papers.

Sixth, on Saturday morning the newsstand distributors picked up papers from the printing plant for distribution to newsstands on Sunday. The hawker edition was distributed at 5:30 A.M. Monday mornings to hawkers. Subscription copies were addressed and mailed on Saturday for delivery to the post office on Monday.

Production of the *Free Paper* followed on Monday, when editorial people altered the layout boards and changed the front page design to conform to the required 20 percent content different regulation. The paper was printed that same day and delivered to college campuses on Tuesday.

Neither composition nor printing facilities were owned by *TRP,* and that work was subcontracted to local, independent firms. "Both of those operations would require substantial capital investments in equipment," Howard Garsh explained.

Control

The comptroller's office consisted of two people, Howard Garsh, the comptroller, and Stanley Korytko, the bookkeeper.

One day, while walking into 10–B Mt. Auburn with the researcher, Howard said, "I don't see how you can do this study without some reference to the figures. Let's talk for a few minutes." The researcher and Garsh walked upstairs, through a small office, and into a connecting closet that served as Garsh's "cubbyhole," as offices were referred to at *TRP*. Garsh proceeded to search for papers in his files and in the clutter on his desk.

> A lot of what I do here deals with keeping track of the company's financial status, either projected or actual. Accordingly, there are several tools I use, the weekly P&L projection according to various book size assumptions, the monthly profit and loss statement, and the semiannual cash and operating budget projections. These budgets tend to be conservative, pessimistic, and possibly just a little extreme. That is, we overestimate expenses and underestimate income just so we don't get cocky and overextend ourselves.
>
> Our auditor says he's never seen such beautiful papers. That's partly because we don't just make broad assumptions of percentage increases but instead get down to the real arithmetic of it. For instance, the budget is based on Bob Williams' projection of revenue from display advertising since that's the source of about 80 percent of our revenue.[9] We ask for the most reasonable, honest estimate that doesn't pull the figures out of the air. He talks to the salespeople, looks at the economy, and maybe talks to some advertisers. And his estimate is usually conservative, as you can see from this [see accompanying table]. Remember, his projections were made one year ago.

1974	Budgeted	Billed
April 5*	$12,000	$14,500
April 12	12,000	12,500
April 19*	12,000	14,000
April 26	12,000	15,000

* Including a $2,000 ad insert.

Our bread and butter is accounts receivable. We stay right on top of them. Our credit allowances are 30 days net. And we allocate 4 percent

---

[9] Regular advertisements from commercial customers, as opposed to classified advertising, for example, notices of apartments for rent.

of revenue to bad debt, although experience shows that 1 percent is sufficient.

And we have virtually no accounts payable. Other than salaries, our
major expenses are printing, composition, subscriber service, mailing, trucking, and editorial free-lance payments. We've never been in a position to
keep any of them waiting. Certainly every account is paid within 30 days.
There are reasons for this: first, we want a top Dun & Bradstreet rating,
a reputation of being a good company to do business with, a company
that pays its bills. Right now our D&B rating is two. D&B told us that
all it would take to get a number one is for us to be in business a little
longer. Second, we have the money so why not pay it; so we try to help
them out by paying on the spot.

The main reason why you'll find differences between actual and projected is in the economics of each week's book, that is, the number of
pages and ad density. In order to consider those very issues in our weekly
business planning, I project the weekly P&L based on assumptions about
number of pages and ad density. We like to see about a $2,000 profit and
not more than 55 percent ad density. Within those parameters we come
to a decision about the number of pages in the book and transmit that
decision to the layout editor who plans the book accordingly.

The economics of our operation greatly affect our performance. For
instance, profitability increases very rapidly with an increase in ad density.
As past weekly projections have shown, most of our costs are fixed, for
example, mailing, trucking, sales expense, art expense. The only variable
costs we have are composition, which really varies only slightly, and editorial
free-lance, which varies because nonstaff articles are used as editorial copy
if we opt for a larger book. Printing costs, which increase by about $1,500
for every eight-page increase we make, and salespeople's commissions (10
percent of collections), which vary with billing but not by size of paper.

For instance, assuming a 56-page paper is average, we will probably
spend a total of $20,000, most of which will be on fixed type costs. Typically
we will get $2,800 from circulation revenue and $3,000 from classified advertising, and that means we'd need about $14,000 from display advertising
to break even. Usually the salespeople can bring in some last-minute advertising if we think we're running low. But there's a danger in thinking you
can cram a lot of advertising into a book, because too much doesn't look
good. So it can cause a problem: At what ad density do you decide you
have to increase the size of the paper? And is increasing the size of the
paper economically profitable? Anything over that $14,000 is gravy until
we have to increase the book size. And increases come only in jumps of
eight pages. Because each jump costs about $1,500, only one full page of
ads (worth about $640) never justifies a book increase of eight pages. But
what is the cutoff? I don't know.

The special supplements are pure gravy. The profit margin varies
between 20 percent and 50 percent because the regular kinds of expenses
are charged against the regular edition, and so that supplement must only
cover its incidental printing, composition, editorial free-lance, artwork, and
mailing expenses.

Garsh's responsibilities also included relationships with the First National Bank of Boston. That bank, since *TRP*'s founding, had financed all major capital needs of the organization.

Circulation Department

Kevin Dawkins, who had joined *TRP* in January of 1973, had just been put in charge of circulation activities.

TRP was distributed through four channels: newsstands, hawkers, subscription, and controlled circulation—that is, free distribution. The percentage breakdown of distribution channels in 1974 was newsstands 30 percent; hawkers, 14 percent; subscription, 4 percent; and controlled, 52 percent. In 1972, Kevin pointed out, the newsstand and hawker percentages had been reversed with hawkers selling over 30 percent and newsstands roughly 15 percent of *TRP* circulation.

Controlled circulation of the *Free Paper* goes to "every conceivable college from here to Worcester, Mass." A formula of one copy per four students was used, and never were more than 50,000 copies distributed. Dawkins commented, "It's gravy. It boosts our circulation which entitles us to boost our advertising rates. Besides, the audience is captive. This edition builds reading habits which can extend to higher newsstand sales. In college towns, though, if we miss delivery to the school for some reason, newsstand sales stay about the same. Sometimes I think the markets are separate."

As for newsstand circulation, two thirds occurred within Route 128 (metropolitan Boston) and one third beyond. *TRP* worked through one distributor, Greater Boston Distributors, Inc., within the Route 128 area. Greater Boston had over 800 outlets including the Union News outlets in subways, railroad stations, and Logan Airport.

TRP was sold at 75 percent of these newsstands. Money was paid only for copies sold. The price to the distributor was 12 cents; the distributor sold it to the independent newsstand operators for 19 cents, and the newsstand price was 25 cents. Greater Boston handled between 1,500 and 2,000 titles, among which were the most profitable in the country. Dawkins felt that *TRP* should be at more newsstands and be featured more prominently.

Newsstand relationships beyond Route 128 were handled through independent distributors. The newsstand circulation area extended as far to the west as Holyoke–Springfield, Massachusetts, as far east as Portland, Maine, and as far south as Providence, Rhode Island. The objective here was to penetrate outlying markets by first reaching college communities and communal areas.

Hawker relationships were one of Kevin's responsibilities. Hawkers were independent operators who bought a paper for 5 cents and sold it for 25 cents on busy street corners throughout Greater Boston.

> In 1970, 200 hawkers used to sell almost 40,000 copies of the *Old Cambridge Phoenix;* now we have 100 hawkers selling 15,000 copies of *TRP.* We used to have 75 hawkers in Boston alone—now there are only 45. There is a very high turnover here, but we have a hard core of about 50 old-timers.
>
> The papers are trucked to a number of distribution points in Boston and Cambridge. The hawkers buy the papers for cash, but if someone is in a rough way we will front him or her for 10 or 20 copies. They can turn unsold copies in the next week for new papers. All hawkers sell both our paper and the *Phoenix.*
>
> The typical hawker is the kind of person you would see at a rock and roll concert—long hair, T-shirt, blue jeans, and sandals. They are street people, and they keep us anchored to that community.
>
> They do pretty well. Richie on the Boston University Bridge must make $80 from *TRP* and the same from the *Phoenix* in a couple of days. Other hawkers can make $100 in two days, and some people living in a group setup can clear $25–$30 in two days, and they can live on that.
>
> And they have their codes too: the oldest one in seniority gets to take the best corner, although the old-timers have the territory well staked out. We don't even know some of their real names. One of them calls himself King Kong. They don't want to have any tax records.
>
> I'm trying to push hawker sales. We are advertising in *TRP,* and I'm preparing posters to put up around the city. Hawkers are great publicity for us, standing at each street corner and practically putting the paper through your car window. Everyone can see that front page, whereas on the newsstands we are buried. I'm trying to extend hawking to the suburbs by promoting hawking through guidance counselors.
>
> They are street people—that community is important to us. And I don't think the *Phoenix* really wants to use them; they aren't sophisticated enough. The *Phoenix,* you know, has hired two former *Herald–American* pros for their circulation department.

Subscriptions had been an increasingly expensive channel of distribution to service. The paper was physically distributed by Hub Mail, Inc. The cost per paper per subscription was about 22 cents, making it the least economic of all channels. Since the mailing service refuses to operate on weekends, a mailed paper arrives at its earliest on Tuesday, whereas *TRP* was delivered to newsstands on Sundays. The one redeeming feature about subscription sales, Kevin noted, was that *TRP* gets "the money up front." Kevin intended to eliminate the discount that subscribers get by subscribing (raising the price from $10 to $13 per year) in an attempt to cover cost increases, and he hoped to negotiate a new mailing agreement which would have the paper in the mail on Saturday and delivered by Monday.

Kevin had growth in *TRP* circulation as one of his primary goals.

He was assisted in this program by a "road man" who visited newsstand owners to "sell" them on the advantages of carrying *TRP*.

> We are one of Greater Boston's top ten best selling accounts. They formerly had sort of a monopoly and weren't aggressive. Terrible things happen to people when they have power. But they are getting competition now and that helps us. We are considering selling papers via machines located in grocery stores.
>
> Our toughest competition is the *Phoenix*. They are supposed to have 110,000 circulation, and their revenues are twice ours—they up their ad density and charge higher advertising rates than we do. But we will catch up with them! Within one year we will be bigger! I get excited about this! Walter Harrison (the former circulation director) has suggested to me that we experiment with a home delivery system.

In the spring of 1974 Bob Williams began to advocate broadcast media promotion as a means of building *TRP*'s visibility and consumer demand. Except for development costs, it was anticipated that the program would operate largely through reciprocal advertising, with commercial radio and television broadcasters.

Kevin concluded:

> I want us to get recognition; we put out the best paper in the country, and I know because I am in touch with lots of them. Our problem is we just aren't taken as seriously as we should be. We want to be an important part of the Cambridge–Boston community in the near future. We want people to use *TRP* as more than just reading material. We want to serve as "the reference" for what goes on here. We want it to be an important part of their lives.

Advertising Sales Department

The advertising sales department was concerned with selling display and classified advertising, and comprised five display salespeople, one classified salesperson, Linda Martin (the advertising traffic controller), and Bob Williams, the department director. Advertising sales accounted for approximately 80 percent of the revenue of *TRP*.

Talking about *TRP*'s advertising market, Williams said:

> There are basically two levels of advertisers we're concerned with. The first group is people who have clubs, restaurants, concert tours, Army-Navy stores, clothing, bookstores, record stores—all the people who sell mainly to college students. These people came in right away. They really had to. They need papers like ours as much as we need them. The second level is the larger companies—GM, stereo companies, Jordan Marsh, and the other big clothing stores, which don't have an immediate relation between advertising money spent and dollars earned. With these people, it's only a matter of time.[10]

---

[10] *Nation,* April 23, 1973, p. 533.

There was no formal system of account assignment, since Williams believed that a strict delineation of "turf" was not healthy. Nevertheless, each salesperson seemed to have specialized in one way or another. For example, one salesman, Steve Cummings, concentrated in cameras, symphony, sex, and religion, for example, Boston Symphony Orchestra, adult bookstores, Indian gurus, and meditation movements. The four most important industries for advertising revenue were stereo components, liquor, phonograph records, and cameras.

The approach each salesperson used was individualized. Price bargaining was allowed which "makes selling tougher," Bob commented. "Otherwise, it is just stating standard rates." A sense of flexibility, of tailoring to the advertiser's needs, seemed to the researcher to be a dominant theme in the advertising efforts of *TRP*. In two instances, the researcher observed that Williams was willing to bend contractual agreements or trade advertising for the specific products of the business. "It's those little guys we've got to help. They're where our future lies." *TRP*'s advertisers were primarily Boston firms, but about 15 percent of display advertisements were placed by national firms.

It seemed to Bob Williams that the *TRP* advertising staff sold access to a special kind of consumer—a youthful, liberal, student market. But "hard" and reliable data were limited. A 1974 company-financed survey of approximately 300 purchasers of *TRP* (*Free Paper* customers were not canvassed) provided the following profile: average age, 23.7; sex, 55 percent male and 45 percent female; 87 percent had some college education and 47 percent were college graduates; 24 percent were professional-technical personnel; 23 percent, full-time students; 12 percent, unemployed; 11 percent, clerical; 10 percent, blue collar; 5 percent, sales; 4 percent, managerial; 1 percent, housewives; and 10 percent, miscellaneous. Thirty-six percent of the papers were sold in Boston, 32 percent in Cambridge, 5 percent in Brookline, 3 percent in Newton, 3 percent in Somerville, and the remainder scattered in other Boston suburbs.

TRP's advertising charges were geared to its circulation rate base of 90,000 copies per week. Rates for display advertisements were $14 per column inch, or $1,120 for a full page. Discounts were given for continuity of placement: 13 weeks, 10 percent; 26 weeks, 15 percent; and 52 weeks, 20 percent. Classified advertisements were $1.90 per line.

> In terms of rates we want to get between $11.00 and $11.50 per thousand readers and stay about 50 cents per thousand under the *Phoenix*. The more specialized your market is, the higher you can charge. Publications get $2 to $3 per thousand for a very general audience, to $5 to $6 for a somewhat specialized audience, up to $30 to $40 for a very specialized group.
>
> We don't cut out stated rates in the summer even though with school vacations, our free circulation drops, but we do make deals. Many of our advertisers are on yearly contract [a total of two thirds of *TRP* advertisers

were on some kind of contractual basis]—they get more power in the fall and winter than in the summer, but it balances out. In this business, one half your customers don't even know what your circulation is; they are only interested in how much response the advertisement gets, and we have a very loyal readership.

With free copies, we don't go above 52 percent at the top; Bob Rotner makes that decision. Free circulation is good, but it makes things a bit more fluffy—particularly for ABC[11] counts. It makes it harder for you to really prove your circulation.

Some of the problems Williams noted were the business community's lack of respect for *TRP* and the staff's prohibition of certain kinds of advertising. With regard to the former, Williams noted that some advertisers regularly abuse credit terms and said, "People don't respect us the first time around. They think we're just a weak underground paper. Meanwhile, the staff prohibits cigarette advertising because it felt that it was detrimental to the paper's image, but that means a loss of revenue."

As for the future, Williams doubted that *TRP* should follow the *Phoenix* to pursue suburban advertisers. He noted that the *Phoenix* was his roughest competition.

I don't think the future is necessarily there. There is a 50 percent bad-debt ratio on advertising beyond Route 128,[12] mostly motorcycle places, bars, and so on. The people who read *TRP* and shop are here in town. We sell our circulation and a kind of readership. It would be foolish not to exploit it here. The *Phoenix* is entering the suburbs and doesn't have the circulation to back it up. That will hurt alternative weeklies in general. Furthermore we're still thrashing around editorially. It would have been unwise to move until we get that straightened out. Finally, we are best sold to small and medium-sized businesses, and they are most concentrated here in town.

The trick is to get local advertisers to transfer ad money from radio to print and more particularly, *TRP*. There are about 50 stations in this area, and ten of them program directly for the youth market. We do some reciprocal advertising with them now.

I love music and have a hi-fit set. The reality of Boston is that there is an important radio market here. If the company were interested, and it isn't, we could go into partnership with one of these stations. It would provide a great new combination for us. Bob Rotner once thought we should go into the newsstand distribution business.

By 1975–76, if my plans work out, we should be in a position to enter the suburbs. I am shooting for advertising sales this year of $1.5 million.

---

[11] Audit Bureau of Circulation, an agency which attested to the circulation figures of newspapers and magazines.

[12] A belt highway, approximately 12 miles west of the central city. Route 128 tended to be a dividing line between the more developed suburbs of Boston and the less developed, higher status suburbs of the city.

Editorial

Editorial offices were located on the second floor at 10–B Mt. Auburn Street. The physical layout consisted of a main room (about one fourth the size of the first floor) and two closet-size offices at the far end; one of the latter also served as a hallway to the back porch. Paul Solman (editor) and Tom Friedman (managing editor) were technically assigned this space, but all members of the department seemed to participate in its use. Jeff Albertson's (the associate publisher) desk was next to Tom's office.

The main room contained five desks, two tables, filing cabinets, and all of the usual paraphernalia of an editorial operation. A chair, with one of its casters off, occupied the center of the room. "We bought all of this equipment secondhand," Paula Childs noted."We sure scrimp around here. Howard buys us discard, advertising promotion pencils but no pens. But we are getting more space in the basement here—that should help a lot."

The researcher agreed that space was needed. Even in a summer lull period, editorial personnel flowed in and out and often there were not enough available desks and chairs. The room had a used and non-cleaned look with papers on the floor and boxes of editorial supplies stacked in every conceivable place. A number of bulletin boards seemed to be a part of the communication system, telling Peter to get a photo at 10:30 and noting that a free-lance writer wanted his check right away— "He is flat broke." Office decor consisted of wall-sized pictures of Katherine Hepburn *et al.*, and advertisements for concerts and artistic events; a somewhat tired and dehydrated plant provided the final touch.

The researcher sought to capture the office tone. Clearly busyness was the order of the day, with editorial personnel constantly using the multiple phones and the limited desk space. Friendliness was another factor. Martha, the receptionist, seemed unflappable despite the constant barrage of questions and calls with which she was confronted. There was an air of informality. Standard dress seemed to be T-shirts, shorts, and sandals; it made the first floor look almost "Establishment."

Editorial proved to be a complex part of *TRP*'s scene to "paint" for the reader. After several abortive attempts the researcher finally decided to look first at "who was in the area and what did they do," next at the "organization and leadership of the work," and finally at *TRP*'s "editorial posture."

TRP's masthead (July) carried the names of 54 individuals, 32 of whom were listed under "Editorial." (See Exhibit 6.) Of those names, Paul Solman commented, "14 are full-time personnel, 8 are part-time members who regularly contribute, and 10 are free-lance or irregular contributors to the book."

The editorial staff tended to specialize by function. On the "support"

EXHIBIT 6: Masthead, July 17, 1974

Real Paper

EDITORIAL
PAUL SOLMAN, EDITOR
TOM FRIEDMAN, MANAGING EDITOR
HENRY ARMETTA
HARPER BARNES
BO BURLINGHAM
STUART BYRON
PAULA CHILDS
STEPHEN DAVIS
CHUCK FAGER
JAN FREEMAN
ARTHUR FRIEDMAN
RUSSELL GERSTEN
ANITA HARRIS
JOE HUNT
JAMES ISAACS
JOE KLEIN, NEWS EDITOR
ANDREW KOPKIND
CHUCK KRAEMER
JON LANDAU
KAY LARSON
JON LIPSKY
DAVE MARSH
JIM MILLER
LILITH MOON
ARNIE REISMAN
LAURA SHAPIRO
BURT SOLOMON
PETER SOUTHWICK, PHOTOGRAPHER
CRAIG UNGER
BRUCE WEINBERG, PRODUCTION
DAVID OMAR WHITE
ED ZUCKERMAN

ADVERTISING
ROBERT WILLIAMS, DIRECTOR
JONATHAN BANNER
STEVE CUMMINGS
MIKE FORMAN
LINDA MARTIN
DONALD MONACK
ELLEN PAUL
RICHARD REITMAN
DICK YOUSOUFIAN

ART
RONN CAMPISI, DIRECTOR
DAVID BROWN
PAT MEARS
REBECCA WELZ

CIRCULATION
KEVIN DAWKINS, DIRECTOR
DON CUMMINGS
CYNDI ROBBINS
MIKE ZEGEL

BUSINESS
HOWARD GARSH, COMPTROLLER
STANLEY KORYTKO
WALTER HARRISON, ASST. TO THE
PUBLISHER
JEFF ALBERTSON, ASSOC. PUBLISHER
ROBERT ROTNER, PUBLISHER

Metropolitan Boston's Weekly Journal of News, Opinion and the
Arts. Address all correspondence to the Real Paper, 10B Mt
Auburn St. Cambridge, Mass 02138 Telephones Editorial and
Art 492-8101, Advertising, Circulation and Business 492-1650
Second-class postage paid at Boston, Mass. Published weekly by
The Real Paper 10B Mt Auburn St. Cambridge Mass 02138
  Copyright © 1974 by The Real Paper All rights reserved
Reproduction by any method whatsoever without permission of
staff is prohibited
  Unsolicited manuscripts should be addressed to Jan Freeman
and must be accompanied by stamped self-addressed envelope
Photographs should be submitted to Jeff Albertson, Photo Editor
  Subscription rates 1 year $10.00, 2 years $18.00

Printing by Arlington Offset

JULY 17, 1974   Vol. 3, No. 29

side, Paul and Tom were assisted by Jan Freeman (copy editor) and Paula Childs (listings and general editorial person), and general assistance to the entire group was given by Peter Southwick (photos) and recently "on board" Bruce Weinberg (production manager).

On the "creative" side the situation was more complicated since most staffers handled multiple assignments. The largest number worked primarily on "back of the book" material—the arts and entertainment section and, in addition, contributed regular columns used throughout the entire paper. The smallest number of full-time masthead personnel were involved with the development of feature stories. "When we came over from the *Phoenix* we had six full-time feature writers," Paul said. "Until recently we had four, but Joe Klein just left to go with *Rolling Stone* at twice what we could pay, and Ed Zuckerman is going back to journalism school. We need to hire another two writers; we're short-handed."

In addition to back of the book and feature writers there were a number of individuals (often part-timers) who specialized in writing a political or news column or, as in the case of Omar White, created a political cartoon. In addition to masthead personnel, there was a pool of free-lance writers who, on occasion, submitted articles to *TRP*. Boston seemed to attract a large number of writers, many of whom could not find, or did not want, a regular organizational relationship.

The editorial group was responsible for the creation and processing of copy with copy coming from staff columnists, staff feature writers, solicited manuscripts from free-lancers, and unsolicited manuscripts. This editorial activity, Tom commented, was organized along the back and front of the book lines.

> Jim Miller is our music editor, and Stuart Byron is our film editor. They, along with Art Friedman, our regular theater columnist, and Kay Larson, our art columnist, hand me back of the book material each week. The back of the book tends to run itself, but Paul is looking for a back of the book editor. Both of us are front of the book oriented, and a good deal more of the budget goes into the front than the back of the book.

All staff members, with whom the researcher spoke, indicated that Paul was the central person in the process of generating or reviewing story concepts, interesting and assigning writers to develop those stories, and finally nurturing and reviewing the resultant manuscript as it evolved. It seemed to the researcher that this was an extremely personal and intuitive process, difficult for all involved to articulate and yet critical for *TRP*'s success.

At a regular Friday morning meeting the editorial staffers gathered with Paul in an informal session to review the copy program. Story ideas were reviewed, modified, or discarded in a free-flowing meeting with staffers sitting on the floor and Paul, his chair tilted against the wall, leading the discussion.

Paul's primary operating pattern, however, seemed to be on an individual-to-individual basis. He often began the process of copy creation by talking with a writer about an idea. "At any given time I expect I am working on 50 story ideas of which 5 may actually come to print. I work at home two days a week because I can concentrate better there and handle the writers more effectively by telephone."

The researcher appreciated the latter comment since Paul's office routine could be described as frenetic. He was constantly on the phone, answering questions, reviewing edit problems with Tom, or working with a writer. Paul's informal style and personal warmth made it easy for all to approach him; and he seemed always to be "in conference" outside the office building, on the stairs, or even walking through the office. "When do you get time to reflect?" the researcher asked. Paul smiled, "It's tough."

With full-time, front of the book personnel, Paul's primary function seemed to be reviewing story ideas that they brought to him. With part-time and free-lance writers, Paul seemed to play a more active role in initiating concepts, but he also reviewed their suggestions and manuscripts. He had a wide acquaintanceship in the Boston community and seemed to the researcher to have knowledge about and interest in a wide range of topics and institutions.

> I handle all of the free-lance work. It is a shifting group of people. Some work for other outfits, some are teachers, some have a cause, most need money—it's hard to make a living free-lancing. We pay them $75 for a short thousand-word story, $250 for a feature article or part thereof. Once in the judge and court system story, where a lot of research work was needed, we paid $600. But we negotiate with each; the budget puts on real limits.

Jan Freeman in commenting on copy development said:

> Paul's job is to think up ideas and then assign them to either regular or free-lance writers, although usually the regular staff generates their own ideas. It is a very difficult job, and I suspect the ratio of ideas to finished stories is about 15 to 1. The process depends a lot upon who is available and whether or not they are interested.
>
> A lot of what Paul wants to do this fall is to make the paper more useful. Tom would probably want more news stories of a political bent. Everyone's ideal would be to do more apartment rental agency stories. Did you read that? They are a real rip-off and take money under false circumstances. We did a lot of research on them. It was both an exposé and a news story.
>
> I want us to do more stories like that or the one in this week's issue on airline safety—more consumer-oriented pieces—but they take lots of time. We should do more local investigatives, like the article on the coroner's

office in Boston's City Hall. We should do stories that make a real difference—a protest that demands a response.

And we need more middle of the book material—material between
the arts and listings and the political and news and feature stories at the
front. We need think pieces, like the story in the *New York Times Magazine*
section. A woman in an apartment house was robbed—bound and gagged.
What was it like? What were her fears? Did she behave bravely enough?
This was a special story, and a woman wrote it from a woman's point of
view. We need more material on ideas and people. I suggested to Paul
that we do an article on people living together—roommates or lovers—or
whatever. It should be funny and yet factual. These aren't news stories—
they are people and idea combinations. And we should do more on scientists
and science articles—the article in the *New York Times* on "black holes" in
space is a good example.

Tom, who had joined *TRP* in November of 1973, had as his prime
objective introducing more organization into the editorial process. He
felt progress had been made in this area, and by July, lead feature articles
had been planned and were in process for the next five months.

It was in my own self-interest to get some planning going—things
were frantic here when I first came. I wish we had more full-time feature
writers; we need at least three now. It would make my job easier. You
get to know the regulars and how to work with them; they have to produce.
But it isn't as cost effective. People don't have story ideas regularly every
week, and so there are bound to be slow times when we won't get stories.

Both Paul and Tom spoke highly of the caliber of *TRP*'s editorial
staff, and conversations with other Boston journalists confirmed that evaluation. Some staffers had achieved awards, national publicity, and peer
recognition from the wider journalistic field.

In trying to pin down *TRP*'s current editorial style and format, the
researcher talked with various members of the staff. Tom Friedman reflected, "Partially it's form—longer paragraphs and in-depth analysis. Partially it's an emphasis on the human dimension. We just don't feed them
information; we create an ambience whereby the reader can relate to
the event. We give them more than historical background, we give them
more than information—we get to the basic reasons."

Joe Klein, who had received several journalist awards, contrasted
TRP's and the *Phoenix*'s editorial style.

Our style strives for both a sense of immediacy and perspective. Our
copy is written more dramatically. We're also much more careful. We want
to write the definitive story on the subject. Paul and I talk it out and
decide what the story should be; it has to have a larger focus than just
what happened last week; we take specific incidents and show how they
reflect on institutions. I don't see that happening with any other publication
in town.

Paul Solman commented:

> Our major articles, in contrast to the *Phoenix,* are long—we do in-depth reporting. Our feature article on selling the Encyclopaedia Britannica was a good example. The writer actually sold Britannicas. We want to be able to help people see why they behave as they do. Why does a blue collar making $14,000 spend 800 bucks on a set of encyclopaedias? Or our article on the hearing aid racket is another good example. We want to be at the cutting edge—what is really going on in that business. We want to answer questions. We want the truth. But the budget limits us; we are small, and they are larger. We can't compete with them in terms of coverage.
>
> The development of a pool of feature article ideas is fairly random. A lot depends on what I read or hear from friends. We get lots of suggestions from people outside the staff. And one of my critical inputs is to gather staff who can contribute ideas. I have a sense of balance for the makeup of the paper, but I don't have a specific formula for a certain amount of political, or human interest, or exposé material in any issue or any month.

Chuck Fager, one of the original staffers, reflected, "We have an ephemeral editorial policy now. Writers just stream in and out. The *Phoenix* does a better job of covering Boston and the State House than we do. But any differences between the *Phoenix* and us now is more individual writer style than editorial strategy."

An Evolving Editorial Posture

In the summer of 1974 the researcher noted, the topic of future editorial direction was the object of considerable discussion, not only within the editorial staff but within the paper at large. Paula Childs commented:

> We're not covering events enough—issues that deal with people's daily lives. We're not covering what's happening with rent control, what's happening in the ecology movement, what's happening in the neighbor-hoods—that kind of stuff. Also, I think we're too Cambridge oriented. Our strongest following is Cambridge. We cover Cambridge things to a much greater extent than Boston. And I think that that's one of the reasons why people on the other side of the river continue to pick up the *Phoenix* instead of *TRP.*

Howard Garsh believed "more hard investigative reporting should be our first priority now." Walter Harrison wanted more emphasis on quality editorial work. Tom Friedman commented feelingly, "I want to have more impact on people's lives. My basic attitude is deep distrust of the people who run our country and our businesses. Some staffers want more emphasis on entertainment; some just want more people to buy it. I want the people to get the information they wouldn't get other-wise. I want more investigations. I want to work on an investigative paper, not just a successful operation. I'm trying to hold on to my sense of moral outrage."

Bob Rotner, from his perspective, saw two approaches to future editorial direction. "The edit people want witty headlines. The business people want headlines that sell. The edit people feel the paper ought to be political, serve the left. The business people see it as the ultimate guide to Boston, serving the consumer element. I want it to do more investigative reporting."

Paul Solman reflected not only on near-term and future editorial direction but plans to get there, noting:

> We are planning some minor modifications for the fall. We will have two long feature stories and a larger number of shorter stories that will provide more information in readable form. And we will expand the number of vignettes from New York City and Washington events. One of the latter might be an interview with the aide of a member of Congress.
>
> And we're trying to figure out what we want the paper to be. The paper is essentially a reflection of the people here, and they are not homogeneous. But in the longer run, we're working toward a personality for this paper that is intelligent, political, which I mean to say politically progressive, interesting to people, compelling, and well written.
>
> We're not real close now, but we're making progress. Our effort now is oriented to four activities. First, we simply want to get more copy available for our use. Copy can always be edited and rewritten. So getting the basic fund is important. This means asking more of our staff people, as well as really pursuing the free-lance sources. This also means we will have to pay higher rates than competitors, pay for research, and make appeals to the really good people based on prestige, personal ties, and even convenience.
>
> Second, we want to tie down regular contributors—good writers who may not be on the staff but can be relied on for quality stuff. We want to create a circle of regular free-lancers.
>
> Third, we have to fight the tendency to diffuse our efforts. Accordingly, we created the position of managing editor which will free me from the day-to-day operational problems.
>
> Fourth, we want to run two or three solid articles per week in the front page of the book that are smart and fascinating.
>
> Success for most people is to be big and powerful. I don't have a specific vision of *TRP* and success, but I want it to be something that serves the people. I want us to be a wing of society—out there after the bad gals and guys. Yet I want it to be entertaining too, for literate people. And I want it to be instructive to the public.

LOOKING AHEAD

The former *Cambridge Phoenix* and *TRP* had been organized and had their early operating years during a period of major societal and youth unrest. Campus stories headlined strikes, riots, and "takeovers," while on the wider scene, the counterculture movement was in full bloom.

Reporters of the mid-70s youth movement indicated that much of the past turbulence seemed to have disappeared. While the president of Ohio University did resign in June of 1974, citing "the mindless destructive events of the past week," most college campuses seemed quiet and the counterculture movement had, in many observers' judgments, "plateaued."

The transition from activism to a more restrained protest pattern was captured for the researcher in Sara Davidson's article on the Symbionese Liberation Army. She interviewed Dan Siegel, a well-known participant in the 1969 Berkeley disturbances about his changing career and life style.

> Siegel is 28, an attractive, modest-looking young man in a sports shirt and slacks. In 1969, when he was student-body president at Berkeley, he gave a speech that sent thousands surging down Telegraph Avenue to reclaim People's Park. Bob Dylan was singing from speaker vans: "You can have your cake and eat it, too."
>
> Siegel says he no longer had "the illusion that revolution will be easy or that a few gallant people can do it. Winning the hearts and minds of tens of thousands of people—that's what making revolution is about." He walks toward the courthouse where he is preparing a test case in which the community is suing the district attorney, and he says that it's funny but in some ways, he feels old.[13]

Given these changes, as well as major developments in the wider environment, the researcher wondered what, if any, impact these forces would have on the future plans of *TRP*. He raised the question of future direction with Paula Childs. She commented:

> I'd like to see this paper eventually be able to own its own composition shop as well as its own printing company. I'd like to see this company own its own other media resources, like its own radio station. And I'd like to see the paper get to a large enough size that we can be covering the things we should be covering. You know. Right now we're in a tug-of-war between whether to be more like a magazine, or whether to be more like a newspaper. Right now, we're much more like a magazine than a newspaper.

Joe Klein, a former staff member, added:

> From here I'd like to see us grow in several ways. First, I want us to develop a broader base of readers and not be read by just street people and hippies. This would mean expanding into older neighborhoods and suburbs, as well as becoming more and more frequently read downtown. I want it to have impact. Furthermore, and I guess this is a second point,

---

[13] *New York Times Magazine,* June 2, 1974, p. 44.

I want us to expand beyond Boston to a regional and even national scope. I want us to have as many readers outside of Boston as the *Village Voice* has outside New York. And third, I want us to become an alternative for top-notch daily journalists.

Bo Burlingham, another staff writer, asked:

Have we reached the end of our growth with this format? It has worked so well. And the answer is so important because it affects so many things. Who do we hire? Young kids just out of college and ask them for a full-time commitment? Or, do we hire older more experienced part-timers who can work here—and write the book they always really wanted to create?

It raises questions as to who our audience is—is it Cambridge, Boston, New England, or ——— ? How we work with that influences Howard's financing plans and Bob Williams's advertising programs. And questions, too, need to be asked editorially. Should we go on primarily with feature stories about current causes or events or institutions? There are lots of reasons why we should. They take less resources and time and are less risky. Or do we become an investigative journal? That's really rough. It takes lots of money and time to do well and it's risky.

Jan Freeman reminisced:

So much of what we are, is what we were—a collection of people who grew up in the late 60s and who, by luck, got into an organization that we like and where we can do what we want.

Our audience is like us—it's growing up! It's no longer the 60s. Our audience isn't clear any more—it is a mixture. Paul knows this. We know we can't just do what we do best. We never have been a doctrinaire leftist paper—we have sort of been, as I told you—a newspaper-magazine. But what's next?

A *Boston Globe* reporter, Nathan Cobb, raised the question of future direction with various members of *TRP* and the *Phoenix* staff. He commented:

Times change. *TRP,* having achieved financial success, wonders where to go. "It's much less clear now what we should be doing than it used to be," says Paul Solman. "It used to be automatic. You didn't have to think about what you did because there was a counterculture not being covered by anyone else. Now we're asking what kinds of things we can provide that no one else can."

*   *   *   *   *

One suspects, though, that the two papers really are still viewed as a legitimate journalistic alternative by the fading remnants of the "youth culture." But out in the great beyond, out in those suburbs where folks are easing into their 30s and 40s, each may indeed be viewed as just another newspaper. "The dailies are getting more like us, and we're getting more like the dailies," says Joe Klein of *TRP*, an experienced and professional newsperson. "And that's all right with me. I'd like to see *TRP* on every doorstep."

Bob Rotner, publisher, in talking with the researcher about his job and responsibilities as publisher, noted:

> But to plan the future of the paper, and to make sure that just because the paper is successful now, it doesn't mean that it's going to be successful in a year or two, and there are certain things happening in the city and the country which need to be understood. We're not making ourselves obsolete. . . . What I hope I can do now is to make the decisions about the future by going to the appropriate places and finding out what is going to happen in the future, and then to make sure that *TRP* is going in the direction it needs to go, so that it doesn't have to worry about the future.

CASE 10

People Express

We're now the biggest air carrier in terms of departures at any New York airport. We've flown almost 3 million passengers and saved the flying public over one quarter of a billion dollars (not including the savings from fares reduced by other airlines trying to compete with us). We expect to see a $3 million profit this year. . . . We have a concept that works and is unique.

But with no growth horizon, people have been disempowered. We've started slowing down, getting sleepy. So, we've decided to set a new growth objective. Instead of adding 4 to 6 aircraft as we planned for this year, we are now thinking in terms of 12 or more new aircraft a year for the next few years.

With this announcement, Don Burr, founder, president and CEO of People Express airline, concluded the business portion of the company's third quarterly financial meeting of 1982, graciously received rousing applause from several hundred of his stockholder/managers there to hear about and celebrate the success of their young company, and signaled for the music to begin.

ORIGINS AND BRIEF HISTORY

People Express had been incorporated on April 7, 1980. In July of that year it had applied to the Civil Aeronautics Board (CAB) for permission to form a new airline to be based in the New York/Newark metropolitan area and dedicated to providing low-cost service in the eastern United States. Organized specifically to take advantage of provisions of the 1978 Airline Deregulation Act, People Express was the first airline to apply for certification since its passage. (The act, which was designed to stimulate competition, allowed greater flexibility in scheduling and pricing and lowered the barriers to new entrants.)

In applying to the CAB for a "determination of fitness and certification of public convenience and necessity," People Express committed itself to:

1.   provide "a broad new choice of flights" with high-frequency service,
2.   keep costs low by "extremely productive use of assets,"
3.   offer "unrestricted deep discount price savings" through productivity gains,
4.   focus on several high-density eastern U.S. markets which had yet to reap the pricing benefits of deregulation,
5.   center operations in the densely populated New York/Newark metropolitan area with service at the underutilized, uncongested, highly accessible Newark International Airport.

The Civil Aeronautics Board was sufficiently impressed with this stated intent that it approved the application in three months (compared to the usual year or more). On October 24, 1980, People Express had its certificate to offer air passenger service between the New York/New Jersey area and 27 major cities in the eastern U.S.

Start-up

People Express's managing officers proceeded to work round the clock for the next six months to turn their plans and ideas into a certificated operating airline. They raised money, leased a terminal, bought planes, recruited, trained, established routes and schedules, and prepared manuals to meet the FAA's fitness and safety standards. "We were here every night . . . from November until April when they [the Federal Aviation Administration (FAA)] gave us our certificate. . . . It was hell" [Burr]. People's operating certificate was granted April 24, 1981.

Operations Begin

Flight service began on April 30, with three planes flying between Newark and Buffalo, New York; Columbus, Ohio; and Norfolk, Virginia. By the following year, the company employed a work force of over 1,200, owned 17 airplanes, and had flown nearly 2 million passengers between the 13 cities it was servicing. People Express had grown faster than any other airline and most businesses. It had managed to survive a start-up year filled with environmental obstacles, a severe national economic recession, a strike of air traffic controllers, and bad winter weather—all of which had serious negative effects on air travel. By June 1982, though the airline industry in general was losing money, and though competition resulting from deregulation was intense, People had begun showing a profit. Exhibit 1 lists milestones in the growth of People Express.

EXHIBIT 1: Major Events

April 1980	Date of incorporation
May 1980	1st external financing—Citicorp venture
October 1980	CAB certificate awarded
November 1980	Initial public offering—$25.5 MM common
March 1981	1st aircraft delivered
April 1981	1st scheduled flight
August 1981	PATCO strike
October 1981	Florida service emphasized
January 1982	One millionth passenger carried
March 1982	17th aircraft delivered
April 1982	Reported first quarterly operating profit
July 1982	Filed 1,500,000 shares of common stock

---

In the spring and summer of 1982 People underwent an extensive review of its infrastructure, added resources to the recruitment function so as to fill a 200-person staffing shortfall, and modified and attempted to implement more systematically a governance and communication system for which there had been little time during start-up. By the fall of 1982 three more planes were about to arrive and three more cities were scheduled to be opened for service.

BACKGROUND AND PRECURSORS

Donald Burr had been president of Texas International Airlines (T.I.) before he left it to found People Express with a group of his colleagues. The airline business was a "hobby business" for Burr; his love of airplanes went back to his childhood and he began flying in college, where as president of the Stanford Flying Club he could get his flight instruction paid for. After receiving an MBA from the Harvard Business School in 1965 he went to work for National Aviation, a company specializing in airline investments, thus combining his affinity for aviation with his interest in finance. In 1971 he was elected president of National Aviation. While at National Aviation, Burr began a venture capital operation which involved him in the start-up of several companies, including one which aimed at taking advantage of the recently deregulated telecommunications industry.

Eighteen months later he decided he wanted to get into the "dirty fingernails" side of the airline business. He left Wall Street and joined Texas International Airlines as a director and chairman of the executive committee. In June 1973 he became executive vice president and in 1976 assumed the responsibilities of chief operations officer. Between 1973 and 1977, Texas International moved from a position close to bankruptcy to become a profitable business. Burr was largely credited in the media for managing the turnaround. In June 1979 he was made president of Texas International. Six months later, he resigned.

Looking for a new challenge, one option he considered at that time was starting a new airline. The day after Burr left T.I., Gerald Gitner, his VP of planning and marketing, and Melrose Dawsey, his own and the CEO's executive secretary at T.I., both submitted their resignations and joined Burr to incorporate People Express.

By the fall of 1980, 15 of Texas International's top managers and several more experienced staff from the ranks followed Burr to become part of the People Express management team and start-up crew. Some gave up their positions even before they knew where the new company would be based, how it would be financed, whether they would be able to acquire planes, or what their exact jobs would be. In spite of the personal and financial risks, the opportunity to start an airline from scratch, with people they liked and respected, was too good to pass up. It was an adventure, a chance to test themselves. Burr at 39 was the oldest of the officers. Even if People Express failed, they assumed that they could pick themselves up and start again.

According to Hap Paretti, former legal counsel and head of government relations at Texas International, who became the fifth managing officer at People Express:

> We weren't talking about my job description or what kind of a budget I would have. It was more, we're friends, we're starting a new airline, you're one of the people we'd like to have join us in starting the company . . . what you do will be determined by what your interests are. The idea of getting involved and letting my personality and talents come through to determine my job appealed to me. I'm not happy doing just one thing.

Bob McAdoo, People's managing officer in charge of finance, had been corporate comptroller at Texas International. For McAdoo, joining People Express "was an easy decision, though I was having a good time at Texas International . . . I happen to be a guy driven by things related to efficiency. This was a chance to build an airline that was the most efficient in the business."

Lori Dubose had become director of human resources at T.I.—the first female director there—within a year after being hired.

When Burr called to offer me the "People" job he explained that we would all be working in different capacities. I'd get to learn operations, get stock—I didn't know anything about stock, never owned any. At 28 how could I pass it up?

She came even though she was married and her husband decided not to move with her to Newark.

FINANCING AND AIRPLANE ACQUISITION

To finance this adventure, Burr put up $355,000, Gitner put in $175,000, and the other managing officers came up with from $20,000 to $50,000 each. Burr secured an additional $200,000 from FNCB Capital Corp., a subsidiary of Citicorp. The papers for the Citicorp money, People Express's first outside funds, were signed on May 8, 1980, Burr's 40th birthday. Subsequently, the investment firm of Hambrecht & Quist agreed to help raise additional start-up funds. Impressed with Burr's record and the quality of his management team, and aware of the opportunities created by airline deregulation, William Hambrecht agreed to Burr's suggestion of taking People Express public. (No other airline had ever gone public to raise start-up money.)

As soon as the CAB application was approved in October 1980 all eight managing officers went on the road explaining their business plan and concepts to potential investors throughout the country. They were able to sell over $24 million worth of stock—3 million shares at $8.50 per share.

The official plan stated in the CAB application had called for raising $4–$5 million, buying or leasing one to three planes, and hiring 200 or so people the first year. According to Hap Paretti, "We thought we'd start by leasing three little DC-9s, and flying them for a few years until we made enough money to buy a plane of our own." According to Burr, however, that plan reflected Gitner's more cautious approach and what most investors would tolerate at the beginning. Even with the additional money raised, Gitner thought they should buy at most 11 planes, but Burr's ideas were more expansive. From the beginning he wanted to start with a large number of planes so as to establish a presence in the industry quickly and support the company's overhead.

With cash in hand they were able to make a very attractive purchase from Lufthansa of an entire fleet of 17 Boeing 737s, all of which would be delivered totally remodeled and redecorated to People's specifications. While other managing officers recalled being a bit stunned, Burr viewed the transaction as being "right on plan."

BURR'S PERSONAL MOTIVATION AND PEOPLE EXPRESS PHILOSOPHY

Government deregulation appeared to provide a "unique moment in history," and was one of several factors which motivated Burr to risk his personal earnings on starting a new airline. At least as important was his strong conviction that people were basically good and trustworthy, that they could be more effectively organized, and if properly trained, were likely to be creative and productive.

> I guess the single predominant reason that I cared about starting a new company was to try and develop a better way for people to work together . . . that's where the name People Express came from [as well as] the whole people focus and thrust. . . . It drives everything else that we do.
>
> Most organizations believe that humans are generally bad and you have to control them and watch them and make sure they work. At People Express, people are trusted to do a good job until they prove they definitely won't.

From its inception, therefore, People Express was seen as a chance for Burr and his management team to experiment with and demonstrate a "better" way of managing not just an airline but any business.

While Burr recognized that his stance was contrary to the majority of organized structures in the United States, he rejected any insinuation that he was optimistic or soft.

> I'm not a goody two-shoes person, I don't view myself as a social scientist, as a minister, as a do-gooder. I perceive myself as a hard-nosed businessman, whose ambitions and aspirations have to do with providing goods and services to other people for a return.

In addition, however, he wanted PE to serve as a role model for other organizations, a concept which carried with it the desire to have an external impact and to contribute to the world's debate about "how the hell to do things well, with good purpose, good intent, and good results for everybody. To me, that's good business, a good way to live. It makes sense, it's logical, it's hopeful, so why not do [it]?"

Prior to starting service, Burr and the other managing officers spent a lot of time discussing their ideas about the "right" way to run an airline. Early on, they retained an outside management consultant to help them work together effectively as a management team and begin to articulate the principles to which they could commit themselves and their company. Over time, the principles evolved into a list of six "precepts," which were written down in December of 1981 and referred to continually from then on in devising and explaining company policies, hiring and training new recruits, structuring and assigning tasks. These precepts were: (1) service, commitment to growth of people; (2) best provider of air transportation; (3) highest quality of management; (4) role model for other airlines and other businesses; (5) simplicity; and (6) maximization of profits.

From Burr's philosophy as well as these precepts and a myriad of how-to-do-it-right ideas, a set of strategies began to evolve. According to People's management consultant, the "path" theory was the modus operandi—management would see what route people took to get somewhere, then pave the paths that had been worn naturally to make them more visible.

Thus, by 1982, one could articulate fairly clearly a set of strategies that had become "the concept," the way things were done at People Express.

THE PEOPLE EXPRESS CONCEPT: THE PHILOSOPHY OPERATIONALIZED

The People Express business concept was broken down and operationalized into three sets of strategies: marketing, cost, and people. (Over Burr's objections, the presentation prepared by investment company Morgan Stanley for PE investors began with the marketing and cost strategies rather than the people strategies.)

Marketing Strategy

Fundamental to People's initial marketing strategy was its view of air travel as a commodity product for which consumers had little or no brand loyalty. (See Exhibit 2 for two representative advertisements.) People Express defined its own version of that product as a basic, cut-rate, no-nonsense, air trip. A People Express ticket entitled a passenger to an airplane seat on a safe trip between two airports, period. The marketing strategy was to build and maintain passenger volume by offering extremely low fares and frequent, dependable service on previously overpriced, underserviced routes. In keeping with this strategy, the following tactics were adopted:

1. **Very low fares**—On any given route, People's fares were substantially below the standard fares prevailing prior to PE's announcement of service on that route. For instance, People entered the Newark-to-Pittsburgh market with a $19 fare in April 1982, when U.S. Air was charging $123 on that route. Typically, peak fares ran from 40 percent to 55 percent below the competition's standard fares and 65 percent to 75 percent below, during off-peak hours (after 6 P.M. and weekends).

2. **Convenient flight schedules**—For any route that its planes flew,

EXHIBIT 2

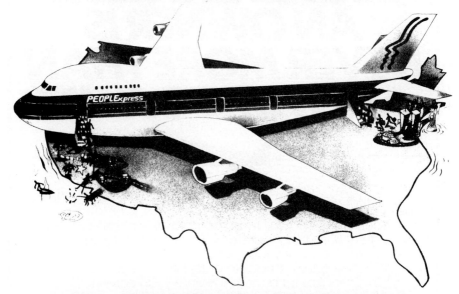

EXHIBIT 2 *(concluded)*

WHEN YOU FLY PEOPLE EXPRESS, AN OWNER IS NEVER MORE THAN A FEW STEPS AWAY.

Our planes are staffed by the most attentive people in the world: stockholders.

Each and every full time member of our staff owns an average of $38,000 of our stock. (That's not including the stock of the company founders.)

Which helps us attract talented people.

Which makes for a more efficiently run airline.

Which enables us to charge less.

Which is how you get both low prices and great service on People Express.

PEOPLExpress
FLY SMART

NEW YORK, NEWARK, BOSTON, WASHINGTON, BALTIMORE, SYRACUSE, BUFFALO, NORFOLK, COLUMBUS, PITTSBURGH, HARTFORD, BURLINGTON, JACKSONVILLE, SARASOTA, MELBOURNE, WEST PALM BEACH

People tried to offer the most frequent flight schedule. With low fares and frequent flights, People could broaden its market segment beyond those of established airlines to include passengers who would ordinarily have used other forms of transportation. In an effort to expand the size of the air travel market, People's ads announcing service in new cities were pitched to automobile drivers, bus riders, and even those who tended not to travel at all. People hoped to capture most of the increase as well as some share of the preexisting market for each route.

3. Regionwide identity—People set out to establish a formidable image in its first year as a major airline servicing the entire eastern U.S. Large, established airlines could easily wage price wars and successfully compete with a new airline in any one city, but they would probably have to absorb some losses and would be hard pressed to mount such a campaign on several fronts at once.

4. Pitch to "smart" air travelers—In keeping with its product definition, People's ads sought to identify People Express not as exotic or delicious or entertaining, but as the smart travel choice for smart, thrifty, busy travelers. The ads were filled with consumer information, as well as information about PE's smart people and policies. Unlike most airlines, for instance, every People Express plane had roomy overhead compartments for passengers' baggage thereby saving them money, time, and the potential inconvenience of loss.

5. Memorable positive atmosphere—Burr's long-term marketing strategy, once the airline was off the ground financially, was to make flying with People Express the most pleasant and memorable travel experience possible. The goal was for passengers to arrive at their destination feeling very well served. Thus, People Express's ultimate marketing strategy was to staff every position with competent, sensitive, respectful, upbeat, high-energy people who would create a contagious positive atmosphere. The message to staff and customers alike was: "At People Express, attitude is as important as altitude."

Cost Structure

People's cost structure was not based on a clear-cut formula so much as on an attitude that encouraged the constant, critical examination of every aspect of the business. According to Bob McAdoo, the management team "literally looked for every possible way to do things more simply and efficiently." McAdoo could point to at least 15 or 20 factors he felt were important in keeping costs down while preserving safety and quality. "If you look for one or two key factors, you miss the point." Cost savings measures affecting every aspect of the business included the following:

1. Aircraft—Since fuel was the biggest single cost for an airline, People chose, redesigned, and deployed its aircraft with fuel efficiency in mind. Its twin engine Boeing 737–100 planes were thought to be the most fuel-efficient planes for their mission in the industry. By eliminating first-class and galley sections, interior redesign increased the number of all coach-class seats from 90 to 118 per plane. Overhead racks were expanded to accommodate more carry-on baggage. The planes were redecorated to convey a modern image and reassure potential passengers that low fares did not mean sacrificing quality or safety.

PE scheduled these planes to squeeze the most possible flying time out of them, 10.36 hours per plane per day, compared with the industry average of 7.08 hours. Finally, plane maintenance work was done by other airlines on a contract basis, a practice seen as less expensive than hiring a maintenance staff.

2. Low labor costs—Labor is an airline's second biggest expense. Though salaries were generally competitive, and in some cases above industry norms, People's labor costs were relatively small. The belief was that if every employee was intelligent, well trained, flexible, and motivated to work hard, fewer people (as much as one-third fewer) would be needed than most airlines employed.

People kept its work force deliberately lean, and expected it to work hard. Each employee carefully selected after an extensive screening process, received training in multiple functions (ticketing, reservations, ground operations, and so on) and was extensively cross-utilized, depending on where the company's needs were at any given time. If a bag needed to be carried to a plane, whoever was heading toward the plane would carry the bag. Thus, peaks and valleys could be handled efficiently. This was in sharp contrast with other airlines which hired people into one of a variety of distinct "classes in craft," (such as flight attendants, reservations, baggage), each of which had a fairly rigid job description, was represented by a different union, and therefore was precluded from being cross-utilized.

3. In-house expertise and problem solving—In addition to keeping the work force small and challenged, cross-utilization and rotation were expected to add the benefits of a de facto ongoing quality and efficiency review. Problems could be identified and solutions and new efficiency measures could be continually invented if people were familiar with all aspects of the business and motivated to take management-like responsibility for improving their company.

The Paxtrac ticketing computer was commonly cited as a successful example of how PE tapped its reservoir of internal brain power rather than calling in outside consultants to solve a company problem. Many of PE's longer routes were combinations of short-haul flights into and out of Newark. The existing ticketing system required a separate ticket for each leg of the trip, resulting in higher fares than PE wanted. Burr spotted the problem when he was flying one day (he tried to spend some time each month on board the planes or in the ground operations area). An ad hoc team of managers was sent off to a hotel in Florida for a week to solve the problem. They came up with a specially designed microprocessor ticketing machine with the flexibility to accommodate the company's marketing plans and fast enough (7 seconds per ticket vs. 20 seconds) to enable on-board ticketing of larger passenger loads.

4. Facilities—Like its aircraft, People Express's work space was low cost and strictly functional. The main Newark terminal was located in the old North Terminal building, significantly cheaper to rent than space at the West and South terminals a mile away. People had no ticket counters. All ticketing was done either by travel agents in advance, or by customer service managers on board the planes once they were airbound. Corporate headquarters, located upstairs over the main terminal had none of the luxurious trappings associated with a major airline. Offices were shared, few had carpeting, and decoration consisted primarily of People Express ads, sometimes blown up poster size, and an occasional framed print of an airplane.

5. Reservations—The reservations system was kept extremely simple, fast, and therefore inexpensive. There were no interline arrangements with other airlines for ticketing or baggage transfer; no assistance was offered with hotel or auto reservations in spite of the potential revenue leverage to be derived from such customer service. Thus, calls could be handled quickly by hundreds of easily trained temporary workers in several of the cities People served, using local lines (a WATS line would cost $8,000 per month) and simple equipment ($900 vs. the standard $3,000 computer terminals).

6. No "freebies"—Costs of convenience services were unbundled from basic transportation costs. People offered none of the usual airline "freebies." Neither snacks nor baggage handling, for example, were included in the price of a ticket, though such extras were available and could be purchased for an additional fee.

People

Burr told his managers repeatedly that it was People's people and its people policies that made the company unique and successful. "The people dimension is the value added to the commodity. Many investors still don't fully appreciate this point, but high commitment and participation, and maximum flexibility and massive creative productivity are the most important strategies in People Express."

STRUCTURE AND POLICIES

As People moved from a set of ideas to an operating business, People's managers took pains to design structures and develop policies consistent with the company's stated precepts and strategies. This resulted in an organization characterized by minimial hierarchy, rotation and cross-utilization, work teams, ownership, self-management, participation, compensation, selective hiring and recruitment, multipurpose training, and team building.

Minimal Hierarchy

People's initial organizational structure consisted of only three formal levels of authority. At the top of the organization was the president/CEO and six managing officers, each of whom provided line as well as staff leadership for more than one of the 13 functional areas (see Exhibit 3 for a listing of functions).

Reporting to and working closely with the managing officers were eight general managers, each of whom provided day-to-day implementation and leadership in at least one functional area, as well as planning for and coordinating with other areas. People's managing officers and general managers worked hard at exemplifying the company's philosophy. They worked in teams, rotated out of their specialties as much as possible to take on line work, filling in at a gate or on a flight. Several had gone through the full "in-flight" training required of customer service managers. They shared office furniture and phones. Burr's office doubled as the all-purpose executive meeting room; if others were using it when he had an appointment, he would move down the hall and borrow someone else's empty space.

There were no executive assistants, secretaries, or support staff of any kind. The managers themselves assumed the activities that such staff would ordinarily perform. Individuals, teams, and committees did their own typing, which kept written communications to a minimum. Everyone answered his or her own phone. (Both practices were seen as promoting direct communication as well as saving money.)

Beyond the top 15 officers all remaining full-time employees were either flight managers, maintenance managers, or customer service managers. The titles indicated distinctions in qualifications and functional emphasis rather than organizational authority. *Flight managers* were pilots. Their primary responsibility was flying, but they also performed various other tasks, such as dispatching, scheduling, and safety checks, on a rotating basis or as needed. *Maintenance managers* were technicians who oversaw and facilitated maintenance of PE's airplanes, equipment, and facilities by contract with other airlines maintenance crews. In addition to monitoring and assuring the quality of the contracted work, maintenance managers were utilized to perform various staff jobs.

The vast majority of People's managers were *customer service managers,* generalists trained to perform all passenger-related tasks, such as security clearance, boarding, flight attending, ticketing, and food service, as well as some staff function activities (see Exhibit 3).

By and large, what few authority distinctions did exist were obscure and informal. Managing officers, general managers, and others with seniority (over one year) had more responsibility for giving direction, motivating, teaching, and perhaps coordinating, but *not* for supervising or managing in the traditional sense.

Ownership, Lifelong Job Security

Everyone in a permanent position at PE was a shareholder, required as a condition of employment to buy, at a greatly discounted price, a

EXHIBIT 3: Organizational Structure, 11/82 (author's rendition)

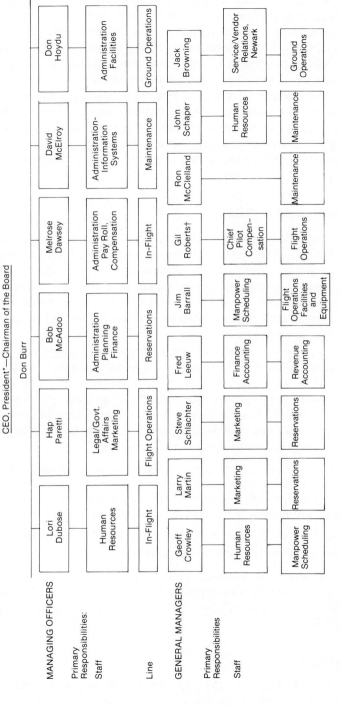

CEO, President*—Chairman of the Board

Don Burr

MANAGING OFFICERS

Lori Dubose | Hap Paretti | Bob McAdoo | Melrose Dawsey | David McElroy | Don Hoydu

Primary Responsibilities:

Staff: Human Resources | Legal/Govt. Affairs Marketing | Administration Planning Finance | Administration Pay Roll, Compensation | Administration-Information Systems | Administration Facilities

Line: In-Flight | Flight Operations | Reservations | In-Flight | Maintenance | Ground Operations

GENERAL MANAGERS

Geoff Crowley | Larry Martin | Steve Schlachter | Fred Leeuw | Jim Barrall | Gil Roberts† | Ron McClelland | John Schaper | Jack Browning

Primary Responsibilities

Staff: Human Resources | Marketing | Marketing | Finance Accounting | Manpower Scheduling | Chief Pilot Compensation | | Human Resources | Service/Vendor Relations, Newark

Manpower Scheduling | Reservations | Reservations | Revenue Accounting | Flight Operations Facilities and Equipment | Flight Operations | Maintenance | Maintenance | Ground Operations

TEAM MANAGERS: 30 appointed, 10/82

CUSTOMER SERVICE MANAGERS

FLIGHT MANAGERS
RESERVATION WORKERS

MAINTENANCE MANAGERS

* Original president, Gerald Gitner, resigned 3/82 and Burr assumed presidency.
† Gil Roberts appointed chief pilot 11/82.

number of shares of common stock, determined on the basis of his or her salary level. It was expected that each employee, in keeping with being a manager/owner, would demonstrate a positive attitude toward work, and participate in the governance of the company. As Managing Officer Lori Dubose pointed out, "We'll fire someone only if it is (absolutely) necessary. . . . For instance, we won't tolerate dishonesty or willful disregard for the company's policies, but we don't punish people for making mistakes." In exchange, People Express promised the security of lifetime employment and opportunities for personal and professional growth though continuing education, cross-utilization, promotion from within the company, and compensation higher than other companies paid for similar skills and experience.

Cross-Utilization and Rotation

No one, regardless of work history, qualifications, or responsibility, was assigned to do the same job all the time. Everyone, including managing officers, was expected to be "cross-utilized" as needed and to rotate monthly between in-flight and ground operations and/or between line and staff functions. (The terms "line" and "staff" in PE differentiated tasks which were directly flight-related from those related to the business of operating the company.)

Seen by some as unnecessarily complicated and troublesome, cross-utilization and rotation were justified by PE in several ways. According to Burr, they were conceived primarily as methods of continuing education, aimed at keeping everyone interested, challenged, and growing. Bob McAdoo appreciated the flexible staff utilization capability which eventually would result from everyone having broad exposure to the company's functions. Rotation did create some difficulties:

> It takes people a while to master each job. It might seem better to have an expert doing a given job. Cross-utilization also means you need high-quality people who are capable of doing several jobs. This in turn limits how fast you can recruit and how fast you can grow.

These were seen, even by McAdoo, the efficiency expert, as short-term inconveniences well worth the long-term payoff.

> When you rotate people often they don't develop procedures that are too complicated for newcomers to learn and master fast. This forces the work to be broken down into short simple packets, easily taught and easily learned.

Self-Management

People were expected to manage themselves and their own work in collaboration with their teams and coworkers. According to Jim Miller, coordinator of training, "We don't want to teach behaviors—we want to teach what the end result should look like and allow each individual to arrive at those results his or her own way. . . . When desired results aren't achieved, we try to guide people and assist them in improving the outcome of their efforts."

The written, though never formalized, guidelines regarding "self-management" read as follows:

> Within the context of our precepts and corporate objectives, and with leadership direction but no supervision, individuals and/or teams have the opportunity (and the obligation) to self-manage, which encompasses the following:
>
> • Setting specific, challenging, but realistic objectives within the organizational context.
>
> • Monitoring and assessing the quantity/quality/timeliness of one's own performance ("how am I doing?") by gathering data and seeking input from other people.
>
> • Inventing and executing activities to remedy performance problems that appear and exploiting opportunities for improved performance.
>
> • Actively seeking the information, resources and/or assistance needed to achieve the performance objectives.

When it came time for performance reviews, each individual distributed forms to those six coworkers from whom feedback would be useful. Again, growth rather than policing was the objective.

Work Teams

Dubose observed that "even with smart, self-managed people, one person can't have all the components to be the answer to every situation." People therefore had decided to organize its work force into small (3–4 person) work groups as an alternative to larger groups with supervisors. "If you don't want a hierarchical structure with 40 levels you have to have some way to manage the numbers of people we were anticipating." Teams were seen as promoting better problem solving and decision making as well as personal growth and learning.

Every customer service manager belonged to a self-chosen ongoing team with which he or she was assigned work by a lottery system on a monthly basis. Though monthly staff assignments were made individually according to interests, skills, and needs, staff work was expected to be performed in teams. This applied to flight managers and maintenance managers as well as customer service managers. Each team was to elect a liaison to communicate with other teams. Each staff function was managed by a team of coordinators, most of whom were members of the start-up team recruited from Texas International. Managing officers also worked in teams and rotated certain responsibilities to share the burden and the growth benefits of primary leadership.

Governance, Broad-based Participation

People's governance structure was designed with several objectives: policy development, problem solving, participation, and communication.

While Burr was the ultimate decision maker, top management decisions, including plans and policies, were to be made by management teams with the assistance of advisory councils. Each of the 6 managing officers and 9 general managers was responsible for at least one of the 13 functional areas (see Exhibit 3) and served on a management team for at least one other function. The 13 function-specific management teams were grouped into 4 umbrella staff committees: Operations, People, Marketing, and Finance and Administration. For each staff committee, composed of managing officers and general managers from the relevant functional areas, there was an advisory council made up of selected customer service managers, flight managers, and maintenance managers serving on relevant line and staff teams. The councils were intended to generate and review policy recommendations, but until August 1982 they followed no written guidelines. A study done by Yale University students under the direction of Professor Richard Hackman showed considerable confusion as to their purposes (influencing, learning, solving, communicating issues) and role (advising vs. making decisions).

To minimize duplication and maximize communication, each advisory council elected a member to sit on an overarching "coordinating council" which was to meet regularly with Don Burr (to transmit information to and from him and among the councils). These ongoing teams and councils were supplemented periodically by ad hoc committees and task forces which could be created at anyone's suggestion to solve a particular problem, conduct a study, and/or develop proposals.

In addition to maximizing productivity, all of the above practices, teams, and committees were seen essential to promote personal growth and keep people interested in and challenged by their work.

Compensation—High Reward for Expected High Performance

People's four-part compensation package was aimed at reinforcing its human resource strategy. Base salaries were determined strictly by job category on a relatively flat scale, ranging in 1981 from $17,000 for customer service managers to $48,000 for the managing officers and CEO. (Competitor airlines averaged only $17,600 for flight attendants after several years of service, but paid nearly double for managing officers and more than four times as much for their chief executives.)

Whereas most companies shared medical expenses with employees, People paid 100 percent of all medical and dental expenses. Life insurance, rather than being pegged to salary level, was $50,000 for everyone.

After one year with PE all managers' base salaries and benefits were augmented by three forms of potential earnings tied to the company's fortunes. There were two profit-sharing plans: (1) a dollar-for-dollar plan, based on quarterly profits and paid quarterly to full-time employees who had been with PE over one year, and (2) a plan based on annual profitability. The former was allocated proportionally, according to salary level and distributed incrementally. If profits were large, those at higher salary levels stood to receive larger bonuses, but only after all eligible managers had received some reward. The sustained profits were distributed annually and in equal amounts to people in all categories. Together, earnings from these plans could total up to 50 percent or more of base salary. The aggregate amount of PE's profit-sharing contributions after the second quarter of 1982 was $311,000.

Finally, PE awarded several stock option bonuses, one nearly every quarter, making it possible for managers who had worked at least half a year to purchase limited quantities of common stock at discounts ranging from 25 percent to 40 percent of market value. The company offered five-year interest-free promissory notes for the full amount of the stock purchase required of new employees, and for two-thirds the amount of any optional purchase. As of July 1982, 651 employees, including the managing officers, held an aggregate 513,000 shares of common stock under a restricted stock purchase plan. Approximately 85 percent were held by employees other than managing officers and general managers. The total number of shares reserved under this plan was, at that time, 900,000.

Selective Hiring of the People Express "Type"

Given the extent and diversity of responsibilities People required of its people, Lori Dubose, managing officer in charge of the company's "people" as well as in-flight functions, believed firmly that it took a certain type of person to do well at People Express. Her recruiters, experienced CSMs themselves, looked for people who were bright, educated, well-groomed, mature, articulate, assertive, creative, energetic, conscientious, and hard working. While they had to be capable of functioning independently and taking initiative, and it was desirable for them to be ambitious in terms of personal development, achievements, and wealth, it was also essential that they be flexible, collaborative rather than competitive with coworkers, excellent team players, and comfortable with PE's horizontal structure. "If someone needed to be a vice president in order to be happy, we'd be concerned and might not hire them" [Miller].

Recruiting efforts for customer service managers were pitched deliberately to service professionals—nurses, social workers, teachers—with an interest in innovative management. No attempt was made to attract those with airline experience or interest per se (see Exhibit 4). Applicants who came from traditional airlines where "everyone memorized the union

EXHIBIT 4

TEAMWORK TAKES ON A WHOLE NEW MEANING AT PEOPLExpress!

TOTAL PROFESSIONALISM

Customer Service Managers

PEOPLExpress has a whole new approach to running an airline! As a Customer Service Manager, you'll be a vital part of our management team, working in all areas from In-Flight Service, Ground Operations, and Reservations to staff support functions such as Marketing, Scheduling, Training, Recruiting, Accounting, and more.

This cross-utilization takes a lot of hard creative work–but it's the best way we know to achieve greater professionalism and productivity! Instead of doing just one limited job, you'll be involved in both line and staff activities–so you can learn the airline business fully. Faced with our variety of challenge, you'll develop and *use* all your decision-making skills. That's how bright people grow at PEOPLExpress... by finding simple creative solutions to complex problems... solutions that contribute to our productivity and growth... and *yours*.

Even better, your productivity can show a direct return. As a Customer Service Manager, you'll have the opportunity to participate in our unique STOCK PURCHASE PROGRAM (subject to legal requirements) and our profit-sharing plan.

If challenge stimulates you, if you really want to pursue management and growth... and are willing to invest the time it takes to achieve TOTAL PROFESSIONALISM, joining PEOPLExpress could be the turning-point in your career (we're already one of the phenomenal success stories in the history of American business).

Our basic requirements are that, preferably, you've had previous business management experience–and that you be poised, personable, have some college education–and be between 5′2″ and 6′4″ with weight proportional.

MEET OUR REPRESENTATIVES AT THE WOMEN'S CAREER CONVENTION ON NOVEMBER 12th & 13th AT THE DAVID LAWRENCE CONVENTION CENTER BOOTH #401

Or send your resume or letter of inquiry to: PEOPLExpress, Newark International Airport, North Terminal, Building #55, Newark, NJ 07114, Attn: Customer Service Manager Recruiting Office

PEOPLExpress

We are an Equal Opportunity Employer M/F

22

contract and knew you were only supposed to work x number of minutes and hours," were often ill-suited to People's style. They were not comfortable with its loose structure and broadly defined, constantly changing job assignments. They were not as flexible as People Express types.

The flight manager positions were somewhat easier to fill. Many pilots had been laid off by other airlines due to economic problems, and People Express had an abundant pool of applicants. All licensed pilots had already met certain intelligence and technical skill criteria, but not every qualifed pilot was suited or even willing to be a People Express flight manager. Though flying time was strictly limited to the FAA's standard 30 hours per week (100/month, 1000/year), and rules regarding pilot rest before flying were carefully followed, additional staff and management responsibilities could bring a flight manager's work week to anywhere from 50 to 70 hours.

Furthermore, FMs were expected to collaborate and share status with others, even nonpilots. In return for being flexible and egalitarian—traits which were typically somewhat in conflict with their previous training and job demands—pilots at PE were offered the opportunity to learn the business, diversify their skills and interests, and benefit from profit sharing and stock ownership, if and when the company succeeded.

Recruitment Process

As many as 1600 would-be CSMs had shown up in response to a recruitment ad. To cull out "good PE types" from such masses, Dubose and her start-up team, eight CSMs whom she recruited directly from T.I., designed a multistep screening process.

Applicants who qualifed after two levels of tests and interviews with recruiters were granted a "board interview" with at least one general manager and two other senior people who reviewed psychological profiles and character data. In a final review after a day-long orientation, selected candidates were invited to become trainees. One out of 100 CSM applicants was hired (see Exhibit 5 for a CSM profile).

In screening pilots, "the interview process was very stringent. Many people who were highly qualified were eliminated." Only one out of three flight manager applicants was hired.

Training and Team Building

The training program for CSMs lasted for five weeks, six days a week, without pay. At the end, candidates went through an in-flight emergency evacuation role-play and took exams for oral competency as well as written procedures. Those who tested at 90 or above were offered a position.

The training was designed to enable CSMs, many without airline

---

EXHIBIT 5: Profile of a Customer Service Manager

Look for candidates who:

1. Appear to pay special attention to personal grooming.
2. Are composed and free of tension.
3. Show self-confidence and self-assurance.
4. Express logically developed thoughts.
5. Ask intelligent questions; show good judgment.
6. Have goals; want to succeed and grow.
7. Have strong educational backgrounds, have substantial work experience, preferably in public contact.
8. Are very mature; self-starter with outgoing personality.
9. Appear to have self-discipline; good planner.
10. Are warm, but assertive personalities; enthusiastic, good listeners.

Appearance Guidelines*

Well-groomed, attractive appearance.
Clean, tastefully worn, appropriate clothing.
Manicured, clean nails.
Reasonably clear complexion.
Hair neatly styled and clean.
Weight strictly in proportion to height.
No offensive body odor.
Good posture.
For women, make up should be applied attractively and neatly.
Good teeth.

* Above-listed guidelines apply to everyone regardless of ethnic background, race, religion, sex, or age.

---

experience, to perform multiple tasks and be knowledgeable about all aspects of an airline. Three full days were devoted to team building, aimed at developing trainees' self-awareness, communication skills, and sense of community. "We try to teach people to respect differences, to work effectively with others, to build synergy" [Miller].

On the last team-building day everybody chose two or three others to start work with. These groups became work teams, People's basic organizational unit. Initially, according to Miller, these decisions tended to be based on personalities and many trainees were reluctant to choose their own work teams. They were afraid of hurting people's feelings or being hurt. Trainers would remind them that People Express gave them more freedom than they would get in most companies, more than they were used to, and that "freedom has its price . . . it means you've got to be direct and you've got to take responsibility."

Over time, trainers learned to emphasize skills over personalities as the basis of team composition and to distinguish work teams from friendship groups. Choosing a work team was a business decision.

BOTTOM LINES: BUSINESS INDICATORS

As of the second quarter of 1982 People was showing a $3 million net profit, one of only five airlines in the industry to show any profit at that time. In addition to short-term profitability, Burr and his people enjoyed pointing out that by several other concrete indicators typically used to judge the health and competitive strength of an airline, their strategies were paying off and their innovative company was succeeding.

Marketing payoff—Over three million passengers had chosen to fly with People Express. The size of air passenger markets in cities serviced by People had increased since People's entrance. In some instances the increase had been immediate and dramatic, over 100 percent. Annual revenue rates were approaching $200 million.

Cost containment—Total costs per available seat-mile were the lowest of any major airline (5.2¢ compared to a 9.4¢ industry average). Fuel costs were 1/2–3/4¢ per-seat-mile lower than other airlines.

Productivity—Aircraft productivity surpassed the industry average by 50 percent (10.36 hours/day/plane compared to 7.06). Employee productivity was 145 percent above the 1981 industry average (1.52 compared to .62 revenue passenger miles per employee) for a 600-mile average trip. Return on revenue was 15.3 percent, second only to, and a mere .9 percent below, Southwest—the country's most successful airline. (Exhibit 6 shows operating statements through June 1982, and Exhibit 7 presents industry comparative data on costs and productivity.)

EXPLANATIONS OF SUCCESS

How could a new little airline with a funny name like People Express become such a formidable force so fast in such difficult times? Burr was fond of posing this question with a semipuzzled expression on his face and answering with a twinkle in his eye! The precepts and policies represented by that "funny" name—People—had made the difference. To back up this assertion, Burr and the other managing officers gave examples of how the people factor was impacting directly on the company's bottom line.

Consumer research showed that, notwithstanding heavy investments in award-winning advertisements, the biggest source of People's success was word of mouth; average customer ratings of passenger courtesy and personal treatment on ground and on board were 4.7 out of 5.

Several journalists had passed on to readers their favorable impres-

EXHIBIT 6

PEOPLE EXPRESS
Statement of operations
(in thousands of dollars, except per share data)

	From April 7, 1980, to March 31, 1981	Nine Months Ended December 31, 1981	Six Months Ended June 30, 1982 (Unaudited)
Operating revenues:			
Passenger	—	$37,046	$59,998
Baggage and other revenue, net.	—	1,337	2,302
Total operating revenues	—	38,383	62,300
Operating expenses:			
Flying operations	—	3,464	4,240
Fuel and oil.	—	16,410	22,238
Maintenance	$ 21	2,131	3,693
Passenger service	—	1,785	2,676
Aircraft and traffic servicing	—	7,833	10,097
Promotion and sales	146	8,076	7,569
General and administrative.	1,685	3,508	2,498
Depreciation and amortization of property and equipment	6	1,898	3,087
Amortization—restricted stock purchase plan	—	479	434
Total operating expenses	1,858	45,584	56,532
Income (loss) from operations	(1,858)	(7,201)	5,768
Interest:			
Interest income.	1,420	1,909	763
Interest expense	14	3,913	5,510
Interest expense (income), net	(1,406)	2,004	4,747
Income (loss) before income taxes and extraordinary item	(452)	(9,205)	1,021
Provision for income taxes	—	—	(470)
Income (loss) before extraordinary item	(452)	(9,205)	551
Extraordinary item—utilization of net operating loss carryforward	—	—	470
Net income (loss).	(452)	(9,205)	1,021
Net income (loss) per common share:			
Income (loss) before extraordinary item.	(.20)	(1.92)	.11
Extraordinary item.	—	—	.09
Net income (loss) per common share	$ (.20)	$ (1.92)	$ .20
Weighted average number of common shares outstanding	2,299	4,805	5,046

sions of People's service: "I have never flown on an airline whose help is so cheerful and interested in their work. This is an airline with verve and an upbeat spirit which rubs off on passengers." Others credited the commitment, creativity, and flexibility of People's people with the company's very survival through its several start-up hurdles and first-year crises.

Perhaps the biggest crisis was the PATCO strike which occurred just months after PE began flying. While the air traffic controllers were on strike, the number of landing slots at major airports, including Newark, were drastically reduced. This made People's original hub-and-spoke short-haul route design unworkable. To overfly Newark and have planes land less frequently without reducing aircraft utilization, People Express took a chance on establishing some new previously unserviced, longer routes between smaller, uncontrolled airports, such as Buffalo, New York, to Jacksonville, Florida. This solution was tantamount to starting a new airline, with several new Florida stations, new advertising, and new route scheduling arrangements. The costs were enormous. According to Hap Paretti:

> We could have run out of $25 million very quickly and there wouldn't be any People Express. The effort people made was astronomical, and it was certainly in their best interest to make that effort. Everybody recognized truly and sincerely that the air traffic controllers' strike was a threat to their very existence. They rearranged their own schedules, worked extra days, really put the extra flying hours in, came in on their off days to do the staff functions, all things of that nature, people just really chipped in and did it and did a damned good job. So when we went into these markets from Buffalo to Florida, we could go in at $69. If we went in at $199 like everybody else we wouldn't have attracted one person. We could go in very low like that because we had a cost structure that allowed us to do that. That's where the people strategy, from a cost standpoint, resulted in our survival. If it wasn't there we'd be in the same situation many other carriers are today, hanging on by a toenail.

By way of comparison, New York Air, a nonunion airline started by others from Texas International around the same time as People Express, with plenty of financial backing, economical planes, and a similar concept of low-cost, high-frequency service, but different people policies, was losing money.

THE HUMAN DIMENSIONS: POSITIVE CLIMATE AND PERSONAL GROWTH

In addition to becoming a financially viable business, People Express had shown positive results in the sphere of personal growth, the number one objective of its "people strategy." High levels of employee satisfaction showed up in first-year surveys done by the University of Michigan.

EXHIBIT 7: Comparative Data—Costs and Productivity

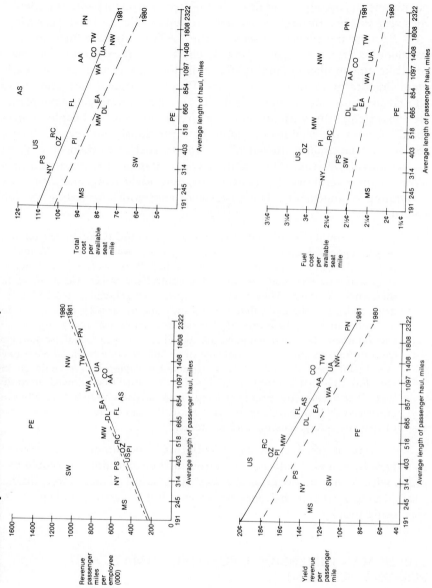

Key to Charts

AA	American	MS	Muse	PI	Piedmont
AS	Alaska	NY	New York Air	RC	Republic
CO	Continental	NW	Northwest Orient	SW	Southwest
DL	Delta	OZ	Ozark	TW	Trans World
EA	Eastern	PN	Pan American	WA	Western
FL	Frontier	PS	Pacific Southwest	UA	United
MW	Midway	PE	People Express	US	USAir

All data have been drawn from calendar 1981 results, except People Express and Muse, for which the first quarter of 1982 is used in order to offer comparisons not influenced by the start-up of operations.

Notes:

- Total cost is operating cost plus interest expense net of capitalized interest and interest income.
- Yield represents passenger revenues divided by revenue passenger miles (RPM).
- Average length of passenger haul is plotted on a logarithmic scale.
- The average line in each graph is a least-squared linear regression curve, based on 16 carriers which evolved in the regulated environment. Southwest, People Express, New York Air, Muse, and Alaska were not used in the calculations to determine the average. The 16 carriers were assigned equal weightings in the average.

Source: Hambrecht and Quist, June 1982, in company prospectus.

Less tangible but nevertheless striking were the nonverbal and anecdotal data. A cheerful, friendly, energetic atmosphere permeated the planes and passenger terminals as well as the private crew lounge and hallways of corporate headquarters. Questions about the company were almost invariably answered articulately, confidently, and enthusiastically. Stories of personal change, profit, and learning were common:

Ted E., customer service manager:

> I was a special education teacher making $12,000 a year, receiving little recognition, getting tired, looking for something else. I started here at $17,000, already have received $600 in profit sharing, and will soon own about 800 shares of stock worth $12 on the open market, all bought at very reduced rates. [Two months after this statement the stock was worth $26 a share.]

Glenn G., customer service manager:

> I was running a hotline and crisis program, then was assistant manager of a health food store before seeing the People Express recruitment ad in the newspaper and coming to check it out. I'm about to sell my car in order to take advantage of the current stock offer to employees.

Both Glenn and Ted had worked primarily in training but had also done "in-flight" and "ground-ops." jobs. They wanted more responsibilities, hoped to get them, but even if they didn't get promoted soon they expected to continue learning from and enjoying their work.

Michael F., a flight captain:

> I'm making $36,000. With my profit-sharing checks so far I've got $43,000 and on top of that I'll get sustained profit-sharing deals . . . I'm doing O.K. . . . Granted, at [another company] a captain might be making $110,000 working 10 days a month [but] they're not really worth it. [In other companies] the top people might make over $100,000 but they throw on 200 guys at the bottom so they can continue to make their salary. Is that fair? [Also, the seniority system would have kept Michael from being a captain at most other airlines.] We're radically different and I believe radically better.
>
> Most pilots know very little about what's going on in their company. In a People flight manager position, the knowledge people gain in this ratty old building is incredible. It's a phenomenal opportunity. It's very stimulating and exciting. I never thought I would have this much fun.

The stories of People's start-up team members and officers were even more dramatic. Each had profited and diversified substantially in their two years with People.

Melrose Dawsey, Burr's secretary at Texas International, was a managing officer at People with primary responsibility for administration. She owned 40,000 shares of stock, purchased at $.50 a share and worth, as of November 1982, over $20/share. For her own career development, she had also begun to assume some line management responsibilities in the in-flight area. In her spare time, she had earned her in-flight certification and run the New York marathon (as had Burr).

Lori Dubose, the youngest officer, had come to People to head the personnel function. In addition, she had taken on primary responsibility for the "in-flight" function as well as assuming the de facto role of key translator and guide vis-à-vis the company's precepts. As others came to see the value and purpose of People's precepts and human resource policies, Dubose's status among the officers had also risen.

Jim Miller had been a flight attendant for a year and base manager of in-flight services for four years at Texas International. As part of Dubose's start-up team, he had been coordinator of training, played a key role in recruitment, and then took on added responsibility for management and organizational development as well.

Hap Paretti, who began as legal counsel and head of government relations, quickly became involved in all aspects of the marketing function, and then went on to head flight operations, a move he acknowledged was "a little out of the ordinary" since he didn't have a technical background as a pilot. He spoke for all of the officers in saying, "As a managing officer you're expected to think about virtually every major decision that comes up for review."

Many spoke of the more subtle aspects of their personal development. Hap Paretti enjoyed the challenge of motivating other people and "managing by example" so as to enhance the growth of others.

Geoff Crowley, general manager in charge of ground operations and manpower scheduling, talked of becoming "less competitive" and "less up tight about winning alone" and more interested in working together with others to accomplish group and company goals.

THE DOWNSIDE OF PEOPLE'S GROWTH AND STRATEGIES

People Express's growth rate and strategies were not without significant organizational, financial, and human costs. By Burr's own observation:

> I would say at best, we're operating at 50 percent of what we'd like to be operating at in terms of the environment for people to do the best in. So we're nowhere near accomplishing what we would really like to accomplish in that regard. [But] I think we're better off today than we ever have been. And I think we're gaining on the problem.

Chronic Understaffing

Lori Dubose saw the hiring rate as the most difficult aspect of the company's growth process, causing many other problems:

If we could get enough people to staff adequately in all three areas of the company so that people got some staff and some line responsibility and would have some time for management development . . . I think things would be a lot different. [There's been] constant pressure to hire, hire, hire, and we just haven't gotten enough.

She was adamant, however, about not relaxing People's requirements.

When Dubose came to PE she expected to have to staff a company flying three planes which would have required rapid hiring of perhaps 200–300 people. The purchase of the Lufthansa fleet meant five to six times as many staff were needed. Given the time consumed by the selective recruiting process, and the low percentage of hires, the staffing demands for supporting and launching 17 planes stretched People's people to the limit. The result was chronic understaffing even by People's own lean staffing standards.

As of November 1982 the 800 permanent "managers" were supplemented with over 400 temporaries, hired to handle telephone reservations, a function trained CSMs were originally expected to cover. Some of these "res" workers had been there a year or more, but still were not considered full-fledged People people, though many would have liked to be. They received little training, did not work in teams, own stock, receive profit-sharing bonuses, or participate in advisory councils. They were just starting to be invited to social activities. For a while those wishing to be considered for permanent CSM positions were required to leave their temporary jobs first on the theory that any bad feelings from being rejected could be contagious and have a bad effect on morale. That policy was eventually seen as unfair, and dropped. Indeed, some managers saw the res area as a training ground for CSM applicants.

In August 1982 several MOs estimated that aside from reservation workers, they were short by about 200 people, though the recruiting staff was working 10 to 12 hours daily, often 6 days a week, as they had since January 1981. This understaffing in turn created other difficulties, limiting profits, policy implementation, and development of the organization's infrastructure.

If we had another 100 to 150 CSMs without adding an additional airplane we could just go out and add probably another half a million to a million dollars a month to the bottom line of the company. . . . There is additional flying out there that we could do with these airplanes . . . we could generate a lot more money . . . almost double the profits of the company. [McAdoo]

The policy of job rotation, critical to keeping everyone challenged and motivated, had been only partially implemented. Initial plans called for universal monthly rotations, with 50 percent of almost everyone's time spent flying, 25 percent on ground line work and another 25 percent in "staff functions." Due to staffing shortages, however, many people had been frozen in either line jobs without staff functions or vice versa. Some had become almost full-time coordinators or staff to a given function like recruiting and training, while others had done mostly line work and had little or no opportunity to do what they expected when they were hired as "managers." Since neither performance appraisal nor governance plans had been fully carried out, many felt inadequately recognized, guided, or involved.

There were also certain inherent human costs of People's people strategies. Rotating generalists were less knowledgeable and sometimes performed less efficiently than specialists on specific tasks. High commitment to the company plus expectations of flexibility in work hours could be costly in terms of individuals' personal and family lives. For many who were single and had moved to Newark to join People Express, there "was no outside life." As one customer service manager described it, "People Express is it . . . you kind of become socially retarded . . . and when you do find yourself in another social atmosphere it's kind of awkward."

For those who were married, the intense involvement and closeness with coworkers and with the company were sometimes threatening to family members who felt left out. Of the initial 15 officers, three had been divorced within a year and a half. The very fact of People's difference, in spite of the benefits, was seen by some as a source of stress; keeping the hierarchy to a minimum meant few titles and few promotions in the conventional sense. As an employee observed:

> You might know personally that you're growing more than you would ever have an opportunity to grow anywhere else but your title doesn't change, [which] doesn't mean that much to you but how does your family react?

Even People's biggest strengths, the upbeat culture, the high-caliber performance, and positive attitude of the work force could be stressful. "It's not a competitive environment, it's highly challenging. Everybody's a star . . . but, you know," said one customer service manager, "maintaining high positive attitude is enough to give you a heart attack."

High commitment and high ambition, together with rapid growth and understaffing, meant that most of People's managers were working long hard hours and were under considerable stress. Said one CSM, "Nobody is ever scheduled for over 40 hours [a week], but I don't know anybody who works just 40 hours."

Dubose recognized that the situation had taken a toll on everybody's health. "I was never sick a day in my life until I worked for People Express and in the last two years I've been sick constantly." Other managing officers, including Burr, had also been sick a lot, as had general managers. "And start-up team members—oh my God, they've got ulcers, high

blood pressure, allergies, a divorce . . . it's one thing after another . . .
we've all been physically run down." She adds, however, "It's not required
that we kill ourselves," asserting that personality traits and an emotionally
rewarding workplace accounted for the long hours many worked.

Burr's stance on this issue was that there were no emotional or
human costs of hard work, "Work is a very misunderstood, underrated
idea. In fact human beings are prepared and can operate at levels far in
excess of what they think they can do. If you let them think they're
tired and ought to go on vacation for two years or so, they will."

By the fall of 1982, though people were still generally satisfied with
their jobs and motivated by their stock ownership to make the company
work, many of People's managers below the top level were not as satisfied
or optimistic as they once were. A University of Michigan 18-month
climate survey taken in September 1982 showed signs of declining morale
since December 1981. "People are feeling frustrated in their work (and
feel they can't raise questions), cross-utilization is not being well-received,
management is viewed as less supportive and consultative, the total compensation package (including pay) is viewed less favorably. Clearly there
is work to be done in several areas." (Exhibit 8 contains excerpts from
the 1982 survey.) The report found significant differences in the percep-
tions of FMs and CSMs: flight managers were more skeptical of cross-
utilization and more uncertain of what self-management meant; they felt
most strongly that management was nonconsultative.

When questioned about such problems, those in leadership positions
were adamant that both business and personal difficulties were short term,
and the costs were well worth the long-term benefits. They felt that
virtually every problem was soluble over time with better self-management skills—including time management and stress management, which
everyone was being helped to develop—and with evolving improvements
in organizational structure. Even those responsible for recruitment insisted, "The challenge is that it seems impossible and there's a way to
do it."

> I don't think the long-term effects on the individual are going to be
> disastrous because we are learning how to cope with it. And I think the
> short-term effects on the organization will not be real bad because I think
> we're trying to put in place all the structure modifications at the same
> time that we're continuing the growth. That makes it take longer to get
> the structure modifications on the road. Which isn't real good. But they'll
> get there. Long term I think they will have a positive effect. I think. I
> wish I knew, for sure. [Dubose]

Within two months of the climate survey report, Dubose and others
from the People advisory council made a video presentation to address
many of the items raised in the report. For almost every major item a
solution had been formulated.

EXHIBIT 8: Excerpts from the 1982 Survey, Showing Changes since the December 1981 Climate Survey

In comparing the responses from the December 1981 and September 1982 surveys, the following significant changes have apparently taken place:*

- Getting help or advice about a work-related problem is not as easy.
- What is expected of people is not as clear.
- People are not being kept as well informed about the performance and plans of the airline.
- Satisfaction with work schedules has decreased.
- The number of perceived opportunities to exercise self-management is lower.
- The process used to create initial work teams is viewed less favorably.
- The work is generally perceived to be less challenging and involving.
- The overall quality of upper management is being questioned more.
- Fewer opportunities for personal growth and career development are apparent.
- People are not very comfortable about using the "open door" policy at People Express.
- People feel that their efforts have less of an influence on the price of People Express stock.
- The buying of discounted company stock is being perceived as less of a part of the pay program.
- The compensation package is thought to be less equitable considering the work people do.
- People feel they have to work too hard to accomplish what is expected of them.
- The team concept at People Express is being questioned more.
- Officers and General Managers are thought to be nonconsultative on important decisions.
- People Express is thought to be growing and expanding too fast.
- There is a stronger perception that asking questions about how the airline is managed may lead to trouble.

All of these changes are in a negative direction. Clearly, people are frustrated with the "climate" at People Express; morale and satisfaction are on the decline.

On the positive side, people's expectations of profiting financially are somewhat greater.

* Responses on many of these items were still quite positive in an absolute sense, though, showing a statistically significant decline from earlier studies.

In spite of all the new initiatives, each of which would entail considerable time and energy to implement, People's officers did not believe they should slow down the company's rate of growth while attending to internal problems. Their standard explanations were as follows:

> If you don't keep growing then the individual growth won't happen. People here have a very high level of expectation anyway, I mean unrealistic, I mean there's no way it's going to happen. They're not going to be general managers tomorrow, they're not going to learn each area of the airline by next month. But they all want to. And even a reasonable rate of growth isn't going to be attainable for the individual if we don't continue to grow as a company. And the momentum is with us now we're on a roll. If we lose the momentum now we might never be able to pick it up again. [Dubose]

Burr put it even more strongly:

> Now there are a lot of people who argue that you ought to slow down and take stock and that everything would be a whole lot nicer and easier and all that; I don't believe that. People get more fatigued and stressed when they don't have a lot to do. I really believe that, and I think I have tested it. I think it's obvious as hell and I feel pretty strongly about it.

He was convinced that the decrease in energy and decline in morale evident even among the officers were not reason to slow down but to speed up. For himself, he had taken a lot of time to think about things in his early years and had only really begun to know what was important to him between his 35th and 40th years. Then he had entered what he hoped would be an enormous growth period, accelerating "between now and when I get senile. It's sensational what direction does. The beauty of the human condition is the magic people are capable of when there's direction. When there's no direction, you're not capable of much."

Approaching 1983, the big issue ahead for People Express, as Burr saw it, was not the speed or costs of growth. Rather, it was how he and People's other leaders would "keep in touch with what's important" and "not lose sight of their humanity."

CASE 11

Polaroid–Kodak

On April 20, 1976, Eastman Kodak Company announced that it would challenge Polaroid Corporation's 28-year monopoly of the instant photographic field. At a press conference held that day in the grand ballroom of the Pierre Hotel in New York City, Walter A. Fallon, president of Kodak, demonstrated two new cameras and an instant film which he described as offering "remarkable color quality" to the consumer. Dr. Albert Fieg, leader of the company's 7-year development effort, stated that the chemistry of the new film was "fundamentally new."

The earliest responses from Polaroid Corporation were varied. Several days before the Kodak announcement, one Polaroid employee had been quoted in the press as saying, "I've seen it. It's primitive, but it works." Later, on the afternoon of the Kodak demonstration, Polaroid issued a formal statement: "We have had a chance to make a brief comparison between the Polaroid instant picture system and the new Kodak system. The comparison renews our confidence that our leadership in the field of instant photography remains unchallenged."

At the Polaroid annual meeting, held one week after the Kodak announcement, Edwin Land, founder, director of research, and chairman of the board of the company, informed his stockholders that their company had filed suit in federal court charging Kodak with the infringement of 10 Polaroid patents. In an emotional session, during which there were periods of prolonged applause from the crowd, Land commented on the situation: "This is our very soul that we are involved with. This is our whole life. For them it's just another field. . . . The only thing that keeps us alive is our brilliance, and the only thing protecting our brilliance is our patents. . . . We will stay in our lot and protect that lot. . . . How serious this is remains to be seen. That's for the courts to decide."[1]

With what some reporters described as a strange blend of ridicule and outrage, Land went on to say that since the introduction of the Kodak system, Polaroid had been "in a state of euphoria" and that their real fear had been that Kodak's product "might incorporate some of the really brilliant ideas we've had but never incorporated ourselves."[2]

Other events at the Polaroid annual meeting centered on several new products then in the late planning or preproduction stages, including instant color transparencies; instant color movies; 8-by-10-inch instant camera and film; and, finally, a camera the size of a room for making full color, instant, life-size copies of museum paintings. This device, Land said, would "change the whole world of Art . . . make great paintings available in every high school . . . [and] bring museums into the home."[3] Land also demonstrated an improved SX–70 film which had a coating that reduced surface reflections and which would develop properly over a wider temperature range.

POLAROID CORPORATION

Origins and Growth

The Polaroid camera was introduced in 1948 as a 5-pound, $90 revolutionary product that produced brown and white pictures one minute after exposure. In 1949, the first full year of sales for the product, company sales reached $6.7 million, more than four times the level of the previous year. Twenty-seven years later the company's sales broke the $800 million mark, proving to skeptics that what they had considered a mere fad was actually one of the most dramatic achievements in the history of photography. From 1947 to 1975, Polaroid's sales grew at an average annual compounded rate of more than 25 percent, while profits and common stock price advanced by more than 17 percent per year (see Exhibit 1). In an accomplishment matched by only a handful of companies, Polaroid achieved an average price-earnings ratio of 44 during this period. By 1969 each dollar invested in Polaroid common stock in 1948 had grown to more than $500. This consistent and clearly outstanding financial performance could be broken down into several distinct phases.

Although for most people the story of Polaroid began in Boston, Massachusetts, in November 1948, with the first retail sales of the "picture in a minute" Polaroid Land Camera, in reality Polaroid (or more accurately

---

[1] *New York Times,* April 28, 1976.

[2] *Wall Street Journal,* April 28, 1976.

[3] *Boston Globe,* April 28, 1976.

EXHIBIT 1: Sales Volume, Earnings per Share, and Stock Price—Polaroid Corporation, 1948–1975

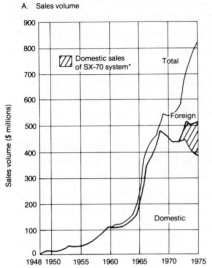

A. Sales volume

B. Earnings per share and stock price

* Researcher's estimate.

Source: Company annual reports.

* $0.32 per share loss.

† Average of high and low by years.

Source: Company annual reports; Merrill Lynch, Inc., historical library.

Edwin Land) had been in business for almost 20 years by that time. Land's initial research dealt with means of polarizing light. In 1932 he and an associate created the Land–Wheelwright Laboratories, Inc., to develop, manufacture, and sell light-polarizing filters. The name of the company's first product, the "Polaroid" filter, was derived from the fact that the filter was composed of cellul*oid* material which *polar*ized light.

The first two customers of any great size for Land and Wheelwright were Eastman Kodak Company, which signed a contract in 1934 for the purchase of "Polascreens," and American Optical Company, which signed a contract in 1935 for the purchase of filter material to be used in "Polaroid Day Glasses" (sunglasses). The money from these contracts provided the young company with funds to continue its development of Polaroid filter products. An additional $750,000 supplied by two investment banking firms in 1937 enabled the company to continue its search for profitable applications for the filter. At that time, the most promising applications appeared to be in 3-D movies (which required that each viewer wear special polarized glasses) and automobile headlights and windshields

(where it was thought the product could reduce the glare from the head-
lights of oncoming vehicles at night).

Polaroid's sales grew from $142,000 in 1937 to $1,481,000 in 1948,[4]
most of the increase represented by sales of Polaroid filter material for
use in sunglasses. The filters, however, never gained widespread use and,
as a result, the company remained much smaller than Land was comfortable with. In 1943 Land began working on the ideas that would form
the basis for an "instant" photographic process and camera. He appears
to have made his first related patent application in June 1944, and by
that time work on the "Land Camera" must have been under way at
Polaroid. In 1945, the company raised $2 million by means of a rights
offering to existing stockholders.

From 1947 to 1962, Polaroid's revolutionary instant photographic
product was essentially a black and white print system for amateur use.
While the product as first introduced fell short of conventional materials
in several respects, it did offer the consumer a truly unique way of making
pictures. Until 1950 the large and bulky roll-film camera could produce
only sepia (brown and white) pictures of sometimes uneven quality from
a comparatively slow film. From 1950 to 1959, however, Polaroid introduced progressively faster films (higher ASAs), which included panchro-
matic film. (See Appendix B.)

In 1960 the time needed to develop a finished print was reduced
for all films from the original 60 seconds to 10 seconds. In the same
year, the company introduced its first camera with automatic exposure
control. By the end of 1962, the company had sold four million Polaroid
cameras. (See Appendix A for information on the market for amateur
photographic products.)

Major Strategic Policies

During Polaroid's exploitation of the market for its black and white
instant photographic system, the company's financial strategy appeared
to be always to preserve capital for investment in the aspects of its business
that would yield the highest possible returns. Plants and equipment were
usually rented or leased; camera manufacture was always subcontracted
to others; and negative material, although developed by Polaroid itself,
was always purchased under long-term contracts from Eastman Kodak.
Capital investments were made only in the critical or truly proprietary
aspects of manufacturing. The company never made any significant use
of long-term debt.

In the marketplace, the company reached out directly to the consumer by advertising. It concentrated on direct sales to large retailers;

---

[4] Sales made to the government during World War II are not included in these figures.

dealers and distributors were looked upon merely as means to deliver the product to the consumer. Industry observers were always amazed by the company's willingness to have its products sold nearly at cost by outlets using them to build retail traffic. Moreover, the company never appeared to be concerned by the high turnover in its sales staff, which, in the opinion of many observers, it treated more as "order-takers" than true salespeople. The company rarely offered dealers sales incentives such as co-op advertising programs, mixed-case discounts, or introductory specials. Product improvements were often introduced with surprising suddenness. New products were generally made available to dealers on an allocated basis during the first few months following their introduction. As a result, dealers were quite often left to dispose of obsolete merchandise as best they could, before they were able to replace it with the newer form.

Polaroid remained apart from the other companies in the industry. It never licensed others to manufacture cameras for its highly profitable films. Indeed, the company built an extensive wall of patent protection around its camera designs and diligently defended its position as the sole manufacturer of instant cameras and films.

Perhaps most importantly, the company never appeared to be at all interested in diversification. Every product introduced since 1948 related solely to the photographic process in its instant form.

An important aspect of Polaroid was Edwin Land's total involvement and identification with his company, of which he owned about 20 percent during the early 1960s. Land's management style seemed to be almost a philosophy. Annual meetings were a unique experience for stockholders; sales and earnings figures were rarely mentioned. At typical meetings Land would demonstrate one or more new products or processes he and his large research team had developed. Most often these demonstrations were totally unrelated to the products the company intended to introduce in the future. Land would occasionally remind his stockholders why Polaroid existed: "Our function is to sense a deep human need . . . then satisfy it. . . . Our company has been dedicated throughout its life to making only those things which others cannot make. . . . We proceed from basic science to highly desirable products."

Results by 1962

Polaroid had achieved impressive financial success by 1962. Since 1947, sales had grown at an average of 42 percent per year compounded, profits at 25 percent per year, and the common stock price had advanced at a rate of 41 percent per year. By the end of 1962, Polaroid had become the second largest photographic products company in the United States. Sales had remained almost level for three years, however, implying that Polaroid had perhaps saturated the market for its black and white product in all its forms (amateur roll films, professional sheet films, x-ray film, and transparencies) and that the total market was not growing very rapidly.

The Introduction of Instant Color

On January 28, 1963, the stock market analysts' dreams came true: Polaroid introduced a color print film with a development time of 60 seconds. The film was compatible with all existing Polaroid cameras. Like the earlier black and white system, "Polacolor" represented a major technological achievement. In the past, conventional color film had had to be printed by highly sophisticated film-developing laboratories in a process that required more than 20 steps and 93 minutes. The new film not only offered color to the owners of Polaroid cameras, but produced its own protective plastic coating as a part of the development process. At that time, all of Polaroid's black and white films required the application of a protective coating by hand, a messy and often difficult procedure.

In June 1963 the company introduced a convenient pack form for its ASA 3000 black and white print and Polacolor films. The new films were designed to be used with a new automatic exposure Colorpack camera, the Automatic 100, priced at $100 retail. Following much the same strategy it had used with black and white, the company gradually reduced the prices of its cameras. In 1964 a lower-priced version of the Colorpack was introduced at a suggested list price of $75, followed a year later by a full line of cameras carrying suggested list prices ranging from $50 to more than $150. In 1967 a second generation of Colorpack cameras was introduced with slightly lower prices overall. In April 1969 the company introduced its first truly low-priced color camera, the $29.95 Colorpack. All of these cameras used Polacolor film, ASA 75, in the same easy-to-load pack size.

During this same period the company began to emphasize foreign sales of its products; its selling strategy abroad closely resembled that employed domestically (see Exhibit 1).

In an effort to gain distribution for its products in drugstores, supermarkets, and other unconventional photo outlets, the company introduced its Swinger camera and film in 1965. The Swinger was a $19.95 (list price) semiautomatic-exposure, fixed-focus, plastic-bodied camera that used a low-cost black and white roll film that did not require coating after processing. Several million of these cameras were sold in just three years. In 1968 the company completely phased out the Swinger by introducing its Big Swinger at a suggested list price of $24.95. The Big Swinger was identical in every respect to the previous model, with the exception of price and the fact that it used ASA 3000 speed film in the same packs as Polaroid's other cameras. The introduction of the Colorpack camera in 1969 virtually halted all sales of the Big Swinger. The Colorpack offered fully automatic exposure and the ability to use Polacolor film at a list price of only $5 more (and a retail price differential of about $3 on the average). By 1970 all traces of the Swinger and Big Swinger had been removed from retailer's shelves. Even the roll film for the original Swinger became almost impossible to obtain.

Results by 1972

As with the previous success in black and white, color caused explosive growth at Polaroid. By 1969, however, the company was once again facing softness in the demand for its products, as may be seen from Exhibit 1. Fortunately, foreign sales expanded rapidly during this period as a result of the gradual introduction of the same products that had given the company its growth in the domestic market during the 1960s.

The SX–70 System Is Introduced

In November 1969 Polaroid raised $99 million through a rights offering to existing stockholders. The prospectus stated that the company was about to undertake another step in its search for the absolute form of one-step photography: The money was to be used to help finance the research, development, and manufacture of a totally new instant color film and camera system. Three years later, in November 1972, the first SX–70 cameras and film went on limited sale in the Miami area. The camera, available in only one model, carried a suggested list price of $180, six times that of the company's Colorpack model, while the film was priced at $6.90 (list) for 10 exposures, compared with $5.49 for Polacolor pack film's 8 exposures.

Shrouded in the greatest of secrecy from the beginning of its design, the SX–70 system was another truly revolutionary product. Polaroid expected it to alter the fundamentals of the industry and eventually make obsolete both earlier instant camera systems (i.e., roll and pack film types). In Land's words, "Photography will never be the same. . . . With the gargantuan effort of bringing SX–70 into being, the company has come fully of age." With a romantic flair that only Land could have fully appreciated, the name SX–70 was chosen because it had been the code name of the original camera project in 1944.

From the consumer's point of view the SX–70 was indeed a different kind of Polaroid camera and film. While earlier systems had generated large quantities of chemically coated waste paper (used negative material and related paper goods), the SX–70 was totally litter-free. Of perhaps equal importance, it was no longer necessary to time the development of the picture. Other features included automatic ejection of the picture by a small electric motor (powered by a fresh battery present in each film pack), single lens reflex viewing and focusing, a folding design that allowed the camera to be carried in a large pocket or purse, and less need for periodic cleaning of critical mechanical components inside the camera.

The SX–70 Program

As originally conceived, the SX–70 program was designed to accomplish two major changes at Polaroid. The first of these was the total integration of the company. All of the manufacturing for SX–70 would be carried out within Polaroid. Toward this end a color negative manufacturing plant and camera assembly plant were designed and built. The program also required an expansion of the firm's existing chemical production facilities and film packaging operation. The total cost of these additions to plant and equipment was estimated, by most observers in 1969, to be $150 million, including the cost of research and engineering for the SX–70 camera and film.

Although the company never formally disclosed the cost of the SX–70 program, Land once referred to it in an interview as "a half-billion-dollar investment." Some outside estimates have placed the actual figure at much more than that. Speculations as to the source of the $350 million additional investment requirement have centered on two items. First, the company admitted publicly that it was not until January 1974 that the SX–70 product was breaking even on a variable manufacturing cost basis. It was not until early 1976 that most outside observers felt that the product was profitable in a conventional accounting sense. The total cost of these manufacturing-related expenses from 1969 to 1976 was estimated at $250 million. Second, some outside observers concluded that the design and development costs of the film and particularly the camera were much higher than anticipated. Both of these factors were related to the second major change SX–70 was intended to bring to Polaroid: the perfection of photography.

For Edwin Land, SX–70 was the realization of a dream, not merely a new product. He often referred to it as "absolute one-step photography." As he stated in a booklet entitled "The SX–70 Experience" (included with the annual report for shareholders in 1974):

> A new kind of relationship between people in groups is brought into being by SX–70 when the members of the group are photographing and being photographed and sharing the photographs: it turns out that buried within us—God knows beneath how many pregenital and Freudian and Calvinistic strata—there is a latent interest in each other; there is tenderness, curiosity, excitement, affection, companionability and humor; it turns out, in this cold world where man grows distant from man, and even lovers can reach each other only briefly, that we have a yen for a primordial competence, for a quiet good-humored delight in each other; we have a prehistoric tribal competence for a non-physical, non-emotional, non-sexual satisfaction in being partners in the lonely exploration of a once empty planet.

Thus, at age 63, Edwin Land brought into existence his highly personalized message to civilization in the form of the SX–70 system.

The design criteria for the SX–70 had been straightforward: The photographer need only compose a picture and press a button; the photographic process was to be totally separated from the creative act. This philosophically ordained task created a number of practical problems for designers. Rather than use the company's successful $30 Colorpack camera as a starting point, Land ordered his engineers to start from scratch on a totally new design. The parameters of the camera were startling: It must fold to a size appropriate for a pocket or purse; be a single lens reflex viewing and focusing design; focus from less than a foot to infinity; and be totally automatic (exposure, processing, and so forth) and litter-free.

The result, after more than three years of intense development work, was a $180 masterpiece of design. The reflex viewing system alone cost millions; a single mirror, one of three in the camera, took over two and one-half years of full-time computer work to engineer. The eyepiece design alone cost $2 million to develop. Capacity decisions for the plants under construction during the camera's design stage were made on the basis of company projections that first-year sales would be at least several million cameras (up to five million by some accounts). Long before the camera design was complete, the company's color negative pilot plant began turning out finished packs of SX–70 film.

Marketing the SX–70

In 1973, the first full year of sales for the SX–70 system, 470,000 cameras and 4.5 million packs of film were sold. The company reported that the system had contributed $75 million to its sales that year. During the year the company grappled with several technical problems. The camera factory, still in its infancy, was turning out a disturbing number of defective cameras even though it was operating at only a fraction of its capacity. At one point the company began to open Polaroid service centers in major cities across the United States in an effort to help consumers with their problems.

A more troublesome technical problem involved the battery built into each film pack. Packaging the battery in the film rather than the camera itself spared users the need to change batteries. But fumes from the battery seriously degraded the color quality of the pictures. Moreover, the battery had a shelf life of only several months. After working with the battery manufacturer for some time, Polaroid decided to build a plant and produce its own batteries. Within a few months the shelf life of the film was extended to six months and color quality improved dramatically.

By far the greatest problem facing Polaroid at the end of 1973 was the fact that camera sales were nowhere near the projected level. Both camera and film manufacturing operations were running at only a fraction of their rated capacity. Although the company sold about four million Colorpacks and an estimated 100 million packs of Polacolor film in 1973, both negative and camera manufacturing for this product line were sub-contracted to others.

In 1974, in an attempt to stimulate SX–70 sales, the company introduced an SX–70 Model II camera. Identical to the original in every respect except for price ($140 suggested retail) and exterior finish (all plastic versus chrome-plated plastic and genuine leather for the original), this model helped to boost 1974 SX–70 camera sales to about 750,000 units, trade sources estimated. The researcher estimated factory sales of the SX–70 system in 1974 at $100 million domestically.

In May 1975, faced with continuing consumer resistance to the product, the company introduced an SX–70 Model III camera, which carried a suggested list price of $99. The Model III replaced the reflex viewing arrangement of the earlier models with a conventional, and far simpler, viewfinder type. The company reported that it sold a total of about one million SX–70 cameras during 1975. The researcher's estimate of the 1975 sales volume of the SX–70 system was $150 million, about 80 percent of this from domestic sales.

In 1975 the company reported that it had sold about four million Colorpack cameras for the third year in a row. In March 1975, Polaroid introduced its Supershooter Colorpack camera at a suggested retail price of $24.95. In the same month the company introduced Polacolor II Color-pack film, the first instant film to offer the consumer excellent color. Earlier instant prints had tended to be somewhat subdued and lacked saturation in comparison with conventional color prints and slides. Both Supershooter and Polacolor II were manufactured by Polaroid in its own plants.

In January 1976, Polaroid introduced a Model IV SX–70 called the Pronto!, which was a nonfolding, nonreflex, molded-plastic-body camera with a suggested list price of $66. This model was widely discounted by retailers to $49 (only a few dollars over cost), and by late April 1976, sales and advance orders of Pronto! had exceeded 400,000 units. Industry observers began predicting that as many as two million SX–70 cameras might be sold during 1976.

Polaroid in April 1976

The suggested retail and common discount prices of the most popular models in Polaroid's two instant systems, as of April 1976, were as follows:

	List	Discount
Camera Prices:		
SX–70 (Pronto!)	$66.00	$49.00
Colorpack (Supershooter). . . .	$28.00	$23.00
Film Prices:		
SX–70 (Pronto!)	$ 6.99	$ 5.50
Colorpack (Supershooter). . . .	$ 6.75	$ 5.50

There were three major differences between the systems. First, while the price of the Supershooter was less than half that of the Pronto!, a Supershooter print cost about 25 percent more than a Pronto! print. Second, pictures made from Polacolor II film had far better color quality than was possible with SX–70 film.[5] Polacolor II prints rivaled conventional color prints in quality. Finally, the Pronto! offered far simpler camera operation. The user just focused and pressed a button, and the camera ejected the print, which developed automatically in about 12 minutes with no litter. The Supershooter user, on the other hand, had to pull each exposure from the camera, time the development for 60 seconds, and then dispose of the used negative (which was covered with a highly alkaline processing jelly).

In terms of manufacturing processes, the two film types were similar, in that both required a negative, a processing reagent, and print material. Each SX–70 pack, however, also required a battery to power the camera's flash, exposure, and print ejection motor. The Pronto! was essentially a Supershooter with a mirror and an electric motor added.

By April 1976, about 25 million Colorpack cameras were in use worldwide, compared with an estimated 2 million SX–70s. Most industry observers agreed that the Colorpack system was the more profitable of the two, contributing at least 95 percent to the company's earnings. (See Exhibit 2 for Polaroid's 1975 financial statement.)

EASTMAN KODAK COMPANY

Origins and Growth

George Eastman had a bit of a jump on Edwin Land; he marketed his first camera in 1888. Kodak's motto, "You press the button, we do the rest," and the ubiquitous "yellow box" were revolutionary developments of their time, sweeping America and the world for 60 years before the first Land camera appeared. Kodak was the world's first integrated photographic firm, so fully integrated at one point that it owned its own

---

[5] Or the new Kodak instant film (researcher's personal judgment, and assessment of industry opinion).

EXHIBIT 2

POLAROID–KODAK
Consolidated Financial Statements, Year Ending December 31, 1975
(in millions of dollars)

INCOME STATEMENT

	Polaroid	Kodak
Net sales	$813	$4,959
Less: Cost of goods sold	468	2,927
Advertising expense	52	*
Research and development	64	313
Administrative expenses	121	632
Operating profit	108	1,087
Less: Interest expense	1	15
Plus: Interest income	9	40
Other income	7	−6
Profit before tax	123	1,106
Less: Income taxes	61	493
Net profit	62	613
Cash dividends paid	10	332

BALANCE SHEET

Assets	Polaroid	Kodak
Current:		
Cash	$ 22	$ 76†
Marketable securities, at cost	158	672
Receivables	181	804
Inventories	244	986
Prepaid expenses	26	82
Total current assets	631	2,620
Fixed:		
Property, plant and equipment, at cost	435	4,348
Less accumulated depreciation	232	1,970
Net property, plant and equipment	203	2,378
Total assets	$834	$5,056†

Liabilities and Equity		
Current liabilities:		
Dividends payable	0	143
Notes payable to banks	12	0
Payables and accruals	80	688
Taxes payable	53	246
Total current liabilities	145	1,077
Stockholders' equity:		
Common stock at par value	33	404
Additional paid-in capital	122	268
Retained earnings	534	3,037
Total stockholders' equity	689	3,709
Total liabilities and equity	$834	$5,056

* Not included separately, included with "Administrative expenses."
† Includes $58 million of miscellaneous assets.

Source: 1975 annual reports for Eastman Kodak Company and Polaroid Corporation.

stockyards to assure a high-quality source for its substantial photographic-grade gelatin needs.

As a trip to the average corner drugstore would have revealed, Kodak products, film, and cameras clearly dominated the U.S. market for conventional amateur products in 1976. Most estimates of Kodak's market shares were 90 percent for film and 85 percent for cameras at that time. The firm's share of the expenditures for processing and printing of amateur films was only about 15 percent, largely because of a 1954 consent decree with the U.S. Justice Department which stipulated that Kodak sell its films and processing separately. If the dollar value of the print paper, chemicals, and processing equipment sold by Kodak to independent photofinishers is included, however, the company's effective market share of processing was probably closer to 50 percent overall.

Kodak was active in many markets beyond those for conventional amateur still films, cameras, and processing. For example, through its Eastman Chemicals Division (1975 sales $1 billion) it sold a wide variety of chemicals, fibers, and plastics to industrial customers. The company's domestic and foreign photographic divisions (1975 sales $4.5 billion combined) marketed a wide range of products including amateur movie films and equipment, professional still and motion picture films and equipment, medical and industrial x-ray films and equipment, various graphic arts and audiovisual products, microfilm, and other business products. Kodak was, with rare exceptions, the leader in each market in which it competed. Compared with Agfa-Gavaert of Belgium, the only other full-line photographic products company in the world, Kodak was a giant; its photographic sales alone were three times those of Agfa in 1975.

Major Strategic Policies

Kodak's dominance of the photographic industry stemmed primarily from its leadership in film technology. To Kodak's competitors, the firm's complete mastery of all aspects of the photographic art was a mighty barrier. Since the 1935 introduction of Kodachrome (with an ASA speed of 10), the first color film for amateur use, Kodak had managed to keep ahead of every other company in almost every aspect of photography. It was Kodak that foresaw and nurtured the color slide and color print for the amateur market. It was not until 1954, when the Justice Department forced it to sell film and processing separately, that other companies were even allowed to participate in Kodak's lucrative color products. In the 20-year period during which it captured all of the profits from both film manufacturing and processing (a situation *all* film manufacturers agree is the ideal), Kodak also prevented the formation of independent photofinishing laboratories equipped to process color products sold by its competitors. The net effect of the tied-in sale of processing was thus to retard the dispersion of color film technology and to allow Kodak to become the dominant company in amateur color photography.

Even after 1954, Kodak was able to capitalize on its previous success by constantly forcing competitors to upgrade the quality of their color film products. Most firms simply did not have the research expertise to continue the fight. During the 1950s Kodak effectively displaced all foreign and domestic competitors from the U.S. market. In addition it successfully defended itself from formidable would-be competitors. In the early 1960s, a joint venture between Bell & Howell[6] and Du Pont failed completely. Du Pont described its color film research program as an exasperating effort: Each time it was able to improve its film to meet Kodak's high quality, Kodak film mysteriously became even better. In 1961, when Du Pont's film was finally ready for introduction, at a total cost to both companies estimated by some to be in the tens of millions of dollars, Kodak responded to the threat with Kodachrome II, a color slide film with an ASA speed of 25 and far better color quality than the original against which the Du Pont entry was targeted. The Du Pont product was withdrawn before it ever reached the market.

For a time some competitors attempted to increase their share of the market by lowering their prices slightly. Consumers' failure to respond positively was interpreted as an unwillingness to accept less quality, or less assurance of quality, under almost any circumstance. In 1976 most competitive color film products were sold for a slight premium over Kodak's prices. Most of Kodak's competitors apparently owed their existence to a small following of users who wished to avoid the supersaturated colors, extremely high resolution, or mass market image of Kodak's color films.

1963: The First Kodak System

Since the introduction of the company's Instamatic camera and film products, Kodak's emphasis in the amateur photographic market had been on "systems"—unique film formats packaged in a cartridge or magazine usable only in cameras designed expressly for that configuration. On February 28, 1963, the Instamatic system hit the market, with complete availability of the product on that day to 75,000 retailers in 147 countries supported by major advertising in eight languages. Prices for the camera, available in five models, ranged from $20 to more than $100 (list). Ten million Instamatic cameras were sold in the 26 months following their introduction.

In that same year Kodak also introduced Kodachrome-X (ASA 64) color slide film for 35mm and Instamatic cameras and the Super 8 film

---

[6] At the time, Kodak's film and camera business alone was about 10 times the size of Bell & Howell's total sales.

and camera system for the amateur movie market. The major feature of the Super 8 and Instamatic systems was that the films were cartridge-loaded into cameras equipped, in most models, with automatic exposure. For the first time in conventional amateur photography, consumers were relieved of two major obstacles to their picture-taking: the manual dexterity required for loading roll-film cameras, and the problem of setting proper exposure. The Instamatic cameras also featured a more convenient flashbulb device, the Flashcube, which provided four flashbulbs in an easy-to-insert configuration (including a disposable reflector for each bulb). Earlier flashbulb devices had been rather bulky and unrealiable.

As one might have predicted, the introduction of the Instamatic and Super 8 systems resulted in not only a dramatic increase in the sales of Kodak's cameras, but an equally impressive increase in film use.

1972: The Second Kodak System

In May 1972 Kodak introduced its Pocket Instamatic system in a manner similar to that used in 1963 with the original system. The major improvement in the Pocket Instamatics was the dramatic reduction in the size of the camera, which was about one-third as large as the original model. Prices for the camera, available in five models, ranged from $25 to more than $200 (list).

In the same month, Kodak introduced its XL Super 8 amateur movie system, which allowed the user to film under most existing light conditions. For example, the light from a single candle on a birthday cake was, in most instances, adequate for proper exposure of subjects within several feet of the cake. In the fall of 1972, Kodak added sound movie cameras to its XL Super 8 line, bringing the total number of Kodak Super 8 movie cameras to five, ranging in price from $35 to $200 (list).

In April 1975 Kodak introduced a new generation of Pocket Instamatics, the Trimlite series. The major improvement in this version of the Instamatic was the use of a small piezoelectric crystal to generate electricity to fire a new form of flashbulb, the Flipflash. One of the cameras in the line was also equipped with a telephoto lens which could be brought into position by moving a small slide at the top of the camera. On the basis of the product name, and the fact that the most expensive camera in the line had been designed to be able to use an ASA 400 color print film, industry observers inferred that Kodak was close to bringing out its long-awaited XL still camera color film, which would eliminate the need for flashbulbs almost entirely.

Industry Reactions

The effect of the two Instamatic waves on the conventional amateur market was significant. By the end of 1975 it was estimated that Kodak had sold more than 60 million Instamatic cameras in just a little more than a decade. During this same period all of Kodak's competitors combined had sold, by most estimates, no more than 10 million Instamatic-type cameras. By surprising the industry with radical changes in both camera design and film requirements, the company was able to consolidate its position in the marketplace. Independent camera manufacturers were faced with a need to invest in increasingly complex production equipment to remain price competitive with Kodak. Kodak's expanding use of precision plastic optics, integrated circuits, and piezoelectric-type devices left many manufacturers dumbfounded. Film manufacturers were equally amazed by Kodak's ability to push film technology to new limits by the use of smaller negatives and higher ASA speeds in both color print and transparency films without significant reductions in quality. Independent processors were forced to buy new processing equipment and learn new techniques to stay in business. In addition, Kodak's competitors had to face the fact that Kodak's product would be on sale for a year or more before they were able to react effectively.

To counteract some of the criticism it was receiving from other manufacturers, Kodak freely licensed its systems. For Kodak, the benefits were twofold. First, of course, licensing probably lessened Kodak's vulnerability to antitrust suits. More importantly, perhaps, the major effect of licensing was to increase the number of cameras that could use Kodak's highly profitable films. In the still film amateur market, the Pocket Instamatic format, which used a negative only 25 percent of the size used until that time, had substantially eliminated all but one or two of Kodak's film sales competitors.

Kodak's Instant System

In February 1976 Eastman Kodak had announced that sometime in April it would demonstrate its own instant photographic product for the amateur market. Not until the day of the demonstration, April 20, did the company reveal that its product would go on sale first in Canada on May 1, 1976, and in the United States on July 5, 1976. Rumors of a Kodak instant product had been circulating in the industry for more than a decade, peaking at one point in 1969 when various publications reported a Kodak–Polaroid agreement to allow the former to market a Colorpack-compatible film of its own by sometime in 1975. But it was not until early 1970 that Kodak formally announced that work on a Colorpack-type film was under way.

In its 1973 annual report, however, Kodak indicated that it had altered its research goals somewhat: "In the field of rapid-access photography, the basic decisions have . . . made feasible a film that will yield dry prints of high quality without waste, to be used in equipment priced for a wide spectrum of consumers."

This announcement left some industry observers puzzled as to whether Kodak's film was still intended for use in Colorpack-type cameras. The company's 1974 annual report offered some clarification: "During the year, Kodak completed the design of its own instant cameras and finalized the format and characteristics of a litter-free film for instant prints." Thus Kodak had, within a comparatively brief period, moved away from the idea of making a film for existing cameras. It now intended to market a system of its own design.

In its 1975 annual report, the company devoted four pages to a detailed explanation of its progress in instant photography, as well as two full pages describing its new Ektaprint 100 Xerox-type copier which had been on limited sale since October 1975.

Some observers, noting that most of Polaroid's basic patent protection had run out by 1969, were concerned by the seemingly ponderous method by which Kodak finally reached the market with an instant product of its own. But others, as they compared the Kodak system with its competition (see Exhibits 3, 4, and 5), were more impressed by Kodak's decision to bring out a completely new system, and the company's stated

EXHIBIT 3: Comparison of Cameras

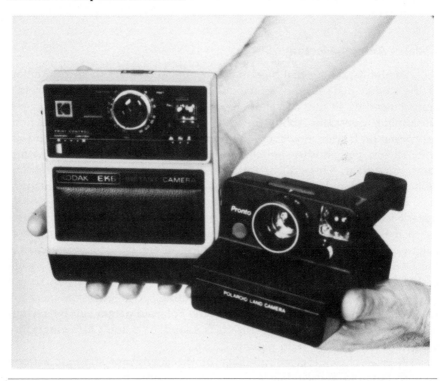

EXHIBIT 4: Comparison of Polaroid and Kodak Instant Color Print Films

	Polaroid SX–70	Kodak PR–10
Format.	Square	Rectangular
ASA speed	100	150
Image size	3.13 inches by 3.13 inches	2.63 inches by 3.56 inches
Image area	9.77 square inches	9.35 square inches
Development time	About 12 minutes	About 10 minutes
Color quality*	Good	Good
Color stability*	Good	Good
Exposures per pack	10	10
List price per pack.	$6.99	$7.45
Average retail price	$5.50	$5.50
Exposed through	Front	Rear

* Researcher's personal judgment and assessment of industry opinion.

Source: Published specifications. Photograph courtesy of *Modern Photography*.

intention of freely licensing others to build cameras that could use the film. With respect to licensing the production of film cartridges and film itself for its instant product, however, Kodak was silent. As one executive of a competing film manufacturing company commented, "It would take us three to five years and a lot of money to come up with a film for that camera."

Kodak's Annual Meeting

At the Kodak annual meeting held one week after the introduction of the Kodak Instant, and coincidentally on the same day as Polaroid's annual meeting, Walter A. Fallon, Kodak's president, responded to several stockholder questions about the new product. "There will be no time for resting on laurels, however," he stated. "I can tell you that the curtain will rise on yet another member of the Kodak Instant family within the coming year. This will be the Kodak EK8 Instant Camera, a folding model designed and built at the Kodak Camera Works in West Germany."

Fallon continued by saying that expressions of interest in the Kodak Instant from the trade were "at a high and very positive pitch." When asked if Kodak planned to introduce an under-$20 EK2 instant camera, Fallon declined to comment. At that point, however, he confirmed that the EK8 would probably be available early in the fall of 1976 for a suggested retail price of about $140.

Later on the day of the annual meeting, at a luncheon held for security analysts, Fallon commented on the Polaroid patent suit by saying, "We believe that our patent position is sound. We don't knowingly infringe anybody else's valid patents."

A brief chronological summary of the significant strategic actions of both Polaroid and Kodak is shown in Appendix B.

EXHIBIT 5: Price Comparison of Polaroid and Kodak Instant Systems

	List Price	Average Retail Price*
Polaroid		
Camera: Pronto!	$66.00	$49.00
Film: SX–70	6.99	5.50
Flash: Flashbar	3.28	1.89
Cost per picture:		
Available light	.70	.55
Flash	1.03	.74
Reprints (by mail from Polaroid, $.88 handling charge per order):		
Wallet size	.39	same
Same size.	.49	same
5 inches by 5 inches	2.25	same
8 inches by 8 inches	5.50	same
11 inches by 11 inches	9.95	same
Kodak		
Camera: EK4	$53.50	$39.00
Camera: EK6	69.50	49.00
Film: PR–10	7.45	5.50
Flash: Flipflash	2.30	1.19
Cost per picture:		
Available light	.75	.55
Flash	1.04	.70
Reprints (available from any Kodak dealer):		
Same size.	.85	.68
3½ inches by 4½ inches	1.00	.80
5 inches by 7 inches	2.25	1.80
8 inches by 10 inches	5.35	4.28
11 inches by 14 inches	10.75	8.60

* Based upon interviews with camera dealers in the greater Boston area in May 1976.

Source: Researcher's fieldwork.

APPENDIX A

A Brief Note on the Amateur Photographic Products Market

Because the photographic industry was highly concentrated, it was very difficult to obtain precise data on the size and character of the segments that made up the total market for amateur photographic products. Most firms treated their market data with the same secrecy as their film and camera designs. This note is a composite picture assembled from a wide variety of public sources.

APPENDIX A *(continued)*

THE MARKET IN 1962

In 1962 the total U.S. domestic market for amateur photographic products was about $1.4 billion at the retail level. In that year some 2.2 billion snapshots were taken by amateur photographers.

The total U.S. domestic factory sales of Eastman Kodak for all of its photographic products were estimated to be $600 million at that time. Polaroid Corporation's reported domestic sales were $100 million in 1962, about 40 percent of this volume related to film sales.

About half of the pictures taken in 1962 were in color, half in black and white. The average consumer used about four rolls of film per year. Women took roughly 60 percent of the pictures.

THE MARKET IN 1969

In 1969 the total U.S. domestic market for amateur photographic products was about $3.5 billion at the retail level. About 4.5 billion snapshots were taken by amateur photographers that year.

Kodak's domestic sales for all of its photographic products were about $1.5 billion in 1969. Polaroid reported domestic sales of $466 million that same year. Kodak's domestic sales of still camera films to the amateur market were about $265 million at the time, about $140 million of this from sales of Kodacolor film, about $100 million from Kodachrome and Ektachrome, and about $25 million from its black and white films. Polaroid's domestic sales of film to the same market were estimated to be $240 million, about $135 million of this from Polacolor and about $105 million from ASA 3000 speed film. The Kodak figure excluded the company's sales of processing services and its sales of equipment and supplies to the photofinishing industry.

Kodak did all of its own manufacturing for film and camera products, and enjoyed an estimated pretax profit margin on these items of about 70 percent. Polaroid, which subcontracted both negative and camera manufacturing, was thought to gross about 45 percent pretax on its cameras and films.

THE MARKET IN 1975

In 1975 the total U.S. domestic market for amateur photographic products was about $6.6 billion at the retail level. In that year about 7 billion snapshots were taken by amateur photographers.

Kodak's domestic sales for all of its photographic products were estimated at $2.5 billion. Polaroid reported total domestic sales of $500 million. One analyst estimated Kodak's and Polaroid's film sales to the

APPENDIX A *(concluded)*

domestic amateur still film market at "about $500 million for each," which was obviously a bit high for Polaroid.

About 90 percent of the pictures taken in 1975 were in color, 10 percent in black and white. The average consumer used about eight rolls of film per year. Again, 60 percent of the pictures were taken by women. Market data suggested that 92 percent of America's homes owned at least one conventional camera, 49 percent owned at least one Polaroid camera. Surveys taken by Kodak suggested that as many as 24 million American homes would buy an instant camera with "improved features."

In 1975 the total world market for amateur photographic products was about $14 billion at the retail level. Worldwide sales of cameras and films were estimated at $2 billion for Kodak, $800 million for Polaroid, and $2 billion for all other companies combined. About $1 billion in retail sales was related to sophisticated equipment.[6] Most of the remaining $8 billion or so was related to the photofinishing industry, which was composed of a multitude of retail outlets and processing laboratories worldwide.

RETAILING AMATEUR PRODUCTS IN 1975

Sales of sophisticated equipment excepted, the average photographic products dealership made its money primarily from processing services. The use of film and cameras of all types as traffic builders and loss leaders had consistently forced dealer margins on both of these items down to minimal levels, in many cases to no more than 5 percent or 10 percent above cost. Retailers, however, seemed to be holding the line on processing prices, where margins of 25 percent or more were common.

---

[6] Sophisticated equipment included cameras, projectors, and various accessory items which were usually only available in stores where more than 50 percent of sales came from photographic products. Prices for this equipment were much higher than those for mass market items.

APPENDIX B

Dates of Significant Strategic Actions

Polaroid

1934	Contract with Kodak for Polascreens
1944	Instant photographic research begun
1948	Contract with Kodak for negative
	First camera introduced at $90
1950	True B&W film introduced, ASA 100
1955	ASA 200 and 400 B&W films introduced
1959	ASA 3000 B&W film introduced
1960	B&W film development time reduced from 60 to 10 seconds
	First auto-exposure camera introduced
1963	Contract with Kodak for color negative January, Polacolor film introduced June, ASA 3000 and Polacolor films introduced in pack format for new, $100 auto-exposure pack camera

Kodak

1934	Contract with Polaroid for Polascreens
1935	Kodachrome color film introduced, ASA 10
1948	Contract with Polaroid for negative
1954	Film and processing sales split apart
1961	Kodachrome II introduced, ASA 25
1963	Contract with Polaroid for color negative February, Instamatic introduced, five models, $20 to $100+
	Super 8 introduced
	Kodachrome-X introduced for 35mm and Instamatic cameras

1964 Cheaper Colorpack camera at $75

1965 Full line of Colorpacks, $50 to $150
     Swinger, $20 B&W roll film camera

1967 Second-generation Colorpacks, $45 and up

1968 Big Swinger $25, ASA 3000 in packs

1969 April, $30 Colorpack camera introduced
     November, $99 million raised for R&D and
     total integration of company

1972 November, SX–70 camera introduced at $180

1974 SX–70 Model II introduced at $140

1975 March, Supershooter introduced at $25
     March, Polacolor II introduced
     May, SX–70 Model III introduced at $99

1976 January, Pronto! announced
     March, Pronto! introduced at $66

1969 Polaroid's basic patents expiring
     Rumors of Kodak ability to market
     Colorpack-compatible film by 1975

1972 February, Pocket Instamatic introduced—
     five models from $25 to $200+
     May, XL Super 8 system introduced
     Fall, Sound XL system introduced, giving
     company total of five movie cameras priced
     from $35 to $200

1975 May, Trimlite series introduced, including
     telephoto model

1976 February, announced April demonstration
     April, demonstrated and announced May
     sales in Canada, July sales in United States
     April, announced folding model at $140 for
     possible fall 1976 introduction

Part II

POLICY ADMINISTRATION

CHAPTER 7

Designing and Managing the Overall Organization

In Part II we ask you to shift your attention to the task the general manager faces in leading the organization in the accomplishment of the purposes identified and decided upon by the process described in Part I. We are passing from the formulation of strategy to the implementation of that strategy via the people in the organization. The focus will be on the broader tasks of designing the appropriate structure and processes and managing the overall organization in the context of the strategy of the company.

The first part of the book is analytical in the usual sense of that word because it deals primarily with the economic environment of the firm and with the functional areas of the business such as marketing, production, and finance in the development of the firm's strategy. Quantitative analyses and techniques are of greater help with strategic issues than with the administrative tasks involved in leading the organization in the accomplishment of its strategy. What you have learned in organizational behavior, accounting and control, and from your own experience in organizations will be the most relevant inputs to the administrative challenges that face the general manager.

The concern of this chapter is one about which a great deal has been written. The challenges of motivating people to contribute their best efforts in the pursuit of purposes for the most part established by others for the benefit of others have been the subject of thought, research, and writings for thousands of years. Academic disciplines such as psychology and organizational behavior have developed which have much to say about these problems. Specific courses dealing with the behavior of people in organizations and methods of measuring their performance exist in every school of business, and any business library is likely to have hundreds of books and thousands of articles which treat these problems.

OBJECTIVES

The preceding should lead any sensible reader to ask what we need to add at this point to the knowledge you already have been exposed to in your courses and readings concerning the behavior of people in organizations. Our objectives are not to repeat what you have learned elsewhere. Instead, we want to emphasize three factors that should strongly influence the manner in which you apply what you have learned, in courses as well as from your own experiences in working with people, to the problems of the cases:

1.   We are dealing with specific companies with specific problems, administrative histories, and strategies which define purposes, key tasks, and constraints. It is highly desirable to attempt to generalize about how categories of problems similar to those in the case should be solved, but this should come after you address the problems at hand, not before. Your task is to suggest what steps Mr. Millman should take in The Adams Corporation (the first case in Part II) to bring about the changes he desires, and not to discuss the characteristics of the ideal management control system, compensation system, or decentralized organization structure for geographically decentralized firms without ever addressing Mr. Millman's specific problems.

2.   In dealing with the specific case situation, you will have to keep in mind that you are also dealing with real people, not idealized or typical people. Frequently you will not know as much about the individuals in the case as you would like, and as you would know in real life, but at least do not ignore what information is available. In the BCI case you do not have to know much more about either Mr. Lampton or Mr. Denham than can be gleaned from the case in order to deal with the problems that exist between these two very real people. Similarly, it will be essential to understand as best you can what it is that influences the American and Japanese managers in the Showa-Packard case, and what Mr. Stafford in the Struthers and Williamson case should consider before he sets about remedying what he thinks are the ills of the company he has just joined.

3.   Most important, your task will be the design of organization structure and processes and the management of its members as a means of achieving the overall purposes of the organization. We all desire a humane and satisfying work environment, but that environment must be effective in meeting organizational as well as individual goals. In the Lincoln Electric case you will find an explicit and unusual attempt to address both of these goals. Organizations in which individual efforts do not contribute sufficiently to the attainment of organizational goals

seldom prosper and sometimes fail, at least in the private sector. If an organization depends upon the voluntary support of its customers, the feedback from the marketplace ultimately will have an impact.

What you have learned elsewhere about interpersonal relationships, human motivation, measurement and control systems, organizational design, and leadership should surely be applicable to the general manager's task of leading the organization to the achievement of its strategy. We will be interested in the application of this knowledge, however, and not in the knowledge itself. In this sense, your task in this part of the book will differ somewhat from what you are likely to have been exposed to in other courses dealing with the topics described above.

We also hope that in this section you will develop for yourself some of the skills essential to the manager, and not just an understanding of the job and the intellectual ability to analyze problems and recommend action to someone else. The development of your personal skills can be facilitated by your classroom discussion of administrative situations. Listening to others, learning to understand what they mean as well as why they are saying it, and convincing them of the merits of your position are important skills to learn. Acting out, where appropriate, exactly what you would say or do in the specific situation is useful practice. Even a brief attempt to *be* the person involved and to talk as though you are that person, not simply to advise him what to say, will emphasize the difference between recommending to another and acting yourself in the situation. You will find that it is very much easier to tell your fellow students what Mr. Lampton of BCI should say to Mr. Denham, his recalcitrant subordinate, than to say it yourself to one of your classmates who is playing the role of Mr. Denham.

FRAMEWORK

To assist you in the task of designing and managing the overall organization, we shall suggest a simple framework, or approach, just as we did for the problem of strategy formulation in Part I. We will emphasize again that these two tasks of formulation and implementation are separate largely in the minds and writings of observers; no manager can focus on one without considering the other. He will concentrate his attention on one aspect or the other as the occasion demands, but the overall achievement of purpose requires a blending of formulation and administration suitable to the company. A brilliant strategy without a means of accomplishing it is of no greater value than a superb organization without a purpose.

We suggest that you think of the problem of managing the overall organization in terms of the sources of influence available to the manager in working with the organization. The tasks to be accomplished will be, in large part, the result of the objectives chosen and the strategies developed. The sources of influence that the manager has in leading the organization in the accomplishment of these tasks can be grouped into five categories:

1. The organization structure: the definition of responsibilities and the establishment of reporting relationships among individuals and subunits.
2. The information systems: the collection, flow, and presentation of information concerning the operations of the organization.
3. The reward systems: the multiple forms of rewards which can be earned (or foregone) by the members of the organization, including pay, incentives of all kinds, praise and personal satisfaction, promotion, and so on.
4. The allocation of resources: the allocation of sufficient resources to units or projects, which not only is essential to the accomplishment of the objectives set out, but also often becomes a source of personal satisfaction to the individuals involved.
5. The most intangible source of influence of all, but perhaps the most important, is what we commonly lump under the catchall of *leadership*: the overall behavior of the manager as it affects the desires and the abilities of the members of the organization to work toward the accomplishment of the organization's goals.

The totality of the general manager's job, then, can be thought of as developing and maintaining a strategy that is a creative and productive fit of the various elements that affect the formulation and the implementation of that strategy. It can be shown graphically in Exhibit 7-1.

Organization structure, information systems, reward systems and human motivation, resource allocation procedures, and leadership are all

EXHIBIT 7-1: Formulation and Implementation of Strategy

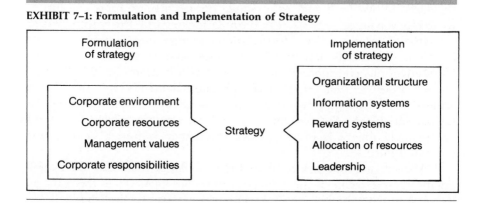

familiar topics. With the exception of the nature of effective leadership, the sources of influence available are in themselves not overly complicated. Experts in various aspects such as organization structure, compensation schemes, or information systems are always ready to advise on the latest developments in their specialties. What is both complex and less common is the judgment required to combine the tools available to all in such a manner that they are effective over a long period of time. The test of effectiveness from the viewpoint of the general manager does not lie in the sophistication or even "correctness" of any one element but in the way that they fit together and reinforce each other to serve the broader purposes dictated by the strategy of the company. Rather than expand upon these topics individually, we would like to direct your attention instead to some of the challenges that arise in combining all of these elements into a coherent, consistent overall approach that is suitable for the organization and the purposes it seeks to achieve.

FORMAL AND INFORMAL ORGANIZATION

The familiar black lines on the organization chart, along with titles and job descriptions that describe what the inhabitants of the boxes are supposed to do, portray a far neater and more rational world than exists in real life. Actual activities, if not formal job descriptions, must accommodate to some degree the skills, interests, and power positions of those who inhabit the boxes as well as what needs to be done if the organization is to perform effectively.

In most organizations there are far more relationships that need to be taken into account than those represented by connecting solid lines. Where alternate or dual reporting relationships are fairly clear, we tend to represent them by means of dotted lines. The term *dotted line relationship to* is often used, for example, with regard to division controllers who may have a solid line relationship to (be a direct subordinate of) the division general manager, but who have a dotted line relationship to the group or corporate controller.

When the multiple relationships become so numerous that a chart showing all the appropriate dotted lines would resemble a drawing of a battle-scarred spider web, we sometimes drop the lines altogether and describe it as a matrix organization, in which responsibilities for results are far more explicit than lines of authority. Such organizational forms are common in industries where large projects exist which require many months or years to complete, as in the defense industry. The product manager form of organization, in which the person "responsible" for the success of a product line does not have much, if any, authority over the product development, manufacturing, or marketing functions that affect the success of his product line, can also be thought of as a matrix form of organization. In such organizations, results are expected to come less from reliance on formal lines of authority than from a common commitment to work together to do what needs to be done, with each party expected to resolve, in a constructive way, the conflicting demands often placed on him or on the resources under his control.

There is also a separate category of relationships brought about by the existence of staff personnel at various levels. The manager of facilities planning can be a subordinate of one of a number of executives, including the president. He is unlikely to have any direct authority over others reporting to those executives or to those who are below him in the organization. His opinions and advice do carry some weight with others in the organization who have no formal reporting relationship with him, however, and in a manner which is seldom spelled out explicitly. Perhaps the most striking example of the importance of the sometimes unclear but often significant role a staff man can play is the case of the executive assistant to a busy president.

Beyond the complexities we try to represent by terms such as *line, staff, solid lines, dotted lines,* and *matrix organization* lies what we commonly call *the informal organization.* That is a euphemism for "the way things really work," and it covers everything about which we cannot be more explicit. It consists of the pattern of relationships and ways of working with each other that build up in conjunction with any formal organization structure and process or that arise even in the absence of such prescribed patterns of interaction.

As you deal with the cases in this section, your challenge will be to go beyond the formalities of the organization structure to discern how the organization actually does work in the particular situation with which you are concerned. Your objective should be to develop the ability to work with and influence the organization in all its complexities and, at times, seeming inertia and apparent "irrationalities." Your goal is to elicit individual behavior that will further rather than hinder the attainment of the corporate objectives. In both BCI and Lincoln you will encounter managers who appear to understand very well what makes the members of the organization work hard. And it is, after all, people who make organizations work effectively, not the reverse.

To consider formal reporting relationships and titles unimportant is of course a mistake; they constitute a starting point. Without some degree of formal structure and definition of tasks and reporting relationships, an organization, even if committed to a purpose, is little more than a crowd. To believe the formalities can be so well specified that the informal workings of any organization can be ignored, however, is unrealistic. The Voltamp case will present you with ample opportunity to elaborate upon the formal arrangements in order to solve a specific interdivisional problem, or else to seek a solution by less formal means.

Authority and Responsibility

If one person could actually perform all of the tasks necessary in the conduct of a business, the problems of management would be simplified considerably. The sole proprietor does not need organization charts, job descriptions, or formalized compensation systems. Most of the things we talk about in this chapter would have little relevance to the manager who works for himself.

As the demands of the business require the addition of people, however, problems of splitting up what needs to be done unavoidably arise. Our largest companies have thousands of people classified as managers, each responsible for the actions of units reporting to them. When the managerial tasks have expanded and then been subdivided, problems of coordination and reintegration follow. Information on what various units are doing is necessary not only to ensure that the efforts are complementary but to monitor progress, help in planning for the future, and evaluate the performance of the people involved so that they can be properly rewarded for their efforts.

It would, of course, be ideal if the overall needs of the company could be subdivided into tasks that were perfectly clear, with sufficient authority given to each subordinate manager so that he could control all of the key factors affecting the performance for which he will be held responsible. Under these conditions we could then evaluate and reward him on the basis of clear objectives related to performance. Authority would be commensurate with responsibility, rewards would be based on explicit and controllable performance measures, and the principles of management would have been complied with.

The preceding is a better description of the goals of an organization structure, information system, and reward system than it is the result of such systems in practice. Because of the unavoidable complexities of most management jobs, such ideal conditions are seldom attained.

A more realistic set of observations about the relationships between authority, responsibility, and evaluation that exist in most organizations and that you are likely to encounter as you move up through the management ranks is the following:

1. Your responsibilities are likely to exceed your authority for a long time. You will be expected to work with the people and the organization to secure by means of persuasion and logic the cooperation and resources you cannot command.

2. The evaluation of your performance will seldom be completely explicit. Judgments and opinions not clarified either before or after the evaluation period will be important. Furthermore, the basis of evaluation is likely to become less clear and explicit the higher up in management you progress.

3. Your superiors will always talk about the importance of not

sacrificing the future in order to achieve short-range goals. If your time perspective is longer than that of your superiors, however, you are likely to find yourself in trouble for failing to meet short-run goals important to them. You have the difficult job of achieving an acceptable balance between these conflicting objectives.

4. Decisions concerning evaluation and reward systems may often be influenced more by what will improve performance than matters of fairness or logic. Giving a person conflicting objectives or holding him responsible for more than he can control may be neither fair nor logical, but this is done at times in most organizations because it is often both unavoidable and effective.

5. Your boss probably knows better than you do the conflicts, illogicalities, and possible unfairness of the system under which you have to work. Probably he is now operating under more pressures and conflicts than you are. He learned to perform well in your environment, perhaps by not becoming overly disturbed by the matters discussed above but by concentrating instead on doing what needed to be done, trusting that in the responsible and effective organization competent effort would be recognized and rewarded regardless of the formalities of the system.

As you move on to jobs of increasing responsibility, you may be able to use your increased power, wisdom, and experience to change some of the inconsistent or frustrating factors you experienced in earlier positions. If so, your subordinates will surely thank you for it. On the other hand, you may also come to the conclusion that such conflicts and frustrations are not necessarily undesirable from the viewpoint of the organization as a whole, that they can in few cases be resolved completely, and that your most constructive role is to strive for a balance between rationality and practicality.

It might be useful to ask yourself periodically just what you think your boss really expects of you, and not just what the formalities of the measurement system are. Most likely he is just as smart as you are, has more experience than you do in the organization, and probably understands your position and pressures better than you give him credit for. He knows as well as you do that there are actions you could take to look good in the formal measurement systems that would be unwise from a broader perspective, and he has some of the same pressures himself. It is easy to lose sight of the fact that good performance on your part very likely helps him with his problems, and that you have many goals in common.

Evaluation and Rewards

Just as most of us want to have the authority to influence the results for which we will be held responsible, we also would like our rewards to be based on clear and explicit measures of our performance. Rewards, both monetary and nonmonetary, are of considerable importance to most people. Of the various sources of influence available to the manager, rewards are probably the most significant as well as the most studied and discussed.

The rewards one gains from employment are of course much broader and more complex than just the monetary benefits earned, and these other satisfactions may compensate for, or at least distract attention from, what are perceived as shortcomings in the financial arrangements.

You will have been exposed to much in your organizational behavior courses concerning the many factors that make for satisfaction in a job environment, and we urge you to draw upon that knowledge. Not the least of these other factors will be the signals you give to your subordinates concerning your opinions of them and their work. When you become engaged full time in your career, it will be useful to reflect upon how much time you spend thinking about what your superior thinks of you and why he made this suggestion or that comment concerning your work. Your subordinates will be just as concerned with your opinions of them, no less inclined to read more meaning into your actions and comments than you intended them to convey, and no less inclined to feel better after receiving justified praise and to feel worse when ignored or criticized unfairly.

Just because financial rewards are but one aspect of the ways in which the manager can reward his subordinates for past performance and thereby provide incentives for the future, it does not follow that financial rewards are unimportant. Most people do, after all, depend on their jobs for their livelihood, no matter how much they might also enjoy their work and appreciate recognition for a job well done. Even when the money itself takes on less importance because of the effect of taxes or diminished personal needs or the high levels of compensation being earned, the level of compensation takes on importance as a way of "keeping score" and measuring success in the job itself as well as position and progress with regard to others in the organization. It is naive to think that compensation is the only thing a manager has to reward his subordinates with, but it is also naive to think that the level of compensation is not important to most people.

There are a number of issues related to compensation and incentives that continue to plague practitioners. How much should you take into account either the personal aggressiveness or the personal needs of individual managers? How often should you match the offer a manager has secured from the outside, perhaps as a way of improving his internal bargaining power? How much should you reward a manager for past contributions or excellent efforts, even if the current performance is not up to expectations, perhaps for factors over which he has little control? We all like to be measured only on matters that we can control, but the general manager is often held responsible for results, not effort. At what level do we expect managers to share in the risks of the enterprise and not just be measured and rewarded for performance with regard to matters they can control?

In any large organization there is of course the need for some rationality and comparability in job descriptions, compensation plans, and pay levels. Much effort has been expended both by companies and consulting firms to deal with these problems. Managers often are caught in a dilemma: they would like to make the rewards as objective as possible to avoid the unpleasantness of having to justify their own decisions to those who performed poorly, as well as to remove the suspicion that personal feelings or biases may have entered into the judgment. On the other hand, totally formula-based and objective measures frequently are unable to capture the full measure of the job done by the specific individual, and most managers feel the need to have some discretionary bonus available as well.

Partly because of the different needs of various organizations and partly because of the common dilemmas all managers face, the variety of basic compensation schemes and incentive-pay packages that have been developed is huge. It includes endless combinations of cash, deferred cash, stock, and fringe benefits. The phrase *cafeteria approach to compensation* has even come into common use to describe plans which enable employees to choose that combination which most suits their tastes.

The Adams Corporation will give you some opportunity to explore just what it is that should be rewarded in the behavior, performance, potential, or personal situation of subordinates. In settling the vexing interdivisional problems of the Voltamp Electrical Corporation, you will surely have to allow for the impact on executive bonuses of various solutions. And in the Lincoln Electric Company you will find a highly unusual as well as effective combination of great attention to the motivation of the work force with the strategy which takes advantage of the higher productivity that results from their generous incentive plan and the important aspects that accompany it. It will be useful to examine some of the statements of James Lincoln concerning what makes people put forth their best efforts to see if there is some application to other situations you will encounter.

It is unfortunate, however, that the establishment of high rewards for narrowly defined performance, whether in monetary terms or with regard to opportunities for promotion, can lead to behavior clearly not in the best interests of the corporation. The temptation to emphasize short-run profits at the expense of long-run development is but one familiar manifestation of this. Every once in a while there are articles in the press on serious aberrant behavior that high pressure for performance can lead to. In a recent example, division personnel falsified records over a period of years to show increased profits of $8.5 million, which was sufficient to result in the involvement of the SEC, delay of the annual meeting, and much publicity and consequent embarrassment to the company. "When we didn't meet our growth targets, the top brass really came down on us," one former executive stated. "Everybody knew that if you missed the targets enough, you were out on your ear."

Similar pressures have led, for example, to instances of falsification of automobile exhaust emission tests, violation of pollution laws, and illegal payments of bribes in violation of corporate policy and (later) the law in efforts to secure business, all without the knowledge of higher levels of management. Many observers have attributed much of the reason for the extensive price fixing that took place in the electrical equipment industry in the 1960s, as well as many later violations in other industries, to the desire on the part of managers to earn bonuses or promotions by performing well in the measures established, or, in some cases, to avoid demotions or even loss of jobs.

As the rewards and punishments associated with performance increase, the temptation to do what is not in the best interests of the company or what is ethically or legally wrong increases. The challenge for you as a manager is to find that productive middle ground in which people will be motivated to expend their best efforts, but not in such a manner as to bring trouble to their companies or themselves. The means by which you can increase or decrease the pressures for performance are much simpler and better understood than the means by which you can determine and maintain the appropriate balance.

Cooperation versus Competition

The responsible, effective general manager will want to keep track of the cooperative-competitive dimension of the working relationships within the organization. It is unavoidable that some will progress faster and farther than others in all organizations; the traditional pyramidal form of organization ensures that. Since the positions higher in the organizational pyramid generally involve more money, prestige, power and (hopefully) personal satisfaction, the matter of who is chosen for promotion is seldom a matter of indifference to the contenders. Even if promotion is not a factor, current pay and incentives are often structured to provide the maximum rewards to those performing the best on the measures used. That is the purpose of reward systems: to provide an incentive to continued good performance in the future by rewarding good performance in the present.

As in any field of competitive endeavor, however, it is necessary to establish limits as to what kind of behavior or degree of competition is acceptable. The question of what constitutes "acceptable competitive behavior" has surely arisen for each of you with regard to the various organizations and groups of which you have chosen to be a member. Parents learn to establish and enforce standards of behavior within the family; referees and umpires enforce the rules in sports; the manager, who unavoidably has such a strong influence on the "rules of the game," must do likewise. If he does not, he will soon find that rewards for individual performance can combine with personal ambitions to create an atmosphere which discourages cooperation and which is less than satisfying to many with useful contributions to make to the organization.

As an example of the power of simple techniques to affect both the competitive relationships and the working environment within an organization, consider the approach which was followed by a major consulting firm for a period of time in scheduling the work loads of their staff, deciding what new engagements they could accept, and planning their hiring requirements.

It was the practice to appoint project leaders for each of the engagements for clients, and these project leaders would then plan the amount and type of work that would have to be done and assemble the people they would need to finish the job on time and under budget. The assignment of consultants to jobs was done by the various project leaders, who had to decide which consultants to "employ," taking into account the rates they would be charged for different consultants as well as when and for how long the consultants would be available to work on that project. The work schedule for individual consultants would then consist of their backlog of commitments to various project leaders, with unallocated time charged to "personal development" or "new business development."

The project leaders did not bargain with the consultants available on the basis of rates; these were determined periodically by the company. The internal rate charged for each consultant was influenced by demand, however, as were the pay and promotion prospects. It was, in effect, an internal market system under which project leaders bid against one another for the use of resources already under the control of the firm.

As a means of helping the project leaders in their scheduling task as well as collecting information useful in coordinating the new commitments of the firm with the available resources and the planned hiring schedule, charts were kept showing the workload by consultant and by project. At one point it was decided to post these charts for all to see and to update them once a week. Who was in demand and who was not therefore became public knowledge within the firm. The weekly posting understandably became an item of considerable interest to all and embarrassment to some. What do you suppose the effects of this simple decision to post this information were? Did it encourage cooperation, or did it not matter in this case? Did it encourage greater effort by all? How would you like to work under such a visible control mechanism? It is questions such as these to which you will want to apply your judgment—not just the technical aspects of evaluation or reward systems.

We face the paradox that we want the organization to be highly competitive in its external relationships with other organizations, but we wish to limit the internal competition so that it does not affect the incentives for individuals to work cooperatively as they do battle with the external world. We want the marketing department to develop a team spirit and work together to gain sales from their competitors, much as we expect a football team to consider the opponent an enemy to be beaten. We do not, however, want this attitude to affect the ability of the marketing people to work with each other, even though we may offer individual sales commissions. Neither do we want our own manufacturing and marketing departments to overlook the corporate interest as one department fights to keep manufacturing costs and inventories down while the other wants a variety of products available in the field.

Unavoidably we seek to measure and reward individual performance within the organization, which may sometimes be achieved at the cost of—or at least without regard for—the performance of others and the overall objectives of the company. Balancing the cooperative-competitive dimension is a difficult judgmental task and one which requires continuing attention. The issues are raised clearly in the Adams case, where you will deal with how to convert the increasingly ineffective "old Adams" into a more competitive and effective "new Adams." The tools and techniques by which you can increase or reduce the amount of internal competition and affect the broader working environment are well known, and the challenge is to employ them wisely and responsibly.

SUMMARY

The accomplishment of purpose is achieved by means of people working together on a voluntary basis. As a manager you will have considerable opportunity to influence or guide that behavior, but only in rare instances can you direct it on a continuing basis. The challenge is to devise structures, procedures, rewards, and an overall working environment that make possible the enthusiastic support for what needs to be done, and not just compliance with what the boss dictates or what the policy manual says. The former describes an organization made up of individuals for whom the achievement of personal goals contributes significantly to the overall goals of the organization. If you can relate the needs of your people to the needs of the organization, success cannot be far behind.

We have said little about leadership as a separate topic. We know, however, that throughout history the personal skills of the leader have had a major impact on the willingness of people to commit themselves to his purposes and his plans. The study of the characteristics of effective leaders in politics, the church, the military, as well as business has long fascinated observers.

The major observation we might offer at this point, as you try to apply what you already have learned about leadership, is that effective leadership depends upon a successful matching of the needs of the situation with the skills and personality of the leader. We urge you to examine both the cases to come and your own skills and development with this in mind. Individuals are limited in the extent to which they can modify their behavior or acquire new skills. Success as a leader is more likely to come from a steady development of skills and the matching of those skills to the requirements of the job than from a blind pursuit of a style that happens to have been successful for others with different skills in different situations.

Technical abilities and skills are likely to be of relatively less importance as you rise through the managerial ranks. More important will be the ability to recognize and deal with issues beyond your own experience and specialized training. You will need to develop the ability to conceptualize and communicate the problems in such a way that others can understand and be convinced of their importance. Progress will come from organizing and motivating those with specialized knowledge and skills to apply their efforts to the constructive solution of the problems. In addition to conceptual skills, effective leadership requires the ability to break down problems into manageable parts for which tasks and goals can be assigned and progress measured. You will need to be good at gaining support and commitment for what you think needs to be done, in spite of the different interests and positions of those on whose help you rely.

In the cases that follow, we will generally be looking at the problems from the viewpoint of the general manager, seeking to understand how he can use the sources of influence available to him in order to motivate the members of the organization to work toward the achievement of the organization's goals. To understand this task better however, we suggest that you form the habit of always putting yourself in the place of a subordinate as well. How would you respond to the incentives or changes being proposed? How long before you would see through changes that are presented in a less-than-honest fashion? Even if the changes and reasons for them are well understood, what other actions might those changes induce you to take? We do not need to feel that we are pandering to the needs of subordinates in order to give some thought to how their jobs and careers could be affected by changes stemming from the organization's needs.

As you work your way through the approach we have suggested for your analysis of the cases in Part II of the book, your objective should be to develop a set of recommendations for each specific situation which has the following characteristics:

1.   Your recommendations flow from your analysis of the case facts.
2.   Your recommendations include a program of action and specify,

to the best of your ability, how the resources required—people and money—will be obtained.

3.   Your recommendations recognize that you are most often dealing with an existing, ongoing business rather than a completely new situation, and that you do not often have the luxury of starting anew. Frequently your changes will of necessity be incremental to an existing pattern of doing business. The more drastic the changes you recommend, the stronger the argument will have to be to gain their acceptance by people on whose cooperation and support you depend.

CASE 12

The Adams Corporation (A)

In January 1972 the board of directors of The Adams Corporation simultaneously announced the highest sales in the company's history, the lowest aftertax profits (as a percentage of sales) of the World War II era, and the retirement (for personal reasons) of its long-tenure president and chief executive officer.

Founded in St. Louis in 1848 the Adams Brothers Company had long been identified as a family firm both in name and operating philosophy. Writing in a business history journal, a former family senior manager comments: "My grandfather wanted to lead a business organization with ethical standards. He wanted to produce a quality product and a quality working climate for both employees and managers. He thought the Holy Bible and the concept of family stewardship provided him with all the guidelines needed to lead his company. A belief in the fundamental goodness of mankind, in the power of fair play, and in the importance of personal and corporate integrity were his trademarks. Those traditions exist today in the 1960s."

In the early 1950s, two significant corporate events occurred. First, the name of the firm was changed to The Adams Corporation. Second, somewhat over 50 percent of the corporation shares were sold by various family groups to the wider public. In 1970 all branches of the family owned or influenced less than one fifth of the outstanding shares of Adams.

The Adams Corporation was widely known and respected as a manufacturer and distributor of quality, branded, and consumer products for the American, Canadian, and European (export) markets. Adams products were processed in four regional plants located near raw material sources, were stored and distributed in a series of recently constructed or renovated distribution centers located in key cities throughout North America, and were sold by a company sales force to thousands of retail outlets—primarily supermarkets.[1]

In explaining the original long-term financial success of the company, a former officer commented: "Adams led the industry in the development of unique production processes that produced a quality product at a very low cost. The company has always been production oriented and volume oriented, and it paid off for a long time. During those decades the Adams brand was all that was needed to sell our product; we didn't do anything but a little advertising. Competition was limited, and our production efficiency and raw material sources enabled us to outpace the industry in sales and profit. Our strategy was to make a quality product, distribute it, and sell it cheap.

"But that has all changed in the past 20 years," he continued. "Our three major competitors have outdistanced us in net profits and market aggressiveness. One of them—a first-class marketing group—has doubled to almost $250 million, but our net profits have dropped continuously during that same period. While a consumer action group just designated us as 'best value,' we have fallen behind in marketing techniques, for example, our packaging is just out of date."

Structurally, Adams was organized into eight major divisions (see Exhibit 1). Seven of these were regional sales divisions, with responsibility for distribution and sales of the company's consumer products to retail stores in their area. Each regional sales division was further divided into organizational units at the state and county and/or trading area level. Each sales division was governed by a corporate price list in the selling of company products but had some leeway to meet the local competitive price developments. Each sales division was also assigned (by the home office) a quota of salesmen it could hire and was given the salary ranges within which these men could be employed. All salesmen were on straight salary and expense reimbursement salary plan, whcih resulted in compensation under industry averages.

A small central accounting office accumulated sales and expense information for each of the several sales divisions on a quarterly basis and prepared the overall company financial statements. Each sales division received, without commentary, a quarterly statement showing the number of cases processed and sold for the overall division, sales revenue per case of the overall division, and local expenses per case for the overall division.

Somewhat similar information was obtained from the manufacturing

---

[1] No single plant processed the full line of Adams products, but each plant processed the main items in the line.

EXHIBIT 1

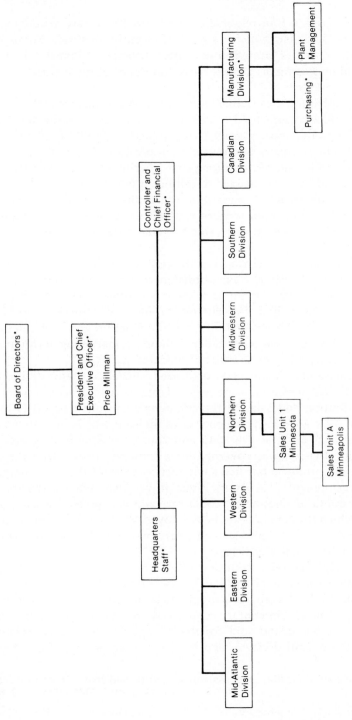

* Located in St. Louis.

division. Manufacturing division accounting was complicated by variations in the cost of obtaining and processing the basic materials used in Adams products. These variations—particularly in procurement—were largely beyond the control of that division. The accounting office did have, however, one rough external check on manufacturing division effectiveness. A crude market price for case lot goods, sold by smaller firms to some large national chains, did exist.

Once a quarter, the seven senior sales vice presidents met with general management in St. Louis. Typically, management discussion focused on divisional sales results and expense control. The company's objective of being number one, the largest selling line in its field, directed group attention to sales versus budget. All knew that last year's sales targets had to be exceeded—"no matter what." The manufacturing division vice president sat in on these meetings to explain the product availability situation. Because of his St. Louis office location, he frequently talked with Jerome Adams about overall manufacturing operations and specifically about large procurement decisions.

The Adams Company, Mr. Millman knew, had a trade reputation for being very conservative with its compensation program. All officers were on a straight salary program. An officer might expect a modest salary increase every two or three years; these increases tended to be in the thousand-dollar range regardless of divisional performance or company profit position. Salaries among the seven sales divisional vice presidents ranged from $32,000 to $42,000, with the higher amounts going to more senior officers. Jerome Adams's salary of $48,000 was the highest in the company. There was no corporate bonus plan. A very limited stock option program was in operation, but the depressed price of Adams stock meant that few officers exercised their options.

Of considerable pride to Jerome Adams had been the corporate climate at Adams. "We take care of our family" was his oft-repeated phrase at company banquets honoring long-service employees. "We are a team, and it is a team spirit that has built Adams into its leading position in this industry." No member of first-line, middle, or senior management could be discharged (except in cases of moral crime or dishonesty) without a personal review of his case by Mr. Adams. In matter of fact, executive turnover at Adams was very low. Executives at all levels viewed their jobs as a lifetime career. There was no compulsory retirement plan, and some managers were still active in their mid-70s.

The operational extension of this organizational philosophy was quite evident to employees and managers. For over 75 years, a private family trust provided emergency assistance to all members of the Adams organization. Adams led its industry in the granting of educational scholarships, in medical insurance for employees and managers, and in the encouragement of its "members" to give corporate and personal time and effort to community problems and organizations.

Mr. Adams noted two positive aspects of this organizational philosophy. "We have a high percentage of long-term employees—Joe Girly, a guard at East St. Louis, completes 55 years with us this year, and every one of his brothers and sisters has worked here. And it is not uncommon for a vice president to retire with a blue pin—that means 40 years of service. We have led this industry in manufacturing process innovation, quality control, and value for low price for decades. I am proud of our accomplishments, and this pride is shown by everyone—from janitors to directors." Industry sources noted that there was no question that Adams was number one in terms of manufacturing and logistic efficiency.

In December of 1971 the annual Adams management conference gathered over 80 of Adams's senior management in St. Louis. Most expected the usual formal routines—the announcement of 1971 results and 1972 budgets, the award of the "Gold Flag" to the top processing plant and sales division for exceeding targets, and the award of service pins to executives. All expected the usual social good times. It was an opportunity to meet and drink with "old buddies."

After a series of task force meetings, the managers gathered in a banquet room—good naturedly referred to as the Rib Room since a local singer, Eve, was to provide entertainment. At the front of the room, in the usual fashion, was a dais with a long, elaborately decorated head table. Sitting at the center of that table was Jerome Adams. Following tradition, Mr. Adams's vice presidents, in order of seniority with the company, sat on his right. On his left, sat major family shareholders, corporate staff, and—a newcomer—soon to be introduced.

After awarding service pins and the Gold Flags of achievement, Mr. Adams announced formally what had been a corporate secret for several months. First, a new investing group had assumed a control position on the board of Adams. Second, that Price Millman would take over as president and chief executive officer of Adams.

Introducing Mr. Millman, Adams pointed out the outstanding record of the firm's new president. "Price got his MBA in 1958, spent four years in control and marketing, and then was named as the youngest divisional president in the history of the Tenny Corporation. In the past years, he has made his division the most profitable in Tenny and the industry leader in its field. We are fortunate to have him with us. Please give him your complete support."

In a later informal meeting with the divisional vice presidents, Mr. Millman spoke about his respect for past Adams's accomplishments and the pressing need to infuse Adams with "fighting spirit" and "competitiveness." "My personal and organizational philosophy are the same—the name of the game is to fight and win. I almost drowned, but I won my first swimming race at 11 years of age! That philosophy of always winning is what enabled me to build the Ajax Division into Tenny's most profitable operation. We are going to do this at Adams."

In conclusion, he commented, "The new owner group wants results. They have advised me to take some time to think through a new format for Adams's operations—to get a corporate design that will improve our effectiveness. Once we get that new format, gentlemen, I have but one goal—each month must be better than the past."

CASE 13

The Rose Company

James Pierce had recently received word of his appointment as plant manager of Plant X, one of the older established units of the Rose Company. As such, Mr. Pierce was to be responsible for the management and administration at Plant X of all functions and personnel except sales.

Both top management and Mr. Pierce realized that there were several unique factors about his new assignment. Mr. Pierce decided to assess his new situation and relationships before undertaking his assignment. He was personally acquainted with the home office executives, but had met few of the plant personnel. This case contains some of his reflections regarding the new assignment.

The Rose Company conducted marketing activities throughout the United States and in certain foreign countries. These activities were directed from the home office by a vice president in charge of sales.

Manufacturing operations and certain other departments were under the supervision and control of a senior vice president. These are shown in Exhibit 1. For many years the company had operated a highly centralized functional type of manufacturing organization. There was no general manager at any plant; each of the departments in a plant reported on a line basis to its functional counterpart at the home office. For instance, the industrial relations manager of a particular plant reported to the vice president in charge of industrial relations at the home office, the plant controller to the vice president and controller, and so on.

Mr. Pierce stated that in the opinion of the top management the record of Plant X had not been satisfactory for several years. The board had recently approved the erection of a new plant in a different part of

Copyright © 1972 by the President and Fellows of Harvard College. Harvard Business School case 9–453–002. Reproduced by permission.

EXHIBIT 1: Old Organization

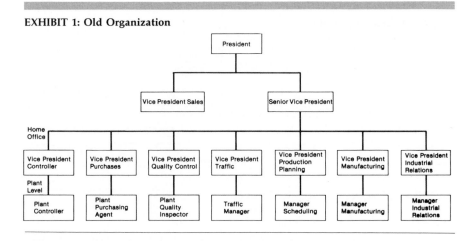

the city and the use of new methods of production. Lower costs of processing and a reduced personnel requirement at the new plant were expected.
Reduction of costs and improved quality of products were needed to
maintain competitive leadership and gain some slight product advantage.
The proposed combination of methods of manufacturing and mixing materials had not been tried elsewhere in the company. Some features would
be entirely new to employees.

According to Mr. Pierce the top management of the Rose Company
was beginning to question the advisability of the central control of manufacturing operations. The officers decided to test the value of a decentralized operation in connection with Plant X. They apparently believed that
a general management representative in Plant X was needed if the new
equipment in manufacturing methods and the required rebuilding of the
organization were to succeed.

Prior to the new assignment Mr. Pierce had been an accounting
executive in the controller's department of the company. From independent sources the casewriter learned that Mr. Pierce had demonstrated
analytical ability and general administrative capacity. He was generally
liked by people. From top management's point of view he had an essential
toughness described as an ability to see anything important through. By
some he was regarded as the company's efficiency expert. Others thought
he was a perfectionist and aggressive in reaching the goals that had been
set. Mr. Pierce was aware of these opinions about his personal behavior.

Mr. Pierce summarized his problem in part as follows:

> I am going into a situation involving a large number of changes. I
> will have a new plant—new methods and processes—but most of all I will
> be dealing with a set of changed relationships. Heretofore all the heads
> of departments in the plant reported to their functional counterparts in

EXHIBIT 2: New Organization

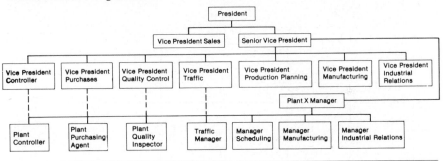

the home office. Now they will report to me. I am a complete stranger and in addition this is my first assignment in a major "line" job. The men will know this.

When I was called into the senior vice president's office to be informed of my new assignment, he asked me to talk with each of the functional members of his staff. The vice presidents in charge of production planning, manufacturing, and industrial relations said they were going to issue all headquarters instructions to me as plant manager and they were going to cut off their connections with their counterparts in my plant. The other home office executives admitted their functional counterparts would report to me in line capacity. They should obey my orders, and I would be responsible for their pay and promotion. But these executives proposed to follow the common practice of many companies of maintaining a dotted line or functional relationship with these men. I realize that these two different patterns of home office–plant relationships will create real administrative problems for me.

Exhibit 2 shows the organization relationships as defined in these conferences.

CASE 14

Voltamp Electrical Corporation

Voltamp Electrical Corporation was a nationwide organization engaged in the design, manufacture, sale, and servicing of a wide variety of electrical and allied products. It had been incorporated in 1909 to manufacture only a specialized line of electric motors, but since that time it had grown substantially, and it had become highly diversified in its output through acquisition of, or merger with, a number of small electrical companies. Except for two years during the Depression, Voltamp's operations had always been profitable, and it had been able to compete successfully within the electrical industry. Voltamp had net sales of almost $1 billion and employed slightly over 100,000 people.

Over the years the company had expanded its operations considerably, by increasing its sales effort on existing products, by further diversifying its products, and by erecting an increased number of manufacturing and assembly plants; there were sales outlets in all major cities in the country, and design, manufacturing, and/or assembly operations in 44 states. As this expansion continued, the top officials of Voltamp insisted more and more on decentralized management of operations.

Originally, the company had operated along general functional lines. Responsibility for production, marketing, finance, and accounting had been vested in separate divisions which cut across product lines. Each division had been headed by an executive vice president. As Voltamp continued to expand its operations and to become more diversified along product lines, top management had come to believe that a centralized functional organization was severely limiting the efficiency of current operations, and would cause even more problems as the company continued to expand. Operating decisions were requiring too much time and those responsible for making these decisions were often not as conversant as they should be with the local situations where the decisions had to be carried out. The result was an increasing number of serious misunderstandings between those at the operating level and those responsible for making decisions. Therefore, after considerable study, it had been decided to shift from a centralized organization along functional lines to a decentralized organization along product lines.

To help implement this policy of decentralization, the company had been reorganized along product lines into a pyramid of operating sections, departments, and divisions (see Exhibit 1). Very simply, Voltamp's concept of decentralization required that "authority, accountability, and responsibility" for making and carrying out decisions be placed as close as possible to the actual level of operations.

Within 5 years of reorganization the policy of decentralization had been implemented through all the operating divisions and their component departments. The executive vice presidents of the divisions were accountable to the president of Voltamp for the profits of their respective divisions, and they had the authority to make broad policy decisions within the charters that allotted and described their general product lines. In like manner, the executive vice presidents of the divisions held their department vice presidents responsible for the profits of their respective departments. (Each of the 14 departments of the company had an average sales volume of almost $70 million per year.)

Every effort was being made by the department vice presidents to carry out the policy of decentralization in their operating sections. All of the numerous possible questions concerning the "authority, responsibility, and accountability" of the section manager had not yet been clearly defined or resolved, but the company president had set forth the following policy and objectives: "It is planned to make the section manager as much like the president of his own small business as possible, within the framework of company policy. He should be constantly thinking about what's best for his own section and then frame this question within the broader question of what's best for Voltamp." Each section manager was accountable to his department vice president for his section's profit and return on investment. Each section's charter broadly defined the product lines for which it was responsible, and, within the limits of this charter, a section manager had the responsibility for determining and implementing policies and practices related to such areas as: development of new products, discontinuation or expansion of particular product lines, production facilities and processes for its products, and the costing, pricing, and sales of its products. General accounting and personnel policies were standardized throughout the company, but each section was responsible for the interpretation and execution of these policies.

Responsibility for a particular product line, as defined in a specific

EXHIBIT 1: Voltamp Electrical Corporation, Organization Chart of Operating Divisions*

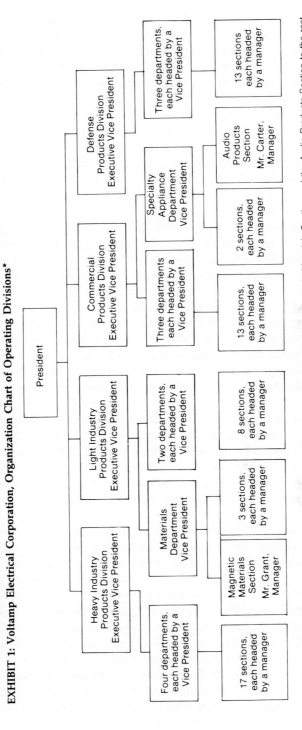

* This is a partial organization chart, designed primarily to emphasize the relationship of the Magnetic Materials Section and the Audio Products Section to the rest of the operating divisions.

section's charter, meant that only this section could sell this product to customers *outside* the company or license other manufacturers to produce it. However, other sections using that product as a component part of their own products had the authority either to purchase the component from the section responsible for producing it, or to produce it themselves; each section was expected to decide in favor of the procedure which would most benefit the company as a whole. Under the decentralization policy, sections selling products within the company could expect to make a "reasonable profit" on these sales. It was Voltamp's general policy not to purchase component parts from outside the company unless the company did not produce the parts itself, or could not produce them to meet necessary standards of quality or within the necessary limits of cost and time.

The section charters were drawn up with the intention of precluding competition among the sections on the sale of general product lines to customers *outside* the company. They were not designed, however, to diminish competition among the sections in such areas as product development, production, and sales of any of their products *within* the company. The department vice presidents realized that this kind of competition among the sections could be at once both a valuable asset and a severe liability of a decentralization policy. They anticipated that there would be numerous problems to be resolved among the sections, but they agreed that if the sections could be encouraged to resolve these problems for themselves, the long-range benefits of decentralization would be best realized. They concluded that clarification of many aspects of how the decentralization policy should work at the section level should come as a result of the sections' efforts to wrestle with their own problems. The department vice presidents were, therefore, urging their section managers to make as many decisions on their own and among themselves as possible. It was clear that only in this way would the section managers learn to accept responsibility commensurate with the authority which they had been granted.

About the same time, Mr. John Carter, manager of the Audio Products Section, recalled the president's statement quoted above, as he deliberated on how to resolve a problem which had arisen between his section and the Magnetic Materials Section. The Audio Products Section manufactured and sold a wide variety of products related to sound amplification, such as: hearing aids, phonograph pickups, microphones, and special-purpose amplifiers. This section had net sales of slightly under $25 million and employed over 2,000 people. It had been operating profitably since its organization as part of the Specialty Appliance Department.

The problem facing Mr. Carter began when the Advanced Development Laboratory of the company developed the theoretical concept of a new kind of magnetic material which would have properties that might permit the manufacture, for existing products and processes, of magnets with considerably more strength than those now being made, but in a smaller size and at less cost than any existing magnets. It was also anticipated that this magnetic material might open up many new uses for magnets in products and processes where conventional magnets could not now be used, and might also lead to the development of new products which were not now commercially feasible.

In conformity with company policy, the facilities of the Advanced Development Laboratory were completely committed to basic and theoretical research. The research laboratories within each of the operating sections were responsible for developmental research on concepts and ideas passed on to them by the Advanced Development Laboratory. Under the decentralization policy of the company, each section had the authority to determine whether or not to go ahead with developmental research on a particular idea that was referred to it by the Advanced Development Laboratory. This decision was usually based on the anticipated feasibility of the idea for commercial development and production.

The Magnetic Materials Section of the Materials Department was primarily engaged in the manufacture of magnets and magnetic materials. By its charter it was responsible for the sale of all magnets and magnetic materials to customers outside the company, and it also sold its products to some of the other operating sections within the company which used magnets as component parts of their own products. About three-quarters of its net sales of $20 million were to customers outside the company. Like the Audio Products Section, the Magnetic Materials Section had operated at a profit each year since its organization as part of the Materials Department some years before.

It was natural, therefore, for the Advanced Development Laboratory to have approached the Magnetic Materials Section as the proper operating section within the company to do the developmental research on the new magnetic material. However, this section had then been engaged in developmental research on a number of other magnetic products, and its engineers had seriously questioned whether the concept could be even developed into a magnetic material, let alone produced commercially. Therefore, the Magnetic Materials Section had declined the opportunity to do developmental research on the new idea for a magnetic material.

The Audio Products Section used magnets as component parts of three-quarters of the 200 different products which it manufactured and sold. About half of these magnets were purchased from the Magnetic Materials Section and the rest were manufactured in Audio Products' own foundry. Because magnets were such an important component part to the Audio Products Section, the Advanced Development Laboratory had offered this section the opportunity to do developmental research on the new magnetic material concept after it had been turned down by the Magnetic Materials Section. Mr. Carter, after reviewing the possibilities of the new material with his staff, had agreed to accept this responsibility.

Developmental research on the new material had continued in the laboratory of the Audio Products Section over the next five years. After considerable trial and error, the concept originated by the Advanced Development Laboratory had been proven valid, and a pilot plant operation set up in the Audio Products Section had clearly indicated commercial applications of the new material far greater than those originally envisioned. It appeared to Mr. Carter that the new material might eventually replace almost all other magnetic materials now used by Voltamp, although he realized that it would be several years before all interested sections could make full use of the material. Most of Voltamp's products that used magnets would have to be redesigned to take full advantage of the unique properties of the new magnetic material, and Mr. Carter realized that the process of redesign would take considerable time.

The developmental work leading to the discovery of the new material had cost the Audio Products Section almost $500,000. A patent covering the process of manufacturing the new magnetic material had been granted to the company within a year, and the material had been given the registered trademark of "TGW."

Mr. Carter had then been faced with the problem of how best to exploit the commercial possibilities of the new magnetic material. As he tried to resolve this problem, he kept in mind that all of the operating sections of Voltamp that used magnets as component parts of their own products should have complete access to TGW. On the other hand, he was also interested in protecting his own section against its many competitors outside the company in the field of audio products by preventing them from buying the new material, and thereby enabling themselves to match Audio's prices on products using the new material. Further, Mr. Carter desired to recoup the development costs of $500,000 which, in accordance with the company's decentralization policy, had been charged directly to his section.

While mulling over various courses open to him in his effort to resolve this problem, Mr. Carter was approached by Mr. Samuel Grant, manager of the Magnetic Materials Section. Mr. Grant congratulated Mr. Carter on the outstanding success of the developmental research on TGW. He went on to say that of course the techniques and procedures for manufacturing TGW would now be turned over to the Magnetic Materials Section as the best and most logical operating section of the company to exploit all of the commercial possibilities of the new material. Mr. Carter replied that this action would allow the outside competitors of the Audio Products Section and all other Voltamp operating sections using magnets as components of their products to buy TGW directly from the Magnetic Materials Section. He asserted that this arrangement clearly would not be best for Voltamp and certainly would not be acceptable to the Audio Products Section.

Thus began a series of discussions between Mr. Carter and Mr. Grant on what action to take regarding the exploitation of TGW. They agreed in the initial stages that the focus of the problem should be the question of what was best for their two sections within the framework of what was best for Voltamp.

Mr. Carter argued that the Audio Products Section had taken a sizeable risk in accepting the responsibility for developmental research on a concept which might easily have proven commercially useless—a risk which the Magnetic Materials Section had not been willing to assume. Therefore, he felt that Audio Products should reap the benefits of having taken this risk, by being given protection against its competitors for a period of at least five years—a period during which Audio Products could establish product leadership in the field. Moreover, Mr. Carter pointed out, Audio Products should be allowed to recoup its developmental investment of $500,000 by manufacturing TGW itself and selling it at a "profit" to those other operating sections of Voltamp that used magnets as component parts of their products. He stated that Audio Products, because of its years of development work with the new material, could manufacture it more easily and with less expense than could Magnetic Materials, for the new manufacturing process was radically different from that used for traditional magnets. While Audio Products did not have the facilities to produce TGW for the general magnet market outside the company, Mr. Carter said that it could easily supply the needs of the operating sections of Voltamp.

Mr. Carter went on to point out that the decentralization policy of the company encouraged the operating sections to take initiative and responsibility for new developments. He wondered whether there would be any incentive for development if a section which took the initiative for development ran the risk that another section might dispute its right to benefit from what it had developed. He feared that a section which took such initiative not only might not benefit fully from any results achieved, but might in fact be penalized.

Mr. Grant argued, on the other hand, that the $500,000 which Audio Products had spent in developing TGW was, in the final analysis, shareholders' money. Therefore, a particular section incurring development costs should look upon them as its contribution to the total company effort. Moreover, he suggested that a new product developed at shareholders' expense should be exploited in such a way as to maximize profits for the company as a whole.

Mr. Grant then pointed out that Audio Products' sales of magnetic components within Voltamp amounted to only $1 million, while Magnetic Materials' sales of magnets and magnetic components within the company amounted to $5 million in addition to his section's $15 million in sales outside the company. He called it to Mr. Carter's attention that only about $750,000 worth of magnetic materials were needed for the products that comprised the remaining $24 million of Audio's sales. He further asserted that his section's variable costs on the manufacture of magnets averaged only 60 percent of sales, and that its after-tax earnings were 5.5 percent of sales. Mr. Carter acknowledged that Audio's earnings after taxes on magnets and magnetic components sold within the company were 4.5 percent of sales and its earnings after taxes on products sold outside the company were 5 percent of sales. Audio's variable costs on magnets sold within the company, Mr. Carter noted, were 65 percent of sales.

TGW, Mr. Grant continued, could be produced at about one-third the cost of traditional magnets of similar strength, but he estimated that the demand for the new material would be so great, because of its superior physical properties, that it could be sold at a price equal to that of traditional magnets. He argued that the profits to Magnetic Materials would thus be far more than those which would accrue to Audio Products. Mr. Grant added that this consideration did not even take into account the fact that the sales volume of Magnetic Materials would undoubtedly be increased substantially because of the anticipated demand for TGW.

Mr. Grant also questioned whether Audio Products was the best section to manufacture TGW in the long run. He pointed out that once Magnetic Materials had trained its personnel and set up production facilities, the fact that its major business was magnets would undoubtedly enable it to achieve more efficient and economical production in the long run. Furthermore, he noted, even if Voltamp decided not to sell TGW outside the company for a given period, such as the five-year protection period that Mr. Carter wanted, production facilities would eventually have to be located in the Magnetic Materials Section. This section, because of its charter, was the only section that would be allowed to handle the anticipated long-run sales volume. Both men agreed that under their section charters, only Magnetic Materials could sell magnets to customers outside the company. It was also clear to them that their section charters should not be changed (see Exhibit 2).

Mr. Carter agreed that in the long run TGW probably could best be produced by Magnetic Materials, and he knew that the $500,000 development cost now on Audio Products' books could theoretically be transferred to Magnetic Materials' books. However, although Mr. Grant acknowledged that a bookkeeping procedure of this sort was theoretically in accordance with general company policy, he now raised the question of whether such a transfer would meet the facts of the present situation. Mr. Grant doubted that, if Magnetic Materials did take over the exploitation of TGW, the transfer of development charges would be a proper course of action under the circumstances. He pointed out that after all it was Audio Products' decision to incur these development costs, and

EXHIBIT 2: Excerpts from Charter, Audio Products Section

I. General Area of Product Interest

The general area of product interest of the Audio Products Section consists of devices and systems, including components thereof, that are used for the amplification of sound and for the improvement of audio transmission and reception.

II. Specific Product Responsibility

Within the general area of product interest described in Part I, product responsibility of the Audio Products Section includes the following products and components thereof:

A. Hearing aids. . . .   D. Microphones. . . .
B. Phonograph pickups. . . .   E. Special purpose amplifiers. . . .
C. Loudspeaker systems. . . .   (etcetera) . . . .

Product responsibility for these products means that only the Audio Products Section may sell these products to customers outside the company.

III. Component Interrelationships

Where a product, for which responsibility has been assigned to another section, is included as a component in any of the products covered by the Audio Products Section's "Specific Product Responsibility," it will not be offered for sale to customers outside the company by the Audio Products Section except as an integral and component part of the section's products or as required in maintenance and repair service. The Audio Products Section may manufacture its own component parts, purchase them from other sections within the company, or, within the limits of company policy, purchase them from sources outside the company. The Audio Products Section is responsible for determining the best source of supply for its component parts, and is held accountable for this decision in terms of the best interest of the company as a whole.

---

he argued that Magnetic Materials should not be held responsible for the apparent fact that a section other than Audio Products was better situated to exploit TGW's commercial possibilities for the overall benefit of Voltamp.

In the continuing discussions, Mr. Carter emphasized the importance of TGW as a component in the development of new products. Its strength and stability so far surpassed magnets currently in use that a whole new range of products, now commercially impractical, could be developed which would take advantage of these properties. Moreover, many existing products could be radically changed by TGW. Mr. Carter illustrated his argument by pointing out that hearing aids could not now help in many types and stages of deafness because the hearing aid could not be made powerful enough or small enough to be practical. He further argued that

Mr. Grant had forgotten that several other sections of Voltamp besides Audio Products and Magnetic Materials used magnets as component parts of their products and that magnets were used as component parts of some 20–30 percent of Voltamp's products. Magnetic supplied $5 million worth of these magnets, and Audio $1 million worth, but other sections of the company also purchased an additional $2 million worth of magnets from outside sources, because the sections that needed them could get them at lower cost by buying from outside specialty manufacturers than by manufacturing them in the sections' own facilities or by purchasing them within Voltamp. The interests of these sections, Mr. Carter contended, would surely be affected by the discovery of TGW. Mr. Carter noted that TGW would certainly increase the demand for, and sales of, all Voltamp products using magnets as component parts, regardless of which section manufactured these products. He suggested that Mr. Grant had the responsibility for protecting the interests not only of Magnetic Materials and Audio Products, but of all the operating sections.

Mr. Carter further emphasized that for many years one of the cornerstones of Voltamp policy had been to establish the company as a leader in the design, development, and improvement of electrical products. Voltamp had sought to be regarded as making the most advanced and refined electrical products on the market. To take full advantage of the benefits that TGW could confer in enhancing Voltamp's position of leadership in the industry by using the new magnet as a component part in existing products and new products, Mr. Carter said, would take five years. A considerable amount of design work and retooling would be necessary, he pointed out, to adjust the products themselves to the unique properties of TGW, and Voltamp would then have to get these products established in the market, before it could be sure that it had fully capitalized on TGW's potentialities.

Mr. Grant agreed on the importance of product leadership to Voltamp, but pointed out that such leadership was important not only in products using magnets as components, but in magnets themselves. He suggested that while Audio Products was preparing to make magnets serve as component parts for its own products, and thus retain its leadership in these products, Magnetic Materials could also gain product leadership in magnets, and realize the resulting profits for the company immediately, by selling TGW to customers outside the company. With such an arrangement there would be no need to wait for possibly five years for profits while design work was completed on products using TGW as a component. Mr. Grant also pointed out that some other operating sections using magnetic components in their products had indicated that enough design work to give them a head start on their competitors in developing some products using TGW could be accomplished in 18 months. Mr. Grant suggested that these facts especially made the five-year protection period requested by Audio Products seem unnecessarily long. Mr. Carter agreed that some progress toward developing new products could be made in a shorter period of time, but argued that the maximum period of protection would be in the best interests of Voltamp in the long run.

Mr. Grant suggested that perhaps part of their problem could be resolved if Magnetic Materials agreed to sell TGW only to customers whose product lines did not compete with Voltamp products using magnets as components. Mr. Grant added that at this time Magnetic Materials' sales outside the company were primarily to industrial distributors of noncompetitive lines and to wholesalers who sold directly to dealers and to magnet users. Most manufacturers competing with Voltamp who used magnets as components of their own products preferred either to manufacture their own magnets or to purchase them from a noncompeting company.

Mr. Carter questioned whether Voltamp's competition would wish to continue this policy in view of the unique and highly desirable properties of TGW. He wondered also whether Magnetic Materials' willingness to sell to some potential customers and not to others would not be construed as restraint of trade. He knew that a company of Voltamp's size was under constant scrutiny by the Antitrust Division of the Department of Justice. Further, Mr. Carter was not sure that Magnetic Materials could police its sales closely enough to avoid having TGW finally reach one or more of Voltamp's competitors who used magnets as component parts of their own products.

Mr. Grant then raised the possibility that Magnetic Materials, besides manufacturing TGW itself, might license the manufacturing process for TGW to competing companies. He pointed out that the royalty payments would reimburse Voltamp, and perhaps Audio Products directly (under a special agreement which Audio Products could make with Magnetic Materials), for the development costs. Further, production costs to Voltamp's competitors would be higher than they would be for Voltamp because of royalty payments, and this situation would give Voltamp the kind of protection and competitive position it wanted. Mr. Carter was not convinced of the validity of this argument as it described the consequences of the licensing arrangement for Audio Products and other operating sections using magnetic components. He pointed out that the magnetic component was a relatively insignificant cost factor in most products using it. He argued that product leadership was the important determinant to the success of his operation. On the other hand, Mr. Carter recognized that for Magnetic Materials whose major product was the magnet itself, the cost differential due to royalty payments could be a significant competitive factor.

While Mr. Carter was fairly sure that licensing the manufacturing process of TGW would not give Audio Products the protection it wanted, he confessed some doubts as to whether Voltamp could long resist the pressure from its competitors for licensing if Voltamp refused to sell TGW to them directly through Magnetic Materials. Mr. Carter thought that competitors could publicize unfavorably the refusal of Voltamp to license or sell the product; they could make it seem as if Voltamp, by withholding TGW, was arbitrarily preventing others from manufacturing and selling products that might improve living standards, strengthen the economy, and promote the national defense effort. Mr. Carter wondered how long a company like Voltamp could, regardless of such pressures, keep a revolutionary product like TGW under wraps and out of the mainstream of competition. He recalled that both Voltamp and many of its competitors had large defense contracts involving products with magnetic components. Mr. Carter admitted that he thought competitors would prefer licensing to direct purchase from Voltamp, since the former procedure would give them control over their own supply of TGW.

At the conclusion of several discussions Mr. Carter and Mr. Grant agreed that they had raised most of the important considerations bearing on their problem. It did not appear possible for them at the time to make a detailed analysis of potential sales and profits for Voltamp or for their sections that would result from the exploitation of TGW, because at that stage the obvious potential of TGW in new and existing products in the industry could not be accurately forecast. Moreover, they agreed that the product leadership which the successful exploitation of TGW would bring to Voltamp could not at this time be translated accurately into anticipated increases in sales and profits. They knew from past experience that similar new products developed by Voltamp had indirectly enhanced the prestige and reputation of the company in the electrical industry, thereby improving the overall competitive position of the company in a variety of ways not directly associated with the specific development.

They were not in agreement, however, on the relative importance and significance of the considerations they had discussed in searching for the decision on how best to exploit TGW. Mr. Grant pointed out that he and Mr. Carter were naturally looking at the problem from the point of view of what was best for their respective sections, and that this preoccupation probably slanted their opinions of what was best for Voltamp. Mr. Carter wryly recalled that a few years earlier, before the company had been reorganized to carry out the decentralization policy, they both might have been reporting to the same vice president who would have resolved their problem for them. Both men agreed, however, that if the effort to push decentralization down to the operating sections was to be successful, they should do their best to resolve the question themselves. They knew that, as managers of the two operating sections most concerned with the new material, they had the authority to act in this matter as they thought right, if in their decision they took properly into account what was best for Voltamp. Mr. Carter, looking at the organization chart of operating divisions within the company, noted that their respective department vice presidents would be faced with the same problem if it were passed up to them.

Mr. Carter and Mr. Grant agreed to give the matter further study and to meet again the following week. They knew that there was no precedent in the company for their decision, since they were confronted with a problem related to an aspect of the company decentralization policy which had not as yet been clarified. Each of the two men promised to bring to the next conference a recommendation concerning the action they might take.

CASE 15

BCI Ltd.

"In today's world, we do not think that our subsidiary companies can expand to their full potential without some help from central advisory services provided by our headquarters staffs," stated Mr. Henry Lampton, one of BCI's executives and a leading contender to succeed the BCI managing director, who would retire within one year. British Commercial Investments Ltd. (BCI), a London-based industrial holding company, comprised 16 subsidiary companies, with operations ranging from the manufacture of oil drilling equipment to electrical components and from special steel fabrication to the construction of agricultural buildings. Originally, the company had been involved solely with Malayan rubber plantations, but in the 50s it was decided to diversify entirely out of these politically risky activities through acquisition of small- to medium-size private companies, mainly in the United Kingdom. During the preceding seven years, partly through acquisition and partly through internal growth, gross tangible assets had risen from £9 million to £31 million and pretax profits from £900,000 to £3.4 million. A recent shift in emphasis had occurred, however. According to one executive:

> Our present investment effort is directed mainly towards internal expansion by existing subsidiaries, and the acquisition of no new subsidiaries, unless they complement technologically those we already have. These two efforts, growth from within and acquisition of *related* companies, is what will produce the kind of profit we are interested in. Also, we have instituted what we call the BCI Three-Year Forecast, which involves much forward-thinking-in-detail. This kind of planning is accepted as essential in modern company planning, but even if it wasn't, something very similar would be needed to ensure the continued strength of BCI.

PARENT–SUBSIDIARY RELATIONSHIPS

The shift in emphasis in corporate objectives as well as the increased attention to formal planning had also led to changes in the relationships between BCI and its subsidiaries. According to Mr. Lampton, who had been instrumental in bringing about these changes:

> We have been trying recently to provide additional help to our subsidiary companies. Until very recently, however, we were rather diffident about providing these services to give specialized advice in particular fields; it would be fatal to try and force them on unwilling subsidiary managements. But recently the success of our operations research group, the welcome accorded to the monthly economic bulletins of our chief economist, and the demand for the services of our BCI marketing adviser, all attest to the need felt by subsidiary managers. Only in the last three weeks a computer adviser has joined our staff and has begun to familiarize himself with existing EDP installations and projects. We have been too slow in recognizing the part which EDP techniques will play in the future. We hope to provide companies individually too small to justify their own EDP units with access to facilities, and to reduce costs for all by organizing a coordinated network available on a BCI-wide basis.
>
> It is, however, a part of our philosophy that our underlying principal subsidiaries (or, if you like, divisions) should be of a size that they can support their own local functional staff of a high caliber. We are not suffering under the delusion that we can operate a large central services team capable of resolving the local problems of such a diverse organization. Our advisory staff are used as catalysts.
>
> Finally, I would like to say something about the services rendered to subsidiary operating companies by our BCI nominee director. We like to think that the personalities, experience, and sometimes wider contacts which our directors have are an important source of help to managements of BCI subsidiary companies.

Another executive elaborated:

> BCI maintains a [nonexecutive] director on the board of each of its subsidiaries, usually as chairman. Although nonexecutive, the BCI nominee normally visits each of his two or three companies about once a week, or twice every three weeks. The BCI nominee typically has had considerable industrial experience before joining our organization, either with a firm of accountants or management consultants, or with some other industrial corporation in an executive capacity. Many of them have university education, and have also attended advanced management programs such as the Administrative Staff College at Henley, Harvard Business School, Stanford Business School, or IMEDE in Lausanne.

Mr. Lampton continued:

> The position of a BCI nominee director involves a rather heavy responsibility. We are not bankers, interested only in the financial aspects of

the business. We are not there to take a normal dividend and let it go at that. In some financial holding companies, the local managements have the idea that they are entirely self-sufficient, except for dividends. At the same time, the directors nominated by the parent company to the boards of those subsidiaries create the impression that they are banker types— somewhat superior to getting into real operating problems. I personally believe that, in some such holding companies, the subsidiary managers are being supine; they sit there with talent which could add to operations, but which they abdicate. Specifically, I am certain that in this day of complex technology and society, the director has a moral responsibility to help his managers—to encourage them to do planning for the future, to aid them in selecting and staffing their operations, and to give advice where the director has talent or knowledge.

I can give you one example. Most recently, BCI acquired the L. M. Trowbridge Company from the Trowbridge family. This company special- izes in construction projects using asphalt products—parking lots, tennis courts, large industrial asphalt areas. It is to the benefit of everyone—BCI, Harrogate [another subsidiary which produces asphalt materials] and Trow- bridge managers, and employees of both companies—to merge the opera- tions of the two companies. In this way, both will be more profitable, enjoy more growth, and stand a much better chance of survival in the British economy. Next year we plan to form a company to hold both Harro- gate and Trowbridge, in the interest of better all-round operations. The move was, inevitably, initiated by the BCI nominee chairman; the managers of Harrogate and Trowbridge don't have the same chance of standing back and taking an overall view of their operations. Without our BCI man, the merger would never have been initiated.

This shows how far we have moved from our position when BCI was still mainly involved in Malayan plantations and when our United Kingdom subsidiaries were regarded merely as diversified investments to be bought and sold, managerial responsibilities resting wholly with the underlying unit. Gradually we have come to acknowledge that this is an untenable position, and have taken on full responsibility for the underlying units, while allowing them a very wide degree of local autonomy in the main areas of their businesses.

THE ACQUISITION OF HARROGATE

Seven years ago, Mr. Jack Stanley, a man of 82, and the owner of a number of family companies including Harrogate Asphalt, wanted to put his estate in order so that it could be passed on to his heirs. His brother approached a member of BCI management in London, with the idea that BCI might be interested in acquiring Harrogate Asphalt. Mr. Lampton, then 31 years old and living in Birmingham as the BCI Midlands representative, was assigned the job of doing a management evaluation of the Harrogate company, which was located in Frampton, a small town in Yorkshire near Harrogate.

Lampton's general conclusion was that Harrogate represented an excellent investment. He based this on a thorough analysis of finances, management, marketing, production, and raw material procurement. He also found that the Harrogate management had sold a less profitable coal business some years earlier, had concentrated on the more profitable asphalt operations, had introduced a revolutionary technological process in the late 50s, and had expanded production and sales. He found that the company was in sound financial condition and that profits had increased at a fast pace.

Mr. Lampton's management evaluation report described Mr. Paul Denham, Harrogate's managing director and secretary, as follows:

> Mr. Denham is 48 years old. He has spent the last 25 years with Mr. Stanley and has grown up with the business. He has been the prime mover in the expansion of Harrogate over the past several years. Despite Harrogate's rapid growth, the company is still relatively easy to administer and Denham has a tight personal control over it. He has a very pleasant personality. He is a strict disciplinarian and is respected for it. As the company is in a rural area and there is a very low labor turnover, Denham regards the employees with Edwardian paternalism. He has three sons at public school; the eldest (at 16) works in the company during vacations. Denham hopes one of the three will join him in the business later.

The works, transport, and sales managers were seen by Lampton as capable but "only one is likely to grow to sufficient stature."

Lampton pointed out that the workers in the plant earned very good wages compared to general conditions in British industry. The wages were exceptionally high in relation to the surrounding agricultural area. Wages of between £30 and £40 per week were due to the fact that when the new revolutionary production machinery was purchased, neither the manufacturer of the machinery nor the Harrogate management knew that it would be so productive. Piece rates were established based on the machines, estimated production, but these were "grossly wrong."

Lampton continued:

> The company (in the event, wisely) did not change these rates, but reserved the undisputed right to trim all production units to a bare minimum of labor. As the company has constantly expanded, no surplus labor has been laid off, but merely transferred to new units.
>
> Needless to say, at these rates competition for jobs at Harrogate is very high. There was an intensely "brisk" air about the whole place. It is nonunion labor. There is no pension scheme. Hours worked are long (normally 07:30 to 18:30) and annual holidays are split, a week in the summer and another in the winter. The work is arduous and in the winter conditions are not good by the very nature of the business. As the rates are all fixed by team output, there is no room for individual slacking. Relations with management appear to be good. Total labor force has risen rapidly in the past year to around 100.

Lampton concluded his report:

> The reason for the company's success is probably due to its geographi-
> cal position (both for raw materials and markets), the fact that it invested
> early in a revolutionary production machinery (outside engineers reckon
> that Harrogate has more of these than anyone else, but Denham has no
> proof of this), very efficient management (mainly by Denham), and because
> it is supplying a material in increasing demand over the past decade.

As a result of his report, BCI made an offer to Mr. Jack Stanley
for his company. This was accepted, and Harrogate became a subsidiary
of the London holding company. At the time of acquisition, Jack Stanley,
with his wife, daughters, and grandchildren, owned 90 percent of Harrogate, and Paul Denham and his wife owned 10 percent. This latter represented an interest which Stanley had permitted Denham to buy. During
the first three years of BCI ownership, Denham retained his minority
ownership, but this was subsequently sold to BCI on recommendation
of his own financial adviser.

Because the future of the company's sales and profits looked so
good, Stanley had proposed that Denham receive £4,000 net salary per
year, and 2.5 percent of net profits over £100,000. Previously, he had
received a lower salary (£2,000) plus 5 percent of total net profits. Lampton stated that Denham agreed with this, and that at the time it meant
a total take-home of £5,000. His total earnings had risen consistently
over the years, culminating in £17,000. This was considered by the casewriter to be a relatively high remuneration in British industry.

THE FIRST FIVE YEARS OF OPERATION

During the first year, the board of directors of Harrogate consisted
of Jack Stanley, Paul Denham, and Gerald Kemp, a full-time executive
in BCI who was assigned as the parent company representative.

During those years, Mr. Henry Lampton was serving as BCI representative in the Midlands and as nominee director of two BCI subsidiaries
located near Birmingham. Mr. Lampton recalled certain things which he
knew went on during the first five years.

> In that period, the new equipment installed from Mason & Grant
> gave Harrogate an overwhelming competitive advantage in a business
> mainly served by fairly small companies, with the result that profits, sales,
> and return on new capital increased dramatically. Here is a company whose
> return on net worth was among the highest of any BCI company. Neverthe-
> less, in my judgment, there were definite signs of trouble. Stanley died at
> the end of the second year. This left the BCI director and Paul Denham.
> About a year later, these two directors recommended as the third director
> Roger Sample, a young man who was hired by Denham in the second

year of our ownership. I'll have more to say about him later, but I acknowledge Roger from the first time I met him to be a capable chap, though his experience in Harrogate was limited.

The board meetings of those days consisted of a rather formal, cut-and-dried reporting of figures, once a month.

The casewriter, at this point, asked: "Was Paul Denham making the policy decisions?" Mr. Lampton responded: "If there were any policy decisions being made—though I doubt there were."

Lampton continued:

Also, in about the second year, Harrogate suddenly found itself with a strike on its hands. Denham was at loggerheads with the union and he was at a loss as to what to do. The BCI director had to go up there and deal with the union, and a settlement was reached. As I recall, Denham simply gave up and said that he could not deal with them.

Also, Denham operated by turning up at 8 A.M., opening the mail, then sitting in the sales [internal] office for two hours, returning to his own office where he would incarcerate himself and merely look at figures of past performance. He rarely went to see customers off site, or saw customers when they came in.

RECENT EVENTS

About two years ago, while some other changes were being made in the BCI organization, Mr. Lampton, at age 36, returned from Birmingham to the BCI London head office as a director of BCI; at the same time he was also assigned to the board of the Harrogate subsidiary. Mr. Lampton commented on his new Harrogate assignment as follows:

I arrived on the scene of this highly successful company (60 percent on net worth is remarkable by any criteria) full of youthful bounce and asking why they don't look at the situation in the building products industries for growth. I knew that the company was doing no real forward planning, and that with the addition of a lot of hard work along this line the company could do much better. I also had a certain amount of good will and ambition—and the knowledge that I would have a delicate time with Paul Denham.

But I soon found that it was an unusual company. I saw a managing director making £15,000 a year, but no other men of responsibility. His four top men, including Roger Sample, were making £3,000 or under. This came as a surprise. Here was an outstandingly successful company, profit-wise, with no staff in depth. In fact, in additon to Roger Sample, the only talent I could see was a good production assistant who had just given notice of his termination.

First let me say that I am not averse to local autonomy—I believe it is best—but not for one local autocrat. Let me also say that my relationship with Denham was a good relationship, personally speaking, but when I tried to bring some things up for improvement around the board table (I had instituted more frequent board meetings and insisted that we discuss company policy problems rather than just review figures of past performance) he did not want to discuss them. Instead, he would say, "This is not a matter for formal board—why don't you come around to my office and let's talk about them informally." Nevertheless, I thought that all three board members (including Sample) should be in on important matters, and that there should be formal board meetings, with the board having the responsibility for making decisions.

Let me give you an example. Our operators in the plant were getting very high piece rates, but it was physically very hard work, 58 hours a week, and two one-and-a-half-week holidays that had to be split, one-and-a-half weeks in summer and one-and-a-half in winter: anyone absent without a doctor's note got instant dismissal. When Denham asked me not to bring this up in the board, but to come to his office, I said, "No, this is a board matter." I could see that these conditions would mean trouble, and Roger Sample was telling me—not as a moral issue at all, but as a practical issue—we couldn't keep things this way. For my own part, I regarded it as a practical issue *and* a moral issue. In a way, we were blackmailing the workers with high pay and not providing opportunity for recreation. They were spending money in considerable amounts in gambling and drinking (this seemed to be a problem in the town). So I proposed that we allow them to take their two one-and-a-half weeks together, thus affording more of a real holiday and rest away from the job.

As I persisted in placing this matter before the board, Denham finally said: "I don't want any part of this discussion. If you want to make board policy, do it." Notice that he wasn't saying, "I am the managing director, I will think and be responsible about this." Instead, he was abdicating the managing directorship to us.

I mentioned Roger Sample. Denham had hired him some years ago from a local construction firm, and he subsequently became production manager. While he had rather narrow experience, working locally up there in Yorkshire, he is a man of talent. He knew I thought highly of him, but he was reticent with me at first because he didn't know what kind of game I was playing. He did not have much confidence in pushing his ideas, because when Denham resisted he did not know if I would back him. Gradually, however, we established a relationship of trust. It came about through situations like the following. On my side, I could see great need for looking beyond the narrow confines of present products and processes. The company needed market research and research on new technology. On Roger's side, he had been reading magazines of the industry and had become aware of some new processes which were being developed in Sweden. He wanted to go there to investigate, but had been forbidden by the managing director. Later, I raised this at the board table, but Denham's reaction was, "Don't let's meddle outside the company now. We have a system which is producing high profit." Why he took this attitude I don't know. I suspect that the real trouble lay in the fact that Denham had been outgrown by the company he managed, and he was afraid that anything new might put him still further out of his depth. Harrogate's very success was against him.

Some time later, the accountant for the plant quit. I think it was because he was mistreated by Denham. At this point, I tried to get Denham to go out and find a really top-flight managerial accountant, one who could think and plan rather than simply be an audit clerk. As things proceeded, I could see that Denham just wasn't capable of doing this, so I persuaded him that we should go out and hire an outside firm of consultants to do the recruiting. The consultants presented four candidates for our approval. I was party to interviewing them. We rejected two immediately, and there were two left, in my opinion, who were suitable. About this time I left to attend the 13-week Advanced Management Program of Harvard University in the U.S. When I returned, I found to my amazement that he had rejected both of them and instead had hired a local accountant at £1,800 a year rather than the £4,000 man I had envisaged.

About this time I recognized that Paul Denham was a man who was going to reject any sort of idea, and any sort of talent, that he was not familiar with. I was utterly disenchanted with what he was doing. When I got back from Harvard, Paul Denham also recognized that I was a chap who was going to stick to his guns. I could see trouble ahead, and was determined to do something about it, even though the company's profit record continued to be outstanding.

Mr. Lampton continued:

At the second board meeting after I returned, Roger Sample brought up a subject which I had encouraged him to study. (I had encouraged him to look at all facets of the business.) Our office staff had very high turnover. The staff was working on Saturday mornings, but there was no need, no work, for this. When Roger proposed it, Paul again said he wanted no part of it. He wasn't even fighting it. I suspect it was because he knew it was going to be put into effect anyway.

At any rate, I was intent on pursuing this to some sort of conclusion. The meeting became heated and intense. Denham said: "Hell, why do we waste our time on these matters; go out and find out what the order position is and let's get down to work." At this point, and in front of Roger, I blew my top. "This is real business," I said, "and if we don't pursue it, we have a real crisis."

One BCI executive commented that, during this time,

Lampton was very conscious that the company's success was in some measure due to the tremendous pace which Denham set for the company in earlier years. Indeed, the competitive edge which Harrogate had gained came largely from the fact that the company utilized its machines so intensively—the credit for which, at any rate initially, was Denham's.

(See Exhibit 1 for Harrogate's sales and profit performance.)

After the above incident, upon returning to London, Mr. Lampton wrote Denham a letter stating:

I have given myself some cooling time since our last meeting to consider its implications. I believe that it is most important that you and I meet away from Harrogate to discuss both the future of the business and the way in which you and I can operate together constructively for its good.

The letter then requested Denham to come to London for a meeting. According to Lampton:

> I felt that it was stupid to keep this up, and that we must resolve it somehow. Anyway, Denham had not once been to London in all the years we owned the company. I always invited him to the annual dinner we hold for subsidiary managing directors, but he always accepted and then sent a last-minute excuse.

EXHIBIT 1: BCI Ltd., Selected Financial and Operating Results of Harrogate Asphalt Products Ltd.

Year	Sales	Profits before Taxes
−14	£ 31,000*	n.a.
−13	55,000	£ 22,000
−12	83,000	28,000
−11	110,000	39,000
−10	178,000	62,000
− 9	224,000	87,000
− 8	361,000	136,000
− 7	520,000	150,000
− 6	867,000	260,000
− 5	1,053,000	310,000
− 4	1,096,000	300,000
− 3	1,638,000	450,000
− 2	1,922,000	595,000
− 1	2,050,000	600,000
Current year	2,500,000	750,000†

* Figures are rounded to nearest £1,000.
† Estimated.

Source: Company records.

The night before the meeting was to take place here at head office, Paul Denham telephoned to say that he was not feeling well. He had shut himself off and did not realize that someone else owns the company and that he was not, as he thought, master of his own domain. I drove all the way to Yorkshire the next day. He was surprised to see me. I said that it is intolerable to go on this way and that we must cooperate if the company is going to progress. I told him also that we must educate Roger Sample in a wider sphere, that we must move him out of the production manager position and give him experience on the commercial side. He agreed to this, and to promote Roger's assistant to production manager.

On his return from Yorkshire, Mr. Lampton also sent to Denham the letter which appears as Exhibit 2. He continued:

EXHIBIT 2

BCI LTD.

Mr. Paul Denham, Managing Director
Harrogate Asphalt Products Company
Frampton, Yorkshire

Dear Paul:

Although I was disappointed that you did not feel fit enough to come down here yesterday, I am glad that we had our discussion about the future, and I hope that you now understand and sympathize with our determination to strengthen the management at Harrogate so that it can be in a position to maintain its leadership in its own field, and to exploit other opportunities in allied fields. I am sure that our decision to put Roger in full charge of sales is sound.

At the same time I hope that you understood that the BCI management is insisting that the individual subsidiaries institute, this year, a formal approach towards three-year planning and forecasting (the majority of the companies did this last year, of course). This is not an academic exercise but, in our opinion, an essential step both for operating companies and for BCI. The preparation of such a report must essentially be a team effort that has your full backing, and as it is sometimes difficult to start viewing the future in this way I have, as I told you, arranged for James Kemp, our management accountant and planning specialist, to be free for a week (or more, if necessary) at the end of this month or in September to give you any help you may need. I sincerely hope that I have managed to persuade you that one is not just looking for a "figure pledge" that you would consider you had broken were it not achieved. When you look at the framework around which such a report is constructed, you will see that it requires the participation of the whole management team.

Naturally, I am anxious about your health and I do hope that you can soon discover what is wrong with your arm. What you said about overworking and the need for a really worthwhile break of two months or more seems to me not only desirable but necessary if you are going to be able to maintain your energies in the future. You have our complete backing for this, and I hope you can manage this as soon as possible.

Yours,

Henry Lampton

During this entire period I had been getting close to Roger Sample, but at this point I got very close. He said, "I don't want to be disloyal to the managing director. You are moving me from an area where I know the work and feel secure, to an area where I do not. But I am going to be of no use to anybody if I go on not being allowed to be in contact with customers. I wonder if Paul, who is 54, knows that, at 38, I am cornered?"

Mr. Lampton said that he then offered Sample a service agreement (contract) to insure that he would not be summarily fired. Sample responded, according to Lampton, "No, that is not what I want. I will give you a pledge to stay three years, but I will leave if there aren't some changes in the way the company is running."

Mr. Lampton continued:

Naturally, I did not put it to Denham that way. I told him it would be a good thing to send Roger to a three-week marketing course I knew about at the University of Glasgow. He said that this is not productive for the company, but that if Roger wants it and I approve, he would go along.

On the very day that Roger left, Paul Denham took sick. Roger phoned from Glasgow (Paul had phoned him) and wanted to know if he should go back to Frampton. I said no.

CASE 16

Showa-Packard, Ltd. (A)

When Richard Johnson, president of the International Division of Packard Foods, Inc. got on a JAL flight from Kennedy Airport to Tokyo, he was still undecided as to how best he could approach several delicate issues with the Japanese company which was a joint-venture partner. He planned to make good use of the grueling eleven-hour flight to Tokyo to formulate his policy. In many ways, he considered this trip of vital importance. For one thing, the nature of the problems to be discussed was such that they were likely to affect the long-term relationship between the Packard company and the Japanese partner in the management of their joint venture in Japan. Moreover, this was his first trip to Japan in the capacity of president of the International Division and he was anxious to make a good impression and to begin to build a personal relationship with senior executives of the Japanese firm.

Mr. Johnson had assumed the position of president several months previously. He was forty-two years old and was considered to be one of the most promising senior executives in the company. He had graduated from a well-known eastern business school in 1954. After two years of military service, he had entered a prominent consulting firm. In 1959, he joined the marketing group of Packard Foods, Inc. Prior to his promotion to the presidency of the International Division, he served as managing director of Packard's wholly owned subsidiary in Great Britain.

Packard was a major manufacturer of breakfast cereals, canned products, instant coffee, frozen foods, and pet foods. The company's total sales for 1972 were roughly $1.5 billion and it had 15 manufacturing subsidiaries and 20 sales subsidiaries throughout the world. International operations, including exporting, accounted for roughly 25 percent of the company's total sales. International sales had been growing at a rapid rate during the previous decade and the company's top management felt that this represented a major thrust for future growth.

The company, after about two years of difficult and often frustrating negotiations, was successful in establishing a joint venture in Japan with Showa Foods, a leading Japanese foods manufacturer. The arrangement was formalized in the summer of 1971 and the venture went into operation in the spring of the following year.

Prior to the establishment of this joint venture, Packard had had limited export operations in Japan through a major trading company, but the company's management recognized that in order to capitalize on the rapidly growing Japanese market for processed foods, the changing diet pattern, and the emerging mass market, more extensive local presence was essential. By the late 1960s, the company began to receive a number of inquiries from major Japanese corporations concerning licensing as well as the possibility of establishing a joint manufacturing venture.

Showa was one of the companies that approached Packard initially for licensing. It appeared to be an attractive potential partner. Showa Foods, Inc. had been a major producer of canned fish. In the early 1960s the company began an active program of diversification into new food products. The company successively entered into new product fields, including ketchup, mayonnaise, salad dressing, and a number of other lines. The company had established a reputation for high quality, and its brands were well established. Moreover, the company had built one of the most effective distribution systems in the industry, using a myriad of wholesalers and small retailers.

In the late 1960s, Showa began to seek still more new products. It was particularly interested in breakfast cereal, nondairy coffee creamer, canned soup, frozen foods, and pet foods. The company's management felt that these products would be a field for major growth. The management, after some investigation concluded that the quickest and most efficient way to achieve entry into these product lines was through either licensing or a joint venture with a leading American company. The Showa management felt that the timing was of particular importance, since its major competitors were also considering a similar move. Showa's expression of interest to Packard was indeed timely, since the latter company, having enjoyed considerable success in Europe, had become increasingly interested in Japan as the only untapped major market. Showa was at first interested in a licensing arrangement, but Packard, anxious to establish a permanent presence in Japan, wished to establish a joint manufacturing venture.

The negotiations concerning this joint venture were difficult in part because it was the first experience of the kind for both companies. Packard had had virtually no prior experience in Japan, and for Showa this was the first joint venture with a foreign company, although it had engaged in licensing agreements with several American and European firms.

The ownership of the joint venture was equally divided between the two companies. In addition to the predetermined level of cash contribution, the agreement stipulated that Packard was to provide technology and the Japanese partner was to make available part of the plant facilities. The joint venture was at first to produce and market breakfast cereal and instant coffee, and later was to introduce pet foods and frozen foods. The products were to be marketed under the joint brands of Packard and Showa. The agreement also stipulated that both companies would have equal representation on the board of directors, with four persons each, and that Showa would provide the entire personnel for the joint venture from top management down to production workers. Such a practice is quite common among foreign joint ventures in Japan since, given the almost total lack of mobility among personnel in large corporations, recruiting would represent a major, often almost insurmountable, problem for foreign companies. The companies also agreed that the Japanese partner would nominate the president of the joint venture, subject to the approval of the board, and the American company would nominate a person for the position of executive vice president. Packard agreed to supply, for the time being, a technical director on a full-time basis.

Representing Packard on the board were the executive vice president of the joint venture, Mr. Johnson, as well as the president and executive vice president of the parent corporation. Representing the Japanese company were the president and executive vice president of Showa, and two senior executives of the joint venture, namely, the president and vice president for finance.

By the spring of 1973 the operations were well under way. Production began and a reasonably effective sales organization had been built. Although the operating plans were progressing reasonably well, Mr. Johnson had become quite concerned about several issues that had come to his attention during the previous two months. The first and perhaps the most urgent of these was the selection of a new president for the joint venture.

The first president had died suddenly about three months before at the age of 64. He had been managing director of the parent company and had been the chief representative in Showa's negotiations with Packard. When the joint venture was established it appeared only natural for him to assume the presidency; Packard management had no objection.

About a month after his death, Showa, in accordance with the agreement, nominated Mr. Kenzo Tanaka as the new president. Mr. Johnson, when he heard Mr. Tanaka's qualifications, concluded he was not suitable for the presidency of the joint venture. He became even more disturbed when he received further information about how he was selected from Jack Harper, the executive vice president of the joint venture and one of Packard's representatives on the board. Mr. Tanaka had joined Showa forty years before upon graduation from Tokyo University. He had held a variety of positions in the Showa company, but during the previous fifteen years, had served almost exclusively in staff functions. He had been manager of administrative services at the company's major plant, manager of the General Affairs Department at the corporate headquarters, and personnel director. When he was promoted to that position, he was admitted to the company's board of directors. When he later became managing director, his responsibility was expanded to include overseeing several service-oriented staff departments, including personnel, industrial relations, administrative services, and the legal department. Mr. Johnson was concerned that Mr. Tanaka had had virtually no line experience, and could not understand why Showa would propose such a person for the presidency of the joint venture, particularly when it was at a critical stage of development.

Even more disturbing to Mr. Johnson was the manner in which Mr. Tanaka was selected. This first came to Mr. Johnson's attention when he received a letter from Mr. Harper, which included the following description.

By now you have undoubtedly examined the background information forwarded to you regarding Mr. Tanaka, nominated by our Japanese partner for the presidency of the joint venture.

I have subsequently learned the manner in which Mr. Tanaka was chosen for the position, which I am sure would be of great interest to you. I must point out at the outset that what I am going to describe, though shocking by our standard, is quite commonplace among Japanese corporations; in fact, it is well accepted.

Before describing the specific practice, I must give you a brief background of the Japanese personnel system. As you know, the major companies follow the so-called lifetime employment where all managerial personnel are recruited directly from universities, and they remain with the company until they reach their compulsory retirement age which is typically around 57. Career advancement in the Japanese system comes slowly, primarily by seniority. Advancement to middle management is well paced, highly predictable, and virtually assured for every college graduate. Competence and performance become important as they reach upper-middle management and top management. Obviously, not everyone will be promoted automatically beyond middle management, but whatever the degree to which competence and qualifications are considered in career advancement, chronological age is the single most important factor.

A select few within the ranks of upper-middle management will be promoted to top management positions, that is, they will be given memberships in the board of directors. In large Japanese companies, the board typically consists exclusively of full-time operating executives. Showa's board is no exception. Moreover, there is a clear-cut hierarchy among the members. The Showa board consists of chairman of the board, president, executive vice president, three managing directors, five ordinary directors, and two statutory auditors.

Typically, ordinary directors have specific operating responsibility such as head of a staff department, a plant, or a division. Managing directors are comparable to our group vice presidents. Each will have two or three functional or staff groups or product divisions reporting to them. Japanese commercial law stipulates that the members are to be elected by stockholders for a two-year term. Obviously, under the system described, the members are designated by the chairman of the board or the president and serve at their pleasure. Stockholders have very little voice in the actual selection of the board members. Thus, in some cases it is quite conceivable that board membership is considered as a reward for many years of faithful and loyal service.

As you are well aware, a Japanese corporation is well known for its paternalistic practices in return for lifetime service, and they do assume obligation, particularly for those in middle management or above, even after they reach their compulsory retirement age, not just during their working careers. Appropriate positions are generally found for them in the company's subsidiaries, related firms, or major suppliers where they can occupy positions commensurate to their last position in the parent corporation for several more years.

A similar practice applies to the board members. Though there is no compulsory retirement age for board members, the average tenure for board membership is usually around six years. This is particularly true for those who are ordinary or managing directors. Directorship being highly coveted positions, there must be regular turnover to allow others to be promoted to board membership. As a result, all but a fortunate few who are earmarked as heirs apparent to the chairmanship, presidency, or executive vice presidency, must be "retired." Since most of these men are in their late 50s or early 60s, they do not yet wish to retire. Moveover, even among major Japanese corporations, the compensation for top management positions is quite low compared with the American standard and pension plans being still quite inadequate, they will need respectable positions with a reasonable income upon leaving the company. Thus, it is a common practice among Japanese corporations to transfer senior executives of the parent company to the chairmanship or presidency of the company's subsidiaries or affiliated companies. Typically, these men will serve in these positions for several years before they retire. Showa has a dozen subsidiaries and you might be interested in knowing that every top management position is held by those who have retired from the parent corporation. Such a system is well routinized.

Our friend, Mr. Tanaka, is clearly not the caliber that would qualify for further advancement in the parent company, and his position must be vacated for another person. Showa's top management must have decided that the presidency of the joint venture was the appropriate position for him to "retire" into. This is the circumstance under which Mr. Tanaka has been nominated for our consideration.

Mr. Harper's letter then went on to discuss other matters.

When he had read this letter, Mr. Johnson instructed Mr. Harper to indicate to the Showa management that Mr. Tanaka was not acceptable. Not only did Mr. Johnson feel that Mr. Tanaka lacked the qualifications and experience for the presidency, but he resented the fact that Showa was using the joint venture as a haven to accommodate a retired executive. It would be justifiable for Showa to use one of its wholly owned subsidiaries for that purpose, for understandably Mr. Tanaka had been a loyal, effective employee who had made significant contributions to Showa, but there was no reason why the joint venture should take him on. On the contrary, the joint venture needed dynamic leadership to establish a viable market position.

In his response to Mr. Harper, Mr. Johnson suggested as president another person, Mr. Shigeru Abe, marketing manager of the joint venture. Mr. Abe was fifty years old and had been transferred to the joint venture from Showa, where he had held a number of key marketing positions, including regional sales manager and assistant marketing director. Shortly after he was appointed to the latter position, Mr. Abe was sent to Packard headquarters to become acquainted with the company's marketing operations. He spent roughly three months in the United States, during which time Mr. Johnson met him. Though he had not gone beyond a casual acquaintance, Mr. Johnson was much impressed by Mr. Abe. He appeared to be dynamic, highly motivated, and pragmatic, qualities which Mr. Johnson admired. Moreover, Mr. Abe had a reasonable command of English. While communication was not easy, at least it was possible to have conversations on substantive matters. From what Mr. Johnson was able to gather, Mr. Abe impressed everyone he saw favorably and gained the confidence of not only the International Division staff, but those in the corporate marketing group as well as sales executives in the field.

Mr. Johnson was aware that Mr. Abe was a little too young to be acceptable to Showa, but he felt that it was critical to press for his appointment for two reasons. First, he was far from convinced of the wisdom of employing Japanese managerial practices blindly in the joint venture. Some of the Japanese executives he met in New York had told him of the pitfalls and weaknesses of Japanese management practices. He was disturbed over the fact that, as he was becoming familiar with the joint venture, he was finding that in every critical aspect such as organization structure, personnel practices, and decision making, the company was managed as though it were a Japanese company. Mr. Harper had had little success in introducing American practices. Mr. Johnson had noticed in the past that the joint venture had been consistently slow in making decisions because it engaged in a typical Japanese group-oriented and consensus-based process. He also learned that a control and reporting system was virtually nonexistent, and felt that Packard's sophisticated planning and control system should be introduced. It had proved successful in the company's wholly owned European subsidiaries, and there seemed to be no reason why such a system could not improve the operating efficiency of the joint venture. He recalled from his British experience that American management practices, if judiciously applied, could give American subsidiaries abroad a significant competitive advantage over local firms.

Secondly, Mr. Johnson felt that the rejection of Mr. Tanaka and appointment of Mr. Abe might be important as a demonstration to the Japanese partner that Showa-Packard, Ltd., was indeed a 50–50 joint venture and not a microcosm of the Japanese parent company. He was also concerned that Packard had lost the initiative in the management of the joint venture. This move would help Packard regain that initiative.

Showa's reaction to Mr. Johnson's proposal was swift; they rejected it totally. Showa management was polite, but made it clear that they considered Mr. Johnson unfair in judging Mr. Tanaka's suitability for the presidency without even having met him. They requested Mr. Harper to assure Mr. Johnson that their company, as half-owner, indeed had an important stake in the joint venture and certainly would not have recommended Mr. Tanaka unless it had been convinced of his qualifications. Showa management also told Mr. Johnson, in no uncertain terms through Mr. Harper, that the selection of Mr. Abe was totally unacceptable because in the Japanese corporate system such a promotion was unheard of, and would be detrimental not only to the joint venture, but to Mr. Abe himself, who was believed to have a promising future in the company.

Another related issue which concerned Mr. Johnson was the effectiveness of Mr. Harper as executive vice president. Mr. Johnson appreciated the difficulties, but began to question Mr. Harper's qualifications for his position and his ability to work with Japanese top management. Mr. Johnson had no concrete evidence but nevertheless had formed a definite impression of ineffectiveness in the last two or three months through correspondence and from two visits Mr. Harper made to the home office. During the last visit, for example, Mr. Harper had complained of his inability to integrate himself with the Japanese top management team. He indicated that he felt he was still very much an outsider to the company, not only because he was a foreigner, but also because the Japanese executives, having come from the parent company, had known each other and in many cases had worked together, for at least twenty years. He also indicated that none of the executives spoke English well enough to achieve effective communication beyond the most rudimentary level and that his Japanese was too limited to be of practical use. In fact, his secretary, hired specifically for him, was the only one with whom he could communicate easily. He also expressed frustration over the fact that his functions were very ill defined and his experience and competence were not really being well utilized by the Japanese.

Mr. Johnson discovered after he assumed the presidency that Mr. Harper had been chosen for this assignment ostensibly for his knowledge of Japan. Mr. Harper had graduated from a small midwestern college in 1943 and when he was inducted into the Army he was sent to the Japanese language school, where he underwent a year's full-time, intensive language program. He was among the first language officers to go to Japan with the Occupation in the fall of 1945. He spent a year in the Counter Intelligence unit in Yokohama. Upon returning home, he joined Packard as a management trainee. He spent many of the ensuing years in the field. In 1968 he became assistant district sales manager in three Western states, California, Oregon, and Washington. When the company began to search for a candidate for executive vice president for the new joint venture, Mr. Harper's name came up quite accidentally. Reportedly, when Mr. Albert Gardner, Mr. Johnson's predecessor, mentioned the problem to Mr. George Vance, corporate vice president for marketing, in a casual conversation, the latter recommended Mr. Harper. Mr. Harper had worked under Mr. Vance in the field in the early 1960s, and Mr. Vance had known his background. Mr. Gardner called Mr. Harper into New York to meet with him and explore the latter's interest in assuming the new position. Mr. Gardner felt that Mr. Harper would be an excellent choice because of his age (53 years), his experience in sales, and his previous language training. Mr. Harper, although somewhat ambivalent about the new opportunity at first, soon became persuaded that this would represent a major challenge and opportunity. He was sure that his advancement opportunity in the company was limited if he stayed on in his present position. Moreover, he thought it would be pleasant to get back to Japan after some twenty-odd years. The fact that his children were all grown made the move less complicated. He was still able to carry on a simple conversation in Japanese and believed that with some effort he might be able to regain his language competence.

Mr. Johnson was wondering by what means he could find out how effective Mr. Harper was in working with Japanese management and how the Japanese regarded him. Mr. Johnson was also considering, if Mr. Harper had to be replaced, what qualifications would be required for another person to be effective in this unfamiliar environment.

CASE 17

Struthers and Williamson Manufacturing Company

Mr. John Stafford was reviewing his first two weeks on the job at Struthers and Williamson (S&W). He had just joined the firm after lengthy negotiations and considerable soul-searching. He had left the strategic consulting firm with which he had been associated for the past twelve years and was wondering if he had made a mistake. At the firm, he was a partner, well compensated and highly visible. He had accepted a cut in current income in order to get the experience in an administrative position and in order to get the equity ownership of 3 percent of S&W. He had thought that he was to be in charge of all financial and administrative affairs of the company. He was sure that both his training and background had prepared him well technically to meet the challenges, but he was beginning to question whether he had the administrative sense to survive. Nevertheless, the opportunity to be one of the top managers of a highly profitable company with over $65 million in sales had attracted him. The company had grown at a compound rate of 20 percent over the 15-year period since it became independent and had 1,300 employees. The challenge, together with a relatively unsuccessful search to find a happy 55-year-old consultant, had caused him to make his move. He had known the president and principal owner of the company for almost 10 years. Their backgrounds of Ivy League education and their common interests had made them into good friends and he had worked with one of the current division presidents at the consulting firm. He had studied the company's financial statements carefully, but had not had an opportunity to meet any of the people who would be working for him until he arrived on the scene. He had made some notes for his own analysis (see Exhibit 1).

Since arriving he had had a series of shocks. He ran through them in his own mind without giving them any particular priority.

- The new computer which he had seen before joining was found to have been in place for 10 months and no programs were operational.
- The corporate controller, through whom all the division's controllers reported to Stafford, was paid at a rate less than 40 percent of Stafford's.

EXHIBIT 1: Notes from Stafford's File on Struthers and Williamson Strategic Analysis*

The company is highly profitable relative to its industry. The basic profitability seems to stem from two factors: its gross margin is higher than competition reflecting both lower labor costs and better than average price realization in a semicommodity market. The latter may be a result of Jack's (the president's) unusual style and close personal contact with major customers. All major accounts are handled by him with frequent social and business meetings.

The company has grown through both internal development and acquisition. The internal development has been based upon intensive capital investment. Over 120 percent of after-tax profits have been invested in capital equipment in the period of the last 10 years. Depreciation as a percentage of sales is increasing. The plant may in fact be underdepreciated based upon replacement cost so that once the initial purchased assets are in need of replacement, the reported profits will be severely impaired, although the cash flow before capital expenditures should improve.

External growth through acquisition has been based upon targets of financial opportunity within the basic product/market commitment of the original S&W. Each of the acquisitions had represented some form of vertical forward or backward integration. There have been four such acquisitions in the past 10 years.

The company has two major profit centers through which 13 separate legal entities are controlled. The profit centers report to division presidents who in turn report to the S&W president. The staff functions report to the division presidents nominally, but due to both interest and historical precedent, there is a dual reporting relationship to Morgan.

All capital needs have been met through incurring additional debt both in the form of purchase money mortgages and through institutional borrowing. Conversion of variable rate debt to fixed rate debt offers considerable cost saving potential.

The management has not been willing to stray from a tightly defined geographic and product base. Jack's view of the world requires the company to stay within areas where he is personally comfortable with his own ability to understand and impact the marketing activities.

EXHIBIT 1 *(concluded)*

Putting Ron as division president of Xtolite and hiring Charles from Multico as division president of Mohegan Products brings operational strength that the retirement of Mr. Whiting requires.

The major risks are the ability of the organization to absorb three new players into new senior positions and the impact of a burdensome debt structure on the company in case of either a market downturn or a technical misjudgment.

* Casewriter's note:

Jack (age 55) is the president and majority shareholder of S&W.

Ron was Stafford's friend at the consulting firm whom he had recruited for S&W. He is president of a major division and like Stafford a 3 percent shareholder.

Charles was recruited at the same time as Stafford from Multico where he was division manager of a division with approximately three times the sales of S&W. He had also been given a 3 percent share interest.

Mr. Whiting had been the production partner of the original threesome. He had retired the year before at age 66 and had resold his stock to the company for notes to be paid out over a nine-year period.

- The operating reports were prepared on a completely different basis than the financial reports and could only be reconciled through adjustments which amounted to several hundred thousand dollars per month.
- The audited financial statements for the previous year end (December 31) had not yet been released by the auditors as of June 15. No qualifications were expected, but the audit process was not working.
- Over $1.5 million of property insurance claims remained outstanding from losses which occurred 18 months previously. The last letters in the file were two months old with no responses from the insurance company.
- Cash was tight from a book basis, but Stafford's analysis of the bank statements showed that the company had drawn down its credit line excessively by covering checks as soon as they were written rather than waiting until they were expected to be presented for payment. As much as $2 million in borrowings might be paid off if a different procedure were adopted.

With all of the important technical issues facing Stafford he still believed that his most critical problem was his relationship with the old treasurer, Mr. Morgan. Mr. Morgan was a fixture at S&W. It was he whom Stafford had been hired to replace. He had worked at S&W for 52 years and was going to celebrate his 75th birthday in October. Although Stafford had been told that he was retiring, recent conversations gave no indication that that was his plan. He owned 33 percent of the stock, had no children, and had taken a hard-line position regarding repurchase of the stock. He indicated that he wanted to stay active and would allow the company to repurchase his stock upon his death at a 75 percent discount from the contractual book value repurchase. This offer was condi-

EXHIBIT 2*

Inter-Office Memo	FROM R.M.	DATE April 27, 1947

TO   CFC   JP
       GEW   Blue File
       SSN
       AL
	SUBJECT
	    Mill Supervisors	

Inasmuch as you and myself are responsible for S&W, I suppose we are jointly responsible for the things enumerated later on which I discovered around the plant yesterday.

Last week, a $30 a week clerk lost her job because she wouldn't assume the responsibility of putting the right letters in the right envelopes and attaching the correct postage to the envelopes. Is it possible that we have men in the $3,000-$4,000 a year bracket who are in the same category?

It makes my blood boil to think that we are paying some $10,000 a year to 3 supervisors who either haven't the capacity to handle their jobs or are indifferent about the company's welfare.

Upon examining the steam meter yesterday afternoon between half-past four and five o'clock, I discovered that it was merrily rolling up steam consumption at almost 1,000 lbs. an hour, even though there was no steam pressure in the boiler.

I came back at 8 o'clock last evening and found that the meter was still adding up 1,000 lbs. an hour. Mr. John Petrelli, the watchman, said that the meter had been out of order for some time, although apparently none of our mill supervisors had even checked whether or not the thing was working properly.

At 8 o'clock I went all over the plant to see if anybody was working and found no one. Mr. Petrelli stated that no one was working.

All of the lights in the corridor at the Westerly end of the office and the Machine Shop were on. *Whose responsibility?*

The door to the plant supply room was wide open.

The lights were all on in the plant supply room.

Luigi's Sea Chest was unlocked and opened.

The cupboard over the sea chest was also unlocked and opened. *Charles Ferreri was working after men went home.*

There were 11 light fixtures lit in the inspection room and near the horizontal boring machine.

There were 2 light fixtures in the polishing department on. *Always left on for watchman, had been corrected.*

There were 10 fixtures lit in the raw material pen. *— Anne Hallery left on.*

There were 12 fixtures lit in finished goods and shipping department. *— Ray Schenk crew probably brought up parts late.*

tional upon his being given a lifetime employment agreement. The difference to the remaining stockholders was a cost of almost $5 million. The president of the company to whom Stafford reported had a very strong personal relationship with Morgan since they had jointly acquired the company in 1966 from a large public company. Many times, cash crunches in the company had been met by Morgan lending personal funds. The three original partners were very close and Morgan's change of heart

EXHIBIT 2 *(concluded)*

Inter-Office Memo	**FROM** R.M.	**DATE** April 27, 1947
TO CFC JP GEW Blue File SSN AL	**SUBJECT** Mill Supervisors--page 2	

This total, some 40 fixtures which were lit with a probable average of 150 watts per fixture or 6 kilowats per hour. The watchman claims that the lights had been that way ever since he came on at 3 o'clock. He also claims that he did not lock up the supply room or turn off the lights because he thought someone must be going to do some work, inasmuch as everything was wide open.

Incidentally, this was a golden opportunity for anyone to have walked into the supply room and carried off several hundred dollars worth of tools.

The fact that it has happened once could be indicative that it has happened in the past.

Yesterday's occurrence indicated weakness somewhere in our plant supervisory group.

I am attaching copies of these for the three supervisors if you care to pass them along. I think that you and myself should discuss this matter at length and see what should be done to correct this and any other supervisory conditions which have not been up to par in the plant even if it may be unpleasant.

RM/mm

* **Casewriter's note:**

RM* = President
CFC = Mill manager
GEW = President of parent company
SSN = Maintenance foreman
AL = Plant superintendent
JP = Section foreman
Blue = Personnel file

was unlikely to be reversed by any forceful intervention by the president.

Looking ahead Stafford was very concerned about what he should do first and how he should assert his authority. He was to share a secretary, Mrs. Mary Monegan, with Mr. Morgan. Mrs. Monegan was a legend within the company. She had worked with Morgan for 46 years. It was she who had guarded the company stores. Until an office union had begun organizing attempts two years previously, all office workers had to get replacement pencils from Mrs. Monegan by bringing in the old pencils. File folders were handed out as specific needs were identified and all accounts payable were specifically released for payment by Mr. Morgan working with Mrs. Monegan.

Mrs. Monegan had indicated that she wished to retire in 22 months, which would be her 66th birthday.

One evening, Stafford had run across a memo in the file which Mr. Morgan had written one Sunday in 1947 (see Exhibit 2). Three of the names on the memo were still in the home division of S&W. Stafford had heard from one of the division controllers about Morgan's approach to management, but this was the first concrete piece of written documentation which he had found.

As he thought about the problem, he picked up the phone to call one of his consulting friends. The company operator responded since she had to place all calls. His mental image was of the ancient patchboard PBX with its spaghetti-like entanglement and of the slips being sent to Mr. Morgan showing whom he called and how long he talked. All calls were logged.

His questions remained: What had he learned and what should he do?

CASE 18

Ideal Standard France: Pat Paterson

In late August 1974, Raymond "Pat" Paterson had been in his job as general manager of Ideal Standard France for only a few weeks. It had taken little time to discover that the recession was hurting the company badly, and losses of over $1 million per month were being registered. The imminent visit of Bill Marquard, president of American Standard Inc., Ideal Standard's U.S.-based parent, provided Paterson with a strong incentive to clarify his ideas on what the problems were and what action might be taken. The question that kept going around in Pat's mind was, "*Can* the company be saved?" Given the parent company's results-oriented attitude and portfolio view of its strategy, he knew Mr. Marquard would be asking the same question—and would want to know why and how as well!

THE PARENT COMPANY: AMERICAN STANDARD

American Standard (AS) grew from the 1929 merger of American Radiator with the Standard Sanitary Corporation, and by the 1970s the heating and sanitary businesses developed by these predecessor companies were still important to AS. The company's proud boast was that its name was in "one out of every five bathrooms in the free world." However, the profitability of the building products group (including doors and fireplaces that had been added to plumbing product line) was generally low for the company and also tended to fluctuate with the cyclical construction cycle.

In an effort to reduce its dependence on this core business, AS had embarked on an aggressive acquisition campaign in the 1960s. Among other businesses, it acquired Westinghouse Air Brake Company (WABCO) and the Mosler Safe Company. By 1970, the company had established three new business groups to counterbalance its basic building products group: transportation systems, industrial and construction, and security systems and graphic arts. Together these three groups accounted for slightly more than 50 percent of sales in 1970.

However, with the 1970 recession came some financial problems that caused AS to pull back on its aggressive, diversification strategy. Operating income on building products dropped below 2 percent on sales, causing that group to contribute only 14 percent of corporate profits on 48 percent of the total sales. Furthermore, the new debt that the company had assumed to undertake its acquisitions proved a major strain at this time, and AS's net income dropped from $39 million on $1.4 billion in sales in 1969 to $2 million on $1.5 billion sales in 1970.

In early 1971, the board asked Bill Marquard, manager of AS's recently acquired Mosler Safe Company to accept the job of CEO and help straighten out the problems. With the aid of the Boston Consulting Group, the company began a review of its various businesses. Heading the list of operations that seemed to consume too much cash for the growth they promised was the venerable heating business (boilers and radiators) and the corporate planning managers were proposing that the company exit this business.

Marquard also made an early impact on the company's management style. He made it clear to his management group that he wanted them to boost their market shares and achieve low-cost manufacturing positions. He indicated that performance would be measured according to a manager's ability to improve cash flows and return on net assets (RONA). In calculating RONA, Marquard insisted that inventories be valued by the LIFO method, that depreciation be based on replacement cost, and that operations be charged 10 percent p.a. for their use of corporate funds. Throughout the corporation, managers soon felt the heat of these new tough demands, and within a couple of years profits had begun to rebound and the balance sheet looked considerably healthier.

Exhibit 1 gives summary earnings, funds flow, and balance sheet data. Exhibit 2 shows the company organization chart.

IDEAL STANDARD EUROPE

American Radiator established its first foreign plant in France in 1901, and before World War I had set up operations in the United Kingdom, Germany, Belgium, Italy, and Austria. Standard Sanitary also had a German plant at the time of the 1929 merger.

Organization

After World War II, the European operations were reorganized into nine national subsidiary companies, each of which was renamed Ideal Standard. These Ideal Standard subsidiaries were responsible only for the company's traditional building products, and all reported to a European headquarters in Brussels.[1] Given their long-standing independence and freedom, general managers of the nine country subsidiaries tended to guard their autonomy jealously, and resented intervention from Brussels or Pittsburgh. One country manager summed up the relationship with the Brussels headquarters in this way:

> Certainly we listen to Brussels. Just one word from them and we go ahead and do what we planned!

EXHIBIT 1: American Standard Financial Statements

Five-Year Income Summary
(in thousands of dollars)

	1969*	1970*	1971*	1972*	1973
Revenues:					
United States .	$ 938,399	$ 994,620	$ 987,851	$ 891,472	$ 811,394
Foreign .	436,247	512,276	532,734	563,687	717,949
Total .	1,374,646	1,506,896	1,520,585	1,455,159	1,529,343
Income before extraordinary items:					
United States .	20,715	7,665	7,588	15,402	17,075
Foreign .	14,732	4,289	3,905	9,847	22,448
Total .	35,447	11,954	11,493	25,249	39,523
Per common and common share equivalents.	1.90	.15	.11	1.15	2.16
Net income (loss) .	39,312	1,954	(85,507)	25,249	39,523
Per common and common share equivalents	2.11	(.62)	(7.26)	1.15	2.16
Dividends paid on common stock.	11,208	12,770	7,171	5,217	6,657
Per common share.	1.00	1.00	.55	.40	.525
Working capital .	364,821	320,114	317,431	261,405	264,054
Facilities, net.	318,491	336,590	322,292	291,987	300,802
Expenditures for facilities.	57,681	68,609	41,108	40,405	52,712
Provision for depreciation	38,613	38,780	38,473	35,829	37,736
Employment costs .	499,920	550,419	531,659	534,333	603,852
Number of employees at year-end	75,000	71,200	66,600	59,900	60,500

* Restated to include Land and Shelter operations.

---

[1] Several of AS's other businesses also had foreign operations but these were managed separately. For example WABCO had a very large French subsidiary that won a major brake systems contract from the government-owned railway in 1973.

EXHIBIT 1 *(continued)*

Balance Sheets: 1972–1973
(in thousands of dollars)

	At December 31	
	1972 Restated	**1973**
Assets		
Current assets:		
Cash	$ 34,638	$ 23,923
Accounts receivable	226,095	238,579
Inventories	282,641	321,631
Future income tax benefits	32,478	44,878
Other current assets	10,142	9,569
Total current assets.	585,994	638,580
Land and shelter	108,725	96,043
Rental equipment, at cost	5,268	5,777
Less: Accumulated depreciation	2,621	1,140
	2,647	4,637
Facilities, at cost	686,453	711,903
Less: Accumulated depreciation	396,182	411,872
	290,271	300,031
Investments	33,058	30,867
Other assets.	112,946	101,809
Total assets	$1,133,641	$1,171,967
Liabilities and Stockholders' Equity		
Current liabilities:		
Loans payable to banks	$ 28,504	$ 23,633
Accounts payable	106,903	129,508
Accrued payrolls	39,121	47,844
Other accrued liabilities	97,251	114,746
Taxes on income	16,907	22,378
Current maturities of long-term debt	35,903	36,417
Total current liabilities	324,589	374,526
Land and shelter	89,065	81,428
Long-term debt.	247,482	238,975
Reserves:		
Foreign operations.	12,093	11,528
Foreign pensions and termination indemnities	21,139	27,981
Product lines and facilities reevaluation.	84,313	64,927
Deferred taxes on income	—	5,899
Minority interests in subsidiaries	5,828	5,691
Stockholders' equity:		
7% preferred stock	2,388	2,365
$4.75 convertible preferred stock.	41,574	41,574
Common stock	64,961	60,785
Capital surplus	59,565	55,920
Earned surplus	180,644	200,368
Total stockholders' equity.	349,132	361,012
Total liabilities and stockholders' equity	$1,133,641	$1,171,967

EXHIBIT 1 *(concluded)*

Statement of Changes in Financial Position
(in thousands of dollars)

	Year Ended December 31	
	1972 **Restated**	**1973**
Source of funds:		
Operations:		
Net income.	$ 25,249	$ 39,523
Income of finance subsidiary.	(1,046)	(1,038)
Depreciation	35,563	37,633
Provision for foreign pensions and		
termination indemnities .	4,181	6,985
Noncurrent income taxes .	12,134	15,335
Amortization of excess of cost over net		
assets of businesses purchased.	1,263	361
Total from operations.	77,344	98,799
Sale and disposal of facilities	36,822	6,401
Sale of rental equipment .	5,334	2,406
Land and shelter:		
Collections of receivables (net of repay-		
ments of related loans of $3,534 in		
1972 and $4,580 in 1973).	5,513	1,450
Proceeds from other loans	19,060	19,700
Cost of real estate project sales (less		
repayments of related loans of $71,182		
in 1972 and $31,069 in 1973)	46,495	15,848
Proceeds from issuance of long-term debt.	—	27,910
Decrease in investment in finance subsidiary .	1,000	3,800
Other	9,555	1,593
	201,123	177,907
Application of funds:		
Expenditures for facilities.	40,271	52,611
Additions to rental equipment	4,128	5,579
Land and shelter:		
Expenditures for real estate projects (less		
proceeds from related loans of $33,752		
in 1972 and $16,035 in 1973)	39,060	26,208
Payments of other loans	12,367	583
Decrease in accounts payable and other		
liabilities .	10,486	3,054
Other.	8,906	2,108
Long-term debt transferred to current		
liabilities.	35,903	36,417
Repayment of long-term debt	59,851	—
Charges for foreign pensions and termination		
indemnities.	1,802	1,669
Losses (net of gains) resulting from reevalua-		
tion of certain product lines and facilities	25,846	19,386
Transactions in capital stock	3,141	10,945
Dividends paid	15,388	16,698
	257,149	175,258
Increase (decrease) in working capital .	$ (56,026)	$ 2,649

EXHIBIT 2: American Standard, Organization of Plumbing and Heating Group (1974)

```
                    ┌─────────────────────┐
                    │     President       │
                    │  American Standard  │
                    │  William A. Marquard│
                    └─────────────────────┘
```

Western Hemisphere Plumbing and Heating Group Bryce S. Durant Executive Vice President	Ideal Standard European Plumbing and Heating Group Fergus W. O'Donnell Executive Vice President

Headquarters: New Brunswick, New Jersey	Headquarters: Brussels, Belgium
American Standard Plumbing and Heating, Inc. (U.S.A.)	Ideal-Standard GmbH (Austria)
American Standard S.A. (Brazil)	Ideal-Standard S.A. (Benelux)
American Standard Ltd. (Canada)	Ideal-Standard Ltd. (U.K.)
Ideal-Standard S.A. de C.V. (Mexico)	Ideal-Standard S.A. (France)
ICS S.A. (Guatemala)	Ideal-Standard GmbH (Germany)
ICC S.A. (Nicaragua)	Ideal-Standard S.A.I. (Greece)
ICC Ltda. (Costa Rica)	Ideal-Standard S.p.a. (Italy)
Sanitary Wares Corp. (Philippines)	Ideal-Standard A.G. (Switzerland)
American-Standard Ltd. (Thailand)	CRR S.A. (Spain)

Strategy

Fergus O'Donnell had been president of Ideal Standard Europe since 1970, having previously served most of his career in the financial function. Although O'Donnell supported the new measurement and control systems being implemented by Bill Marquard's corporate staff, he was less enthusiastic about the proposal that the company exit the heating business.

He argued that the market situation in Europe was different and that there was no strong trend toward warm air heat as there had been in the United States. He did acknowledge, however, that generally in Europe there appeared to be some shift in demand away from cast-iron radiators (AS's traditional strength) toward steel and aluminum products.

O'Donnell pointed out that the heating business was a large and important one in Europe, accounting for some $220 million of Ideal Standard Europe's $350 million sales in 1973. Although the boiler product line had been experiencing difficulty in several countries, the radiator line had posted an excellent year in 1973. O'Donnell believed the heating business could be made viable given sufficient time, investment, and management attention.

Not wishing to demoralize the Ideal Standard European organization, AS's top management decided to give Fergus O'Donnell the time to justify his optimism. Following the strong performance in 1973, O'Donnell began to implement a plan of European manufacturing rationalization with early focus on the French and Belgian plants.

The largest boiler plant in Europe was in Aulnay, France, and this facility was chosen to become the primary boiler plant for Europe. The choice hinged partly on the fact that Aulnay was large enough to accept this role, but also in part because it would have been more difficult to close down than the Belgian boiler plant. In 1973 some $6 million was spent on new equipment and machinery to expand the capacity of Aulnay by almost 50 percent by 1974.

Problem: Ideal Standard France

The French subsidiary was a very important one for Ideal Standard Europe, contributing about one-third of total sales and accounting for almost half the heating business. It was with some concern, therefore, that Fergus O'Donnell viewed a rapid deterioration in Ideal Standard France's results in the first half of 1974 (see Exhibits 3 and 4).

EXHIBIT 3: ISF Summary Income Data: 1969 to June 30, 1974 (in thousands of dollars)

	1969	1970	1971	1972	1973	Jan.–June 1974
Sales.	82,440	82,662	81,587	93,360	121,347	65,731
Cost of goods sold	61,672	71,788	69,377	78,632	102,900	62,480
Gross margin . . .	20,768	10,874	12,260	14,728	18,447	3,251
Administrative expenses . . .	3,852	4,644	4,258	3,341	4,249	1,954
Marketing expenses . . .	7,589	4,541	4,113	4,451	5,489	3,100
Other overhead expenses . . .	—	—	—	—	—	585
Operating income .	9,327	1,930	3,370	6,369	7,465	(2,388)
Other expense . .	2,514	3,699	2,273	2,087	2,856	1,632
Before-tax income .	6,813	(1,769)	1,097	4,282	4,609	(4,020)
Net income . . .	3,473	(1,769)	142	2,031	2,275	(4,020)
Number of employees . . .	7,058	5,572	5,209	5,269	5,528	5,421

After 1973's record sales of $120 million, and the strongest profit performance in five years, O'Donnell was shocked at the rapidity with which ISF had dropped into a loss position, and was equally concerned about the marked deterioration in the company's balance sheet. As the year progressed, he became increasingly skeptical of French general manager Georges Frehis's claim that things would improve in the last two quarters and that the company just had to "weather the storm."

EXHIBIT 4

ISF Summary Balance Sheets: 1969 to June 1974
(in thousands of dollars)
Assets

	1969	1970	1971	1972	1973	June 1974
Cash	$ 4,009	$ 780	$ 311	$ 5,193	$ 6,075	$ 130
Accounts receivable .	21,107	19,247	18,227	17,740	21,457	23,869
Inventory	23,596	21,163	19,263	16,901	21,990	27,125
Other assets . . .	141	341	134	110	2,467	2,644
Current assets . . .	48,853	41,531	37,935	39,944	51,989	53,768
Facilities	53,721	53,191	60,259	61,667	65,029	66,109
Accumulated depreciation . . .	(41,562)	(39,857)	(45,455)	(46,288)	(47,833)	(48,991)
Other	342	412	602	363	365	371
Total assets. . . .	$61,354	$55,277	$53,341	$55,686	$69,550	$71,257

Liabilities

	1969	1970	1971	1972	1973	June 1974
Accounts payable and accrued liabilities	17,520	17,715	18,577	18,084	24,542	28,406
Taxes accrued. . .	0	(872)	103	279	2,939	(1,856)
Other payables . .	12,500	10,959	2,453	362	1,199	7,476
Current liabilities . .	30,020	27,802	21,133	18,725	28,680	34,026
Long-term debt . .	0	230	246	250	313	338
Other liabilities. . .	121	(2,253)*	18	171	1,425	1,425
Capital and R.E. . .	31,213	29,498	31,944	36,540	39,132	35,468
Total liabilities . . .	$61,354	$55,277	$53,341	$55,686	$69,550	$71,257

* Contingent liability.

After several unsatisfactory meetings with Frehis during the spring, O'Donnell finally sent one of his senior staff to France to investigate in early July. The report he got back was far from encouraging. The recession in the building industry had softened demand considerably and as inventories grew in the plants and at distributor locations, the company had been forced to discount heavily to move product. While this had helped sales early in the recession, the pipeline was now very full and sales in recent months were sagging despite these efforts.

Margins were also being squeezed by cost increases in an economy with an inflation rate of around 12 percent. Prices were controlled by the government and were lagged six to nine months behind the cost increases. The plant-by-plant cost breakout revealed a bleak picture (Exhibit 5). In short, the staff analyst reported, he did not see how Frehis could be optimistic about the next two quarters.

O'Donnell decided he would have to replace Frehis. As he cast around for names of a suitable replacement, the one he kept coming

EXHIBIT 5: Cost of Goods Sold: ISF Radiator and Boiler Plants, January–June 1974 (in thousands of dollars)

	Boiler Plants		Radiator Plants		
	Aulnay	**Blanc-Mesnil**	**Autun**	**Dammarie**	**Argenteuil**
Sales					
Manufacturing cost (at Standard):	17,340	4,790	19,102	12,862	4,002
Direct labor.	742	270	762	811	226
Direct material.	6,362	1,895	4,098	3,025	412
Manufacturing overhead-variable	2,774	425	1,825	1,760	805
Manufacturing overhead-fixed	1,095	336	2,665	1,395	558
Cost of goods sold at standard	10,973	2,926	9,350	6,991	2,001
Manufacturing Cost Variables:					
Material price variance . . .	1,862	280	3,430	1,925	220
Material use variance . . .	311	(15)	281	296	(60)
Labor rate variance	279	32	182	265	85
Labor performance variance	(77)	—	(18)	62	—
Rework variance	62	14	132	182	—
Spoilage variance	896	—	568	384	60
Overhead spending variance	2,628	335	1,189	1,050	524
Overhead volume variance	872	340	296	995	201
Other variance	(90)	—	138	210	(18)
Total variances	6,743	986	6,198	5,369	1,012
Other manufacturing expense:					
Start-up expense (Aulnay)	440				
Inventory adjustment	1,220		(175)		
Total manufacturing cost	23,288		30,746		
Distribution cost	1,832		1,606		
Service and warranty.	1,122		—		
Total cost of goods sold	26,242		32,342		

back to was the managing director of Ideal Standard U.K., Raymond (Pat) Paterson.

PAT PATERSON

Pat Paterson was a 52-year-old Scot of medium height, sturdy build and erect posture. His soft voice had a "filter tipped" quality to it— perhaps a consequence of smoking some four packs of cigarettes a day. Pat projected a certain warmth that revealed his fondness for people, but his strong, engaging personality also left one feeling that he was in command and could be very hard-nosed when circumstances demanded. Paterson had left school at 16 to join the Territorial Army, and spent World War II as an officer in the Royal Engineers. After a distinguished military service he returned to University College of London, where he graduated with an economics degree in 1949.

Reflecting on his own management philosophy and style, Pat felt they probably owed more to his military experience than to his economics training.

> I still love a good fight. And I like to put together a good team and lead them in a tough situation. My style tends to be to get into action first, then decide what to do.
>
> There is just no way you can know the full consequences of an action before you take it, and I tend to trust my gut reaction in many circumstances. Perhaps that makes me an old-fashioned kind of a manager, but I still believe I can "feel" a situation and exercise good judgment based on experience.
>
> I think a sense of urgency is important, and that means you can't run a business as a democracy. People need to feel they are participating and they must be kept informed all the way, but it is the leader's responsibility to decide on action and priorities.

Pat had experienced many challenges and "good fights" in his 25 years as a manager. He had worked as an export manager for Olivetti from 1949 to 1952, before joining Burroughs for two years. He worked as divisional financial controller for Ford U.K. from 1954 to 1957, then joining SCM, first as their managing director in the United Kingdom, then as their deputy chairman in Switzerland. In 1963 he took a job running the Avery Label franchise in Britain, before joining Ideal Standard U.K. in 1968 as marketing director. He had been appointed managing director in 1970.

In his four years as managing director of the U.K. subsidiary, Pat had made considerable change. Recognizing that the market was moving away from cast-iron baths to plastic, he decided to close down the plant. Believing that the company's steel radiator plant was only one-tenth the size it needed to be to achieve any reasonable level of efficiency, he closed this plant also. Fortunately the British economy was strong at the time these closures were made and most employees were able to find alternative work.

After cutting out 20 product lines, Pat set about rebuilding the strong core that remained. With a drastically rationalized product line he was able to convert the domestic heater operations from a job shop to more of a production line operation. By 1974 their domestic heater market share had increased from 4 percent to 43 percent. Overall, the company was profitable.

In late July 1974, Fergus O'Donnell called Paterson to say he had to meet with him urgently. At a meeting in London the next day O'Donnell outlined the French situation to Paterson and asked him to take the job. He asked Pat if he could give him a reply within 24 hours. Paterson's response was that he didn't need that long—he was ready to accept.

Things in the United Kingdom were under control and he needed a new challenge.

IDEAL STANDARD FRANCE

Having been in operation for 75 years, Ideal Standard France (ISF) was a well-established company in France. That long tradition was reflected in the company's two main lines: heating products and sanitary china products. Heating products consisted of boilers and radiators and represented almost 90 percent of ISF's sales. Boilers were a fairly standardized mature product that varied by size depending on whether they were intended for residential or commercial use. The radiator market was segmented by design and fabricating material. Although there had been a worldwide trend from cast-iron to steel, copper, or aluminum radiators, the French and Italian markets had remained steadfastly cast-iron markets. While most French consumers believed cast iron was more durable, other materials had been making inroads. Industry size and share estimates are presented in Exhibit 6.

Manufacturing

The company employed some 5,500 people, 5,000 of whom worked in one of ISF's six plants (see map, Exhibit 7). Boilers were manufactured at Aulnay (which had been modernized and expanded to European scale during 1973) and at Blanc-Mesnil. All casting was done at Aulnay, while Blanc-Mesnil was a smaller assembly plant which also housed ISF's research and development group.

Despite its expanded physical facilities, Aulnay had been unable to realize its potential as a European source for boilers in 1974. The main impediment was low plant productivity. The Aulnay plant was in a strongly Communistic area and labor relations had long been difficult. In addition, the engineers necessary to run the expanded capacity were not available in this location. As a result, the planned third shift was not operational since it could not be run economically. Furthermore, subsidiary managers in other countries protested that the French boiler design was unsuitable for their markets and seemed unwilling to send orders to Aulnay.

Cast-iron radiators were built at the Autun and Dammarie plants. Autun was felt by ISF management to be the most efficient radiator plant in Europe. A modern, highly automated plant at Argenteuil specialized in the manufacture of malleable iron nipples used on cast-iron radiators.[2]

---

[2] Although the company filled out its line with some copper and aluminum radiators, these were acquired from outside manufacturers.

EXHIBIT 6: Product and Market Share Estimates ($ million)

Business	1969	1970	1971	1972	1973
A. Plumbing (sanitary)					
Total industry sales	$126.6	$117.3	$109.3	$184.5	$230.7
ISF market share.	10.0%	7.9%	7.2%	6.4%	6.7%
Sales.	$ 12.66	$ 9.27	$ 7.87	$ 11.81	$ 15.46
Operating income	1.08	(.008)	(.583)	1.35	1.81
Return on net assets . . .	10.4%	—	—	23.5%	22.5%
B. Boilers:					
1. Residential:					
Total industry sales . . .	$110.3	$122.7	$111.6	$140.1	$181.3
ISF market share	20.8%	20.2%	18.4%	16.8%	14.8%
ISF sales	$ 22.94	$ 24.79	$ 20.53	$ 23.54	$ 26.83
2. Commercial:					
Total industry sales . . .	$ 33.19	$ 31.32	$ 53.62	$ 51.83	$ 76.57
ISF market share . . .	33.2%	34.2%	28.7%	32.3%	28.3%
ISF sales	$ 11.02	$ 10.71	$ 15.39	$ 16.74	$ 21.67
Total ISF boiler:					
Sales.	$ 33.96	$ 35.50	$ 35.92	$ 40.28	$ 48.50
Operating income	3.59	(1.79)	1.16	.66	(1.04)
Return on net assets . . .	12.1%	—	1.1%	.5%	—
C. Radiators:					
1. Cast iron:					
Total industry sales . . .	$ 53.45	$ 54.90	$ 59.95	$ 68.28	$ 99.72
ISF market share . . .	67.0%	69.0%	63.0%	60.0%	56.8%
ISF sales	$ 35.81	$ 37.88	$ 37.77	$ 40.97	$ 56.64
2. Steel:					
Total industry sales . . .	$ 48.8	$ 51.1	$ 47.6	$ 59.3	$ 76.3
ISF market share . . .	0	0	0	0	0
ISF sales	0	0	0	0	0
3. Copper and aluminum:					
Total industry sales . . .	$ 4.0	$ 5.0	$ 7.4	$ 14.0	$ 19.1
ISF market share . . .	0	0	0	2.1%	3.9%
ISF sales	0	0	0	$ .29	$ .74
Total ISF radiator:					
Sales.	$ 35.81	$ 37.88	$ 37.77	$ 41.26	$ 57.38
Operating income	4.65	3.72	3.61	4.97	6.99
Return on net assets . . .	19.2%	16.0%	19.3%	28.9%	39.0%
ISF total sales	82.44	82.66	81.59	93.36	121.35

Porcelain sanitary equipment (basins, bowls, etc.) was manufactured at the Dôle plant. Market pressure to expand the variety of shapes and colors of bathroom fittings had resulted in a proliferation of models in the 1960s and 1970s, a trend that had reduced the efficiency of the Dôle plant.[3] An industry upturn in 1972–73, however, had lifted this product line back into profitability, and subsequent strong demand had maintained the momentum.

---

[3] Brass fittings that completed the sanitary line were also acquired from outside suppliers since the closure of ISF's large brass plant in 1969.

EXHIBIT 7: ISF's Manufacturing Facilities

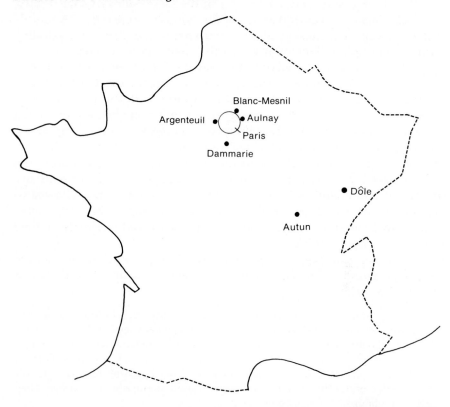

Plant	Product Line	Number of Employees*	Capacity† ($000)	Break-event ($000)	1973 Sales ($000)
Argenteuil	Radiator nipples	274			
Autun	Radiators	1,089	65,000	52,000	57,380
Dammarie	Radiators	1,171			
Aulnay	Boilers (casting)	1,545	55,000‡	48,000	48,500
Blanc-Mesnil	Boilers (assembly)	212			
Dôle	Sanitary products	640	18,000	14,000	15,460

* In addition, there were 494 employees in ISF's headquarters in Paris.
† Capacity and break-even figures are calculated at 1973 prices and cost levels, and represent an estimate only.
‡ Before completion of $6 million expansion; 1974 capacity planned to be up to 50 percent higher.

Labor Relations

In all ISF plants, and particularly in the large Aulnay boiler facility, labor relations were a critical aspect of the company's operation. A considerable amount of management time and energy was focused on dealing with the multiple unions with which the company negotiated.

The largest national labor union was the Communist-led CGT with over one million members. The other major union, the CGR–FO, had around 500,000 members and aligned itself more with the Socialist party. However, in any company location, either union might be represented by two locals—one for hourly employees, and one for weekly employees. Furthermore, many white collar workers, including engineers, salesmen, and even some managers, were members of a separate organization, the CGC. Under French law, the company was obliged to bargain with any union that had members in its organization. Each union was allowed to appoint two delegates to represent its interests, no matter how few members it had. Delegates were entitled to office space and work release time to attend to union business.

One senior manager in the company's European headquarters gave his perspectives on French unions as compared to others with which the company dealt:

> Unions in France are stronger than in most other European countries and relationships between unions and management tend to be rougher for several reasons. First, there are more laws relating to labor relations in France than in most other countries, and the unions are well protected. Perhaps more important is the fact that delegates from opposing unions often try to outdo each other, making competing claims about what concessions they have obtained for their members.
>
> Finally, French unions tend to have strong political and ideological objectives in addition to their worker representation role. Strikes are often called for purely political reasons, with the success being gauged by the size and disruption of the accompanying demonstrations.

Competition

In the French marketplace, ISF's major competitors were the French companies—DeDietrich and SGF. The former was an old family-owned firm which manufactured a wide range of products, including equipment for the chemical industry and railway equipment. Its heating business was specialized in the large boiler segment, although it did offer a full line by acquiring radiators from SGF or ISF. DeDietrich was thought to be a very efficient producer in large boilers.

SGF focused its product line more on the sanitary equipment segment, manufacturing bathroom fittings and heating equipment. SGF also owned a share of an Italian radiator manufacturer.

ISF sold its full line under its own well-known and reputable brand through building product wholesalers. In the French distribution channels, it was normal for these wholesalers to carry competitive lines. They played a passive marketing role, their major function being to break bulk, carry inventory, and finance their retail and trade customers. Most heating equipment was sold to the trade for original installation, but in the sanitary equipment business, the emergence of a replacement market could be seen, and retail outlets were beginning to play a role.

Manufacturers' credit terms to wholesalers were typically 60 to 90 days. However, when inventories began to accumulate at the plant, extended credit terms were often the major weapon used to move product out into wholesaler inventory.

Price cutting had not been an important practice, mainly due to the fact that the industry was under the jurisdiction of the National Price Control Board. Price increases were allowed only when justified by an application backed by documented evidence of increases in material costs. Labor cost increases were not regarded as justification for price increases by the board, since they assumed such cost increases were offset by increases in productivity. Even when a price increase could be justified, the processing and granting of such increase could take six to nine months. As a result of such price restrictions, companies were unwilling to cut prices, even under tight economic conditions. The basis of competition was much more on brand reputation and product design and, occasionally, on credit terms.

PAT PATERSON IN FRANCE

True to his management philosophy, Pat Paterson hit the ground running when he arrived in ISF on August 1, 1974. The following represent the major decisions and actions he took in his first four weeks.

Early Action

August being the vacation month in France, almost all of the ten-man senior management team were on vacation. Paterson sent telegrams summoning them back to a management meeting, where he outlined his early assessment of the situation and his plans to take quick and drastic action. Judging the reaction of the individual managers to his presentation, he selected a team of three to work with him (the finance manager and the heating and plumbing division managers) and terminated the others. Pat explained his actions:

> I conveyed my sense of urgency and indicated some of the drastic steps I thought needed to be taken. The three who picked themselves off

the floor first became my team. This was no time to be working through an unwieldy and timid management group. I needed a lean and determined team to help turn this thing around.

Within 24 hours of his arrival in Paris, Paterson had a delegation of union officials at his door demanding to know if he had been brought in to close down the business. Pat assured them that this was not the case and that his family and his furniture were on their way from England. He was planning to save the company and hoped to be living in France for many years. He promised to meet with the unions within the following two weeks to outline his plans for ISF.

At the subsequent meeting Paterson was confronted by 35 delegates representing three unions and six plants, plus officials from union headquarters. The meeting lasted 10 hours, during which time Paterson outlined the company's financial and market position and explained the consequences of not responding to such a serious situation. Fearing a possibility of a large-scale cutback (and a consequent collective dismissal, as large-scale layoffs were known), the unions asked for a postponement of any such action. Paterson realized that permission for a collective dismissal could take months to get through the labor courts anyhow, and so agreed to this request. Furthermore, he needed time to reflect on the economic impact of such a move. Severance payments could easily average FF 15,000 ($3,500) per employee. The meeting concluded on a vague note with the unions clearly concerned that cutbacks were on the way. Continuing consultation was agreed to.[4]

Another early priority was to try to get some relief on prices from the Price Control Board. His feeling was that even an immediate 5 percent price increase could restore ISF's economic viability, and he made his reasoned plea to the government officials. Despite his plea, the board refused to make concessions and advised the company that increases would have to be fully documented and justified, and approved by the system. In Pat's view, price controls were the government's way of having business pay for the social costs of inflation.

Undaunted by his inability to win price increases, the new country manager began work on another area of possible relief. Recognizing that each of his competitors also had some less efficient plants, Paterson felt that the present difficult economic climate might provide an opportune moment to propose a rationalization of manufacturing within the industry. He therefore petitioned the Ministries of Industry and Finance for permission to open such negotiations with competitive companies. The ministries

---

[4] The relations were not always cordial, but Paterson claimed he was trying to let the unions see the economic reality. After one meeting at Aulnay, he emerged from the small hut next to the plant where negotiations were being held to find it was surrounded by some 800 workers who began chanting, "Paterson into the smelter! Paterson into the smelter!" Pat relieved a tense moment when he called out, "Hell no! You'll spoil the iron!"

agreed to allow the discussion but stopped short of offering either assistance or endorsement.

His initial contacts with SGF and DeDietrich were disappointing. Although they were willing to talk generally about industry problems, when it came to the decision of which facilities to close, neither competitor seemed willing to take action. Their main objection was that the labor relations problems accompanying plant rationalization was something they were unwilling to take on. They also alluded to the possible impact a shutdown might have on wholesaler and contractor confidence. They did, however, encourage ISF to pursue its own plans to close inefficient operations.

Not only did Pat face external resistance to his thoughts about cutting back manufacturing, but many of his own ISF managers also seemed unwilling to endorse such proposals. In one early meeting, he suggested that the company try to sell the Argenteuil plant, which was producing malleable iron nipples for ISF's radiators, and purchase less expensive steel nipples from a supplier in Germany. Several of his managers objected, claiming that although such a product might be used in Germany, French contractors were accustomed to the iron nipple and would not buy radiators with steel nipples.

Decision Options

Despite these early frustrations, by the end of August Pat felt he was beginning to understand the problems and to identify some alternate courses of action.

One of the toughest judgments to make concerned the direction of the economy generally and the building industry in particular. Government forecasts seemed to indicate an economic turnaround was near. Among their published estimates were the following:

- anti-inflationary policies would cut the increase in the retail price index from 12 percent in 1974 to 9 percent in 1975, and 7.5 percent by 1976;

- housing completions would continue to decline by 2 percent a year in 1975 and 1976, but would increase 7 percent in 1977;

- nonresidential construction would increase 4 percent in 1975 (compared to 6.5 percent growth in 1974), but would build to a 7.5 percent annual growth rate by 1977.

Paterson felt the government forecasts were politically motivated and therefore likely to be optimistic.

In discussions with competitors, Pat was told by SGF and DeDietrich managers that business was off slightly but that they were optimistic that the situation would turn around. Neither company would concede that it was experiencing any real difficulty. Since his personal assessment was that the recession would be longer and deeper than either the government or his competitors were indicating, Pat was cautious about the information he was getting.

Within the Ideal Standard France organization there was also a diverse range of views. Some felt that ISF's current problems were rooted in the company's outmoded product line and inefficient plants. In the view of this group, ISF should use the current crisis as the lever to make some major changes in repositioning and rebuilding ISF for the next upturn in the construction cycle. They argued that Pat should use his credibility and position to get funds from American Standard to change the product line and rationalize and modernize the manufacturing facilities.

Another group argued that while M. Frehis, the previous manager, had not always been right, his policy of tightening the ship to weather the storm was appropriate in the current environment. They urged Pat to trim, squeeze, and tighten controls, but to keep his powder dry for the upturn in the economy. Further studies of the sources of inefficiencies could be initiated so that stronger action could be taken in the event an upturn did not occur in the next 6 to 12 months.

Despite this advice, Pat Paterson's gut was telling him that stronger action was needed. A report from his personnel manager indicated that at current prices, sales projections, and inventory levels, ISF would have to dismiss around 1,500 workers to become profitable. From his U.K. experiences, Pat recognized that such a major cut would be bitter medicine, but might well be what was needed to make the patient well. However, he was well aware that this was not the United Kingdom, and that the consequences of such action might be quite different.

One thing Pat was sure of. American Standard's CEO, Bill Marquard, was booked into the Ritz in Paris the next week and would be expecting a good analysis of the situation and its causes, a strong recommendation of what to do, the results that could be expected, and an action plan that Pat and his managers planned to implement.

CASE 19

Peter Olson

Peter Olson was 37 years old, and an assistant to the head of the Plastics Division of United Chemical Corporation. Peter had been with UCC for 14 years. UCC was a large chemical company with annual sales of approximately $1.25 billion; the Plastics Division, with sales of over $200 million, was one of UCC's fastest growing divisions.

Peter Olson graduated from Case University in 1956 and went to work for UCC immediately upon graduation as a research and engineering assistant. He held various positions in the fields of production and engineering, did well in all of them, and management let Pete know on many occasions that he was regarded as potential top-management material. In 1967 Pete was asked to move into the Plastics Division in charge of production planning. In 1968 he moved to the division's headquarters office, which was located in a small city about 30 miles from New York City, as head of long-range planning for the division. Early in 1970 he became assistant to the president of the Plastics Division. His salary was $27,000.

Peter Olson and his wife Toni had been married in 1959. Toni was a graduate of Wellesley and had lived on the East Coast all her life. Pete's career with UCC required the Olsons to make a number of moves, and although Toni made them without complaint, Pete knew that she had not been happy at the need for so many changes and did not enjoy their assignments in the South and Midwest. So far as the Olsons could tell, their two children made the adjustments to new surroundings very easily. Peter Jr., was 9, and Karen was 7.

When Pete took his job at divisional headquarters in 1968, both

Copyright © 1970 by the President and Fellows of Harvard College. Harvard Business School case 9–371–143. Reproduced by permission.

he and Toni were delighted to find an old salt-box colonial in the country three miles from the outskirts of Littleton. Littleton itself was a city of about 50,000 people and was a "bedroom" community for New York City. Both Toni and Pete found it easy to make friends in Littleton, and Toni was particularly happy to find so many women her age with interests similar to hers. Littleton's school system was excellent, and young Pete and Karen seemed completely happy in the Littleton environment.

Peter found that his new job as assistant to the president of the Plastics Division placed heavy demands on his time. Frequent trips to divisional plants were required, as were visits to large customers and branch sales offices. Pete believed that he was away from home on an average of 1½ weeks each month. During the remainder of his time, Peter Olson found that the demands of his office work were also heavy. His boss was a driver who expected a lot from his subordinates, and Pete spent many evenings at the division office and many others working at home. The work itself, however, was exciting, and Pete knew that he was doing a good job; he had been told that a nice raise would be forthcoming if his contribution continued high.

The Olsons had always been a close knit family, and Pete had realized for months that his absence from home and his long working hours created some strains on his relationship with Toni. Occasional minor frictions developed, and Toni said on several occasions that she was not sure whether "it's worth the rat race," but Peter's enthusiasm for his work, his evident love for his family, and Toni's own sense of balance succeeded in avoiding any serious problems. On two or three occasions Pete and Toni discussed how they might guide their activities to do more than simply offset the demands of Pete's job—they sought positive ways to build their own lives together. But the demands of Pete's job proved to be a more powerful force than the outcomes of these discussions.

In the late spring of 1970, UCC made some major organizational changes which were designed to create more authority at lower levels. Use of the profit-center concept was pushed further down in the organization. The Plastics Division itself was affected by the changes. Both UCC headquarters and the president of the division agreed that it should be split into four profit centers, though the structure and details of the changes had not yet been worked out.

On a pleasant spring evening in May, Peter Olson got home at about 9:45 to tell Toni that he had just been offered a position as head of one of the new profit centers. Annual sales would be in the neighborhood of $70 million, and the demand for the center's new lines of products was growing rapidly. Pete talked delightedly about the "million and a half" problems of sales, production, engineering, and organization that would be his responsibility, and the opportunity for advancement that the job represented. He was so excited that he talked without stopping for 40 minutes.

It dawned on Peter Olson that his wife had said nothing. Trying to find some way to wind down his oration, he said lamely, "Of course, we'll have to move out to St. Louis. I've got to go out week after next, but you and the kids don't have to come until school finishes here."

Toni stared fixedly at her husband. Finally she said "Peter, dinner is cold. I'll have to warm it up." She rose and turned to go to the kitchen. As she got to the kitchen door, she turned and said, "Peter, who the hell wants to live in St. Louis?"

CASE 20

The Lincoln Electric Company

> We're not a marketing company, we're not an R&D company, and
> we're not a service company. We're a manufacturing company, and I believe
> that we are the best manufacturing company in the world.

With these words, George E. Willis, president of The Lincoln Electric
Company, described what he saw as his company's distinctive competence. For more than 30 years, Lincoln had been the world's largest manufacturer of arc welding products (Exhibit 1). In 1974, the company was
believed to have manufactured more than 40 percent of the arc welding
equipment and supplies sold in the United States. In addition to its welding
products, Lincoln produced a line of three-phase alternating-current industrial electric motors, but these accounted for less than 10 percent of
sales and profits.

Lincoln's 1974 domestic net income was $17.5 million on sales of
$237 million (Exhibit 2). Perhaps more significant than a single year's
results was Lincoln's record of steady growth over the preceding four
decades, as shown in Exhibit 3.

During this period, after-tax return on equity had ranged between
10 percent and 15 percent. Lincoln's growth had been achieved without
benefit of acquisition and had been financed with internally generated
funds. The company's historical dividend payout policy had been to pay
to the suppliers of capital a fair return each year for its use.

EXHIBIT 1: Arc Welding

   Arc welding is a group of joining processes that utilize an electric current produced by a transformer or motor generator (electric or engine powered) to fuse various metals. The temperature at the arc is approximately 10,000 Fahrenheit.
   The welding circuit consists of a welding machine, ground clamp, and electrode holder. The electrode carries electricity to the metal being welded and the heat from the arc causes the base metals to join together. The electrode may or may not act as a filler metal during the process; however, nearly 60 percent of all arc welding that is done in the United States utilizes a covered electrode that acts as a very high quality filler metal.
   The Lincoln Electric Company manufactures a wide variety of covered electrodes, submerged arc welding wires and fluxes, and a unique self-shielded, flux-cored electrode called Innershield. The company also manufactures welding machines, wire feeders, and other supplies that are needed for arc welding.

Lincoln Arc Welding Machines

COMPANY HISTORY

Lincoln Electric was founded by John C. Lincoln in 1895 to manufacture electric motors and generators. James F. Lincoln, John's younger brother, joined the company in 1907. The brothers' skills and interests were complementary. John was a technical genius. During his lifetime he was awarded more than 50 patents for inventions as diverse as an

EXHIBIT 2: Lincoln's Status in 1974

Statement of Financial Condition
(foreign subsidiaries not included)

	December 31, 1974
Assets	
Current assets:	
Cash and certificates of deposit	$ 5,691,120
Government securities	6,073,919
Notes and accounts receivable	29,451,161
Inventories (LIFO basis)	29,995,694
Deferred taxes and prepaid expenses	2,266,409
Total	73,478,303
Other assets:	
Trustee—notes and interest receivable	1,906,871
Miscellaneous	384,572
Total	2,291,443
Intercompany:	
Investment in foreign subsidiaries	4,695,610
Notes receivable	0
Total	4,695,610
Property, plant, and equipment:	
Land	825,376
Buildings*	9,555,562
Machinery, tools, and equipment*	11,273,155
Total	21,654,093
Total assets	$102,119,449

Liabilities and Shareholders' Equity

Current liabilities:	
Accounts payable	$ 13,658,063
Accrued wages	1,554,225
Taxes, including income taxes	13,262,178
Dividends payable	3,373,524
Total	31,847,990
Shareholders' equity:	
Common capital stock, stated value	281,127
Additional paid-in capital	3,374,570
Retained earnings	66,615,762
Total	70,271,459
Total liabilities and shareholders' equity	$102,119,449

EXHIBIT 2 *(concluded)*

Income and Retained Earnings

	Year Ended December 31, 1974
Income:	
Net sales	$232,771,475
Interest	1,048,561
Overhead and development charges	
to subsidiaries	1,452,877
Dividend income	843,533
Other income	515,034
Total	236,631,480
Costs and expenses:	
Cost of products sold	154,752,735
Selling, administrative, and general	
expenses and freight out	20,791,301
Year-end incentive bonus	24,707,297
Pension expense	2,186,932
Total	202,438,265
Income before income taxes	34,193,215
Provision for income taxes:	
Federal	14,800,000
State and local	1,866,000
	16,666,000
Net income	$ 17,527,215

* After depreciation.

apparatus for curing meat, an electric drill, a mine-door-activating mechanism, and an electric arc lamp. James's skills were in management and administration. He began as a salesman but soon took over as general manager. The Lincoln Electric Company was undeniably built in his image.

In 1911, the company introduced its first arc welding machine. Both brothers were fascinated by welding, which was then in its infancy. They recognized it as an alternative use for the motor-generator sets they were already producing to recharge the batteries for electric automobiles. The success of Ford, Buick, and others indicated that the days of the electric auto might be numbered, and the brothers were anxious to find other markets for their skills and products.

John's mechanical talents gave the company a head start in welding machines which it never relinquished. He developed a portable welding machine (a significant improvement over existing stationary models) and incorporated a transformer to allow regulation of the current. As his biographer noted, "This functional industrial development gave Lincoln Electric a lead in the field that it has always maintained, although the two

EXHIBIT 3

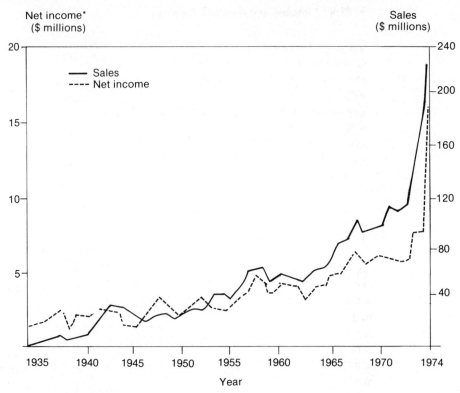

Net income*
($ millions)

Sales
($ millions)

—— Sales
---- Net income

* Excludes foreign operations.

giants—Westinghouse and General Electric—soon entered the market."[1]

By World War II, Lincoln Electric was the leading American manufacturer of arc welding equipment. Because of the importance of welding
to the war effort, the company stopped producing electric motors and
devoted its full capacity to welding products. Demand continued to outpace production, and the government asked the welding equipment manufacturers to add capacity. As described by Lincoln's president, George
Willis:

> Mr. Lincoln responded to the government's call by going to Washing-
> ton and telling them that there was enough manufacturing capacity but it
> was being used inefficiently by everyone. He offered to share proprietary
> manufacturing methods and equipment designs with the rest of the industry.

[1] Raymond Moley, *The American Century of John C. Lincoln* (New York: Duell, Sloan &
Pearce, 1962), p. 71.

Washington took him up on it and that solved the problem. As a result of Mr. Lincoln's patriotic decision, our competitors had costs which were close to ours for a short period after the war, but we soon were outperforming them like before.

In 1955, Lincoln once again began manufacturing electric motors, and since then its position in the market had expanded steadily.

Through the years, Lincoln stock had been sold to employees and associates of the Lincoln brothers. In 1975, approximately 48 percent of employees were shareholders. About 80 percent of the outstanding stock was held by employees, the Lincoln family, and their foundations.

In its 80-year history, Lincoln had had only three board chairmen: John C. Lincoln, James F. Lincoln, and William Irrgang, who became chairman in 1972.

STRATEGY

Lincoln Electric's strategy was simple and unwavering. The company's strength was in manufacturing. Management believed that Lincoln could build quality products at a lower cost than their competitors. Their strategy was to concentrate on reducing costs and passing the savings through to the customer by continuously lowering prices. Management had adhered to this policy even when products were on allocation because of shortages in productive capacity. The result had been an expansion of both market share and primary demand for arc welding equipment and supplies over the past half-century. Lincoln's strategy had also encouraged the exit of several major companies (including General Electric) from the industry and had caused others to seek more specialized market niches.

Management believed its incentive system and the climate it fostered were responsible in large part for the continual increase in productivity upon which this strategy depended. Under the Lincoln incentive system, employees were handsomely rewarded for their productivity, high quality, cost reduction ideas, and individual contributions to the company. Year-end bonuses averaged close to 100 percent of regular compensation, and some workers on the factory floor had earned more than $45,000 in a single year.[2]

Lincoln's strategy had remained virtually unchanged for decades. In a 1947 Harvard Business School case study on the company, James F. Lincoln described the firm's strategy as follows:

---

[2] By contrast, the median income for U.S. manufacturing employees in 1974 was less than $9,200, according to Bureau of Labor Statistics data.

It is the job of The Lincoln Electric Company to give its customers more and more of a better product at a lower and lower price. This will also make it possible for the company to give to the worker and the stockholder a higher and higher return.

In 1975, Chairman William Irrgang's description was remarkably similar:

The success of The Lincoln Electric Company has been built on two basic ideas. One is producing more and more of a progressively better product at a lower and lower price for a larger and larger group of customers. The other is that an employee's earnings and promotion are in direct proportion to his individual contribution toward the company's success.[3]

Management felt it had achieved an enviable record in following this strategy faithfully and saw no need to modify it in the future. Lincoln Electric's record of increasing productivity and declining costs and prices is shown in Exhibit 4.

COMPANY PHILOSOPHY

Lincoln Electric's corporate strategy was rooted in the management philosophy of James F. Lincoln, a rugged individualist who believed that through competition and adequate incentives every person could develop to his or her fullest potential. In one of his numerous books and articles he wrote:

Competition is the foundation of man's development. It has made the human race what it is. It is the spur that makes progress. Every nation that has eliminated it as the controlling force in its economy has disappeared, or will. We will do the same if we eliminate it by trying to give security, and for the same reason. Competition means that there will be losers as well as winners in the game. Competition will mean the disappearance of the lazy and incompetent, be they workers, industrialists, or distributors. Competition promotes progress. Competition determines who will be the leader. It is the only known way that leadership and progress can be developed if history means anything. It is a hard taskmaster. It is completely necessary for anyone, be he worker, user, distributor or boss, if he is to grow.

If some way could be found so that competition could be eliminated from life, the result would be disastrous. Any nation and any people disappear if life becomes too easy. There is no danger from a hard life as all history shows. Danger is from a life that is made soft by lack of competition.[4]

Lincoln's faith in the individual was almost unbounded. His personal

---

[3] *Employee's Handbook* (Cleveland: The Lincoln Electric Company, 1974).

[4] James F. Lincoln, *Incentive Management* (Cleveland: The Lincoln Electric Company, 1951), p. 33.

EXHIBIT 4: Lincoln Electric's Record of Pricing and Productivity

A. Lincoln Prices* Relative to Commodity Prices,† 1934–1971

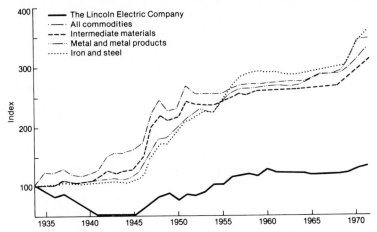

* Index of annual selling prices of ³⁄₁₆-inch diameter electrode in No. 5 and No. 5P in 3,000 pound quantities.
† Indexes of wholesale prices.

B. Lincoln Prices* Relative to Wholesale Machinery and Equipment Prices, 1939–1971

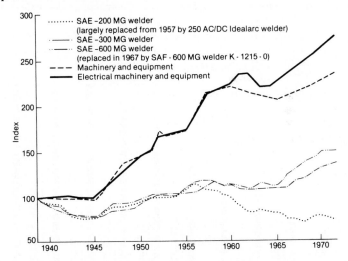

* Average annual prices of specific Lincoln welders.

EXHIBIT 4 *(concluded)*

C. Productivity of Lincoln Production Workers Relative to Workers in Manufacturing and Durable Goods Industries, 1934–1971

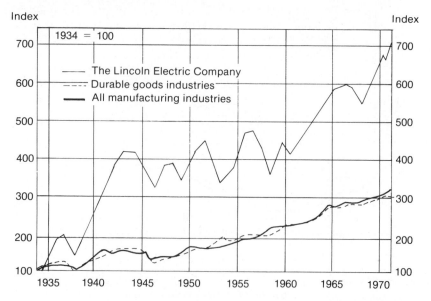

D. Lincoln Productivity Relative to Three Other Companies: Sales Value* of Products per Employee, 1934–1971

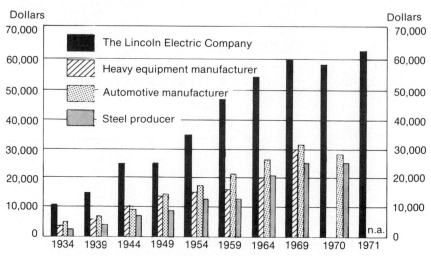

* At current prices.

Source: Company records. Adapted from "How Lincoln Motivated Men," *Civil Engineering*, January 1973.

experience with the success of Lincoln Electric reinforced his faith in what could be accomplished under the proper conditions. In 1951 he wrote:

> Development in many directions is latent in every person. The difficulty has been that few recognize that fact. Fewer still will put themselves under the pressure or by chance are put under the pressure that will develop them greatly. Their latent abilities remain latent, hence useless. . . .
>
> It is of course obvious that the development of man, on which the success of incentive management depends, is a progressive process. Any results, no matter how good, that come from the application of incentive management cannot be considered final. There will always be greater growth of man under continued proper incentive. . . .
>
> Such increase of efficiency poses a very real problem to management. The profit that will result from such efficiency obviously will be enormous. The output per dollar of investment will be many times that of the usual shop which practices output limitation. The labor cost per piece will be relatively small and the overhead will be still less.
>
> The profits at competitive selling prices resulting from such efficiency will be far beyond any possible need for proper return and growth of an industry. . . .
>
> How, then, should the enormous extra profit resulting from incentive management be split? The problems that are inherent in incentive dictate the answer. If the worker does not get a proper share, he does not desire to develop himself or his skill. Incentive, therefore, would not succeed. The worker must have a reward that he feels is commensurate with his contribution.
>
> If the customer does not have a part of the saving in lower prices, he will not buy the increased output. The size of the market is a decisive factor in costs of products. Therefore, the consumer must get a proper share of the saving.
>
> Management and ownership are usually considered as a unit. This is far from a fact, but in the problem here, they can be considered together. They must get a part of the saving in larger salaries and perhaps larger dividends.
>
> There is no hard and fast rule to cover this division, other than the following. The worker (which includes management), the customer, the owner, and all those involved must be satisfied that they are properly recognized or they will not cooperate, and cooperation is essential to any and all successful applications of incentives.[5]

Additional comments by James F. Lincoln are presented in Exhibit 5.

---

[5] "Incentive Management in Action." Reprinted from *Assembly Engineering,* March 1967. By permission of the publisher, © 1967 Hitchcock Publishing Co. All rights reserved.

EXHIBIT 5: James F. Lincoln's Observations on Management

- Some think paying a man more money will produce cooperation. Not true. Many incentives are far more effective than money. Robert MacNamara gave up millions to become Secretary of Defense. Status is a much greater incentive.
- If those crying loudest about the inefficiencies of labor were put in the position of the wage earner, they would react as he does. The worker is not a man apart. He has the same needs, aspirations, and reactions as the industrialist. A worker will not cooperate on any program that will penalize him. Does any manager?
- The industrial manager is very conscious of his company's need of uninterrupted income. He is completely oblivious, though, to the worker's same need. Management fails—i.e., profits fall off—and gets no punishment. The wage earner does not fail but is fired. Such injustice!
- Higher efficiency means fewer manhours to do a job. If the worker loses his job more quickly, he will oppose higher efficiency.
- There never will be enthusiasm for greater efficiency if the resulting profits are not properly distributed. If we continue to give it to the average stockholder, the worker will not cooperate.
- Most companies are run by hired managers, under the control of stockholders. As a result, the goal of the company has shifted from service to the customer to making larger dividends for stockholders.
- The public will not yet believe that our standard of living could be doubled immediately if labor and management would cooperate.
- The manager is dealing with expert workers far more skillful. While you can boss these experts around in the usual lofty way, their eager cooperation will not be won.
- A wage earner is no more interested than a manager in making money for other people. The worker's job doesn't depend on pleasing stockholders, so he has no interest in dividends. Neither is he interested in increasing efficiency if he may lose his job because management has failed to get more orders.
- If a manager received the same treatment in matters of income, security, advancement, and dignity as the hourly worker, he would soon understand the real problem of management.
- The first question management should ask is: What is the company trying to do? In the minds of the average worker the answer is: "The company is trying to make the largest possible profits by any method. Profits go to absentee stockholders and top management."
- There is all the difference imaginable between the grudging, distrustful, half-forced cooperation and the eager, whole-hearted, vigorous, happy cooperation of men working together for a common purpose.
- Continuous employment of workers is essential to industrial efficiency. This is a management responsibility. Laying off workers during slack times is death to efficiency. The worker thrown out is a trained man. To replace him when business picks up will cost much more than the savings of wages during the layoff. Solution? The worker must have a guarantee that if he works properly his income will be continuous.

EXHIBIT 5 *(concluded)*

- Continuous employment is the first step to efficiency. But how? First, during slack periods, manufacture to build up inventory; costs will usually be less because of lower material costs. Second, develop new machines and methods of manufacturing; plans should be waiting on the shelf. Third, reduce prices by getting lower costs. When slack times come, workers are eager to help cut costs. Fourth, explore markets passed over when times are good. Fifth, hours of work can be reduced if the worker is agreeable. Sixth, develop new products. In sum, management should plan for slumps. They are useful.
- The incentives that are most potent when properly offered are:

  Money in proportion to production.
  Status as a reward for achievement.
  Publicity of the worker's contributions and skill.

- The calling of the minister, the doctor, the lawyer, as well as the manager, contains incentive to excel. Excellence brings rewards, self-esteem, respect. Only the hourly worker has no reason to excel.
- Resistance to efficiency is not normal. It is present only when we are hired workers.
- Do unto others as you would have them do unto you. This is not just a Sunday school ideal, but a proper labor-management policy.
- An incentive plan should reward a man not only for the number of pieces turned out, but also for the accuracy of his work, his cooperation in improving methods of production, his attendance.
- The progress in industry so far stems from the developed potentialities of managers. Wage earners, who because of their greater numbers have far greater potential, are overlooked. Here is where the manager must look for his greatest progress.
- There should be an overall bonus based on the contribution each person makes to efficiency. If each person is properly rated and paid, there will not only be a fair reward to each worker but friendly and exciting competition.
- The present policy of operating industry for stockholders is unreasonable. The rewards now given to him are far too much. He gets income that should really go to the worker and the management. The usual absentee stockholder contributes nothing to efficiency. He buys a stock today and sells it tomorrow. He often doesn't even know what the company makes. Why should he be rewarded by large dividends?
- There are many forms and degrees of cooperation between the worker and the management. The worker's attitude can vary all the way from passivity to highly imaginative contributions to efficiency and progress.

Source: *Civil Engineering,* January 1973.

COMPENSATION POLICIES

Compensation policies were the key element of James F. Lincoln's philosophy of "incentive management." Lincoln Electric's compensation system had three components:

- wages based solely on piecework output for most factory jobs,
- a year-end bonus which could equal or exceed an individual's full annual regular pay, and
- guaranteed employment for all workers

Almost all production workers at Lincoln were paid on a straight piecework plan. They had no base salary or hourly wage but were paid a set "price" for each item they produced. William Irrgang explained:

> Wherever practical, we use the piecework system. This system can be effective, and it can be destructive. The important part of the system is that it is completely fair to the worker. When we set a piecework price, that price cannot be changed just because, in management's opinion, the worker is making too much money. Whether he earns two times or three times his normal amount makes no difference. Piecework prices can only be changed when management has made a change in the method of doing that particular job and under no other conditions. If this is not carried out 100 percent, piecework cannot work.
>
> Today piecework is confined to production operations, although at one time we also used it for work done in our stenographic pool. Each typewriter was equipped with a counter that registered the number of times the typewriter keys were operated. This seemed to work all right for a time until it was noticed that one girl was earning much more than any of the others. This was looked into, and it was found that this young lady ate her lunch at her desk, using one hand for eating purposes and the other for punching the most convenient key on the typewriter as fast as she could; which simply goes to show that no matter how good a program you may have, it still needs careful supervision.[6]

A Time Study Department established piecework prices which were guaranteed by the company, until methods were changed or a new process introduced. Employees could challenge the price if they felt it was unfair. The Time Study Department would then retime the job and set a new rate. This could be higher or lower but was still open to challenge if an employee remained dissatisfied. Employees were expected to guarantee their own quality. They were not paid for defective work until it had been repaired on their own time.

Each job in the company was rated according to skill, required effort, responsibility, and so on, and a base wage rate for the job was assigned.

---

[6] William Irrgang, "The Lincoln Incentive Management Program," Lincoln Lecture Series, Arizona State University, 1972, p. 13.

Wage rates were comparable to those for similar jobs in the Cleveland area and were adjusted annually on the basis of Department of Labor statistics and quarterly to reflect changes in the cost of living. In this way, salaries or hourly wages were determined. For piecework jobs, the Time Study Department set piece prices so that an employee producing at a standard rate would earn the base rate for his or her job.

The second element of the compensation system was a year-end bonus, which had been paid each year since 1934. As explained in the *Employee's Handbook*, "The bonus, paid at the discretion of the company, is not a gift, but rather it is the sharing of the results of efficient operation on the basis of the contribution of each person to the success of the company for that year." In 1974, the bonus pool totaled $26 million, an average of approximately $10,700 per employee, or 90 percent of pre-bonus wages.

The total amount to be paid out in bonuses each year was determined by the board of directors. Lincoln's concentration on cost reduction kept costs low enough that prices could generally be set (and not upset by competition) on the basis of costs at the beginning of the year to produce a target return for stockholders and to give employees a bonus of approximately 100 percent of wages. The variance from the planned profits was usually added to (or subtracted from) the bonus pool to be distributed at year-end. Since 1945, the average bonus had varied from 78 percent to 129 percent of wages. In the past few years, it had been between 40 percent and 55 percent of pretax, prebonus profit, or as high as twice the net income after taxes.

An individual's share of the bonus pool was determined by a semiannual "merit rating" which measured individual performance compared to that of other members of the department or work group. Ratings for all employees had to average out to 100 on this relative scale. If, because of some unusual contribution, an individual deserved a rating above 110, he or she could be rewarded from a special corporate pool of bonus points, without any penalty to co-workers. Ratings above 110 were thus reviewed by a corporate committee or vice presidents who evaluated the individual's contribution. Merit ratings varied widely, from as low as 45 to as high as 160.

In determining an employee's merit rating, four factors were evaluated separately:

- Dependability
- Quality
- Output
- Ideas and cooperation

Foremen were responsible for the rating of all factory workers. They could request help from assistant foremen (dependability), the Production

Control Department (output), the Inspection Department (quality), and the Methods Department (ideas and cooperation). In the office, supervisors rated their people on the same items. At least one executive reviewed all ratings. All employees were urged to discuss their ratings with their department heads if they were dissatisfied or unclear about them.

Lincoln complemented its rating and pay system with a Guaranteed Continuous Employment Plan. This plan provided security against layoffs and assured continuity of employment. Every full-time employee who had been with the company at least two years was guaranteed employment for at least 75 percent of the standard 40-hour week. In fact, the company had not had any layoffs since 1951 when initial trials for the plan were put into effect. It was formally established in 1958.

The guarantee of employment was seen by the company as an essential element in the incentive plan. Without such a guarantee, it was believed that employees would be more likely to resist improved production and efficiency for fear of losing their jobs. In accepting the guaranteed continuous employment plan, employees agreed to perform any job that was assigned as conditions required, and to work overtime during periods of high activity.

The philosophy and procedures regarding the incentive plan were the same for management and workers, except that William Irrgang and George Willis did not share in the bonus.

EMPLOYEE VIEWS

To the researchers, it appeared that employees generally liked working at Lincoln. The employee turnover rate was far below that of most other companies, and once a new employee made it through the first month or so, he rarely left for another firm (see Exhibit 6). One employee explained, "It's like trying out for a high school football team. If you make it through the first few practices, you're usually going to stay the whole season, especially after the games start."

One long-time employee who liked working at Lincoln was John "Tiny" Carrillo, an armature bander on the welding machine line, who had been with the company for 24 years. Tiny explained why:

> The thing I like here is that you're pretty much your own boss as long as you do your job. You're responsible for your own work and you even put your stencil on every machine you work on. That way if it breaks down in the field and they have to take it back, they know who's responsible.
>
> Before I came here, I worked at Cadillac as a welder. After two months there I had the top hourly rate. I wasn't allowed to tell anyone because there were guys who still had the starting rate after a year. But, I couldn't go any higher after two months.
>
> I've done well. My rating is usually around 110, but I work hard,

EXHIBIT 6: Stability of Employment

A. Lincoln and Industry Labor Turnover Rates, 1958–1970

Percent

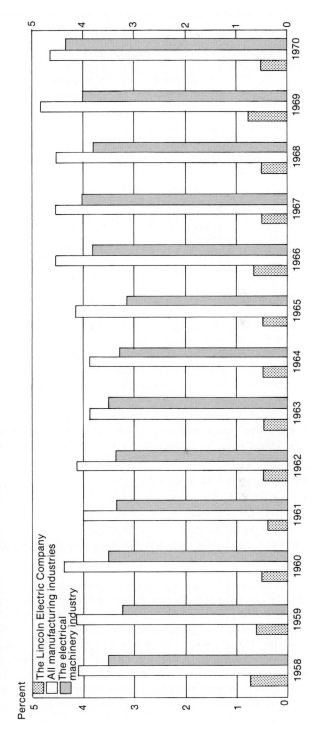

EXHIBIT 6 *(concluded)*

B. Employee Distribution by Years of Service, 1975

Employee Years of Service	Number of Employees
Less than 1	153
1	311
2	201
3	93
4	34
5	90
6–10	545
11–20	439
21–30	274
31–40	197
41–50	27
51 or more	1
Total	2,365

right through the smoke breaks. The only time I stop is a half-hour for lunch. I make good money. I have two houses, one which I rent out, and four cars. They're all paid for. When I get my bills, I pay them the next day. That's the main thing, I don't owe anyone.

Sure, there are problems. There's sometimes a bind between the guys with low grades and the guys with high ones, like in school. And there are guys who sway everything their way so they'll get the points, but they [management] have good tabs on what's going on. . . .

A lot of new guys come in and leave right away. Most of them are just mamma's boys and don't want to do the work. We had a new guy who was a produce manager at a supermarket. He worked a couple of weeks, then quit and went back to his old job.

At the end of the interview, the researcher thanked Tiny for his time. He responded by pointing out that it had cost him $7.00 in lost time, but that he was glad to be of assistance.

Another piece worker, Jorge Espinoza, a fine-wire operator in the Electrode Division, had been with the company for six years. He explained his feelings:

I believe in being my own man. I want to use my drive for my own gain. It's worked. I built my family a house and have an acre of land, with a low mortgage. I have a car and an old truck I play around with. The money I get is because I earn it. I don't want anything given to me.

The thing I don't like is having to depend on other people on the line and suppliers. We're getting bad steel occasionally. Our output is down as a result and my rating will suffer.

There are men who have great drive here and can push for a job. They are not leaders and never will be, but they move up. That's a problem. . . .

The first few times around, the ratings were painful for me. But now I stick near 100. You really make what you want. We just had a methods change and our base rate went from 83 to 89 coils a day. This job is tougher now and more complex. But, it's all what you want. If you want 110 coils you can get it. You just take less breaks. Today, I gambled and won. I didn't change my dies and made over a hundred coils. If I had lost, and the die plugged up, it would have cost me at least half an hour. But, today I made it.

MANAGEMENT STYLE

Lincoln's incentive scheme was reinforced by top management's attitude toward the men on the factory floor. In 1951, James Lincoln wrote:

> It becomes perfectly true to anyone who will think this thing through that there is no such thing in an industrial activity as Management and Men having different functions or being two different kinds of people. Why can't we think and why don't we think that all people are Management? Can you imagine any president of any factory or machine shop who can go down and manage a turret lathe as well as the machinist can? Can you imagine any manager of any organization who can go down and manage a broom—let us get down to that—who can manage a broom as well as a sweeper can? Can you imagine any secretary of any company who can go down and fire a furnace and manage that boiler as well as the man who does the job? Obviously, all are Management.[7]

Lincoln's president, George Willis, stressed the equality in the company:

> We try to avoid barriers between management and workers. We're treated equally as much as possible. When I got to work this morning at 7:30, the parking lot was three-quarters full. I parked way out there like anyone else would. I don't have a special reserved spot. The same principle holds true in our cafeteria. There's no executive dining room. We eat with everyone else.[8]

Willis felt that open and frank communication between management and workers had been a critical factor in Lincoln's success, and he believed that the company's Advisory Board, consisting of elected employee representatives, had played a very important role in achieving this. Established by James F. Lincoln in 1914, the board met twice a month, providing a forum in which employees could bring issues of concern to top manage-

---

[7] James F. Lincoln, *What Makes Workers Work?* (Cleveland: The Lincoln Electric Company, 1951), pp. 3–4.

[8] The cafeteria had large rectangular and round tables. In general, factory workers gravitated toward the rectangular tables. There were no strict rules, however, and management personnel often sat with factory workers. Toward the center was a square table that seated only four. This was reserved for William Irrgang, George Willis, and their guests when they were having a working lunch.

ment's attention, question company policies, and make suggestions for their improvement. As described in the *Employee's Handbook:*

> Board service is a privilege and responsibility of importance to the entire organization. In discussions or in reaching decisions Board members must be guided by the best interests of the Company. These also serve the best interests of its workers. They should seek at all times to improve the cooperative attitude of all workers and see that all realize they have an important part in our final results.

All Advisory Board meetings were chaired by either the chairman or the president of Lincoln. Usually both were present. Issues brought up at board meetings were either resolved on the spot or assigned to an executive. After each meeting, William Irrgang or George Willis would send a memo to the executive responsible for each unanswered question, no matter how trivial, and he was expected to respond by the next meeting if possible.

Minutes of all board meetings were posted on bulletin boards in each department and members explained the board's actions to the other workers in their department. The questions raised in the minutes of a given meeting were usually answered in the next set of minutes. This procedure had not changed significantly since the first meeting in 1914, and the types of issues raised had remained much the same (see Exhibit 7).

Workers felt that the Advisory Board provided a way of getting immediate attention for their problems. It was clear, however, that management still made the final decisions.[9] A former member of the Advisory Board commented:

> There are certain areas which are brought up in the meetings which Mr. Irrgang doesn't want to get into. He's adept at steering the conversation away from these. It's definitely not a negotiating meeting. But, generally, you really get action or an answer on why action isn't being taken.

In addition to the Advisory Board, there was a 12-member board of middle managers which met with Irrgang and Willis once a month. The topics discussed here were broader than those of the Advisory Board. The primary function of these meetings was to allow top management to get better acquainted with these individuals and to encourage cooperation between departments.

Lincoln's two top executives, Irrgang and Willis, continued the practice of James F. Lincoln in maintaining an open door to all employees.

---

[9] In some cases, management allowed issues to be decided by a vote of employees. Recently, for example, employees had voted down a proposal that the company give them dental benefits, recognizing that the cost of the program would come directly out of their bonuses.

EXHIBIT 7: Management Advisory Board Minutes

September 26, 1944

Absent: William Dillmuth

A discussion on piecework was again taken up. There was enough detail so it was thought best to appoint a committee to study it and bring a report into the meeting when that study is complete. That committee is composed of Messrs. Gilletly, Semko, Kneen and Steingass. Messrs. Erickson and White will be called in consultation, and the group will meet next Wednesday, October 4th.

The request was made that the members be permitted to bring guests to the meetings. The request was granted. Let's make sure we don't get too many at one time.

The point was made that materials are not being brought to the operation properly and promptly. There is no doubt of this difficulty. The matter was referred to Mr. Kneen for action. It is to be noted that conditions of deliveries from our suppliers have introduced a tremendous problem which has helped to increase this difficulty.

The request was made that over-time penalty be paid with the straight time. This will be done. There are some administrative difficulties which we will discuss at the next meeting but the over-time payment will start with the first pay in October.

Beginning October 1st employees' badges will be discontinued. Please turn them in to the watchmen.

It was requested that piecework prices be put on repair work in Dept. J. This matter was referred to Mr. Kneen for action.

A request was made that a plaque showing the names of those who died in action, separate from the present plaques, be put in the lobby. This was referred to Mr. Davis for action.

The question was asked as to what method for upgrading men is used. The ability of the individual is the sole reason for his progress. It was felt this is proper.

J. F. Lincoln
President

September 23, 1974 (excerpts)

Members absent: Tom Borkowski, Albert Sinn

Mr. Kupetz had asked about the Christmas and Thanksgiving schedules. These are being reviewed and we will have them available at the next meeting.

Mr. Howell had reported that the time clocks and the bells do not coincide. This is still being checked.

Mr. Sharpe had asked what the possibility would be to have a time clock installed in or near the Clean Room. This is being checked.

Mr. Joosten had raised the question of the pliability of the wrapping material used in the Chemical Department for wrapping slugs. The material we use at the present time is the best we can obtain at this time. . . .

Mr. Kostelac asked the question again whether the vacation arrangements could be changed, reducing the fifteen year period to some shorter period. It was pointed

EXHIBIT 7 *(concluded)*

out that at the present time, where we have radically changing conditions every day, it is not the time to go into this. We will review this matter at some later date. . . .

Mr. Martucci brought out the fact that there was considerable objection by the people involved to having to work on Saturday night to make up for holiday shutdowns. This was referred to Mr. Willis to be taken into consideration in schedule planning. . . .

Mr. Joosten reported that in the Chemical Department on the Saturday midnight shift they have a setup where individuals do not have sufficient work so that it is an uneconomical situation. This has been referred to Mr. Willis to be reviewed.

Mr. Joosten asked whether there would be some way to get chest x-rays for people who work in dusty areas. Mr. Loughridge was asked to check a schedule of where chest x-rays are available at various times. . . .

Mr. Robinson asked what the procedure is for merit raises. The procedure is that the foreman recommends the individual for a merit raise if by his performance he has shown that he merits the increase. . . .

                                                                        Chairman
William Irrgang: MW
September 25, 1974

George Willis estimated that at least twice a week factory employees took advantage of this opportunity to talk with him.

Middle managers also felt that communication with Willis and Irrgang was open and direct. Often it bypassed intermediate levels of the organization. Most saw this as an advantage, but one commented:

> This company is run strictly by the two men at the top. Mr. Lincoln trained Mr. Irrgang in his image. It's very authoritarian and decisions flow top down. It never became a big company. There is very little delegated and top people are making too many small decisions. Mr. Irrgang and Mr. Willis work 80 hours a week, and no one I know in this company can say that his boss doesn't work harder than he does.

Willis saw management's concern for the worker as an essential ingredient in his company's formula for success. He knew at least 500 employees personally. In leading the researcher through the plant, he greeted workers by name and paused several times to tell anecdotes about them.

At one point, an older man yelled to Willis good-naturedly, "Where's my raise?" Willis explained that this man had worked for 40 years in a job requiring him to lift up to 20 tons of material a day. His earnings had been quite high because of his rapid work pace, but Willis had been afraid that as he was advancing in age he could injure himself working in that job. After months of Willis's urging, the worker switched to an easier but lower paying job. He was disappointed in taking the earnings cut and even after several years let the president know whenever he saw him.

Willis pointed out another employee, whose wife had recently died, and noted that for several weeks he had been drinking heavily and reporting to work late. Willis had earlier spent about half an hour discussing the situation with him to console him and see if the company could help in any way. He explained:

> I made a definite point of talking to him on the floor of the plant, near his work station. I wanted to make sure that other employees who knew the situation could see me with him. Speaking to him had symbolic value. It is important for employees to know that the president is interested in their welfare.

Management's philosophy was also reflected in the company's physical facilities. A no-nonsense atmosphere was firmly established at the gate to the parking lot where the only mention of the company name was in a sign reading:

> $1,000 REWARD for information leading to the arrest and conviction of persons stealing from the Lincoln Electric parking lot.

There was a single entrance to the offices and plant for workers, management, and visitors. Entering, one could not avoid being struck by the company motto, in large stainless steel letters extending 30 feet across the wall:

THE ACTUAL IS LIMITED
THE POSSIBLE IS IMMENSE

A flight of stairs led down to a tunnel system for pedestrian traffic which ran under the single-story plant. At the base of the stairs was a large bronze plaque on which were inscribed the names of the 8 employees who had served more than 50 years, and the more than 350 active employees with 25 or more years of service (the Quarter Century Club).

The long tunnel leading to the offices was clean and well lit. The executive offices were located in a windowless, two-story cement-block office building which sat like a box in the center of the plant. At the base of the staircase leading up to the offices, a Lincoln automatic welding machine and portraits of J. C. Lincoln and J. F. Lincoln welcomed visitors. The handrail on the staircase was welded into place, as were the ashtrays in the tunnel.

In the center of the office building was a simple, undecorated reception room. A switchboard operator/receptionist greeted visitors between filing and phone calls. Throughout the building, decor was Spartan. The reception room was furnished with a metal coat rack, a wooden bookcase, and several plain wooden tables and chairs. All of the available reading material dealt with Lincoln Electric Company or welding.

From the reception room, seven doors each led almost directly to the various offices and departments. Most of the departments were large open rooms with closely spaced desks. One manager explained that "Mr. Lincoln didn't believe in walls. He felt they interrupted the flow of communications and paperwork." Most of the desks and files were plain, old, and well worn, and there was little modern office equipment. Expenditures on equipment had to meet the same criteria in the office as in the plant: The Maintenance Department had to certify that the equipment replaced could not be repaired, and any equipment acquired for cost reduction had to have a one-year payback.[10] Even Xerox machines were hidden. Copying costs were tightly controlled and only certain individuals could use the Xerox copiers. Customer order forms which required eight copies were run on a duplicating machine, for example.

The private offices were small, uncarpeted, and separated by green metal partitions. The president's office was slightly larger than the others, but still retained a Spartan appearance. There was only one carpeted office. Willis explained: "That office was occupied by Mr. Lincoln until he died in 1965. For the next five years it was left vacant and now it is Mr. Irrgang's office and also the Board of Directors' and Advisory Board meeting room."

PERSONNEL

Lincoln Electric had a strict policy of filling all but entry level positions by promoting from within the company. Whenever an opening occurred, a notice was posted on the 25 bulletin boards in the plant and offices. Any interested employee could apply for an open position. Because of the company's sustained growth and policy of promoting from within, employees had substantial opportunity for advancement.

An outsider generally could join the company in one of two ways: either taking a factory job at an hourly or piece rate, or entering Lincoln's training programs in sales or engineering.[11] The company recruited its trainees at colleges and graduate schools, including Harvard Business School. Starting salary in 1975 for a trainee with a bachelor's degree was $5.50 an hour plus a year-end bonus at an average of 40 percent of the normal rate. Wages for trainees with either a master's degree or several years of relevant experience were 5 percent higher.

Although Lincoln's president, vice president of sales, and personnel

---

[10] Willis explained that capital projects with paybacks of up to two years were sometimes funded when they involved a product for which demand was growing.

[11] Lincoln's chairman and president both advanced through the ranks in manufacturing. Irrgang began as a pieceworker in the Armature Winding Department, and Willis began in Plant Engineering. (See Exhibit 8 for employment history of Lincoln's top management.)

EXHIBIT 8: Employment History of Top Executives

William Irrgang, Board Chairman
1929   Hired, Repair Department
1930   Final inspection
1934   Inspection, Wire Department
1946   Director of factory engineering
1951   Executive vice president for manufacturing and engineering
1954   President and general manager
1972   Chairman of the board of directors

George E. Willis, President
1947   Hired, factory engineering
1951   Superintendent, Electrode Division
1959   Vice president
1969   Executive vice president of manufacturing and associated functions
1972   President

William Miskoe, Vice President, International
1932   Hired, Chicago sales office
1941   President of Australian plant
1969   To Cleveland as vice president, international

Edwin M. Miller, Vice President and Assistant to the President
1923   Hired, factory worker
1925   Assistant foreman
1929   Production Department
1940   Assistant department head, Production Department
1952   Superintendent, Machine Division
1959   Vice president
1973   Vice president and assistant to the president

D. Neal Manross, Vice President, Machine and Motor Divisions
1941   Hired, factory worker
1942   Welding inspector
1952   General foreman, Extruding Department, and assistant plant superintendent
1953   Foreman, Special Products Department, Machine Division
1956   Superintendent, Special Products Division
1959   Superintendent, motor manufacturing
1966   Vice president, Motor Division
1973   Vice president in charge of Motor and Machine divisions

Albert S. Patnik, Vice President of Sales Development
1940   Hired, sales student
1940   Welder, New London, Conn.
1941   Junior salesman, Los Angeles office
1942   Salesman, Seattle office
1945   Military service
1945   Reinstated to Seattle

EXHIBIT 8 *(concluded)*

1951   Rural dealer manager, Cleveland sales office
1964   Assistant to the vice president of sales
1972   Vice president

Donald F. Hastings, Vice President and General Sales Manager
1953   Hired, sales trainee
1954   Welding engineer, Emeryville, Cal.
1959   District manager, Moline office
1970   General sales manager, Cleveland
1972   Vice president and general sales manager

director were all Harvard Business School graduates, the company had not hired many recent graduates. Clyde Loughridge, the personnel director, explained:

> We don't offer them fancy staff positions and we don't pretend to. Our starting pay is less than average, probably $17,000–$18,000[12] including bonus, and the work is harder than average. We start our trainees off by putting them in overalls and they spend up to seven weeks in the welding school. In a lot of ways it's like boot camp. Rather than leading them along by the hand, we like to let the self-starters show themselves.

The policy of promoting from within had rarely been violated, and then only in cases where a specialized skill was required. Loughridge commented:

> In most cases we've been able to stick to it, even where the required skills are entirely new to the company. Our employees have a lot of varied skills, and usually someone can fit the job. For example, when we recently got our first computer, we needed a programmer and systems analyst. We had twenty employees apply who had experience or training in computers. We chose two, and it really helps that they know the company and understand our business.

The company did not send its employees to outside management development programs and did not provide tuition grants for educational purposes.

Lincoln Electric had no formal organization chart and management did not feel that one was necessary. (The chart in Exhibit 9 was drawn for the purposes of this case.) As explained by one executive:

> People retire and their jobs are parceled out. We are very successful in overloading our overhead departments. We make sure this way that

---

[12] In 1975, the median starting salary for Harvard Business School graduates who took positions in industrial manufacturing was $19,800.

EXHIBIT 9

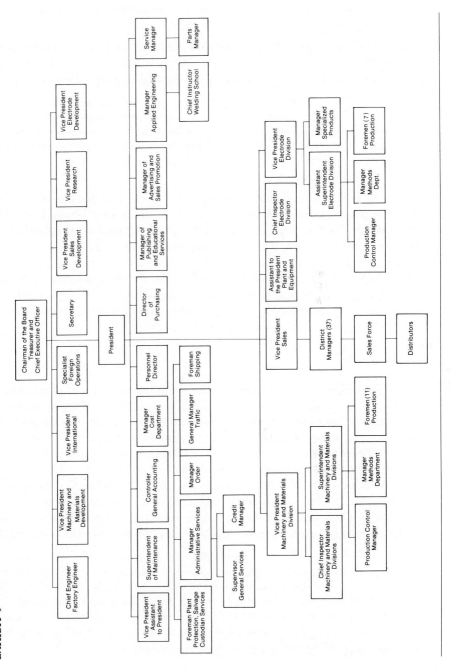

no unnecessary work is done and jobs which are not absolutely essential are eliminated. A disadvantage is that planning may suffer, as may outside development to keep up with your field.

Lincoln's organizational hierarchy was flat, with few levels between the bottom and the top. For example, Don Hastings, the vice president of sales, had 37 regional sales managers reporting to him. He commented:

> I have to work hard, there's no question about that. There are only four of us in the home office plus two secretaries. I could easily use three more people. I work every Saturday, at least half a day. Most of our regional men do too, and they like me to know it. You should see the switchboard light up when 37 regional managers call in at five minutes to twelve on Saturday.

The president and chairman kept a tight rein over personnel matters. All changes in status of employees, even at the lowest levels, had to be approved by Willis. Irrgang also had to give his approval if salaried employees were involved. Raises or promotions had to be approved in advance. An employee could be fired by his supervisor on the spot for cause, but if the grounds were questionable, the decision had to be approved afterward by either Willis or Irrgang. Usually the supervisor was supported, but there had been cases where a firing decision was reversed.

MARKETING

Welding machines and electrodes were like razors and razor blades. A Lincoln welding machine often had a useful life of 30 years or more, while electrodes (and fluxes) were consumed immediately in the welding process. The ratio of machine cost to annual consumables cost varied widely, from perhaps $7:1$ for a hand welder used in a small shop to $1:5$ or more for an automatic welder used in a shipyard.

Although certain competitors might meet Lincoln's costs and quality in selected products, management believed that no company could match the line overall. Another important competitive edge for Lincoln was its sales force. Al Patnik, vice president of sales development, explained:

> Most competitors operate through distributors. We have our own top field sales force.[13] We start out with engineering graduates and put them through our seven-month training program. They learn how to weld, and we teach them everything we can about equipment, metallurgy, and design. Then they spend time on the rebuild line [where machines brought in from the field are rebuilt] and even spend time in the office seeing how orders are processed. Finally, before the trainees go out into the field, they

---

[13] The sales force was supplemented in some areas by distributors. Sales abroad were handled by wholly owned subsidiaries or Armco's International Division.

have to go into our plant and find a better way of making something. Then they make a presentation to Mr. Irrgang, just as if he were one of our customers.

Our approach to the customer is to go in and learn what he is doing and show him how to do it better. For many companies our people become their experts in welding. They go in and talk to a foreman. They might say, "Let me put on a headshield and show you what I'm talking about." That's how we sell them.

George Ward, a salesman in the San Francisco office, commented:

The competition hires graduates with business degrees (without engineering backgrounds) and that's how they get hurt. This job is getting more technical every day. . . . A customer in California who is using our equipment to weld offshore oil rigs had a problem with one of our products. I couldn't get the solution for them over the phone, so I flew in to the plant Monday morning and showed it to our engineers. Mr. Willis said to me, "Don't go back to California until this problem is solved. . . ." We use a "working together to solve your problem" approach. This, plus sticking to published prices, shows you're not interested in taking advantage of them.

I had a boss who used to say: "Once we're in, Lincoln never loses a customer except on delivery." It's basically true. The orders I lost last year were because we couldn't deliver fast enough. Lincoln gets hurt when there are shortages because of our guaranteed employment. We don't hire short-term factory workers when sales take off, and other companies beat us on delivery.

The sales force was paid a salary plus bonus. Ward believed that Lincoln's sales force was the best paid and hardest working in the industry. He said, "We're aggressive, and want to work and get paid for it. The sales force prides itself on working more hours than anyone else. . . . My wife wonders sometimes if you can work for Lincoln and have a family too."

MANUFACTURING

Lincoln's plant was unusual in several respects. It seemed crowded with materials and equipment, with surprisingly few workers. It was obvious that employees worked very fast and efficiently with few breaks. Even during the 10-minute smoke breaks in the morning and afternoon, employees often continued to work.

An innovative plant layout was partly responsible for the crowded appearance. Raw materials entered one side of the plant and finished goods came out the other side. There was no central stockroom for materials or work-in-process. Instead, everything that entered the plant was transported directly to the work station where it would be used. At a work station, a single worker or group operated in effect as a subcontractor. All required materials were piled around the station, allowing visual inventory control, and workers were paid a piece price for their production. Wherever possible, the work flow followed a straight line through the plant from the side where raw materials entered to the side where finished goods exited. Because there was no union, the company had great flexibility in deciding what could be performed at a work station. For example, foundry work and metal stamping could be carried out together by the same workers when necessary. Thus, work could flow almost directly along a line through the plant. Intermediate material handling was avoided to a great extent. The major exception arose when multiple production lines shared a large or expensive piece of machinery, and the work had to be brought to the machines.

Many of the operations in the plant were automated. Much of the manufacturing equipment was proprietary,[14] designed and built by Lincoln. In some cases, the company had modified machines built by others to run two or three times as fast as when originally delivered.

From the time a product was first conceived, close coordination was maintained between product design engineers and the Methods Department; this was seen as a key factor in reducing costs and rationalizing manufacturing. William Irrgang explained:

> After we have [an] idea . . . we start thinking about manufacturing costs, before anything leaves the Design Engineering Department. At that point, there is a complete "getting together" of manufacturing and design engineers—and plant engineers, too, if new equipment is involved.
>
> Our tooling, for instance, is going to be looked at carefully while the design of a product is still in process. Obviously, we can increase or decrease the tooling very materially by certain considerations in the design of a product, and we can go on the basis of total costs at all times. In fact, as far as total cost is concerned, we even think about such matters as shipping, warehousing, etc. All of these factors are taken into consideration when we're still at the design stage. It's very essential that this be done: otherwise, you can lock yourself out from a lot of potential economies.[15]

In 1974, Lincoln's plant had reached full capacity, operating nearly around the clock. Land bordering its present location was unavailable and management was moving ahead with plans to build a second plant 15 miles away on the same freeway as the present plant.

Over the years, Lincoln had come to make rather than buy an increasing proportion of its components. For example, even though its unit volume of gasoline engines was only a fraction of its suppliers', Lincoln

---

[14] Visitors were barred from the Electrode Division unless they had a pass signed by Willis or Irrgang.

[15] "Incentive Management in Action," *Assembly Engineering*, March 1967.

purchased engine blocks and components and assembled them rather than buying completed engines. Management was continually evaluating opportunities for backward integration and had not arbitrarily ruled out manufacturing any of Lincoln's components or raw materials.

ADMINISTRATIVE PRODUCTIVITY

Lincoln's high productivity was not limited to manufacturing. Clyde Loughridge pointed to the Personnel Department as an example: "Normally, for 2,300 employees you would need a personnel department of about 20, but we have only 6, and that includes the nurse, and our responsibilities go beyond those of the typical personnel department."

Once a year, Loughridge had to outline his objectives for the upcoming year to the president of the company, but as he explained, "I don't get a budget. There would be no point to it. I just spend as little as possible. I operate this just like my home. I don't spend on anything I don't need."

In the Traffic Department, workers also seemed very busy. There, a staff of 12 controlled the shipment of 2.5 million pounds of material a day. Their task was complex. Delivery was included in the price of their products. They thus could reduce the overall cost to the customer by mixing products in most loads and shipping the most efficient way possible to the company's 39 warehouses. Jim Biek, general traffic manager, explained how they accomplished this:

> For every order, we decide whether it would be cheaper by rail or truck. Then we consolidate orders so that over 90 percent of what goes out of here is full carload or full truckload, as compared to perhaps 50 percent for most companies. We also mix products so that we come in at the top of the weight brackets. For example, if a rate is for 20,000 to 40,000 pounds, we will mix orders to bring the weight right up to that 40,000 limit. All this is computed manually. In fact, my old boss used to say, "We run Traffic like a ma and pa grocery store."

As in the rest of Lincoln, the employees in the Traffic Department worked their way up from entry level positions. Jim Biek had become general traffic manager after nine years as a purchasing engineer. He had received an M.B.A. degree from Northwestern after a B.S. in mechanical engineering from Purdue, started in the engineering training program, and then spent five years in Product Development and Methods before going to Purchasing and finally to Traffic. Lack of experience in Traffic was a disadvantage, but the policy of promoting from within also had its advantages. Biek explained:

> One of my first tasks was to go to Washington and fight to get welders reclassified as motors to qualify for a lower freight rate. With my engineering

experience and knowledge of welders, I was in a better position to argue this than a straight traffic man. . . .

Just about everybody in here was new to Traffic. One of my assistant traffic managers had worked on the loading platform here for 10 years before he came into the department. He had to go to night school to learn about rates, but his experience is invaluable. He knows how to load trucks and rail cars backwards and forward. Who could do a better job of consolidating orders than he does? He can look at an order and think of it as rows of pallets.

Some day we'll outgrow this way of operating, but right now I can't imagine a computer juggling loads like some of our employees do.

Lincoln's Order Department had recently begun computerizing its operations. It was the first time a computer had been used anywhere in the company (except in engineering and research), and according to Russell Stauffer, head of the Order Department, "It was a three-year job for me to sell this to top management." The computer was expected to replace 12 or 13 employees who would gradually be moved into new jobs. There had been some resistance to the computer, Stauffer noted:

It's like anything new. People get scared. Not all the people affected have been here for the two years required to be eligible for guaranteed employment. And even though the others are assured a job, they don't know what it will be and will have to take what's offered.

The computer was expected to produce savings of $100,000 a year, and to allow a greater degree of control. Stauffer explained:

We're getting information out of this that we never knew before. The job here is very complex. We're sending out more than two million pounds of consumables a day. Each order might have 30 or 40 items, and each item has a bracket price arrangement based on total order size. A clerk has to remember or determine quickly whether we are out of stock on any items and calculate whether the stock-out brings the order down into another bracket. This means they have to remember the prices and items out of stock. This way of operating was okay up to about $200 million in sales, but now we've outgrown the human capability to handle the problem.

Although he had no previous experience in computers, Stauffer had full responsibility for the conversion.

I've been here for 35 years. The first day I started, I unloaded coal cars and painted fences. Then I went to the assembly line, first on small parts, then large ones. I've been running the Order Department for 12 years. Since I've been here, we've had studies on computers every year or two and it always came out that we couldn't save money. Finally, when it looked like we'd make the switch, I took some courses at IBM. Over the last year and a half, they've totaled eight and a half weeks, which is supposed to equal a full semester of college.

To date, the conversion had gone well, but much slower than antici-pated. Order pressure had been so high that many mistakes would have been catastrophic. Management thus had emphasized assuring 100 percent quality operations rather than faster conversion.

LINCOLN'S FUTURE

The 1947 Harvard Business School case study of Lincoln Electric ended with a prediction by a union leader from the Cleveland area:

> The real test of Lincoln will come when the going gets tough. The thing Lincoln holds out to the men is high earnings. They work like dogs at Lincoln, but it pays off. . . .
>
> I think [Mr. Lincoln] puts too much store by monetary incentives—but then, there's no denying he has attracted people who respond to that type of incentive. But I think that very thing is a danger Lincoln faces. If the day comes when they can't offer those big bonuses, or his people decide there's more to life than killing yourself making money, I predict the Lincoln Electric Company is in for trouble.

Lincoln's president, George Willis, joined the company the year that this comment was made. Reflecting on his 28 years with the company, Willis observed:

> The company hasn't changed very much since I've been here. It's still run pretty much like Mr. Lincoln ran it. But today's workers are differ-ent. They're more outspoken and interested in why things are being done, not just how. We have nothing to hide and never did, so we can give them the answers to their questions.

Looking forward, Willis saw no need to alter Lincoln's strategy or its policies:

> My job will continue to be to have everyone in the organization recognize that a common goal all of us can and must support is to give the customer the quality he needs, when he needs it, at the lowest cost. To do this, we have to have everyone's understanding of this goal and their effort to accomplish it. In one way or another, I have to motivate the organization to meet this goal. The basic forms of the motivation have evolved over the last 40 years. However, keeping the system honed so that everyone understands it, agrees with it, and brings out disagreements so improvements can be made or thinking changed becomes my major re-sponsibility.
>
> If our employees did not believe that management was trustworthy, honest, and impartial, the system could not operate. We've worked out the mechanics. They are not secret. A good part of my responsibility is to make sure the mechanics are followed. This ties back to a trust and understanding between individuals at all levels of the organization.
>
> I don't see any real limits to our size. Look at a world with a present

population of just under four billion now and six and a quarter billion by the year 2000. Those people aren't going to tolerate a low standard of living. So there will be a lot of construction, cars, bridges, oil, and all those things that have got to be to support a population that large.

My job will still be just the traditional things of assuring that we keep up with the technology and have sufficient profit to pay the suppliers of capital. Then, I have to make sure communication can be maintained adequately. That last task may be the biggest and most important part of my job in the years ahead as we grow larger and still more complex.

APPENDIX A

Lincoln Comment on the Case

After reading the 1975 Harvard case study, Richard S. Sabo, manager of publicity and educational services, sent the following letter to the case writer:

July 31, 1975

To: Mr. Norman Fast

Dear Mr. Fast:

I believe that you have summarized the Incentive Management System of The Lincoln Electric Company very well; however, readers may feel that the success of the Company is due only to the psychological principles included in your presentation.

Please consider adding the efforts of our executives who devote a great deal of time to the following items that are so important to the consistent profit and long range growth of the Company.

I. Management has limited research, development and manufacturing to a standard product line designed to meet the major needs of the welding industry.

II. New products must be reviewed by manufacturing and all production costs verified before being approved by management.

III. Purchasing is challenged to not only procure materials at the lowest cost, but also to work closely with engineering and manufacturing to assure that the latest innovations are implemented.

IV. Manufacturing supervision and all personnel are held accountable for reduction of scrap, energy conservation, and maintenance of product quality.

V. Production control, material handling and methods of engineering are closely supervised by top management.

VI. Material and finished goods inventory control, accurate cost accounting and attention to sales costs, credit and other financial areas have constantly reduced overhead and led to excellent profitability.

VII. Management has made cost reduction a way of life at Lincoln and definite programs are established in many areas, including traffic and shipping, where tremendous savings can result.

VIII. Management has established a sales department that is technically trained to reduce customer welding cost. This sales technique and other real customer services have eliminated non-essential frills and resulted in long term benefits to all concerned.

IX. Management has encouraged education, technical publishing and long range programs that have resulted in industry growth, thereby assuring market potential for The Lincoln Electric Company.

Richard S. Sabo

bjs

CASE 21

Data Resources, Inc.

HISTORY

DRI was founded in December 1968 as an outgrowth of a consulting project at Mitchell, Hutchins, an investment advisory and brokerage concern. The project consisted of the retention of leading experts in the fields of economics, politics, and foreign policy, to advise corporations and financial institutions on the economic and political environment. One of these experts was Dr. Otto Eckstein, Paul M. Warburg Professor of Economics at Harvard University, and a former member of President Lyndon Johnson's Council of Economic Advisers.

Dr. Eckstein became president of DRI (while retaining his Harvard professorship), and Donald B. Marron, the president of Mitchell, Hutchins, became chairman of DRI. Mitchell, Hutchins arranged the initial financing of DRI and also provided business expertise.

In November 1976, DRI became a public company, offering its stock in the over-the-counter market. At that time its projected 1976 revenues were $17 million, and projected net income was about $1.5 million. The equivalent 1971 figures had been $1.9 million and $44,500. Revenue growth since 1971 had averaged over 50 percent per year, and net income growth over 30 percent per year. The initial offering price was $7.67[1] a share, and 450,000 of the 1,950,000 shares outstanding were offered. Existing shareholders (before the offering) had paid an average of 53 cents a share.

---

[1] Adjusted for a 3-for-2 split in March 1979.

The distribution of share ownership before and after the offering was as follows:

	Percent	
	Before	**After**
Mitchell, Hutchins . . .	22.6	15.3
First Security Co. . . .	17.3	10.3
Otto Eckstein,		
family and trusts . . .	22.1	20.5
Other	38.0	53.9
	100.0	100.0

First Security Company was an investment holding company, and had a representative on DRI's board of directors.

After going public, DRI continued to grow: its 1977 and 1978 revenues were $23.8 million and $31.5 million, and its 1977 and 1978 net earnings were $2.5 million and $3.1 million. Its stock price had also risen dramatically to a level of about $32 per share in July of 1979, while the Dow Jones Industrial Average had fallen over that period.

DRI'S BUSINESS[2]

DRI called itself an integrated economic information service company and described its business as combining econometric models and forecasting, computer-accessible economic data banks, associated data processing services, and consulting to support customer management information systems. DRI had over 600 customers in manufacturing, finance, other businesses, governments, and universities. Manufacturing and retailing customer applications of DRI's services included forecasting prices and sales volumes of specific product lines, budget setting and variance analysis, investment allocation among corporate divisions, and merger analysis. Banks and other financial institutions used DRI for loan, deposit, and interest rate estimations, securities analysis, and profit planning. Federal and state government agencies used DRI to forecast tax revenues and treasury disbursements, and for policy simulations. Universities and research organizations used the DRI system for testing hypotheses with statistical data and for building simulation models for scientific purposes. The emphasis in all these applications was to provide a system which kept customers up-to-date on how they were being affected by the economic environment. DRI offered each customer a package of services for which it paid an annual subscription fee. Typically, a subscriber received periodic "macro" forecasts in textual form of the U.S. or other economies, as well as industry forecasts, and was entitled to use the

---

[2] Source: DRI prospectuses, 10Ks, and annual reports.

macro- and micromodels through access to the computer on which they were stored. In July of 1979 the annual subscription fee for the basic U.S. "macro" service was $15,000. Other services had subscription fees of up to $35,000. The subscriber received consulting support in his use and analysis of DRI-provided information and had access to various computerized data banks. Computer access was billed separately, based on central processor usage, connect time, and storage.

The four areas of service offered by Data Resources included economic data banking, econometric models and forecasting, associated data processing services, and consulting.

Economic Data

The data banks maintained by DRI included national, industrial, regional, international, financial, company, and special-purpose data, totalling millions of time series. DRI believed that this was the largest collection of economic data in the world which was computer-accessible on a commercial basis. DRI's data banks were collected from numerous U.S. and foreign government and nongovernment sources, and could be accessed through a system of computer software specially designed for use in various kinds of quantitative analysis.

The data banks contained macroeconomic variables such as gross national product, total employment, profits, interest rates, investment and consumption, as well as statistics on many specific segments of an economy, e.g., steel production, nondurables consumption, and bond interest rates. Over 25,000 weekly, monthly, quarterly, and annual series were stored in the U.S. central data bank. All U.S. national data were available on-line in the data banks within at most 24 hours of release by reporting agencies, and usually within an hour. Other data banks were for regions, industries, Western Europe, Japan, Canada, and other nations and special purposes such as daily stock price, commodity, weather, and foreign exchange data analysis. Various cross-section data banks, such as consumer surveys, were also stored on-line.

DRI's data banks were of two types. The first consisted of data which were entered manually and updated continuously by the DRI data bank staff from publicly available source documents. A staff of 50 kept the data current. The second type of data bank consisted of material obtained in machine-readable form from source organizations. DRI provided report writing, analytical programs, and documentation to assist subscribers in using these data banks.

Econometric Models and Forecasting

Econometric models portray economies and industries through sets of interactive simultaneous equations derived from a historical record and founded on economic theory. DRI's models were built and stored on the computer and encoded in simulation software which made it possible to solve the models for a given set of policy assumptions and to display the results.

The model solutions were developed for the purposes of forecasting and testing the impact of alternative assumptions. Generally, DRI's models were solved by the company's staff to produce a forecast as well as optimistic and pessimistic alternatives. These estimates were designed to bracket the range within which the actual outcomes were most likely to occur. The customer had the option of changing the assumptions by commands to the computer and solving the model to produce his own forecasts.

The most widely used model in the DRI system was its macromodel of the U.S. economy. This forecast over 1,000 variables through a system of equations. Forecasts were provided each month for the succeeding 8 to 12 quarters, and were provided at least once each quarter for the succeeding 10 years or longer intervals.

With the use of this model, DRI prepared short-term and long-term forecasts of the major dimensions of the U.S. economy. These forecasts projected detailed breakdowns of consumer spending, business investment in plant, equipment and inventories, construction activity, government receipts and expenditures, wages, profits, breakdowns of major price indexes, and the composition of exports and imports. A complete set of financial projections, such as interest rates, monetary aggregates, household and corporate flows of funds and balance sheets, and mortgage activity was also included.

By using this model, changes in national variables such as monetary policies, budget policies, population growth, consumer attitudes, costs of capital, raw material prices and international economic trends could be analyzed in terms of their impact upon the major dimensions of the economy as a whole and on specific industries.

The DRI staff provided a regular flow of textual memos analyzing current economic developments and policy proposals. These were also available through the computer and communications system and through publications distributed to subscribers.

In addition to its macromodel of the U.S. economy, DRI had developed and maintained a variety of other models. Foreign economy models were used by multinational companies for market analysis and as inputs for industry analysis. Energy models projected key energy demands and prices. State models were used by state governments for budgeting, revenue estimation, and for the analysis of programs. Regional models were used by retail organizations and other firms to project regional market growth and to help assess regional location choices.

Detailed models of particular industries were used to forecast and analyze industry product markets, prices, input costs, and capacity expansion requirements. Models for particular industries included U.S. agriculture, petrochemicals, wood products, paper, automotive, steel, casualty insurance, and banking. Other DRI models included a cost forecasting service for purchasing executives, and a consumer age-income service projecting the composition of income change by age group. DRI maintained an ongoing program of new model development.

Models could be linked on the DRI computer system, with the solutions of the macromodels frequently used as inputs for solutions of the regional and industry models. Each model had its own staff of economists for its development and operation. Most of the models had associated data banks and periodic publications, and some had regular conference programs. The most rapid means of disseminating the materials was the time-shared computer system with its communications network.

Associated Data Processing Services

The use of the DRI information system generally involved the use of the DRI computer and communications network. DRI's software packages used English language commands to communicate with the computer in order to access data, perform statistical analyses, build and simulate models, and develop and display forecasts. DRI's own software included programs known as EPS, MODEL, AID, CSS, FAS, and SURVEY. These programs, which were written by DRI's software groups, enabled users to employ a wide range of techniques without requiring specialized knowledge about computer and programming languages. This software focused on applications which permitted the customer to analyze exposure to various potential economic changes in the light of alternative simulations of the overall economy provided by DRI's models. DRI maintained ongoing software development acitivities. DRI also provided standard software packages such as APL, SPSS, EMPIRE, and various compilers.

Service Consulting

DRI believed that its growth was attributable in part to its consulting support of client applications. Approximately 160 consultants were located in nine regional offices (including offices in Brussels and Toronto) to provide close support of customer work. This support included direct attention to specific customer applications, and education in the techniques and applications of DRI's services.

In what DRI considered a unique consulting approach, its consultants worked with clients on a continuing basis rather than on single projects. DRI consultants helped identify decisions whose outcomes would be influenced by economic events, formulated research to address those decisions, and helped the customer's staff perform the necessary research work. Consultants worked with customer management and staff to interpret the research results for their decisions, and to establish monitoring systems to identify when the economy might signal for a change in the organization's plans. The consultants' goal was to help the client make more effective use of DRI's data, models, and time-shared computer services.

The DRI educational program helped clients develop their own skills at several levels. An initial three-day course of seminars, case discussions, and computer sessions introduced new clients to econometric methods using the DRI data and software. DRI's Quarterly Education Seminars provided a curriculum of courses taught by noted academic economists to improve client sophistication in econometric modeling techniques. Applications seminars showed customers how to use DRI services to solve problems facing their organizations. Each of these components of DRI's education program was oriented to helping customers become self-sustaining users of DRI's models and data.

Marketing

DRI's services were marketed by about 40 salespersons, almost all of whom held advanced degrees in economics or business. In 1976, DRI's U.S. customers included 52 of the 100 largest industrial corporations, 32 of the 50 largest commercial banks, 9 of the largest insurance companies, and 19 of the 50 largest securities firms. Other clients included foreign corporations and governments, retail companies, state and local governments, universities, research organizations, and various other businesses. DRI contracted separately with various agencies and departments of the U.S. government. All U.S. government agencies and departments in the aggregate accounted for about 15 percent of total revenues for 1978. No single customer of DRI accounted for 10 percent or more of its revenues.

An extract from *Dun's Review* on the marketing approach and skills of DRI is shown in Exhibit 1.

Competition

DRI believed that its integrated economic information system, consisting of its extensive data banks, its ability to provide computer time-shared access to its data, its collection of econometric models, and its large organization made it a unique economic information service company. Nevertheless, DRI recognized that it had a number of competitors in significant areas of its business. In the area of econometric modeling and forecasting, it considered its principal competitors to be Wharton EFA, Inc., a nonprofit corporation owned by the University of Pennsylvania, and Chase Econometric Associates, Inc., a subsidiary of the Chase Manhattan Bank, N.A. Both of these companies had a macromodel of

---

EXHIBIT 1: Extract from "DRI—Selling the Future Now" (by Paula Smith, *Dun's Review*, February 1976)

Apart from the reputation of Eckstein himself, a major reason for DRI's dominance of the field is skillful marketing. Many buyers who have heard the sales pitches of all three major services—DRI, Wharton, and Chase—say that DRI is one of the most aggressive marketers they have ever encountered in any business. "We wanted to buy a model of the state of Wisconsin so we called in all three services to see what they had to offer," says Eugene Smolensky, economics professor at the University of Wisconsin and a member of the governor's Council of Economic Advisers. "The guy from Chase was earnest, sober, straightforward. Then we saw the Wharton representative, all tweedy and so soft-sell, he kept telling us we couldn't expect all that much from a model. And then there was DRI, just about the slickest operators I ever saw. They were PhD used-car salesmen, hucksters in the latest Brooks suits, tall, thin, and very Harvard with a persuasive well-developed patter about their modelling expertise and the genius of Dr. Eckstein. We found the presentation a little frightening, but we had to go with DRI because they had done state models before."

It is not easy to find MBA's and PhD's who both know econometric modelling and can sell. But with its Lexington, Massachusetts headquarters, just a stone's throw from Harvard, Massachusetts Institute of Technology, and other colleges in the Boston area, DRI has its pick of bright, young prospects. Constantly adding new staff, DRI now has twenty front-line salesmen and 120 consultants who work directly with customers on the models. Most of the staff is under thirty, and around the DRI offices such words as "brilliant" and "high-IQ minds," which is a pet Eckstein phrase, are often used to describe the people who work there.

---

the U.S. economy as well as models of some other economic areas covered by DRI models, together with related data banks. Certain of their models and data banks could be accessed through time-sharing arrangements with general-purpose time-sharing firms. DRI believed that a number of its customers also subscribed to the services offered by its principal competitors. In addition, several other firms were engaged in providing economic data or forecasts, principally in printed form. These included Merrill Lynch Economics, Townsend-Greenspan, Inc., and Evans Economics. Merrill Lynch Economics was a subsidiary of the U.S.'s largest investment brokerage company. Townsend-Greenspan was headed by Alan Greenspan, chairman of the U.S. President's Council of Economic Advisers during the Ford administration. Evans Economics had been formed in March 1979 by Michael Evans after selling his interest in Chase Econometrics to the Chase Manhattan Bank.

Comments by *Business Week* on the principal economic forecasters are shown in Exhibit 2.

EXHIBIT 2: "Right or Wrong, Forecasts Pay" (*Business Week*, May 28, 1979)

"You know my motto," says economic forecaster Michael K. Evans with his promoter's chuckle. "Often wrong but never in doubt."

Mike Evans can afford to joke when twitted about some major forecasting errors he has made, such as predicting bottlenecks and shortages in 1977 and a recession for 1978. In February, the 40-year-old economist sold his remaining 20% interest in Chase Econometric Associates Inc., of Bala Cynwyd, PA., to Chase Manhattan Bank for $2.8 million.

Besides, almost everyone in economic forecasting has been wrong on some count lately, especially on predicting the gross national product and the inflation rates for the last two quarters. And the error column includes not only Chase but also the other two leaders in forecasting based on large computerized models— Data Resources Inc. (DRI), of Lexington, Mass., headed by Otto Eckstein, and Wharton Econometric Forecasting Associates, led by Lawrence R. Klein.

Nevertheless, the Big Three continue to lead the way in a thriving little growth industry whose impact on government and business far outweighs their combined volume of less than $100 million a year. Despite the miscues, their clients are buying bigger bundles of services each year. And with pretax profits typically running to 20% of sales, an increasing number of companies and universities are competing for a share of what looks like an expanding pie.

The balance sheets. Comparing the finances of the Big Three is even trickier than evaluating their forecasts, because DRI is publicly owned, Chase is a subsidiary of the bank, and Wharton is part of the University of Pennsylvania. For 1978, DRI had revenues of $31.5 million, of which 34% came from fees for its forecasts and most of the remainder from its huge data bank and time-sharing service. Chase Econometric's sales by one count are only $10 million, but a company source says, "They would be far in excess of $50 million, making us bigger than DRI, if you counted us with the other parts of the bank's information services department."

Unpretentious Wharton, which rents its time-sharing facilities, comes in third with sales of only $4 million. Wharton managed to lose $800,000 last year by expensing several capital costs, including the purchase of a data bank, the start-up of new offices, and development of a world forecasting service in conjunction with SRI International. Klein expects to break well into the black this year.

Chase, with 600 clients, holds a slight edge over DRI at 550, and Wharton has 200. DRI's average revenue per subscriber rose 20% last year, to $51,000. Chase's prices range from $10,000 for the printed forecasts to $25,000 for time-sharing and access to the model.

The personalities. How can a business do so well when its best-known products—the GNP and inflation forecasts—have been so flawed lately? In large part, the answer is that the Big Three sell a lot more than their macroeconomic forecasts. To Stephen McNees, of the Federal Reserve Bank of Boston, the hottest items of the Big Three are their big-name chiefs, all of whom have powerful connections with Washington. (On July 1, Evans will leave Chase and be succeeded as chief macro forecaster by Lawrence T. Chimerine, 38, now with International Business Machines Corp. Evans will be bound by contract not to sell a competing forecast until March, 1980.)

EXHIBIT 2 *(continued)*

The styles of the individuals are vital, says McNees, "because the distinction between judgmental and computer-based forecasting has been blurred. The judgmental forecasters all look at what the models are saying, while the model builders all add personal judgment to the numbers their models produce." So the client buying basic quarterly or annual forecasts is "really buying ebullient Otto Eckstein, scholarly Larry Klein, or flamboyant Mike Evans."

This "cult of personality" is not a light matter in a world of highly imperfect information and increasingly confusing economic turns. McNees says, "What executives and government officials are interested in are not the numbers but the story you tell, your view of the world and the economy. They want a reasonable, coherent scenario or alternative scenarios that make sense of things."

Mass-produced data. Although the Big Three do have trouble making consistently correct forecasts, the range of their undertakings, poses perhaps a greater threat to their basic credibility. DRI and Chase, especially, have become mass-production factories, churning out studies as fast as the issues of political economy change these days. And signs of shoddy workmanship have been cropping up.

One DRI customer, for example, complains that "Otto may be delighted with adding U.S. and foreign weather reports to his fabulous data banks, but I'm finding errors in some bread-and-butter series." He cites some state employment data that failed to reflect a major "rebenchmarking of the whole series."

Eckstein concedes that he no longer has time "to check everything as it goes out the door." But the oversights include more than occasional data errors. A recent DRI study for St. Joe Minerals Co., which sought to show that U.S. prices for lead and zinc are closely linked to prices on the London Metals Exchange, was blasted by economists at the Council on Wage & Price Stability. The reason: DRI used the wrong time frame, leading to "spurious results."

Capital gains. DRI also came in for some criticism last fall when Eckstein joined Evans in supporting legislation to reduce the top tax rate on capital gains to 25% from 49.1% (the measure was passed with a 28% lid). But Eckstein was careful to distinguish his own shop's assumptions from those made by his client, the Securities Industry Assn., and he never claimed as much good would come from a capital gains cut as Evans did. Evans asserted that the bill would have unleashed huge amounts of stock trading and boosted the market by 40% in a few years, bringing the Treasury more revenue than it cost.

Arthur M. Okun, chairman of the Council of Economic Advisers under President Johnson, did not comment on his old CEA colleague Eckstein's study, but he called Evans' work "wholly without scientific merit." Klein criticizes both studies because "we don't have a good history of changes in capital gains taxes. The 1969 increase did not generate enough data to conclude that a cut would yield a boom on Wall Street."

Politicization. Perhaps the most disturbing aspect of the capital gains flap is the question of politicization—whether the forecasters' work has been slanted to fit their politics. But such suspicions are inevitable: Part of the appeal to customers of the Big Three has been that Eckstein, Evans, and Klein are all wired in to Washington decision makers—Eckstein through his old CEA ties, Evans as the darling of Capitol Hill conservatives, and Klein as President Carter's chief economic

EXHIBIT 2 *(continued)*

adviser during the 1976 campaign. Their frequent testimony on the Hill, roles as advisers to lawmakers or the administration, and work on special projects, make them conduits for high-powered economic information.

All of this is obviously good for business. Several months ago Chase won a $248,000 contract, at the behest of former Senator Carl Curtis (R–Neb.), to have Evans develop a "supply side" model of the economy for use by the Senate Finance Committee. Since Keynesian models already can be programmed to show the impact of tax reductions on output, Hill economists are questioning the purpose of the Evans project.

But Evans' politicking may have been the final cause of his break with Chase Manhattan. According to one top government economist, "Mike was embarrassing the bank. It has to be tough for David Rockefeller to break bread with administration officials and [Fed Chairman G. William] Miller, when his own economist is calling Miller 'a tool of the administration.' "

Bank officials indicate that Evans was pushed out. He replies: "I could have stayed, taken the money ($175,000 a year), and shut up, but that's not my style." Now Evans clearly will be heard from as he starts a commodities consulting firm cater-corner from the White House. Other economists predict that when he returns to forecasting, the Big Three or Four will again include Evans. But after nine years as manager of forecasting at IBM, Chimerine has the proven credentials and reputation to be a strong successor to Evans at Chase—without making waves.

An array of services. Chase will clearly survive without Evans, for the Big Three still offer services that are hard to match. These include: desk-top terminal access via time-sharing lines to huge data banks (DRI's contains millions of historical series), regional and industry studies, educational seminars, frequent workshop meetings with other economists and financial officers (a specialty of Wharton), teams of analysts, software, and use of the macromodels as input to industry or company models. Perhaps most important to many economists is the ability to plug into the big models and play the "what if" game, varying assumptions for different government policies, oil price changes, or different market outlooks.

Says Ben E. Laden, chief economist of T. Rowe Price Associates Inc., a Baltimore-based investment house: "The big models provide government and business economists with a powerful tool for analyzing what is going on in the economy and catching the interactions of many economic variables through their hundreds of interrelated equations."

Says Richard G. Kjeldsen, senior corporate economist for Security Pacific National Bank in Los Angeles: "It's the vehicle and the package that are valuable." Kjeldsen "fine tunes" the basic DRI model with the bank's own assumptions in order to give the bank a customized forecast. In addition, he uses DRI's macromodel "to drive individual forecasts" for the bank's marketing, research, institutional investment, corporate planning, and economics departments.

An administration economist puts it this way: "Easy access to all that data and analytical support not only is a powerful tool but also makes economists look powerful to their supporters. They can come up with fast answers at relatively low cost."

Thus, it pays the administration to spend $3 million a year and Congress

EXHIBIT 2 *(concluded)*

more than $500,000 for the services of the Big Three, even though the government has several models of its own—at the Federal Reserve Board, the Commerce Dept.'s Bureau of Economic Analysis, and the Treasury Dept.—for internal use to handle sensitive materials.

The competition. But the Big Three are beginning to get some competition. Merrill Lynch Economics Inc., one of a batch of relative newcomers to the field, claims to be catching up with Wharton in sales, but as a unit of a big brokerage house it declines to disclose numbers. In addition, sellers of model-based forecasts include the University of California at Los Angeles, the University of Michigan, Georgia State University, the University of North Carolina, Kent State, and Claremont College. Other models for hire in banking and industry include those at General Electric; Fidelity Bank of Philadelphia; and First National Bank of Boston. Citibank, of New York, is now test-marketing a model-based forecast.

No one in the forecasting business sees these operations as a real threat to the Big Three so far. There is more than enough business to go around, with untapped markets especially inviting overseas. On that front, DRI currently holds a lead in market development, with six people in its European headquarters in Brussels compared with one for Chase and none for Wharton, although Klein's operation should get some lift from its new SRI International affiliation and a lineup of foreign consultants in several countries.

The Evans buy-out at Chase raised speculation in the forecasting field about the future of DRI and Eckstein, who is under pressure by Harvard University to teach full time rather than part time. Eckstein will only acknowledge that "large companies are perpetually interested in us, and as a publicly owned company we have a responsibility to look at all such offers. But personally, I have no desire to leave for the Bahamas."

Reprinted from the May 28, 1979, issue of Business Week *by special persmission.*
© *1979 by McGraw-Hill, Inc.*

Property

DRI's central administrative office and computer facilities were in Lexington, Massachusetts. In 1978, DRI had purchased its office building and land for $1,200,000. DRI also owned the central processors of its Burroughs 7700 computer systems. In 1979 DRI expected to take delivery of computer equipment costing almost $2,000,000.

DRI maintained a communications network which permitted each of its customers to have direct access to its computer system. This system employed both telephone lines leased from American Telephone & Telegraph Co. enhanced by concentrators owned and installed by DRI and for customers in areas not covered by the lines so leased, networks operated by communications vendors.

Employees

As of June 30, 1976, DRI had 280 employees. The most advanced degrees held by these employees included 30 Ph.D. degrees, 40 MBA degrees, 47 other master's degrees and 84 bachelor's degrees. Of the 280 employees, 90 were engaged primarily in model development and forecasting, 18 in marketing, 79 in service consulting, 47 in data processing and other related internal computer activities, and 46 in general and administrative work. By the beginning of 1979, DRI had 574 employees, of whom 208 held advanced degrees and 228 held bachelor's degrees.

Officers and Directors

Dr. Eckstein, who was aged 51 in 1979, had reporting to him three senior vice presidents: Donald McLagan, Dennis O'Brien, and Edward Siegfried. McLagan, aged 36, had joined DRI in 1969, having previously worked as director of the Advanced Computer Techniques Division of the United States Department of Defense. McLagan had an MBA from the Harvard Business School. O'Brien, aged 35, had joined DRI in 1971, and, prior to that, had been an economist at Union Carbide, a leading industrial concern. Siegfried, aged 34, was the chief financial officer of DRI, having joined in 1974 from Arthur Andersen & Co., a major public accounting firm. There were also twenty vice presidents.

DRI's board of directors consisted of Donald B. Marron, chairman; Otto Eckstein, president and chief executive officer; T. Stanton Armour, and Robert J. Denison. Marron was the president of Paine Webber Inc., a leading brokerage firm which had recently acquired Mitchell, Hutchins, Marron's previous firm. Stanton Armour was a senior vice president of Paine Webber Mitchell Hutchins, Inc., and Robert Denison was general partner of the First Security Company.

The Future

Financial information on DRI is shown in Exhibits 3 through 7. Recent developments in the price of the stock and in the sudden departure of five of DRI's senior executives are described in Exhibits 8 through 10.

Data Resources, Inc. Five-Year Summary of Operations For the Year Ended December 31, Data Resources, Inc. and Subsidiary

	1978	1977	1976	1975	1974
Revenues.	$31,470,700	$23,871,200	$17,175,600	$12,742,700	$8,741,700
Operating expenses . .	25,726,100	19,146,600	14,403,300	11,314,000	7,440,700
Operating income . .	5,744,600	4,724,600	2,772,300	1,428,700	1,301,000
as percent of revenues .	18.3	19.8	16.1	11.2	14.9
Interest income . . .	162,200	143,100	68,200	44,200	14,100
Interest expense . . .	—	—	59,800	17,900	43,400
Income before income taxes	5,906,800	4,867,700	2,780,700	1,455,000	1,271,700
Provision for income taxes .	2,758,000	2,323,000	1,279,000	571,000	615,000
Net income	3,148,800	2,544,700	1,501,700	884,000	656,700
as percent of revenues .	10.0	10.7	8.7	6.9	7.5
Net income per share of common stock . . .	1.55	1.26	.80	.49	.38
Weighted average number of shares outstanding . .	2,035,959	2,027,124	1,869,724	1,801,294	1,747,887
Dividends declared per share:					
6% convertible income preferred stock . .	—	—	—	—	—
Common stock	.21	.08	.02	.47	1.00

Source: DRI Annual Report, 1978.

EXHIBIT 4

Data Resources, Inc. Second Quarter Results, 1979

	Six Months Ending June 30	
	1979	**1978**
Revenues	$18,639,500	$15,045,300
Operating expenses	15,197,800	12,206,900
Operating income	3,441,700	2,838,400
Income before income taxes . . .	3,563,300	2,893,100
Net income	1,897,300	1,506,100
Net income per share.	.93	.74
Average shares outstanding . . .	2,039,890	2,034,864

Source: Company records.

EXHIBIT 5

Data Resources, Inc.
Consolidated Balance Sheet

Assets	1978	1977
Current assets:		
Cash	$ 476,300	$ 293,200
Short-term investments.	2,500,000	1,100,000
Accounts receivable.	5,905,900	4,685,000
Unbilled contract costs	355,800	269,200
Prepaid expenses	201,100	164,300
Total current assets	9,439,100	6,511,700
Property and equipment, at cost:		
Computer equipment	7,064,200	3,777,100
Computer support and communications equipment .	2,840,000	1,834,900
Computer equipment in process of installation. . .	420,000	1,520,600
Land, building, and improvements	1,604,700	—
Office furniture and equipment	1,295,700	784,100
Leasehold improvements	456,500	659,000
	13,681,100	8,575,700
Less: Accumulated depreciation and amortization . .	3,435,200	1,917,700
	10,245,900	6,658,000
Prepaid federal and state income taxes	72,000	72,000
Total assets	$19,757,000	$13,241,700

Liabilities and Stockholders' Investment

	1978	1977
Current liabilities:		
Accounts payable:		
Trade	$ 570,200	$ 586,400
Computer equipment.	2,583,900	1,283,000
Dividends payable	107,200	39,800
Accrued federal and state income taxes	982,400	30,900
Other accrued expenses	546,400	412,900
Deferred subscription income	885,700	671,300
Deferred federal and state income taxes.	2,349,000	1,813,000
Total current liabilities.	$ 8,024,800	$ 4,837,300
Deferred taxes.	1,740,000	1,187,000
Total stockholders' investment	9,992,200	7,217,400
Total liabilities and stockholders' investment	$19,757,000	$13,241,700

Source: Company records.

EXHIBIT 6: Five-Year Growth Record

Revenue ($000)

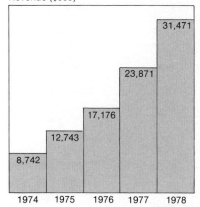

Net income ($000)

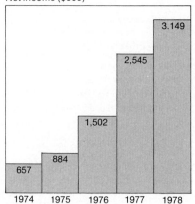

Net income per share ($)*

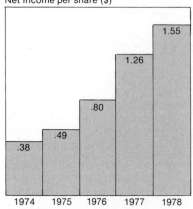

Stockholders' equity ($000)

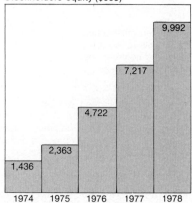

* Adjusted to reflect a 3-for-2 stock split declared February 14, 1979.
Source: DRI Annual Report, 1978.

EXHIBIT 7

Data Resources, Inc.
Breakdown of DRI Revenues
(in thousands of dollars)

Year Ended December 31,

	1971		1972		1973		1974		1975		1976		1977		1978	
Subscription fees	$ 723	38%	$1,068	35%	$1,704	33%	$2,975	34%	$ 4,587	36%	$ 6,209	36%	$ 8,487	35%	$10,709	34%
Associated data processing services	1,011	53	1,779	58	3,014	58	4,834	55	7,087	56	9,609	56	13,115	55%	17,452	55
Other services	159	9	229	7	459	9	933	11	1,069	8	1,358	8	2,269	10%	3,310	11
Total revenues	$1,893	100%	$3,076	100%	$5,177	100%	$8,742	100%	$12,743	100%	$17,176	100%	$23,871	100%	$31,471	100%

Note: DRI's standard commercial contract provided for an initial noncancellable term of 12 months; thereafter, the contract was cancellable by the customer upon 10 days' prior notice. Customers terminating DRI's services in the five years ended December 31, 1975 had accounted for 4%, 8%, 4%, 6%, and 4%, respectively, of total DRI revenues for the calendar year preceding cancellation.

EXHIBIT 7 (concluded)

Analysis of Subscribers

Year Ended December 31,

	1971	1972	1973	1974	1975	1976	1977	1978
Number of subscribers at* start of period	78	132	184	285	320	382	472	528
Number of subscribers at end of period	132	184	285	320	382	472	528	586
Average number of subscribers†	111	157	229	307	360	426	506	550
Average revenue per subscriber‡	$15,625	$18,134	$20,603	$25,436	$32,427	$37,132	$42,692	$51,203

* The term "subscribers" refers to customer organizations (other than those for whom DRI does only nonrecurring special projects) and not to the number of individual users of DRI's system within those organizations.
† As determined by an average of the number of subscribers at the end of each month within any given year.
‡ As determined by dividing total revenues (excluding revenue from nonrecurring special projects) by the average number of subscribers.
Source: Company records.

EXHIBIT 8
DRI Stock Price History*

On July 12, 1979, DRI's stock had closed at $31–1/2 bid, $33–1/2 asked. The stock price's past and recent history was as follows:

	Bid	Asked
11/76†	$7.04	$7.67
10/78	28	
3/79	18	
6/15/79	27	28
6/22/79	26–3/4	27–3/4
6/29/79	30–1/2	32–1/2
7/2/79‡	29	31
7/3/79	24–1/2	26–1/2
7/5/79	26	28
7/6/79	27–1/2	29–1/2
7/9/79	27	29
7/10/79	30	32
7/11/79	31–1/2	33–1/2
7/12/79	33	35

* Adjusted for 3-for-2 split in March 1979.
† Initial offering.
‡ Defection announced on 7/2/79.
Source: Company records.

EXHIBIT 9: "Economic Forecasting Company Loses Five of Its Senior Executives" (by Leonard Sloane, *The New York Times*, July 3, 1979)

Five senior executives resigned yesterday from Data Resources, Inc., the econometric forecasting company headed by Otto Eckstein, a Harvard professor. A spokesman for the company confirmed the resignations but would not say more.

Those who resigned were Stephen Browne, vice president; Alan Cody, vice president and head of the eastern region; William Kassner, vice president, financial marketing; Ferris Taylor, regional manager of the West Coast office, and Robert West, vice president, marketing.

Mr. Cody, speaking for the group, said, "We have no immediate comment other than to confirm that we resigned." He added tantalizingly: "We will in the near future, perhaps in several days, announce where we plan to go. We will also be able to tell you the whole story about Data Resources, and it will be very interesting."

Some of their former colleagues said the five were expected either to form their own forecasting company or to join a competitor.

Data Resources, which was founded a decade ago by Mr. Eckstein, has many of the nation's largest corporations as clients. They pay an average of $51,000 a year for monthly forecasts on inflation, gross national product, unemployment and other key factors in the economy. The company has developed one of the nation's most respected macroeconomic models, a data system designed to show the direction of the economy.

Apparently, few of the other Data Resources employees knew about the departure of their five associates until they left. As one economist said, "I saw Mr. Cody walking out the door this morning. If I had known he was leaving for good, I would have talked with him."

EXHIBIT 10: "Eckstein Returns, Sees No Problem in Resignations" (by Robert Lenzner, Globe Staff, *The Boston Globe,* July 6, 1979)

The main challenge to Data Resources, Inc., from the sudden departure this week of five marketing executives, is to "continue its information service to government and business without interruption," President Otto Eckstein said yesterday.

Eckstein interrupted a trip with several Harvard University professors in Japan to return to Boston, and spent the holiday meeting with his staff.

Eckstein was more philosophic than bitter about the departure of the five employees, who left Tuesday without notice. They did not have contracts, and "obviously had lots of legal advice, because they went through elaborate procedures to show they took nothing with them," Eckstein said in a telephone interview.

"We are talking to lawyers about their rights," he added.

Eckstein said he viewed the resignations as "the development of young, ambitious marketing-based people, who want to establish their own thing." He added: "I don't like losing bright young people. Some of them had just been given new responsibility.

The Globe could not locate any of the five. The resignations Tuesday included Alan Cody, vice president, head of the eastern region; Robert West, vice president, marketing; William Kassner, vice president, financial marketing; Ferris Taylor, regional manager of the West Coast office in San Francisco, and Stephen Browne.

The Harvard economist and former member of the Council of Economic Advisers still doesn't know if the five former officers will start an independent firm or join with an organization already in the economic forecasting business.

"DRI has 600 employees, a more enormous data base than anyone else, and we should remain untouchable," Eckstein said yesterday. "We have no real full-scale competition," he added.

Considering the event and his fast return from Japan, Eckstein said: "The competitive economy has some strains. But it's still the best system in the world."

No other forecasting firm publishes as many studies about the course of the economy, interest rates, and other financial data. Data Resources was started by Mitchell, Hutchins, the brokerage firm, now merged into Paine, Webber, to give investment managers a running commentary on the economy that was not available elsewhere.

One major competitor is Townsend-Greenspan & Co., an economic forecasting firm in New York that is run by Alan Greenspan, chairman of the Council of Economic Advisers in the Nixon administration.

PART III

POLICY FORMULATION AND ADMINISTRATION IN DIVERSIFIED FORMS

PART II

POLICY FORMULATION AND ADMINISTRATION IN DIVERSIFIED FORMS

CHAPTER 8

New Tasks and Complexities

In Part III we would like to direct your attention to the general management problems of the diversified firm. The preceding text and cases, with but a few exceptions, have been largely concerned with the strategic and organizational problems of essentially single-business firms, rather than the general management tasks in the much more complex environment of the corporate level of the multibusiness firm.

Although uniformly accepted measures of diversification do not exist, the evidence is clear that the extent of diversification in American industry is both high and increasing. Recent estimates place the proportion of the Fortune 500 that are still "single-business" companies (95 percent of their revenues from the largest business unit) at about 15 to 20 percent, and continuing to decline, as shown in Exhibit 8-1.

Since the Fortune 500 firms characteristically account for about two thirds of the industrial output, investment, and employment, and three quarters of the industrial profits in the American economy, the diversified firm is clearly the major and most important form of industrial organization in this country. The same trends are occurring in other industrialized economies as well, as may be seen from the results of research in a number of European countries as summarized in an article by Scott.[1]

An understanding of the general management task at the corporate level of the diversified firm is clearly helpful to those who aspire to, and the even fewer who will eventually reach, that position themselves. An understanding of these companies and the tasks their managers face is also important to the far greater number who will serve in specialist capacities in such organizations; act as management consultants to them; deal with them as suppliers, investment bankers, financial analysts, or loan officers; or even seek to influence the behavior of such large compa-

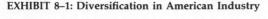

EXHIBIT 8-1: Diversification in American Industry

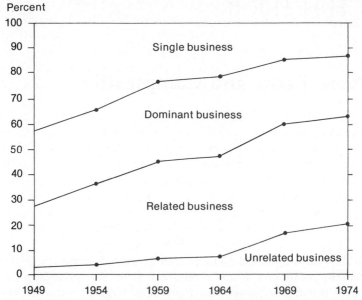

Source: Richard P. Rumelt. "Diversification Strategy and Profitability." Strategic Management Journal (1982), p. 361. Reprinted by permission of John Wiley & Sons. Ltd.

nies via public policy. And to understand the job, there is no substitute for placing yourself in the position of the involved general manager to as great an extent as you can.

This chapter will describe the additional complexities that strategies of diversification have brought to the general management task in such organizations. The next chapter will then show how the framework of analysis you have developed and applied to the general management problems of the single-business firm can be expanded and supplemented to be useful in dealing with general management problems at the corporate level in the diversified firm as well.

LEVELS OF GENERAL MANAGEMENT

Historically we have tended to think of the general manager as the executive to whom the functional managers report. The job evolved in this manner, and much of the literature, research, and teaching on management historically has made the implicit, if not explicit, assumption that general managers are responsible for a single business in an identifiable market and have the assistance of a number of functional managers in marketing, production, finance, and so on, to help them do what they cannot do all by themselves. Indeed, one of the essential tasks of general managers is often described as coordinating the activities of their functional managers in the achievement of the product/market strategy of the firm, an activity for which they are principally but not solely responsible. Most of the cases in this book have dealt with single-business organizations, or else essentially single-business issues in "the middle" of larger organizations.

This conception of the job of the general manager has quite properly had an extensive influence on both research and teaching in the field of General Management or Business Policy. In addition to focusing our attention on a particular set of tasks, it has also resulted in the tendency to think of general management as taking place at a single organizational level. It is a natural outgrowth of thinking of the job of the general manager in terms of the single business for which he or she does —or should—have considerable knowledge of both the industry, major competitors, his or her own company and people.

Such a conception of the general manager's position is inaccurate for virtually all of our larger corporations. The trend to diversification and therefore divisionalization and decentralization has created several new layers of general management above the traditional manager of the single business. General managers in diversified firms may have subordinates who are themselves general managers of businesses with hundreds of millions of dollars in sales volume.

There is a clear relationship between this increasing managerial complexity, brought on by strategies of product diversification, and the movement to the product division form of organization, brought on by the attempts to deal with this increasing complexity. The new organizational positions and levels created by the movement to product divisions present different challenges than the old positions and structure, which best served the needs of the single-business organization.

Scott [2] has developed a conceptual scheme and a set of terms which describe the evolution in a useful way. He characterizes the small, entrepreneurially managed firm without clear functional departments as a "Stage 1" firm, the traditional functional organization as a "Stage 2" firm, and the firm organized along product division lines as a "Stage 3" firm. Scott's projected scheme is a developmental model of organizations in that firms over time tend to move from one identifiable stage to another as they diversify. The model is useful in that it emphasizes that the differences in the management tasks and the increases in complexity are more associated with the "stage" and therefore product diversity of the firm than they are with its size at any given stage. Finally, it provides a framework for discussing how the characteristics of organization change from one stage to another.

What Chandler [3] described so well are the difficulties that companies encountered in trying to administer a number of different products by means of the single functional organization. The natural tendency as products were added was first to assign responsibility for functions such as R&D, production, and marketing in the new businesses to the well-established functional departments that already existed. The difficulties for managers in comprehending the overall business and coordinating the functional activities increased rapidly as new businesses were added. The eventual solution of having separate businesses report to a new and higher level of general management evolved from the traditional structure of functional units reporting to the top management of the company.

An intermediate step is often followed as companies add new activities to an existing predominantly single-business operation. Instead of moving directly to the product division form of organization, a more gradual transition can be made by retaining the functional organization for the historic bulk of the business, while having the new activities report as separate business units to the existing corporate management. For a variety of reasons such a structure generally evolves into the product division form of organization. The addition of more new activities would obviously push the organization in that direction, but even if no new activities were added, it leaves the president in the somewhat ambiguous position of having functional managers as well as business managers report to him.

As a result of this addition of new businesses and organizational levels, the task of the general manager of a division in the diversified company is in many ways more like that of his or her counterpart in the single-business independent company. In the typical large diversified company there will be one or more levels of management above the division manager, as well as varying amounts of staff personnel at the different levels. As one proceeds up through the levels to a group vice president (commonly responsible for a number of divisions) and to the president or chief executive officer of the entire organization, new tasks and complexities arise.

The demands placed on the top managers of diversified companies are not only complex but also different. As diversity increases, these demands would at some point seem to exceed the capacities of both people and organizations to deal with them effectively. Responsibility and power become increasingly removed from the reality of the business operations and the people running them. The connecting links between the two increasingly become quantitative reports, written summaries, conferences, staff assistants, and more abstract models of the various businesses and their environments. Economists and social scientists discuss the problem in terms of the managerial inefficiencies which unavoidably accompany increased size and diversity and which ultimately negate whatever other economic advantages growth via diversification might bring to the organization. Lammot Copeland, when he was president of Du Pont, stated his opinion in a more direct way: "Running a conglomerate is a job for management geniuses, not ordinary mortals such as we at Du Pont."

INCREASED STRATEGIC OPTIONS

The most dramatic new task which ordinary mortals must nevertheless master arises from the fact that both the present and potential strategic options of the firm have by definition been broadened considerably. The manager of the diversified firm (or the firm considering diversification) is no longer concerned with the attendant opportunity for involvement in the development of the strategy for that business and the allocation of resources to various functional areas and programs in support of that strategy. The manager must now make, or at least assume responsibility for, decisions as to the products and markets in which to compete, and not just how to compete in given product markets.

The fundamental notion of "our industry" obviously loses its meaning as the company diversifies. For the highly diversified company it becomes almost meaningless in the traditional product-market sense. The more a company diversifies, the less attention the corporate level can pay to any one industry, and the more they will be forced to rely on the judgments of others or on abstractions which try to capture the important characteristics of an industry for someone who is not intimately familiar with it. This may be useful in that it can result in a broader look across a number of industries than might otherwise be possible. An unavoidable shortcoming, however, is the loss of the ability to be as close to the trends and people and happenings of a specific industry as any good operating manager should be.

The new and critical strategic choice that faces the general manager at the corporate level then becomes the selection of products and markets in which to engage, and the development of a rationale for that particular choice as well as a means of making that choice effective. General managers of diversified firms can no longer be primarily concerned with the development of strategy for a single business, but neither can they ignore the strategic position and performance of their existing units as they consider the broader issues of the product-market portfolio. Therein lies a substantial dilemma to which we shall return later.

This enlarged strategic horizon for the firm complicates the job of the general manager in the search for and evaluation of new activities. Without some guidelines as to what businesses to consider, the manager would be faced with the prospect of investigating the whole world of business activity. The development of such guidelines which must be tailored to the needs and capabilities of the individual company, is not easy however. If the guidelines are to permit one to go beyond the present businesses, as is their purpose, they will require an understanding on the part of someone of the opportunities that exist for that company in new products and markets. One extensive discussion of the development of acquisition guidelines that go beyond financial criteria to emphasize strategic and managerial factors may be found in the book *Diversification Through Acquisition* by Salter and Weinhold.[4]

Questions of the divestment of existing operations—a necessary option to consider if one is to view the products and divisions of a company as elements of a portfolio—may not be as difficult analytically because of the greater familiarity of corporate management with any operation which has been a part of the company. The analytical benefits the manager possesses because of greater familiarity, however, are no doubt more than offset by the administrative difficulties of selling a segment of the company which may include many long-tenure workers and managers.

There is also the unavoidable need to consider the effects of the divestment of an ailing division on the balance sheet as well as the reported earnings of the company. Any sale of assets below the value of those assets as they are carried on the books of the corporation will result in a charge against current earnings unless a reserve account has been set up, which also entails a charge against earnings. Sometimes the stock price will increase on the announcement of such write-offs, as analysts see the prospect of improved earnings in the future. Divestment may also have an adverse effect on the stock, however, especially if the write-off was not anticipated by the financial community.

ALLOCATION OF RESOURCES TO OPERATIONS

Additions to and deletions from the portfolio of a corporation represent dramatic but (for most companies) periodic and perhaps infrequent major resource allocation decisions. The allocation of resources to the various subunits of the corporation is another new and continuing task, however, influenced by every budget, capital appropriation request, incentive plan, and profit goal. The question is no longer the allocation of resources among the functional departments of a single business, with some requirements of balance among the departments in order to achieve the overall goals of the business. Instead, the president now has the option of channeling financial resources from one division to another, in accordance with that executive's perception of the best opportunities for spending the corporation's limited resources. The old challenge of allocating resources to their most productive use is raised to the level of choosing among separate and often dissimilar businesses. In broad terms this can be described as substituting an internal capital market for the traditional external capital markets.

Allocating resources is a task the corporate level can in no way avoid, since even "objective" decision rules, profit goals, or capital hurdle rates will influence the pattern of cash flows into or out of divisions. From the corporate point of view, there is no reason to assume that the divisions with the highest cash flow or profits are also those which should have the most money to spend on their own futures. Neither is there any reason to believe that the establishment of uniform profit goals for all divisions, or the establishment of incentive plans which are based on divisions profits, will result in the best allocation of resources to divisions in view of the long-run opportunities facing the corporation. The nature of these problems will become much more evident to you as you study the Imperial Corporation case, which deals primarily with the appropriate rationale for making resource allocation decisions at the corporate level.

The objective is not just to evaluate each division's plans on its own merits but to evaluate each relative to the others. This poses very considerable analytical and administrative problems. A thorough review of a division is not something that can be done either quickly or frequently. If the goal is to evaluate the opportunities facing any one division in relation to the opportunities in all of the divisions, however, it is necessary to have the reviews close enough together so that comparisons can be made and remembered before the decisions are final. Analogies which compare the virtually instantaneous analysis of a large sample of common stocks to construct the most efficient investment portfolio, based as they are on the processing by computer of large amounts of readily available quantified data, are of little help for this substantial managerial task.

The more the corporate level seeks to actively influence the allocation of funds among the divisions, or what is even more difficult, to also influence the content of the strategy at the division level, the more someone must make trade-offs among unlike and little-known alternatives. It may be that no one of these problems is different in principle from the traditional single-business problems more familiar to all of us.

Adding greatly to the number of problems, however, as well as attempting to evaluate the alternatives in relation to each other, creates a formidable intellectual and administrative task, as is well demonstrated by the problems posed in the Imperial Corporation case. The process is complicated by the fact that the various levels and units in the organization have different interests, perspectives, and biases, and obtaining objective data—whether historical data or forecasts and judgments—is not easy. The past can be as difficult to ascertain as the future is uncertain.

In addition, just because a company adopts the product division form of organization, it does not follow that the strategy and operations of each division are necessarily independent of all the other divisions except for the allocation of financial resources. Depending on the nature of the businesses of the various divisions and the approach of the corporate level to the relationships among the divisions, there may be numerous opportunities or even requirements for the coordination of R&D, manufacturing, or marketing activities of divisions with each other. Some companies prefer to let the self-interests of the individual divisions govern such matters; others prefer to play a more active role. In either event, interrelationships complicate the strategic evaluations and the allocation of resources.

MANAGING MANAGERS

A third task that arises for the chief executive in the diversified corporation is the training, selection, evaluation, motivation, and reward of general managers (division presidents) rather than functional specialists (vice presidents of manufacturing, etc.).

The job of the general manager of the single business is more complex in many ways than that of his or her functional subordinates in that it involves more numerous as well as more complex variables than most functional responsibilities entail. In addition, the impact of many of the general manager's most important decisions can best be measured in terms of several years, or even decades; functional decisions and managers can usually be evaluated over a shorter period of time.

One can of course evaluate a division manager very largely on "the numbers," but this can incur many long-run risks and costs. If he is to do his job well, the general manager at the corporate or group level should be able to understand the performance and the potential of division managers of businesses different from each other and located physically away from headquarters. This is a more difficult job than a division president faces in evaluating the six or so functional managers that report directly to him, where they are all in the same industry, organization, and (probably) location.

CORPORATE LEVEL STRATEGY

The fourth new task is an outgrowth of all that has been mentioned: the need to conceptualize a strategy for the corporation as a whole which is something more than the sum of the division strategies. The president of the diversified company has the task of defining and communicating just what the "central theme," "core skill," or "concept of the corporation" is in operational terms that go beyond a listing of the product-market strategies of the individual divisions. Financial goals unaccompanied by some notion of how they can be achieved are not likely to be very useful. Neither are product definitions as broad as "products of value to people," a definition used for several years by one large diversified company.

An essential part of the concept of strategy in the diversified firm is the role played by the corporate level and the specific structure and processes they adopt in managing the overall organization. We tend to think of strategy as encompassing primarily product-market choices and strategies. You need only recall the case of Lincoln Electric Company to appreciate the impressive results that can come from combining an approach to organization and motivation which strongly supports the basic product-market strategy of the firm. The role and contribution of the corporate management in the implementation of strategy, an issue we shall return to in the next chapter, is an equally important element of the overall strategy for the diversified firm.

Developing a statement of strategy for the diversified firm that is a useful guide to action for those within the firm, and not just an attractive statement for outside consumption, is a most challenging intellectual exercise. This will become evident to you as you study the attempts of the management in the Voltamp Electrical Corporation and Imperial Corporation cases to deal with specific problems with major strategic implications for their divisions. You will also have a chance to identify and evaluate the concept of strategy for the diversified firm as you study several of the other cases in this book. In the next chapter we will suggest a framework of analysis that will assist you in this.

MERGER MOTIVES

Much has been written about the motives of management which have led to such a clear and pronounced trend away from concentration on a single line of business, with the resultant great increase in the task of managing the enterprise. The search for such motives has been heightened by the fact that neither traditional arguments favoring the economies of scale, financial theory, nor empirical financial research provide satisfactory explanations for the observed trends of diversification and acquisition activity.

Underlying motives for any action are always difficult to prove; it is only the resulting actions which are directly observable. It seems apparent, however, that the underlying reasons for diversification have been the desires of management for some combination of increased growth, profits, and stability for the firm. Chandler found that diversification occurred historically when companies accumulated resources in excess of what was needed to fully exploit their historic lines of business, and then applied these resources to new fields of endeavor in order to continue their growth. He noted that organizations, just as individuals, develop goals of their own, and in healthy organizations these goals include continued growth.

Paul Davies, then chairman of FMC Corporation, a large company which diversified aggressively in the late 1970s, stated his reasons very simply: "To make sure everything doesn't go to hell at once." Royal Little, the founder of Textron, frequently justified his wide-ranging diversification efforts in terms of the constant redeployment of assets from areas of lower return to those of higher return in order to earn the highest possible profits for the stockholders. Litton executives often justified their ambitious acquisition program in terms of the benefits to be gained from combining new technologies with existing businesses to achieve dramatic rather than incremental commercial advantages. Many firms have cited the advantages of size and increased stability of earnings as justification for acquisitions.

The trend to diversification can be thought of in even broader terms. It is another manifestation of the increasing professionalization of management which has occurred since World War II, at first in the United States, and now elsewhere. Just as the corporate form of management provides a means to efficiently extend the life cycle of the single business beyond the lifetime of the individual owners, the strategy of diversification represents a means to extend the life cycle of the corporation beyond the hazards and limitations of the single industry. The development of management skills which transcend specific industries has made diversification feasible.

Just because countless business executives have repeated these themes in one variation or another in explaining their actions does not mean that personal ambitions are not also involved, that the actions will always turn out to have been in the stockholder's interest, or that the manager's and the stockholder's interests are always congruent. As in all fields of human endeavor, motives are mixed and not always clear, and results are not always as hoped for. To consider the motives we have suggested as being important, however, is a useful starting point.

Growth and reasonable stability are often commented on by managers as being essential to the building of a successful organization. One can observe that nonbusiness organizations as well often seem to be guided by similar goals. It is not unheard of for government agencies and congressional staffs to aggressively seek larger and larger budgets and mandates. Even the highly respected March of Dimes charity, first started when Franklin Delano Roosevelt was president, changed its goals from the prevention and treatment of polio to research on and the treatment of congenital birth defects when the development of the Salk vaccine effectively put the original March of Dimes out of business.

It is useful to think of the great trend to diversification, then, as arising largely from the natural and widespread desire to make use of excess—or obtainable—resources in order to take advantage of an opportunity or solve a problem. Although this may describe the motives in broad terms, you will surely want to look carefully at each situation you encounter to discern just what that particular management was trying to accomplish, and how they went about it. That the motives that lead various managements to diversify may have much in common at the general level of a desire for some combination of increased stability, growth, and profits, in no way lessens the need to look carefully at the reasons for diversifying in the individual situation.

The key issue for the general manager is not whether certain generic diversification strategies seem to be associated with high or low returns on average, but whether certain actions are likely to present a solution to the problems, opportunities, and aspirations of that particular company. To increase the stability of earnings or to improve from below average to average in growth or profitability over time by means of the shifting of assets from declining businesses to areas of more promise may not meet the standards of some financial theorists for the ideal use of the shareholder's resources. It does represent a substantial accomplishment to most business executives, however, and an objective which explains much diversification activity.

SUMMARY

New problems always prompt the development of new tools, techniques, conceptual schemes, and organizational arrangements. So it is with diversification. Divisionalization and decentralization were the solutions to the managerial problems created by product diversity, which was in itself a response to other problems and opportunities. The creation of additional levels of general management above the product divisions resulted in new jobs at the corporate and group levels as well as the redefinition of the general manager's job at the division level. Many years ago the development of the teaching area of business policy represented a jump in the level of abstraction from that of the specialist and the functional manager to the generalist responsible for the enterprise as a whole. In some ways we now have similar adjustments to make in our thinking about these new levels of general management created in the diversified company.

It is unfortunate but unavoidable that as the territory becomes more complex and the problems to be dealt with more numerous, as happens when a company diversifies, the president is forced to view the territory from increasingly higher levels of abstraction. At the same time that we are proudly adding layers to the beehive and constructing all kinds of elaborate tunnels within it, the queen bee is becoming more and more removed from the workers and their daily forays for pollen. But it is at the operating level that continuing contributions must be made in the ongoing industrial concern. As an experienced division manager in one highly diversified company remarked:

We have got to keep in mind what makes the corporation go. It isn't head-quarters; I never have seen a headquarters that generated income by itself. The foundation for the whole operation is in the divisions; it is in the divisions that the money is spent and the money is earned. That is mainly where we have to worry about selling things for more than they cost to make. Headquarters, of course, has an important role to play, but it is too easy for them to get preoccupied with their own needs.[5]

In the next chapter we will turn to suggestions as to how you might build on the analytical and administrative skills you have already learned in order to deal with the general management problems of the diversified company.

CHAPTER 9

A Framework for Analysis

The purpose of this chapter is to describe an analytical approach to the corporate level general management problems of diversified companies that will be useful to you as you study the cases in the final section of the book. As has been explained in the preceding two chapters, diversified companies are the most important form of business institution in this country, and product diversity and the consequent development of divisional structures have created some significant additional complexities in the general manager's job at the corporate level.

In your role of manager, or advisor to the manager, your task is to *identify* the strategic position, problems, and opportunities of the company; to *evaluate* these in terms of the aspirations of the management and the seriousness of the problems or the attractiveness of the opportunities; and to *recommend* to the general manager a strategy, including the approach to organization, which will facilitate over time the achievement of a set of objectives.

STRATEGIC AND ORGANIZATIONAL ISSUES

You will find that the cases in this section will, to a greater degree than most of the other cases in this book, include considerable data on both the strategic and organizational issues facing each company. The approach to organization in diversified firms is even more intertwined with the corporate strategy than in the single-business firm. The cases developed for examining the general management problems of diversified firms have therefore not followed the more traditional approach of many business policy courses of considering problems of strategy formulation and implementation largely in a sequential order. This admittedly complicates your tasks of identification, evaluation, and recommendation—a complexity brought on by the nature of the problems with which you are dealing.

You will need to be concerned with the overall strategy and the approach to organization of the multibusiness firm over time, not just with specific acquisition decisions or other large resource allocations to a specific business. Such decisions are obviously important, and the larger the commitment in relation to the resources of the company, the more important they become. The single acquisition or major resource allocation decision is to the corporate strategy of the diversified company what the single capital expenditure project in a functional area is to the strategy of the single-business company. Both must be done well, but both must be part of a much larger mosaic.

A practice of making individual acquisition or investment decisions without a concept of how the resulting business units will be managed, how they will relate to each other, and how they will contribute to the overall goals of the corporation is not any more likely to be successful than a capital budgeting program in the single-business company that is unrelated to the strategy of the company. In matters of corporate strategy, it is often what cannot be reflected accurately in the numbers that becomes important, not just the careful analysis of the numbers. Individual acquisition or investment decisions often become the specific issues by which the overall strategies are tested for both their utility and relevance. They should be made in the context of a strategy and a plan for how they will be managed, however; they should not be the determinants of a strategy.

ANALYTICAL APPROACH

The most fruitful way for you to extend to diversified firms your understanding of the job of the general manager derived from your study of the single-business company is to build on the approach and models that you have already developed. To do so we will need to examine some of the ways in which the main elements of that policy model, as we may call it, need to be modified or thought of differently in order to make them useful for this purpose. We will also look briefly at the portfolio planning model, an analytical technique that has been developed to deal with the resource allocation problems of the diversified firm. Insights and questions generated through use of such a model can provide useful inputs to the broader analytical framework described in this book.

The basic policy model, most easily applied to the general management problems of the single-business firm, was developed in Parts I and II and portrayed graphically in Exhibit 9-1. In applying that basic approach, we will make use of the concepts already developed but will

EXHIBIT 9-1: Multibusiness Organization Chart

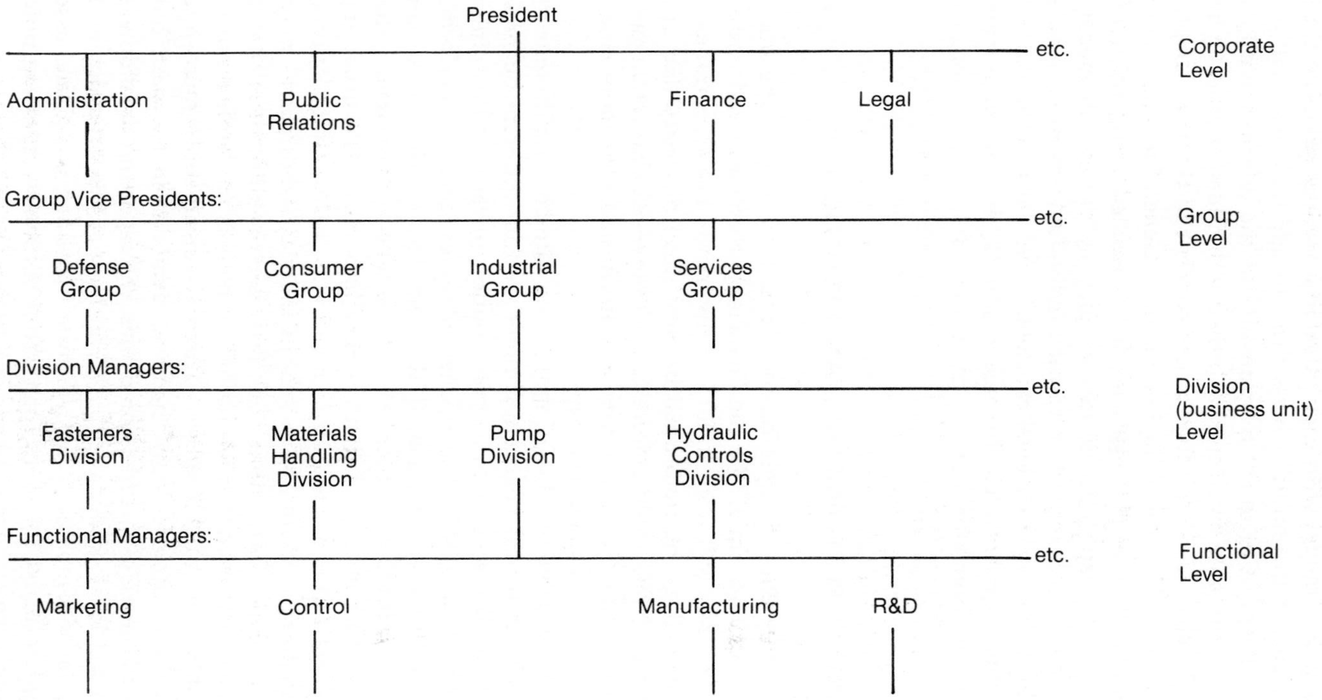

President

| Administration | Public Relations | Finance | Legal | etc. | Corporate Level |

Group Vice Presidents:

| Defense Group | Consumer Group | Industrial Group | Services Group | etc. | Group Level |

Division Managers:

| Fasteners Division | Materials Handling Division | Pump Division | Hydraulic Controls Division | etc. | Division (business unit) Level |

Functional Managers:

| Marketing | Control | Manufacturing | R&D | etc. | Functional Level |

emphasize the importance of the *fit* or *consistency* of the various elements of the policy model with each other in a manner suited to the problems and needs of the multibusiness firm. In addition, we shall extend this same concept of fit to the relationships of the divisions with each other, with the corporate level, and with their individual external environments.

We shall also introduce a new concept in the next chapter, that of the *corporate role* in diversified companies. General management tasks are performed at multiple levels in the diversified company, and the role that the corporate level decides to play in the overall management of the corporation is important to each individual company. It is the means by which the corporate level can seek as well as maintain a *fit* or pattern of relationships between the business units, the corporate level, and the external environment that contributes effectively to the corporate objectives.

FINANCIAL PERFORMANCE AND POSITION

Just as with a single-business company, one of the first elements in your analysis should be the financial performance and position of the company. You will want to look at the trend of sales, earnings, and margins, as well as the traditional balance sheet measures that apply to all companies. You should be forewarned, however, that intelligent financial analysis of the diversified company is considerably more complex than for the single-business company.

One reason for this is simply the number of different businesses in which the firm is engaged. If there are four different businesses, each important with respect to its contribution to sales and earnings and use of assets, you will feel compelled to investigate the performance and prospects for each of them. If the company consists of 40 such units, you cannot investigate them all, but neither can you ignore them all on the basis that no one of them is very important. The usual approach is to aggregate the businesses in some way for analytical purposes, but then important factors or details in individual businesses may be lost.

A second reason that your task is more difficult is that often the kind of information you would like to have is not broken out separately for public reporting purposes. There is considerably more information on business segments now than was available in the past, but for the larger and more diversified companies, the reporting breakdowns seldom get to the level of divisions. As you look at the breakdowns for some of our large companies, you will note that sales, profit, and asset figures are seldom listed for more than about six major reporting units, which may not even correspond to organizational units.

If you then concentrate your attention on overall corporate figures rather than product-market breakdowns, you will need to be careful that still a third difficulty does not lead you astray. For companies that have been engaged in acquisitions, it is often difficult to ascertain just what portion of the performance can be attributed to internal growth and what portion was simply due to the arithmetic of the acquisitions. Financial data and the prices paid for acquisitions are not always reported publicly, and even if they were, pulling this data together can be a major task. The sources of the sales and earnings growth therefore can be difficult to trace. In addition, both profit and loss and balance sheet items are affected by the accounting treatments used as well as by the terms of the acquisitions. None of this is intended to dissuade you from attempting a financial analysis of the diversified company as a part of your overall evaluation. If anything, it is more important to do this carefully with the diversified company, because the basic split of performance due to internal growth, as opposed to acquisition, and the health and prospects for major business segments are very useful to know. You will want to draw upon your knowledge of financial accounting and reporting practices, including how they have changed at times, to do the best job possible. The text by Weston and Brigham is but one of many that deal with some of the complexities of financial reporting in diversified companies.[1]

The difficulty of doing a careful job of financial analysis, however, explains in part why financial analysts do not like dealing with highly diversified companies. Obtaining and analyzing the information necessary to truly understand their operations is considerably more burdensome than for a single-business company.

We are specifically *not* viewing the management problems of the diversified company solely, or even primarily, from the standpoint of the investor or of financial theory. We hope that good theory and responsible practice would not be in significant conflict. The reason for continuing with the managerial viewpoint that was introduced at the beginning of the book is simply that it is the most useful one to adopt if you wish to understand and influence actual managerial behavior and develop your own managerial skills.

CONCEPT OF STRATEGY

Let us look at how we can apply the concept of strategy from the basic policy framework to the corporate level in the diversified company, as portrayed in Exhibit 9-1.

We will use the term *corporate level* to refer to those units and people above the level of the specific business units. Product groups—organizational units made up of several divisions—are in fact an intermediate level between the business and true corporate levels, but this distinction need not concern us at this point. The main distinction to be made is that product-market strategies exist at the business level, as do general managers and functional organizations responsible for a traditional business. The corporate level has responsibility for a portfolio of businesses, as well as the traditional financial, legal, and administrative tasks common to all corporations.

In Chapter 1 we suggested that a statement of strategy

> should convey both what a company is trying to achieve and how it hopes to achieve it. The plan for achievement should include attention to the important factors influencing that achievement, as mentioned, and it should specify what major steps are to be taken, in what rough time frame, by whom, what resources will be required, and how the resources will be obtained. It should communicate, in as tangible a way as possible, just how this particular company has chosen to compete in the marketplace.

This general prescription applies to the corporate level as well as the business level. The main adjustment that has to be made is in the level of detail concerning specific businesses with which the corporate level strategy concerns itself. For the single business, it is important for the manager to be familiar with, and then to understand strategy to deal with, specific products, markets, competitors, functional policies, and so on, as we emphasized in the earlier cases and text. At the corporate level in the diversified company, comparable detail is not possible. The corporation, however, still needs to have its own longer term objectives and plans for achieving them. These objectives and plans unavoidably depend upon and in turn influence the strategies of the individual divisions. A corporate level strategy that is no more than a compilation of the strategies of the various divisions, however, is neither useful nor interesting.

A key change is that instead of devoting attention to how the corporation will compete in its many specific businesses, more attention now must be paid to what the resources, skills, and the underlying strategic thinking are that led to that particular set of activities. Just as a business-level strategy can be thought of as an organizing concept that helps relate the activities of the functional departments to the opportunities in the external environment, the corporate strategy in the multibusiness corporation can be thought of as the organizing concept which both explains and guides the activities of the many separate businesses within the corporation. The corporate strategy in the diversified company is more concerned with where the corporation is going to spend its money, and why; business-level strategies deal with the plans for spending it. Neither can be arrived at independently of the other.

There is a view that the overall corporate strategy can be largely the sum of the product-market opportunities and strategic plans at that business unit level, and that therefore there is not much need for a broader, corporate-level strategy that should be communicated to the divisions and be of use to them in devising their plans. In this view, the role of the corporate level is largely to assign priorities for claims on the limited corporate resources, allocating money to the divisions according to their promise.

A more commonly held view, and one which we support, is that even the most diversified company needs a broader conception of itself than as an allocator of resources to the most promising opportunities that arise. If there is little effort to influence what arises or little attention paid to why that particular corporation should be better than anyone else in pursuing a particular market opportunity, superior performance is unlikely to result. A strategy for the overall corporation is just as important as a strategy for the individual division, and they need to be formulated and revised in relation to each other.[2]

If we must forsake most of the product-market components of strategy familiar at the business level when we move to the corporate level, what is changed, what remains, and what new is added?

The concept of strategy at the corporate level in the diversified company should address long-term growth and profitability goals, just as in the single-business company. The derivation of these may range from somewhat arbitrarily selected goals arrived at by a "top-down" process to a consolidation of the plans submitted by the existing units, adjusted downward through conservatism or nudged upward as a form of encouragement or pressure.

The overall financial objectives are not derived from conditions in the existing businesses as readily as in the single-business company, however, since the limitations of any single industry do not apply. Indeed, it is the desire to avoid the constraints arising from the conditions in a single industry that often causes companies to seek profits and growth elsewhere. It should be apparent, however, that just because the pharmaceutical industry has for decades ranked at or near the top of all industries in return on equity, or because Xerox or IBM or McDonald's have been highly profitable and growing companies, neither their financial achievements nor their lines of business are necessarily appropriate goals for any other company.

Corporate goals stated purely in financial terms do not, it should be noted, provide much operational guidance for the corporation with regard to the lines of business to engage in, nor for the divisions with regard to how to compete in the businesses they are already in. Such goals have more of an effect on the degree of risk that managers feel compelled to undertake in both product decisions and financing decisions. They also affect the pressure felt within the organization to achieve current goals, which may influence behavior in many ways, some of them to the detriment of the long-term health and reputation of the company.

The degree of risk that a company management is willing to undertake is an element of its strategy and becomes evident in the actions of the company. Historically companies tended to diversify when they had an excess of resources over what they felt they could profitably apply to their traditional businesses, even though those base businesses might not have been in trouble. When faced with trouble and declining prospects in the base business, companies have often sought to reduce their overall risk by diversifying, with whatever resources they could spare, into areas that seemed more attractive.

In the 1960s, however, a new category of risk taking appeared, in which companies were very aggressive in obtaining resources for expansion and were willing to subject themselves to both highly leveraged capital structures as well as unknown and possibly risky new businesses in their pursuit of growth. The Leisure Group, which you will encounter later, is an example of highly ambitious but risky financial as well as operating strategies, with consequent high risk to investors and managers alike. Textron, a large and well-known conglomerate, was quite highly leveraged in its early days but has for decades maintained a conservative ratio of debt to capitalization.

The point is not that one approach or the other is always the preferred one but that management's choice of the level of financial and operating risk that is acceptable—or, what is more important, the combination of the two—is an essential factor influencing other aspects of both corporate-and business-level strategies. You need to be sensitive to what the preferences are for any given company, and most of all, to ensure that the risks actually taken do not unknowingly exceed the comfort level of either management or stockholders.

A difficult component of the concept of strategy at the corporate level of the diversified company is that which addresses the kinds of businesses the company will engage in, and why. The allocation of funds to competing businesses presently within the corporation is an aspect of this problem, but it is much more amenable to analysis by means of various portfolio planning models that have been developed (and will be discussed later) than is the rationale for the product range of the company as a whole.

The range of product diversification can be viewed primarily in financial terms such as profitability, growth, cash flow patterns, degree of risk in the operations of the business, and so on. These measures can be applied to existing as well as potential businesses. In the case of possible acquisitions, the immediate impact of the acquisition on the earnings, earnings per share, and balance sheet of the acquirer are also of interest to managers and investors.

Although financial measures invariably need to be considered, they do not themselves constitute a sufficient basis for deciding upon the degree and type of diversification that should be pursued. If only financial criteria are applied, there would be little difference between the range of products within the company and the variety of stocks in a nonspecialized common stock mutual fund. Given such a variety of businesses, it is unlikely that the corporate level would be able to make any significant contributions to the operations of the various businesses. Such a corporation could more accurately be thought of as a financial holding company than an operating company.

Related versus Unrelated Diversification

The way in which a particular acquisition or a diversification strategy can be justified in terms of R&D, manufacturing, marketing, or management skills that are related or complementary is important to examine. One type of relatedness can be viewed as what the corporation can contribute because of a general management ability that will be useful as an addition to, not a substitute for, the management of certain kinds of product divisions. Perhaps more frequently, relatedness is defined in terms of useful and more tangible skills in functional areas, an excess of physical resources, or technology that can be applied to an acquisition. In any event, the degree of relatedness of both present and prospective businesses is an element of the corporate strategy that you will want to examine.

In considering diversification alternatives, it is natural to look first at those areas most closely related to the existing businesses. Indeed, management would be remiss not to do so, since there is every reason to believe that familiarity is an advantage in evaluating and managing new opportunities and that it is easier to apply existing resources and skills to new opportunities if they are related in some manner. In addition, Rumelt's findings indicate that firms that engage in related diversification tend to have better performance than others, and those that engage in "passive-unrelated" have the worst records.[3]

It does not follow that a strategy of unrelated diversification is preferable, however. Part of the difficulty stems from the problems of classification, especially for an outside observer. What is *related* in a meaningful sense, and what is not? The concept is surely more than a pair of boxes, one marked *related* and one marked *unrelated*; it is more like a continuum or a spectrum. In addition, new businesses can be related in some aspects— a common manufacturing process, for example, such as familiarity with precision plastic injection molding techniques—and totally unrelated in other important aspects of the business such as product design or marketing. One has to judge both the degree of relatedness and the overall importance of the areas in which relatedness exists.

Apart from the difficulties of classification, the problem of assuming a cause-and-effect relationship from a correlation study also exists. The profitability of expansion into any field depends in part on the skills and resources of both the parent and the acquisition and the extent to which each can contribute to the other. It also depends to a significant extent on the profitability of the field entered. If the base industry is profitable, related fields may also be, as Rumelt demonstrated in his later research.[4] This tends to be true especially for companies with a significant

core technology which provides the basis for related diversification, although other types of barriers to entry may have similar effects.

One needs to look to the base industry and company to determine
whether the admitted risks of moving to less-familiar territories outweigh
the disadvantages of remaining close to the original business, continuing
to apply skills and resources to related and familiar areas that may unfortunately have many of the very problems from which the company is trying
to escape. The arguments favoring a strategy of related diversification
are surely less applicable to a textile company than to companies like
Xerox or Polaroid, both of which have very substantial technical skills
and (historically) extremely successful core businesses.

In spite of the difficulties we have with both classification and cause-
and-effect as far as the related-unrelated dimension is concerned, it is
important to think about present as well as future activities in terms of
how they are, or can be, related to each other. The main benefits of
doing so lie in three areas:

1.   The degree of relatedness is some evidence of how good the
judgment and knowledge of the parent are likely to be with regard to
the requirements for success in the new industry, as well as its ability
to evaluate the positions and potential of a prospective acquisition. Indeed,
the most important aspect of relatedness may be whether the parent
has a strategic understanding of the needs of the new business which
is insightful enough to enable it to see opportunities to improve the strategy or operations that others may have overlooked, and not primarily
whether one activity is related to another in a functional or market or
technological sense. A corporate management that is thoroughly familiar
with consumer packaged goods, for example, may have much to contribute
to a venture in that field, even though there are no specific activities in
any of the existing divisions that would be of value or could supply
resources to the new company. Similarly, basic technical skills and experience in dealing with the problems of small, high technology companies
may represent a highly useful resource, even though there are no specific
technical skills or facilities or patents that are directly applicable.

2.   The more related the functional aspects of the possible diversification effort are, the more likely it is that the functional skills and resources
of the parent will be of value to the acquisition. If one activity is to
make a contribution to the other, the skills or resources have to be both
applicable and available.

3.   The more related the various businesses of the corporation are,
the easier it is likely to be for the corporate level to understand the
basic characteristics of each of their businesses. In addition, it will simplify
the task of developing an appropriate role for the corporate level with
respect to the management of these businesses, an issue which we shall
discuss later.

It is important to look beyond the popular concept of synergy to investigate just what the advantages will be that stem from relatedness. Perhaps the most important thing is to avoid the illusion of relatedness, which has been used to justify almost any kind of diversification. An extreme but perhaps apocryphal example is that of the manufacturer of fork lift trucks that decided its real business and basic skill was in providing vertical transportation and therefore diversified into escalators, with disastrous results.

Although the related-unrelated dimension does not provide us with an explicit guideline for selecting the best diversification strategy in the individual situation, it is a very useful way to begin investigating alternatives. We all find it more comfortable, although perhaps less interesting, to remain with familiar activities. We have to remember that the very reason companies diversify, however, is that the present activities no longer meet the longer term objectives. The more closely related the new activities are to the existing operations, the greater the chance that they will evidence similar problems. Carried to its logical extreme, the most "related" diversification is no diversification at all.

STRATEGY FORMULATION AND CORPORATE RESOURCES

In Chapter 4 we discussed the need to base a company's strategy on its distinctive strengths as well its opportunities and aspirations. Successful strategies build upon the strengths and avoid the weaknesses of the specific company. The need to explicitly consider just what the resources of the company are and what the distinctive strengths are, or can be, is just as important when considering corporate-level strategies as business-level strategies.

The problem at the corporate level is more complex because the distinctive strengths, just as the strategy, generally have to be stated at a higher level of abstraction to be useful. It may be that a company wishes to define its basic competitive advantage in terms of a distinctive competence in supplying and selling mass-produced consumer packaged goods, for example, or in working with high technology firms, or specific kinds of technologies, and to develop and transmit these skills within the corporation in a way that results in a competitive advantage for the corporation.

Financial Resources and Skills

One must not, of course, minimize the importance of financial resources as an important strength. They are the most readily applied resource of all. Such resources can come from many sources in a diversified company: a predictable cash flow in excess of current division needs, additional borrowing capacity, cash that could be freed up by better asset management or the sale of some businesses, and so on.

An important (but temporary) financial resource in the development of some of the conglomerates in the 1960s was a reception in the capital markets that bestowed upon them a price/earnings ratio high enough to make the issuance of stock for cash or for other companies unusually attractive. The Leisure Group is an example of a company that was able to obtain the financial resources necessary to support their rapid growth in part because of a very favorable market reaction to their strategy and performance. The integrated petroleum industry in the late 1970s and early 1980s is a prime example of an industry in which predictably large cash flows could provide resources for diversification on a scale far beyond that available to other industries and companies. The steel industry would be an example of an industry suffering not from a cash surplus, but a cash shortage; just as existing or obtainable resources are an advantage, a shortage is a clear liability.

As you study the cases in the book as well as think about the diversification opportunities of other companies and industries, it is essential to examine the financial resources available to support diversification strategy. A strategy of diversification which does not take into account the amount and source of the financial resources required is just as deficient as a strategy for a single business which identifies great opportunity but neglects to put a price tag on the effort and to identify the source of the funds.

Allocating Financial Resources

The diversified corporation cannot avoid playing a continuing role in the allocation of funds within the existing businesses, and this can constitute a significant competitive advantage if done well. Whether allocations of capital or, more broadly, cash flow is based on judgment, formula, or a combination of the two, the procedure chosen will have an effect on current profits as well as which business units receive resources for future growth and which units supply these resources.

Encouraging and rewarding high current profits from all may encourage divisions which have good opportunity to invest in R&D or gain-share market strategies to neglect such long-run development in favor of good current returns. Formulas or approaches which in effect permit each division to spend whatever cash flow they develop may well result in more capital investment than is warranted from a corporate viewpoint in declining areas and less than is warranted in areas of higher promise.

It is only natural for divisions and companies to want to spend themselves whatever resources they develop, but there is no reason to believe all areas are, from the corporate viewpoint, equally worthy of support. Neither is there any reason to believe that any single factor such as current profits or profitability, market size or growth, capital project hurdle rates, or level of technology will result in an "optimum" strategic allocation. No matter what the formula chosen, some unintended adverse consequences are likely to ensue, as will become evident to you in the Imperial Corporation case.

This opportunity to influence the allocation of funds to the divisions by means of an internal capital market, by-passing the traditional private capital markets and avoiding the loss of both taxes and transaction costs, is a significant potential advantage for the diversified company. The ability to do this well is an important skill and one which companies have spent much time and effort trying to improve. The more diverse the company and the more numerous the units, the more difficult the task becomes, and the more necessary it becomes to develop a more abstract framework or method of analysis to make up for the lack of first-hand knowledge of the divisions and industries themselves. An analytical method to deal with problems of this kind which has become popular in the last decade or so is the portfolio planning model, which we will discuss in more detail later in the chapter.

Undervalued Situations

It is tempting to believe that the corporate level can develop a distinctive competence at finding and buying undervalued situations, or companies that are available at a price that makes them attractive candidates without changes in their operations. It is the modern-day version of the "buy low and sell high" recipe for success in the stock market, with the additional handicap that premiums of from 25 percent to 100 percent over the market price will almost surely have to be offered to gain control and ultimately ownership.

The results of numerous empirical studies on investment results should make you careful about believing too strongly in the ability of management to develop and exploit this skill on a consistent basis over a period of time, however. There is very little evidence that *any* particular investment strategy (other than buying and holding a diversified portfolio) is superior, after adjustment for risk, to any other for the passive investor buying securities on the public market.[5] There is no reason to believe companies should be better at this than individuals or financial institutions. Just as with investing in the stock market, there are many examples of specific acquisitions which did, in fact, turn out to be undervalued at the time. Still, these examples should not obscure the low probability that such a skill can provide a competitive advantage over time for an operating company.

General Management Skills

A most important potential advantage of the diversified company, claimed by many but difficult to verify, is the ability of the corporate level to provide both strategic and operational guidance to disparate business units because of the general management abilities of the group and corporate officers and staff, as well as the ability to design the appropriate organizational structure and processes so that these skills may be brought to bear in the individual situation. You will find explicit statements as well as unstated assumptions concerning the impact of these general management skills on the operations of the acquired businesses in all of the cases in Part III, as well as in the public statements of executives of diversified companies.

The contribution made by such general management skills has been much debated in the investigations of diversified companies, with little evidence developed concerning its value that is convincing to those who hold opposing views. Most of us would likely agree that there are a number of general management skills that can usefully be applied without deep knowledge on the manager's part of the specific business, as is evidenced by the success with which some managers are able to oversee or even move into new businesses. At a more personal level, are you not now investing your own time and money in learning management skills that transcend industry boundaries in the hopes that they can be usefully applied to whatever industry in which you end up working?

There are also strong arguments that a knowledgeable and experienced group executive who will take the time to learn a reasonable amount about his specific divisions can be more useful, with regard to both advice and direction, than the typical board of directors of the independent company. The group vice president has the advantage of broad experience, has access to funds from the corporate office, and has considerably more power to enforce more planning, reward good performance, and penalize poor performance than most outside directors or any outside consultant. As you study the cases in this last section, you should reflect upon just what the contributions—and limits to the contributions—of the group vice president or the corporate office can be to the operations of the division.

Strategic and Operational Improvements

Quite apart from the ability to find undervalued companies in the marketplace, when viewed as passive investments, is the ability to find companies which will be worth more as a result of whatever changes or additions the acquiring company seeks to accomplish. This ability is largely the consequence of the general management skills discussed above. This is the true creation of value and not just the recognition of undervalued situations. The changes to be made can be of considerable variety—new strategies not contemplated, or at least not likely to be pursued, by the present owners or other potential acquirers; the pooling of resources or skills already existing within the corporation with the acquired company; the more effective management of existing operations; and so on. The flow need not be all one way; acquisitions are often sought for what they can do for the acquiring corporation and not just for what the acquiring corporation can do to improve the operations of the acquisition.

Summary of Resources and Skills

The purpose of this discussion of company resources and possible distinctive skills has not been to develop an exhaustive listing of these items but rather to suggest ways in which the basic concept of corporate resources as they influence the selection of a strategy needs to be modified in its application to the corporate level of the diversified company. You will need to think carefully about each individual situation that you encounter to determine what the resources are that might be applied to new opportunities and what the distinctive strengths are that enable the company to exploit most fully its present opportunities. The task is not an easy one, and even highly successful companies make mistakes.

Heublein, for example, a very successful marketer of distilled spirits (especially Smirnoff vodka), entered the beer business and the California wine business by acquisition largely because they believed their marketing skills, which had formed the basis for their success in a closely related business, would be of great help to them in their new businesses. The acquisition of United Vintners was very successful for a long period of time; the acquisition of Hamm's Brewery was a disaster from the beginning. Heublein eventually sold Hamm's at a substantial loss after a decade of unsuccessful attempts to apply their skills at marketing liquor and wine to the marketing of beer.

The challenge for the corporate level is to develop the distinctive strengths and acquire the resources needed to enable it to capitalize on the opportunities in the environment, not just uncover such opportunities or note that others have been able to exploit them successfully. If all a steel company management had to do was buy a pharmaceutical company in order to obtain the higher returns and growth of that industry for their own shareholders, there would not for long be either low-margin steel companies or high-margin pharmaceutical companies.

In the diversified company, just as in the single-business company, successful results come not just from finding opportunity or developing competencies but from the fit which follows the creative and successful matching of the two. Such matching can only stem from a concept of what the distinctive resources or skills are of that particular company that will enable it to take advantage of specific existing opportunities.

The point is not that certain definitions are inherently better than others, but rather that it is important to think through very carefully just what the rationale will be for choosing activities in which to engage and for managing those activities most effectively. In the absence of guidelines based on product, market, or technology characteristics, selection is likely to stem largely from financial criteria, which can result in a very strange collection of businesses indeed. Such financial guidelines and stock market opportunities can combine to create companies no industrial logic can justify.

MANAGEMENT VALUES AND CORPORATE RESPONSIBILITY

The concepts of management values and corporate responsibility as we developed them in the earlier sections need little further elaboration or modification here. They are just as important in the diversified corporation as in the single-business corporation. With regard to management values, the major complicating factor is that more levels of management, with different perspectives and personal interests, have been added. As far as corporate responsibility is concerned, several new issues arise because of the nature of the diversified corporation.

One new issue is the responsibility the corporation has to local employees and communities. Whether or not divisions or multiunit companies are in fact better or worse citizens of their local communities than local companies is at present a matter of debate. Also important from a public policy point of view is whether society is better served by a shutdown or phasing out of the less promising operations in the portfolio of the parent's activities, as must sometimes happen, as opposed to letting those businesses continue to struggle along with marginal results until bankruptcy overtakes them.

It is clear, however, that local communities have often been against the acquisition of local businesses by distant conglomerates, and a number of states have enacted antitakeover laws designed to make such acquisitions much more difficult. As a result of recent court cases, it appears that federal laws will override state laws restricting takeovers, and this avenue of local defense is likely to be ineffective.

At a broader level, the concentration of ownership of widespread and often seemingly disparate operating units that formerly were independent business units, and perhaps could again be independent, has concerned many observers. Large and distant corporations are understandably viewed as more remote from local needs and control as well as more powerful politically on the national level because of their size and geographic dispersion. This point is raised periodically in congressional hearings and has also been argued very strongly with regard to ITT on a worldwide basis, for example, in a book by Sampson.[6] The lack of clear empirical data as yet that such concentration results in improved economic performance for investors or for society eliminates one important counter-argument to those who would restrict or break up such concentrations of power for social and political reasons.

PORTFOLIO PLANNING MODELS

As we mentioned earlier, one of the significant advantages a diversi-fied company has relative to the single-business company is the greater variety of opportunities it has to invest its financial resources. The diversi-fied company can contribute to the cash needs of some divisions with the resources obtained from other divisions, whereas the single-business company must obtain any long-term net cash inflow that its operations require by acquiring the funds—equity or debt—on whatever terms the capital markets will provide them. The diversified company has internal-ized the traditional capital market function with regard to the allocation of funds among its own businesses, and the invisible hand of the market becomes the visible hand of the corporate management.

The objective of earning a maximum return on the resources avail-able or on the effort expended is neither new nor revolutionary; credit for the first attempts to do so must go to our ancestors who sought out more fertile gamelands or gaming areas. Neither is the idea of using the resources of an older and established business to support the expansion of a more promising newer one within the same corporation. The accounts of early diversification attempts describe clearly the pattern of applying resources earned in existing businesses to more promising areas elsewhere.

Several developments have occurred in the last 15 years or so which provide considerable assistance to the manager in thinking about the nature of the resource allocation problem at the corporate level as well as in providing guidelines for the actual allocations themselves. These developments consist of a basic conceptual scheme, a simple language system, and the collection of empirical data that can lend quantitative support to efforts to identify preferred mixes of business within the prod-uct portfolio and to the allocation of resources to those businesses on a continuing basis.

The basic concept with which you should be familiar is the portfolio planning model, or PPM, as it has come to be called. Learning to think about the resource allocation problem in this manner is far more important than mastering the details of its application in specific situations, which requires considerable experience as well as more detailed market and cost information than companies themselves normally possess at the time they initiate such planning efforts.

Portfolio planning models combine measures of industry attractive-ness with measures of a division's position in that industry to provide help to the manager who needs to make a judgment concerning the attractiveness of investment in that division relative to other divisions. The widest popularization of this approach has been by the Boston Consulting Group. Their 2x2 matrix, as well as the logic supporting it and the implications of the model, has been explained extensively in their own literature and elsewhere.[7] The essential elements of their matrix, and the terms they have applied to the various quadrants, are shown in Exhibit 9-2.

EXHIBIT 9–2: Market Share/Market Growth Matrix

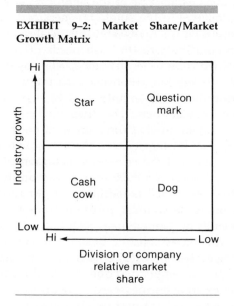

The matrix seeks to establish measures of relative industry attractiveness along the left-hand vertical scale and of the division's competitive position within the industry along the horizontal scale. In this simple format, the principal determinant of industry attractiveness is assumed to be the rate of growth of the industry. For the company position, the relative market share of the particular company or division is considered the single most important variable. The objective is to portray businesses in terms of their potential for generating cash flow; no substantive information about the nature of the industry influences or appears on the matrix.

With regard to the level of abstraction, then, this particular matrix is just as much removed from the details of the individual business as is the experience curve and the PIMS study of determinants of market profitability discussed in Chapter 3. They all seek to build models and derive hypotheses concerning the profit potential of businesses and business strategies that can apply to any business, and that therefore can be used to compare businesses otherwise quite dissimilar. The advantages of being able to do so are great, especially when many diverse businesses must be considered. The hazards of making judgments on the basis of such abstract data should also be apparent.

McKinsey & Company and Arthur D. Little, Inc., both leading management consultants, employ similar graphic models to assist the manager in conceptualizing and analyzing problems. Their models are more detailed and qualitative in that they include more factors than just market growth and market share in arriving at judgments about industry attractiveness and company competence to succeed in that industry. In this respect, the models are more like the policy model to which you were exposed in the earlier parts of this book.

A term that has come into use to describe groupings of businesses that are useful for portfolio planning purposes is *strategic business units* or SBUs.[8] Companies that have seriously pursued portfolio planning methods have first had to study carefully their number of SBUs and collect market and cost data to fit these new definitions, as is described in some detail in the Imperial Corporation case. Interestingly enough, this number seems to seldom exceed 30, even in large and diverse companies with a far greater number of divisions and profit centers. It appears that if the number of units to be considered at the top level becomes too large, the task once again becomes unmanageable, even with the assistance of these more abstract analytical approaches.

There are many elaborations that are made in the models, and their representation in graphic form is limited only by the ingenuity and budget of the graphic arts department. One refinement is to portray the various divisions of the company on the chart in terms of circles, with the area of the circles representing the relative size of the units in terms of sales or profits or assets. Another is to construct such a chart for several points in time, so that trends in the development of businesses can be observed. To assist in assessing what countermoves important competitors are likely to make, charts can be prepared on competitors in order to assess what their options and likely responses will be.

The usefulness of this type of matrix is based on the assumption that specific patterns of cash flows are associated with each of the various quadrants, and that the primary measure of the attractiveness of a business is the pattern of cash flows over time. For example, to maintain a dominant position in a growing industry (a *star*) will probably require a high cash input to support the rapid growth. As the growth slows, the high profits presumed to accompany high market share should result in a high positive cash flow (a *cash cow*) while still maintaining a strong market position. Companies with a small market share in slowly growing industries are considered to be *cash traps* or *dogs*, where the potential is unlikely to merit the investment required. The *question marks* are those that are uncertain, either because of the industry or the company position or both. They may require much cash to bring them into the star category; they may also end up in the dog category if events do not turn out well.

The objective is to build a portfolio which is balanced in the sense that there are sufficient cash cows to provide the cash flow to support the question marks and possibly the stars, if they need it, and to ensure the continued emergence of stars as companies and industries decline and become less attractive for all participants over time.

A very substantial management problem that the portfolio planning models do not address, and which the facile terminology does little to ease, is that of the administrative difficulties of implementing whatever allocation decisions are made. It is all well and good to decide as a result of portfolio analysis that a given division is a dog, but how would you like to be the division manager of an operation so categorized? How would you explain the corporation's view of your division to your management team, understandably concerned with their own careers? It is for reasons such as this that companies are often not as explicit in the communication of their decisions, and the reasons for them, as the analytical framework would permit them to be. Even without labels or reasons, the resulting allocations can cause unproductive anxiety and opposition which require both skill and tact to overcome. Publicly identifying winners and losers has high costs, and companies look for ways to make the judgments and resulting allocations less threatening to everyone.

Another important assumption implicit in such models is that the businesses plotted can be considered as separate units for the purposes of such analysis. In practice, this makes the consideration of interdependencies among divisions, if there are any, difficult to handle. It may also require the specification of business units for strategic planning purposes that differ from present organizational structure and reporting relationships and which therefore also are likely to be different than established patterns of accounting data and spending responsibility.

It should be apparent that the same cautions and reservations that apply to the application of experience curve data and PIMS analyses for the individual business apply to the application of a product portfolio approach built on these concepts. Unforeseen and uncontrollable external changes or disruptions can have a major strategic impact. In addition, the experience curve in particular is most relevant in cases where manufacturing costs are important and products are well defined. Seemingly minor changes in product characteristics or in marketing policies can sometimes counter the overall trend of the industry as well as the history of that specific product. A very helpful discussion of the use, evolution, and impact of portfolio planning models in the large diversified company, based on detailed clinical research as well as survey data from a sample of several hundred companies drawn from the Fortune 500, is contained in an article by Haspeslagh.[9]

Portfolio planning models, then, represent a way to estimate what the cash flows into or out of divisions could be under various assumptions. A portfolio model is therefore also useful in helping to identify the cash flow characteristics of businesses that possibly should be added to the product portfolio. This does not differ conceptually from the objective of basic strategic planning for the single-business company, which is also to provide a means for estimating potential cash flows under a variety of possible strategies. The advantage of the portfolio model for the diversified company is that it facilitates the comparison of many alternatives and highlights the advantages of moving resources from one activity to another. It also makes clearer the need to have a portfolio in which there are adequate sources to supply the essential needs. For the corporation as a whole, simple arithmetic indicates that cash needs which cannot be met from the divisions themselves can only come from corporate resources or external capital markets.

The data necessary to do a thorough job of applying a portfolio planning model to the problems of a specific company in cases for classroom use exist in only a few specialized cases designed for that purpose. As you study the diversified companies in this book, however, you should find it useful to keep in mind the concepts underlying the portfolio planning model, using whatever data are available to you and making assumptions where necessary. Questions of relative promise, cash resources, and cash needs are important elements for all of those companies. The Leisure Group, Inc., is perhaps the best example of demands exceeding resources and of the catastrophic consequences that can follow.

CHAPTER 10

The Corporate Role in Implementation

In this final chapter dealing with the diversified company we will address the important issue of the corporate role in both the formulation and the implementation of strategy.

For the diversified company, a major element of the corporate strategy is what the role of the corporate office will be in contributing to the operations of the divisions and to the overall performance of the corporation. It affects the formulation of strategy at the corporate and division levels as well as the organization structure and processes by which the strategies—corporate and divisional—are implemented. Even more so than in the single-business company, corporate strategy and the approach to the implementation of that strategy via organization structure and management processes are highly interdependent, and are influenced by the role that the corporate office chooses to define for itself.

The job of the general manager in the single-business organization was created when the burden of managing each of the functional activities, in addition to performing the necessary corporate level tasks, became too much for one person. In a similar manner, the corporate role and positions in diversified companies evolved in response to the added managerial complexities brought on by strategies of product diversification. As you study cases such as BCI Ltd., The Leisure Group, Inc., the CML Group, Inc., and Imperial Corporation, you will find that the issue of what role the corporate or group levels should play in division matters is one of continuing concern. The problems are not just what is the best solution to issues of division investments or strategy or pricing or interdivisional cooperation, but who decides what the best solution is, using what criteria, and how such problems should be decided on a continuing basis.

The degree of involvement of the corporate level in the affairs of the divisions can be thought of in terms of a spectrum, with "laissez-faire" or "hands-off" at one end and "managed" at the other as shown in Exhibit 10-1.

EXHIBIT 10–1: Role of Corporate Staff

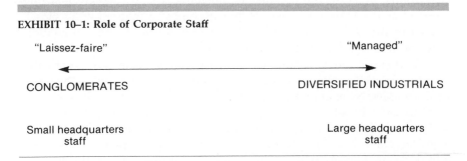

"Laissez-faire"   "Managed"

CONGLOMERATES   DIVERSIFIED INDUSTRIALS

Small headquarters   Large headquarters
staff   staff

Companies commonly referred to as conglomerates tend to be at the left end of this spectrum. Such companies tend to have diversified primarily by acquisition, often of seemingly unrelated activities, and usually within the past 20 years or so. Textron and Gulf & Western are two well-known examples of this category. Companies that tend to fall into the right-hand category of "managed" are more likely to be older industrial companies whose acquisitions took place long ago, if at all, and which have diversified primarily through building upon existing and often technically based skills into related areas. General Electric and Westinghouse are excellent examples of this category of "diversified industrials."

The important point is not that companies can be distinguished from each other in terms of the way in which they became diversified, but that different ways of managing the divisions and the approach to tasks and staffing at the corporate level are often associated with the history of diversification. Conglomerates tend to have much smaller corporate staffs in all areas than the older diversified companies. The disparity is especially true with regard to functions such as R&D, marketing, and production, which are frequently not present at all at the corporate level in conglomerates but widely prevalent in the diversified industrials. These differences have persisted over time, as shown by two studies conducted over a decade apart.[1]

These two categories are presented not because all companies fall into one category or the other, or even remain where they presently are. Companies inhabit the spectrum with the majority somewhere in the middle. The issue of just what the role of the corporate level should be is a recurring question for many companies, however, since the evils of the present system and the advantages of an alternative approach often seem most apparent.

It is not too difficult to draw up a list of functions that can be performed more cheaply and with greater expertise at the corporate level than at the division level. Matters such as dealings with the SEC, stockholder and investor relations, awareness of and reporting on government regulations affecting the conduct of business, and so on, are generally handled at the corporate level. When it comes to matters more closely related to the strategy and operations of the divisions and the relations between them, however, the approaches diverge.

If there is much commonality in the manufacturing or marketing activities of the various divisions, for example, even though they may be in completely separate businesses, it becomes difficult for the corporate level to assist by offering its expertise and advice to the operating units and to actively encourage, if not require, interdivisional cooperation. In addition, there may simply be the temptation to want to oversee and advise on all important decisions made in the divisions in the hope of improving their quality, in addition to ensuring that the decisions made are best from the corporate point of view. As you may remember from the discussion of the problems of rationally allocating resources among competing divisions and the unavoidable fact that division self-interests will not always coincide with corporate interests, there is ample incentive to centralize and build staff.

Even the most casual observation of organizations indicates that the pressures for centralization and the establishment of staff units are widespread. Top managers are under severe time pressures. One solution to these time pressures, as well as the complexity and the remoteness caused by the number and variety of divisions to be dealt with, is to create more staff at the corporate level. That staff will then be able to spend the time that the corporate officers are unable to spare to become familiar with the divisions. The staff can then analyze the problem and recommend action, brief the line management, or act in their stead.

In addition, whenever trouble arises the temptation is to centralize, even if lack of centralization is not what caused the trouble in the first place. It is also far easier to demonstrate the sharp-pencil economies that can be achieved by coordinating purchasing or transportation or computer services or dozens of other activities than to demonstrate the adverse effects of more central staff and direction on the initiative, flexibility, and accountability of the divisions.

The challenge is not just to arrive at the *best* answer to the *immediate* problem. More important in the long run is to develop the best way for problems of this nature to be solved, recognizing the severe time constraints on corporate top management. For the president to immerse himself in the affairs of any single division, either directly or vicariously through the mechanism of a staff, is no permanent solution to the problem. There *is* a general manager in the division. The reason the product division form of organization developed was to separate the management of the product division from the management of the overall corporation, not to combine them. The lack of separation is what led to a new form of organization in the first place.

Corporate management in the diversified company can influence the organization by means of the same variables as the manager of the single-business company. As we discussed in Chapter 7, the organization structure, the information systems, the policies on the measurement and reward of managers, the allocation of resources, and the intangible but vitally important matter of personal leadership are all important in leading and guiding the organization in the accomplishment of its strategic goals.

The appropriate fit of these influences available to the general manager is more complex but not different in kind in the diversified company. Just as for the earlier cases, you will want to concentrate on what is most appropriate for the given situation. Organization structures inevitably reflect a compromise between the desire to have as few levels of management as possible in the chain of command while not letting the number of units reporting to any one individual exceed six or so.

Information systems of course need to balance the amount and type of information given to higher levels with the cost of assembling it. It is even more important to consider whose responsibility it should be to monitor and take action on such information, on what matters various levels of management should be spending their time, and how much information higher levels of management can assimilate. It is quite possible to provide the chairman of General Electric with a video console on which he can call up the number of TV sets sold in Seattle the day before, but it does not follow that looking at such information is a good use of the chairman's time, nor a useful influence on the eight or so levels of management between the chairman and the local sales manager.

With regard to the system of incentives and rewards, it is clear that the greater the degree to which individual incentives reward performance that clearly is in the corporate benefit, the less the amount of involvement required by the corporate level to ensure that decisions made throughout the corporation are in the interest of the corporation interest and not just of the subunit or the individual manager. The problem, of course, is that it is difficult to structure reward systems so that little oversight is needed, and the more such systems attempt to be congruent with the corporate interests in all respects, the more cumbersome and detailed they become. Once again it is a trade-off, not one right answer, with the balance appropriate to the businesses and the culture of the company that is to be sought. It is clear that the opportunity for first-hand observation of managers by the corporate president decreases as the company grows and diversifies, which makes more reliance either on the judgments of intermediate managers, staff, or formal performance measures inevitable.

The dilemma is clear with regard to the role of the corporate level in the innumerable decisions and issues in which it could become involved. The more the corporate level wishes to become involved in the substance of decisions in the divisions, the more information they will need if they are not to act capriciously and "shoot from the hip."

As more information is gathered, however, the greater the temptation is to assemble staff to check, analyze, and interpret it for the corporate manager. More people then are also needed at the division level, not only to assemble the reports, but to deal with the questions of the corporate staff so that the division manager can remain free to spend his time on the demanding job of running the division. Before long there will be staffs talking largely to staffs, hardly a happy arrangement. But with no staff and scanty information at the corporate level, the company is little more than a financial holding company, hardly a happy arrangement either.

CML's planned approach, for example, would clearly place them at the left-hand side of the spectrum shown in Exhibit 10-1, with a very small corporate staff and a strong preference for divisions that can deal with most of their problems themselves. An essential element of the strategy of The Leisure Group was a belief in what a relatively large, professional, and powerful corporate staff could do to improve the operations of the companies that were purchased. Imperial is an example of a much larger and older company with a far more extensive corporate staff, and clearly at the right-hand side of the scale.

Your challenge is not to settle upon one approach as better than the others for all situations, but to try to think through what the most useful role of the corporate office is in the particular situation. The choices made are not just a matter of style or personal preference, but depend upon the history of the company, the kinds of businesses the corporation is in, and the strategy for competing in them.

SUMMARY

"If a company doesn't continue to do new and exciting things, its management dies. So does the company. You have to keep growing. Stagnation in management makes you just as vulnerable as stagnation in the market."[2]

The above statement was made by Stuart Watson, then president of Heublein, a company which experienced decades of growth at far above average rates. It would be supported by hundreds of other presidents. Sentiments similar to his are the driving force behind most of the companies we regard as successful, and the diversification strategies to which we have introduced you in this part of the book are one major way in which companies have sought to continue their growth.

As you deal with the problems of the manager at the corporate level in the diversified company, it is essential for you to keep in mind that the way any one problem can be solved is not necessarily the way such problems can or should be solved on a continuing basis. It is the diversity of the operations and the number of decisions that need to be made that led to the creation of more levels of management to compensate for the impossibility of the top management becoming as involved in operating affairs on a continuing basis as is possible in the single-business company. New roles had to be worked out, partly to handle the large number of familiar types of problems and partly to deal with entirely new problems.

The nature of the corporate role in the overall management of the diversified firm is but one of the elements which need to be consistent with each other. We have discussed the main elements involved in the strategy formulation process and in the challenge of leading the organization in the implementation of that strategy. Your concern should be the degree to which these elements are supportive of each other—the degree of *fit* or *consistency* among them. There are no strategies or organizational approaches that are "best" in isolation. Your challenge is to find the creative fit among these elements that best reconciles the goals management is seeking with the opportunities in the environment and the administrative history and the resources of the company. Just as with each of us as individual persons, goals, resources, opportunities, and strategies will differ.

The challenge for you is to perceive the ways in which the firm, whether diversified or not, can manage its affairs so that management, employees, investors, and the public are all satisfactorily rewarded. As you attempt to do so, you will not have the benefit of a rigorous or comprehensive general theory. You will have to rely on the application of the basic but imprecise analytical approach we have developed, plus a generous application of common sense, judgment, and whatever experience you can bring to bear. These, fortunately, are commodities which companies reward far more handsomely than theories and concepts useful in the disciplines but limited in their application to practice.

CASE 22

CML Group, Inc.

In early January 1971, John Morgan, general manager of Hood Sailmakers, Inc., the world's largest and most prestigious manufacturer of sails for big ocean racing yachts, was trying to make a final decision on whether to recommend to Hood's board of directors that $314,000 be requested for the establishment of a sailcloth weaving mill in Ireland. Hood had been a wholly owned subsidiary of the CML Group since February of 1970 but still operated with its own board of directors.[1] The project, even if recommended, would require approval by CML Group management, however, because of its size and nature. Hood was but one of the four recent acquisitions in the "leisure time" field that made up the CML Group, a company which had attained an annual sales volume of over $11 million in its first year and a half of operations.

In Mr. Morgan's opinion, several factors favored the investment. It represented a 13 percent aftertax return (based on cash flow) for the division, substantially better than Hood was making on its present asset base. Perhaps more important, both Ted Hood, founder and current president of the division, and his father, R. S. Hood, an influential Hood board member and general manager of the Hood cloth manufacturing operation, were in favor of the project, as they both felt that it would significantly enhance the long-run competitive position of the company and was therefore an important strategic move.

Mr. Morgan recognized that going ahead with the investment presented certain difficulties, however, and that several of these were of particular concern to CML corporate management. Most significant was

[1] Hood's board included five members, three chosen by the Hood family and two by CML.

Hood's sales and profits slump during fiscal 1970, when earnings had dropped about 30 percent from their peak year level. Though profitability was considerably better in the current year, sales had not risen appreciably above the prior year. As Hood had doubled its weaving capacity in 1968, only about 50 percent of existing weaving capacity was currently being utilized. Under such circumstances, corporate management's reluctance to invest in substantially increased capacity for Hood was understandable, especially in view of opportunties to invest in other divisions. Corporate management also questioned Hood's ability to take on a major new commitment in light of the many pressing issues already demanding management time and energy. Secrecy surrounding Hood's unique weaving process presented a further problem. All Hood sailcloth was currently woven in the very closely guarded Marblehead facility. A second mill naturally increased Hood's risk of exposure. Finally, uncertainties such as future tariff levels, fluctuation in domestic demand, and possible competitive moves and reactions complicated the economic analysis.

Since Mr. Morgan had joined Hood as general manager only nine months earlier and had no prior experience in the industry, he recognized that he was still in a transition period with regard to learning an entirely new business and establishing his own position within the company. Several factors made it important to come to some decision on the Irish project fairly soon, however. Although the Industrial Development Authority (IDA) of the Irish government had agreed to supply as a nonrepayable grant $266,000 of the $580,000 total funds required, Hood had already requested several extensions of the original deadline for purchasing land and commencing construction. While Mr. Morgan felt that a further extension could probably be obtained, he sensed that an increasingly wide credibility gap was developing on the part of IDA over Hood's real intentions in Ireland. In addition, preliminary planning for the Irish facility, which had already cost Hood about $20,000 since early 1969, was currently being funded by Hood at the rate of $1,000 per month in retainer fees and travel expenses. Further delay was therefore both risky and expensive.

CML GROUP DEVELOPMENT

In May 1969 Charles Leighton, Robert Tod, and Sam Frederick[2] resigned from the Willard Corporation, a large diversified manufacturing

---

[2] *Charles Leighton* (36 in 1971); MBA, Harvard Business School, 1960; product line manager, Mine Safety Appliances Corporation, 1963–64; instructor in management of new enterprises at the Harvard Business School, 1964–65; group vice president, Willard Corporation Leisure Time Group, 1965–69.

Robert Tod (32); MBA, Harvard Business School, 1967; project engineer, Hooker Chemical, January–September 1967; group operations manager, Willard Corporation Leisure Time Group, 1967–69.

Sam Frederick (36); MBA, Columbia, 1962; accounting with Arthur Andersen & Co., 1962–68; group controller, Willard Corporation Leisure Time Group, 1968–69.

company which had grown largely by acquisition, in order to establish their own company in the leisure time field.

Mr. Leighton had joined Willard in 1965 as group officer in charge of three divisions (a jewelry manufacturer and two boat manufacturers) with total sales of $7 million per year. Throughout the next four years internal growth and six acquisitions had raised the sales of the renamed "Leisure Time Group" to about $70 million; profits grew at about 25 percent per year during this period. By the time Mr. Leighton and his colleagues left the Willard Corporation in 1969 their group was one of the largest, most profitable, and most rapidly growing groups in the company, which then had sales of several hundred million dollars.

In the spring of 1969, Mr. Leighton described the original objectives of CML in a short pamphlet prepared for prospective investors:[3]

> We want to build an organization devoted to self-expression and individual creativity for profit. Basically, we intend to use the skills demonstrated by our success at Willard to build our own diversified company in the leisure time field. Our plan is to acquire companies and to operate them on a decentralized basis so that chief executives of acquired companies retain full authority for management of their business, with us at the corporate level providing supplementary assistance in the form of long-range planning help, marketing and manufacturing consultation, accounting, and most importantly, strong financial control and support. We are looking for companies with top-quality product lines and excellent trade names in businesses where management experience and creativity are more important to success than bricks and mortar. Companies we'll be interested in will generally have been founded by men with great creativity from a product standpoint, but who basically dislike the administrative burdens of running a growing business. A key element of our strategy is therefore to provide administrative assistance to these companies, thereby freeing up more of an owner-manager's time for the really creative things he's most interested in. Another key aspect is motivation. We plan to acquire companies only on an earn-out basis so that the owner-manager is fully motivated to realize the growth and profit potential which we feel are in the business when we buy it.
>
> From a financial standpoint our objectives are the following: growth in corporate earnings per share of at least 20 percent per year, a pretax return on CML's investment in acquired companies of at least 20 percent, and a 12½ percent annual profit growth of acquired companies.

With these objectives in mind CML's cofounders established the new company in early June 1969. Two million dollars of outside equity funds were raised in just 10 days by selling 50 percent of the company to 18 large investors.[4] The best known of these was a major national

---

[3] See Exhibit 1 for further discussion of objectives appearing in CML's first annual report.

[4] A total of 800 shares of convertible preferred stock (convertible on a 1-for-1 basis) and 3,200 shares of common stock were sold to outside investors for $500 per share. As no investment banking fees were paid, total cost of the issue was only $364.

EXHIBIT 1: Excerpt from a Letter to the Stockholders, July 30, 1970

To our stockholders:

A little over a year ago, the CML Group, Inc., was founded on the premise that a variety of new skills will be needed for business success in the 1970s. The ability to provide an environment which would encourage creative product development and innovative marketing will become a key success factor. Our previous business experience led us to believe that the orientation of business toward individual creativity could attract imaginative entrepreneurs and result in a high rate of profitable growth. Of course, financial control, production, and the other customary management skills will remain critical to the success of any business.

The leisure time industry is the best candidate for the implementation of this theory because it contains a number of very creative people who founded companies with interesting products. As a result of increasing discretionary income in all levels of society, this industry also has a high growth rate. It was decided to group several of these companies into one corporation emphasizing performance and quality.

Widespead equity ownership among the managers of the companies would provide strong motivation for capital growth and act as a measure of their common success. The creative leaders could become even more productive by delegating their administrative burdens and financial problems to qualified persons. An active corporate management team would be able to introduce modern control systems and other management tools to support long-term growth. The diversity of experience and skills of the CML management team would be an advantage in this effort. Accordingly, the CML Group was incorporated in June of 1969.

The principal objectives of the Group were established at the outset as follows:

> First of all, the Group would seek several outstanding leisure time companies to provide a base for business operations. At the same time, the Group would keep itself in a strong financial position. Bank relationships would be developed and lines of credit established. A pattern would be established for the integration of new members into the Group; this would include the strengthening of autonomous management whenever necessary and the introduction of an extensive, but easily administered, control system.

> Second, the Group would begin immediately to prepare itself for a public offering of its stock at the most favorable opportunity in the next few years. Improved marketability of the Group's common stock would provide a better tool for use in attracting additional companies and employees and would improve the original subscribers' return on their capital investment. The Group determined that a high rate growth in sales and profits of each company after joining the Group would be the most important factor in valuing the Group's stock at the time of public sale. Also important would be a record of making prudent acquisitions.

> Ultimately and most importantly, the Group would begin to build for the long term. The desired environment would be developed slowly to ensure that creativity and innovation became permanent characteristics of the Group. The best management teams take time to form, particularly when business practices are considered a complement to innovation and art rather than the dominant force. The control systems would have to be structured so that the effect of changes within and without the business could easily be assessed and recognized.

Source: A letter to the stockholders appearing in CML Group, Inc.'s, July 31, 1970, annual report.

foundation which invested $400,000 in the company, choosing CML Group for one of its first attempts to invest in new ventures. The four cofounders paid a total of $40,000 for the remaining 50 percent of the equity.[5] Mr. Leighton described as follows the relative ease with which outside equity funds were obtained despite the unfavorable economic climate prevailing at the time:

> At that time, we hadn't made any attempt yet to negotiate with prospective acquisitions, so we couldn't talk specific companies to financial backers. Despite this, we felt we had several things to offer. First, we represented a team whose combined skills balanced out any individual weaknesses. I've always maintained that covering yourself on weaknesses is far more important than having outstanding but spotty strengths. Second, we had a very good four-year track record at Willard. Third, we had a concept of management which we had spelled out in detail in a recent *Harvard Business Review* article and which had already proved itself at Willard. Finally, we had two very influential men behind us. One was my father-in-law, Dan Smith,[6] who provided invaluable advice and experience. Homer Luther was the other. At 29 he was already an extremely successful and influential investment manager. I had met him in 1964 while he was an MBA student at Harvard. We got to know each other as a result of a creative marketing study he made of the product line I handled at Mine Safety Appliances. We had kept in touch off and on since then, and after we decided to leave Willard we called him, since he had told me that if we ever needed money we should come to him. His introductions to potential investors and his assistance in general were invaluable. Dan Smith and Homer also became substantial investors in CML, and both are very active directors of the company.

Acquired Businesses

Exhibit 2 shows CML's balance sheet as of July 31, 1969, shortly after registration of the new company and before any acquisitions had been made, and as of July 31, 1970, following one year of operations. During its first year CML acquired four companies and reported fiscal 1970 sales of approximately $11 million (see Exhibit 3 for the first year's operating results). Terms of purchase for acquired companies appear in Exhibit 4. A brief account of each acquired company follows.

Boston Whaler, Inc.   Boston Whaler, CML's largest division, was estimated to be the 10th largest U.S. manufacturer of outboard boats. CML's 1970 annual report described this division as follows:

> The first company to join the CML Group was Boston Whaler, Inc., of Rockland, Massachusetts, in September 1969. Their principal product

---

[5] A total of 4,000 shares of common stock were sold to the four cofounders at $10 per share.

[6] Dan T. Smith, professor emeritus of finance, Harvard Business School.

EXHIBIT 2

CML GROUP, INC.
Consolidated Balance Sheet as of July 31, 1969 and 1970
(in thousands of dollars)

	1969	1970
Assets		
Current assets:		
Cash	$ 242	$ 731
Short-term commercial paper	1,787	—
Net receivables	—	1,217
Inventories	—	2,433
Prepaid expenses	14	109
Total current assets	2,042	4,490
Property, plant, and equipment (net)	3	2,143
Investments and other assets:		
Investments	—	876
Excess of cost over net book value of acquisitions	—	1,959
Other assets	7	137
Total assets	$2,052	$9,604
Liabilities and Stockholders' Equity		
Total current liabilities	$ 14	$2,545
Long-term debt	—	3,424
Subordinated convertible debenture	—	498
Stockholders' equity:*		
Preferred stock (par value $0.10)	1	1
Common stock (par value $0.10)	1	1
Capital in excess of par	2,038	2,771
Retained earnings	(2)	364
Total equity	2,038	3,137
Total liabilities and stockholders' equity	$2,052	$9,604

* Stockholders' equity information:

	Convertible Preferred	Common	
		Non-	
Source of Equity	**Nonfounders**	**founders**	**Founders**
Sold during June 1969	800 (Series A)	3,200	4,000
Exchanged to acquire Boston Whaler	1,000 (Series B)		
Exchanged to acquire Hood Sailmakers	4,600 (Series C)		
Sold during summer of 1970		920	
Total outstanding as of 7/31/70	6,400	4,120	4,000

Number of Shares Outstanding

Series A ranks on a parity with common stock with respect to voting and dividend privileges. May be converted by holder into common stock at any time on a share-for-share basis. May be redeemed by CML any time after September 30, 1971, at the original selling price ($500 per share).

Series B ranks on a parity with common stock with respect to voting privileges. Receives a preferential annual dividend of $10 per share. See footnote in Exhibit 4 for conversion privileges.

Series C ranks on a parity with common shares with respect to voting and dividend privileges. See footnote in Exhibit 4 for conversion privileges.

Source: Company records for 1969; annual report for 1970. Errors are due to rounding.

EXHIBIT 3

CML GROUP, INC.
**Consolidated Statement of Income and Retained Earnings
For the Year Ended July 31, 1970
(in thousands of dollars)**

Net sales		$11,109
Less costs and expenses:		
Cost of goods sold	$7,943	
General, selling, and administrative.	2,553	10,496
Income from operations		613
Interest expense (net)		190
Income before income taxes		423
Provision for income taxes*		217
Net income ($21.25 per share)†		206
Deficit, beginning of year		(2)
Retained earnings of pooled companies		161
Retained earnings, end of year		$ 365

* Represents a reserve against future income tax payments. No income taxes were paid in 1970. Income for tax purposes had been reduced to zero as a result of—

a. A tax loss carry-forward in connection with a relatively minor portion of one subsidiary's business spun off at the time of acquisition.
b. Amortization charges in connection with certain assets revalued for tax purposes at the time of acquisition.

† The annual report comments as follows upon earnings per share: Net income per common share and common equivalent share is based on the 9,675 weighted-average number of shares outstanding. For purposes of computing net income per share, the convertible preferred shares—Series A, B, and C—are considered to be common stock equivalents. The weighted-average number of common and common equivalent shares assume conversion of the Series A on a share-for-share basis and the Series B and C on the basis of the number of shares issuable at the last sales price of common stock and the current level of income affecting the conversion rate of these securities.

    The 7 percent subordinated convertible debentures and stock options are not included in the net income per share computations, as their effect is not dilutive.

Source: 1970 annual report.

is the Boston Whaler outboard motor boat. A 30 percent interest in Boston Whaler Bearcat, Inc., manufacturer of nonpolluting four-cycle outboard engines, was acquired at the same time. Dick Fisher, the chairman of Boston Whaler, has been instrumental in the founding of several companies requiring a high level of technical skill. The creativity and innovative talents of Mr. Fisher made this company particularly attractive as the first member of the Group.

    The Boston Whaler meets the high quality criteria of the group. [A well-known consumer report] has rated Boston Whaler as the most outstanding outboard boat produced in the United States. The boats are easily identified by their distinctive and functional shape and a well-regarded trademark. Boston Whalers are made of a monolithic casting of plastic foam with a smooth molded fiberglass "crust" on both sides. This construction causes the Boston Whaler to be extremely durable and unsinkable. No

EXHIBIT 4: Terms of Payment for Companies Acquired

Accounting Treatment	Acquisition Date	Name of Company	Original Payment in Shares of CML Stock		Original Payment in Cash and Notes (in thousands of dollars)		Additional Earn-out (in thousands of dollars)	
			Common	Convertible Preferred	Cash	Notes	Minimum	Maximum
Pooling	9/30/69	Boston Whaler	250	1,000			$ 500*	$2,975*
Pooling	2/25/70	Hood Sailmakers	400	4,600			1,600†	5,000†
Purchase	10/1/70	Carroll Reed			$700	$ 600		400‡
Purchase	5/1/70	Mason & Sullivan			450	1,050		1,100‡

* Represents conversion value of 1,000 shares of convertible preferred stock. Conversion value is contingent upon the earnings of Boston Whaler, Inc., for the period beginning 8/1/69 and ending 7/31/74, and on the market price of CML's common stock at the time of conversion.
† Represents conversion value of 4,600 shares of convertible preferred stock. Conversion value is contingent upon the earnings of Hood Sailmakers, Inc., for the period beginning 8/1/70 and ending 7/31/75, and on the market price of CML's common stock at the time of conversion.
‡ Additional cash amount payable through 1974 contingent upon achievement of certain earnings by the purchased company.

Source: 1970 annual report.

other boat manufacturing company has developed the technical skills needed to build a comparable product.

An asset with long-term growth implications is the Boston Whaler marketing organization. There are eight sales representatives whose principal products are the Boston Whaler and Bearcat engines. More than 700 dealers are located throughout the world. The dealers are known to be the most reputable in the industry. Obviously, other products can be sold through this system as they are developed or acquired by Boston Whaler.

During the current fiscal year, Boston Whaler has introduced a new product, the "Outrage," a larger outboard boat with a new and distinctive hull configuration. A patent application is pending to cover the boat design. It is expected that the boat will have a pronounced effect on the design of larger outboard boats.

Major programs now under way in cost savings, manufacturing efficiency, and overhead reductions are expected to improve profitability to a level in excess of all previous years.

Despite modest volume and profit declines during 1970, Boston Whaler's long-term sales growth was expected to run somewhat above the 8 percent average for the industry. In addition, significant profit increases at current sales levels were expected reasonably quickly through improving margins. These had consistently run well under half the level of Willard's outboard runabout divisions of equivalent size, which CML management knew well from their previous experience.

Carroll Reed Ski Shops.   This division was described as follows in CML's 1970 annual report:

> The [Carroll Reed] Ski Shops, which joined the Group in October 1969, are a series of retail stores and a national mail-order business headquartered in North Conway, New Hampshire.
>
> The business was founded by Carroll Reed in 1936 to service the burgeoning ski areas in northern New England. Mr. Reed's creative merchandising skills are the principal reason for the store's development into one of the country's best-known ski shops. The company has become known for its extremely high-quality merchandise, excellent service, and unique "country store" style that appeals to both men and women.
>
> In the early spring, an executive vice president [and general manager] was employed by Mr. Reed. The new individual has had significant merchandising experience and will be of value in the day-to-day management of the business. This new management depth will better allow Mr. Reed to concentrate on the future expansion of the business. The Group believes that the company employees are a major asset who provide an excellent foundation for future growth.
>
> During the fiscal year, the mail-order handling systems were substantially improved by the construction of a 6,000-square-foot addition in North Conway for order processing and additional storage space. The order processing was improved by introducing computerized equipment on a limited basis. A new ski shop of approximately 4,000 square feet is about to open

in Simsbury, Connecticut, as the first in a planned program of store expansion.

Three residents of the northern New England area have been elected to the board of directors of Carroll Reed Ski Shops, Inc., and participate actively in the long-term planning for the business. They are Tom Corcoran [MBA, Harvard Business School, 1959], a former Olympic skier and president of Waterville Valley ski area; Malcolm McNair, professor emeritus of retailing at Harvard Business School; and Leon Gorman, president of L. L. Bean, Inc., in Freeport, Maine.

Growth opportunities exist for Carroll Reed Ski Shops in the gradual expansion of the retail store business. The mail-order business can be further expanded without significant addition of facilities or personnel. Carroll Reed Ski Shops also provides a vantage point to study several fast-growing sectors of the leisure time industry.

Mr. Reed had played a leading role as one of the early pioneers in recreational skiing in this country and had opened the first U.S. ski lift and school, headed by the world-famous Hans Schneider, in Jackson, New Hampshire, in the early 1930s. Several years later he sold his interest in the ski area and founded Carroll Reed Ski Shops (CRSS) in nearby North Conway. Not long after joining CML, Mr. Reed described CRSS's success over the years to the casewriter, as follows:

> When my wife and I began this business in 1936, we had no idea it would ever grow to what it has become. We simply did not want to go back to Boston, liked the Conway area very much, and felt we could make a living here in this kind of business by treating customers well so that they would stop in and buy something from us the next time they passed through the area. I feel that many of our customers have come to feel a personal closeness to Kay and me and like the way we do business, and that this is what has brought them back over the years. It's this personal touch, a certain integrity in what we stand for in each transaction, that gives us something special to offer. This is the main basis on which we are able to compete with large city stores selling much the same type of merchandise as we do.

During the summer of 1970, Mr. Tod made the following observations about CRSS:

> Carroll Reed has a number of important strengths. Most important are its reputation, based upon the quality and style of the items sold; its interesting, well-laid-out store in North Conway, which accounts for nearly half of total sales; its masculine image, despite the fact that 70 percent of all merchandise sold is for women; and the courteous, service-oriented manner of its retail people. They have unusually capable people with exceptionally high employee morale compared to others in their industry.
>
> Carroll Reed's mailing list for catalog sales, which account for about half of total sales, is another valuable asset. Average order size is nearly four times that of the mail-order industry as a whole, and about double that for small specialty houses like Carroll Reed. Another strength is Carroll's

wide delegation of buying responsibility to six buyers. In most operations of their size, the top person tries to do all the buying personally.

The division's primary weakness, however, is its geographical dependence on one region—North Conway. This is alleviated somewhat by a couple of factors. Catalog sales reach a customer group scattered across the country. Even retail sales are not confined to North Conway residents. Because of its location as both a winter and summer resort, North Conway draws large numbers throughout the year from all over New England and Middle Atlantic states. Partly as a result of these factors their product line has shifted significantly from almost 100 percent ski equipment in the early years to an increasing percentage of primarily women's fashion sportswear, and now less than one third of their volume is ski related.

Another weakness is their dependence on one retail outlet for selling marked-down merchandise from the catalog business. This problem is particularly pressing because of the current push to expand catalog sales. Retail outlets are needed to dispose of unsold merchandise at the end of the catalog season. The current procedure is to turn much of this over to the discount basement of a large downtown Boston department store at about 17 percent of Carroll Reed's retail price.[7]

Mr. Tod felt there were several additional areas of CRSS's operation in need of some strengthening, including internal controls (such as inventory and catalog order processing) and market knowledge in the mail-order area. He thought that an expansion of mail-order sales was CRSS's greatest opportunity for profit growth. The second major retail store, which was being planned for Simsbury, Connecticut, would provide both a non–New Hampshire retail outlet and an additional retail outlet for the resulting increase in markdowns.

Mason & Sullivan Company.   CML's 1970 annual report described this division as follows:

> The projected growth rate for the hobby sector is among the highest of the leisure time market because of early retirement and a renewed interest in hand work. The Group entered one of the fastest growing segments of the industry when Mason & Sullivan of Osterville, Massachusetts, joined in June. This business sells clocks, barometers, and music boxes in kit form and by mail.
>
> The founder, Ed Lebo, purchases the working parts of the various items in Europe. Wood, metal trim, and other parts are purchased from numerous suppliers in the New England area. Because the designs are largely antique reproductions with handcrafted movements, there is virtually no model obsolescence.
>
> The company has two unique aspects. It has a high-quality reputation among woodworking hobbyists throughout the United States and Canada;

---

[7] Approximately 10 percent (at retail valuation) of total sales were made at markdown prices.

it also has established relationships with craftsmen-suppliers in Austria, Germany, Switzerland, and England.

Shortly after Mason & Sullivan joined the Group, the former chief executive of a large mail-order house was employed as vice president and general manager to assist in the day-to-day operations of the business. Efforts are being made to introduce control and information systems to support future profitable growth.

Mr. Lebo plans to expand the product line to include other related items.

Hood Sailmakers, Inc. By any index, Hood was clearly the leading supplier of sails for large ocean yachts (over 40 feet in length), commanding over 50 percent of the U.S. market. Exhibit 5 shows the text of a *Yachting* magazine article describing the company and its products.

EXHIBIT 5: Ted Hood: Sailmaker to the Twelves (by B. D. Burrill)

"They are the ultimate teaching and testing ground as far as we're concerned. A Twelve is under sail as much in three months as the average cruising boat in five years." Speaking was Frederick E. "Ted" Hood, the 43-year-old Marblehead, Mass., sailmaker who has made more sails for 12-Meter yachts than any man alive. And perhaps no man in the years since 1958, with the possible exception of Olin Stephens, has contributed more to keeping the America's Cup firmly bolted in the New York YC's trophy room than this genius of boat speed. During these years a small sailmaking operation that started in 1950 has grown into one of the world's largest, to a great extent as a result of the success his 12-Meter sails have enjoyed.

Ted Hood's involvement with the America's Cup and 12-Meter boats began in 1958 when he served in the cockpit of *Vim* during her brilliant bid to become the Cup defender. He served as an advisor to skipper Bus Mosbacher on sail trim and tactics, and generally made himself useful where help was needed. One day, when working on a coffee grinder, he somehow managed to loosen the bolted-down winch—Ted would be a good man aboard any boat on the basis of his physical strength alone.

Hood got his chance to make sails for *Vim* after her owner, the late Capt. Jack Matthews, had seen the sails he produced for the 5.5-Meter *Quixotic,* a Ray Hunt design built and sailed by Ted, which narrowly missed becoming the 1956 U.S. Olympic representative. In spite of a DSQ in the next to last race, *Quixotic* had only to beat one boat in the final race to win the trials. Well up in the fleet on the final leg, the main halyard shackle unaccountably opened, the sail came down, and she finished last. So Ted's first experience with Meter boats wasn't very happy. But he also made sails for *Easterner* and *Weatherly* in 1958 and two famous red-top spinnakers borrowed from *Vim,* "Big Harry" and "Little Harry," were used by *Columbia* in her successful defense of the Cup.

In 1962 Ted designed and made just about everything except the hull and winches for *Nefertiti* which was the last boat eliminated in the trials by *Weatherly,* which had Bus Mosbacher at the helm. All of the Twelves, including the Australian challenger *Gretel,* used Hood sails that summer. *Gretel,* in fact, used a mainsail

EXHIBIT 5 *(continued)*

made in 1957 for *Vim* in the race she won over *Weatherly* in '62. This would seem ultimate proof of a theory which Ted still believes strongly, particularly with respect to mainsails, that good sails get better with age if they receive proper care. A Dacron sail develops a certain "set" much like the old cotton sails. After a few years the fabric has settled down and the stretch is gone.

One anecdote of the '62 campaign bears repeating. Just before the final trial races between *Weatherly* and *Nefertiti,* Ted Hood spent a whole day, at Mosbacher's request, on the rival Twelve making sure her sails were the best possible. Some sails even went off to Marblehead for recutting and were rushed back in time to be used against him. Some of *Nefy's* crew felt this hurt their chances, but it's a mark of the man that he only wanted to win over the best possible boat, and he'd rather have been beaten by *Weatherly* than the Aussies. Hood now doubts that he'd ever again have the time to get involved in designing and campaigning a Twelve, business being what it is.

Not long after the '62 defense, the New York YC's Trustees passed a resolution interpreting the Cup's Deed of Gift to mean that challengers not only had to be designed and built in the challenging country but that gear and sails should come from there too. This has effectively cut off the challenging nations from Hood sails but they continue to order them from Marblehead as yardsticks. Many of the early pictures of the French trial horse *Chancegger* showed a lovely Hood main with one lower panel of a distinctly different color. Obviously the section had been removed for testing the Hood-woven cloth which continues to be one of the secrets of any Hood sail.

Hood sailmakers now have lofts in Canada, England, France, Australia, and New Zealand. And while a challenging Twelve from any one of these countries would be allowed to have sails made at the local Hood loft, they cannot use the fabric produced in Marblehead. Largely due to the great success of the English loft, there is a plan afoot to weave Hood cloth in Ireland. If this ever reaches fulfillment, the sail gap will almost certainly be narrowed.

Back in 1964, with future challenges in mind, the Australians sent their top sailmaker, the late Joe Pearce, to spend a year with Hood, and he became a top assistant. With Ted preoccupied by a second unsuccessful attempt with *Nefertiti,* Pearce became the man who dealt with the sails for the defender, *Constellation,* during the trials. Pearce may have learned quite a bit about the cut, but said his boss, "we didn't tell him much about the cloth."

Following this, and until his untimely death, Joe Pearce became the Hood sailmaker in Australia. He made *Dame Pattie's* sails in 1967 but by mutual agreement there was no communication with Marblehead on the subject of 12-Meter sails. The same arrangement applies with Peter Cole, the present Aussie Hood sailmaker, who has supplied the motive power for *Gretel II.* The Hood loft in France, newest of the foreign operations, has not been involved in Baron Bich's undertaking.

Although nearly all of the technical improvements and lessons learned are applicable to Hood's normal business of making sails for cruising/racing yachts, there are some special problems and differences in making sails for the Twelves. To begin with, a 12-Meter has a ¾ foretriangle rig (the maximum allowable under the rule) while most boats today have masthead rigs. Mainsails must be fitted to

EXHIBIT 5 *(continued)*

masts and booms that are designed to bend to a far greater degree than on any cruising boat. Spinnakers are not made to the maximum size the 12-Meter rule permits—experience has shown time and again that shape is more important than sheer size when it comes to making a Twelve go downwind. Nevertheless, a maximum chute is made every Cup summer just to be sure that the theory still holds.

In preparing for a Cup summer, the Hood loft is looking for ways to make their sails lighter, smoother and stronger. The Twelves put tremendous strains on their sails and it is essential that they be strong and durable. But still, to save weight, less provision is made to prevent chafing than in a normal sail. As to the weight of sailcloth, there is continuous research into ways of making it lighter but still strong enough to retain its shape-holding ability. This work comes under the supervision of Ted's father, Steadman, known to everybody as "The Professor," who has done much over the years to insure the success of his son's business. The Professor's research is continuous and he says that progress is slow. But the following table on mainsail cloth weights used by the Twelves would seem to belie this claim:

Year	Weight
1958	14 oz.
1962	12 oz.
1964	10 oz.
1967	7.5 oz.
1970	6.9 oz. (or slightly less)

One characteristic of every U.S. defender since 1958 has been a tendency to hobby-horse less than her rival in the seas off Newport. While hull design is all important in this respect, there is little doubt that lightweight sails—weight saved up high where it really counts—have also contributed significantly to this advantage.

One recent development of Hood research that has reached a sufficiently advanced stage to be used on 12-Meter sails this summer is the Hood Ring, a replacement for the large hand-worked grommets in the corners of sails. Hood Rings have proved to be almost twice as strong as the best hand-sewn equivalent even though they are considerably lighter in weight. Hood Rings are inserted by special high-pressure hydraulic tooling and now there is virtually no handwork in a typical Hood clew since roping has also been eliminated.

Other new wrinkles in 12-Meter sails this season include Cunningham holes for draft control in both genoas and mainsails. The latter have Cunninghams along the foot as well as the luff. When this was written, experimental zippers (two of them, side-by-side) seemed to have proved their worth as a further means of draft control along the luffs of mainsails. Hood and others have been using foot zippers on mainsails for many years. This year's lightest polypropylene spinnaker cloth is even lighter than *Intrepid*'s much talked-about Floater of '67, but The Professor won't say by how much. Mainsail headboards are now made of titanium for the ultimate in strength without weight.

EXHIBIT 5 *(concluded)*

Valiant and *Heritage* have the recently developed Hood Sea Stay, a hollow grooved rod in which the genoa luff is hoisted. This item eliminates hanks as well as the space between headstay and sail, thereby significantly reducing turbulence at the leading edge.

In perfecting 12-Meter sails, spinnakers and jibs are recut often. There has been a definite trend among U.S. Cup sailors toward working for perfection with the sails at hand rather than ordering one after another and trying to decide which of the lot is best, as was popular until 1964. *Intrepid,* for example, went through the entire '67 campaign with only two mainsails in her inventory. Hood has had great luck in making mainsails right the first time and thus virtually eliminating recutting. The 7.5-oz. main *Intrepid* used most only had one seam let out near the head. *Valiant's* first Hood main had not been touched, at least through the Preliminary Trials. Ted points out that owners often will get him out to look at sails believing they need to be recut when what is really needed may be a proper knowledge of how to adjust luff and sheet tension or how tight to carry a leech line. Hood personnel spend long hours discussing and demonstrating adjustment techniques to 12-Meter crews.

The problem is trying to find enough time to satisfy everybody. There can be little doubt that over the long haul Ted Hood's success in making 12-Meter sails has meant much to his business, even though it is now quite a small part of the total. But one of the ironies of a Cup summer for Hood is that much less other work comes in. Many owners apparently feel that the loft will be too busy with the Twelves to pay much attention to them. This is not true—a 12-Meter sail goes through the same manufacturing process as any other. But what is certainly true is that what started as a bedroom sail repair business during college years would never have grown to be the international enterprise it is today had Ted Hood not become sailmaker to the Twelves.

Some of the reasons behind the company's success were discussed in CML's 1970 annual report:

> In every major ocean race of recent years, the winning boats (including *Intrepid* in the recent America's Cup Race) have consistently used Hood Sails. When Hood Sailmakers of Marblehead, Massachusetts, joined the Group in February [1970], the Group became a very important factor in the marine accessories segment of the leisure time industry.
>
> The business was started by Ted Hood as a hobby when he was a boy. Now there are sail lofts in Massachusetts, California, Canada, England, France, New Zealand, and Australia. The company weaves and finishes its own cloth in mills in Massachusetts, and, as such, it is the only fully integrated sailmaker in the world. Hood Yacht Systems, a division of Hood Sailmakers, manufactures masts, rigging, and specialty marine hardware.
>
> The principal asset of the company is its technological and inventive skill. No other sailcloth maker has the technical ability to make such light

yet strong cloth without the use of plastic resins. These innovative skills have also been applied in the design of sails and the manufacture of specialty marine hardware.

During the year, an entirely new style of sailcloth was introduced for use in the America's Cup. The company also began to extrude its own fibers for use in its "Floater" spinnaker cloths. The "Sea Stay" style of rod rigging became commercially available. Sail lofts were opened in France and California. A new [executive] vice president and general manager was employed to give additional depth in administration and production management.

Additional lofts are planned in the United States, and substantial sales growth is expected in the foreign markets. New marine accessory products are being developed for Hood Yacht Systems.

Competition for Hood came mainly from dozens of small local manufacturers, which generally had strong market coverage in particular regions of the country only. Hood in fact had itself been established in the late 1930s as a strictly local loft supplying the Marblehead market. Over the years it had grown both nationally and internationally to its current position of preeminence. Mr. Morgan, the new division general manager, described the company's success as follows:

> Hood's success can be attributed to a couple of factors. The most important of course is Ted Hood himself. Ted is a soft-spoken, modest kind of guy with an amazing knowledge of sailing and racing. He exudes confidence. What an ocean racer wants most from a sailmaker Ted Hood can supply in abundance . . . expert consultation in sail design and individual help in getting the best out of sails once they're made. Since the CML merger much of Ted's administrative load has been reduced and he now spends much more of his time testing new designs and out working with customers. Not only is this the kind of thing he enjoys most but it's where Ted's time is most valuable to the company.
>
> Hood Sailcloth is also a key competitive factor. Hood has a real product edge as the only U.S. sailmaker with its own weaving capability. In a very closely guarded process here in Marblehead we produce a tight-weave cloth of unusual lightness and strength. In fact, many in racing circles attribute *Intrepid*'s victory over Australia's *Gretel* in the 1970 America's Cup Race at least in part to the fact that *Intrepid*'s sails [using Hood cloth] weighed about half those of *Gretel.*

Hood sails were sold by five salaried salesmen and Mr. Hood himself through a variety of channels: direct to sailors (about half) and to dealers, naval architects, yacht builders, and the federal government. Hood competed only slightly in areas other than the large yacht market.

CML'S OPERATING PHILOSOPHY AND POLICIES

Hood's Irish investment was being considered in the context of an intricate set of relationships between CML and its divisions. According to Mr. Leighton, these relationships typically began taking shape even prior to acquisition itself and were strongly affected by personal factors:

> It would have been very difficult to have acquired any of our companies without our personal interest in their products. Bob Tod, for instance, is a great hydroplane enthusiast and for a time even held the U.S. Class B hydroplane speed record. This, together with our outboard boat experience at Willard, made it much easier to approach Dick Fisher about joining us. My own sailing background gave us some immediate rapport with Ted Hood. Ted and I had even competed once in the 1956 New England Men's Sailing Championships. I had come in second behind Ted, who went on to win the U.S. Men's Championships that year. All of us in the group are skiers, so Carroll Reed's business was not completely foreign to us. Learning Carroll Reed's mail-order business in turn provided a background for rapport with Ed Lebo when we first approached him about selling Mason & Sullivan.

Mr. Leighton considered preacquisition discussions to be extremely important because they provided an opportunity for both parties to get to know each other. This involved both discovering the owner-manager's underlying needs and aspirations and outlining clearly what joining CML would mean in terms of policies, procedures, authority and responsibility relationships, management changes, and so forth. This "foundation building" period was considered of prime importance because it paved the way for changes to be made after acquisition. According to Mr. Leighton, only by letting an owner-manager know beforehand what changes to expect could a transition be made smoothly. He commented:

> Most companies in our industry can benefit substantially from association with a larger, more sophisticated firm such as CML. We can provide capital and management know-how usually not available to a small company. We provide a vehicle for taking a small company public at favorable values and minimum expense. We can also provide a valuable environment for the top man in these companies. The independent businessman typically feels alone and would like someone to recognize his achievements and exchange ideas. His board of directors (if he has one) usually is not made up of professional managers who can give real guidance. He has no one to turn to for advice on a continuing basis. Therefore, he is typically a very lonely man under extreme pressure from long hours, and surrounded by subordinates he may not wish to confide in. About the only persons around to motivate and console him are his wife, banker, and accountant, and they may not be close enough to the business to do this effectively.
>
> Countering this strong need for association is, of course, an equally strong need for autonomy. This creates an antagonism of forces which inevitably causes an owner anxiety during early stages of discussion with us. He has normally spent years building up his business and wants to make sure he will remain in control after acquisition. Our big initial job is to subdue these anxieties. For this reason we deliberately don't talk price or even ask for financial statements during early contacts. Instead, we try

to get to know the owner's business, problems, and personality. We explain to him in detail what life will be like with us and exactly what changes in his operation he can expect. The whole emphasis is one of building up trust and understanding. At some point along the way he inevitably brings out his financial statements to show us. As a result of our emphasis on mutual understanding, we are less apt to get involved in a bidding match than if we were to negotiate mainly on a price basis.

According to Mr. Leighton, the acquisition process itself had varied considerably among companies acquired so far:

One of our companies first came to us about joining CML. Another I had heard might be available. I simply phoned the president and set up a meeting to talk. For a third company we had to make overtures over a number of months before we finally got anywhere. Another acquisition came to us in an interesting way. Last spring an acquaintance of mine and the former president of a medium-sized mail-order company phoned to say that he had a company he wanted to buy personally, but that the purchase price was above his financial means, and he wondered whether CML might like to buy it in partnership with him. We liked the company so much we bought it outright and put him in as general manager, with the former owner's concurrence, of course. This route is one we may use more frequently both for hiring new managers and acquiring new companies. I had a very qualified fellow in here not long ago who said he wanted to work for us. I told him we simply didn't have an opening at present, but that if he could bring us an attractive company we might acquire it and with the owner's approval put him in as general manager with attractive financial alternatives. He's working on one right now.

The Corporate Office

In January 1971 CML's corporate office consisted of four officers. Mr. Leighton, chairman of the board, focused mainly on relationships external to operations, concentrating primarily on new acquisitions, investor relations, and the raising of new capital. Mr. Tod, president, spent an estimated 90 percent of this time working directly with divisions and was the corporate officer immediately responsible for operations. Mr. Chaffee,[8] treasurer, worked closely with divisional controllers in preparing accounting statements and various management studies, such as cost-volume relationships, product mix contribution analyses, and so forth. He also handled companywide cash control, auditor relations, tax form preparation, and corporate office accounting. Management felt that the existing corporate staff was sufficient to handle expected growth for the

---

[8] Philip Chaffee (32): BS, University of Vermont, 1962; Financial Management Program, 1962–65, and then traveling audit staff, 1965–67, of the General Electric Company; manager of corporate auditing, ITEK Corporation, 1968–70. Mr. Chaffee had joined CML as controller in June 1970, and had assumed Mr. Frederick's duties as treasurer upon the latter's resignation in December 1970.

next three or four years, with perhaps the addition of a financial controller to share some of Mr. Chaffee's current responsibilities.

Since July 1970, borrowing and cash receipts for the entire corporation had been consolidated at the corporate level. Divisions could therefore no longer borrow on their own or build up their own cash balances; all funds passed through central CML accounts. Each division paid (or received) interest on funds received from (or advanced to) CML. Apart from interest payments there were no corporate charges.

Financial Control

Mr. Tod commented as follows on the company's philosophy regarding divisional autonomy:

> We want to give divisions their heads and let them make their own decisions within the broad policy constraints set at the corporate level. This much autonomy is workable only in the presence of complete, accurate, timely information on operations. Such data come in several forms. Prior to the beginning of our fiscal year each division submits three forecasts: monthly profit and loss for each of the following 12 months, end-of-month balance sheets for each of the following 12 months, and an annual capital budget showing forecasted expenditures by month. As the year proceeds, forecasts are compared on a monthly basis with actual operating figures.
>
> In addition to strictly accounting data we receive a number of key indicators from divisions on a monthly basis. These are vital measures of each division's performance. For instance, from one division I get catalog and retail sales and open-to-buy figures. For another I get bookings (orders), shipments, and discount levels for both dealer and direct sales, while another supplies order backlog, production, and inventory figures in addition to about six or eight others. For one division I look hardest at advertising response figures. Any variances are discussed in detail at regular meetings with division managements. Meetings are summarized in memo form and then sent back to divisions. If divisions don't agree with opinions or decisions stated in these memos, they are supposed to let me know right away. With this system I feel we have about as tight a control system as we could get without our actually making the decisions ourselves.

Part of the reason for the emphasis on close control, Mr. Tod explained, stemmed from a desire to avoid an experience CML management had had at Willard. One of their divisions that had been reporting adequate profits for several years had suddenly shown considerable red ink following an examination of inventories which had precipitated large writedowns. This situation had come as a complete surprise to both group and division management, and in management's opinion was simply the result of inadequate controls.

Mr. Leighton offered the following comments on operating control:

We have two main operating policies: "No closets to hide in" and "No surprises." Together they spell full decentralization of operations *except for* financial information flows. If things go wrong in a division, division management has nowhere to hide because we've given them complete authority and responsibility for their operations. On the other hand, if things go well they take the bows. We don't want surprises either good or bad from divisions, and we try to ensure this by getting complete and frequent information on operations.

Division controllers were considered an important link in providing information flow from divisions to the corporate level, and CML had inherited what corporate management considered to be experienced men within three of the acquired companies. (The fourth required only a part-time bookkeeper.) Two of these men were CPAs, while the third was an MBA from the Tuck School at Dartmouth. All had extensive backgrounds in either public or corporate accounting.

Divisional General Managers

Another important ingredient in CML's operating strategy was the division general manager. Professionally trained, experienced general managers had been hired to complement all four division presidents, partially relieving them of administrative duties and thereby giving them more time to do what they were best at. While several of the general managers hired so far were still quite new to the company, Mr. Tod felt that they were already proving to be valuable additions to the divisions.[9] He stated that one of the most significant ways in which CML could benefit an acquired company was by recruiting for it people who would not normally be attracted to small companies, which often offered little opportunity for equity participation and promotion. Compensation of general managers was tied to earnings growth formulas similar to those of owner-managers, and involved liberal cash bonus and stock option

---

[9] Fred Snow (35), executive vice president and general manager of Carroll Reed Ski Shops since March 1970; AB, Babson College, 1958; salesman, sales manager, promotions manager, and marketing vice president of Fieldcrest Company, 1959–70.

John Morgan (33), executive vice president and general manager of Hood Sailmakers, Inc., since April 1970; Princeton, electrical engineering, 1959; MBA, Harvard, 1966; prior to joining Hood, had had a number of technical and management positions at General Electric Company over a 10-year period.

Bob Lavery (49), vice president and general manager of Mason & Sullivan Company since July 1970; BS, Kansas State College, 1940; 25 years' experience in catalog sales, first with Montgomery Ward and more recently with a successful medium-sized mail-order firm where he had been president since 1961.

Dave Wilson (33), vice president and general manager of Boston Whaler, Inc., since January 1971; Cambridge, England, chemical engineering, 1961; MBA, Harvard, 1968; had worked for six years as a process engineer with a major U.S. chemical company, and since 1968 as president of a Canadian manufacturing concern where he had achieved profitable operations of the company for the first time since 1960.

possibilities based on performance. The relationship of a division general manager to an owner-manager was determined partly by this congruence of compensation interests, partly by the fact that each general manager had been selected by the owner-manager of the division involved from among several candidates prescreened by CML management, and partly by the understanding that the owner-manager ultimately had final say on all decisions affecting a division and in fact could fire the general manager if it became apparent that the two could not work together. All these arrangements had, of course, been discussed at length with owner-managers during the "foundation setting" stage preceding acquisition. All four general managers hired so far were still with the company in January 1971.

Financial controls and other influences ushered in by CML appeared to have caused some changes within acquired companies. Middle management personnel from various divisions described some of these as follows:

> It's not at all like it used to be around here. [The owner-manager] had always been an easygoing guy running the business pretty much on a day-to-day basis. I liked this myself. It suited my style. Unfortunately, all this is changing now. Things are becoming much more systematic and "big business" around here. We're feeling this most in cost reduction and in sales promotion, but every one is feeling it to a certain extent. I don't think this will cause people to quit, though. Most of the workers are very unskilled and easy to train, so they aren't likely to do much better elsewhere. Most of the management people are like me. They've come here because they love [boating, sailing, skiing] and will stick it out because they love the sport.

> *   *   *   *   *

> [The new general manager] is a good man. We had about nine different men around here doing his job before he came. He made a 10th, but because he has just a little more finesse plus the authority of the job behind him things have been running much more smoothly around here since he came. I'm not sure, though, that any of the other nine couldn't have done just as well if they had been given the position.

> *   *   *   *   *

> I think people are happier and things are running more smoothly since we joined CML. Previously; it was hard to get big decisions made. Problems would frequently just float along without ever being resolved. This was frustrating. [The new general manager] is the kind of guy who looks at the facts and comes to a decision on them. This has made life easier for all of us.

Mr. Tod's Role

An additional important corporate link with divisions was provided by Mr. Tod himself. Mr. Tod tried to visit each division at least once every two weeks, and to spend not less than 50 percent of his time physically on-site with division personnel. These visits enabled him to participate on an ongoing basis in divisional developments. According to Mr. Tod, discussion during these visits ranged over every aspect of a division's business: pricing policy, marketing strategy, expansion requirements, personnel problems, production scheduling, and so on. He stated:

> It's hard to generalize about this relationship because it's so different in each specific instance. How I deal with a division depends upon the division involved, its key man, its employees, its particular problems, and so forth. One division president, for instance, is constantly after me to spend more time with him and his people. Until recently another division has been quite reluctant to seek any help.
>
> There do seem to be certain patterns, however. When a new division first comes on board, Charlie and I try to schedule a luncheon for all its employees at which we introduce ourselves and discuss CML and our plans for the division. We deliberately wait two or three weeks after original announcement of the acquisition before having this luncheon in order to let division personnel get used to the idea prior to meeting us. During this period, we intentionally stay away from the division; this helps convey the impression that we don't intend to meddle too much in divisional operations. Before the luncheon meeting, Charlie and I try to learn as much as we can about the 12 or 15 key people in the division. We feel this is useful for getting to know a new division better and for establishing relationships with its key people.

While the above described the usual procedure, not every acquisition had had an initiation luncheon. One division president had objected to the custom so no luncheon had been held for that division.

Because, in principle, divisions operated relatively autonomously, Mr. Tod felt his influence upon operations was based less on exerting direct authority than on the confidence and respect he inspired as a manager. He commented on this situation to the casewriter as follows:

> The influence I can exert comes in preparation, really. I must have intimate knowledge of the business of each division, and must have the numbers involved in any particular situation at my fingertips. This means doing my homework. Otherwise, division people won't listen. They may pay lip service, but they'll make their own decisions in the final analysis. Of course, if they do, they'll have to live with them.
>
> I have to be able to understand our divisions' businesses as well as division presidents themselves in order to do my job. I think I will be able to continue to do this as we expand the number of divisions. Keep in mind that all our divisions are in the leisure time industry and in many ways aren't really that different from one another. Our two mail-order businesses have a number of similarities, for example. The same is true, though to a lesser extent, of our two marine divisions.
>
> I realize I have to walk a fine line most of the time between supervisor and boss, consultant, and advisor. The key to this role of course is working

with people, and the key to that is flexibility . . . listening to people, getting to know their capabilities, and correctly evaluating their judgments. All this of course requires intimate knowledge of the facts of specific situations. Again, doing your homework is essential!

When asked to comment upon the kinds of divisional situations he became involved in apart from those involving routine financial control, Mr. Tod replied that these could be best classified according to the role he played in the development or solution of each. He saw himself playing several roles, but primarily those of—

1. Management consultant.

2. Management recruiter.

3. Participant in key decisions.

Mr. Tod described several situations as examples of each.

1. Management Consultant.   The role typically involved the collection and analysis of information in such a way that it shed light on some important aspect of a division's operation. Mr. Tod described several instances in which he had played this role.

Consumer Analysis.   Dick Fisher, himself an avid fisherman, had deliberately designed the Boston Whaler for the fisherman's every need. As a result, the product combined the general advantages of stability, maneuverability, unsinkability, safety, and performance with specific fishing-oriented features, such as a built-in bait box and a rack for fishing rods. Given this background and orientation, the company naturally directed advertising toward fishermen. Soon after acquisition Mr. Tod began to question whether such an orientation was really justified, however. He commented on this situation as follows:

> Working closely with the Boston Whaler sales organization during the months following acquisition, I came increasingly to feel that a significant percentage of Whaler owners were using the boat for family and recreational in addition to strictly fishing purposes. If this were true, I felt that Boston Whaler advertising copy should reflect the fact. One problem was that there wasn't really much product-in-use data available within the division. During my visits there I had plenty of opportunity to discuss my feelings, though, and suggested from time to time that a customer survey might be made to get a better feel for who bought Whalers and just how the boats were used. It took a while before anything happened, but gradually people began to get interested. During this period I spent quite a lot of time with the division advertising manager talking about what information might be helpful and how it might be obtained. After a while he began putting together a questionnaire, and we discussed this and revised it several times. Finally, by September [1970] a completed questionnaire was mailed out to about 400 customers. Responses have shown a significant family recreational clientele, and recent ad copy is already beginning to reflect this.

Winter Catalog Program.   Mail-order catalogs of one division had traditionally been published and mailed twice a year. The winter catalog consisted of 32 pages; the spring catalog, typically a less ambitious project, contained 24 pages. Each had a total mailing of several hundred thousand copies.

A review of catalog sales in past years had convinced Mr. Tod that an expansion of the spring catalog, in terms of pages, items, or mailings, or any combination of the three, could add to profits substantially. To demonstrate this he reconstructed from divisional accounting data a detailed analysis of the company's catalog experience to date, showing how past changes in pages, items, and mailings had affected volume, tying in enough cost data to provide estimates of profitability. This analysis indicated an optimum mix consisting of a 10 percent increase in total items offered, an increase in the number of pages from 24 to 32, and a continuance of mailings at their former level.

Getting the division to implement this increase was another matter, however. Mr. Tod stated:

> Division personnel just didn't feel there was enough time to produce the eight additional pages before the deadline for mailings. It took a little pushing on our part to get this through, but eventually the division made it. I was able to help a little on a bottleneck situation involving page layout. By setting up a very simple PERT chart with deadlines for the various activities involved, I was able to persuade division personnel to farm out certain layout functions. As it turned out, by following the PERT chart, the catalog was completed three days before the mailing deadline. Partly as a result of the page increase, profits from the 1970 spring catalog were about $50,000 higher than the previous year.

The division president had the following to say about this situation:

> I didn't feel we were geared up at the time to handle the increased volume. One reason I sold to CML was to get their professional help in solving some of our internal systems problems like order processing and inventory control. We haven't had too much help on this so far, however. The increase in catalog volume before straightening out these problems inevitably caused some foul-ups with customers. I'm a little afraid that this kind of thing may undercut some of the goodwill and close personal contact with customers we've worked so hard to build over the years.

2. Management Recruiter.   A second corporate role vis-à-vis divisions in which Mr. Leighton and Mr. Tod appeared to be equally active was that of management recruiter. Mr. Leighton described this role as follows:

> In talking with prospective acquisitions we typically find that the presidents really don't enjoy what they're doing. They have to be concerned with banking relations, accounting, marketing, production, and sales, but what they really want to do is develop more and better products.

To reduce the administrative load on division presidents, CML had helped recruit general managers for all four divisions, leaving the final hiring decision in the hands of division presidents themselves.

Mr. Leighton added:

> We try to get division presidents to hire a man who will complement them. Generally, we try to get an MBA who's been out and gotten six or seven years' experience. We would rather go out and pay someone in his early 30s a lot of money because he has tremendous potential and good background than to get someone with less experience more cheaply or someone with more experience but with less potential.
>
> We want the man that every company wants. We spend as much time trying to meet and recruit a man as we do a company. For example, we went night and day after John Morgan.

Mr. Morgan had graduated from Princeton in 1959 with a degree in electrical engineering and had joined the General Electric Company shortly afterwards. He worked there until 1964 in a number of technical and supervisory positions, including foreman of shop operations and project supervisor for the transfer of products from U.S. to European factories. Mr. Morgan then entered the Harvard Business School, graduating as a Baker Scholar with High Distinction in 1966. Following graduation Mr. Morgan returned to GE, where he subsequently held positions as manager of business planning, manager of marketing administration (both at the division level), and finally as manager of resource planning for a $600 million product group. He resigned in the spring of 1970 to become general manager of Hood Sailmakers.

Mr. Leighton commented as follows on the process of recruiting a Hood general manager:

> We had heard some very good things about John from his professors at Harvard. The feedback we got about his work at GE was also excellent. We heard that he was considered one of their most able young men. We decided that if he was that good, we would like him to join our team, so we went after him.

Mr. Morgan offered the following remarks on this situation:

> I really hadn't been thinking of leaving GE when Bob and Charlie approached me. I had recently been promoted for the third time since leaving the Business School in 1966. I was getting all the right signals from higher management, and I felt I was on the way up.
>
> I think what really appealed to me in CML's offer was the opportunity to build something on my own. Financially, I'm at about the same level as at GE. Of course there's a possibility of building some equity here, but the risks are great too. Over the long run GE probably offered about as good an opportunity for building a personal estate. What I couldn't resist about the Hood offer was the excitement of working in a small operation where I could really influence the future of the company.

3. Participant in Key Decisions. A third important role played by corporate management was that of participant in key decisions facing divisions. Mr. Tod offered the following as an example of the kind of decision he typically became involved in.

Production Cutback. During the third quarter of fiscal 1970, Mr. Tod and one division president had held quite different opinions over what constituted a wise production level for the division. Each side claimed a good case for its position. Division management argued that sales for January and February had been well ahead of forecast, indicating that another good year was in the making. Corporate management feared that trends in the general economy might significantly reduce fourth-quarter shipments and was urging sizable production cutbacks. Mr. Tod was unsuccessful in getting division management to accept his view, however, and production continued at high levels throughout the first three quarters. Mr. Tod noted:

> I made my voice heard, but I couldn't convince anyone to follow me. In fact, I'm not sure whether if I'd been in the division's shoes I would have cut production myself, given the demoralizing impact this has on a division if high sales eventually materialize. From our standpoint, however, the risk of overproduction seemed sizable, and we were advocating a path of prudence.
>
> As it turned out, an unexpected stock market slide caused May and June sales to drop well below forecast. Inventories rose substantially as a result, requiring much more CML financing than originally budgeted. The division became dependent on us because it had to ask for additional financing to carry inventory. This puts us in a good position to exert our influence. At our urging, the division is reducing next year's forecast well below the level originally planned. In addition, it is making contingency plans to cover a further sales drop next year, and is cutting overhead substantially.

Hood's Irish Project

Corporate management's involvement in Hood's Irish weaving mill project constituted yet a further example of its role as participant in key decisions facing divisions.

Hood's organization had grown rapidly in recent years. As recently as early 1967, production facilities had been limited to one weaving and one sailmaking facility, both located at Marblehead, and all sales (already 30 percent foreign in 1967) had been made by Mr. Hood and three sales consultants working out of Marblehead. To reduce tariff expenses on sails shipped abroad and to give better service to foreign customers, Hood had begun setting up foreign lofts, first in England (1967) and later in France, New Zealand, Australia, and Canada. In the United States a West Coast loft had been opened during this period, and the Marblehead weaving capacity had been nearly doubled. This expansion had naturally been

EXHIBIT 6: Organization Chart of Hood Sailmakers, Inc.

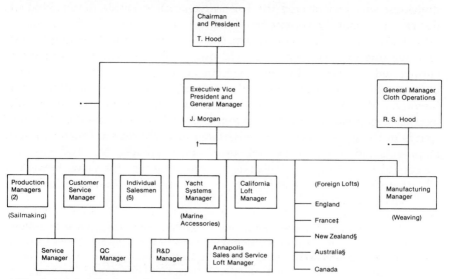

* Primarily technical direction and control.
† Primarily administrative direction and control.
‡ Owned 80 percent by Hood Sailmakers, 20 percent by the loft general manager.
§ Owned 50 percent by Hood Sailmakers, 50 percent by the loft general manager.

Source: Sketch prepared by John Morgan, general manager of Hood Sailmakers, in early January 1971.

accompanied by an increase in the number of Hood employees, from a total of about 165 in 1967, all located in Marblehead, to approximately 300 by 1971, 175 in the United States and 125 abroad. The organization had also become increasingly complex, as evidenced by Mr. Morgan's sketch appearing as Exhibit 6.

The concept of a European-based weaving mill had originated in 1968 with the manager of the newly established English loft, which paid a 20 percent tariff on all sailcloth imported from Marblehead. Hood's interest in a European mill naturally increased with the opening of additional foreign lofts in 1968 and 1969, since duties on the sailcloth they imported ranged as high as 35 percent in France and 31 percent in Australia. The ad valorem value of cloth represented approximately 25 percent of the final selling price of Hood sails; import tariffs therefore constituted a significant percentage of each foreign sales dollar—from 5 percent in England to more than 8 percent in Australia and France.

Because of increasing pressure from the managers of foreign lofts, Mr. Hood in early 1969 hired a brother-in-law of the English loft manager to begin site studies for a European mill. The desirability of an Irish site soon became evident because the Republic of Ireland's inclusion in the British Commonwealth permitted tariff-free export to all Common-wealth countries, because the Irish government offered to underwrite 50 percent of capital costs for the new facility and to waive all tax on profits earned in Ireland, and because of low labor rates in Ireland. By August 1970 the Irish Development Authority (IDA) had agreed to fund $266,000 of the total $554,000 fixed capital required by the project, and quotes for the necessary equipment were already being solicited.

As shown in detail in Exhibit 7, the project called for a total invest-ment of $580,000. Mr. Morgan calculated that the cash flow savings result-ing from the new mill (shown in part B of Exhibit 7) represented a 13 percent aftertax return on CML's $314,000 investment in the project. Cash flow savings were expected in three areas:

1. Elimination of tariffs on cloth currently woven in Marblehead and shipped to lofts in Commonwealth countries.
2. A reduction in variable cost of manufacture arising mainly from lower labor rates in Ireland.

EXHIBIT 7

A. Capital Requirements for Irish Weaving Mill (in thousands of dollars)

	Total Cost	Sources of Funds	
		IDA Grant	CML
Land	$ 8.4	$ 4.2	$ 4.2
Building	216.0	108.0	108.0
Equipment	329.6	154.1	175.5
Working capital (net)*	26.0	0.0	26.0
Total funds required	580.0	266.3	313.7

B. Aftertax Cash Flow Savings Resulting from Transferring to Ireland All Weaving of Cloth Sold Outside the United States (in thousands of dollars)

	1971	1972	1973	1974	1975
Cash flow increase resulting from decreases in—					
Tariffs	$ 16	$ 18	$ 20	$ 23	$ 27
Variable costs of manufacture . . .	56	63	65	83	96
U.S. corporation profit taxes	74	85	87	110	128
Subtotal	146	166	172	216	251
Cash flow decrease resulting from an increase in—					
Fixed cost of manufacture†	98	97	96	96	96
Net cash flow increase (net cash flow savings)	48	69	76	120	155

Note: Discounted cash flow return on $314,000 investment = 13 percent.
* Net of working capital freed in the United States as a result of moving a portion of the weaving operation to Ireland.
† Excludes depreciation.
Source: Company records.

3. A reduction in U.S. corporate profits tax arising because the Marble-
    head mill would suffer a significant loss of contribution margin (ap-
    proximately 40 percent) as a result of moving production to Ireland.
    The resulting reduction in profits reported in the United States would
    reduce U.S. taxes on corporate profits.

The only recurring cash outflow resulting from the investment arose
from an increase in fixed manufacturing expenses. While no reduction
in Marblehead's fixed expenses was expected despite the 40 percent reduction in throughput, Ireland would itself incur $98,000 of additional fixed
costs (after depreciation).

Mr. Morgan offered the following comments on the Irish project:

> From my standpoint, the big advantage of the project is strictly finan-
> cial . . . the 13 percent aftertax return it represents for us. There are minor
> strategic advantages, of course. The investment will protect our positions
> in England and France, where duties have pushed prices about as high as
> they can go. If duties should go even higher, which we feel could happen,
> we might be pushed out of these markets if we are still shipping cloth
> from Marblehead.

Hood's board of directors was scheduled to meet on January 15 to
decide on a recommendation with regard to the Irish investment. Mr.
Tod saw three alternatives open to the board: (1) dropping the project
outright, (2) going ahead with it full speed, or (3) delaying it until Hood's
domestic market improved. The more he considered the many factors
involved, the more he came to favor the third alternative. First, cash
inflows were relatively small during early years of the project. They would
therefore not significantly contribute to the earnings track record CML
hoped to establish prior to going public in 1972. Second, the tax status
of profits earned in Ireland raised a complex set of questions including
(1) whether or not future investors would be evaluating CML's earnings
on a before-tax or an aftertax basis, (2) future cash needs in Europe
providing a use for profits earned abroad, (3) difficulties and costs associated with eventual repatriation of profits earned abroad, and (4) possible
legal complications arising from the fact that earn-out for former Hood
owners was based on before-tax rather than aftertax profits. Third, Hood
was showing a somewhat lower return on the funds currently being advanced by CML[10] than some of the other divisions of the company. Therefore, while Hood profits had improved somewhat in recent months, the
division had not yet entirely demonstrated an ability to achieve its full
profit potential. Fourth, the continued slump in domestic sales had reduced
Hood's Marblehead operation to 50 percent of capacity. This made a
sizable investment in additional capacity difficult to justify. Fifth, and
most important, Hood management was already spread extremely thin

---

[10] Totaling $800,000 in early January 1971.

over a great number of activities and did not appear to have the time and energy at present to take on a major new commitment.

There were, of course, disadvantages to delay. The IDA grant might be lost. Hood funds and management energy would be expended just maintaining status quo on the project. The Hoods themselves, concerned with the long-run competitive advantages of the investment and eager to get under way, might be disappointed.

Mr. Tod commented on his position as follows:

> I just feel we can get a quicker payout by putting our money in other areas . . . expanding one company's product line, for instance, or improving another company's sales organization.

Mr. Leighton offered the following comments:

> I think over the long run it makes sense for Hood to begin weaving abroad. It's a question of timing, really. With sales down, plus an over-capacity situation, I'm afraid of what the Irish investment will do to Hood's current profit picture. In addition, I wonder whether at this point in time Hood has enough management time and energy to take on something like this. A start-up situation is never easy.

ACHIEVEMENTS TO DATE: FUTURE PROBLEMS AND OPPORTUNITIES

Hood's Irish investment was under consideration just 18 months after the formation of CML and 15 months since its first acquisition in September 1969. Mr. Leighton had the following to say about CML's achievements to date and the problems and opportunities facing the company in the months to come:

> Progress so far has been excellent. Three out of four companies will show significant profit increases this year over last—20 percent or more. In the case of one division profits will fall somewhat, but mainly because we are deliberately scheduling manufacturing below break-even in order to work off excess inventory built up last year. Fiscal 1972 should bring a big profit increase for this division.
>
> As for further acquisitions, the biggest constraint at this point is pressure on Bob Tod. Right now, for instance, we are looking at three companies as possible acquisitions this spring. All are out of state and only one is in New England. This is quite different from our existing divisions, which are all easily accessible from Boston. The big question on further acquisitions becomes how many companies one man can handle at once. This depends, of course, on how spread out they are geographically, and on the quality of division management. If our divisions can more or less run themselves, we can spread Bob a lot thinner. The real key to further growth then becomes the development of good management teams within divisions, and this in turn depends heavily on the quality of people we can bring into CML

Group companies. As a matter of fact, after acquiring our fourth company last July we completely stopped all acquisition search and spent six months just looking for people. Now that general managers have been installed in all divisions and we've got four really good division management teams, we're back looking at acquisitions again.

There are other ways of easing the pressure on Bob, of course. One would be to limit acquisitions to businesses very similar to existing divisions. This would reduce the learning effort required at our level. Another would be to eventually develop several Bob Tods as Group vice presidents for our three main areas: marine, sporting equipment and related accessories, and hobby crafts. An advantage of this would be the increased promotion opportunities it would open to new employees now being brought into the company. A disadvantage is that it would necessarily reduce the tremendous fun and personal involvement we are now having with our companies. How we go on this is a personal decision we'll have to make at some point. A third possibility would be to bring new companies in under existing divisions.

A long-term objective is to take CML public sometime after the fall of 1972. This would provide the three full years of audited operations required by the SEC. We'd like a major "quality" brokerage firm to handle the public offering, and want a large enough offering in our shares to provide for after-market trading. To achieve this we feel we will need from $750,000 to $1 million in aftertax profits.

As far as we're concerned, the current economic downturn couldn't have been timed better. It has pushed us to trim deadweight in divisions to a point where they are now lean and hungry. When the economy finally turns around, we should be in a position to show attractive internal earnings increases. This of course is the real key to the long-run success of CML Group: Our ability to show earnings per share increases through internal growth rather than through newly acquired earnings. Stated another way, we believe that our future success will depend far more on our ability to successfully manage than on our ability to successfully acquire.

CASE 23

The Leisure Group, Inc.

The Leisure Group, Inc., a once-bustling Los Angeles conglomerate that produced a wide range of products for leisure time use, had grown from sales of $10 million in 1965 to sales of $66 million in 1970. But in 1971 The Leisure Group (TLG) suffered a financial crisis which resulted in losses of $31 million on sales of $58 million. TLG common, which traded over-the-counter for as much as $36 in 1969, sank to $1¼ by the end of 1971 and subsequently declined to 6 cents per share by the end of 1974. Exhibit 1 shows TLG's past ten years' sales and the price range of its common stock since it became a public company in 1968 (see Exhibit 2).

Merle Banta and Stephen Hinchliffe, the founders and co-chief executive officers, controlled about 10 percent of TLG's 3.2 million outstanding shares of common stock. Miraculously enough, they were not only still managing TLG but had managed to show $1 million in profits on $27 million in sales for 1974. Now, however, confident that they had pulled TLG out of the crisis, they both felt they were faced with a new challenge:

> The biggest risk now is in doing nothing. We could sit back, draw a salary, and grow modestly; but that is most risky. We would still be unable to really grow or raise new capital since after three years of survival management, the bankers feel we are resourceful and can do without additional funds. But the truth is that the operations are lean—the rabbits coming out of the hat are awfully thin. There are limits to being resourceful, and we're approaching them. We must now go on the attack instead of defense.

EXHIBIT 1: Sales and Stock Price

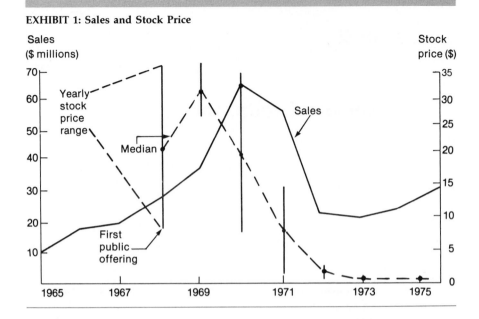

BACKGROUND

In 1964 Hinchliffe and Banta left McKinsey & Company, a large management consulting firm, to look for a company they could buy and manage. After five months of search, they bought Thompson Manufacturing Company, a manufacturer of lawn and garden sprinklers in Los Angeles, using only $8,000 of their own money and borrowing $550,000. With that heavily mortgaged base, they set about showing the business world how a couple of bright young MBAs could achieve fame and fortune while constructing a dynamic business enterprise around the concept of leisure. Hinchliffe and Banta subsequently broadened product lines and acquired other businesses, combining the various activities into The Leisure Group, Inc. By 1969 they were self-made millionaires.

The period from 1965 to 1970 was one of rapid growth for TLG in the manufacturing and marketing of leisure time products. It also represented an aggressive acquisition strategy which had led to the integration of 12 firms into the TLG management system and growth from 2 to 17 factories accounting for an increase in employees from 120 in 1965 to 2,600 in 1969.

Their goals for 15 percent increased annual sales through internal growth had been met except in 1968 when they had cut back their Planet Junior farm and garden product line. Their goal of 50 percent annual sales growth through acquisitions had also been met except for 1967

EXHIBIT 2

THE LEISURE GROUP, INC
Selected 10-Year Operating Results
(in thousands of dollars)

	1974	1973	1972	1971	1970	1969	1968	1967	1966	1965
Operating results:										
Net sales	$26,952	$21,911	$23,713	$57,702	$66,480	$39,694	$30,427	$22,161	$19,069	$10,234
Gross margin	8,345	6,727	6,912	3,002	12,612	10,528	7,572	5,403	4,051	2,068
Operating expenses	5,608	5,294	7,426	15,561	9,438	6,111	4,755	3,756	3,239	1,659
Interest	1,718	1,404	2,023	3,297	2,900	1,308	717	550	423	128
Net income	1,019	222	(7,727)	(31,399)	219	1,678	1,053	571	191	89
Earnings per share	0.13	0.03	(2.46)	(10.16)	0.08	0.73	0.54	0.36	0.14	0.10
Average shares outstanding (in thousands)	3,123.4	3,143.7	3,143.7	3,092.0	3,087.2	2,387.2	2,241.0	n.a.	n.a.	n.a.
Financial position:										
Working capital	2,946	2,531	3,770	5,942	11,504	9,339	5,883	2,777	2,328	489
Net property, plant, and equipment	5,562	6,976	8,072	13,818	20,879	15,060	8,026	3,635	3,326	1,479

EXHIBIT 2 *(concluded)*

THE LEISURE GROUP, INC
Selected 10-Year Operating Results
(in thousands of dollars)

	1974	1973	1972	1971	1970	1969	1968	1967	1966	1965
Shareholders' equity	6,427	5,231	5,453	8,957	30,705	13,841	8,989	1,723	1,037	521
Retained earnings	(34,145)	(35,386)	(35,164)	(27,659)	3,740	3,300	1,622	n.a.	n.a.	n.a.
Total debt	12,447	21,072	14,860	38,510	43,152	25,801	15,711	n.a.	n.a.	n.a.
Short term†	5,379	8,695	5,287	20,559	24,179	10,369	8,058			
Long term	7,068	12,377	9,573	13,951	9,973	9,342	7,653			
7% convertible subordinated notes	—	—	—	4,000	9,000	6,000	—			
Current assets	12,778	17,958	11,533	32,636	50,953	30,583	20,581	n.a.	n.a.	n.a.
Other information:										
Number of plants	7	10	8	14	19	17	7	4	3	2
Number of employees	1,000	1,000	1,000	1,500	3,300	2,600	1,700	700	530	120
Space occupied (square feet)	492,000	593,000	527,000	1,128,000	2,075,000	1,370,000	750,000	491,000	281,000	50,000

n.a. = not available.

* As stated in annual reports of 1969–74.

† Includes current position of long-term debt.

when management efforts were devoted to integrating the Ben Pearson product line. They surpassed their goal of 25 percent increase in earnings per share each year. The major problems had been in meeting their goal of 6 percent aftertax profit. Management time and cost of integrating new acquisitions were making it difficult to achieve profit targets. Exhibit 3 gives a summary of TLG performance to those goals through 1969, as reported.

EXHIBIT 3: TLG Five-Year Performance Compared to Financial Goals

	Performance (percent)				
Goal	1969	1968	1967	1966	1965
15 percent internal sales growth*. . .	17	3	21	25	9
50 percent acquisition sales growth† .	82	68	32	175	84
6 percent aftertax profit‡	4.3	5.5	5.6	3.2	6.3
25 percent increase in EPS§	35	42	90	74	—

* Sales of product lines owned by TLG for the entire year divided by sales of such product lines for most recent prior audited fiscal year whether or not owned by TLG for that entire year (starting one year after acquisition in the case of new product lines).
† Sales during most recent audited fiscal year of product lines acquired during year divided by sales of product lines owned by TLG at beginning of year.
‡ Aftertax profits as reported.
§ EPS compared with prior fiscal year as reported.

Source: 1969 annual report.

STRATEGY

TLG's business strategy had been to sell leisure time products through mass-merchandising channels. With professional management, TLG was concentrating on acquisitions of recognized brands which could be integrated into TLG's new merchandising channels.

Sales. By 1966 Banta and Hinchliffe had zeroed in on the growing demand for leisure products and on new opportunities to mass market them through large outlets rather than small specialty shops. They recognized that with shorter workweeks, younger families, rising incomes, and higher levels of education, Americans were becoming more involved in free-time activities. This trend, coupled with increasingly sophisticated promotional techniques for mass merchandising and self-service, provided the impetus for TLG's strategy of capitalizing on the opportunities by marketing various leisure time products through a single sales force. As Banta commented in 1969:

> This choice is more significant than might seem to be the case at first glance. The most obvious result is, of course, the economies of selling

effort spread over several products. Because the products are not highly technical, one salesman can handle the various lines. Equally significant, however, is an ability to provide the buyers at large distributors with facts and data quickly and concisely. What we are working toward is a two-tiered sales force: (1) a small number of expert salesmen who can provide the benefits of our centralized information on several product groups, and (2) a larger number of "retail detail" people who stock shelves, handle promotional material, and so on, at the various retail outlets. The result is that we are able to overpower most of our competitors in dealing with buyers; these competitors are still organized as though they were selling to a network of small retailers. In fact, over 50 percent of the sales of products such as ours are sold through mass merchandisers.

Stephen Hinchliffe also commented in 1969 on their long-run strategy:

> In terms of where we hope to take TLG, we are really still in Phase I. Our present lines can easily be handled by one sales force. The questions I grapple with are what happens when sales of our present groups (and acquisitions to be made in these existing lines) reach $100 million or more and we move into fields such as travel, education, or entertainment. We might have to leave TLG at that time as a separate organization and start almost from scratch with the added services. You know, we can go a long way under the umbrella "leisure time" and "recreation."

Acquisitions. TLG's acquisition strategy was aimed basically at achieving economies of scale through integration of all products into a common sales channel of mass merchandisers. To make this work, it was felt that "brand leadership" was essential for marketing with a single nationwide sales force handling all products. As a result, an acquired firm's operating performance or size was of less importance than its position of product leadership or brand image.

This acquisition policy had led TLG to market leisure-related products in three principal areas: *youth recreation* toys, play equipment, and snow play equipment and sleds; *lawn and garden* sprinklers, sprayers, indoor plant care, and power mower products; and *sporting goods* including firearms, archery equipment, camping equipment, toboggans, trophies, and camouflage hunting wear. (See Exhibit 4 for acquisitions.) The product list had expanded to 10,500 items by 1970.

In analyzing operations of potential acquisitions, TLG concentrated on three major areas: cost of goods sold, manufacturing methods, and technologies that capitalize on the company's design know-how. These areas, more than earnings history, were particularly pertinent because of TLG's policy of total integration of acquired companies.

1. Cost of goods sold: TLG preferred operations with high manufacturing overhead and a high labor content as they represented the greatest potential for improved gross margins.
2. Manufacturing methods: Acquisitions which had not applied profes-

sional management techniques in the area of inventory control, production planning, work simplification, and value engineering provided the best opportunity for TLG to make significant improvement.

3. Design and manufacturing technologies: TLG considered plants as a center of specific manufacturing capability and was interested in acquiring new technologies that might subsequently be applied to existing product lines.

Stephen Hinchliffe described the acquisition process in 1969:

> We've had enough experience at making acquisitions to have distilled a few generalizations. The process can be visualized in four stages.
>
> First, Merle and I evaluate the opportunity in the context of our established strategy. Does this situation fit? Can it take us where we want to go? Next we enter a period of negotiating with the present owners as to the value of the firm. Being human, these owners generally want more than a firm is worth; sometimes they seem to expect us to pay them for value we intend to introduce by making changes.
>
> The third stage is probably the most critical: that is to arrange for integrating an acquisition into The Leisure Group, Inc. We take a *task force* into the new firm; usually someone from marketing, operations, and control. Each of these men analyzes the situation he finds and is responsible for developing an "action plan." This plan should tell us, in specific language, what has to be done to turn this company into a contributor to the company. We spend quite a bit of time as a task unit, preparing changes we believe necessary.

The action plans indicated what types of inputs TLG expected to inject into an acquisition, both in the immediate future and over the long term. In most cases to date the immediate emphasis was on reducing general overhead expenses and instituting cost control measures in the plants. More significant were the sophisticated marketing ideas and techniques which TLG brought to bear; products were added and others discontinued to strengthen the line; some products were altered and improved to be more attuned to changes in the markets; and more emphasis was placed on providing retail outlets with data helpful in making their decisions as to product mix and space allocations.

Professional Management. The key element of TLG's concept was the integration of product lines into a single professionally managed organization which would enhance these product lines. Advanced techniques for gathering and analyzing information, establishing objectives, and measuring performance against goals were critical to TLG's management system.

In developing a professionally managed organization, by 1970 TLG had employed 30 men with MBAs from leading business schools. Of the 37 members of the executive staff, 40 percent were under 30 years

EXHIBIT 4: Acquisitions

Date of Acquisition (divestiture)	Former Name (location)	Business Description (product group)	Approximate Terms (accounting method)
1964 (October 1973)	Thompson Mfg. Co. (Los Angeles, Cal.)	Small area sprinklers for lawns and gardens (Lawn and Garden Products)	$555,000 in cash and $350,000 in notes (purchase)
July 1965	Hayes Spray Gun Co. (Los Angeles, Cal.)	Hose and garden sprayers for insecticides and fertilizers (Lawn and Garden Products)	$505,000 in cash and $470,000 in notes (purchase)
February 1966 (November 1971)	Ben Pearson, Inc. (Pine Bluff, Ark.)	Archery equipment [and a line of mechanical harvesting equipment which was disposed of in 1967] (Sporting Goods Products)	$3 million in cash (pooling of interests) [sold in 1971 for $3,289,000 plus $380,000 in liabilities]
September 1967 (May 1971—Planet Junior) (February 1973)	S. L. Allen & Co., Inc. (Philadelphia, Pa.)	Flexible Flyer and Yankee Clipper sleds; Planet Junior farm and garden tools (Youth Recreation Products)	$1,760,000 in notes and common stock (purchase)
November 1967 (October 1973)	Rain Spray Sprinkler, division of Abro Mfg. Co., Inc. (Los Angeles, Cal.)	Underground lawn and garden sprinklers (Lawn and Garden Products)	$63,000 in cash and $127,000 in notes (purchase)
March 1968	Black Magic, Inc. (Los Angeles, Cal.)	Indoor plant care products (Lawn and Garden Products)	$193,872 in common stock (purchase)
June 1968	The High Standard Mfg. Corp. (New Haven, Conn.)	Sporting firearms (Sporting Goods Products)	$5,300,000 in cash (purchase)
October 1968 (June 1973)	Werlich Industries Ltd. (Preston, Ontario, Canada)	Toboggans, sleds, and snow saucers (Youth Recreation Products)	$460,000 in cash and $690,000 in notes (purchase)
March 1969	Sierra Bullets, Inc. (Santa Fe Springs, Cal.)	Bullets for target and hunting rifles (Sporting Goods Products)	$4.5 million in cash (purchase)

Date	Company	Description	Consideration
July 1969 (February 1973)	Blazon, Inc. (Jamestown, Pa., and West Point, Miss.)	Play gyms and hobby horses. Sales: $12.5 million (Youth Recreation Products)	$4.5 million in common stock (pooling of interests)
September 1969 (February 1973)	Mascon Toy Co., division of Masco Corp.	Toy telephones and toys for young children. Sales: $3 million (Youth Recreation Products)	$800,000 in cash and $2 million in notes (purchase)
September 1969	The Lyman Gun Sight Corp. (Middlefield, Conn.)	Gunsights and accessories for sporting firearms (Sporting Goods Products)	$2 million in cash (purchase)
September 1969 (October 1973)	Himalayan Industries (Monterey, Cal.)	Backpacks (Sporting Goods Products)	$480,000 in common stock (pooling of interests)
February 1970 (November 1971)	Yard-Man Incorporated (Jackson, Mich., and Sullivan, Ill.)	Powered lawn, garden, and yard maintenance equipment. Sales: 9 months, $22.9 million (Lawn and Garden Products)	$15.5 million in common stock (purchase resulting in cost of $10.2 million in excess of net asset valuation) [sold for $9 million in notes to be paid over five years]
October 1970	Dodge Trophy (Crystal Lake, Ill.)	Manufacturer of sporting trophies, awards (Oscar, Emmy), trophy cases, plaques, etc. Sales: $6 million (Sporting Goods Products)	$937,167 in common stock (purchase)
October 1970	Kamo	Camouflage hunting wear. Sales: $1.4 million (Sporting Goods Products)	$210,000 in common stock (pooling of interests)

of age; 58 percent had been employed by corporations in the *Fortune* 500; 30 percent had been with TLG over two years; and, of those, 90 percent had been promoted at least once, had stock options, and had earned incentive bonuses. TLG preferred candidates with past experience in leading packaged goods companies, with successful records, and high motivation toward rapid advancement.

In addition to semiannual salary and stock option reviews, performance bonuses accounted for 10 to 40 percent of salary. Additional motivations were derived from (1) interaction with higher level managers and the chief executive officers; (2) task force assignments to select, negotiate, and integrate acquisitions; and (3) exposure to the financial and business communities. Advancement was based on performance as was compensation.

ORGANIZATION

TLG's organization had been in a constant state of transition, and no formal organization charts were available. (Exhibit 5 is the casewriter's description developed from TLG's 1970 profile.) In 1970 TLG reorganized from a purely functional organization to concentrate efforts in specific market areas. The product groups, reporting to two corporate vice presidents, had marketing and operations responsibility. The functional areas of sales, product development, and control were all centralized to achieve greater efficiencies. These functional activities had to be coordinated with the product groups to achieve corporate goals. This coordinating function was explained in TLG's 1970 profile:

> Two TLG vice presidents handle coordination of all functional activities, in addition to their specific product line responsibilities. This organizational structure has two objectives: (1) it permits effective coordination and integration of acquisitions into functional areas, and (2) strengthens the entrepreneurial spirit at all TLG management levels by allowing freedom of access by the co-chief executives to all managerial employees, regardless of organizational relationships.

Planning. TLG's management system was a continual cycle of gathering and analyzing information, establishing objectives, and monitoring operations. More and more functions were being centralized at the corporate level so as to develop relevant data and controls. However, data processing facilities were still being "debugged" in 1969, and operations people and product managers were not getting timely data. This problem was forcing consideration of having plant controllers report to their respective plants, instead of to the corporate controller, to provide managers with more responsive information.

For purposes of financial control and planning, a computer model

EXHIBIT 5: Organization Chart, 1970

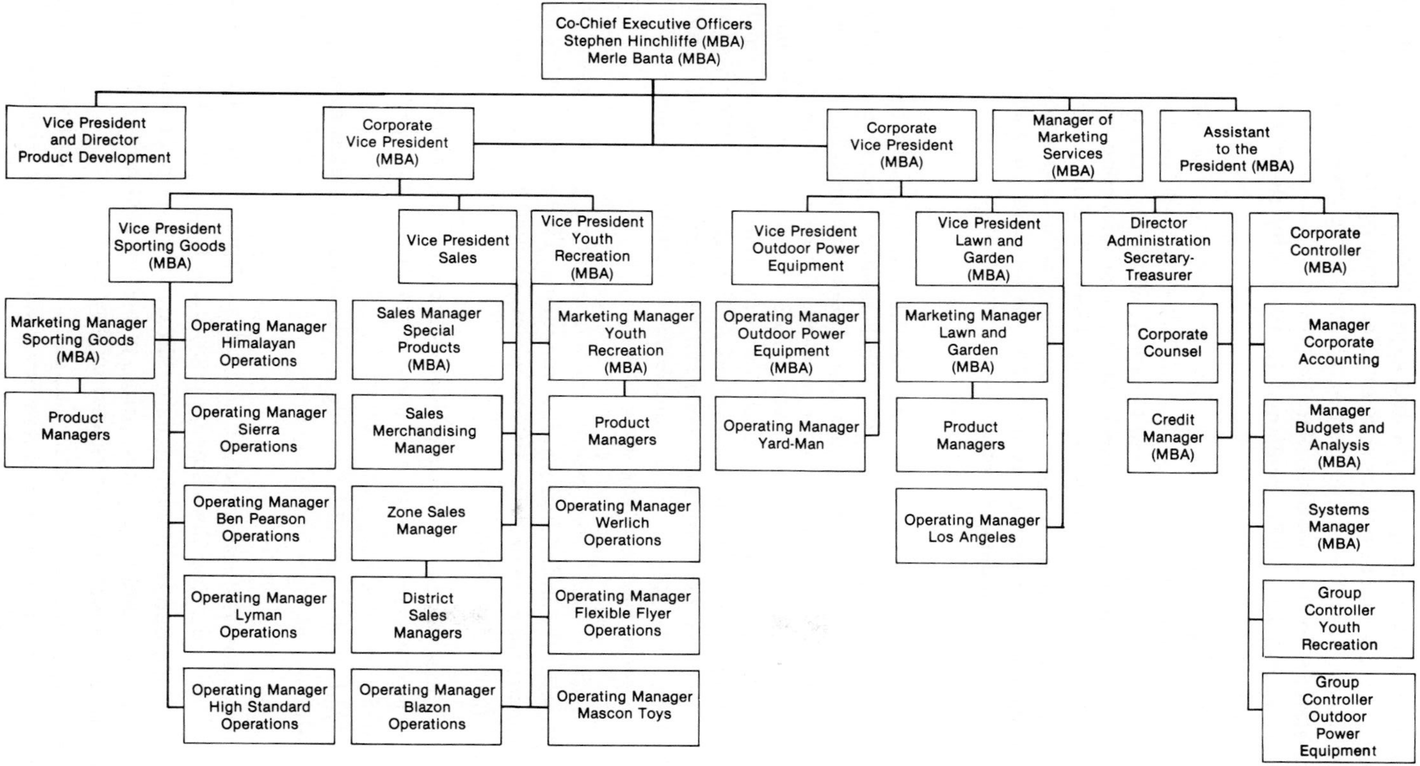

Co-Chief Executive Officers
Stephen Hinchliffe (MBA)
Merle Banta (MBA)

- Corporate Vice President (MBA)
  - Vice President and Director Product Development
  - Vice President Sporting Goods (MBA)
    - Marketing Manager Sporting Goods (MBA)
    - Product Managers
  - Vice President Sales
    - Sales Manager Special Products (MBA)
    - Sales Merchandising Manager
    - Zone Sales Manager
    - District Sales Managers
    - Operating Manager Blazon Operations
    - Operating Manager Himalayan Operations
    - Operating Manager Sierra Operations
    - Operating Manager Ben Pearson Operations
    - Operating Manager Lyman Operations
    - Operating Manager High Standard Operations
  - Vice President Youth Recreation (MBA)
    - Marketing Manager Youth Recreation (MBA)
    - Product Managers
    - Operating Manager Werlich Operations
    - Operating Manager Flexible Flyer Operations
    - Operating Manager Mascon Toys

- Corporate Vice President (MBA)
  - Manager of Marketing Services (MBA)
  - Vice President Outdoor Power Equipment
    - Operating Manager Outdoor Power Equipment (MBA)
    - Operating Manager Yard-Man
  - Vice President Lawn and Garden (MBA)
    - Marketing Manager Lawn and Garden (MBA)
    - Product Managers
    - Operating Manager Los Angeles

- Assistant to the President (MBA)
  - Director Administration Secretary-Treasurer
    - Corporate Counsel
    - Credit Manager (MBA)
  - Corporate Controller (MBA)
    - Manager Corporate Accounting (MBA)
    - Manager Budgets and Analysis (MBA)
    - Systems Manager (MBA)
    - Group Controller Youth Recreation
    - Group Controller Outdoor Power Equipment

was developed to project sales and expenditures for each manufacturing operation and functional department. Resulting operating statements, balance sheets, cash flows, and pertinent ratios were reviewed by the corporate staff to correct possible plan variances.

Stephen Hinchliffe explained in 1969 why there was an emphasis on planning at TLG:

> Given our backgrounds, it's not hard to understand why we are so thorough in our planning efforts around here. Merle and I were consultants, exposed to a broad range of situations where we could observe a number of different planning systems. Most of our marketing organization comes from companies like General Foods, Procter & Gamble, and Xerox—so we have the benefit of knowing how these rather sophisticated firms went about it. And most of us are MBAs, so I'm sure we're all still recovering from the pounding of "planning is a way of life."

He continued:

> Detailed emphasis on planning fits integrally with the style of Merle and myself here at TLG. We both believe it is possible to make certain types of decisions once, and then disseminate procedures for how these recurring problems should be handled. We have seen so many examples of rather simple decisions being made over and over, each time with a new analysis. In this vein, we are convinced that a strong emphasis on planning forces our people to think in strategic terms. With well-thought-out plans, the everyday events can be interpreted in the context of the larger plan. Planning also contributes to setting goals and specific action routes to accomplishing these goals.

Because TLG was essentially a marketing organization, planning began with the individual product managers. These men were responsible for the preparation of marketing programs derived from five major interrelated marketing plans:

1. Annual product plan: Specified strategies and action for achieving goals by setting long- and short-term profit, market share, and sales goals by specific product group.

2. Product line introduction report (annual): Detailed every product in the line, along with selling prices, cost factors, and the resulting "merchandising profit."

3. Sales forecast: Set product unit sales estimates and set targets against which all other departments coordinate their programs.

4. Annual budget: Listed all expenditures for product support, including specific promotions, advertising, publicity, packaging, research, advertising allowances, and related expenses.

5. Annual promotion plan: Supplied detail on actions to be taken throughout the year and described timing, theme, strategy, and implementation of each program.

The bottom line figure for product managers was one which measured sales dollars minus all marketing expenses controllable by PMs, such as advertising and promotion. PMs were held entirely responsible for their product lines.

The managers of operations were given full responsibility for the plant or plants under their supervision. They were responsible for translating marketing forecasts into production quotas and for monitoring ongoing operations to assure they met these goals.

In discussing the internal functioning of TLG's organization, Steve Hinchliffe explained in 1969:

> Clearly the most general fact is our informal communications and the access everyone has to everyone else. Being MBAs, Merle and I expect these men to have an orientation broad enough to fit their job into the more general picture. We also expect them to be problem oriented: to go where they have to and speak to whomever they need, to solve their particular problem.
>
> Secondly, our detailed emphasis on planning and review allows each unit to operate without being totally dependent on other functional units. Once our annual plans are established, the product and operating managers practically live with each other, going across the functional boundaries. And since product managers have responsibility meeting sales forecasts, they have what I believe to be a very strong incentive to keep in touch with everyone necessary to do so, everyone being other managers at TLG, the sales force, customers, suppliers.
>
> Last, Merle and I have mentioned our belief that a lot of decisions in any firm can be procedurized. We hope to have made the process easier for our people by disseminating procedures and criteria. This provides a framework within which our managers can work.

1970 OPERATING RESULTS

While the results for fiscal 1970 were satisfactory in terms of sales and acquisitions of new product lines, it was a disappointing year for profits and earnings per share. Compared with 1969, sales went from $41 million to $66 million; but net income fell from $1.7 million to $219,000, a drop from 75 cents to 8 cents in earnings per share.

The increase in 1970 sales was from acquisitions of Kamo camouflage hunting wear, Dodge Trophy, a manufacturer of trophies, and Yard-Man outdoor power equipment. Yard-Man accounted for almost $23 million of the $26 million sales increase in 1970.

Part of the problem had come from a 4 percent decline in sales of product lines owned more than one year. This sales slump was seen as a consequence of the economic climate, but the more significant profit decline was caused by the failure to adequately plan for and control changes initiated in operating facilities of acquired product lines. The 1970 annual report listed the major failures as:

Unanticipated labor and overhead costs associated with the consolidation of Blazon play gyms and hobby horse manufacturing and administrative activities from four sites into a single location.

Direct labor, scrap, and manufacturing overhead costs significantly higher than budget in the Flexible Flyer sled plant.

Lower than planned sales of Blazon outdoor play equipment.

A decline in sales of certain High Standard sporting firearms below 1969 levels.

Higher than planned marketing and sales costs, due in part to significant price competition experienced in 1970.

Blazon Plant Consolidation.   The managers of Youth Recreation Products explained in the 1970 annual report that the unanticipated decline in Blazon gross margins was in large part a function of cost overruns in labor, materials, and manufacturing overhead and in lower than planned sales.

As part of the action plan to integrate and consolidate Blazon operations into TLG, it was decided to close three warehouses and three manufacturing plants, while expanding the remaining Mississippi plant. Reduced overhead costs and production efficiencies were estimated to more than offset increased transport costs. However, estimates for the time required to close facilities, transfer equipment and personnel, negotiate with union employees, and institute accounting and control procedures was longer than expected. As explained:

> The net effect was a failure to meet planned manufacturing cost standards. Concurrently, the cost system in use at Blazon plants combined with changes in personnel, manufacturing methods, and locations resulted in a significant portion of these cost overruns being accounted for as "inventory." Because of the numerous changes taking place at the operations level throughout 1970, physical inventories were not taken until year-end, and the difference between book and actual inventory was not identified until November 1970.

Flexible Flyer Sled Manufacturing.   The second major factor affecting Youth Recreation Products' gross margins was also explained:

> This plant was constructed in 1969, and substantial plant start-up costs were incurred. The start-up problems resulted in late shipments of sleds in 1969, and, accordingly, attention was directed toward avoiding similar delivery and customer service problems in 1970.
>
> A combination of failure to develop an adequate inventory mix of sales and an unanticipated increase in sled orders created serious production capacity problems in late 1970. In an effort to meet our customers' delivery

requirements, we placed the Medina plant on three-shift operation, six days a week with maintenance and limited production on Sundays. The labor and cost inefficiencies resulting from the influx of new and inadequately trained employees, shift and overtime premiums, and insufficient supervision caused actual manufacturing costs to exceed standard.

Failure to meet standard manufacturing costs and the expensing of earlier labor, overhead, and material costs incurred in 1970 and associated with bringing the Medina plant on-stream added over $1 million to the decline in Youth Recreation Products' gross margins.

Financial Problems

In January 1970, TLG acquired Yard-Man for common stock valued at $15.5 million. As part of the integration program of Yard-Man into TLG, approximately 50 separate capital programs were planned for product-line engineering, development, and appearance changes. These programs, plus the added working capital requirements of Yard-Man, led TLG to open a $26 million revolving short-term loan agreement with a group of six banks. This financing arrangement, requiring a minimum of $10.5 million in working capital, eventually led to the crisis of "Black Wednesday."

Merle Banta explained how the situation developed:

> In February of 1971 we needed $26 million to finance operations. We needed $10 million in working capital for Yard-Man plus an additional $16 million in working capital for the other product lines. We had already issued a "Red Herring"[1] to raise additional capital, but the day before we were to meet with the Boston investment community, Nixon invaded Cambodia. Few analysts showed up at the meeting since the brokers were all concerned about the effects of the invasion on the market and were watching their stocks. Well, the Dow Jones dropped sharply, and TLG's stock price fell from $24 to $16. We decided not to go through with the issue. However, that meant that we had no cushion in case anything went wrong.

1971 OPERATING RESULTS

In early 1971, sales of lawn and garden products, principally Yard-Man lawn mowers, dropped substantially and continued to decline through the summer of 1971. At the same time, anticipated improvements in shipping levels and operating efficiencies at Blazon and High Standard plants were not achieved. The combination of lower sales and higher operating costs resulted in a pretax operating loss at nine months of approximately $4.3 million, which placed the company in default under its bank line of credit. Merle Banta explained the default:

---

[1] Preliminary prospectus.

> Since our lead bank had a legal loan limit of $6 million, we ended up with a consortium of six banks. Then in our third quarter (May, June, and July), we missed our sales forecast of $18 million with actual sales of $12 million. Had it been just Yard-Man the banks would have understood, but it was across the board—sales were down in sprayers, archery, and 15 other product lines. The banks lost confidence in the management and in the lead bank. They panicked and wanted out.

TLG was required to begin reducing its outstanding bank loans in August. This severely curtailed operating cash at the time of peak seasonal requirements for production and shipping. For several weeks in September and October production at virtually all TLG plants was essentially suspended until interim short-term financing was arranged. Merle Banta explained the events that followed:

> When the banks panicked, we were under the gun. We had proposed to sell some businesses, but the banks felt that would take too long. We had tremendous back orders in archery, shotguns, sleds, and so on, but the banks extracted $10 million in working capital, and we couldn't produce the products. We had a commitment for an additional $3 million in long-term debt, but the new lender would not fund if the banks were going to continue to pull down the working capital line.
>
> On September 28, 1971, we arranged a meeting with the banks in Detroit, but our lead banker didn't attend. The meeting was a debacle and cut off any hope for additional funds. On September 29, "Black Wednesday," we closed all 19 plants and laid off all 3,000 employees. We contacted our bank, but couldn't get any help from the loan officer or their assigned "work out" officer. We finally went to the bank's president, whom we knew, and found out he didn't know much about our problem. We showed him our back orders and said we wanted financing to enable us to ship until December. Using half the collateral we had left and the president's faith in us, we ended up with an additional $750,000. The $750,000 wouldn't go very far—by the time we paid past-due utilities, rents, taxes, expenses, and salaries, we would have enough to keep only three people per plant for one week. It seemed rather hopeless. Nevertheless, we got the money on Monday, and it kept us alive for one more week. During that period, other senior officers of the participating banks focused on the problem and brought in a team of consultants to assess the situation. Based on the outside advice and the judgments of the new senior officers, the banks reversed their position. They commenced funding again at minimal levels. By November, we had sold Yard-Man and Ben Pearson as we had originally proposed in August, and the crisis started to fade.

As a result of these conditions, many orders could not be shipped in time to meet seasonal schedules. Accordingly, sales in the fourth quarter, ending October 31, 1971, were substantially below forecast with pretax operating losses of $11,580,000, bringing the operating loss for the full year to $15,886,000.

Financial Program

TLG's inability to finance its production requirements for the fourth quarter of fiscal 1971 made necessary a new financial program. This plan included the aforementioned sale of Yard-Man and Ben Pearson, renegotiation of existing indebtedness, the conversion of long-term debt to equity, and the establishment of a new line of credit for working capital.

The sale of Yard-Man to Montgomery Ward and Ben Pearson to Brunswick resulted in special charges of $1.5 million plus another $12 million in goodwill associated with the sale of Yard-Man to be written off. The sale of Planet Junior farm implements in May had also resulted in a $942,000 loss. Total losses resulting from the sale of these divisions, including refinancing costs, were $15,515,000.

The cash and notes received from the sale of Yard-Man and Ben Pearson were used to reduce bank borrowings to about $2 million from $16 million and allowed TLG to obtain an additional one-year agreement with its banks. Past-due trade debt of over $10 million was consolidated into long-term debt through agreement with TLG creditors.

As part of TLG's refinancing program, holders of $9.5 million in 7 percent convertible subordinated notes exchanged their debt for $7 noncumulative junior convertible preferred stock. The remaining $4 million of subordinated notes was converted in 1973 to noncumulative senior convertible preferred stock which had priority over the junior preferred stock in case of liquidation or dividends. (See Exhibit 6 for details.)

To obtain needed flexibility in meeting seasonal production requirements, a credit line of $3,750,000 was negotiated with a commercial finance company. The resulting interest rates were 6 percent over prime rate.

A summary of the total restrictions on TLG resulting from the various debt agreements is listed in Exhibit 7.

EXHIBIT 6: Shareholders' Equity

Preferred Stock

The Board of Directors has established the rights and preferences of 150,000 shares of the authorized preferred stock, of which 110,000 shares are $7 Noncumulative Convertible Preferred Stock (Junior Preferred Stock), 95,000 shares of which were issued in November 1971, and 40,000 shares are $7 Noncumulative Senior Convertible Preferred Stock (Senior Preferred Stock) which were issued in April 1973. These shares have an aggregate mandatory redemption and liquidation value of $13,500,000. The Board of Directors has the authority to establish the rights and preferences of the remaining 350,000 shares of authorized but unissued preferred stock.

Holders of Junior Preferred Stock have the same voting rights as holders of the Company's common stock, have votes equal to the shares of

EXHIBIT 6 *(concluded)*

common stock they would receive upon conversion, and are entitled to a $7 per share noncumulative annual dividend, commencing February 1, 1974, when and as declared by the Board of Directors. Such dividends are payable before dividends may be paid on the common stock. The Junior Preferred Stock is redeemable at the Company's option at $100 per share, plus a premium of $6.30 per share, such premium reducing annually through 1991. Redemption cannot occur prior to November 1, 1976, unless the market price of common stock is equivalent to at least 150 percent of the per share conversion price. Beginning in 1982, the Company is required to redeem, at $100 per share, 10 percent of the then outstanding Junior Preferred Stock each year through 1991. In the event of involuntary liquidation, holders of Junior Preferred Stock are entitled to $100 per share. Each share of Junior Preferred Stock is convertible into common stock at any time prior to November 1, 1991, on the basis of $2.74 per common share (subject to antidilution adjustments) divided into the redemption price of $100.

The rights and preferences of the holders of the Senior Preferred Stock are the same as the Junior Preferred Stock, except (1) they have preference with respect to dividends and in liquidation, (2) they may convert into common shares on the basis of $3 per common share (subject to antidilution adjustments) divided into the redemption price of $100, and (3) they may preclude the Company from selling a substantial portion of the business or its assets.

Common Stock

In 1971 the Company issued seven-year warrants to purchase 670,000 shares of the Company's common stock at $2 per share and 27,671 shares at $2.50 per share. In February 1974 the holders of warrants to purchase 697,671 shares returned them to the Company for cancellation.

In May 1974, 45,000 shares of the Company's stock were received from the former owner of an acquired business in connection with a settlement relating to the acquisition. Accordingly, "cost of purchased businesses in excess of net assets acquired" has been reduced by the stated value of the returned shares.

At October 31, 1974, 4,800,000 shares of common stock were reserved for conversion of $7 Noncumulative Senior and Junior Preferred Stock, and 290,780 shares were reserved for exercise of employee stock options. At October 31, 1974, 51,810 options were exercisable.

EXHIBIT 7: TLG Debt Restrictions

THE LEISURE GROUP, INC., AND SUBSIDIARIES
Notes to Consolidated Financial Statements
October 31, 1974

In 1974 and 1973 the Company negotiated repayment schedules and certain other conditions and features of substantially all of its major debt agreements and exchanged $4 million of 7 percent Convertible Subordinated Notes for $7 Noncumulative Senior Converti-

EXHIBIT 7 *(concluded)*

ble Preferred Stock. These negotiations resulted in forgiveness of indebtedness and accrued interest which has been reflected as an extraordinary credit to income in the accompanying financial statements but did not result in any obligation to issue additional common stock. The following summarizes the components of long-term debt:

	1974	**1973**
Working capital term loan, bearing interest at 6% over prime rate, payable in equal monthly installments to July 15, 1978	$1,470,000	$ 2,798,000
Subordinated bank loans, bearing interest at 1½% over prime rate, payable in equal quarterly installments to October 31, 1983.	1,055,000	1,175,000
Extended unsecured trade debt, bearing interest at 7¾%, payable in equal monthly installments to October 15, 1980	2,218,000	2,535,000
Other long-term debt, bearing interest at rates to 6% over prime rate with installments to December 1987:		
Secured	1,275,000	2,058,000
Unsecured	2,214,000	2,647,000
Other	319,000	447,000
	8,551,000	11,660,000
Less: Current portion	1,483,000	2,087,000
	$7,068,000	$ 9,573,000

Minimum principal payments due on long-term debt in the next five years are $1,483,000 in 1975, $1,659,000 in 1976, $1,784,000 in 1977, $1,453,000 in 1978, and $1,004,000 in 1979.

All of the Company's assets are collateral for the working capital, bank, and other secured loans. Many of the agreements containing cross-default provisions may be terminated if the lender shall reasonably determine that it is insecure with respect to payment of its loans or may be declared due and payable if a material adverse change in the financial position or results of operations of the Company occurs.

The Company's working capital agreement, with a commercial finance company, provides for short-term loans equal to 80 percent of eligible accounts receivable plus $850,000, bearing interest at 6 percent over prime rate. During 1974, outstanding short-term borrowings averaged $4,559,000 (borrowings ranged from $3,458,000 to $5,264,000) with interest rates averaging 16¾ percent.

The Company's various debt agreements place certain restrictions on the Company with respect to mergers, divestitures, borrowings, leasing, and other activities, and restrict the Company from paying dividends or purchasing or retiring shares of its capital stock.

Under the most restrictive covenants of its debt instruments, the Company must maintain the following financial ratios and conditions, all of which were met at October 31, 1974: *(a)* A minimum working capital of $1 million; at October 31, 1974, working capital was $2,946,000. *(b)* A minimum consolidated net worth of $4.5 million; at October 31, 1974, consolidated net worth was $6,427,000. *(c)* A tangible net worth, as defined, of not less than $1 million; at October 31, 1974, tangible net worth, as defined, was $1,973,000. *(d)* Maintain inventories of not less than $4 million; at October 31, 1974, inventories were $7,258,000.

NEW DIRECTIONS: 1973 AND BEYOND

After the 1971 crisis, TLG's operations were reorganized to decentralize product management. In order to improve customer coordination and communication, and to improve the profitability of each operation, the previously centralized general management, sales, and marketing functions were transferred to the operating headquarters of each product division.

The decentralization and reorganization in January 1972 restructured TLG into six divisions. By 1975 two more divisions had been sold for financial reasons and four divisions remained, including the following (see Exhibit 8):

1. Sporting Firearms Products, which had responsibility for High Standard sporting firearms and Kamo products.
2. Reloading Products, having responsibility for Lyman and Sierra products.

EXHIBIT 8: Organization Chart, 1975

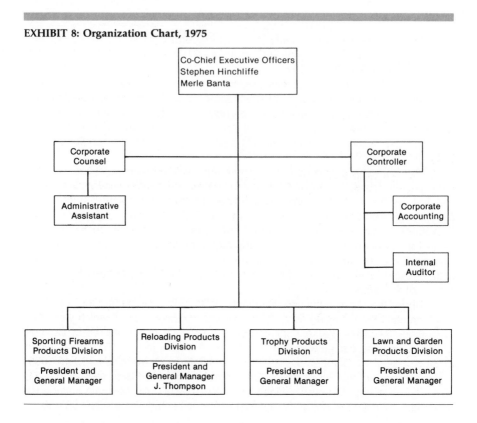

3. Trophy Products, responsible for Dodge Trophy products.

4. Lawn and Garden Products, responsible for Black Magic plant care products and Hayes spray guns.

The reduction in the size of TLG's corporate staff obtained through the reorganization and decentralization of operations had reduced corporate general and administrative expenses from $4.6 million in 1971 to $1.3 million in 1974. TLG's professional staff at corporate included seven members in 1975, down from 37 in 1971.

Growth in sales of sporting goods, including firearms, reloading, and trophy products, increased from $14.5 million in 1971 to $20.9 million in 1974. Lawn and Garden accounted for the remaining $1 million in 1971 and $6.1 million in 1974, as seen in Exhibit 9.

EXHIBIT 9: Five-Year Sales Results

	1974	1973	1972	1971	1970
Sales by product class (in thousands of dollars):					
Sporting goods	$20,900	$17,900	$17,250	$14,550	$11,500
Others	6,100	4,000	3,250	1,050	4,200
	27,000	21,900	20,500	15,600	15,700
Discontinued operations . . .	—	2,200	14,000	42,100	50,800
	27,000	24,100	34,500	57,700	66,500

Management Philosophy

Division Management. James (Mace) Thompson, president of Reloading Products Division, was one of the few managers who remained through the turnaround. He joined TLG in June 1968, as product manager for High Standard. In November 1969 he became marketing manager for High Standard, Sierra Bullets (acquired May 1969), and Lyman products (acquired October 1969). Mace Thompson related in 1975 his early precrisis experience of integrating the new acquisitions:

> After acquiring a self-sufficient company, we would split it into three units. The operations manager would report to the vice president of operations who reported to Merle Banta. The product manager reported to the vice president of marketing who reported to Steve Hinchliffe. And the sales manager reported to the national sales manager who reported to the vice president of marketing.
>
> There was a functional organization, but the operations manager was located at the factory, the product manager was in Los Angeles, and sales were all over the United States.
>
> An integrating team would go into the company and decide on the

changes. The strong-willed MBAs would tend to win any argument, and the acquired companies felt like a herd of elephants ran over them—young guys running in, canning people, changing policy, asking penetrating questions—and morale would be bad until the TLG operations man came in to try and pull it together.

By June 1970 Mace Thompson had additional product responsibilities as marketing manager of Sporting Goods, with product, not sales, responsibility. Products added were Ben Pearson archery, Himalayan back-packs, Werlich toboggans, and Dodge Trophy. In December 1970 he was appointed general manager of Shooting and Sports Products with product and operating responsibilities, but not sales. He explained in 1975 some of the difficulties he had:

> Was there really synergy in a common sales force? We were mistaken in what we thought our strengths were. We had 50 salesmen who could make five calls per day and sell x units, and so on, but the mix was wrong, the selling features were different, the sales methods were different. Product managers had no authority over sales. Having sales and marketing report to a vice president may be all right for Proctor & Gamble who use a common channel and a "pull" strategy, but not for a sales force calling on back-pack, reloading, gun, lawn and garden, and toys customers—they are all different.
>
> Management controls and MIS were ineffective and not available in a given company or to a sales manager. We were flying by the seat of our pants, and good decisions were still based on bad data. We were moving too fast in acquiring new companies—reality was lost.
>
> Forecasts were bad. Backlogs on seasonal products were added to forecasts. But once it was budgeted, there was no turning back—you couldn't cut back on inventories and get financing as fast as you could change a forecast. Management had a "can do" attitude that didn't allow for much change. Once the backlog was so high, advertising was cut substantially.

The company was reorganized after the crisis, but true decentralization occurred in January 1972, when sales responsibility was given back to the divisions. Mace Thompson explained in 1975 the importance of this move:

> Decentralization! This is the key as to why we're in business today and why we almost weren't in 1971. We had lost our control over receivables, collections, and sales. We had lost the intimacy of an individual company.
>
> In the gun market, for example, you needed to know guns. When I was product manager I wrote a product knowledge manual for salesman training. There was no way we could expect salesmen to be able to sell guns without knowing anything about them. We were also vulnerable to competition since we weren't in some segments and weren't number one in others. For example, target pistols, where we are strong, had little growth, so market share was important. We weren't even in the rim fire segment. Shotguns were the key market, but we were private branding and didn't

even have a position. We couldn't expect 15 percent sales increase across the board, we had to look at segments.

By 1971 people were getting dissatisfied unless they were moving rapidly. The corporate group was on a "high"; they were working so hard they lost touch with reality. Salesmen didn't know what to do—missing goals was a deflating experience. It was an invigorating environment as long as you could cope with it, but it tore up a lot of good people. I'm sure they have changed their goals since then. You adopt your personal policy to the environment you're in. For me it was a stimulating, invigorating experience—"doing the impossible dream." I enjoyed it!

A major reduction in corporate overhead expenses came from the shift of responsibilities to the divisions. In addition to moving sales, marketing, and general management back to the divisions, the control and administrative functions were also decentralized. Now, accounts receivable, credit, collections, and data processing were divisional responsibilities. TLG's headquarters' functions were basically reduced to that of financial management. Merle Banta describes the change in management's methods.

We made a 180-degree flip from centralization to decentralization. We now have four divisions which report to Steve or me. They each have a president, controller, marketing staff, and sales force. The divisions run independently though we have mini-board meetings with the division management where we require more than just numbers by digging into what they are doing and why. Cash is also managed centrally. All collections come into corporate headquarters and are then disbursed to fund divisions on a weekly basis. We also set policy on borrowing and allocation of funds, logos, insurance, salaries, hiring and firing, lease agreements, and budgets. Any capital expenditures over $5,000 come to us for authorization.

In elaborating the changes in business philosophy and management methods, Merle Banta explained the shift to a more conservative business approach and the emphasis on experience rather than education.

Though it's not company policy, the 30-year-old, bright MBA hasn't been hired since Black Wednesday. Having an MBA is not in itself a sufficient criterion for success. This became obvious in the Blazon plant consolidation where the chain of command responsible for that project was five MBAs, four of whom had graduated with honors. We now look for mature, experienced people from the appropriate industry or functional area. Many of the people hired since 1971 have been over 40 and wouldn't know a button-down-collared MBA if they were bitten by one.

We've become extremely cautious and even conservative. We've been so close to the brink that our budgets, plans, and forecasts have had to be more realistic.

We're more concerned about the long term. In the 60s, people saw themselves growing fast and weren't in a job over six months. You couldn't evaluate them because they would change jobs too often—never looked at long-term consequences of decisions. Today we are most conscious in marketing—we had really damaged our image when deliveries weren't made.

We have good relations now and make long-term decisions first priority.

Motivation is different now, and harder. In the 60s, TLG was a glamorous and exciting company—people clamored to come to work even at a pay cut—it was the "in" place to be. Now that's not the case, especially for the kind of people we want to hire—experienced, tough-minded managers. They report to us, but we don't tell them what to do the way we used to—now we discuss it in much greater depth.

We review objectives quarterly now instead of annually. We sit down with managers and assign their bonus target and set qualitative and quantitative objectives. We started this in 1972 to restore employee confidence and make certain they were working in the right direction.

Morale seems to be good now, but it has been bad during periods of tight cash. Any sales slump would cut receivables, and low cash resulted in a need to delay paying vendors. Everyone has been a part of it.

MBAs are not as salable today as they were in the 60s. They have the image of not being the type who wants to plug away over the long run. That isn't the kind of a guy we want.

The Leisure Industry. There had also been a change in TLG's concept of the leisure industry and the approach that would be taken in entering new product areas.

In the 60s we saw it as manufactured products, branded, and sold by mass merchandisers. Now we see it as anything that people do or use during leisure, not necessarily sold by mass merchandisers, manufactured, or branded. The Atlantic Braves could be an example. Being practical, we'll probably stay in areas related to what we have now.

We didn't care before if a product was in a good or bad industry, whether the firm was profitable or not, or whether it was a growing or dying market. Flexible Flyer was a good brand but a dying market. Today we are more traditional—we want a profitable, growing product, unique technology, or manufacturing, and so on—we want some advantage. We would also operate them independently unless it made sense to fold it in with an existing division.

Much of the change in management philosophy had come from a recognition of the fundamental importance of "cash flow" as reflected in the attitudes of "Wall Street" and the increasing importance of "financial institutions." Merle Banta explained in 1975 this shift and its impact on TLG:

Running a growth business today is totally different from the 60s. Then you had a market that thrived on optimism. Our youth, the MBA and McKinsey background, the excitement of leisure time markets—all sounded great to the young analysts of Wall Street. By 1972 it was a different market, all the hard-assed bankers wanted to see was the cash flow.

During the 60s, you needed earnings growth, a sexy story like leisure time, MBAs, and acquisitions. Now the bankers require a profitable business with good cash flow—we've had to deal with the cash flow to survive. We've had to watch day-to-day working capital while we regained trade creditors' confidence. We went from cash in advance to C.O.D., but now we're at 30–90 days' credit. We've reduced our long-term debt from $40 million to $7 million. Our short-term borrowings were $25 million; now they are $4 million. Our profits plus depreciation exceed the required debt amortization, so we have a positive cash flow! [See Exhibits 10 and 11 for recent financial data.]

EXHIBIT 10

THE LEISURE GROUP, INC.
Consolidated Statements of Operations
For the years Ended October 31, 1974, and 1973

	1974	1973
Continuing operations:		
Net sales	$26,952,000	$21,911,000
Cost of sales	18,607,000	15,184,000
Gross margin	8,345,000	6,727,000
Selling, general, and administrative expenses excluding corporate expenses	4,397,000	4,444,000
Income from continuing operations before corporate expenses	3,948,000	2,283,000
Loss from discontinued operations before corporate expenses	—	(753,000)
Corporate expenses:		
General, administrative, and other expenses	1,211,000	850,000
Interest (including $756,000 and $583,000 on short-term obligations in 1974 and 1973)	1,718,000	1,404,000
Income (loss) before income taxes and extraordinary items	1,019,000	(724,000)
Provision for income taxes	519,000	—
Income (loss) before extraordinary items	500,000	(724,000)
Extraordinary items	519,000	946,000
Net income	$ 1,019,000	$ 222,000
Income (loss) per share:		
Assuming full dilution:		
Income (loss) before extraordinary items	0.06	(0.09)
Extraordinary items	0.07	0.12
Net income	$0.13	$0.03

In reflecting about the problems that TLG had incurred and rethinking what might have been done differently to have avoided the crisis, Merle Banta felt that the major problem had been in TLG's handling of its banking relations. When asked what they would do differently if they could do it over again, Banta replied:

Our approach would be similar, but we would avoid the mistakes. We went too fast. We uprooted acquisitions and tried to integrate them in 30 days—now we would take six months or six years, if necessary. The loss of coordination caused by short-term upheavals must be minimized

EXHIBIT 11

THE LEISURE GROUP, INC.
Consolidated Balance Sheets
October 31, 1974, and 1973

Assets	1974	1973
Current assets:		
Cash	$ 330,000	$ 267,000
Accounts receivable, less reserves of $586,000 in 1974 and $430,000 in 1973	4,861,000	4,397,000
Receivable from sales of discontinued operations	—	466,000
Federal income tax refunds	—	282,000
Notes receivable	13,000	138,000
Inventories, at the lower of cost (first-in, first-out) or market	7,258,000	5,758,000
Prepaid expenses	316,000	294,000
Total current assets	12,778,000	11,602,000
Property, plant, and equipment (at cost):		
Land	562,000	804,000
Buildings and improvements	2,638,000	3,558,000
Machinery and equipment	4,920,000	4,728,000
Office furniture and fixtures	482,000	486,000
	8,602,000	9,576,000
Less: Accumulated depreciation and amortization	3,040,000	2,600,000
Total property, plant, and equipment	5,562,000	6,976,000

Liabilities and Shareholders' Equity	1974	1973
Current liabilities:		
Loan payable	$ 3,896,000	$ 3,202,000
Current portion of long-term debt	1,483,000	2,087,000
Accounts payable	1,904,000	1,286,000
Accrued liabilities	2,549,000	2,427,000
Total current liabilities	9,832,000	9,002,000
Long-term debt:		
Secured	3,800,000	6,031,000
Unsecured	4,432,000	5,182,000
Other	319,000	447,000
	8,551,000	11,660,000
Less: Current portion included above	1,483,000	2,087,000
Total long-term debt	7,068,000	9,573,000
Commitments and contingencies:		
Shareholders' equity (see Exhibit 6):		
Preferred stock, $5 par value:		
Authorized—500,000 shares		
Outstanding—135,000 shares, stated at		
Common stock, no par value:		
Authorized—10,000,000 shares	13,500,000	13,500,000

	1974	1973
Other assets:		
Cost of purchased businesses in excess of net assets acquired	4,454,000	4,499,000
Long-term receivables	218,000	629,000
Cash surrender value of life insurance policies and deposits	315,000	322,000
Total other assets	4,987,000	5,450,000
Total assets	$23,327,000	$24,028,000
Outstanding—3,098,684 shares in 1974 and 3,143,684 shares in 1973, stated at	3,099,000	3,144,000
Capital surplus	23,973,000	23,973,000
Retained earnings (deficit)	(34,145,000)	(35,164,000)
Total shareholders' equity	6,427,000	5,453,000
Total liabilities and shareholders' equity	$23,327,000	$24,028,000

to achieve long-term integration. We would meld the aggressive MBA with the old-time experienced manager. Maybe this change in attitude comes from age—I was 31 when we started The Leisure Group, and you couldn't have anyone older than yourself, could you?

The major difference would be in the way we put together our financing. It was our policy to use the best: auditors—Arthur Andersen; we went to O'Melveny & Myers for counsel; Blyth and Company underwriters. But our lead bank was not a major bank. Moreover, we leaned too heavily—and successfully—on them for short-term financing to avoid further dilution by going to the equity market. In other words, we were too heavily leveraged with too small a bank. As a result, when the crunch came there was no cushion and no real strength leading the bank group. When we go back to the banks, after leaving the Commercial Finance Company, we'll seek a large commercial bank.

Once TLG was caught in the crisis of "Black Wednesday," both Merle Banta and Steve Hinchliffe felt a responsibility to the employees of the acquired companies and were determined to do whatever was possible to work it out. However, by late 1975, their basic entrepreneurial spirit was beginning to come alive again. Banta and Hinchliffe both felt it was necessary to begin looking for new opportunities for growth and had begun looking around for potential acquisitions. Merle Banta explained:

We got everyone into the mess, and we were responsible for getting them out. But as we go on now, it is the chance for economic opportunity that is the motivating factor. I don't have to do more—the economic opportunity line has taken over and that's the motivation. We're basically the same as before—looking for a chance to respond to environmental opportunities. We'll break out of the gate at first chance. Our managerial skills of the 60s are 500 percent better today though our basic beliefs are the same.

CASE 24

Imperial Corporation (A)

With 130 divisions as of 1978, most of which had been developed
internally, the Imperial Corporation was one of the country's most diversified industrial companies. As corporate management teams had succeeded
each other at the helm of Imperial over the past decades, two challenges
seemed to remain: How could they combine the strong decentralized division level management which was necessary to cope with the wide variety
of markets, products, and competitors, with equally strong central strategic
direction? How could they, in the face of growing competition and growing scarcity of resources, decide and influence how much each of the
very often dissimilar divisions should spend for its further growth?

In 1975, in response to the disappointing profits resulting from a
period of rapid, diversifying growth, Imperial's current management had
decided to reorganize the company's divisional structure into *strategic business units*. Two years later, with the new structure in place, they started
to transform Imperial's formal planning system toward a portfolio planning approach. The main impetus behind these changes had come from
Mr. Samuel Peters, vice president for planning.

Though a strategic planning consulting firm was called in to assist
with the portfolio analysis, the consultants provided no guidance with
respect to implementation. As a senior partner of that consulting firm
stated to the casewriter:

> Frankly, let me tell you that I am not interested in the administrative
> implications of our portfolio planning approach. The challenge is really
> analytical, not administrative. The way I see implementation is what I call

the "rule of the Prince": once the analysis is done, a strong CEO should see to it that the portfolio strategy gets implemented.

As the first round of Imperial's business unit plans under the new approach was being presented however, a number of administrative issues demanded Mr. Peters's attention. One concern was that the new business structure might handicap Imperial's competitiveness in both systems sales and the international area. Another problem that soon surfaced was how to monitor the execution of the new segment-oriented plans. Was it desirable and practical to change Imperial's incentive compensation system to support the new planning approach? Should he recommend the establishment of corporate funding of the major gain-share strategies?

Mr. Peters was trying to establish his position and priorities on these administrative issues, when he received a memorandum from Mr. John Rand, vice president for finance, informing him that the total of the five-year capital investment requests were at least 40 percent over what he and Donald Mackenzie, Imperial's CEO, thought the company should spend. But on what basis could Peters ask Mackenzie to allocate more explicitly, to support strategic planning, and down to what level? Peters knew that if the company ended up—as in the past—reverting to a proportional cutback, the whole portfolio planning effort would be undermined.

The Company

Imperial Corporation, which in 1974 had sales and assets in excess of $4 billion and employed over 80,000 people, had grown by both acquisitions and internal development since the turn of the century. The company was active in many different product/markets and technologies, both in the U.S. and abroad. Products included large industrial machinery, automotive products, electronic and electrical components and systems, construction products, industrial motors and controls, and sophisticated defense products.

As a company that diversified in the early 1930s, Imperial was one of the pioneers in adopting a divisionalized structure. To accommodate both its diversity and the increased number of divisions, a group level, consisting of six groups, was created in the 1950s. In the early 60s, in response to a period of plateauing sales, this group structure was broken down into a large number of more focused groups. These were later organized into three different sectors—Industrial Products, Automotive Components, and Electrical Products—whose heads became part of the Management Committee.

In 1974, Imperial had over 100 divisions, ranging in size from $5 million to $100 million in assets, organized into 12 groups with assets anywhere between $50 million and $500 million (see Exhibit 1). Several

EXHIBIT 1: Organization Chart, 1975

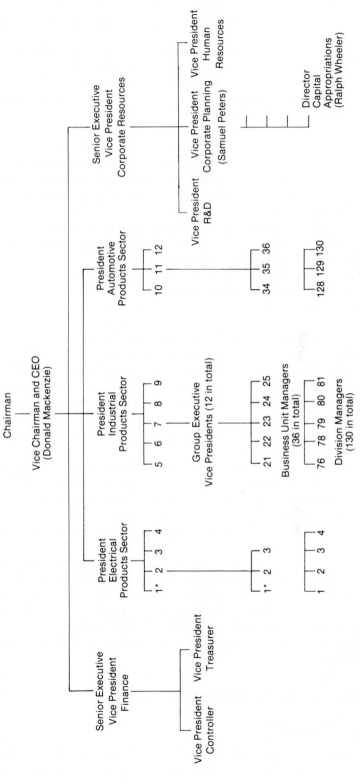

* One business unit had group status.

thousand people were employed at the group and corporate level. Many divisions sold their products through group-level marketing organizations, and a large part of research was done at a corporate research laboratory employing over 1,000 scientists and engineers. In 1974, nonfunded corporate staff operations cost nearly 2 percent of sales. Corporate and group-level staff units had no line authority, except in the controllers' area which had a dual reporting structure. Division managers' autonomy over specific matters was delineated by extensive policy manuals and a history reflecting the groups' unique problems and the various managers' attitudes toward supervision. Significant differences existed among sectors and among groups. The overall corporate culture of the organization was, however, largely defined by the strong engineering background represented in Imperial's management, and the technological and product leadership Imperial enjoyed in most of its businesses.

Corporate strategic guidance for this wide array of activities had at its core a set of explicit corporate financial objectives in terms of earnings growth and dividend policy, as well as a number of key product/market and technological choices, such as the decision to go after the automotive business after World War II, to limit defense products' relative importance, and to get out of an early involvement in computers. In its details, however, the corporate strategy of Imperial Corporation was really the aggregation of hundreds of resource commitment decisions by the various divisions. These decisions involved not only capital spending, but also the degree to which each division's operating profit would be plowed back for future growth in the form of *strategic expenses* such as R&D, engineering, and market development.

In many cases, corporate and even sector managers were too removed to review these decisions in other than financial terms, and the group VP was the highest level manager who could examine these substantively. As most of the higher executives had been with the company over 20 years, they all had firsthand line experience in several of the operating units.

The remainder of this case is divided into three parts. The first part describes the systems through which Imperial's corporate management influenced and controlled the divisions as of 1975. The second part describes the introduction of strategic business units and a portfolio planning approach between 1975 and 1978. The third part describes the immediate impact of these changes and some of the administrative issues that they raised.

I. ADMINISTRATIVE SYSTEMS AS OF 1975

Strategic Planning

Strategic planning at Imperial had always been essentially a line responsibility. Insofar as one person was responsible for monitoring the strategic planning effort, it was the vice president for corporate planning. His corporate planning group traditionally consisted of about 20 managers covering four areas: corporate strategy, business analysis, corporate development and, recently, capital appropriations.

Imperial's formal planning process had been developed in the early 60s and constantly refined. It was quite typical of many of the "long-range planning systems" used by U.S. companies over that period. Each division would use economic data and forecasts provided by the planning group to forecast and analyze trends in the marketplace. Having assessed the divisions' strengths and weaknesses, goals would be stated to allow for the realization of financial objectives. Strategies would be formulated to realize those goals and detailed programs spelled out for each of the strategies. Such programs would cover not only facilities investment but also the strategic expenses described above.

The resulting inch-thick long-range plans were summarized in financial projections consisting of a detailed five-year income statement and balance sheet. The income statement and, in particular, next year's figures, tended to receive much emphasis in the negotiation and review process. Upon approval, the first year of the long-range plan became the annual profit plan for the division, upon which the control system and incentive compensation were based.

Financial Planning and Control

Imperial's approach to financial planning was as formalized as in any diversified company of its size. Performance vis-à-vis the objectives of the profit plan was monitored on a monthly basis, and consolidated at all organizational levels. Mr. Rand, vice president, finance, felt that "the company developed a financial control system which by and large is well organized in providing the information needed for management."

One distinct feature of Imperial's financial planning system was its explicit recognition of a separate category for those R&D, engineering, and marketing expenses which were considered to be an investment in future growth. The realization that *strategic expenses,* both in dollar terms and in terms of impact, were as important as capital expenditures had led Imperial's management to treat such expenses as a reinvestment of profits, putting them "below the line" of operating profit. In practice, however, it was difficult to draw a line between expenses that were truly strategic and other R&D, engineering, and marketing costs. As a result, corporate staff people felt that "many of the strategic expenses were not really strategic."

Capital Appropriations

The capital appropriation system at Imperial again was similar to that of many large diversified companies. It consisted of a level-by-level review process of each project. Limits were set on the spending authority of each level; all projects over $250,000 required approval of the Capital Expenditure Review Committee (CERC), which was composed of Management Committee members and corporate staff vice presidents. Elaborate instructions, bound into an inch-thick "Green Book," guided the evaluation of each project, which was done principally on a discounted cash flow basis at the corporate hurdle rate.

The CERC, at its creation, had been assigned the following role:

> The CERC is essentially a *risk-sharing entity* of diverse functional skills and business experience. It was established to serve and advise the Management Committee on matters pertaining to capital investments and major strategic programs. More specifically, its principal role in the planning, implementation, and control of such investments is to (1) review individual projects, (2) assess probable risks, and (3) recommend appropriate actions.

Sitting on the CERC were most corporate staff vice presidents and, ex officio, the members of the Management Committee. Mr. Peters acted as secretary and Mr. Wheeler, who headed a three-man staff within the corporate planning group, was responsible for the administration of CERC procedures.

The company had classified capital expenditures into three categories, with different review and approval procedures.

The first category, Maintenance Investments, comprised those capital expenditures which maintain the competitive nature of a facility, such as replacements, continuing regular cost improvement, minor capacity increases, OSHA, EPA and other regulatory items.

A second category, Growth Investments, comprised expenditures for major expansions, new products, quantum increases in capacity or reduction in cost, new processes, and new plants.

A third category of Special Growth Investments consisted of investments and acquisitions of new businesses, joint ventures, etc.

Both Maintenance Investments and Growth Investments were further classified in four risk categories as follows:

	Risk Categories	Hurdle Rate (percent)
A.	Projects—for *existing* facility and *existing* market and *existing* products or technology.	15
B.	Projects—*One* of above *new*.	17.5
C.	Projects—*Two* of above *new*.	20
D.	Projects—*Three* of above *new*, or any acquisition, joint venture, equity investment, new business formation.	22.5

Recently, to make the procedure less burdensome, it had been decided the CERC would only review Growth Investments on a project-

by-project basis. Sector presidents would approve the Maintenance Investments proposals which represented about 50 percent of the capital
investment budget. The limits for approval at different levels also had
been significantly raised. This reduced the number of projects to be reviewed from over a thousand to about two hundred a year.

Meetings of the CERC typically lasted a whole morning. They started
off with a review of the corporate cash position and capital expenditure
approval to date. A few days after the CERC meeting the committee
typically would send a brief written statement of support or questions
to the respective sector presidents.

There was no formal link between the strategic planning process
and investment project approval process except that the administration
of both had recently become the responsibility of the vice president of
planning. Before that, investment project approval was administered by
a corporate vice president of manufacturing. Most, but not all, of the
investment proposals considered had previously been announced or described in the long-range plans.

In practice, projects rarely got turned down at the CERC level. As
Mr. Wheeler, director of capital appropriations, put it: "As a matter of
fact, both Sam Peters and I would consider it to reflect on us if a project
comes to the CERC and gets chewed up. That shouldn't happen. Projects
should be in better shape by then."

The Appropriation Request for a project was the responsibility of
the division. Within the division, most requests were initiated by a manager in the manufacturing organization and the actual writing and assembling of the proposal was carried out by manufacturing and controller
personnel. Within the capital expenditure chain of approval, the two
key people were the division manager and the group vice president. The
division manager was responsible for the preparation of the request and
was the sponsor. The group vice president was the individual who said
yes or no. As for the sector presidents, as one division manager put it:
"I don't recall any appropriation that was not approved by the sector
president after the group vice president approved it."

When surveyed on their opinion about the capital expenditures procedures, the group vice presidents' response was positive. They felt the
key strength of the approach was that "it places resource allocation decisions in the hands of those most knowledgeable about the needs of the
businesses."

Incentive Compensation

Imperial's incentive compensation system consisted of two parts,
the standard incentive compensation program and a stock option program.

The *standard incentive compensation* program applied to over 1,000 people,
including those reporting directly to division managers. Incentive compen-

sation was determined by performance vis-à-vis objectives on a number of short-run criteria such as return on investment, total investment, and operating margin of the unit, as well as corporate earnings per share. The relative weight of corporate performance rose from 10 percent for division people to 35 percent for group-level managers. The multiplier curves were steep within a narrow range around the financial objectives, but flat beyond a certain performance level. Most managers regarded the level at which their objectives were negotiated as reasonable. In fact, groups tended to have a set of internal target figures which were higher than the official objectives.

The *stock option* program applied to over 200 people, starting at the level of division manager. Formally, this system was completely judgmental. The corporate compensation services staff established standard amounts per job level, and the supervisor had the option to revise these downward for a given individual. In practice, this meant that 90 percent got virtually the full amount.

Human Resources Management

The average stay of a manager in a particular position at Imperial was between three and four years, with about one-third of the promotions crossing group lines, and practically none of the appointments filled from the outside. Group vice presidents played a strong role in all appointment decisions at divisional level. Corporate management kept track of the management development process through a system of replacement tables, and through the annual management review process.

Though the extent of profit pressures weighing on division general managers varied over time, it was clear that most group vice presidents were there because they were good operators who had demonstrated their ability to deliver earnings.

II. INTRODUCING STRATEGIC BUSINESS UNITS AND PORTFOLIO PLANNING, 1974–1978

A Corporate Reexamination

Imperial's performance over the last 25 years had alternated between periods of high earnings but limited sales growth and periods of fast sales growth with mediocre earnings. Corporate management had responded by shifting from a more centralized approach to more decentralization and back.

The recent period from 1969 to 1973 had resulted in a mixed performance record for Imperial. Company sales and investment grew over 50 percent as new and largely unrelated businesses were entered, putting the company in markets such as health care, leisure, housing components, computers, and construction. Corporate earnings, however, were essentially flat over the period and as of 1973, a score of divisions were in a loss or downtrend situation.

This unsatifactory earnings performance triggered a thorough corporate self-examination and led to a revision of the corporate approach to both strategy and organizational structure. At the 1974 management meeting, the basic issues of future development were summed up as follows:

> The corporate strategies we develop and the performance we attain will result, in large measure, from the way we organize and manage the corporation. This interdependence between strategy, structure, and results is fundamental, yet complex.
>
> In evaluating past corporate performance we can discern strengths as well as weaknesses that are a direct result of our organization and management philosophy. There are at least two elements that need reexamination.
> 1.   Decentralization—our decentralized structure has contributed to our ability to focus technical and management strength on diverse businesses and has facilitated more rapid decision making. Yet, this same decentralization, coupled with our size, has too often *insulated top management from the true direction and performance of our businesses* and made control and corporate resource allocation dangerously difficult. Often, it is difficult for corporate management to assess the full implications of division plans until the plans are well under way, requiring, in some cases, large commitments of corporate funds for completion or causing wasted resources if the plans need to be truncated or terminated. We should reexamine our profit center concept to determine whether the 100-plus profit centers we now have are the optimum number from a commercial and organizational efficiency and control viewpoint.
> 2.   Diversity—our diverse business posture has insulated us from cyclical swings and has generated significant potential for technology and know-how transfer within the corporation. At the same time, this diversity has spread our strategic funds and management resources very thin. The result has been an inordinate amount of top management "problem solving" rather than "opportunity pursuit." Moreover, we have too often failed to anticipate the proper time to phase out or sell product lines or businesses that no longer fit our performance requirements, partially as a result of our diversity and the diverted management attention span that can result from such a posture. . . .

Reemphasizing the Core Businesses

While a Planning Council was set up to review the basic strategies and the structure of the company, the more immediate reaction of corporate management to the 1973 earnings dip was to reemphasize the company's traditional core businesses and fix the profit drain. Resource allocation priority was given to "the consistent improvement of existing successful businesses trading in existing markets, over allocation of resources to new businesses in new markets."

On the basis of criteria such an investment turnover, level and trend in ROI, net income (NI), and cash flow, a "fix or eliminate" list of over 15 divisions was drawn up, composed mostly of recent entries or acquisitions. Between 1974 and 1977, a number of these were sold. Others were turned around, and a few remained marginal performers. Over that period also a strong corporate emphasis weighed on the divisions to attain their objectives with respect to earnings, cash flow, and price realization.

Restructuring into Strategic Business Units

The Planning Council also undertook a study of the organizational structure of Imperial. Though the current structure was regarded as appropriate from an operating point of view, many believed its size and diversity would be obstacles in strategic decision making. The sheer number of divisions and resulting number of plans strained the capacity of the corporate level to review and to trade off among them. More important, in many instances several divisions were active in the same broad product categories or sold to the same markets. Most of the groups, on the other hand, were very heterogeneous. Moreover, group management tended to focus on controlling operations and on short-term objectives, such as delivering next year's net income.

The Planning Council established a list of characteristics of an "ideal" business unit and reviewed the whole structure of the company. Their key consideration was the "need for minimal interaction with other business units," as Mr. Peters said, "on the premise that once you structure this way, you will not get coordination across business units even if you would need it."

More practical considerations were that the appropriate total number of SBUs should probably not exceed 40, and that each should have sufficient size to stand on its own in most support functions.

Another issue was the reporting structure within which these newly created structures would fit. In that respect, the Planning Council reported:

> The ideal reporting location for a business unit would appear to be the chief executive office, i.e., to a member of the [corporate] Policy Committee. Any intermediate reporting location creates problems in defining the job of the intermediate manager. He is not running operations because this is the business unit manager's job. He is not coordinating two or more business units toward a common business goal because the business unit should have been structured with minimum need for such coordination. He is not a part of the corporate policy team that governs personnel and financial policies and definition of business unit characters. Such an executive is literally an intermediary. He functions primarily as a communications line between top management of the corporation and top management of

the business unit. He can also function as a coach and counsellor to the business unit general manager and as a troubleshooter for corporate management. Such a position might be justified on these bases plus administrative convenience for grouping smaller business units. However, it is believed that the number of such positions should be as small as possible and that the job content of each requires individual tailoring.

After acceptance of the Planning Council proposals, Mr. Mackenzie, Imperial's CEO, announced the new management structure at the 1975 management meeting. Thirty-six business units were created. A few coincided with an existing division, but most grouped several divisions. None crossed divisional lines, though a few small charter adjustments were made. The newly appointed SBU general managers would have *worldwide* strategic planning and long-range resource management responsibility for the division(s) under them. Each was authorized to recruit a strategic planning manager to assist in this responsibility. The divisions, now numbering 130, would continue to be the primary organizational units with respect to operations and financial reporting. Above the business unit level, the group structure was retained (see Exhibit 1). Though Mr. Mackenzie stated that "group vice presidents will serve more as extensions of top management rather than line operating people," no formal changes in the role of authority of group VPs were made.

Resource Allocation Imbalance

By 1976, with the major problem divisions fixed and with the new SBU structure in place as a vehicle, the time seemed appropriate to try to correct what many managers felt were the fundamental problems of their company.

First of all, the organization was basically quite risk averse. New growth opportunities, with risk levels which the company as a whole would be willing to assume, never got to the stage of corporate review because the reward structure made it unattractive for individual unit managers to develop these. This problem was an old one for Imperial—as a matter of fact the CERC had originally been introduced to create some "risk sharing"—but the recent emphasis on earnings had made it worse.

Secondly, a major imbalance in the current resource allocation pattern gave least weight to the profitable business units and those with good opportunities for investment. This imbalance extended up to the level of group and even sectors.

The company's problem businesses, on the other hand, tended to receive capital injections each time a new divisional manager was put in charge to turn them around. The company's mature low-return businesses, mostly in the very capital-intensive Industrial Products Sector, tended to reinvest substantially. The company's high-return businesses in the Electrical Products Sector by contrast invested very little even though they had more technological and market opportunities.

Introducing Portfolio Planning

A task force was created to examine how the company's strategic planning effort could be improved to address these problems. Upon recommendation of the task force, a number of changes were made in the planning process, which increased the amount of management review and focused the review on those activities where strategic decisions would play a key role in the future of a business unit. For each business unit a review team was set up composed of other business unit managers and corporate staff people who had experience in an area that might be relevant for the business unit. It was decided to spread out the review of business unit plans over a two-year period.

In the course of 1977, Mr. Peters, who had managed one of Imperial's largest divisions before becoming involved in the Planning Council, became vice president for planning. He set out to further transform both the format and content of planning at Imperial into a portfolio planning approach for better resource allocation decisions.

His early efforts directed attention to strategic and competitive analysis by dissociating strategic planning from financial planning, and increased exposure to portfolio planning "technology" throughout the organization.

A strategy consulting firm was called in to do a corporatewide portfolio analysis. Over a period of six months a four-man team analyzed the competitive position of the company's SBUs into the detail of the major strategic segments. The consultants' presentation confirmed and clarified the resource allocation problems, pointing out the impact on the market positions which the company's investment patterns were having. In addition, they identified a small number of SBUs which would need a drastic decision for a major gain-share commitment or eventual divestment.

Given the fact that the 36 business units in reality represented several hundred product/market segments, this first cut at portfolio analysis was by necessity simplified and lumped a lot of businesses together. Subsequently, the consultants were asked to perform specific studies on some of the SBUs they had identified as requiring major decisions.

With respect to the technology of portfolio planning, Mr. Peters used an educational approach. A first exposure to these techniques had come to SBU managers through participation in the corporate portfolio analysis. Subsequently, the corporate planning group organized a two-day workshop in each of the SBUs, covering topics such as segmentation, experience curve analysis, and portfolio displays. The pilot SBUs, those that had been singled out in the corporate portfolio analysis, would be able to build on the consultants' data gathering and analysis to present their strategic plans. Rather than prescribing what the strategic plans should contain and how the analysis should be done, the six-page manual for the 1978 strategic planning format emphasized the purpose of the exercise and briefly outlined the format: The format called for an identification of the strategically significant segments within each business unit, a detailed analysis of those that were important or posed strategic questions, and an identification of key issues for the SBU as a whole. The manual also stated that "except in very special cases, a document of more than 40 pages would be regarded as excessively long." The only numbers required in the strategic plan were cumulative net income (NI), changes in working capital and in fixed assets, and cumulative cash flow.

Though it absorbed most of his time, improving the strategic planning process was only Mr. Peters's second priority. His first priority was to use his influence to man the positions of business unit manager with the right people. This meant promoting from among the division managers those who, besides being good operators, were good strategists, and then giving them support when they needed it.

III. IMPACT AND ADMINISTRATIVE IMPLICATIONS OF THE NEW APPROACH WORKING WITHIN THE BUSINESS UNIT STRUCTURE

By 1978, managers at Imperial generally felt that the Strategic Business Unit structure had succeeded in its original purpose: to focus strategic planning at the appropriate level, thereby improving the quality of business planning, and to better enable corporate management to focus on setting priorities and allocating resources for the separate businesses.

There were also a number of drawbacks to the present SBU structure. One corporate concern, for instance, was that the company might be losing its capability to serve certain industrial markets such as the petrochemical industry, where it was important to sell a packaged system, including the products of many SBUs, belonging to different groups. The Management Committee was currently studying a proposal to establish a Systems and Projects Division for large multidivisional projects, to coordinate technical evaluations, assess risks, make the pricing decisions, and manage the contract. The new unit would also have responsibility for developing strategic plans to increase Imperial's participation in related key industries. The policies for pricing product and supplying cost data, however, were still to be formulated. So was the issue whether such a unit should be allowed to fund development expenses.

A second concern of Imperial's management was the effect that assigning worldwide responsibility to the business units was having on the company's international competitiveness. As the treasurer of Imperial International commented:

The argument for worldwide SBU responsibility is that it would provide the international operations with good technical support, which is important in our kinds of businesses. It would also focus the SBU strategy on a worldwide level. In practice, only a few SBUs have the outlook and expertise to take up this worldwide responsibility. Moreover, it leads every SBU to reinvent the wheel in a particular country. Maybe to cover the international scene you really need some sort of matrix organization.

A third concern was the adaptation of the existing SBU structure as technologies and markets evolved. The original set of business units had been designed to create fairly autonomous units from a strategic point of view. Where that was not possible, given the multiple interdependencies in Imperial's businesses, trade-offs had been made in favor of what was seen as the key dimension for a given business. As such, some SBUs had been created around markets, others around technologies. Sometimes a choice had to be made between incorporating a division into a SBU, emphasizing its role as internal supplier and support activity, or leaving it autonomous. As time passed, however, some of these trade-offs came into question. For example, Imperial had created a semiconductor and electronic components SBU (SIAC) which was fairly successful in its markets. Since then, solid state design had become increasingly central to the technological development of many of Imperial's businesses in all three sectors. Some businesses did not pay sufficient attention to this development. Others built up their own capability duplicating SIAC. Others again asked SIAC for technical input.

Impact of the Portfolio Planning Approach

As the first round of the new business unit plans was being submitted throughout 1978, it became clear that the quality of strategic analysis at the business level had considerably improved. The controller of the Automotive Products Sector commented:

> In the past, a parody of how strategic plans were written would be as follows: the controllers went in one room and projected some numbers. At the same time, a bunch of writers, mostly marketing people, in another room would write programs to go with it. This year the strategic plan was such a new concept that the business unit manager and his whole management team got involved. The result is both better analysis and more commitment.

Ultimately, the proof of the pudding would be whether better planning translated into a better resource demand pattern. On this, however, the preliminary score was mixed. As the Automotive Products controller observed:

> The big difference strategic planning made so far is psychological. People are less reluctant to sell a lower ROI objective in return for a stronger

market position. They know it will be acceptable if based on sound competitive analysis. However, though the concept of reducing ROI for share gain went over, the concept of reducing NI for share gain did less so. Here, the earnings improvement goal still takes precedence. As a result, we get some improvements in the capital investment picture but not in the strategic expenditures.

These improvements in the capital investment picture were not uniform either. A few business units presented strategic plans which called for the pursuit of major growth opportunities. An even larger amount of investment was called for by business units that faced up to the instability of a weak competitive situation and proposed major gain share strategies in selected segments. Both types of business units were typically "noncore" businesses in the Automotive Products Sector.

The new planning approach seemed to have had a lesser immediate impact on the investment plans of the company's mature core businesses, however. The highly capital-intensive, low-return businesses in the Industry Products Sector were still requesting substantial investment funds, though at a lower level than in the past. The high-return businesses typical of the Electrical Products Sector, on the other hand, had increased their planned investment level somewhat, but not considerably. One group in particular seemed to feel little need to absorb the new planning philosophy. A business unit general manager in that group remarked: "One of the things that concerns me is that the best strategic plans were generally from the less successful operations and the worst strategic plans were from those with the highest performance."

On the whole, the business unit plans seemed to call for substantially more investment than in the past. That would become clearer when the businesses presented their five-year financial plans.

That portfolio planning would not be an automatic panacea had always been evident to executives at Imperial. The assistant to the president of the Industrial Products Sector commented:

> Portfolio analysis has some limitations, in that it is really impossible for the corporate level to look at all segments at the same time, which is what you would need to do. This for instance is the portfolio for just our company [showing a portfolio display with at least a hundred circles]. What the approach does, however, is to provide a common language and a way to state the issues. What the issues are and how you solve them has not changed, however.

Not only was the sheer magnitude of the analytical problem a constraint to be overcome by the administrative process, but that same process also limited the actual impact of the planning "philosophy," as some of the other formal systems were hardly compatible with or supportive of the planning system.

Link with Financial Planning

The separation of financial planning and strategic planning had clearly been a major ingredient in the success of and quality of the latter. As Mr. Peters commented: "What we have done is take advantage of people's hate for numbers to get acceptance for a major change. Leaving out the numbers was an exclamation mark behind the strategic thinking."

As the new strategic plans were accepted, however, the issue of how they could be monitored became more pressing. As one sector controller posed the problem: "Our strategic plans rightfully concentrate on segments. We do not account that way, however: our financial plan is by division."

Besides the issue of how to monitor, there was also the question of who should do so: strategic planners or the controllers' organization?

Mr. Peters felt it was important to get the controllers' organization closely involved in or at least informed of the efforts of his strategic planning group:

> An important element is to have the controllers' organization think in that direction because, ultimately, they will have to be the link. There is no reason why 15 years from now, there should be separate strategic and financial control. What we are doing is making sure they are familiar with the strategic planning ideas. That is why, whenever we have a strategy meeting we invite them, and they mostly come. As a matter of fact, I hope they will try to steal some of our functions. . . . Their involvement will be key to the change.

Link with Incentive Compensation

"The current incentive compensation is counterproductive to strategic planning," said one group controller. "It is purely operational, focusing on this year only, and only considers performance against objective. It has more of the character of a supplementary salary and a punishment for faltering badly than a true incentive."

Corporate staff managers, however, felt that it would not be easy to conceive of a system that would give more emphasis to strategic considerations and also be practical and seem fair. Two types of approach appeared possible. One would be to develop a system that would track performance over a longer period of time; the other would establish a system on the basis of criteria corresponding with the basic "strategic mission" of the business unit.

One corporate staff member had worked out a proposal based on the idea of long-term performance, to replace the stock option plan. The procedure was basically that of a phantom stock plan. A business unit manager would be given "equity" in his business. Every year his business would be valued by applying a price/earnings ratio to the earnings of the unit. The price/earnings ratio would be selected on the basis of earnings growth and return on investment, using weighted moving averages. Awards would be made every two years, based on a four-year horizon, and they would follow the manager into his next job.

Though business unit managers had not been exposed to this or any other proposal in particular, they were skeptical about the general possibility of rewarding long-run performance. Their major objections concerned the short tenure of business unit managers, coupled with the unfairness of being held responsible for a successor's decisions, especially as they felt they had little control over the selection of their successors. One business unit manager even questioned the fairness of measuring long-term performance during a manager's tenure: "Many of the things that I suffer from or benefit from are the results of my predecessor's decisions, only some are the result of my decisions."

Like his colleagues, this SBU manager was more receptive to the other approach. "We could have a system based on a set of factors which management agrees upon as the true points of concentration for success in a particular business unit."

Mr. Peters felt that such a system could eventually be envisaged and applied flexibly:

> The current system is clearly designed for operating performance and, as such, fits the divisional managers. It was not designed for business unit managers.
>
> The system we would like to see for them should be geared toward the building of business unit competitive *strength*. We could have a system in which we can change the mix of criteria according to the judgment of the strategic content of a business unit manager's job. Some business units which have a certain market share, and which will have the same share 15 years from now unless they make a big mistake, present little strategic opportunity for the business unit manager's job, and he should be rewarded basically like division managers. Other business units represent a mix of both operating and strategic challenges. Some business units, finally, are pure strategic gambles where the question is not what next year's loss situation will be but whether they will become a billion dollar business 20 years out.

Most business unit managers saw a lot of problems with the actual implementation of such a system, however. As one of them stated:

> In our group we have no reliable outside statistics. Our market share data can be nothing but approximations, based on such inputs as customer interviews and monitoring of competitors' component and raw materials purchasing. On a year-to-year basis the variations in our market share fall within the "noise" level of those data. So it would be very difficult to negotiate and monitor a market share objective or even to agree on the scope of the "served" market. It's not as clear a concept as ROI or NI.

Another problem raised by a business unit manager was the fact that SBUs' missions were a composite of often widely different segments:

> Our strategic plan identifies 12 distinct segments. Though our business unit could be considered overall as being in the "hold" category, our strategic plan actually designates three of these segments as "growth" opportunities, and calls for harvesting two others. How does such a system reward me for my success in realizing those segment strategies?

Corporate Funding of Major Growth Strategies

Given the reluctance on behalf of line managers to cloud their earnings record with the large increases in strategic expenses vital to any gain-share strategy, the managers of the Automotive Products Sector advocated the establishment of corporate funding for major growth strategies. As the sector controller argued:

> Our sector has a lot of the potential growth businesses. They also did a great job over the last years in terms of improving earnings and ROI. If they invest, their financial records will look bad. What really is the issue here is pride.
>
> The way to overcome that and to motivate people is to establish funding for major investments for gain-share strategies at the sector level, which is what we did. The result, of course, is that now my boss looks bad. It really should be done at the corporate level. At the group level also, they are funding some strategic expenses that way. If you move it up to the corporate level, you may lose some control but you can overcome that by setting up a group of people and proper procedures. The reason you have to do it is that there is no substitute for motivating business unit people.

Other managers, however, felt that establishing a corporate fund would not be a good idea. A group controller commented:

> There may be a good reason for a pot of corporate money. Some projects may be outside the realm of the business units. For growth investments *within* business units, however, all expenditures should go through the financial statements. Otherwise, it distorts the financial figures too much, and makes control difficult.

Formal Capital Allocation

Corporate managers had dual reactions to the emerging capital requests picture.

Some managers pointed out the considerable improvements and stressed that one should not expect planning effort to have a more immediate impact. A member of the corporate finance department said:

> I think what counts is really the thought process of this year's strategic plan. You shouldn't expect the impact on capital allocation to come in

the first year of the new process. As long as there is a commitment to a
strategy, that gets transmitted down through the line to where the proposals
originate. So, in later years, you will see the projects coming up which fit
the strategic thinking of this year's plan. The value of strategic planning
is the thinking, and the subsequent focus and commitment.

Other managers, including Mr. Peters, agreed that it would take
time, but argued that it was necessary to make the capital allocation
process more supportive of the strategic planning effort, and hoped that
the urgency created by the increased investment demands might precipitate a decision for corporate management to allocate resouces more explicitly.

*   *   *   *   *

At this point in late 1978, Mr. Mackenzie called Mr. Peters about
the preliminary totals in the five-year financial plans.

> The capital requests come to $1.4 billion, way over the $1 billion
> we thought we could afford without compromising our dividend and debt
> policy. I agree with you that we certainly shouldn't give in to the easy
> solution of proportional cutbacks: I want to give the capital to those units
> that will contribute the most for us! Why don't you come up with some
> proposals for me to look at?

Though Mr. Peters sensed this first corporate effort to allocate capital
could be a big step, he knew it would not be easy. Mr. Mackenzie was
very much his own man and would expect to be presented with a set
of alternatives; he even might settle on a different one. A lot would
depend on how saleable the proposal was and on Mr. Mackenzie's commitment to make it stick.

Mr. Peters asked his secretary to order sandwiches and alert his
people to stay after 6 P.M. to discuss the matter. He then called Mr. Wheeler
to ask him to bring some data for the discussion that would reflect relative
strengths of sample business groups in the three sectors (Industrial Products, Electrical Products, and Automotive Components), and show how
their capital expenditure requests compared with current expenditures
(see Exhibit 2). He also asked Mr. Wheeler to bring the market share/
market growth matrices for the three groups with the SBUs plotted individually (see Exhibit 3).

As managers filled the conference room, Mr. Peters explained the
purpose of the meeting and started them off with the issue of the level
down to which they should propose to allocate.

Opinions were quite divided as to whether it should be to the groups
or the SBUs. One of the young consultants argued strongly for the SBUs
as the appropriate level to focus on—that's what they were created for
in the first place. He argued that leaving decisions on cutbacks up to

EXHIBIT 2: Comparative Data for Sample Groups

Sectors	1979–1983 Net Income (% corporate)	1978 Depreciation (% corporate)	Planned ROI (% corporate average)	Planned Sales Growth (% corporate average)
Industrial Products	35	46	72	98
Group A	12	20	80	100
Electrical Products	46	31	141	99
Group B	14	5	275	85
Automatic Components. . .	19	22	100	104
Group C	5	8	68	190
Imperial Corporation. . . .	100	100	100	100

Capital Expenditures

Corporate funding available: $1,000M.
Total requested, 1979–1983 financial plans: $1,400M.

	Capital Expenditures 1978 ($ millions)	Strategic Expenses 1978 (% of sales)	Capital Expenditures Requested 1979–1983 ($ millions)	Strategic Expenses 1984 (% of sales)
Industrial Products	$ 75	7.0	$ 650	6.4
Group A	25	7.0	275	6.8
Electrical Products	50	3.2	450	3.2
Group B	5	5.0	75	4.8
AutomotiveComponents . .	30	5.0	300	6.0
Group C	8	4.8	100	6.2
Imperial Corporation . . .	$155	5.2	$1,400	4.9

Source: Disguised from company records.

the group VPs would result in proportional cutbacks within the groups and a lot of effort for nothing.

A senior consultant pointed out that it would be very hard to get that accepted by the group VPs and that the benefits were not worth the risk of getting nowhere. Allocating to the groups would capture most of the redistribution which was sought. Actually, shifting the investment across the sectors would help a lot. He also said that, for a lot of the business units, he would not feel comfortable deciding how much they should get—even for those on whose review team he was, let alone just on the basis of the strategic plans.

After quite some discussion, Mr. Peters suggested that they leave the issue unsettled for the moment and discuss which criteria they would propose as the basis to allocate capital investment to either the groups or business units. From the ensuing conversation three principles quickly emerged: Capital investment should somehow take into account (1) the size of the unit, (2) its contribution to corporate performance, and (3) its "strategic priority," based on managers' judgment of its investment

EXHIBIT 3: Market Share/Market Growth Data for Three Groups

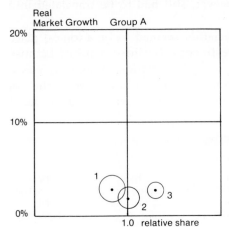

Real
Market Growth   Group A

Group A: Industrial Products Sector

SBU	ROI 1978	Plan ROI 1984	Number Segments	Strategy
# 1	7	15	5	Hold
# 2	17	20	5	Grow*
# 3	17	20	2	Hold

* SBU plan not yet reviewed. Stated growth goal: 30 percent higher than market. Corporate planning staff favored a hold strategy.

Real
Market Growth   Group B

Group B: Electrical Products Sector

SBU	ROI 1978	Plan ROI 1984	Number Segments	Strategy
# 1	35	40	4	Hold*
# 2	50	52	7	Hold*
# 3	20	25	9	Hold*

* Corporate planning staff doubted whether relative market share would be held given ROI targets. Corporate planning staff favored a selective growth strategy.

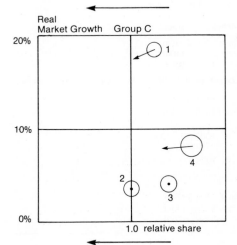

Real
Market Growth   Group C

Group C: Automotive Components Sector

SBU	ROI 1978	Plan ROI 1984	Number Segments	Strategy
# 1	40	30	1	Grow
# 2	18	20	3	Hold
# 3	10	12	6	Hold
# 4	0	5	2	Grow

opportunities. These principles, however, still had to be translated into actual criteria.

To most people present, depreciation seemed to be a logical place to start figuring out how much investment a business required because of its *size*. The ratio of investment over depreciation, moreover, was a widely used one throughout the company. One consultant, nevertheless, pointed out that using depreciation meant that the older, more depreciated

EXHIBIT 4: Effects of Four Alternative Proposals for 1979–1983 Allocations

Criteria	I	II	III	IV
Size:	Sales	Sales	Depreciation	Depreciation
Contribution:	NI	NI	NI	NI
Strategic Priority:	—	Strategic factor		Strategic factor
Group A (Industrial Products Sector)	$120m	$ 96m	$160m	$128m
Group B (Electrical Products Sector)	$100m	$410m	$ 95m	$133m
Group C (Automotive Products Sector)	$ 85m	$102m	$ 65m	$ 78m

Note: Each alternative was calculated as follows:

I. [(1978 group sales as % of corporate sales + 1979–1983 planned group NI as % of corporate NI)/2] × total funding available.

$$\text{Group A: } \frac{.12 + .12}{2} \times \$1000m = \$120m$$

$$\text{Group B: } \frac{.16 + .14}{2} \times \ 1000m = \ 100m$$

$$\text{Group C: } \frac{.12 + .05}{2} \times \ 1000m = \ 85m$$

II. Multiply I by strategic factor (.8, 1.4, 1.2 respectively for Groups A, B, and C).

$$\text{Group A: } \$120m \times \ .8 = \$ 96m$$
$$\text{Group B: } \ 100m \times 1.4 = \ 140m$$
$$\text{Group C: } \ 85m \times 1.2 = \ 102m$$

III. [(1978 group depreciation as % of corporate depreciation + 1979–1983 planned group NI as % of corporate NI)/2] × total funding available.

$$\text{Group A: } \frac{.20 + .12}{2} \times \$1000m = \$160m$$

$$\text{Group B: } \frac{.14 + .05}{2} \times \ 1000m = \ 95m$$

$$\text{Group C: } \frac{.08 + .05}{2} \times \ 1000m = \ 65m$$

IV. Multiply III by strategic factor for each group:

$$\text{Group A: } \$160m \times \ .8 = \$128m$$
$$\text{Group B: } \ 95m \times 1.4 = \ 133m$$
$$\text{Group C: } \ 65m \times 1.2 = \ 78m$$

units, which supposedly needed more maintenance investment, would get less than those which had a lot of new plant and equipment. It would also result in higher capital allocation for the capital-intensive businesses, exactly what the company wanted to deemphasize. For what they were trying to accomplish, he felt sales figures would be as good a measure of size as depreciation.

With respect to *contribution,* the discussion was brief. Only net income and operating margins were put forward, and people felt they were only marginally different.

As they came to the issue of *strategic priority* of the units, Mr. Peters suggested that they somehow try to quantify the relative investment priority of the company's businesses, taking into account not only what the opportunities of the businesses were, but also their need to defend their current position. He suggested they take a break from the discussion so that each could go down the list of business units and groups individually and quantify his judgment, given a factor of 1.0 as average for the company.

As they reconvened, it appeared that there was quite a lot of convergence in the numbers, certainly at the level of groups. After a brief discussion and some questions addressed to the corporate planner who was on a given business unit's review committee, Mr. Peters quickly got nods for compromise figures. Having decided to leave a few odd businesses such as leasing and insurance aside, the group had by 8:30 a list of "strategic factors," which they added to Mr. Wheeler's data sheet. The senior consultant again asked whether they would feel confident enough about those judgments to allocate capital on that basis. In the meantime, Ralph Wheeler, who had been pushing his calculator at the far end of the table, put on the blackboard some examples of the allocation which the various criteria implied (see Exhibit 4). These showed, for example, that if sales rather than depreciation were used as the size criterion, the allocation would be lower for the sample group in Industrial Products and higher for the sample groups in Electrical Products and Automotive Components. Multiplying by the agreed-upon strategic factors would mean a further reduction for Industrial Products, but increase allocations for each sample group in the other two sectors.

As it was already 9:00 P.M., Mr. Peters decided to end it there and meet again the next afternoon. He asked his people to think it over again and to come up with a proposal to cut the five-year capital investment requests by $400 million bringing the total down to the $1 billion, which would be acceptable to Mr. Mackenzie.

PART IV

POLICY FORMULATION AND ADMINISTRATION IN THE ENTREPRENEURIAL FIRM

CHAPTER 11

Policy Formulation and Administration in the Entrepreneurial Firm

Although many authors have identified entrepreneurship with the individual entrepreneur, increasing attention is focusing on the dynamics of entrepreneurial behavior within the firm. The importance of maintaining an "entrepreneurial spirit" of view is obvious in the face of a rapidly changing environment which poses serious threats and creates important new opportunities. This section is designed to help you understand the role of strategy and policies in an entrepreneurial firm and to provide you with an opportunity to set entrepreneurial strategies.

WHAT IS THE ENTREPRENEURIAL FIRM?

Many authors have attempted to define entrepreneurship as either risk taking or as a particular psychological profile. As you will see, the notion of a swashbuckling risk taker does not fit the character of many of the most successful entrepreneurs. Long-term success requires management of risk, not wildly seeking it out in the hopes of great reward. Many of you who do not presently think of yourself as being entrepreneurial will sometime be faced with the opportunity of going into business for yourself or of joining with friends and acquaintances in the launching of a new business venture. The fundamental difference between those who launch a new venture and those who do not can be regarded as a fundamental strategic choice: Will I be driven by a desire to capitalize upon the opportunities I see, or will I choose to build and protect the resources that I currently control?

Identifying a sound entrepreneurial strategy will require you to address five questions:

1. What is an opportunity for me and for the company?
2. What resources will I need in order to pursue the opportunity which I have identified?
3. How will I gain control over the necessary resources?
4. How will I coordinate and control the resources while I am pursuing the identified opportunity?
5. How will I realize the value which has been created?

These questions are deceptively simple, but the cases in this section will help to build the skills which are necessary in order to answer them. As you study the cases, it is critical to remember than no single question can be answered in isolation. As with almost all strategic problems, the answers are interdependent. As you will see, you will not often be faced with the choice of entrepreneurship. You will, however, frequently be forced to address whether resource limitations will prevent you from pursuing an otherwise attractive opportunity. It is often the answer to the third question above which determines the degree of entrepreneurship present in a firm.

DEFINING AN OPPORTUNITY

The most important job of top management is to identify and to assess opportunity. We believe that the capability of creatively identifying opportunity is the starting place of entrepreneurship for both the individual and the business organization. In order for a potential business to be seen as an opportunity, it must meet two conditions: (1) it must carry the organization into a desired future state which involves change and (2) it must be seen as a realistic possibility. The cases in this section will help you to be specific about the nature of the future state which is desired and will enable you to use the skills developed previously in order to assess whether it is possible for the organization to achieve the desired goals.

One of the major characteristics which separates entrepreneurial firms and individuals from those which are less entrepreneurial is the refusal to let a lack of currently controlled resources stop them from attempting to pursue an opportunity. Thus on balance the strategy of entrepreneurial firms is said to be opportunity driven, whereas others become driven by the resources which they currently control.

In examining the Hudepohl Brewing Company case, you will want to be very specific about the examination of the opportunity which Mr. Pohl has identified. You will want to see the components of the opportunity and attempt to understand why the future state is so desirable. You may even wish to ask whether there are other possible future states which are equally desirable or even more desirable from his point of view. You must then ask whether it is possible to achieve the future which he has outlined in light of the present state of the organization.

In order for a firm to remain entrepreneurial, management must constantly be on guard against allowing the current resources and activities to totally determine strategy. The current resource base of technology, distribution, skills, and product may not be adequate for the future being brought to pass by environmental change. You must examine the future to identify new opportunity and then go to the second step of assessing the resources required to pursue the opportunity. You can conceptualize this as follows:

This is not to say that entrepreneurs should look only at opportunity. In general you must seek those areas in which you have a particularly strong advantage in one or more major aspects of the opportunity. Technology, distribution, product, and cost structure are often the basis of an entrepreneurial move. It is rare that simply working harder is sufficient to ensure entrepreneurial success. The good entrepreneur seeks in some way to have an "unfair advantage" in order to ensure success. If that unfair advantage can be clearly identified, then the entrepreneur can proceed to the next stage, which is outlining the resources that will be required in order to achieve success.

IDENTIFYING THE REQUIRED RESOURCES

The entrepreneurial firm starts with identifying an opportunity. Stopping there leaves one *only* with dreams. As a manager, one of the most important skills you need to develop is the ability to set out a time-phased plan which identifies milestones to be accomplished and the resources which will be required in order to achieve each milestone. Entrepreneurial firms are often required to do more with less. Almost by definition, they are attempting to achieve goals which will require considerably more resources than they currently possess. Two issues rise to paramount importance: How do I commit to the pursuit of the opportunity, and how do I know what resource I will need when?

While acknowledging the importance of the opportunity, you cannot forget the need to make an accurate assessment of the resources currently controlled and the resources needed to pursue the identified opportunities. Accurate resource assessment must be made relative to those of the competitors and the time-based goals of the organization which you are studying. The unique difference among entrepreneurial firms is seeing the acquisition of resources as one of the tasks to be accomplished rather than as a barrier to change. Most entrepreneurial firms must be constantly in the resource acquisition mode. Change which creates opportunity also creates the need for new organizational, technological, productive, distributive, and human resources. The best firms, such as IBM, Hewlett-Packard, and 3M, recognize the need for change but help to cushion the cost of change for their employees.

Not allowing the lack of resources to stop strategic change forces you as a manager to adapt a style toward accomplishment of intermediate goals. We suggest that one of the skills which entrepreneurial firms develop is a *bias toward action.* They are prepared to tentatively pursue many opportunities. They are prepared to make strategic experiments. By this we mean that management frequently takes actions which can have a long-term impact on the company, but management is prepared to reassess and to pursue opportunistic availability of resources. Both in the Hudepohl and in the Electrodec cases, you will need to ask yourself what resources will be required to pursue the desired opportunities. One of the clear differences between the cases is the scale required. You must address the question as to whether you can pursue either the beer or the electric utility industry in a small way. You will then want to identify the milestones which Mr. Pohl and Mr. Nolan should set for their respective companies in order to measure the success of the strategic experiments which are proposed.

Often as we look at entrepreneurial firms and more classically administered firms, we see differences in the following dimensions:

You will see that often the entrepreneurial firm must commit all of its available resources in order to get to even the next stage of development. The need for full commitment is often cited as the risk-taking characteristic of the entrepreneurial firm. Often entrepreneurs see the risk subjectively. They believe that they control the critical skills or resources. If they can just achieve the next milestone, they will have access to the required resources. One of the most important skills which you can develop is the ability to set your milestones in such a way that achievement of a milestone will attract additional resources and will help the firm to pursue its ambitious goals. You must then be certain that you have sufficient resources under control in order to achieve this proximate milestone.

GAINING CONTROL OVER RESOURCES

Once you have identified the resources you will need to pursue your opportunity, only a part of the job is done. As we have said, entrepreneurial firms are often faced with a scarcity of resources. As a manager, you must decide how to lever that which you currently control in order to proceed. The term *resources* encompasses far more than money, as you will discover by studying the first two cases in this section. Resources include technology, management talent, distribution channels, as well as financial strength. Not all of these resources need to be a financial strength. Not all of these resources need to be a formal part of the firm. Areas such as Silicon Valley, Triangle Park, or Route 128 are full of firms which provide specialized resources to emerging businesses. Major metropolitan areas often are fertile ground for growing organizations as well, because of the availability of critical skills which need not be integrated into the structure of the firm. One of the major skills you develop as a manager will be achieving success through resources which you do not own or control hierarchically.

We have seen that the entrepreneurial firm often has a different concept of control than the administratively driven firm. This different concept of control lets the company pursue opportunities more readily, but it also changes the risk profile and the required management style. Two of the differences are shown below:

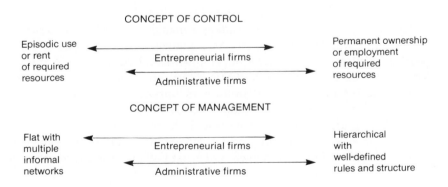

CONCEPT OF CONTROL

| Episodic use or rent of required resources | ←——— Entrepreneurial firms ———→ | Permanent ownership or employment of required resources |
| | ←——— Administrative firms ———→ | |

CONCEPT OF MANAGEMENT

| Flat with multiple informal networks | ←——— Entrepreneurial firms ———→ | Hierarchical with well-defined rules and structure |
| | ←——— Administrative firms ———→ | |

As you study the Michael Bregman case, you must keep in mind the nature of the opportunities which his company is facing, the kind of resources which will be required in order to pursue the opportunities and the risks and rewards. You can then examine two different techniques for gaining control over the resources. It is important for you to consider the managerial implications of these two fundamentally different approaches. Going with looser legal control will call for more persuasive skills. You will have to ask whether the experiences of Michael Bregman to date have prepared him for leadership without formal authority. On the other hand, you must ask yourself whether attempting to own and control directly all of the geographically disbursed units will increase or decrease the risk of failure.

As more skills become highly specialized, companies have to recognize that only the largest can afford to have the best specialists available as part of the permanent staff. Just as the entrepreneur has recognized the need to use outside resources, so too are many companies having to face up to this need and to develop the requisite management skills. Many important staff skills will always lie outside of the formal hierarchical boundaries of your companies. These "staffs" need to be managed just as much as if they were part of the firm. Goals must be set, performance measured and rewarded, personnel selected and trained in the appropriate problem definition. Even some line skills will often lie outside the organization. Critical factors in research, production, and distribution are often provided by independent contractors. You as managers must challenge the logic of efficiency which says that they must be owned or employed. Even more critically, if the decision is made to have these resources controlled by independent outsiders, you must develop appropriate techniques for managing them. The contrast between management and purchase of service must be seen to be artificial. You will need to develop the informal power and influence networks which allow you to accomplish your purpose through others.

MANAGING THE OPPORTUNITY LIFE CYCLE

We believe that any opportunity has a finite life. One of the greatest and most frequently occurring mistakes is management's failure to support a continuing process of renewal. As a manager, you have the ultimate responsibility for ensuring the development and continuity of the firm for which you are responsible. One critical step for an entrepreneur is to separate his or her own definition of opportunity from that of the enterprise. For you as an individual, success need not always be defined as continuing organizational growth and change. Once a certain base of resources is achieved, the individual entrepreneur has to examine both what is good for himself or herself and what will ensure continuing benefits for the others within and without the organization who depend on it for both financial security and intrinsic self-worth.

There are often three choices which you might face as a manager: selling out, administering stability, or pursuing continuous change. Each of these choices has its own set of risks and rewards. The achievement of continuous dynamism is often considered to be the highest form of management accomplishment. The final case in this section allows you to examine one of the most successful companies in the United States as it attempts to reorganize and yet to continue to support its entrepreneurial culture. Hewlett-Packard's management has achieved remarkable success. It is often cited as an excellent company because of its remarkable record of growth, innovation and continuous profitability. For many students of business, it epitomizes the entrepreneurial dream. It has allowed considerable freedom and responsibility at all levels in the organization. Its managers at all levels have participated in the development of an industry and an industrial climate which has been studied and envied worldwide.

As you read this case, you will be faced with numerous questions. You will need to examine the opportunity which Hewlett-Packard recognized in the computer industry. You will need to examine the organization change which is proposed in order to see if it will improve the responsiveness of the company to the market. At the same time you must face the dilemma often faced by professional managers: additional control and coordination might put at risk the entrepreneurial spirit which has been at the root of the organization's magnificent success.

We do not propose that there is a single answer to the question of how management can preserve an opportunity-driven culture. You need to address the delicate balance which must be preserved. As a manager, you must recognize that some of the most sophisticated techniques available may have severe and unfortunate side effects. Tight control, budgeting, and planning systems are powerful medicines for firms. Before prescribing additional integration, management must be conscious of the benefits of differentiation.

SUMMARY

The search for entrepreneurial management is critically important to the survival of independent business organizations. The rate of change in technology, society, and markets increased dramatically in the late 70s and early 80s. At the same time the opportunity streams which fueled postwar economic growth may largely have played out. The first 30 years of the postwar period in the United States were characterized by an abundance of opportunity brought about by expanding markets, high investment in the national infrastructure, and mushrooming debt for individuals, corporations, and governments. In this environment it was possible to prosper even with the sloppiest of practices, but this is no longer true. Access to cheap international resources is no longer guaranteed. Increased government regulation has brought a recognition of the full costs of doing business. Foreign competition has put an end to American dominance in numerous industries. Technological change has reduced product life in many industries. For you to manage a successful firm, you must either be capable of rapid responses to changes which are beyond your control or else you must contribute to innovation which causes the changes in the competitive environment.

We believe that many of the practices in what are considered to be well-managed firms tend to inhibit entrepreneurial behavior in both managers and their subordinates. These practices developed in the context of abundant opportunity and were adequate in that context. The long-term efficacy of these practices is in doubt, however.

As you think about your business practice, you must address the question clearly: How do I pursue opportunity for which my currently controlled resources are not adequate or appropriate? You must look at the question of good management as both initiative and quick reaction. The material on entrepreneurial management should raise some questions in your mind:

How do I organize so that opportunity for the managers and opportunities for the company are the same and thus managers have incentive to pursue opportunities for the firm?

How do I conduct "strategic experiments" which will create commitment to new opportunities and yet minimize danger to the existing businesses?

How do we deal with failure so that individuals will be encouraged to take the risk required to pursue new opportunities?

How will the company develop a diversified portfolio of risk when managers within the organization cannot diversify their own risk structure?

How do we ensure that everyone will try to do more with less so that perceived resource constraints will not prevent new opportunities from being pursued?

How do we ensure that adequate resources will be available for use when needed without the firm bearing the risk of obsolescence and exposure to continuing overhead?

How do we reward intelligent use of other organizations' resources and not simply reward managers for justifying the purchase of additional assets or the employment of additional personnel?

How do I manage without the tools available in formal hierarchies and yet coordinate critical resources needed for success?

The entrepreneurial firm faces many dilemmas. Tensions exist between the goals which have been set in the pursuit of recognized opportunities and the resources available to the firm. The entrepreneurial practices identified above are relevant to today's business practice. You will often be facing the choices outlined above and be forced to address these questions.

A changing business environment requires new commitments and great flexibility; otherwise strengths become weaknesses and weaknesses strengths. As you address the cases in this section, focus upon opportunity. Do not view the lack of resources as the analytical answer and therefore a convenient stopping place. Develop an understanding of the dynamic balance which can be achieved as goals are set and met, resources attracted, and the availability of new resources allow further goals to be set.

Finally, maintaining the entrepreneurial spirit within your organization requires a very personal commitment on your part. Try to place yourself in Michael Bregman's or Kirk Nolan's shoes. What would it feel like to be in their position? A good analysis of these cases requires understanding equilibrium of opportunity and resources through time. You must decide what is critical and when the need will be critical. As you gain insight into how all of the participants' interests can be served over time, you will be focusing on the dynamic world of entrepreneurial management.

CASE 25

Hudepohl Brewing Company

Bob Pohl, age 32, was appointed general manager of the Hudepohl Brewing Company following the unexpected death of the company's president in March 1980. Since 1975, Pohl had managed Hudepohl's marketing response to rapidly changing conditions in the brewing industry. The death of the president, a relative, left Pohl as the only member of the founder's family active in the day-to-day activities of the business.

Based in Cincinnati, Ohio, Hudepohl was the twentieth largest brewery in the United States. From 1978 to 1980 the brewery operated at less than 40 percent of its one million barrel[1] capacity, and in 1978 the company experienced the largest operating loss in its history—$538,000. After adjusting for gains on Hudepohl's securities portfolio and a tax loss carryback, net income for that fiscal year was $95,161, down from $268,611 in 1977. Additional financial information is presented in Exhibits 1, 2, and 3.

After three months as general manager, Pohl was predicting improved earnings in the near future. A 7 percent gain in sales during the first four months of 1980 seemed to confirm his expectations. Pohl felt that by 1983 Hudepohl would achieve a 10 percent growth in sales.

BACKGROUND ON THE COMPANY

Ownership and Organization

Hudepohl's board of directors consisted of seven members, all of whom were descendants of founder Louis Hudepohl. Chairman John Hes-

---

[1] The term "barrel" refers to a full barrel, which has a volume of 31 gallons.

EXHIBIT 1

HUDEPOHL BREWING COMPANY
Financial Analysis
(in thousands of dollars except per share and per barrel data)

	1978	1977	1976	1975	1974	1973	1972	1971	Percent Growth Rates per Annum
Gross sales	$17,168	$16,972	$18,629	$19,097	$18,188	$16,708	$12,931	$14,578	
Net sales	13,070	12,615	13,544	13,611	13,261	11,005	8,340	9,431	
Cost of goods sold	10,204	9,668	10,150	10,516	10,084	8,357	6,208	6,692	6.2
Gross profit	2,866	2,947	3,394	3,094	3,178	2,648	2,132	2,739	
Selling, general, and administrative	3,404	3,153	2,929	2,537	2,105	2,272	1,651	1,837	9.2
Income from operations	(538)	(207)	465	557	1,072	376	481	901	
Number of shares	48,000	48,000	48,000	48,000	48,000	48,000	48,000	48,000	
Income from operations/share	(11.21)	(4.31)	9.69	11.60	22.33	7.83	10.02	18.77	
Barrels sold	334	355	407	436	469	468	367	391	
Sales per barrel	51.40	47.81	45.77	43.80	41.09	35.70	35.23	37.28	4.7

EXHIBIT 2

HUDEPOHL BREWING COMPANY
Net Income Analysis
(in thousands of dollars)

	1978	1977	1976	1975	1974	1973	1972	1971
Operating income.	$(538)	$(207)	$ 465	$ 557	$1,072	$ 376	$ 481	$ 901
Other credits:								
Municipal interest	203	192	184	161	124	123	193	210
Corp. dividends	154	153	145	135	119	96	81	69
Bank interest	45	37	93	134	202	125		
Miscellaneous	40	24	129	100	104	99	82	124
Other charges:								
Goodwill	(25)	(25)	(25)	(25)	(25)	(20)	(51)	(54)
Miscellaneous	(5)	(7)	(8)	(7)	(48)	(79)		
PBT	(126)	167	983	1,055	1,548	720	786	1,250
(Taxes due) tax loss carryback.	221	101	(320)	(366)	(657)	(227)	(255)	(514)
Net income .	$ 95	$ 268	$ 663	$ 689	$ 891	$ 493	$ 531	$ 736

EXHIBIT 3

HUDEPOHL BREWING COMPANY
Comparative Balance Sheets

Assets	1978	1970
Current assets:		
Cash.	$ 822,627	$ 1,942,308
Certificates of deposit	750,000	1,250,000
Accounts receivable	372,027	170,132
Inventories .	1,039,381	675,708
Refundable income taxes.	203,546	—
Other.	61,528	59,099
Total Current Assets .	3,249,109	4,095,247
Investments (at cost) .	5,160,556	4,062,357
Property, plant, and equipment:		
Land and improvements	414,133	390,676
Buildings	4,573,369	4,471,407
Machinery and equipment	6,630,814	6,017,214
Total	11,618,316	10,879,297
Less accumulated depreciation	8,270,747	6,205,512
Net property, plant, and equipment	3,347,569	4,673,785
Other assets:		
Goodwill	103,619	—
Surrender value of insurance	27,976	35,681
Deposits	3,000	17,800
Miscellaneous.	74,875	75,765
Total other	209,470	129,246
Total assets	$11,966,704	$12,960,635

Liabilities		
Current liabilities:		
Accounts payable	$ 236,980	$ 187,591
Federal, state beer taxes .	130,546	195,928
Customers' deposits	205,909	266,132
Salaries, wages .	180,865	121,139
Other taxes	139,788	191,481
Other.	106,490	15,922
Total Current Liabilities .	1,000,578	978,193
Shareholders' equity:		
Common stock	4,122,000	4,800,000
Retained earnings	6,844,126	7,182,442
Total shareholders' equity .	10,966,126	11,982,442
Total liabilities	$11,966,704	$12,960,635

selbrock, age 73 and the uncle of Bob Pohl, held almost total control over the board but did not take an active role in daily management decisions. The board which made the final decision on major expenditures, was generally conservative. Pohl felt that this had been appropriate in the past, when other breweries were also conservative, but that a far more aggressive approach was necessary in every area now.

Pohl's first major change as general manager involved the organizational structure. Fifteen people in charge of various areas had reported directly to the former president. Pohl's reorganization delegated responsibility to managers of functional areas (purchasing, personnel, marketing, comptroller, and plant) and was designed to free Pohl himself to concentrate on planning, an area he felt had been neglected in the past.

Key supervisors felt that under Pohl they had the authority needed to manage their operations effectively. Those in marketing and distribution were excited by being part of a young, aggressive team. Other older functional area managers were less enthusiastic about the changes they saw.

Hudepohl's Marketing Strategy

In 1980, Hudepohl marketed five brands of beer. Tap, Hudepohl, and Burger accounted for nearly 80 percent of Hudepohl's sales in Cincinnati. Hudy Delight, the company's recent entrant into the rapidly growing light beer field, accounted for most of the remaining 20 percent. Hofbrau, an all-malt premium beer sold only on draft, contributed under 1 percent. Compared with competitors' products, all Hudepohl products were sold with low retail prices.

Much of Hudepohl's sales occurred in the city of Cincinnati (55 percent) and the metropolitan area (80 percent). Although the population of the metropolitan area had been growing at 1 percent per year from 1970 to 1978, the city's population had declined by 1 percent annually over the same period. During this time the ethnic groups represented in the metropolitan area remained the same, but the percentage of minorities in the city increased from approximately one-quarter to one-third. The effective buying power per household in metropolitan Cincinnati consistently ranked above the Ohio and U.S. averages, yet the buying power of inner-city households lagged significantly behind state and national levels. These trends were expected to continue in the 1980s.

The Cincinnati beer market displayed several unique characteristics. At 18 gallons per person per year, the average Cincinnatian drank less beer annually than the average Ohioan (23 gallons) or American (25 gallons). Nonetheless, Cincinnati enjoyed a solid reputation as a beer-drinking town because of its unusually large draft beer market. Draft beer accounted for 17 percent of total Cincinnati beer sales (versus 11 percent nationwide) and 41 percent of Hudepohl's Cincinnati sales (versus 20 percent of its non-Cincinnati sales).

The company used a heavy push and pull communications strategy in Cincinnati. Twelve salesmen, supported by a $200,000 expense budget, called on current and potential accounts. Sales calls at bars typically involved buying drinks for the house to promote goodwill, but in recent years this form of promotion had been discontinued by most of Hudepohl's competition. Over half of Hudepohl's advertising budget was devoted to the Cincinnati market, as shown in Exhibit 4.

EXHIBIT 4: Hudepohl's Sales and Advertising Expense by Market

	Sales		Advertising Expense	
	1979	1978	1979	1978
Cincinnati. . .	81%	80%	52%	52%
Dayton. . . .	8	9	17	14
Columbus. . .	4	4	27	17
Lexington. . .	1	1	4	4
Other	6	6	1	13

Hudepohl's $700,000 advertising expenditure in Cincinnati in 1979 exceeded that of Miller, the next largest advertiser, by $300,000; in Columbus, Hudepohl's advertising expenditure was less than half of Miller's $400,000; and in Dayton four companies spent from two to four times as much as Hudepohl's $100,000.

Until 1979, Hudepohl's advertising dollars were distributed somewhat randomly across product offerings and were mostly for sports-related advertising, such as spots during Cincinnati Reds games. Hudepohl's emphasis on popularly priced products, barroom sales, sports-dominated advertising, and reliance on city sales was aimed at urban, blue collar workers. Action Data, a local market research organization, described the average Hudepohl drinker as follows: "white, lower income, blue collar, middle-aged, male city residents who have a union affiliation and are the outdoor sportsman type."

Bob Pohl implemented a number of changes in this policy in 1979. For example, advertising was split 75/25 between Hudepohl and Hudy Delight. Arte Johnson, a nationally known comedian, was hired to depict a comic German Hudepohl beer drinker. Management felt that this approach would capitalize on Cincinnati's strong German heritage (25 percent of the population).

Production

All of Hudepohl's operations were conducted at its Cincinnati plant, an older facility that included a coal-burning power plant capable of supplying steam and electricity for the company's operations.

The Process. Hudepohl made its beer by a process utilized by all commercial beer makers. Barley mash was cleaned and ground to a coarse grist, weighed and placed in a mash tub, and then mixed with water. Simultaneously, a mixture of hot water, additional malt, and cooked grits consisting of rice, corn, and/or flakes was heated in a cooker to liquefy the starch. This cereal mash was then added to the malt in the mash tub. The malt's enzymes converted the starch into fermentable sugars (maltose and dextrin) and the resultant liquid, called wort, was then filtered. This mixture was moved to the brew kettle where hops were added and boiled for several hours. Then the wort was filtered to remove the hops and funneled to a hot wort tank. The filtered liquid was pumped through a cooler as it approached the fermentation and finishing stage.

The wort entered the fermentation vat and yeast was added. After fermentation took place, the beer was stored in tanks at controlled temperatures for six weeks or longer so that mellowing and sedimentation could occur. Before the beer was packaged, it was filtered; CO_2 that had been removed during fermentation was reintroduced to the beer at this time. Draft beer, intended for quick consumption, was put in barrels and sold without further processing. Beer intended for bottles or cans, which had a shelf life of four to six months, was pasteurized before being packaged.

The Brewing Cycle. At Hudepohl six men (two per shift) were scheduled to brew round the clock Monday through Friday. The maximum output was 35 batches a week, and each batch contained about 610 barrels. A batch moved from the mash tub to the cooler in about half a day. The next cycle, fermentation, required at least 10 days per brew, yielding a maximum of 36 fermentation cycles per year. Hudepohl's present fermentation tank capacity was 21,155 barrels. Available tanks not in use in 1980 could provide another 3,845 barrels per cycle.

Since demand for Hudepohl's beer was well below manufacturing capacity, the last brew of the week was typically started on Tuesday. Hence, all brewing was finished by noon on Wednesday. The use of a continuous process during the first part of the week obviated the cleaning required for idle tanks. The six men who brewed during the beginning of the week performed the cleaning and maintenance tasks in the brewing area when their primary work was completed. These men, according to the union contract, could also be used in other areas of the brewhouse.

Besides the 6 brewing employees, there were 38 other employees involved in production. Approximately 28 of them worked on aspects of the fermentation cycle and the remaining 10 were involved in the racking operations. The interchangeability of workers was limited only by the hierarchy of skill required.

Six salaried employees—three brewmasters, a chemist, and two others—handled the managerial and quality-control functions in the brewhouse. The job of brewmaster required the talents of a master scheduler, a thorough knoweldge of brewing, and a discriminating palate. Supervision of the work force and scheduling the brewing and finishing operations were the most time-consuming tasks for the brewmasters. The brewmasters also performed numerous tasting and other sensory tests on each batch of beer as the beer aged, since beer testing for quality control was a major responsibility of the brewmaster.

Racking and Packaging. The racking area of the brewhouse was where the unpasteurized beer was put into full, half, and quarter barrels. Typically only one or two employees at a time actually filled barrels. The others cleaned returned barrels, positioned barrels so that they could be quickly grabbed by those filling, or rolled newly filled barrels to a storage area. The racking area was currently operating at 68.8 percent of capacity.

All beer that was not racked was packaged in cans or bottles within the bottle shop. For bottles, the brewery used returnable quarts and 12-ounce containers (called "pints"), and nonreturnable quarts and 12-ounce containers (called "glass cans"). The cans were made of tinplate and held 12 ounces. The bottle shop was a major user of the brewery's resources, employing 42 production workers and 5 supervisors. There were four packaging lines, including the canning operation, and the overall capacity rate for the bottle shop in 1980 was 40 percent.

Scheduling the packaging operation was a somewhat complicated process. Since production workers were on two shifts, only half the labor force was available at any given time. Vacations (about 10 percent of paid time in the bottle shop) and absences for other reasons also reduced the work force. As a result, on days when the pint line was operating, no other lines could be run; on days when the quart or glass can lines were running, cans could also be filled. Scheduling was complicated by the necessity of making quick changes from one package type to another in response to market demand. Flexibility was achieved by transferring workers among bottle shop tasks, a practice allowed by the employee's union. Some tasks required more skill than others; thus, 100 percent interchangeability was not possible. Since all workers were paid at the same rate, the rotation policies in brewing and packaging tended to lower the morale of the older, more skilled workers.

After the beer was racked or packaged, it was transferred to a warehouse. The unpasteurized draft beer was held in cold storage to prevent spoilage. Beer in bottles and cans was stacked on pallets at room temperature.

Distribution

Hudepohl's beer was distributed outside Cincinnati by independent distributors, who picked up the beer at Hudepohl's dock, warehoused it, and then delivered it. In 1978, independent distributors handled 47.3

percent of the company's barrels sold. Hudepohl's own drivers made the deliveries within Cincinnnati; these deliveries represented 21.4 percent of draft beer and 31.2 percent of packaged beer volume sales in 1978 (see Exhibit 5).

EXHIBIT 5: Sales Data by Package Type and Distribution Method, 1978

	Number of Barrels	Revenue Received
Draft:		
Sold to independents	50,265	$ 1,161,233
Sold via own distribution network	73,513	2,842,792
Bottles or cans:		
Sold to independents	112,403	5,712,595
Sold via own distribution network	107,169	7,451,535
Total.	343,350	$17,168,155

Hudepohl's distribution network consisted of 23 bottle routes and 10 draft routes. Bottle deliveries were handled by a driver/sales representative whose job included taking an order, filling it from supplies that had been placed on the truck the day before, collecting cash for the order,[2] and picking up empty returnable bottles held by the customer. Bottle drivers were compensated with a base salary of $277 per week, plus incentive compensation of 4 cents per case on the first 750 cases and 26 cents per case for each case above 750 delivered in a week.

Roy Nixon, the shipping department supervisor, estimated that the average driver delivered about 1,200 cases per week. Nixon had recently reorganized the routes so that distinct territories for bottle drivers were developed. He balanced the routes so that a typical driver would make about 15 stops a day. The new system tried to cluster accounts served in any given day so that daily driving was limited to an average of less than 50 miles.

Unlike bottle orders, draft beer was preordered, but draft drivers were responsible for delivering the orders, collecting empty barrels, and obtaining the cash payment for the beer they delivered. Draft deliveries were made by two men and often to barroom storage areas that were not readily accessible. With full barrels weighing over 300 pounds, draft delivery was a strenuous task even for two men. After making a delivery, the crew would frequently have a beer or two and chat with the bartender while waiting for payment. The typical five half-barrel delivery took about 1.1 hours, and during that time the truck sat idle.

---

[2] Ohio law required payment upon delivery.

Summary of Operating Revenues and Expenses

It was through this chain of brewing, packaging, and distribution that Hudepohl earned all of its operating revenue. The price that Hudepohl received for its products varied significantly, depending on container type and whether the beer was delivered by the company or an independent distributor (see Exhibit 5).

While federal and state taxes averaged $11.95 per barrel regardless of package type and method of delivery, other costs associated with these sales differed considerably. For example, the costs associated with the sale of a barrel of draft beer to an independent distributor were less than the cost of pasteurizing and packaging the barrel's 31 gallons in bottles and cans and then delivering it.

Expenses incurred by Hudepohl during 1978 are listed in Exhibit 6.

EXHIBIT 6: Expenses by Principal Operation, 1978

Brewing (variable and associated fixed costs)	$2,778,103
Racking (variable and associated fixed costs)	256,220
Bottling and canning (variable and associated fixed costs) . . .	5,564,694
Distribution:	
Draft (variable cost)	485,921
Packaged (variable cost)	738,394
Associated fixed costs	145,289
Other operating expenses	203,424
Selling expenses	2,692,652
General and administrative expenses	697,324

THE LARGER ENVIRONMENT: THE U.S. BREWING INDUSTRY

Historically, the U.S. brewing industry has been characterized by a growing market increasingly supplied by fewer brewers. This concentration of the industry has occurred partly due to economies of scale in the production, distribution, and marketing of beer. The degree of industry concentration accelerated rapidly during the most recent decade; by 1978, the top 10 American brewers accounted for 94 percent of beer sales, leaving only 6 percent or 10 million barrels to the remaining competitors. The big sales winners between 1969 and 1979 were Anheuser-Busch, Miller, and Heileman. The laggards appeared to be Schaefer and the smaller regional companies. Overall, of the 750 breweries operating after the end of Prohibition (1933), only 44 remained by 1978. Exhibit 7 presents relevant volume and market share data. Exhibit 8 describes the production capabilities of the leading companies.

EXHIBIT 7: Industry Statistics

I. Top Ten American Brewers

Company	Rank	1978 Barrels (in thousands)	1978 SOM (by volume)	1969 Barrels (in thousands)	1969 SOM (by volume)	Compound Growth Rate
Anheuser-Busch.	1	41,610	25.7%	18,860	16.2	9.4
Miller	2	31,274	19.3	4,189	4.5	21.3
Schlitz	3	19,600	12.1	13,709	11.8	2.1
Pabst	4	15,367	9.5	10,250	8.8	4.0
Coors	5	12,566	7.7	6,350	5.5	7.4
Heileman	6	7,112	4.4	2,215	1.9	17.9
Olympia	7	6,662	4.1	3,375	2.9	6.0
Stroh	8	6,329	3.9	2,939	2.5	7.4
Schmidt	9	3,792	2.3	2,950	2.5	2.7
Schaefer	10	3,429	2.1	5,450	4.7	(4.2)
Total Industry		162,174		116,271		

II. Brewing Industry Leaders*

Company	1978 Sales	1978 Net Income	1974 Sales	1974 Net Income
Anheuser-Busch	2,701,611	111,040	1,791,863	64,019
Miller	1,834,526	n.a.	403,551	n.a.
Schlitz	1,083,272	11,961	1,015,978	48,982
Pabst	753,770	11,086	558,852	18,330
Coors	624,804	54,774	466,297	41,051
Heileman	393,454	18,038	182,192	4,833
Olympia	372,229	6,259	237,948	3,702
Stroh	365,000	6,300	n.a.	n.a.
Schmidt	n.a.	n.a.	n.a.	n.a.
Schaefer	172,792	(63,038)	211,134	675

III. 1978 Financial—Top Ten U.S. Breweries*

Company	Total Assets	Equity	Long-term Debt
Anheuser-Busch.	1,600,000	754,000	
Miller	1,200,000†	—	—
Schlitz	692,000	355,000	140,000
Pabst	425,000	271,000	26,000
Coors	752,000	598,000	none
Heileman	147,000	78,000	17,000
Olympia	125,000	71,000	20,000
Stroh	105,000	63,000	460
Schmidt	—	—	—
Schaefer	86,000	(44,000)	97,000

* In thousands of dollars.
† Wholly owned subsidiary of Philip Morris, Inc.
Source: Compiled from company and industry information.

EXHIBIT 8: Production Facilities

Brewery	Capacity (thousands of barrels per year)	# Breweries	Average Capacity per Brewery (millions of barrels)	Location
Anheuser-Busch .	46,400	10	4.6	California (2), Florida (2), Missouri, New Hampshire, New Jersey, Ohio, Texas, Virginia
Miller	32,000	5	6.4	Wisconsin, New York, California, Texas, North Carolina
Schlitz	31,400	8	3.9	California, Hawaii, Florida, North Carolina, New York, Tennessee, Texas, Wisconsin
Pabst	19,000	5	3.8	California, Georgia, Illinois, New Jersey, Wisconsin
Coors	15,000	1	15.0	Colorado
Heileman. . . .	14,000	9	1.6	Wisconsin, Kentucky, Minnesota, Indiana, Washington, Michigan, Illinois, Arizona, Maryland
Olympia	9,450	3	3.2	Minnesota, Texas, Washington
Stroh	6,000	1	6.0	Michigan
F&M Schaefer . .	5,000	1*	5.0	Pennsylvania
Hudepohl . . .	1,000	1	1.0	Ohio

* Reputed to be one of the most efficient brew and packaging plants in the industry.
Source: Compiled from company and industry information.

Industry Economics

There were five major cost components in beer production in 1980: purchase of raw materials, production costs, labor, packaging, and general and administrative expenses.

Raw Materials Purchasing. Brewing ingredients and packaging materials made up almost all of the typical brewery's raw materials purchases. Malt, corn, rice, and hops, the major brewing ingredients, were subject to wide fluctuations in price due primarily to crop conditions and international trading. Brewers' major packaging materials purchases were bottles and cans. Draft kegs, paperboard, and corrugated board were relatively minor purchases, and there were significant volume discounts on can purchases up to the 500,000-can lot size. The terms for purchasing glass bottles for beer were similar to those for cans.

Production. Nearly all U.S. breweries used a batch size and technology similar to Hudepohl's, regardless of plant scale. Even though lower-cost production technology had been developed in the past, the traditionally conservative brewing industry was reluctant to change its methods of brewing. This reluctance was reinforced by the experience of one of the large companies, which had abandoned such an attempt after incurring consumer ill will due to quality-control problems. The only significant technological development in recent years had been the increasing automation of the brewing process by the large breweries, which were able to install expensive computers primarily to increase quality control and product consistency.

Labor. Wages in the brewing industry have been consistently higher than the average for all manufacturing firms. Average hourly earnings of brewery employees were $10.90 in 1980, compared with $7.29 for manufacturing employees and $6.86 for food industry workers. Two unions represented brewery workers, the Teamsters and the United Brewery Workers of America. Both unions were powerful and had shown ample capacity to sustain long strikes. Brewery managements perceived strikes as a major threat, because they feared an inability to recover market share lost through a disruption in the supply of their products. Draft beer sales particularly were susceptible to supply shortages, since taverns would not go for long without some beer on tap.

To reduce the cost of labor arbitration, a system of wage leadership had evolved. During the 1950s and 1960s, Anheuser-Busch's wage settlements with both unions provided a guideline for settlements with other unions. That company was aptly suited for the position of wage leader, since its sales and profits were high enough to absorb occasional unexpected costs without serious hardship. Anheuser-Busch's wage leadership could work against the smaller regional breweries, however. As the larger breweries expanded, they increasingly invested in capital-intensive equipment, which meant that they could set wages at a higher rate than the smaller companies with labor-intensive manufacturing techniques could afford. Exhibit 9 shows the shift in labor costs before and after automation at Anheuser-Busch, compared with the labor costs of a regional brewery without new equipment.

EXHIBIT 9: Labor Cost as a Percentage of the Cost of Goods Sold

	1971	1955
Anheuser-Busch	0.28	0.42
Regional company (Falstaff)	0.37	0.385

Source: Kenneth Hatten, "Strategic Models in the Brewing Industry" (Ph.D. dissertation, Purdue University, 1974).

Labor productivity improved as new equipment was introduced. For example, Schlitz's labor productivity rose by a compound annual rate of 9.4 percent from 1965 to 1975. This highly capital-intensive company had a 1972 output of 9,110 barrels per year per employee, at a cost of $1.08 per barrel. Falstaff, without new equipment, had an annual output of 2,277 barrels per employee, and a production cost of $4.39.

The system of wage leadership became a subtle competitive tool with which to wrest market shares from regional competitors.[3] For some smaller breweries without sufficient funds to invest in new equipment, the strength of the unions and the wage setting practices of the leaders drove them to the brink of bankruptcy. Still, two New York State breweries operated at a loss for several years because that was cheaper than the union settlement required if the breweries closed down.

Packaging. Owing to technological improvements, between 1960 and 1979 canning line speeds increased 123 percent and labor requirements dropped 42 percent. The can itself improved over this time; the three-piece tinplate can was replaced by a two-piece aluminum one. A new 1,800-cans-per-minute line cost about $3 million in 1979, which was much higher than the price for earlier equipment. Bottle filling also improved over this period given improvements in equipment for the bottle lines. The hicone, a set of plastic rings used to bind six or eight cans, became a cost-effective replacement for paperboard can carriers, while shrink wrapping was economically replacing many of the functions of the corrugated box.

General and Administrative Expenses. The increase in the average plant's scale from 1 million barrels in 1969 to over 2.5 million barrels in 1979 allowed companies to decrease their unit costs, because fixed administrative expenses such as management salaries could be spread over larger volume. Alternatively, this economy of scale allowed companies to attract better management with higher salaries for the same unit cost. Some companies pursued both strategies. Larger overall scale also enabled more economic warehousing and provided the volume necessary to justify investment in expensive equipment. In addition, the large dollar investments in equipment by aggressively expanding companies enabled them to take a larger depreciation expense before calculating their taxes on profits.

Summary. The effects of these components of the industry's production process affected trends in the industry's cost structure, as can be seen in Exhibit 10.

---

[3] Lynn Feldman, "The Brewing Industry 1958–1977" (undergraduate thesis, Harvard University, 1978).

EXHIBIT 10: Brewing Industry's Cost per Barrel in Constant 1977 Dollars

	1977	1972
Brewing materials	$9.00	$4.49
Package materials	16.91	18.90
Production labor	3.75	4.53
Nonproduction labor	1.71	2.70
Selling, general, and administrative expense . .	1.25	1.36
Total	32.62	31.98

Industry Distribution Practices

Although most large brewers distributed a small percentage of their beer directly to retailers, this practice typically represented experimental "branches" or hometown distributorships inherited from their days as local breweries. The small breweries generally self-distributed a much larger portion of their total sales (see Exhibit 11). This disparity could probably be attributed to the economics of the distribution business. The key profitability criteria in beer distribution were: (1) high sales per order, (2) high number of accounts per distribution route, (3) high number of routes per distributor. Generally, unless a single beer had a very high local market share—which would enable its manufacturer to spread out fixed transportation, labor, and warehouse costs over large volume, and to decrease variable transportation and labor between deliveries—it was more cost effective to leave distribution to an independent distributor with more than one product line over which to spread the costs.

EXHIBIT 11: Beer Distributed Directly to Retailers by Manufacturers, 1978

Nationals		Regionals	
Anheuser-Busch . . .	3%	Schaefer	32%
Schlitz	1	Schoenling . . .	65
Pabst	5	Hudepohl	60
Coors	9		
Heileman	6		

To avoid conflicts of interest, breweries with high market shares tended to choose distributors that did not carry another high-market-share beer. Consequently, in most cities there would be two to four profitable distributors, each of whom carried a high-volume seller plus some other brands. Distributors gave a disproportionate amount of support to the large-volume brands, since the companies that manufactured them usually offered an attractive combination of pull advertising to help presell the beer, a cooperative advertising budget for the distributor, and large margins.

Industry Marketing

Marketing in the industry changed dramatically during the 1970s. Until the early 1970s, most domestic beer producers acknowledged only two types of beer drinkers: men who drank popularly priced beer and men who drank premium beer. The popularly priced beer drinkers, by far the most important in terms of per capita consumption, were perceived as primarily young blue collar workers, and barroom purchases accounted for 21 percent of sales in 1958. Consequently, mass advertising was minimized in favor of low retail prices and on-premise promotions.

Changing consumer profiles, a change in where beer was purchased, and a softening regulatory environment argued for a redefinition of the beer market by the early 1970s. While many companies recognized this, the Miller Brewing Company was the first to develop a new marketing strategy, which was oriented toward advertising and focused on selling premium beers. The competitors, noting the company's success, rapidly began imitating Miller's approach.

With regard to consumer preferences, Miller capitalized in its advertising on perhaps the most obvious change—the increasing social acceptability of beer drinking by women. Miller also took note of the decline in draft sales (from 21 percent in 1958 to 11 percent in 1978). The company's move to premium beer sales was prompted partly by the decline in barroom draft beer sales, and by the relaxation of Sunday blue laws coupled with the growth of convenience stores, which made beer more readily available to less price-sensitive, white collar workers. (By 1978 food stores accounted for roughly 60 percent of sales; on-premise sales, 25 percent; other retail establishments, 9 percent; and liquor stores, 6 percent.)

By 1978, total beer sales by market segments were divided as follows: premiums, 48 percent; popular, 30 percent; lights, 10 percent; super premiums, 5 percent; malts and ale, 4 percent; and imports, 3 percent. In percentage terms, the greatest decline since 1973 had occurred in popular beers and the greatest increase in super premium beers. In 1979 almost all the national companies had, or had plans for, premium or super premium products (see Exhibit 12), although the cost of such new product introduction was high. Miller was estimated to have spent over $300 million in advertising to launch Miller Lite.

Premium beers were attractive to beer makers. They cost no more to make and yet commanded a higher price because they had a higher

EXHIBIT 12: Brands by Company and Price Segment

Company	Super Premium	Premium	Popular
Anheuser-Busch .	Michelob Michelob Light Hofbrau (test market 1979)	Budweiser Natural Light Classic Dark	Busch Bavarian
Miller	Lowenbrau Miller Lite	Miller High Life	
Schlitz.	Erlanger (test market 1979)	Schlitz Schlitz Malt Liquor Schlitz Light Beer	Primo Old Milwaukee
Pabst	Andecker Pabst Special Dark (new)	Pabst Light Pabst Extra Light Pabst Blue Ribbon	Eastside Burger Meister Red, White & Blue
Coors	(test market expected 1980)	Coors Banquet Coors Light	
Heileman. . . .	Special Expert Colt 45 Becks Malt Duck	Old Style 11 light beer brands National Premium Ranier Ale Royal Amber Carling Red Cap Tuborg Gold	Ranier Carling Black Label Schmidt Weidemann Falls City Stag Sterling Drewrys Heidelberg Blatz Light Cream Ale Grain Belt National Bohemian Mickey's Malt Liquor Blatz Drummond Bros.
Schoenling . . .		Top Hat	Schoenling Little King
Hudepohl . . .		Hudy Delight Hofbrau	Hudepohl Tap Burger

Source: Compiled from company and industry information.

perceived quality.[4] In 1975, the *Sloan Management Review* published results of an experiment demonstrating that consumers generally could not distinguish between most brands on the basis of taste, but instead formed their preferences by the image projected in advertising and promotion. Higher status beers commanded higher prices and, to support that image, necessitated higher levels of advertising.

---

[4] In 1980, low-priced brands were about $2.00 per six-pack; premiums, $2.50; and super premiums, $2.80 or more.

Due in large part to Miller's aggressive drive for market share, advertising outlays for the top breweries rose from approximately 2 percent of sales in 1974 to 5.3 percent in 1978 (see Exhibit 13).

EXHIBIT 13: Advertising Expenditures as Percentage of Sales

	1978	1974
Anheuser-Busch. . . .	4.2%	.9%
Miller	4.4	3.4
Schlitz	5.4	2.1
Pabst	5.4	1.5
Coors	4.5	.3
Heileman	3.3	1.5
Schaefer	3.9	2.0
Stroh	1.7	n.a.
Olympia	4.1	1.6
Hudepohl	16.0	5.2
Average	2.1	5.3

As breweries began relying more on advertising, the national companies gained an advantage, since national advertising was more cost-effective than local advertising. To illustrate, the cost per viewer impression for a 30-second commercial on a CBS Tuesday night movie ranged from $.0024 on national TV to $.0046 on spot TV.

A trend toward charging higher prices was clearly evident on the part of some nationals, and not just for premium brands. Miller, for example, raised prices by 2.2 percent per year from 1971 to 1976, and by 14.7 percent from 1976 to 1978. Nonetheless, the price of beer adjusted for inflation has been declining steadily since the 1950s.

Profiles of the Top Six Industry Leaders

In 1979 the top six firms sold 82 percent of the beer and, not surprisingly, shared many characteristics. All were vertically integrated into such areas as yeast, malt, grain, can and bottle production, and recycling. They had large-scale plants, advertised heavily, distributed mostly through independent wholesalers, sold at most 10 percent of their output in draft form, and could command substantial financial resources to fund future growth plans. Yet not all of these big firms had prospered during the 1970s. Dollar sales and net income for the top ten American brewers are given in Exhibit 7.

Anheuser-Busch. Anheuser-Busch became the U.S. brewing industry's volume leader after 1957. The company had 10 different brewing locations and a total capacity of 46.4 million barrels a year in 1979. In

1978 management embarked upon an ambitious five-year capital expansion program totalling over $1.5 billion in order to expand capacity to 58 million barrels annually.

Total sales in 1978 exceeded 1977 sales by 21 percent. The company's total assets in 1978 equaled $1.6 billion, of which current assets were $492 million, and net property, plant, and equipment, $1.1 billion. Total current liabilities equaled $255 million, and retained earnings and stockholders' equity, $754 million.

In early 1979, Anheuser-Busch announced its intention to import a 350-year-old German beer from Wurzburg Hofbrau AG in West Germany. The beer was to be brewed in Europe by Wurzburg and shipped in large, insulated 5,100-gallon barrels to the U.S., where it would be bottled by Anheuser-Busch and test marketed in selected cities (including Cincinnati).

Miller Brewing Company.   In general, Miller's five brewing facilities were younger and consequently more efficient than those of Anheuser-Busch. Miller shifted to continuous production (24 hours, 7 days a week) in 1973 and was believed to be running at virtually 100 percent capacity, around 36 million barrels in 1980. Miller's marketing leadership in the 1970s has already been described.

Miller was the rising star among the businesses of its parent, Philip Morris Inc. Acquired in 1970 for approximately $153 million, Miller generated 28 percent of total corporate revenues, 16 percent of operating profits, and represented 24 percent of total assets. Miller relied on the huge cigarette profits to fund its very rapid growth. During 1978, 63 percent of total Philip Morris's capital spending, or $358 million, went to Miller. Over $1 billion was spent to expand brewing capacity between 1973 and 1978. Over $1.5 billion had been budgeted for this purpose during the 1979–1983 period.

Joseph Schlitz Brewing Company.   Schlitz operated eight breweries with a total capacity of 31.4 million barrels. Schlitz's volume in 1978 declined by 12 percent, to 19.6 million barrels. In 1979 volume dropped again, to 16.8 million barrels. This caused Schlitz's market share to decline from 14.1 percent in 1977 to 12.1 percent in 1978, and to 10 percent in 1979. Sales as a percent of capacity dropped from 75 percent in 1977 to 54 by 1979. (A capacity utilization level of 80 percent was regarded as the break-even point for U.S. breweries.) Sales revenues in 1978 increased by 16 percent over 1977, from $937 million to $1.1 billion. Earnings in that period decreased by 40 percent, down from $19.8 million to $12 million.

According to industry analysts, Schlitz was losing market share due to extremely poor advertising copy, lack of a super premium brand, and ignorance of the changing nature of beer marketing. Much of Schlitz's lost market share in the 1970s was captured by Miller. In 1978 the company reshuffled its management, bringing in new talent from Anheuser-Busch and Heileman.

Schlitz had attempted to expand its beer operation internationally by investing $16.5 million in four breweries in Spain. Schlitz's ownership varied from 11 percent to 30 percent. Total dividend income from these subsidiaries in 1978 was approximately $375,000.

Pabst Brewing Company. Pabst had five breweries with a total capacity of 19 million barrels annually. In fourth place with a market share of 9 percent, Pabst's volume decreased from 16 million to 15.1 million barrels during 1978. Sales, however, increased from $726 million to $753 million over the same period due primarily to general price increases of approximately 3.5 percent and higher revenues per barrel from Pabst's successful introduction of its premium low-calorie beer, Pabst Extra Light.

Adolf Coors Company. Coors was not a national brewery, but its proliferation into 16 western states gave the company a ranking of fifth in terms of barrels sold. Revenues in 1978 increased to $625 million from $593 million the year before. Total capacity of Coors' single Colorado brewery was approximately 15 million barrels per year, and in 1978 the company was operating at 81 percent of capacity. Before 1978, the company was engaged in a plant expansion program to increase its annual brewing capacity to approximately 25 million barrels. Reputedly, Coors planned to build a $500 million brewery and canning plant in Virginia with a capacity in the 10–12 million barrel range.

Coors was caught off guard by Miller's market segmentation strategy and by the construction of efficient plants by Busch, Schlitz, and Miller in California, formerly Coors territory. Before 1978, the company had been concentrating on product quality and distribution, and marketing that perpetuated the mystique of Coors—which was enhanced by its unavailability in eastern locations except through bootleggers. Peter Coors explained that "Coors didn't emphasize advertising or price competition." When Coors changed its marketing strategies in 1978 and began concentrating on mass media advertising, the advertising costs per barrel increased from $1.21 to $2.66.

Heileman Brewing Company. In 1978 Heileman's nine breweries produced sales of $393 million on assets of $147 million. In 1979 they were $657 million on assets of $225 million. The increase in sales and assets was due to the purchase in 1979 of Carling-National Brewing Company, which contributed 2.4 million barrels to Heileman's total sales of 11.1 million barrels. Heileman was slowly but steadily gaining market share while maintaining profits. In many years, Heileman's profit rate exceeded the rate of its larger competitors.

Heileman was somewhat unique in that it was expanding its own distribution network, often acquiring companies with a well-established distribution system. In this way Heileman could further the sales of the acquired companies' numerous existing brands as well as acquire local brands with well-developed followings. Heileman's roster of brands climbed to more than two dozen through mergers.

Since antitrust constraints prevented the top five brewers from growing through acquisition, Heileman was often the only bidder on these acquisition properties, which resulted in additional capacity at bargain prices. Heileman was careful to avoid acquiring outmoded union contracts by purchasing only assets and brand name rights. This made operation of labor-intensive older breweries economically viable. Management took a hard line on labor and endured an occasional strike to keep wages down. Because packaging was the most expensive element in production, the company invested in capital-intensive equipment for its canning lines and allowed relatively less costly but inefficient equipment to be utilized for the other phases of production.

The Next Four Competitors

The next four brewing companies—Olympia, Stroh, C. Schmidt & Sons, and F&M Schaefer—together represented 12 percent of the industry's volume sales and, like fifth-ranked Coors, were regional competitors. Principal markets for these brewers were generally located within the same state as the brewery or in neighboring states. Only Schaefer was vertically integrated to any extent.

Total capacity and volume were far below the top six. In fact, total assets available to each of these companies in 1978 came to 12 percent of the average for the top six breweries. The average production capacity was also 21.5 percent less.

Most of these second-tier breweries competed with a narrow line of products in the popularly priced market segment. The exception was Olympia, which imported a super premium from Germany called Grunzguell.

HUDEPOHL'S COMPETITIVE SITUATION AND PROSPECTS IN 1980

Competitors in the Cincinnati Market

Market share statistics for selected companies are given in Exhibit 14. Several of the leading breweries announced plans or made changes

EXHIBIT 14: Selected Market Share Statistics, 1978–1979

Market	Company	1978 Sales (in $ millions)	1978 Market Share (percent)	1979 Sales (in $ millions)	1979 Market Share (percent)	1978–79 Bbl Δ	1978–79 Percent Δ
Cincinnati . .	Miller	138,861	18.2	175,251	23.4	36,390	+26.2
	Stroh	142,318	18.6	97,377	13.0	(44,941)	(31.6)
	Hudepohl	180,248	23.6	180,596	24.1	348	+.2
	Total Cincinnati market	763,543	100.0	749,210	100.0	(14,333)	(1.9)
Columbus . .	Miller	97,540	15.7	168,926	24.2	71,386	+73.2
	Stroh	107,466	17.3	97,665	14.3	(7,801)	(7.3)
	Hudepohl	3,506	.6	2,739	.4	(767)	(21.5)
	Total Columbus market	619,948	100.0	698,400	100.0	78,452	+12.7
Dayton . . .	Miller	116,803	12.1	161,046	17.1	44,243	37.9
	Stroh	256,451	26.6	206,327	21.9	(50,124)	(19.5)
	Hudepohl	24,198	2.6	24,422	2.6	(776)	(3.1)
	Total Dayton market	965,110	100.0	944,202	100.0	(20,908)	(2.2)
Ohio. . . .	Miller	1,265,302	17.0	1,679,577	22.1	414,275	+32.7
	Stroh	1,326,646	17.8	1,104,382	14.5	(222,264)	(16.8)
	Hudepohl	268,900	3.6	274,546	3.6	2,646	+1.0
	Total Ohio market	7,463,654	100.0	7,613,718	100.0	150,064	2.0

Source: Compiled from company and industry information.

that affected the Cincinnati market. In addition to announcing plans to construct a 10-million-barrel facility 45 minutes from Cincinnati, Miller had recently begun raising retail prices significantly. Eleventh-ranked Genesee located a sales representative in Cincinnati to market its products. In an attempt to gain market share, the Stroh company placed a bounty on Hudepohl taps in Cincinnati but discontinued it after one month.

Weidemann a subsidiary of sixth-ranked Heileman, operated solely as a distribution company in the Cincinnati market. Weidemann was supplied from Heileman breweries scattered around the U.S. Some of Heileman's $5.7 million advertising was allocated to Ohio to promote Heileman brands, and Weidemann's share of the advertising budget was $200,000. Beer was delivered to Cincinnati sales outlets directly from Weidemann's warehouses with a minimum required markup of 25 percent. The brands included:

Super premiums.	Becks, Malt Duck
Premiums	Royal Amber, Old Style, Tuborg Gold, Carling Red Cap Ale
Popular.	Weidemann, Blatz, Mickey's Malt Liquor, Heileman Light
Economy	Drewrys, Pfeiffer

Heileman also used local wholesalers to distribute brands of beer not carried by Weidemann. In fact, every independent distributor carried at least one Heileman brand, as did approximately half of the independent distributors in Columbus and Dayton (see Exhibit 15).

Cincinnati-based Schoenling had sales in 1978 of $15 million. The company's capacity was 260,000 barrels a year; actual production volume was not reported. The firm employed 105 workers and conducted business from a plant that was old but well maintained. Schoenling distributed 65 percent of its products via the company's fleet of 50 trucks. Schoenling's territory was confined to a 100-mile radius of Cincinnati, with 40 percent of sales occurring in the metropolitan area. The company marketed three brands: Top Hat (premium), Schoenling (popular), and Little King (popular), a beer targeted to the youth market where it purportedly did quite well. Schoenling management had expressed some interest in selling the company. President and Chairman of the Board Edward Schoenling was 82 years old in 1980.

The General Manager's View of Hudepohl's Prospects

Bob Pohl felt that Hudepohl was not in a position to worry too much about what competitors were doing.

> We plan to watch what they do. Let them produce new products and create the market for them by advertising heavily. We'll watch what's

EXHIBIT 15: Beer Wholesalers by City (1980)

	Sales (in $ millions)	Delivery Vehicles	Domestic Brands
Cincinnati:			
Dayton Heidelbert Dist.	over 10	20 or more	Anheuser-Busch, Schlitz, Heileman, Stroh, Latrobe, Peter Hand
Dennert, H Distributing	over 10	50 or more	Miller, Pabst, Heileman
Ohio Valley Wine Co.	3 to 5	5 to 9	Heileman, Schmidt
Setter Wine Co.	5 to 10	10 to 19	Champale
Columbus:			
Ace Beverage Distributing . .	1 to 2	5 to 9	Heileman
Allied Beverage Dist. Co. . .	1 to 2	5 to 9	Heileman
C & M Distributing Co. . .	3 to 5	5 to 9	Heileman, Olympia, Falstaff, Pearl
Columbus Distributing Co. . .	over 10	20 to 49	Anheuser-Busch
Fay Distributing	2 to 3	10 to 19	Heileman, Schmidt
Hi-State Beverage Co. . .	over 1	50 or more	Miller, Stroh
Hill Distributing Co. . .	5 to 10	20 to 49	Schlitz, Heileman, Latrobe, Van Munching
Moose Beverage Co. . .	over 10	20 to 49	Pabst, Heileman
Dayton:			
B & W Distributing Co. . .	1 to 2	5 to 9	Heileman, Olympia, Pittsburgh
Bonbright Distributors . .	over 10	20 to 49	Miller, Schoenling
Deis Distributing Co. . .	2 to 3	10 to 19	Schlitz, Heileman, Hudepohl, Champale
Heidelberg Distributing . .	over 10	20 to 49	Anheuser-Busch, Pabst, Latrobe
Midwest Beer Distributing . .	3 to 5	10 to 19	Heileman
Quallity Beer Distributors . .	over 10 million	20 to 49	Stroh
United Beverage Co. . .	5 to 10 million	10 to 19	Schlitz, Heileman

Source: Compiled from company and industry information.

selling well for them and then produce products to fill the gap they leave in the market.

Hudepohl is not a low-cost competitor. We can't be; so I think our goal should be to trade up. We are already planning new products—another light beer and perhaps a malt and a premium. There is a possibility that we could go into specialty beers that would be available two or three times a year for a limited time only.

Although he planned to distribute these products nationally, Pohl did not think that national advertising support would be necessary, because independent distributors who would earn high margins would help push their sales.

Escalating costs due to competitive bidding prompted Hudepohl to forego sponsoring Cincinnati Reds games. (Anheuser-Busch won both television and radio contracts for the Reds games in 1980.) Pohl felt that this was a necessary part of Hudepohl's plan to use advertising more effectively. Two marketing segments were now targeted: consumers over 30 and those between 18 and 24.

Pohl believed that the most immediate problem was to increase sales volume in order to justify increased production, because the current overall operating rate was well below the industry's 80 percent break-even standard. To do so, Pohl wanted to analyze those markets where sales had been lagging and try new approaches. For example, Hudepohl had never price promoted its beer outside the Cincinnati area.

Pohl intended to capitalize on the loyalty of Hudepohl's customers which was considered by observers to be one of Hudepohl's greatest strengths. Other brewers that price promoted in Cincinnati were not successful in capturing Hudepohl's share of the market. People who went away from Cincinnati often arranged to take Hudepohl along or to have it sent at regular intervals by friends, giving Hudepohl the same mystique in the Cincinnati area that Coors enjoyed on a larger scale. Pohl felt that once people in other areas had tried Hudepohl they would develop the same loyalty to it that people in Cincinnati had. Other changes in production would not be necessary, he suggested.

We're going to try to take what we've seen in the past as a disadvantage and make it a plus. We want to sell the fact that we're a small brewery, that we brew the best with tender loving care, the way it was done in Germany 200 years ago. I think we can enhance Hudepohl's image and make it a well respected specialty brewery producing a high-quality beer.

CASE 26

Electrodec

Andy, Tom, and Pete began spring break of their second year at the Northern Business School with a great deal of work ahead of them. The three had spent that winter and spring working on a field study for Electrodec, a small electronics firm. Now their efforts indicated that there was a promising market for one of Electrodec's new products, and each of the men had an offer to join the firm as both an employee *and* equity owner.

Each of them had to decide whether or not this business represented an attractive opportunity for them, and if so, what share of equity ownership was appropriate.

ELECTRODEC

Electrodec was a small firm located in Charlotte, North Carolina, with 1982 sales of approximately $300,000 (see Exhibit 1 for recent income statement and balance sheet). The company designed and manufactured several sophisticated electronic instruments which recorded and analyzed data, and consisted of eight employees (see Exhibit 2).

The president/founder and sole owner of Electrodec, Kirk Nolan, had been responsible for establishing his firm as a true "state-of-the-art" engineering and product development center. Clients included NASA, the Department of Defense, General Electric, and other firms with sophisticated engineering needs. The firm operated in a very informal and open

EXHIBIT 1

ELECTRODEC
Financial Statements

Income Statement

	6 Months 2/28/83	Percent	12 Months 2/28/83	Percent
Sales	$92,590	100.00	$302,380	100.00
Cost of sales	19,605	21.17	109,205	36.12
Gross profit	72,985	78.83	193,175	63.88
Operating expenses:				
Sales expenses	15,158	16.37	35,877	11.86
General and administrative expenses	39,808	42.99	103,480	34.22
Research and development	18,010	19.45	32,383	56.80
Total expenses	72,976	78.82	171,740	56.80
Operating profit	9	0.01	21,435	7.09
Other income	20,099	21.71	22,287	7.37
Other expenses	(12,018)	(12.98)	(18,595)	(6.15)
Net profit	8,090	8.74	25,127	8.31
Income taxes	(388)	(.42)	(2,388)	(.79)
Net income	$ 7,702	8.32	$ 22,739	7.52

Balance Sheet at February 28, 1983

Assets

Current assets:		
Cash	$ 4,519	
Receivables	127,186	
Inventories	112,728	
Prepaid insurance	572	
Due from officers	17,918	
Total current assets		$262,923
Fixed assets:		
Equipment	36,353	
Accumulated depreciation	(12,124)	
Book value		24,229
Total assets		$287,152

Liabilities and Equity

Current liabilities:		
Accounts payable	$ 12,395	
Commissions payable	19,959	
Accrued expenses	21,598	
Notes payable	110,000	
Payroll and sales taxes	19,622	
Income taxes	1,500	
Total current liabilities		$185,074
Equity:		
Common stock	35,100	
Retained earnings	44,238	
Current income (loss)	22,740	
Total equity		102,078
Total liability and equity		$287,152
Working capital		$ 77,849

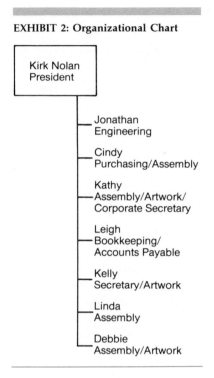

EXHIBIT 2: Organizational Chart

- Kirk Nolan
  President
  - Jonathan
    Engineering
  - Cindy
    Purchasing/Assembly
  - Kathy
    Assembly/Artwork/
    Corporate Secretary
  - Leigh
    Bookkeeping/
    Accounts Payable
  - Kelly
    Secretary/Artwork
  - Linda
    Assembly
  - Debbie
    Assembly/Artwork

manner and, as Exhibit 3 indicates, Kirk Nolan was intimately involved with virtually every aspect of the firm's work.

Historically, Electrodec had derived a majority of its income from custom R&D projects which had subsidized product development efforts. For example, the firm had done a great deal of work for the Electric Power Research Institute, winning these contracts over competition from GE, Hughes Aircraft, and others.

Electrodec had two specific products lines:

1. Laser Doppler Velocimeters (LDV) which provide an accurate means of measuring flow speed without actual contact with the material, i.e., air in a wind tunnel, molten metals in production.
2. An electronic recording and data acquisition (ERDAC) product line, which measured, recorded, and analyzed electric signals. Some of these ERDAC products were geared specifically toward the electric utility environment.

A new ERDAC product, the 1620, was currently in development, and was targeted toward the electric utility market. It was the market potential of the ERDAC 1620 which was the object of their field study and subsequent enthusiasm. The ERDAC 1620 was in the last phase of design, and work on a prototype had begun.

EXHIBIT 3: Typical Job Order Flow, Kirk Nolan

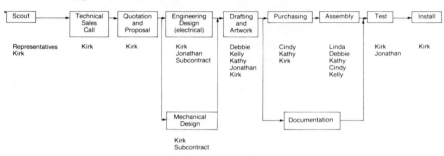

BACKGROUND

Andy Barnes, Tom Templeton, and Pete Rhodes had all been first-year sectionmates at the Northern Business School (NBS). (See Exhibit 4 for resumes.) They worked with one another on a variety of group projects during the first year, and were enthusiastic about the prospect of working together on a field study. They each brought varied experience to the team.

Andy Barnes

Andy, 27, had worked for Electrodec the previous summer. He had met Kirk Nolan, Electrodec's president, during his years at Westinghouse's Advanced Systems Technology Division, where Electrodec had been a subcontractor to Andy on various projects. Andy had extensive experience in the design and development of power systems. He had left Westinghouse to get his MBA because of a long-standing interest in management, and the realization that "I didn't have enough gray hair to get the job I wanted at Westinghouse."

Andy left his summer job at Electrodec convinced that the ERDAC 1620 was a promising product, and relatively certain that he would return to the firm. The field study's purpose was to evaluate the market potential of the ERDAC 1620, and recommend a plan for capitalizing on its potential.

Tom Templeton

Tom Templeton, 24, had received his master's degree in Mechanical Engineering from MIT just prior to starting business school. He had received his BS degree in three years, and worked for Hughes Aircraft before returning to MIT for his master's degree. His experience with

EXHIBIT 4

ANDREW BARNES

Married, one child
Excellent health
Security Clearance: Secret

Experience

Summer 1982   ELECTRODEC   CHARLOTTE, NORTH CAROLINA
Self employed consultant to a high technology venture. Performed duties of chief operating and financial executives including the successful negotiation and structuring of debt financing, establishment of accounting and control policies, and the implementation of a computer based accounting system. Conducted market research and formulated pricing and distribution policies. Supported sales efforts through customer calls and contract negotiation. Supervised production scheduling and generated personnel plans.

1978–1981   WESTINGHOUSE ELECTRIC
CORPORATION   PITTSBURGH, PENNSYLVANIA

1980–1981   *Director of Product Integrity and Productivity, Advanced Systems Technology Division:* Developed and implemented strategic programs to ensure continuing market leadership as a staff assistant to the division General Manager. Initiated the company's first engineering/professional Quality Circle program.

1978–1980   *Senior Engineer and Project Manager, Advanced Systems Technology Division:* Promoted through four engineering levels while functioning as a Project Manager. Directed the technical and financial aspects of a development program for a major product line and large-scale contract research projects. Conducted several smaller consulting efforts oriented toward problem solving in a variety of industries.

1974–1977   VOUGHT CORPORATION OF
LTV, INCORPORATED   DALLAS, TEXAS
Engineer-in-Training/Co-op: Assigned as an Assistant Engineer to various programs to perform circuit and logic design, systems instrumentation, computer systems analysis and programming, and development of life-cycle cost models for logistics purposes.

Education

1981–1983   NORTHERN BUSINESS SCHOOL
Candidate for the degree of Master in Business Administration, June 1983. General management curriculum. Electives in marketing, finance, and technology management. Member of Marketing, Finance, Investment, and International Business Clubs. Intramural athletics.

EXHIBIT 4 *(continued)*

1978–1980	CARNEGIE-MELLON UNIVERSITY PITTSBURGH, PENNSYLVANIA Received Master of Science in Electrical Engineering degree from the Carnegie Institute of Technology, May 1980. Specialized in power and energy related topics.
1973–77	GEORGIA INSTITUTE OF TECHNOLOGY ATLANTA, GEORGIA Received Bachelor of Electrical Engineering, Cooperative Plan degree, December 1977. Emphasis on digital communications and instrumentation. Academic honors include Eta Kappa Nu, Secretary; Omicron Delta Kappa; and Dean's List. Elected President and Secretary of the Society of ANAK, Georgia Tech's highest honorary; named ODK Leader of the Year at Georgia Tech, 1977. Appointed Director and Chairman of the Board of a new $5.5 million student athletic complex: responsible for administrative, policy, and programming matters including a yearly operating budget of $450,000.
Personal background	Author of three technical papers and five engineering reports. Hold two patent disclosures in power related areas. Lecturer at the Westinghouse Advanced School in Power Engineering, 1979. Member of Georgia Tech's Committee of 20 Advisory Board. Have lived in various sections of the United States and Europe. Working knowledge of German and French. Licensed Engineer-in-Training.
References	Personal references available upon request.

November 1982

TOM TEMPLETON

Education

1981–1983	NORTHERN BUSINESS SCHOOL Candidate for the degree of Master in Business Administration in June 1983. Concentration in marketing and finance. Tutor for first-year finance. Member of Management Consulting, Small Business, and Marketing Clubs.
1976–1981	MASSACHUSETTS INSTITUTE OF TECHNOLOGY CAMBRIDGE, MASSACHUSETTS Bachelor of Science and Master of Science degrees in Mechanical Engineering in January 1980 and June 1981 respectively. Concentration in design and dynamics. Master's thesis dealt with advanced manufacturing systems within

EXHIBIT 4 *(continued)*

the East Peoria Plant of Caterpillar Tractor Company and their impact on the "L" series crawler tractor design. Graduate of Engineering Internship Program. President of Pi Tau Sigma, Mechanical Engineering Honor Society. Wunsch Foundation Award for Design Excellence. Hughes Masters Fellowship. Naval Reserve and NROTC Training. Freshman Advisor. Varsity Letterman in Lacrosse.

Business experience

1982   J. MAKOWSKI ASSOCIATES, INC.   BOSTON, MASSACHUSETTS
Consultant, Energy Industry. Coauthor of MBTA Prospectus to solicit private investments in cogeneration projects. Project developer in coal conversion of paper company utilizing fluidized bed combustor and third party financing. Preliminary engineering, logistics and financial analyses presented to Haverhill Gas Board of Directors as a diversification opportunity. Structured and negotiated exclusive contract to sell submetering billing system to northeast utilities. Initiated current investigation to structure and secure third party financing of flash gas recovery and cogeneration project at the Everett LNG storage facility.

1978–1981   HUGHES AIRCRAFT COMPANY   CULVER CITY, CALIFORNIA

1981   *Assistant to Program Manager,* Laser Augmented Airborne Tow (LAAT) Program. Extensive interdepartmental and vendor coordination to resolve system problems. Matrix organizational structure implied dual operating responsibilities of Program Office and Departmental organization. Broader exposure to defense contract preparation and budgeting.

1980   *Member of Technical Staff,* LAAT Program. Coordinated efforts of designers, draftsmen and technicians to identify and implement system revisions facilitating mass production. Follow-up engineering support of manufacturing start-up at alternate plant site.

Summers

1978–1979   *Engineering Analyst,* Fighting Vehicle System. Analyzed boresight specifications of missile launcher, optical elements tolerance study, mirror head balancing, and computer methods in product design.

Other experience

1979–1981   PLOUGHMAN'S PUB   CAMBRIDGE, MASSACHUSETTS
Owner-manager, luncheonette. Duties included inventory

EXHIBIT 4 *(continued)*

	control, bookkeeping, budgeting and hiring. Fifteen part-time employees. Up to three hundred customers daily.
1980	Licensed *Real Estate Salesperson* in California.
Patent	Patent Pending, 1980, "Double-Sided Lockbar," designed for Julius Koch Company, New Bedford, Massachusetts.
Publication	"INDUSTRIAL INNOVATION: The Dynamics of Product and Production Process Change," Master's Thesis, Massachusetts Institute of Technology (Cambridge: MIT Press, 1981). October, 1982

PETER RHODES

Education

1981–1983   NORTHERN BUSINESS SCHOOL
Candidate for the degree of Master in Business Administration in June 1983. Followed general management curriculum in first year. Second-year emphasis directed toward marketing, production, and operations management. Member of the Finance and Marketing Clubs.

1972–76   UNITED STATES
NAVAL ACADEMY   ANNAPOLIS, MD
Awarded Bachelor of Science degree in History. Superintendent's List. Varsity track team letterman. Company Commander responsible for the military training of one hundred men.

Business
experience

summer 1982   THE PROCTER & GAMBLE
DISTRIBUTING COMPANY   CHICAGO, IL
Summer Sales Management Intern. Responsible for fifty retail accounts. Made sales presentations and merchandising recommendations to these accounts. Attended one-week sales training course. Completed special projects for the District and Division managers.

Military
experience

1976–1981   UNITED STATES NAVY, Progressed from Ensign to Lieutenant

11/79–8/81   Weapons Officer on board the nuclear fast attack submarine USS Pargo (SSN 650). Department head, responsible for operation and maintenance of the ship's weapon, sonar,

EXHIBIT 4 *(concluded)*

	and fire control equipment. Supervised thirty men. Department awarded Antisubmarine Warfare (ASW) "A" during this period. Personally awarded two Navy Commendation Medals for superior performance.
11/78–11/79	Communicator on board USS Pargo (SSN 650). Organized and trained ten electronic technicians and radiomen. Molded an effective communications team that was able to meet all communications requirements during a Mediterranean deployment. Awarded Navy Achievement Medal.
3/78–11/78	Reactor Controls Assistant onboard USS Pargo (SSN 650). Responsible for the preventive and corrective maintenance of the reactor control and protection equipment. Led and trained the reactor control electronic technicians. Successfully completed an Operational Reactor Safeguards Examination and qualified in submarines during this period.
9/76–3/78	Student in the Naval Nuclear Power Training Pipeline. Qualified to supervise the operation and maintenance of a naval nuclear power plant.
Personal background	Grew up in Massachusetts. Willing to travel. Interests include athletics, sailing, and literature. Married. Excellent health.
References	Personal references available on request.

Hughes had been focused on prototype design and the start-up of manufacturing operations. Tom had always been interested in business, had owned a luncheonette during college, and was a licensed real estate broker. His summer job with J. Makowski Associates had added to his experience in project management and consulting.

Pete Rhodes

Pete Rhodes, 27, had graduated from the Naval Academy in 1976, and had served for five years in various capacities in the Navy's nuclear submarine program. This experience had given Pete a significant exposure to both engineering and managing people. He chose to concentrate on the latter, and left the Navy to attend NBS. His first-year exposure to marketing had led him to accept a summer job with Procter & Gamble's sales program. He returned from the summer with a strong interest in a career in sales and marketing.

Kirk Nolan

Kirk Nolan, Electrodec's president, 38, had been oriented toward engineering since his high school days, and had even published some technical work prior to attending college.

Kirk attended Rensselaer Polytechnic Institute from 1963–1971, when he was awarded his Ph.D. in Electrical Engineering. Kirk and a partner founded Electrodec as an engineering consulting firm. When his partner suddenly died, Kirk assumed ownership and control.

Kirk was clearly the driving force behind Electrodec, and vital to its operations. Kirk was motivated far more by the engineering challenge of an assignment than by the profit potential. He would frequently fly off on a moment's notice to solve a difficult engineering problem on projects in response to customer requests.

THE MARKET

The ERDAC 1620 was designed specifically for the utility customer. Kirk and Andy felt sophisticated electronic equipment could meet these customers' needs better than existing electromechanical products.

Utility Customer Needs

In order to understand why such equipment was useful, it was necessary to understand how a typical utility's power network was configured.

Power systems consisted of generation stations and load centers. A generation station, such as a nuclear power plant, produced power for several load centers (see Exhibit 5). This power was carried via transmission lines, which were the familiar steel towers with multiple wires that cross the U.S.

Where lines met, or branched out, there existed "mini-hubs" which packaged and monitored the flow of electricity so that it was sent most efficiently. These were called substations.

In order to deliver electricity safely, and with minimum wear and tear on the transmission equipment, the power must be carried in a stable manner—i.e., at a constant frequency and voltage. When there was a significant disturbance on a power line—which could be caused by a falling tree, lightning, equipment failure—relay equipment automatically shut down the line to prevent damage to the system.

At this point, other power sources would be automatically brought on line. On occasion, when the utility could not fill the gap with power of its own, it would purchase electricity from another utility company. In the case of a severe fault in the Florida power system, for instance, the Florida Power & Light Company would purchase electricity from

EXHIBIT 5: Typical Power Grid

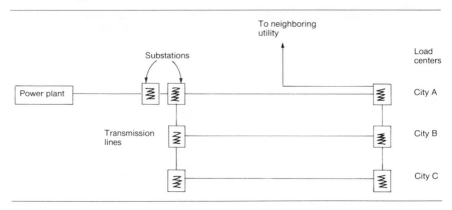

Georgia at a rate which can vary from $10,000 to $50,000 per hour. They would then determine the location of the fault, and repair it. Only a very low percentage of faults, however, necessitated the repurchase of power from other utilities.

The Utility Market

Historically, utilities have been permitted to earn a target Rate of Return on Capital (ROC). Utilities could expand their investment base, and then request rate increases to obtain their target ROC. The utilities costs skyrocketed in the 1970s, due principally to the rise in the price of oil. At the same time, public interest research groups (PIRGs) became more active.

This led to frequent refusals of utility rate increases, a fall in utilities ROC, decreased profitability, a consequent rise in the utilities' cost of capital and ultimately, a decrease in the utilities' ability to spend money on capital equipment.

In response to a shortage of funds, the utilities cut back on installing generating facilities (i.e., power plants) and added additional transmission and distribution facilities to existing generation capacity, rather than build expensive new generation stations. See Exhibit 6 for data on utility company capital spending.

Electric Power Recording Equipment

Electric power recording equipment (EPRE) consisted of several types of equipment which were attached to transmission lines and served varying functions:

- Fault recorders—sensed and recorded variations in current, voltage, and frequency. Typically called oscillographs, these machines would

EXHIBIT 6: Total Electric Industry Power System Capital Expenditures (in $ millions)

Year	Gener- ation	Trans- mission	Distri- bution	Miscel- laneous	Total
1972 . . .	9,737	2,148	3,989	777	16,651
1973 . . .	10,924	2,450	4,434	915	18,723
1974 . . .	12,504	2,451	4,577	1,024	20,556
1975 . . .	12,724	2,379	4,071	981	20,155
1976 . . .	16,612	2,945	4,548	1,084	25,189
1977 . . .	19,094	3,106	4,523	988	27,711
1978 . . .	21,951	2,736	4,347	1,216	30,250
1979 . . .	24,875	3,384	5,329	1,666	35,254
1980 . . .	25,688	3,280	5,307	1,650	35,925
1981 . . .	25,823	3,168	4,950	1,882	35,823
1982 . . .	29,836	3,497	5,228	1,654	40,216
1983*. . .	28,189	4,182	5,496	1,988	39,855

* Prospective.
Source: *Electrical World*, 17th annual T&D construction survey, August 1982, pp. 66 and 68; and 1983 annual statistical report, March 1983, p. 62. Reproduced by permission.

record data for a few seconds after a fault (and in some cases, for a few milliseconds prior to a fault). Permanent records of surges on the power line would then be available for analysis by the utility engineer. These data would not, however, help the power company determine the cause and location of the fault. Further, these data were not remotely accessible and the engineer had to travel to the transmission substation to obtain them.

Essentially, this equipment told the utility that the system protection scheme was operating properly. This equipment typically cost $70,000 to $80,000.

- Event recorders—monitored and logged the operation of transmission and relay equipment during routine operation and system disturbances. This equipment told the utility precisely which pieces of equipment operated, and when. This permitted the utility to monitor the performance of the different components of the transmission and protection system. This equipment typically cost $20,000 to $45,000.

- Fault monitor—a combination of an event recorder and a fault recorder in one cabinet. This provided both the wave form data from the oscillograph and the data on the operation of specific pieces of transmission and relay equipment. This equipment typically cost slightly more than the sum of the individual event and fault recorders, i.e., $80,000 to $100,000.

The Market for EPRE

The market for EPRE was driven by the growth in transmission and distribution substations. These substations exist at the beginning and end of power lines, as well as at other points where lines meet or branch out.

Growth in substations was, in turn, driven by the demand for electric power. When a new area required power service, new lines were laid and substations added. Or, if an existing area demands greater amounts of power, new lines with new substations could be added.

When a new substation was added, there also existed an opportunity to add a piece of EPRE, such as a fault recorder. If the substation was a very major one—carrying power into New York City or Boston, for example—the utility would certainly want to monitor the equipment there. If, on the other hand, the substation was only carrying a small amount of electricity to a remote area, monitoring this equipment would be less important.

Utilities classified substations by the amount of electricity that passes through them. There were standard categories that ran from the largest—765 kilovolts (kv), to the smallest—69kv and less. Generally, most substations of 500kv and up would have EPRE, and some proportion of the smaller substations would also have EPRE. See Exhibit 7 for a forecast of substation growth.

EXHIBIT 7: Utility Market Forecast for Transmission and Distribution Substations (units)

Size (kv)	1981 Actual	1982	1983	1984	1985	1986–88
765	3	1	0	4	1	5
500	15	18	10	6	19	36
345	59	45	41	40	27	78
230	70	84	70	74	67	162
161	38	42	37	34	28	76
138	226	193	227	157	186	376
115	251	239	198	189	175	406
69 and less	581	508	509	435	380	906

Source: *Electrical World*, August 1982, pp. 66, 68. Reproduced by permission.

THE ERDAC

Electrodec's ERDAC 1620 was a sophisticated microcomputer-based system which performed the functions of both fault recorders and event recorders, and also provided the following additional features.

- Greater number of inputs—permitted the monitoring of a greater number of lines and pieces of equipment.

- Remote access to data—information was available on-line; travel to actual transmission line and recording equipment was not required.
- System integration—provided features of fault recorder and event recorder in one instrument.
- Lower maintenance—no mechanical parts to break down.
- Software availability—ERDAC 1620 could be used as a personal computer with commonly available software.
- Fault locating utility—system could pinpoint location of fault.
- Sophistication—better bandwidth, range, resolution, and accuracy in data recording.
- Self-diagnostic ability—identified recording device malfunctions before actual fault.
- Prefault data availability—system recorded data prior to fault occurrence.

The ERDAC system consisted of two units:

- The ERDAC 1620—the monitoring and recording device.
- The ERDAC 1625—the computer which would analyze the data which the 1620 would collect. Each 1625 could monitor and analyze up to fifteen 1620s.

Electrodec planned to design and build the electronic "guts" of the product, but would subcontract the fabrication of printed circuit boards and metal cabinetry. Electrodec would provide a turnkey system which integrated the 1620 with a playback unit which would analyze and print out the data captured by the ERDAC 1620.

THE FIELD STUDY

The field study's major goal was to assess and quantify the market opportunity the ERDAC 1620 represented, and to identify the critical path for capitalizing on it. The team sent out a questionnaire (see Exhibit 8) to the largest 150 independently owned utilities. They received an extremely high response, giving them data on utilities which represented over 50 percent of the operating capacity in the U.S. (See Exhibit 9 for results.) Between January and April 1983, the team identified and addressed several issues with the help of this data.

The Utility Customer

The utility market consisted of a very diverse customer base. Numerous aspects of a utility's operating environment affected the purchase decision for this equipment. Among these were the network's complexity,

EXHIBIT 8: Questionnaire

Dear Sir:

We are doing field research on the market for oscillographic, fault and event recording devices used on utility transmission lines. This research will be used to write a case study for the MBA curriculum. As a user of this equipment, your comments would be invaluable to us in formulating an accurate representation of this market. If you chose to pass this form on to someone with more specific knowledge, please write their name, position and phone number on top of this page.

In light of your busy schedule, we hope that you can provide us with answers to the following questions at your convenience:

(1) How many oscillographic recorders do you presently own?
   13 oscillographs

(2) Who are the manufacturers and what % does each represent?
   Powerpath Exclusive

(3) What is the age distribution of this equipment?
   1967 (10 of 13)   1972 (3 of 13)

(4) What percent of the time is fault/transient activity not recorded because of equipment failure?
   2%

(5) What % of the time are electro-mechanical, oscillographic recorders not functioning because of maintenance or failure?
   5%

(6) Do you consider service good (i.e., spare parts costs and speed of delivery)?
   I would rate the service fair to poor.

(7) How many channels do you use per recorder?
   32 channels

(8) What would you expect to pay for a fault and event recording device with 32 analog channels?
   $60,000

(9) How many fault/event recorders do you expect to buy in the next five years?
   12

service area size, growth, cost of downtime, frequency of faults, its power generation source (i.e., nuclear) and the sophistication of its engineering staff.

Equipment was purchased on the basis of a bidding system, where the engineering staff would specify a list of acceptable suppliers, who would then bid to obtain the business. (See Exhibit 10.)

EXHIBIT 8 *(concluded)*

(10)   How much of a premium (over the price you quoted in #8) would you be willing to pay for a "digital" device which offered the following feature:

Feature	Premium %
A. Remote access, immediate recognition of fault activity and network monitoring. One central computer located at engineering headquarters can monitor 12–20 substations simultaneously.	20%
B. Lower Maintenance. Downtime reduced to less than 5%. No mechanical parts to break down and no ongoing calibration.	10%
C. Self Diagnostics. Identifies equipment malfunction BEFORE fault activity, thereby eliminating the chance of transients not being recorded because of unidentified recorder failure.	0%
D. Much greater # of digital and analog inputs which can be added modularly (up to 64 analog channels and 500–1000 event channels).	5%
E. More selective data, improved resolution, accuracy, intelligence and programmability (40kHz bandwidth to record switching surges, and 72dB dynamic range to record 1% harmonics).	2%
F. Fault "locating" ability. Resolution ≈ 3%.	0%
G. Integration of sequence of events recording and fault recording into one instrument.	5%
H. Availability of supplemental software packages to automatically locate faults on network, perform harmonic analysis, calculate rise times, record inventory, etc.	0%
I. Availability of 1–2 hours of prefault data.	0%

Please feel free to include any additional thoughts you may have on this subject area. Because of our academic requirements, we hope you will be able to respond to these questions some time during the next week. We would be happy to provide you with a summary of our findings.

Thank you for your assistance.

Sincerely,

EXHIBIT 9: Results of Survey

1. Age Distribution of Installed Base

0–5 years	26%
5–10 years	15%
10–15 years	27%
15–20 years	18%
20–50 years	14%

2. Service Response: Utility rating of service as . . .

Good	22.5%
Fair	29.0%
Poor	48.5%

3. Frequency of Unrecorded Fault Activity
Mean = 9.5%

4. Downtime Percentage
Mean = 11%

5. Cost
This survey question was clearly worded ambiguously and caused confusion. Major sources of divergence originated if:

(1) The customer had not purchased equipment for many years
(2) Had last purchased equipment during the 1980–81 price war
(3) Had unusual network requirements
(4) Did not understand what a fault monitor was versus a fault recorder

As best can be deciphered, the following mean expectations of cost were derived:

Event Recorder	= $30,000
Fault Recorder	= $60,000
Fault Monitor	= $85,000

6. Utility Valuation of Features

Feature	Mean (% premium)
A. Remote access	3.9%
B. Maintenance	2.8
C. Self-diagnostics	1.7
D. More inputs	4.5
E. Sophistication.	2.2
F. Fault locating	2.8
G. Integration of S.E.R.	3.1
H. Software availability.	2.8
I. Prefault data	0.5
Cumulative*	24.3%

* Features D and G are not entirely independent; therefore, a 22% cumulative premium is viewed as more accurate.

7. Adjusted Premiums
Because the utilities were asked to provide the above premiums as a percentage of cost, different cost estimates by different utilities make the comparison of premium values like comparing "apples and oranges." Consequently, to provide a uniform basis of comparison, the following adjustments were made to each premium:

Adjusted Premium = Features Premium (%)/Largest Premium (%)

EXHIBIT 9: *(concluded)*

Each features premium was divided by the largest premium assigned by that utility. This procedure essentially ranks each premium from zero to one, with "0" representing a feature of no value to the utility and "1" representing the most important feature to the utility. Features are ranked in order of importance.

		Adjusted Premium
# 1	Remote access	.50
# 2	More inputs	.39
# 3	Maintenance	.36
# 4	Fault locating	.35
# 5	Integration of S.E.R.	.32
# 6	Software availability	.30
# 7	Self-diagnostics	.26
# 8	Sophistication	.23
# 9	Prefault data	.05

Utilities were notoriously conservative and would not use a product that did not have a proven track record. Most design engineers wanted several references before they would consider buying unfamiliar equipment. Risk reduction was a major concern for utility engineering personnel. For this reason performance was seldom compromised for price. Price sensitivity was also reduced because equipment of this nature became part of the utility's rate base (i.e., utilities were permitted to earn a certain percentage rate of return on capital—when their capital base increased, so did their allowable dollar profit).

Value-Added of ERDAC

The ERDAC 1620 had several advantages over competitors' equipment, based on its sophisticated array of features. These advantages provided value to the utility by both lowering costs and improving operations, as shown below:

Lower Costs	**Improved Operations**
Lower Labor Costs	Easier storage of records
Less man-hours repairing equipment	More timely fault analysis
Less man-hours retrieving data	More accurate understanding of network
Fault locating reduces cost of downtime	operation
Purchase of electricity at premium from	Faster fault resolution reduces system risk
neighboring utility	More inputs can be monitored
Community impact	

The study team attempted, based on discussion with the utilities, to derive a "theoretical value-added premium," i.e., how much more would a utility customer be likely to pay for each of the ERDAC's unique features. This premium is expressed as a percentage of the base price

EXHIBIT 10: Buying Model for Fault Monitors

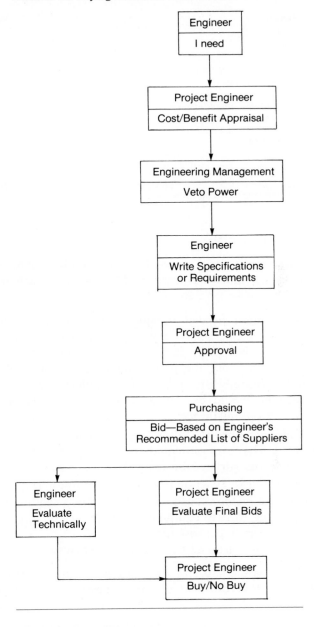

for a standard fault recorder. They identified the following features, and their "theoretical premiums":

Feature	Premium (%)
Remote access to data	5
Lower maintenance costs	10
Self-diagnostic ability	10
Greater number of inputs for analysis*	20
Selectivity, resolution, accuracy	20
Fault locating ability*	25
Integration of event and fault recorder*	5
Use as personal computer availability of software*	5
Availability of prefault data*	5
Total	105
Without special case	45

* These premiums are "special case," i.e., will be valued by only some utilities with certain equipment configurations. Other premiums should be valued by all utilities.

Market Size and Potential

In order to estimate market size, the team divided potential demand into three segments, and then attempted to estimate each one. These segments were:

- Growth—equipment needed because new transmission lines were built: The size of this segment was estimated based on a forecast for substation growth given in Exhibit 7. The team made a series of assumptions both about the percentage of substations of each size which would require EPRE, and about what Electrodec's market share of each segment would be. These assumptions varied between the pessimistic and optimistic scenarios.

- Replacement on failure (R/failure)—equipment which was replaced when it failed. The team estimated an installed base of roughly 2,900 units. Based on its survey, the team then assumed an economic life of 25 (pessimistic) to 10 years (optimistic assumption).

- Replacement on value-Added (R/value-added)—equipment which was replaced due to new equipment with better features. The team assumed that from 1 percent (pessimistic) to 10 percent (optimistic assumption) of the installed base could be replaced.

The team attempted to size the market for the ERDAC 1620 (in units) for 1984 in three different scenarios: pessimistic, best guess, and optimistic.

	Segment	Pessimistic	Best Guess	Optimistic
Size of total segment	Growth	80	91	105
	R/failure	117	194	291
	R/value-added	28	82	262
Total		225	367	658

	Segment	Pessimistic	Best Guess	Optimistic
Electrodec	Growth	15	33	45
Market share of	R/failure	15	33	45
each segment (%)	R/value-added	100	100	100
Total		130	166	190
Resultant	Growth	12	30	47
Electrodec	R/failure	18	64	131
sales (units)	R/value-added	28	82	262
Total		58	176	440

Cost

The team also performed a detailed analysis of the cost for the ERDAC unit:

ERDAC 1620	Material	Total Direct Labor Cost	Material and Labor
Totals	$32,028	$9,420	$41,448
ERDAC 1625			
Playback analysis and central controller	$18,160	$500	$18,680

Competition

The industry, following the utilities' historic conservatism, has been very slow to change technically. The industry was dominated by Powerpath, Inc., although other firms also competed.

Powerpath had been the dominant supplier of recording instrumentation to the utilities for over 40 years. Although they had the dominant market share, Powerpath was generally disliked by utilities because of their

- Exorbitant prices for spare parts.
- Frequent breakdown of equipment.
- Extremely long wait for spare parts.

In addition, Powerpath had recently been involved in an extended price war with Serol, a company founded by an ousted ex-president of Powerpath. Powerpath cut prices drastically, which damaged Serol's profitability severely; after two years of this price war, Powerpath bought Serol, and *doubled* prices the next day.

UNRESOLVED ISSUES

The field study raised several issues which would have to be dealt with if Electrodec were to attempt to enter the market. These included questions of price, sales force, location, and long-term strategy.

Price

The unit (without computer and printer) could be built for roughly $42,000; a standard Powerpath fault recorder sold for $65,000. Yet, the ERDAC unit also filled the role of a fault monitor, which sold for closer to $100,000. And there were 10 times as many fault recorders as fault monitors. If the ERDAC sold for $70,000 to $80,000, they should be able to compete very effectively in the fault recorder market (they had used a price of $76,000 in their market survey). But, they would be leaving *a lot* of money on the table when someone purchased the unit as a fault monitor. If the unit was priced near the $100,000 mark, they would capture this full value, but would be less effective in competing for fault recorder business.

Sales Force

Because the ERDAC is technologically sophisticated, and the selling cycle is a long one, a direct sales force seemed appropriate. Yet, as the team's own analysis showed, this option raised fixed costs tremendously; they could use manufacturers' reps, who would work solely on a commission basis.

Cost of Sales Force Alternatives

Assumptions: Average unit price is $76,000
Base salary $25,000
Commissions: $600/unit for first 10 units
$2500/unit for all others
Five salesmen are hired

Direct Sales Force Costs:

Fixed costs:

Salary (5 × $25,000).	$125,000
Benefits (.5 × 5 × $25,000)	62,500
Travel	
50% on road @ $100/day	
This covers gas, food, and lodging	
125 days × $100 × 5	62,500
Office expenses:	
50% in office @ $20/day	
This covers phone and supplies	
125 days × $20 × 5	30,000
	262,500

Variable costs:
Assume 50 units sold:

50 units × $600 commission	30,000
Total costs of direct sales force	$292,500

Manufacturer's Rep Costs

Variable cost = 10% commission = $7,600/unit

$$\text{Breakeven} = \frac{\$292,500}{\$7,600} = 39 \text{ units}$$

Location

While Charlotte had been a fine place for Kirk himself to run Electrodec as essentially a "consulting engineer's shop," manufacturing would be a different story altogether. Charlotte lacked:

- A major airport, required for quick selling trips to out-of-state locations.
- A stable base of skilled labor.
- An attractive climate and social amenities for attracting and keeping skilled professionals.

These would all be important factors in getting Electrodec's ERDAC off the ground, and would be even more important as the company grew.

The study team had identified Atlanta as a location which met all the above criteria, and was personally preferable as well. Any move would have to occur quickly—Electrodec's current facilities were not large enough to support the building of even one finished unit (the metal cabinetry which houses the unit is very large). But, with the product in the delicate prototype phase, did it make sense to move *away* from the only trained workers that Electrodec had?

Long-Term Strategy

In the short term, Electrodec's strategy was to build a technologically superior product, charge a premium price, and compete against Powerpath based on its poor reputation for reliability and spare parts availability. Electrodec's other product—the LDV—is a completely different line of business altogether. Was Electrodec a "one-trick pony" or did it have the potential to establish itself over the long term with a succession of products?

Keeping All the Balls in the Air

Work on the prototype had begun several months ago, and was proceeding slowly for a number of reasons:

- It was difficult to get Kirk to focus on the project. He was often running off to work on various consulting projects, which provided the cash that the company needed to operate in the short term.
- The final design had yet to be "frozen" so design changes occurred frequently.
- There was a long lead time for parts—a resistor or capacitor which cost a few pennies could delay completion of a $50,000 unit for up to two months.
- The magnitude of the development work was enormous for such a

small company, and hence, cash flow was strained. This forced Electrodec to divert its resources toward projects which would generate short-term revenues.

Still, Electrodec had accepted a few orders for the ERDAC and there were prospects for several more. This made them more confident, and they knew it would help them raise the financing they needed.

Yet, one of Powerpath's really weak points, and a key element of Electrodec's strategy, was a reputation for reliability and on-time delivery. Should they accept orders before the product was perfected?

They knew that capital might be difficult to raise, and were sure that having a working prototype would make the process easier, improve their bargaining position, and enable them to drive a better deal. But, if they didn't get money soon, they would not be able to start making commitments for the upcoming move, wherever it might be. Their pro forma financials had been run under two different assumptions (see Exhibit 11):

1. A $1 million equity investment in September 1983 and an additional $1 million in June 1984.
2. No equity investment.

EXHIBIT 11: Financial Pro Formas

Assumptions

Sales: Beginning in August 1983, only ERDAC 1620 sales projected since it is anticipated the product line will consume virtually all of Electrodec's available resources.

Cost of goods sold: 50% with a 15% decline along experience curve.

Selling costs: Salaries, overhead, and expenses of building a five-person sales force, plus 12% for commissions, advertising, and promotion.

Interest: 12% interest rate. The model is not sensitive to 25% fluctuations in rate.

Taxes: 28% effective rate for $100K or less. 30% effective mid-range rate. 35% effective high-range rate.

Cash: 30% of sales base, minimum.

Receivables: 45 days.

Inventory: 6 turns per year (building to order).

Depreciation: 5 years ACRS.

Accounts payable: 34% of sales base—effectively 30 days with material cost assumptions.

Full-Year Income Statements, Ending Fiscal Year February 28
Assuming $1,000,000 Equity Investments, September 1983 and July 1984

	1984	1985
Sales.	$1,701,700	$11,612,700
Gross margin	793,287	5,768,335
Total SG&A.	555,606	2,119,505
EBIT	237,681	3,648,830
Interest	10,700	20,800
Taxes.	69,199	1,263,932
PAT	$ 157,782	$ 2,364,098

EXHIBIT 11: *(continued)*

Pro Forma Financials Assuming $1,000,000 Equity Investment in September 1983 and $1,000,000 in June 1984

Quarterly Income Statements (in thousands of dollars)

	June–Aug. 1983	Sept.–Nov. 1983	Dec. 1983– Feb. 1984	March–May 1984	June–Aug. 1984	Sept.–Nov. 1984	Dec. 1984– Feb. 1985	March–May 1985
Number of units.	2	7	8	16	26	44	52	60
Sales	194.0	504.0	608.0	1,216.0	1,976.0	3,444.0	3,952.0	4,560.0
Gross margin	92.8	229.5	283.8	579.1	958.5	1,641.7	1,963.0	2,290.8
Selling costs.	36.1	54.5	97.3	174.1	283.0	442.5	508.7	574.9
General and administrative.	71.3	89.3	106.9	121.4	135.7	136.4	154.0	163.6
Total Selling, general and administrative	107.4	143.8	204.2	295.5	418.7	578.9	662.7	738.5
EBIT	−14.6	85.7	79.6	283.6	539.8	1,062.8	1,300.3	1,552.3
Interest.	6.2	1.5	0	2.5	1.5	2.0	0	0
Taxes	—	—	30.9	102.2	188.4	371.3	455.1	543.3
PAT.	−8.1	84.2	48.7	178.9	349.9	689.5	845.2	1,009.0

Pro Forma Financials Assuming $1,000,000 Equity Investment

Quarterly Balance Sheets

	June 1983	August 1983	November 1983	February 1984	May 1984	August 1984	November 1984	February 1985	May 1985
Current assets:									
Cash	$ 12,000	$ 30,000	$ 489,609	$ 438,663	$ 124,200	$ 815,152	$ 303,600	$ 576,933	$1,109,311
Receivables	60,000	150,000	310,500	310,500	621,000	897,000	151,800	1,794,000	2,070,000
Inventory	135,000	200,000	414,000	414,000	828,000	1,196,001	2,024,001	2,392,001	2,760,001
Prepaid expenses	20,000	20,000	20,000	25,000	25,000	30,000	30,000	30,000	35,000
Total current assets	227,000	400,000	1,234,109	1,188,163	1,598,200	2,938,153	3,875,601	4,792,934	5,974,312
Equipment	37,000	45,000	45,000	140,000	200,000	250,000	400,000	450,000	450,000
Depreciation	9,280	9,780	10,530	13,780	20,280	29,980	51,980	75,580	97,180
Net equipment	27,720	35,220	34,470	126,220	179,720	220,020	348,020	374,420	352,820
Total assets	$254,720	$435,220	$1,268,579	$1,314,383	$1,777,920	$3,158,173	$4,223,621	$5,167,354	$6,327,132
Current liabilities:									
Accounts payable	13,600	34,000	70,380	70,380	140,760	203,320	344,080	406,640	469,200
Payroll	15,000	15,000	15,000	20,000	20,000	25,000	25,000	30,000	30,000
Taxes	2,000	2,000	19,824	12,026	64,486	188,950	372,000	455,090	543,308
Total current liabilities	30,600	51,000	105,204	102,406	225,246	417,270	741,080	891,729	1,042,508
Total liabilities	$ 30,600	$ 51,000	$ 105,204	$ 102,406	$ 225,246	$ 417,270	$ 741,080	$ 891,729	$1,042,508
Equity:									
Common	35,100	35,100	1,035,100	1,035,100	1,035,100	2,035,100	2,035,100	2,035,100	2,035,100
Retained earnings	56,836	44,208	128,275	176,877	355,869	705,802	1,395,359	2,240,525	3,249,525
Total equity	$ 91,936	$ 79,308	$1,163,375	$1,211,977	$1,390,969	$2,740,902	$3,430,459	$4,275,625	$5,284,625
S/T Debt	132,184	304,912	0	0	161,705	0	52,083	0	0

EXHIBIT 11 *(continued)*

Pro Forma Financials Assuming No Equity Investment

Quarterly Income Statements (in thousands of dollars)

	June–Aug. 1983	Sept.–Nov. 1983	Dec. 1983– Feb. 1984	March–May 1984	June–Aug. 1984	Sept.–Nov. 1984	Dec. 1984– Feb. 1985	March–May 1985
Number of units	2	4	3	3	4	5	6	7
Sales	194.0	276.0	228.0	228.0	304.0	380.0	456.0	532.0
Gross margin	92.8	124.7	106.4	108.5	147.5	186.6	226.5	267.3
Selling costs.	36.0	29.8	24.9	24.9	49.1	57.4	65.7	74.0
General and administrative . .	72.0	66.0	66.0	66.0	75.0	95.0	75.0	75.0
Total Selling general and administrative	107.5	95.8	90.9	90.9	124.1	132.4	140.7	149.0
EBIT	−14.7	28.9	15.5	17.6	23.4	54.2	85.8	118.3
Interest.	6.2	6.7	5.5	5.4	7.7	9.0	9.0	9.0
Taxes	—	—	3.2	7.8	6.5	16.9	27.9	39.3
PAT.	−20.9	22.2	6.8	4.4	9.2	28.3	48.9	70.0

EXHIBIT 11 *(concluded)*

Pro Forma Financials Assuming No Equity Investment

Quarterly Balance Sheet

	June 1983	August 1983	November 1983	February 1984	May 1984	August 1984	November 1984	February 1985	May 1985
Current assets:									
Cash	$ 12,000	$ 30,000	$ 20,700	$ 20,700	$ 20,700	$ 27,600	$ 34,500	$ 41,400	$ 48,300
Receivables	60,000	150,000	103,500	103,500	103,500	138,000	172,500	207,000	241,500
Inventories	135,000	200,000	138,000	138,000	138,000	184,000	230,000	· 276,000	322,000
Prepaid expenses	20,000	20,000	20,000	20,000	20,000	20,000	20,000	20,000	20,000
Total current assets	227,000	400,000	282,200	282,200	282,200	369,600	457,000	544,400	631,800
Equipment	37,000	45,000	45,000	75,000	75,000	100,000	100,000	100,000	100,000
Depreciation	9,280	9,780	10,530	12,280	14,530	17,530	20,530	23,530	26,530
Net equipment	27,720	35,220	34,470	62,720	60,470	82,470	79,470	76,470	73,470
Total assets	$254,720	$435,220	$316,670	$344,920	$342,670	$452,070	$536,470	$620,870	$705,270
Current liabilities:									
Accounts payable	13,600	34,000	23,460	23,460	23,460	31,280	39,100	46,920	54,740
Payroll	15,000	15,000	15,000	20,000	20,000	25,000	25,000	30,000	30,000
Taxes	2,000	2,000	2,710	4,088	4,630	9,220	20,006	31,087	42,454
Total current liabilities	30,600	51,000	41,170	47,548	48,090	65,500	84,106	108,007	127,194
Total liabilities	$ 30,600	$ 51,000	$ 41,170	$ 47,548	$ 48,090	$ 65,500	$ 84,106	$108,007	127,194
Equity:									
Common	35,100	35,100	35,100	35,100	35,100	35,100	35,100	35,100	35,100
Retained earnings	56,836	45,208	68,987	80,865	88,312	100,430	131,735	183,618	256,611
Total equity	$ 91,936	80,308	104,087	115,965	123,412	135,530	166,835	218,718	291,711
S/T Debt	132,184	303,912	171,413	181,408	171,168	251,040	285,529	294,145	286,365

THE DECISION

Finally, each of the men had to make a decision about how well this opportunity fit their own personal abilities and career plans. They each described their feelings.

Andy

I really believe that this is a terrific opportunity for all of us. Personally, I have a great deal of experience in the power systems area, and I am convinced that there is a market for the product. We do have a lot of work ahead of us—finding a new location, getting a prototype built, and hiring a sales force; but I'm very confident that we will be able to accomplish this. Kirk is a terrific guy and a real engineering talent.

Tom

I was very surprised when Andy called me and offered me a position with Electrodec. It's very tempting—with a piece of the equity, there could be a large financial upside, and I have enjoyed working with Kirk and everyone at Electrodec.

Still, there are plenty of risks. I have no electrical engineering background. Kirk and Andy *say* the product will work, but I don't have the technical competence to make that judgment on my own. It seems to me that we are really in a bind: we don't want to get venture money until we have a prototype, can't build units until we have a new location, but need money for a new location.

Finally, I'm getting married in a couple of months, and my fiancée has a full scholarship to a graduate school in Boston. What will we do in Charlotte or Atlanta? I'm already in over my eyeballs in debt—I'm borrowing money to pay for my honeymoon—and Electrodec won't be generating any cash for quite a while.

I also have some other very attractive offers, including:

- A 1/3 partnership in an area engineering consulting/development firm.
- A position as a general manager of one of the subsidiaries of the consulting firm I worked with last summer.
- A position with a New England conglomerate which is considering entering the robotics area. I would work with the CEO and strategic planning group for a year, and if we decided to proceed, I would be the general manager of the robotics division.

Each of these positions offers the ability to work in an area that I'm very interested in, live in New England, and start making some money right away.

Pete

My offer from Electrodec was a surprise, too. I've been recruiting pretty heavily in the sales and marketing area, and have some attractive offers from Procter & Gamble, General Foods, Bath Iron Works, and Gould. My wife and I are both from outside Boston, and have some very close ties there.

Although this opportunity has gotten me pretty excited about working for a small company—my own company at that—I do have some concerns. Financially, the upside is attractive, but I'm heavily in debt, have a 3-year-old kid and my wife is 7-months pregnant.

I also question whether Electrodec can really handle three MBAs.

Finally, I am less optimistic about the product than Kirk and Andy. I think it's going to be very tough to get a prototype up and working. Kirk just isn't focusing his energies on it. I wonder if he has the discipline to do the kind of work that's required.

Kirk

Kirk summed up his views as well:

The field study has pointed out a market potential far in excess of that which I'd expected. There really is a strong demand from the utility customer for this product. It is an opportunity to use very sophisticated technology in an area that hasn't seen it yet, and the utilities are very excited about it.

For me, this is a very fundamental change in the business: to go from a consultant/tinkerer to a full-fledged manufacturer. There certainly are risks to bringing on the additional overhead, and I will be giving up a good-sized piece of the equity. But I have complete faith in Andy, and I would rather own a smaller percentage of a bigger business.

I hope that Tom and Pete decide to join us. We really need their help in manufacturing and sales, and if they want to have their own business, they should do it now because it gets much more difficult to do it later on.

CASE 27

Michael Bregman

In July 1980, Michael Bregman was preparing a strategy to expand his fledgling Canadian restaurant business. During the last eight months, he had started pilot locations for two different restaurant concepts. The first was "Mmmuffins" (as in, "Mmm, good!"). This was a take-out bakery operation offering a wide variety of fresh, hot muffins (baked on-premises) together with accompanying beverages. The second was "Michel's Baguette," a more elaborate French bakery cafe. Baguette offered a take-out counter for a variety of French croissants and breads (also baked in the restaurant) as well as an on-premises cafe with soups, salads, sandwiches on fresh bread, an omelette bar, and fresh croissants.

Michael hoped to build a substantial restaurant chain with one or both of these concepts. Even though the two pilots were just underway, a flurry of construction of new shopping centers across Canada appeared to offer a unique opportunity for rapid growth. In fact, one major developer was negotiating with Michael for a package of locations right now. The package included some locations Michael felt would be good, but the developer also wanted commitment to some locations Michael felt would do poorly.

Such a deal would be a major undertaking for his young company. It would heavily influence the company's direction during the crucial formative years. Yet Michael was still considering the merits of franchising versus internal growth and evaluating the relative attractiveness of the two restaurant concepts. He wanted to make conscious strategic decisions in these areas before he committed to any course of action.

BACKGROUND

Michael Bregman was a native of Canada. After earning a degree in finance from Wharton at the University of Pennsylvania, he entered directly into the MBA program at Harvard from which he graduated in 1977. Michael sought a job in the food business because of an interest he had developed due to his family's long association with that industry.

Michael's grandfather had built a successful bakery as had Michael's father, Lou Bregman. In 1971, Lou Bregman had purchased Hunt's and Woman's Bakery (Hunt's) division from the Kellogg Company which Lou had been supplying. The division had been losing money on annual sales of about $20 million, but under Lou Bregman's guidance soon prospered. Hunt's sold bakery products to 130 company-owned retail stores and to 370 supermarkets. Michael had worked after school and in summer jobs in various restaurants and bakeries.

> I joined Loblaws, a Canadian chain that was perceived as being a very stodgy supermarket company. Everybody thought I was crazy because I had offers from some of the big consulting companies and investment banks, places that I should be going. But at Loblaws I would be working for a new president with no experience in supermarketing right in the midst of a turnaround. I would call him a marketing genius and really went to work for him rather than the company.

Michael worked on corporate development projects including the launch of NO-NAME (unbranded) products in Canada which was very successful. But things were not going as smoothly at Hunt's. Lou Bregman was having disagreements with his majority partners (who were in the real estate business) as the result of some difficult financial times. The company was in a turmoil and Lou asked Michael to join Hunt's to see if he could help out. Michael agreed in June of 1978, and was put in charge of the retail division. Lou concentrated on the central bakery operations and the other partners attempted to provide overall direction. Michael quickly found himself at odds with the other managers and strongly disagreed with what he thought were stupid decisions. He stayed only at his father's urging until December 1978, then resigned.

> I must say that I felt pretty defeated at the time. I'd worked so hard and had accomplished so little. I'd fought a lot, and I've never been much of a fighter, but I also can't do anything unless I believe in it. It was a difficult time.
>
> I didn't know what I was going to do. I'd always planned all along to start my own business at some time. I didn't know what or when, but I did know I wanted to do it quickly because I think it gets harder and harder as life goes on and you have all sorts of commitments.
>
> I went out for lunch one day with my old boss from Loblaws who suggested I go back to them again. I really hadn't thought of that but

had simply been keeping in touch. I told him I couldn't really make a long-term commitment because my heart was in starting my own business. He said that would be all right, that he could put me on a short-term assignment. It took about five minutes worth of convincing for me to agree.

EVOLUTION OF A START-UP

As his first project, Michael was asked to recommend a strategy for Loblaws' in-store bakeries: What should they be? Should they be bake-off stores of frozen products (baking prefrozen doughs) or scratch bakeries? Should Loblaws have them? He prepared a similar study of the deli department. Michael was then asked to implement his recommendations in the bakery area and became director of Bakery Operations, a new position. He worked closely with the manager of Bakery Operations who was oriented to the day-to-day management more than to strategy and planning for the department. Bakeries became important to Loblaws' new superstores which were designed to provide greater variety and savings than traditional supermarkets. Bakery products were successful in drawing customers to the stores with store-baked crusty bread and rolls.

> Somewhere along the way, a small businessman visited me. He thought we should sell his muffins in our stores. We had taken muffins for granted: they'd been around forever and were sort of stable and unexciting—what do you do with a muffin? All of a sudden this fellow comes in with these giant muffins, much larger than any we'd ever seen. We sold our small muffins for 15 cents each; we'd have to retail his at 45 cents.
>
> Naturally everybody was against them just on price. But I decided to test them in two of the most affluent stores. They went like crazy, it was wild. We kept upping the orders and we could never keep them in stock. We didn't promote them, just put them in the counter, but there was immediate appeal. That triggered something in me. Seeing that here you could take a very drab product and make it exciting. And I thought you could do more with it than I saw him do.

Despite Michael's interest in the food industry and fascination with the performance of the large muffins, he really didn't like the bakery business:

> It always seemed to be an old man's game, a tired industry that was declining and very production-oriented, very unexciting. Over 75 percent of the retail bakeries in North America had closed between the early 60s and mid-70s. Before that, the retail baking industry was comprised of hundreds of independent skilled bakers who had come over from Europe and opened up shops and carried on as they had in Europe. The little shops handled two or three hundred items, mostly, if not all, made by hand. You needed skilled bakers to continue who became very expensive and in short supply.

Mom and Pop were willing to work crazy hours and take low salaries because they wanted their own bakery. But by the mid-70s those same skilled people could get jobs in any supermarket in the country, earn $25,000, work 37–38 hours, have terrific benefits and no headaches. That together with the shift of customers to the shopping centers really put an end to most of that business.

The pressure really began with the bakery chains, like my father's, that were serviced from central plants. But then the supermarkets started doing in-store baking, selling a fresher product at a lower price. Gas had gone crazy and it had become prohibitive to deliver fresh products from a central facility to many small shops daily or twice a day. And the supermarket had a different view of the baking business. They were very price conscious. They weren't in the baking business to make money, but to draw customers to buy other things. The last thing they wanted to do was to draw a customer into the store and see a bakery that had prices that were too high. Their cost systems were often really rather silly and ignored investment and overhead and value of the space used by any individual area. Some supermarket departments, like the bakeries, were really much more expensive marketing tools than they thought. But the supermarkets tended to just look at the total bottom line as a contribution number. Looking at these things, it was easy to be negative about the industry.

Then I started to feel there was a massive opportunity out there! People still liked baked goods and they hadn't been supplied with them in the right fashion. As I thought in general terms of what was going to happen to the retail baking industry, I felt that the stores were going to get smaller and the industry would have to specialize in one or two lines of products. Also you'd surely have to bake on-premises to create the freshness that no one else could duplicate. That's really the key component of quality in our industry. I also reminded myself that the retail baking business is primarily based on impulse sales and location is extremely important.

I guess I had all of this in mind in May 1979 while my father and I were driving to a restaurant show in Chicago. For the first time it really occurred to me: Why don't we open a muffin shop? We sort of chuckled— what a stupid idea. Later I began to think, why not? There's not a lot of money to lose and a lot to gain if it worked. It was totally different than anything we'd seen in North America.

During the summer, I began investigating some space in the Eaton Centre. This was Toronto's principal downtown shopping complex with over 3.7 million square feet of space. The Eaton Centre was directly connected to three subway terminals and had 200,000 office workers within easy walking distance. It was anchored by two major department stores and two office towers. There were over 300 retail shops and restaurants in the complex. Their leasing agent was pretty skeptical, but was willing to lease some space. In August, I committed to lease 350 square feet at $15,000 a year or 8 percent of sales, beginning December 1. Now I needed to develop my shop.

In the meantime, Lou Bregman had sold his interest in Hunt's and had considered retirement. Yet when he had the chance to buy a downtown Bagel Nosh store that had gone bankrupt, he decided to develop a new full-service restaurant and bakery called Bregman's. Michael was helping his father get started with that and Lou Bregman co-guaranteed the lease obligations with Michael for the muffin shop.

In addition to his duties at Loblaws, helping his father's new venture, and planning his muffin shop, Michael found himself drawn into yet another start-up:

> My wife and I had honeymooned in France when we were married in May 1978. I really fell in love with their croissants. I couldn't believe how great they were. I'd never tasted a decent croissant in North America. They were all weak imitations and I thought this would be a great product to bring over here. I had seen a few French bakery stores in Chicago and New York, but very few. I knew that this would be something to pursue in the future.
>
> As we were settling our lease deal for the muffin shop in the Eaton Centre, I mentioned to the leasing agent that I had heard that a French bread chain, Au Bon Pain, was coming to the centre. He was surprised I'd heard of it, but said they had some problems with them. I said I was planning to get in the same business and he got very excited. He called his boss and very quickly offered to negotiate with us. Space in the Eaton Centre was very difficult to obtain and seemed to me to be one of the best possible locations. So we leased the space and decided to do our French bakery, too. Again, we personally guaranteed the leases.

Despite the serendipitous opening at the Eaton Centre, Michael's commitment to the French bakery restaurant was not a spur-of-the-moment decision. He had been actively investigating the possibilities of both the muffin shop and the French bakery since the Chicago show in May. Because the French bakery would require much more capital, Michael had prepared a short business plan which he circulated to three or four people he thought might invest. One was Ralph Scurfield of Calgary, president of the NuWest Group, the largest homebuilder in North America. Michael had met him while Ralph was enrolled in an executive program at Harvard. Michael had done a field study for NuWest and had kept in touch with Ralph. Now Ralph said that he knew very little about the restaurant business, but that he did know Michael Bregman and would be willing to bet some money on him. A long negotiation ensued as Michael sought locations for the muffin shop or for the French bakery. They reached agreement in the fall:

> We capitalized the company with $450,000. My father and I each put in $62,500 in common stock and Ralph put in $125,000 in common stock and an additional $200,000 in preferred shares. I had a net worth of about $8,000 and got a loan for my share. I had to get my wife, mother, and father to co-sign and my parents to put their house up. It scared the daylights out of me. If things went wrong, it wouldn't sink them, but I didn't know how I could live with it.

I would take a salary cut to $25,000 a year, which together with my wife's income would just about let us live and cover the loan. The contract ended up sixty pages long with five pages of basics and the rest disaster clauses. I would have tie-breaking power unless things went wrong and would also have to get Ralph's approval for capital expenditures over $5,000. The initial spending requirements were approved as part of the agreement. There was also a complex redemption plan for the preferred which included penalties for not making the five-year schedule.

The fall of 1979 was frantic as Michael managed to get both of his projects underway. Although he and his father had been in the baking business, neither of them were familiar with the special processes needed for muffins of this type or with French baking. At the same time Michael was working to design the stores, he had to find and test muffin recipes and learn to operate the specialized French baking equipment. Part of his strategy was to use the very best help he could find. For design, he employed Don Watt & Associates, one of Canada's premier designers. The equipment suppliers were also very helpful in the strenuous task of laying out all of the necessary customer service and baking equipment in 350 square feet for the muffin shop. Michael also found a French baker who lived in Washington who agreed to come up just before the bakery opened to teach several bakers how to bake French bakery products.

Somehow they got underway. Michael left Loblaws at the end of November 1979 and Mmmuffins opened December 15. Michel's Baguette began construction at that point and opened in April 1980. It was not a time Michael would like to repeat.

EVALUATING THE FIRST EFFORTS

By July, the two stores were beginning to stabilize and Michael was preparing to expand. He reviewed the sate of each operation to help him decide what directions he might take.

He was pleased with both store designs and concepts. The extra expense and effort he had put in store planning had been well worth the investment. Both facilities were attractive and inviting (Exhibit 1). As for product selections, they had developed recipes for over 15 varieties of muffins which could be made from four different base mixtures. About 10 would be offered at any point in time. At Baguette, the menu appeared workable and was proving to be a popular range of choices (Exhibit 2).

Sales for both stores had been encouraging and costs were beginning to become steady. He now had seven months of experience with Mmmuffins and three months with Baguette. Exhibit 3 is a record of sales and variable costs for the two stores. Exhibit 4 is a year-to-date financial statement showing the total performance and financial position.

EXHIBIT 1: Store Designs

EXHIBIT 1 *(concluded)*

EXHIBIT 2: Michel's Baguette, Product Line Highlights

Bakery		Cafe	
Bread:	Baguette	Salads:	Julienne
	Boule		Nicoise
	Alpine		Spinach
	Mini-Baguette		Side Salad
	Whole Wheat Baguette		Salad du Jour
Croissants:	Butter	Soups:	Yellow Pea
	Almond		with Ham
	Petit Pain au Chocolat		Soup du Jour
	Raisin-Custard	Quiches:	Bacon
	Cream Cheese		Spinach
	Cheddar Cheese		Mushroom
	Ham and Cheese	Omelette Bar:	Cheddar Cheese
	Apple Cinnamon		Ham
	Blueberry		Swiss Cheese
	Cherry		Green Pepper
			Onion
			etc. . . .
		Sandwiches:	Ham & Cheese
			Roast Beef
			Tuna
			Chicken Salad
			Egg Salad
			Cream Cheese
			Swiss Cheese
			Le Hero
			Le Jardin
			Roast Beef &
			Herb Cheese
			etc. . . .
		Beverages:	Coffee
			Tea
			Milk
			Soft Drinks
			Juices
			Perrier
		Croissants:	(as in Bakery)

After hectic start-up periods, the operations of each store were now also satisfactory. As expected, they were very different from each other. The Mmmuffins store had only 350 square feet of space. That small area had to contain supplies storage, preparation of raw materials and mixes, baking, clean-up, and the retail service counters. Michael described how this worked:

> I think our design was one of the very most important reasons behind our early success. Don Watt was able to create the magnet to draw customers in the first time. If they liked our product, liked our service, they'd come

EXHIBIT 3: Initial Operating Results, 1980

Mmmuffins

Period Ending	Number of Weeks	Dollar Sales	Average Dollar Sales per Week	Percent Food, Supplies	Percent Labor	Percent Food, Supplies, and Labor
Jan. 19, 1980 . . .	5	$ 9,010	$ 1,802	38.2	38.8	77.0
Feb. 16	4	10,866	2,716	36.3	29.8	66.1
March 15	4	14,901	3,725	24.5	23.9	48.4
April 12	4	17,250	4,312	28.0	22.5	50.0
May 10	4	16,696	4,174	34.6	25.6	60.2
June 7	4	17,346	4,337	38.5	25.4	63.9
July 5.	4	20,602	5,150	31.1	21.0	52.1
Highest week's sales, June 21: $5,574						51.4%

Michel's Baguette

Period Ending	Number of Weeks	Dollar Sales	Average Dollar Sales per Week	Percent Food, Supplies	Percent Labor	Percent Food, Supplies, and Labor
May 10	4	44,470	11,118	37.7	33.5	68.2
June 7	4	52,921	13,230	27.4	25.4	52.8
July 5.	4	65,487	16,372	25.9	23.1	49.0
Highest week's sales, June 21: $17,289.						48.7%

EXHIBIT 4

MICHAEL BREGMAN
Balance Sheet
June 30, 1980
(unaudited)

Assets

Current assets:
Term deposit	$120,000
Receivables	1,525
Inventory	6,669
Prepaid expenses	15,345
Deferred charges	1,062
Deferred income taxes.	7,250
	151,851
Equipment and leasehold improvements	400,741
Incorporation expense–at cost	7,151
	$559,743

Liabilities

Current liabilities:
Bankers' advances	$ 1,436
Payables and accruals.	124,736
Dividend payable	4,500
	130,672

Shareholders' Equity

Share capital	$450,000
Deficit	(20,929)
	$559,743

EXHIBIT 4 *(continued)*

Statement of Loss and Deficit,
Period from Inception, December 4, 1979 to June 30, 1980
(unaudited)

Sales	$269,428
Cost of sales	169,919
Gross operating profit	99,509
Store expenses	78,473
Income from store operations	21,036
Other income—Interest	14,972
	36,008
Administration expenses	55,187
Net loss before income taxes	19,179
Deferred income taxes	7,250
Net loss	11,929
Dividends	9,000
Deficit, end of period	$ 20,929

Internal Statements of Operations,
Inception to July 5, 1980

	Mmmuffins	Michel's Baguette
Sales	$106,404	$162,745
Food costs	35,090	44,861
Gross profit	71,314	117,884
Operating expense:		
Supplies	6,083	7,259
Labor	29,249	52,333
	35,332	59,592
Gross operating profit	35,982	58,292
General expenses	2,228	1,992
Occupancy costs	19,411	35,609
Administrative costs	5,442	8,137
Total expenses	27,081	45,738
Net profit from operations	8,901	12,554
Add depreciation and amortization	5,367	9,005
Cash flow from operation	$ 14,268	$ 21,559

Note: Slightly different period than prior statements.

back. They came in first because of the color, the lighting, the photography—it's just a different showcase.

The design also worked well functionally. There's just enough space to do everything, but no extra space to become cluttered or dirty and not be corrected. The customer cannot see the preparation area, but the manager can easily keep track of all activities. The total staff complement for the store runs between 6 and 12 people including part-timers, depending on the part-time mix. You need one manager and one assistant to cover the shifts. There are salespeople at the counter and bakers. You can trade-off some during slack buying periods. Service at the counter is fairly simple and you can train a baker in two days from start to finish. You could almost get this down to two hours for most of the functions.

Although we didn't really know what we were doing when we opened, we soon learned better ways to do things. We got better at finding and selecting specialized preparation equipment that fit our particular needs. Since we bake right from scratch using no commercial mixes, every extra efficiency helped. We learned what items we could make ahead of time and better ways to store them. This is really important when you begin baking early in the morning before opening and continue throughout the day.

I knew that if we were going to grow, we'd have to systematize the operation, so during the first months I wrote an operating manual with everything from opening procedures, to how to clean the store, to recipes, to baking procedures, to how to greet customers and work the counter—everything. I found it one of the most grueling experiences I had ever been through in my life. I was working behind the counter myself during those opening months and was learning how important those controls and procedures were.

I also learned how important the manager was. As Baguette opened and I left the Mmmuffins store under the supervision of a manager I had hired, little problems started to arise—fighting among the staff, quality being a little less consistent than it should have been. I'm sure there was fault on both sides, but I found that the manager constantly needed attention.

But all in all, I was very pleased.

As a much larger and more complete bakery and restaurant, Michel's Baguette was much more complex:

Baguette had 2,500 square feet of space which was really a bit too tight. This had a larger food preparation, baking and storage area, a take-out bakery counter, the cafeteria-style serving line, and an on-premises eating area with seats for 35. Once again, our physical design was an important asset. Our store helped attract customers at the same time that it worked well functionally in a very tight space.

With a larger menu, there were many more tasks to perform. There was a total staff of 55 to 60 people, including part-timers. You really need a very qualified head manager to be the general manager of the overall business as well as two assistant managers who have the capability to be the acting general manager when the general manager isn't there. You need a head baker who is a skilled baker and can guide the whole production area of the store. There are kitchen prep people, two kinds of service people, cafeteria counter people who actually prepare your portions, the salads, and sandwiches. Most of these jobs are more complex than those at Mmmuffins and the baking is particularly difficult. It takes 20 steps to make croissants and the breads also have more steps and are more demanding than making muffins. There are many delicate areas where you can ruin the product, but I must say that we brought in the right equipment from France and, with care, can consistently make excellent products. All of the baked goods and other items are made from scratch and are continuously baked throughout the day.

I began to spend most of my time at Baguette once it opened and again had to learn as we went. This would take more effort to systematize and I hadn't written a manual here yet. I was lucky in hiring some good bakers and restaurant managers to help me out. I went after managers that I had heard did a good job for other restaurants in the city and was able to get two to join me. They both worked out very well.

The primary appeal of each concept was absolute freshness and quality of baked goods. As Michael looked at the two operations, he was satisfied that they each properly reflected the key conceptual definitions he felt were critical to their success: hard-to-replicate standards of quality with costs kept to acceptable levels by careful specialization, organization, and store design. Michael described how these worked together:

> For superior quality our recipes are based on using fresh eggs, buttermilk, and other very perishable items—very expensive, very hard-to-handle items. Bakeries don't use fresh eggs; they use powdered or frozen. But we decided we would use fresh: we didn't care about any of the rules; we would be better than anybody. But this created very difficult production problems. You can't make too much at once, and you can't make too little because it's a waste of time. The mixes and products aren't very storeable, you can't freeze them, and you can't keep them for more than one day.
>
> Besides ingredients, we control our quality by specializing. This means making limited types of baked goods in the best possible way and then providing only those menu items needed to support the specialized baking operation. With Mmmuffins this is practically absolute: there are only muffins and beverages. The bakery for Baguette is simply too capital intensive for the menu to remain that simple. So we combine the bakery with a restaurant. Having the fresh croissants and fresh bread to make sandwiches helps the restaurant and the sampling that goes on in the restaurant spills over and helps the bakery. The restaurant and bakery counter also have different peak times, so you have better distribution for the bakery equipment and your service people can sway back and forth. But other than the baking, we do no cooking! It's just an assembly operation. We assemble salads, cut meat, cut cheese. But except for omelettes, we don't fry anything, we don't boil anything, we don't cook. Other than the baking, in terms of the back-of-the-house, it's a very simple restaurant.
>
> The stores' layouts and service delivery systems are designed to efficiently support each menu concept. Both provide efficient preparation areas. Both have ovens prominently situated in view of shoppers and passersby—the sight and aroma of fresh baking are major merchandising tools. At Mmmuffins, we have very efficient customer handling along with some innovative packaging for quantity purchases. At Baguette, we selected a cafeteria line for the restaurant to go along with the counter service for

the take-out bakery. This is one step up from the fast food joint where you have to fight for a seat and eat from a tray with disposables. We use better dinnerware, metal utensils, and glasses. This is a step down from the full-service restaurant where you are served by waitresses. We selected this because I felt strongly that in the mall environment, people want to eat quickly but in some comfort.

CONSIDERING FRANCHISING

With both Mmmuffins and Baguette well started, Michael began to consider expansion. He felt there should be many opportunities for good restaurants and specialty food stores despite competition ranging from retail bakeries and supermarkets, to fast food operations, to full-service restaurants. Almost all of these types of competitors would be present clustered in large shopping areas and malls. This was true for the first Mmmuffins and Baguette locations. Yet both had held their own in the very competitive and highly visible Eaton Centre. The question was how to expand. Michael had two concepts, limited experience, and limited resources. How could he best capitalize on his work to date to build a significant restaurant business?

One avenue of growth he could pursue was franchising. Certainly enough others had chosen this method to make franchising a very important factor in the Canadian and U.S. economies. A *Foodservice & Hospitality Magazine* survey estimated that franchising represented 16.5 percent of the total Canadian food-service and lodging industry in 1979. This market share was increasing. Survey respondents reported a 29 percent increase in total food-service franchise sales resulting from a 10.5 percent increase in total units operating and a 17 percent increase in average sales per unit (to $381,443).

For U.S. firms, franchised units accounted for approximately one quarter of all food-service sales. Exhibit 5 lists several characteristics of U.S.–owned restaurant franchisors for 1978 with projections for 1979 and 1980. About 40 percent of all U.S. franchised restaurants were located in California, Texas, Ohio, Illinois, Michigan, or Florida. A January 1980 study by the U.S. Department of Commerce noted that:

> the entry into the restaurant franchising system mostly by small companies continued in 1978 with a net gain of 38 franchisors, bringing the total to 388. During 1979, 17 franchisors with a total of 227 restaurants, 198 franchisee-owned, went out of business while 13 franchisors with a total of 168 restaurants, 84 franchisee-owned, decided to abandon franchising as a method of marketing.
>
> Big franchisors with over 1,000 units each increased to 11 in 1978

EXHIBIT 5: Characteristics of U.S.-Owned Restaurants (all types)

Table A: Statistics of U.S.-Owned Restaurant Franchisors, 1978–80*

	1978	1979†	1980†	Percent Changes 1978–79	Percent Changes 1979–80
Total number of establishments	55,312	59,928	66,672	8.3	11.3
Company-owned	15,510	16,781	18,549	8.2	10.5
Franchisee-owned	39,802	43,147	48,123	8.4	11.5
Total sales of products and services (in thousands of dollars)	21,100,788	24,591,880	28,990,499	16.5	17.9
Company-owned	6,733,545	7,816,198	9,111,129	16.1	16.6
Franchisee-owned	14,367,243	16,775,682	19,879,370	16.8	18.5
Total sales of products and services by franchisors to franchisees (in thousands of dollars):					
Merchandise (nonfood) for resale	33,013	37,534	48,656	13.7	29.6
Supplies (such as paper goods, etc.)	170,889	231,017	287,379	35.2	24.4
Food ingredients	298,063	383,774	481,004	28.8	25.3
Other	46,817	53,728	40,771	14.8	−24.1
Total	548,782	706,053	857,810	28.7	21.5

* See Tables C and D.
† Data estimated by respondents.

EXHIBIT 5 *(continued)*

Table B: Distribution by Number of Establishments—1978*

Size groups	Number of Franchising Companies	Establishments		Sales	
		Number	Percent	(in thousands of dollars)	Percent
Total.	388	55,312	100.0	21,100,788	100.0
1,001 and greater	11	27,750	50.2	11,400,272	54.0
501–1,000.	11	8,925	16.1	3,513,637	16.7
151–500	34	8,833	16.0	2,928,603	13.9
51–150	59	5,580	10.1	1,712,930	8.1
11–50	153	3,642	6.6	1,360,850	6.4
0–10.	120	582	1.0	184,496	0.9

* See Tables C and D.
Source: U.S. Department of Commerce, "Franchising in the Economy 1978–1980," January 1980.

EXHIBIT 5 *(continued)*

Table C: Distribution of Establishments by Major Activity

Major Activity	Firms	1978			1979*			1980*		
		Total	Company-Owned	Franchisee-Owned	Total	Company-Owned	Franchisee-Owned	Total	Company-Owned	Franchisee-Owned
Total	388	55,312	15,510	39,802	59,928	16,781	43,147	66,672	18,549	48,123
Activity:										
Chicken.	31	6,708	1,870	4,838	7,193	2,011	5,182	7,826	2,197	5,629
Hamburgers, franks, roast beef, etc. . . .	117	26,038	4,648	21,390	27,833	5,077	22,756	30,651	5,695	24,956
Pizza.	66	7,542	3,042	4,500	8,355	3,288	5,067	9,434	3,577	5,857
Mexican (taco, etc.) . .	29	2,329	993	1,336	2,527	1,044	1,483	2,913	1,183	1,730
Seafood	11	2,297	899	1,398	2,444	901	1,543	2,704	966	1,738
Pancakes, waffles . .	15	1,441	363	1,078	1,577	418	1,159	1,770	491	1,279
Steak, full menu . . .	86	7,924	3,479	4,445	8,756	3,813	4,943	9,771	4,180	5,591
Sandwich and other . .	33	1,033	216	817	1,243	229	1,014	1,603	260	1,343

* Data estimated by respondents.

EXHIBIT 5 *(concluded)*

TABLE D: Sales by Major Activity (in thousands of dollars)

Major activity	Firms	1978			1979*			1980*		
		Total	Company-Owned	Franchisee-Owned	Total	Company-Owned	Franchisee-Owned	Total	Company-Owned	Franchisee-Owned
Total	388	$21,100,788	$6,733,545	$14,367,243	$24,591,880	$7,816,198	$16,775,682	$28,990,499	$9,111,129	$19,879,370
Activity:										
Chicken	31	$ 2,034,012	$ 653,977	$ 1,380,035	$2,247,838	$ 765,738	$ 1,482,000	$ 2,563,755	$ 899,485	$ 1,664,270
Hamburgers, franks, roast beef, etc.	117	10,862,837	2,589,465	8,273,372	12,961,887	3,038,923	9,922,964	15,521,446	3,595,801	11,925,645
Pizza	66	1,735,279	696,364	1,038,915	2,007,066	776,902	1,230,164	2,364,317	903,182	1,461,135
Mexican (taco, etc.)	29	602,376	304,697	297,679	648,100	315,922	332,178	766,692	377,652	389,040
Seafood	11	563,827	216,486	347,341	667,098	260,633	406,465	772,794	299,624	473,170
Pancakes, waffles	15	601,029	139,899	461,130	681,728	164,023	517,705	834,135	216,290	617,845
Steak, full menu	86	4,531,709	2,104,623	2,427,086	5,170,218	2,461,797	2,708,421	5,883,140	2,779,340	3,103,800
Sandwich and other	33	169,719	28,034	141,685	207,945	32,260	175,885	284,220	39,755	244,465

* Data estimated by respondents.

from 8 a year earlier. These 11 franchisors had 27,750 restaurants, 50.2% of all franchised restaurants, and accounted for $11.4 billion in sales, 54% of the total. Compared with 1977, the 8 franchisors with over 1,000 units each had 45% of the total units and 47% of the sales.

Menu expansion and diversification continues on the increase to meet the mounting competition from other chains and to enlarge customer counts that have been adversely affected by higher food costs and periodic gasoline shortages. The higher costs of cosmetic and structural construction changes are forcing fast food franchisors to reevaluate their investment in design, and cast their decor changes more and more in marketing terms.

Growth statistics of the 25 largest U.S. franchise restaurant systems are shown in Exhibit 6.

While franchising was one means to achieve growth for either Mmmuffins or Baguette, it would impose additional complexities in doing business. A franchisee is an independent business person with personal capital at risk and a fair amount of management flexibility. In addition to the demands inherent in such relationships, there was increasing government regulation of franchise offerings and operations. In October 21, 1979, a new U.S. Federal Trade Commission rule requiring comprehensive disclosure statements for prospective franchisees became effective. Sixteen separate states also required various types of disclosures (although some states accepted a uniform format). Canada had no such comprehensive disclosure requirement, but many felt there was a need for one and expected such a rule in Canada in the future. Some pressure for such regulation came from established franchisors who were worried about the effect that a few incapable, overconfident, or unscrupulous franchisors might have on the industry.

The areas of disclosure required by the new U.S. law illustrate the many aspects of the business and the relationship that must be considered in franchising. These include:

- Specific background information about the identity, financial position, and business experience of the franchisor company and its key directors and executives.
- Details of the financial relationship including initial and continuing fees and expenses payable to the franchisor.
- Requirements for doing business with the franchisor or affiliates (such as purchase of supplies from a franchisor source), and any realty fees, financing arrangements, or other financial requirements.
- Restrictions and requirements for methods of operation placed on the franchisee.
- Termination, cancellation, and renewal terms.
- Control over future sites.

EXHIBIT 6: Top 25 U.S. Franchise Restaurant Systems
Growth in Systemwide Sales, 1974–79 (sales in $ millions)

Franchise system	1974	1978	1979	1974–79 % Change	1978–79 % Change
McDonald's	$1,943	$4,575	$5,385	177%	17.7%
Kentucky Fried Chicken†	925.5	1,393.4	1,669	80	19.8
Burger King†	467	1,168	1,463	213	25.3
Wendy's	24.2	783	1,000*	4,032	27.8
International Dairy Queen† . . .	590	823.2	926	57	12.5
Pizza Hut	232	702	829	257	18.1
Big Boy	484*	660*	750*	55	13.6
Hardee's†	280	564.6	750	168	32.8
Arby's	120	353	430	258	21.8
Ho Jo's.	300*	425*	425*	42	0.0
Ponderosa†	183	328.5	406.9	122	23.9
Church's	126.9	345	405.7*	220	17.6
Bonanza	190	346	378	99	9.2
Tastee Freez†	267.9*	353.8*	350*	31	(1.1)
Long John Silver's†	45.5	283.4	342	652	20.7
Sonic Drive-ins†	52.1	291.7	336	545	15.2
Burger Chef†	250	301	335	34	11.3
Taco Bell†	71.1*	212*	320*	350	50.9
Western Sizzlin†	100	217.3	278.1	178	28.0
Dunkin' Donuts	163.3	249.4	283.8	74	14.0
A & W	174.4	247.5	255	46	3.0
Arthur Treacher's	48.3	191.5	226.3	369	18.2
Sizzler†	85.5	181.8	225.9	164	24.3
Perkins Cake n Steak.	75*	200*	223*	197	11.5
Pizza Inn	58.6	165.8	189*	223	14.0

Growth in Number of Units, 1974–79

Franchise system	1974	1978	1979	1974–79 % Change	1978–79 % Change
McDonald's	3,232	5,185	5,747	78%	10.8%
Kentucky Fried Chicken†	4,627	5,355	5,444	18	1.7
Burger King†	1,199	2,153	2,439	103	13.3
Wendy's	93	1,407	1,818	1,855	29.2
International Dairy Queen† . . .	4,504	820	4,860	8	0.8
Pizza Hut	1,668	3,541	3,846	131	8.6
Big Boy	881	1,041	1,100	25	5.7
Hardee's†	924	1,125	1,231	33	9.4
Arby's	439	818	928	111	13.4
Ho Jo's.	922	882	867	(6)	(1.7)
Ponderosa†	389	588	636	63	8.2
Church's	565	970	1,125	99	16.0
Bonanza	550	700	675	23	(3.6)
Tastee Freez†	2,215	2,022	2,000*	(10)	(1.1)
Long John Silver's†	208	1,001	1,007	384	0.6
Sonic Drive-ins†	220	1,061	1,182	437	11.4
Burger Chef†	950	853	831	(13)	(2.6)
Taco Bell†	562	877	1,100	96	25.4
Western Sizzlin†	140	319	400	186	25.4
Dunkin' Donuts	780	956	1,007	29	5.3
A & W	1,899	1,500	1,306	(31)	(12.9)
Arthur Treacher's	250	730	777	211	6.4
Sizzler†	256	352	402	57	14.2
Perkins Cake n Steak.	183	342	400*	119	17.0
Pizza Inn	336	743	760	126	2.3

Note: Includes U.S. and foreign sales and units.
* Estimated.
† Fiscal year-end figures (remainder are calendar year-end figures).
Source: *Restaurant Business*, March 1, 1980, p. 130. Reproduced by permission.

- Statistical information about the number of franchises and their rate of terminations.
- Franchisor-provided training programs and other support.

Even without disclosure requirements, it was considered a good idea to develop policies and practices for dealing with franchisees for the long term before opening the first operation. One reason for this was a general desire for consistent treatment of franchisees. Some examples of current practices of Canadian franchisors are summarized in Exhibit 7.

Increased regulation was not the only area of change going on in franchising. There was ever-increasing competition in Canada as more U.S. franchisors sought new markets in other countries. The need for better communication with franchises had started a trend of development of franchisee advisory councils by franchisors. The ultimate roles of these councils were still evolving. There was also a fairly constant trade back and forth between franchisors repurchasing franchised units for company ownership and company-owned units being franchised.

A QUESTION OF STRATEGY

The question of using franchising as a means of expansion was only one aspect Michael needed to consider in planning for growth for his restaurant business. A fundamental question was how suitable were his concepts for wide use? He had started and managed both current units personally. How well would they "travel?" Both concepts depended on fresh baking which made them more demanding than many franchises. Other stores offering similar baked goods (donuts, cookies, or other items) used premixed ingredients, premade frozen products to be baked in the units, or simply distributed centrally baked products.

Michael also had to include the capital requirements and likely performance of additional units of either type in his planning. His estimates of capital requirements for new locations are shown in Exhibit 8. His estimates of stand-alone operating results if operated by a franchisee are shown in Exhibit 9.

Finally, no matter what methods of growth he might choose, his location strategy would be critical. Where would his concepts best fit? One aspect was the type of location and surrounding demographics. Another would be geographic—how far away, and Canada versus the U.S. Even within Canada, there were very different demands between the more stable eastern portion and the rapidly growing western area. Should he concentrate on finding more established and stable locations in the east or should he take advantage of the many openings in new centers a construction boom in the west was creating? What differences were there between good locations for Mmmuffins and good locations for Baguette?

EXHIBIT 7: Sample Canadian Franchise Terms, February 1980

Franchisor (franchise)	History, Current Status, and Expansion Plans	Franchise Requirements and Costs	Services Offered to Franchisee
Mister Donut of Canada Ltd. (Mister Donut)	Established 1955 55 franchised units in Canada, 715 franchised units in U.S., Japan Locations: Ont. 43, Que. 9, B.C. 2, Alta. 1 Canadian sales $10 million 10 operations to open in 1980	Initial fee $10,000 Royalty fee 4.9% of gross sales Advertising fee .5% Current equipment package $50,000	Opening supervision Field supervision Classroom training Newsletter Site selection Lease negotiation
McDonald's Restaurants of Canada Ltd. (McDonald's Restaurants)	Established 1967 in Canada 156 franchised—168 company-owned Total Canadian sales $500 million 45 new units planned across Canada	Franchise fee $10,000, initial investment $190,000, total cost is around $400,000 Percentage rent plus royalty fee Total commitment by sole operator to run operation 4% advertising fee	Continual consultation of operation Marketing Training Personnel Real estate
The Harvest Inn, Inc. (The Pantry Family Restaurant)	Established 1975 5 units company owned, 2 franchised, all in B.C. Full-service restaurant for breakfast, lunch, and dinner 4 additional units are planned for B.C.	$20,000 initial fee Royalty fee 4% gross Advertising fee 2%	Full turnkey service including site selection, interior design Accounting, training, and personnel selection

Company	Details	Fees	Services
Burger King Canada Ltd. (Burger King)	Established 1976. 27 franchised units & 10 company owned. 2,650 worldwide; B.C. 2, Alta. 2, Ont. 30, P.E.I. 1, N.B. 1, N.S. 4 26 franchised units planned for Ont., N.B., B.C., N.S., Alta. Menu includes hamburgers & specialty sandwiches	Initial fee $40,000 4% royalty fee 4% advertising fee	Complete service package
Smitty's Pancake Houses Ltd.	Established 1959. Now has 86 franchised and 6 company owned; 3 in Hawaii Total sales $59 million 16 units planned for 1980	Initial fee $25,000 over 70 seats, $25,000 under 70 seats	
Country Style Donuts Ltd.	Established 1962. 66 franchised, 4 company owned, 4 in U.S., Alta. 5, Sask. 1, Man. 3, Ont. 55, Que. 5, N.S. 1 Total sales $15 million 14 new units planned for Alta., Ont., & Sask. Menu includes coffee & donuts	Initial fee $85,000 ($2,500 deposit, $27,500 for construction, $50,000 equipment contract, $5,000 inventory) Royalty fee 4.5% of gross 2% advertising fee	Turnkey operation 4-week training course Supervisory assistance on opening 20-year franchise term

EXHIBIT 8: Estimated Capital Requirements of Additional Stores

Mmmuffins

Equipment package	$15,000
General construction (including fixtures and leasehold improvements)	40,000–60,000
Opening supplies and inventories	5,000
Miscellaneous (design, insurance, permits, pre-opening salaries, opening promotion, landlord chargebacks, working capital)	10,000
	$70,000–$90,000*

Michel's Baguette

Equipment package	$145,000
General construction (including fixtures and leasehold improvements)	170,000–235,000
Furniture and supplies	35,000–45,000
Miscellaneous (working capital, design, permits, opening promotion, pre-opening salaries, and advance rent)	20,000–40,000
	$370,000–$465,000*

* These are stand-alone estimates. If franchised, any franchise fee would be an additional requirement.

AN OFFER OF LOCATIONS

To help learn about possible locations that might be available, Michael began talking with major Canadian development companies. One important firm was Real Estate Canada (REC) which developed and controlled a large number of shopping malls across Canada. After preliminary discussions, REC offered Michael locations for Mmmuffins stores in one new mall and one mall expansion, both in Toronto suburbs. This was an important developer and Michael felt the locations would be good for Mmmuffins, so he agreed and they shook hands on the deal.

Later, while lawyers were completing the legal paper work, things changed. REC came back and said they wanted to include another location in Manitoba in central Canada in the agreement:

> They said they were creating a package for me: the two Toronto locations and Manitoba in the west or nothing. And being the naive kid that I was, I got extremely upset. But we had a deal! I'd already told my partner about my plans for Toronto and that was OK, but the town in Manitoba had only about 50,000 people and was a thousand miles away. It was a rural environment and difficult to reach.
>
> So I told them that we were just a young chain, and we just wanted to do a few stores at a time. They said no, that's the way it has to be. They had a brand new mall and needed to fill the space.

In the excitement of the offer of the initial two locations, Michael

EXHIBIT 9

MICHAEL BREGMAN
Estimated Earnings Potentials
Mmmuffins Potential Annual Cash Flow*
(350 sq. ft. mall location)

	Weekly sales					
	$3,000		**$4,000**		**$5,000**	
	Dollars	**Percent**	**Dollars**	**Percent**	**Dollars**	**Percent**
Annual sales	156,000		208,000		260,000	
Food cost (1)	48,360	31.0	62,400	30.0	78,000	30.0
Selling supplies	7,020	4.5	9,360	4.5	11,700	4.5
Labor (including benefits) (2)	31,200	20.0	37,440	18.0	41,600	16.0
Gross operating profit	69,420	44.5	98,800	47.5	128,700	49.5
Operating expenses:						
Royalties	9,360	6.0	12,480	6.0	15,600	6.0
Telephone	500	.3	500	.2	500	.2
Utilities	3,500	2.2	3,800	1.8	4,000	1.5
Uniforms and laundry	600	.4	600	.3	650	.3
Advertising	3,120	2.0	4,160	2.0	5,200	2.0
Repairs and maintenance	800	.5	800	.4	800	.3
Insurance	900	.6	900	.4	900	.3
Total occupancy (rent) (3)	16,800	10.8	17,500	8.4	21,000	8.1
Depreciation and amortization (4)	7,000	4.5	7,000	3.4	7,000	2.7
Miscellaneous (5)	1,560	1.0	2,080	1.0	2,600	1.0
Total operating expenses	44,140	28.3	49,820	24.0	58,250	22.4
Earnings before interest and tax (6)	25,280	16.2	48,980	23.5	70,450	27.1
Add: Depreciation and amortization (7)	7,000	4.5	7,000	3.4	7,000	2.7
Cash flow before interest, tax, and franchise compensation	$32,280	20.7%	$55,980	26.9%	$77,450	29.8%

* Post start-up; no operator/franchisee compensation is included.

EXHIBIT 9 (*continued*)

Notes to Mmmuffins Cash Flow Projections:

(1) Based on prices of 60–65¢ per muffin, $3.45 for six, and 40¢ per cup of coffee.

(2) Based on 70-hour weekly selling period with hourly wages of $3.75–$4.75 for baking staff, $3.50–$4.00 for full-time selling staff, and $3.00–$3.50 for part-time staff. Owner-operator's compensation is not included.

(3) Total occupancy includes all services for which landlord invoices: rent, merchants association fees, common area charges, HVAC, realty taxes, etc. Total occupancy may vary depending on location. We have assumed base rent of $40 per square foot for a 350 square foot store or 7 percent of sales (whichever is greater) plus $8 per square foot in "extras."

(4) Depreciation and amortization is calculated by applying the straight-line method on $70,000 over 10 years.

(5) Miscellaneous expense may include cash shortages, licenses and permits, office supplies, professional fees, etc.

(6) Earnings before interest, tax, and franchisee's compensation are expressed as such due to wide variances in compensations paid, amount of debt to service, individual's accounting treatment of expenses, etc.

(7) Depreciation, being a noncash expense, is added back to illustrate total cash generated before interest, tax, and franchisee compensation.

EXHIBIT 9 (*continued*)

Baguette Potential Annual Cash Flow*
(3,000 sq. ft. mall location)

Weekly Sales

	$14,000		$18,000		$22,000	
	Dollars	**Percent**	**Dollars**	**Percent**	**Dollars**	**Percent**
Annual sales	728,000		936,000		1,144,000	
Food cost	232,960	32.0	299,520	32.0	354,640	31.0
Selling supplies	21,840	3.0	28,080	3.0	34,320	3.0
Labor (including benefits) (1)	203,840	28.0	243,360	26.0	286,000	25.0
Gross operating profit	269,360	37.0	365,040	39.0	469,040	41.0
Operating expenses:						
Royalties	43,680	6.0	56,160	6.0	68,640	6.0
Utilities (2)	14,000	1.9	15,000	1.6	17,000	1.5
Telephone	700	.1	700	.1	700	.1
Uniforms and laundry	2,200	.3	2,600	.3	3,000	.3
Advertising (3)	7,280	1.0	9,360	1.0	11,500	1.0
Repairs and maintenance (4)	5,000	.7	6,000	.6	7,000	.6
Replacements (5)	3,500	.5	4,500	.5	5,500	.5
Insurance	3,000	.4	3,000	.3	3,000	.3
Total occupancy (rent) (6)	75,000	10.3	77,000	8.2	89,500	7.8
Depreciation (7)	30,000	4.1	30,000	3.2	30,000	2.6
Miscellaneous (8)	7,280	1.0	9,360	1.0	11,500	1.0
Total operating expenses	191,640	26.3	213,680	22.8	247,340	21.6
Earnings before interest and tax	77,720	10.7	151,360	16.2	221,700	19.4
Add: Depreciation (9)	30,000	4.1	30,000	3.2	30,000	2.6
Cash flow before interest, tax, and franchisee compensation	$107,720	14.8%	$181,360	19.4%	$251,700	22.0%

* After 6-month start-up period; no operator/franchisee compensation is included.

EXHIBIT 9 (concluded)

Notes to Baguette Cash Flow Projections:

(1) Based on 70-hour weekly selling period with hourly wages of $4.00–$5.00 for baking staff, $3.50–$4.50 for full-time service, food preparation, and bussing staff and $3.25–$3.75 for part-time staff. Management salaries included: assistant store manager at $14,500 per year, head baker at $15,600 per year. Owner-operator's salary is not included.

(2) Based on actual experience in Toronto store. Utility expenses may vary widely depending on location, use of gas vs. electric oven, hours of operation, etc.

(3) 1 percent allocation is for local advertising and promotion. At this time the franchisor does not maintain a national advertising fund.

(4) As most equipment is under warranty, first-year repair expenses should be lower than projections. Actual cost in future years will vary considerably due to periodic breakdowns, preventive maintenance program, use of equipment, etc.

(5) Replacements include costs of replenishing supplies of utensils, dishware, cutlery, trays, etc.

(6) Total occupancy includes all services for which landlord invoices: rent, merchants association fees, common area charges, heating, ventilation, and air conditioning, realty taxes, etc. We have assumed a base rent of $18 per square foot for a 3,000 square foot store or 6 percent of sales (whichever is greater) plus $7 per square foot in nonrent "extras." Actual total occupancy costs will vary for each location and should be evaluated individually.

(7) Depreciation is calculated by applying the straight-line method on $360,000 over 12 years.

(8) Miscellaneous expenses may include professional fees, licenses, and permits, cash shortages, office supplies, etc.

(9) Depreciation, being a noncash expense, is added back to illustrate total cash generated before interest, tax, and franchisee's compensation.

had been somewhat swept away with events. Now he was confronted with a more difficult situation than he had anticipated and felt he should pause to rethink his overall company strategy before reacting to this new offer. How should he make his company grow? How fast? How should he divide his efforts between the two concepts? Now he realized he should answer these questions before he went ahead with any expansion deal.

CASE 28

Hewlett-Packard: Challenging the Entrepreneurial Culture

In early 1983, the Hewlett-Packard Company announced the most significant restructuring of its computer organization since the company had entered the information processing business in 1966. This reorganization directly addressed the new demands required for success in the dynamic computer industry. To succeed in the 1980s, companies had to sell integrated hardware and software marketed as packaged solutions to end-user application needs. To achieve this integration various product lines of a firm had to be coordinated. This required an overall strategy to tie the pieces together.

In 1982, Hewlett-Packard was made up of more than 45 product divisions, with 22 directly related to computers. The organization was highly decentralized with the divisions operating much like independent businesses. While fostering a healthy entrepreneurial culture with small-business flexibility, the organization appeared to be inconsistent with the need for overall coordination. This autonomy had resulted in some overlapping products. Customers complained about products developed in one HP division not being compatible with products from other divisions. The company's position in one of the most critical markets, personal computers, was threatened by a lack of cohesive effort between three geographically separated divisions. Each was individually engaged in the design, manufacture, and marketing of personal computers.

A December 1982 *Business Week* cover story discussed these problems concerning HP's computer strategy. The article described some of the company's attempts to achieve the overall coordination of its 22 information processing divisions. Included were a computer strategy council comprised of that business's top management, an experimental "program management" style to provide unified direction on cross-divisional projects, and improved planning through a number of task forces and committees. There had been some very positive outcomes from these efforts recently. *Business Week* reported concern however, particularly from former HP employees now in their own ventures, that these coordinating activities might damage HP's entrepreneurial spirit.

Further, the article suggested these changes might not be sufficient to resolve the company's problems in computers. It indicated that fundamental changes in HP's organizational structure might be needed. The reorganization which soon followed this article had two major purposes. These were included in a letter from Paul C. Ely Jr., executive vice president for computers, to the company's top 150 customers:

> 1. Unify our development and manufacturing activities in three strategic centers; system processors, personal computers and networks. This will increase Hewlett-Packard leverage and efficiency in striving for innovative leadership and will provide a more cohesive product offering for customers.
> 2. Combine the marketing of all HP computers in a single organization to improve our effectiveness in interacting with our customers.

Now the possibility of a deteriorating entrepreneurial culture seemed even more likely. Would tighter control systems and other bureaucratic procedures be the next step for HP? Would employee turnover, then a relatively low 5–10 percent, significantly increase? Or would HP's unique personnel practices and powerful culture be able to absorb these changes without losing the entrepreneurial spirit so essential to its success?

BACKGROUND

In 1939 Bill Hewlett and Dave Packard set up shop in a one-car garage. Their first product was a new type of audio oscillator used to test sound equipment. By 1982, sales of the Hewlett-Packard Company were $4.25 billion from a line of more than 5,000 products. HP's products for the first 20 years were primarily electronic test and measuring instruments for engineers and scientists. Since then, HP had added computers, calculators, medical electronic equipment, instrumentation for chemical analysis, and solid-state components. In 1982, sales had grown at a compounded annual rate of 24.3 percent over the previous 10 years, while earnings had increased tenfold. HP had approximately 68,000 employees worldwide. There were 40 manufacturing locations spread across the U.S. and 10 others around the world. In addition, there were more than 240 sales and service locations. About half of the company's sales were to the U.S. with the rest to other parts of the world. (See Exhibits 1, 2,

EXHIBIT 1

Five-Year Selected Financial Data
For the Years Ended October 31
(in $ millions except per share amounts)

	1982	1981	1980	1979	1978
Domestic orders	$2,283	$1,918	$1,517	$1,280	$ 977
International orders	1,962	1,789	1,623	1,247	898
Total orders	$4,245	$3,707	$3,140	$2,527	$1,875
Net sales	4,254	3,578	3,099	2,361	1,737
Earnings before taxes	676	567	513	391	291
Net earnings	383	305	263	199	150
Per share:					
Net earnings	3.05	2.49	2.19	1.68	1.29
Cash dividends	.24	.22	.20	.17	.12
At year-end:					
Total assets	3,470	2,782	2,350	1,910	1,469
Long-term debt	39	26	29	15	10

Orders ($ millions)

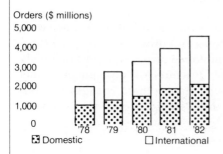

☒ Domestic   ☐ International

Earnings before taxes as a percent of net sales

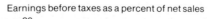
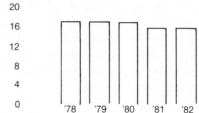

Number of employees at year-end (thousands)

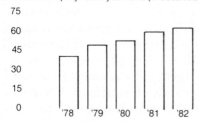

Net sales per employee* ($ thousands)

*Based on average number of employees.

Fiscal years 1978–1981 reflect the restatement for the accrual of compensated absences earned by employees.

Source: Hewlett-Packard Company and subsidiaries annual report, 1982.

EXHIBIT 2

Business Segments

The company operates in four business segments, all of which are engaged in the design and manufacture of precision electronic equipment for measurement, analysis and computation. A brief description of each business segment is given below. In addition, the accompanying tables show financial data for each business segment during the last three years.

Electronic data products consist of the Business Computer, Technical Computer, Computer Peripherals, Computer Terminals, Computer Marketing and Personal Computation Groups. Products include small-to-medium-scale computer systems for business, scientific and industrial applications; desktop, personal and portable computers; personal scientific and business programmable calculators; and computer peripherals. Also included is a wide variety of software and support services.

Electronic test and measurement products consist of the Electronic Measurements, Microwave and Communication Instrument, Instrument Marketing and Components Groups. Products include instruments, systems and components for design, production and maintenance. The prod-

1982 orders by business segment (unaudited) (millions):

Electronic data products $2,218 (52%)

Electronic test and measurement $1,540 (36%)

Medical electronic equipment $315 (8%)

Analytical instrumentation $172 (4%)

(Millions)	1982	1981	1980
Segment sales:			
Electronic data products	$2,212	$1,816	$1,546
Electronic test and measurement	1,606	1,364	1,215
Medical electronic equipment	325	275	230
Analytical instrumentation	177	185	159
	4,320	3,640	3,150
Intersegment sales:			
Electronic data products	(44)	(45)	(36)
Electronic test and measurement	(21)	(15)	(15)
Medical electronic equipment	(1)	(2)	—
	(66)	(62)	(51)
Net sales	$4,254	$3,578	$3,099

EXHIBIT 2 *(concluded)*

(Millions)	1982	1981	1980
Earnings before taxes:			
Electronic data products	370	314	280
Electronic test and measurement.	339	279	267
Medical electronic equipment	60	49	36
Analytical instrumentation	28	31	24
Eliminations and corporate	(121)	(106)	(94)
	$ 676	$ 567	$ 513
Identifiable assets:			
Electronic data products	1,358	1,169	1,000
Electronic test and measurement.	903	817	709
Medical electronic equipment	191	175	146
Analytical instrumentation	104	99	94
Eliminations and corporate	914	522	401
	$3,470	$2,782	$2,350

Fiscal 1981 and 1980 reflect the restatement for the accrual of compensated absences earned by employees.

ucts are primarily used in the communications, electronics manufacturing and aerospace industries.

Medical electronic equipment products perform a number of patient-monitoring, diagnostic, therapeutic, and medical and financial data-management functions for health care providers. Included are measurement and computation systems and a wide variety of software and support services and supplies.

Analytical instrumentation products are used primarily to analyze chemical compounds. Products include gas and liquid chromatographs, mass spectrometers, spectrophotometers, laboratory automation systems and integrators.

Source: Hewlett-Packard Company and subsidiaries annual report, 1982.

EXHIBIT 3: HP Growth by Geographic Area ($ millions)

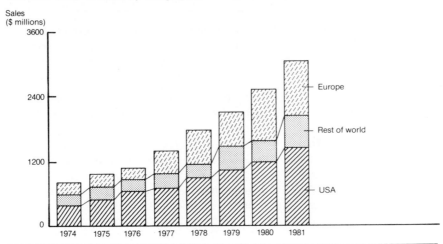

and 3 for five-year selected financial data, and sales by business segments and geographic area.)

During the early years of the company, the founders developed a number of management concepts that evolved into a directing set of corporate objectives. First put into writing in 1957, these objectives remained the most fundamental, active guiding forces at Hewlett-Packard (see Exhibit 4). From these evolved a certain business style, known inside and outside the company as "The HP Way." For a detailed description of the HP Way and the company's human resource practices, see HBS case 9–482–125, *Human Resources At Hewlett-Packard*.

The Move into Computers

The portion of total revenues attributable to computer products increased from 16.8 percent in 1971 to 51 percent in 1982. Exhibit 5 graphically shows HP's expansion into computers between 1971 and 1981. This dramatic shift was especially challenging to HP because of the differences between the instrument and computer businesses. Instruments were essentially stand-alone products, whereas computers required a systems integration. In instruments, HP could rely on its technological superiority to sell customers premium-priced products. Further, customers were often left with the job of tailoring the equipment to their own particular needs. This was acceptable since instrument customers were usually technical people. Those market segments were well defined and HP held the leadership position in most product categories. Information processing markets,

EXHIBIT 4: Excerpts from HP's Statement of Corporate Objectives

---

The achievements of an organization are the result of the combined efforts of each individual in the organization working toward common objectives. These objectives should be clearly understood by everyone in the organization, and should reflect the organization's basic character and personality.

1. PROFIT: To achieve sufficient profit to finance our company growth and to provide the resources we need to achieve our other corporate objectives.

2. CUSTOMERS: To provide products and services of the greatest possible value to our customers, thereby gaining and holding their respect and loyalty.

3. FIELDS OF INTEREST: To enter new fields only when the ideas we have, together with our technical, manufacturing and marketing skills, assure that we can make a needed and profitable contribution to the field.

4. GROWTH: To let our growth be limited only by our profits and our ability to develop and produce technical products that satisfy real customer needs.

5. OUR PEOPLE: To help HP people share in the company's success, which they make possible; to provide job security based on their performance; to recognize their individual achievements; and to help them gain a sense of satisfaction and accomplishment from their work.

6. MANAGEMENT: To foster initiative and creativity by allowing the individual great freedom of action in attaining well-defined objectives.

7. CITIZENSHIP: To honor our obligations to society by being an economic, intellectual and social asset to each nation and each community in which we operate.

---

in contrast, were not as clearly defined and were marked by fierce competition. Computer customers demanded increasingly better performing products at lower prices. They wanted products designed for specific applications that were often ready to use when delivered. These demands required that HP be well in tune with the market, develop products based on customer needs, and strategically position themselves against tough competitors.

The Organization

The product divisions were considered HP's tactical business units, each having responsibility for R&D, manufacturing, marketing, finance, and personnel management of its own products. All sales organizations

EXHIBIT 5: HP Market Diversification and Growth (sales in $ millions by product groups)

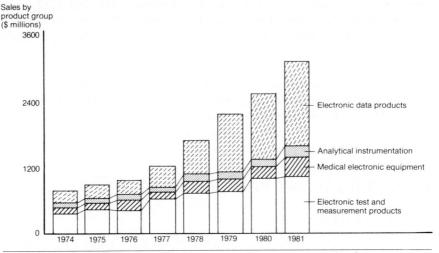

Sales by
product group
($ millions)

Electronic data products

Analytical instrumentation

Medical electronic equipment

Electronic test and
measurement products

reported at the group level (e.g., Computer Group) and were separate from the product divisions. Divisions were kept relatively small (approximately 1,000 people) to allow considerable individual freedom while maintaining a focused business purpose. This decentralization into small work groups provided a great motivation. HP had attempted to preserve a small-business climate while supplying the support of a large company's resources.

As of November 1982, there were over 45 product divisions organized into 12 product groups (see Exhibit 6). Each group was responsible for the overall operations and financial performance of its members. Business strategy was determined at the group level and was heavily dependent on the fundamental corporate objectives discussed earlier. The group strategy then established the short- and long-range objectives for each division via a well-developed management-by-objectives (MBO) system. These broadly stated objectives served as goals, not tactics, which left divisions with substantial freedom in choosing how to accomplish them. Individuals were encouraged to participate in setting overall goals. To ensure that the goals of each group fit with the whole organization, the entire MBO process was part of the annual strategic planning process.

Quality of Management

Much had been written about Hewlett-Packard in the business press, typically praising the firm's commitment to technology, quality, and employee well-being. A January 1983 *Fortune* magazine article presented the results of a "survey of nearly 6,000 executives, outside directors, and financial analysts who were asked to rate the reputations of the ten largest companies in America's twenty largest industries." HP and IBM each received an average score of 8.26 out of 10—higher than any other firm. In the same survey, HP was ranked first in its "ability to attract, develop and keep talented people." These results were largely a reflection of the tremendous influence the HP Way had on the entire organization. Informality, trust, and respect for individual initiative were norms, along with a commitment to teamwork and participative decision making. There was a strict policy of promotion from within, and a strong belief that managers receive exposure to more than one functional area.

HP AND THE DYNAMIC COMPUTER INDUSTRY

Reorganizing for Growth

In 1966, Hewlett-Packard introduced its first "computer," which was designed specifically to work with HP instruments. In fact, it was called an instrumentation computer. Several major reorganizations occurred over the next 14 years in response to HP's growth into computers. The first major restructuring came in 1969, establishing HP's first group structure with a Data Products Group and an Electronic Products Group. Data Products, comprised of just three divisions, was responsible for the design, manufacture, and marketing of computers and computer-related products.

Further growth into several new markets led to a second major regrouping in 1974. The six product categories were: (1) electronic test and measuring instruments, (2) computers and computer-based systems, (3) calculators, (4) solid-state components, (5) medical electronic products, and (6) electronic instrumentation for chemical analysis. These remain HP's basic lines of business today.

After a weak start in 1971 with their initial entrance into business computers, HP reintroduced the HP–3000 minicomputer in 1973. By 1975 this product had firmly established HP as a leading computer manufacturer. In fact, the HP–3000 was a primary contributor to the development of distributed data processing, which expanded computing power beyond the data processing department. By 1976, HP had decided to refocus its computer strategy by separating technical/industrial systems from business/commercial systems. And in 1979, the Computer System Group was reorganized into five groups: (1) Technical Computer, (2) Business Computer, (3) Computer Peripherals, (4) Terminals, and (5) Computer Marketing (see Exhibit 6).

Throughout all these changes in HP's corporate organization, the company remained dedicated to the divisional structure emphasizing decentralized work units. Two unifying forces gave this complex organization common direction and cohesion: shared philosophies (HP Way), and commitment to technological superiority.

Leading Trends in Information Processing[1]

To understand HP's success in the computer business and their future strategy it was necessary to understand the dynamics of this fast-paced industry. After several decades of accelerated growth, the industry was entering an even faster growth period in the early 1980s (see Exhibit 7).

During the 50s and 60s, company data processing was done on huge central mainframes. As processing power needs increased, systems grew through upgrades. In the early 70s, mainframe-attached terminals first gave access to users outside the data center, and then to remote users. This trend was popular throughout the 70s. Complementing this increasing use of terminals on mainframes was the appearance of small, time-sharing minicomputers. This was the beginning of distributed data processing. Hewlett-Packard and the HP–3000 were to become a major force and recognized leader in this movement. By the late 70s this trend had fully evolved.

The next phase of distributed processing would move not only systems, but data bases, out to local departments—such as personnel, marketing, or finance. These systems have data useful for the individuals within that department. By linking the individual systems together in a network, sharing of peer group information would be possible. Finally, there would be links to larger mainframes at regional or corporate headquarters.

Beyond 1985, the dominant industry trend expected was an evolution to include not only these departmental systems, but also networks tied in to individual user work stations. By 1990, there would be entire systems selling for the equivalent of a 1982 $4,000 terminal. And they would include a built-in disc and letter quality printer for word processing. These systems would have the power of a 1980 minicomputer.

The economics of providing information systems had been changing dramatically. The price/performance ratio of hardware had been decreasing at a rate of 20 percent to 30 percent per year, for a given set of capabilities. A change of only 20 percent per year compounded meant that what had cost $1 million in 1970 would be down to $100,000 by 1980, and down to $10,000 by 1990. This trend was mostly the result of large-scale integrated technology. By 1990, there would probably be a mainframe on everyone's desk instead of one for the organization.

The real challenge was what to do about the exploding costs of software, which were primarily a function of people's salaries. System

---

[1] Most of this section was extracted from an HP customer presentation, "Computer Solutions for the '80s."

EXHIBIT 6: Hewlett-Packard Corporate Organization, November 1982

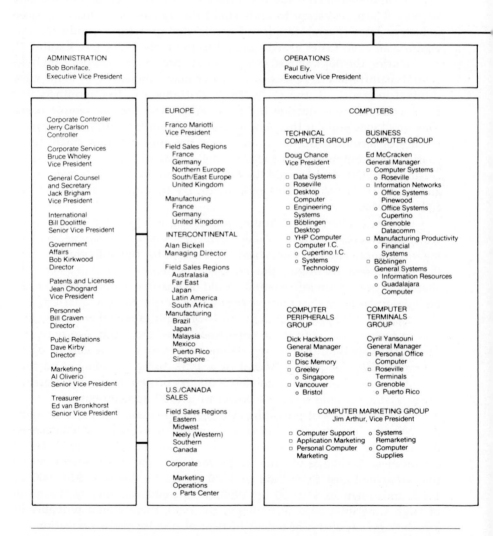

software and application software could cost the user many times more than the hardware they were designed to run on. Yet it would be this software support that would differentiate computer manufacturers as the hardware became continually more standardized.

With the continuing decrease in hardware costs, more industries

EXHIBIT 6 *(concluded)*

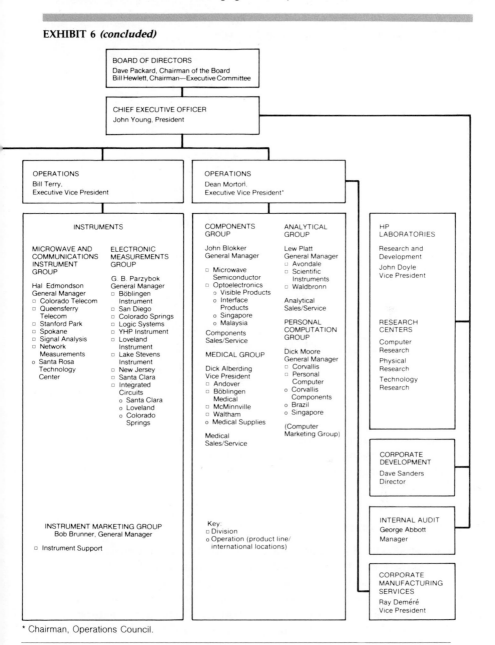

* Chairman, Operations Council.

and application areas were taking advantage of computer technology. As data processing moves from being centralized to being distributed, and beyond, more professional workers would have access to computers. In the 60s, members of the DP profession and accountants were using computers. In the 70s, computer use expanded to include specialists and

EXHIBIT 7: Computer Industry Evolution and Growth

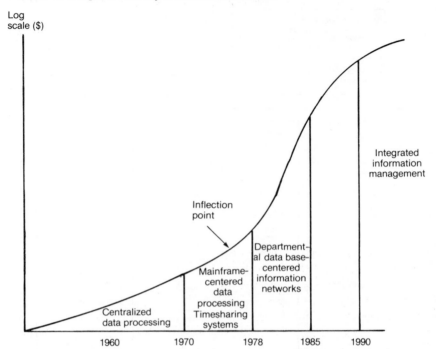

clerks. As the era of integrated information management unfolded, distributed data processing would move toward handling not just data, but information that organizations need in all forms—words, graphics, voice, and video.

HP's Success in Computers

Hewlett-Packard had performed exceedingly well in penetrating the explosive market for small- to medium-sized computers (less than $250 thousand system price). Total 1982 computer products sales for HP were $2.2 billion. Based on 1981 revenues HP had been ranked the seventh largest computer manufacturer in the world (see Exhibit 8). In terms of growth rate, only HP and DEC had grown at more than 30 percent per year between 1978 and 1981.

Having been the pioneer system in the market for interactive business systems for on-line processing, the HP–3000 remained the leader in 1983 with 12,000 systems installed worldwide (as of May 1983). A 1982 survey of minicomputer users, conducted by Datapro Research Corp.,

EXHIBIT 8: World Computer Industry's Top Ten ($ millions)

		1981 Revenues	**3-Year Growth**
1.	IBM	$25,111	14%
2.	DEC	3,586	31
3.	CDC	3,131	19
4.	BURROUGHS.	2,934	11
5.	NCR	2,838	14
6.	SPERRY	2,718	12
7.	HP	1,875	34
8.	FUJITSU	1,811	9
9.	HIS	1,774	11
10.	ICL LTD.	1,487	16
Total.	. . . .	$47,265	14%

Note: Data adjusted for calendar year.

Source: Compiled from The Gartner Group, *Top 100 Almanac*, p. 15 (information processing related revenues).

attested to HP's ability to satisfy its customers. When asked if they would recommend the HP–3000, 95 percent of HP–3000 users said "yes."

HP's ability to manage such phenomenal growth and maintain a healthy working environment was acknowledged in the *Fortune* survey cited earlier. That environment had fostered innovativeness (HP ranked third in survey) which had allowed the continued development of technically outstanding products. An example was the HP–9000, introduced in 1982, which had the power of a mainframe in a desktop unit. Some considered it the ultimate personal computer for scientists and engineers. The HP–9000 incorporated HP's new integrated-circuit technology, which allowed up to 600,000 transistors to be put onto a single quarter-inch silicon chip.

Strategy behind the Success

There had been five basic components to HP's computer strategy:[2]

1. Build high-quality interactive computers ranging from personal to medium-size, multiterminal systems.

2. Provide data base management systems linked in networks.

3. Provide graphics capabilities across all products.

4. Aid personal productivity through application development, office systems, engineering, and decision support systems.

5. Sell user-friendly systems that inexperienced users will find easy to use.

_____
[2] Ibid.

Hewlett-Packard management had always placed great emphasis on product development programs, which they considered a fundamental strength of the company. The 1982 R&D budget was $424 million, representing 10 percent of sales. An indication of the importance of this effort was the fact that more than half of 1982's orders came from products introduced during the prior three years.

Just as the internal management of HP was dictated by the HP Way, there was an "HP Way of Doing Business" that provided guidelines for running the company.[3] First, HP maintained a pay-as-you-go attitude. This meant they had no long-term borrowing which helped maintain a stable financial environment during depressed business periods. Second, any market expansion or leadership was based on new product contributions. Engineering excellence determined market recognition of new products. HP expanded into new markets only with innovative new product ideas. Next was the goal of providing superior customer satisfaction. HP products were thoroughly designed, tested, and specified before being brought to market. The company's extensive sales/support organization provided consulting, training, hardware and software support. Finally, honesty and integrity in all matters was a guiding principle for HP employees. There was no tolerance for dishonest dealings with vendors or customers.

Hewlett-Packard's Future Strategy

Over the next five years, HP intended to become a worldwide leader in providing integrated information solutions for medium to large companies. The strategy to achieve this objective was fourfold:[4]

1. Provide leadership in application development products which improve productivity in software development and maintenance.
2. Increase the productivity of HP computer users by providing easy-to-use, customizable application software.
3. Continue to build upon the leadership in networked, interactive data base systems which are software compatible and have integrated network resources.
4. Provide friendly and easy-to-use access to all forms and types of information: words, data, graphics.

In addition to an outstanding sales/support organization and commitment to R&D, HP management believed the company had three other competitive advantages to help achieve its goals. First, HP was developing high-volume, low-cost manufacturing capabilities. Many of those state-

---

[3] Ibid.
[4] Ibid.

of-the-art capabilities could be transferred to HP's manufacturing customers as an added selling point. Second, HP produced nearly $200 million worth of integrated circuits for internal consumption. Second only to IBM, this captive production was several times larger than any other competitor. Last, and probably most important, HP had long provided computer systems for both technical and business applications. Both would be needed to meet the integrated processing needs of manufacturers. DEC, HP's leading competitor in technical computers, had a limited business computer offering and didn't even have a commercial user sales force. IBM, traditionally a business computer supplier, had substantially less to offer engineering and scientific markets than did HP.

Computer Industry Projections

HP management believed that by 1990 most large companies would standardize on two or three computer suppliers. They felt IBM would probably be one of those suppliers with their tremendous installed base. In support of this projection, a study by an independent market research firm indicated that only four computer firms would exceed $5 billion in sales by 1985 (see Exhibit 9). The study also suggested that HP would maintain the fastest growth rate, nearly 30 percent per year between 1980 and 1985.

To survive the expected industry shakeout, companies would have to position themselves to respond to new market demands as they evolved. This was exactly what Japanese computer manufacturers had been doing for several years. An HP vice president believed that the two facets of the Japanese plan were:

1. Shorten R&D cycles in bringing new products to market. They intend to innovate by utilizing existing technology in creative ways, rather than depending on new inventions. This is much the same strategy the Japanese have used in penetrating, and often dominating, a number of U.S. industries, including automobiles, steel, and color television sets.
2. Listen better to customers to understand their application needs. Combined with shorter R&D cycles the Japanese will be able to quickly respond to, and often predict, customers' needs. Utilizing their skills in low-cost high-quality manufacturing, Japanese computer firms are in a strong position to be among the future industry leaders.

Regardless of which companies survived the shakeout, future winners in the computer industry would be compatible with each other, i.e. their products would be able to communicate with each other through a common network. In 1982, no standard network had been determined by the industry. Nonetheless, since IBM would likely be a winner, a key to success would be to develop systems compatible with IBM. But IBM had not yet announced what network they would standardize on.

EXHIBIT 9: Growth Rate, 1980–1985 ($ millions)

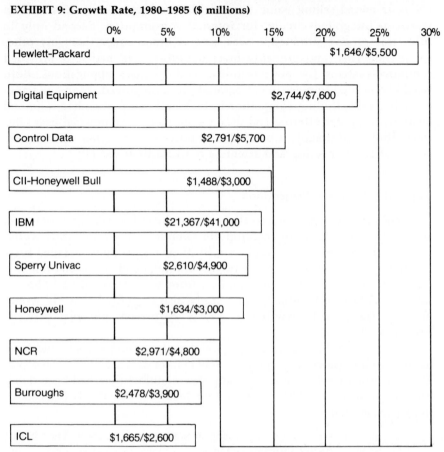

Source: Compiled from Martin Simpson & Co., *Hewlett-Packard: Future Growth in the Minicomputer and Instrumentation Market.*

Thus, a company's selection of a network would have far-reaching implications for their future product strategy.

The New Market Demands

HP's 1977 strategy to separate technical computer from business computer efforts had worked well. Focusing development and marketing on each market individually had positioned HP as a strong player in both. But the 1980s were revealing a new era in information processing. HP's 1983 reorganization was an attempt to confront these changes, which could be summarized as:

1. Dramatic decreases in the cost of hardware are bringing computing power to the desks of every worker. Personal work stations will become as common as the telephone.

2. With productivity improvements increasingly dependent on business information and operating data, the ability of various users to share information requires communication networks. Technical standards for these networks must be developed to allow computers from different manufacturers to be linked, as well as allowing different computers from a single vendor to communicate.

3. Computer customers want solutions to their problems, not just an assortment of hardware and software tools. This demands a shift to vertical marketing to specific industries. Success depends on selling systems supported with solutions-oriented application software. Winners in the new computer business will be as much market-driven as they are engineering-driven.

4. As more people throughout an organization begin using computers there is a need for easy-to-use systems requiring little or no training. This demands the continued development and improvement of user-friendly software.

5. Rapidly developing hardware technology, combined with intense competition, is producing more powerful products at lower prices. These conditions are likely to make computers, particularly personal computers, a commodity item differentiated only by marketing expertise and application software.

Meeting the Challenge

HP had taken several significant steps to confront the new market demands. These actions were attempted to improve overall planning for HP's computer business, and to better coordinate development and marketing across divisions.

Manufacturer's Productivity Network (MPN). A major outcome of the council's effort was an applications-oriented marketing strategy called MPN. Introduced in 1981, MPN addressed the four key manufacturing areas of planning and control, factory automation, office systems, and engineering (see Exhibit 10). Built around HP's business and technical computers, as well as some of its electronic instruments, MPN would allow companies to link computer applications and resources throughout their organization. Departmental sharing of information could improve asset utilization, labor productivity, management information, and quality. The MPN framework would help direct HP's product development efforts as HP attempted to provide most of a customer's information processing

EXHIBIT 10: The HP Manufacturer's Productivity Network

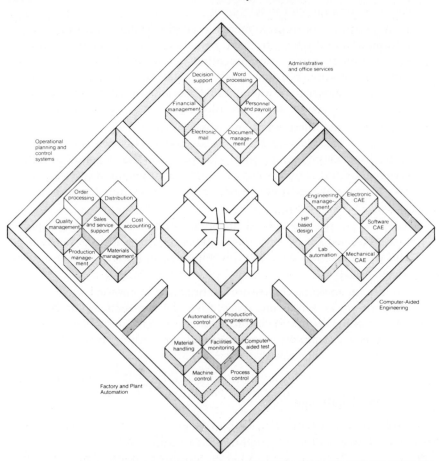

needs. Communication networks would tie together the various pieces of equipment from the many divisions. HP chose to target manufacturers because 40 percent of their computer sales had come from that market.

Program Management. The complexity of computer systems required a coordinated team approach. For example, a printer developed in one HP division had to be compatible with the operating system developed in another division. Also, they both had to be ready for market introduction at the same time. Program management assigned a single "program manager" responsibility for the overall management of such a project. Also, the manager was given authority to utilize the resources from the many divisions involved. In this way, a coordinated development and marketing plan could be executed.

This experimental management process was first used in creating the HP–9000. The HP–9000 was HP's first 32-bit[5] computer system and was a highly integrated product requiring closely coupled joint effort on the part of 10 different HP divisions to complete. The project was begun in 1976, and in 1981 a program manager was assigned overall responsibility and authority for the project across the many HP divisions involved. Less than two years later, the program produced the HP–9000 family.

Applications Marketing Division (AMD).   HP's first applications division, AMD, began work in November 1982 to provide sales support in delivering application software to customers. This was to be implemented through Area Application Centers that were being set up in HP's 17 North American sales offices. The centers were being staffed with specialists from other industries to act as consultants. Customers would be helped in selecting, and later implementing, computer systems for their particular application needs. The software packages, many of which HP had already developed, would come from several new divisions dedicated to specific markets. For example, the Manufacturing Productivity Division was developing software for manufacturing planning and control, materials, management, process control, and quality control.

Task Forces and Committees.   HP utilized a large number of task forces and committees to accomplish specific projects and to discuss issues that involved several divisions. Task forces were temporary assignments with a specified deadline. The task force typically consisted of 5 to 10 people often from different functions and levels within HP. Included were the people most affected by the particular project. Two examples of task force assignments were preparing for a new product introduction, and producing a teleconference for training salespeople.

Committees, or councils, were ongoing teams concerned with issues impacting either a single part of the company or the whole organization. An example, besides the Computer Strategy Council, was HP's fabrication shop committee. Composed of about six fabrication shop managers from throughout HP, the group discussed long-term plans, shared information, and determined job classifications. The task forces and committees were successful largely because the HP culture encouraged teamwork and open communication.

---

[5] 32-bit processing allows additional speed and accuracy. Previously, most computers were 8- or 16-bit machines.

THE REORGANIZATION

The *Business Week* article previously mentioned had suggested that these actions taken by HP would not be sufficient. One computer industry expert claimed HP was "a classic case of the engineering-driven company confronting a marketing-driven world and that they should restructure to acknowledge that."

Phase I

The lack of coordination between HP's three separate divisions selling personal computers had been the most obvious problem. Delays in introducing new products and confusion among customers had hurt HP's competitive position in that market.

In January 1983 HP announced the consolidation of the Personal Computation Group and the Computer Terminals Group. The new group, the Personal Computer Group, would be responsible for developing and manufacturing personal computers, terminals, personal computer peripherals, and other personal computation products such as calculators. This change provided for the first time a cohesive overall strategy for HP's personal computer efforts. Decisions about marketing and R&D could now be made at the group level by a single manager. Before the reorganization, the only common manager for the separated divisions had been the company president.

Phase II

In a February 1983 news release, HP announced a realignment of its computer products organization (see Exhibit 11). This realignment would:

a. provide an improved strategic focus, and
b. strengthen channels of customer interaction.

The reorganization did not alter the top management people in HP's computer business. Only the specific group names and some responsibilities were changed (e.g., the Business Computer Group general manager had become head of the Business Development Group).

Dataquest, Inc., a high-technology market research organization, summarized the reorganization in a February 1983 newsletter.

> Hewlett-Packard's January 13 and February 2 announcements constitute the Company's most fundamental reorganization since it started divisionalizing in the late 1950s. However, whereas previous group structures were merely a collection of more or less related divisions, HP's new structure for its computer operations divides the divisions in much the same way a single computer would be developed and marketed. The new structure in-

cludes a group of CPUs and operation software, a group for peripherals, and data communications, a group for terminals and personal computers, a group for factory marketing, and a group for field marketing. This reorganization directly addresses the problems of overlapping products and piecemeal approaches to markets.

In some ways it follows IBM's restructuring in October of 1981, in that it provides for single sales interface with the customer and common development and manufacturing for all common products. However, the groups for developing vertical markets and personal workstations, which HP added, recognize important new directions in the computer industry.[6]

Paul Ely, head of all HP computer operations said:

The changes reflect a broad-based effort to stay ahead of sweeping changes in the computer marketplace of the 80s. Coupled with the consolidation earlier this year of our personal-computation activities, these latest adjustments will further streamline HP's computer operations and should reinforce our position of innovative leadership among major computer suppliers.

The most undefined of HP's five new computer groups (see Exhibit 11) was the Business Development Group (BDG). Yet BDG probably would play a primary role in executing HP's strategic plan to sell "integrated system solutions." In acknowledging the new market-driven computer world, BDG was responsibile for the strategic marketing and business-development activities for all HP computer products. This would involve generating three-year business plans to position HP in three key markets: computer-integrated manufacturing, office automation/personal computers, and commercial data processing. These plans would be developed in conjunction with the divisions involved in the particular market. For example, the business development manager for commercial data processing would head a council comprised of marketing managers from the divisions involved in data processing. Overlaying these broader markets would be a number of vertical market specialists who would target specific industries with application software. Additionally, the merchandising activities of advertising, promotion, direct mail, and other marketing programs would be centralized in BDG. This would allow for coordinated selling campaigns aimed at the markets selected by the business development councils.

Another significant change that would be part of BDG was the creation of two sales centers, in California and in Germany. The sales centers would consolidate into a single location all the sales development activities previously conducted in each individual division. The primary role of sales development was to support and help motivate the sales force. Sales development provided the interface between the product divisions and the sales force. In the past, when sales representatives or HP

---

[6] Dataquest, Inc., *Newsletter,* February 1983. Reproduced by permission.

EXHIBIT 11: Hewlett-Packard Corporate Organization, June 1983

BOARD OF DIRECTORS   Dave Packard, Chairman   Bill Hewlett, Vice Chairman

CHIEF EXECUTIVE OFFICER   John Young, President*

ADMINISTRATION	OPERATIONS
Bob Boniface, Executive Vice President	Bill Terry, Executive Vice President

CORPORATE STAFF

Corporate Controller
Jerry Carlson
Controller

Corporate Services
Bruce Wholey
Vice President

General Counsel
and Secretary
Jack Brigham
Vice President

International
Dick Alberding
Senior Vice President

Government
Affairs
Bob Kirkwood
Director

Public Relations
Dave Kirby
Director

Patents and Licenses
Jean Chognard
Vice President

Personnel
Bill Craven
Director

Marketing
Al Oliverio
Senior Vice President

Treasurer
Ed van Bronkhorst
Senior Vice President

EUROPE

Franco Mariotti
Vice President

Field Sales Regions
France
Germany
Northern Europe
South/East
Europe
United Kingdom

Manufacturing
France
Germany
United Kingdom

Manufacturing
France
Germany
United Kingdom

INTERCONTINENTAL

Alan Bickell
Managing Director

Field Sales Regions
Australasia
Far East
Japan
Latin America
South Africa

Manufacturing
Brazil
Canada
Japan
Malaysia
Mexico
Puerto Rico
Singapore

U.S./CANADA SALES

Field Sales Regions
Eastern
Midwest
Neely (Western)
Southern
Canada

Corporate

Marketing Operations
o Parts Center

INSTRUMENTS

ELECTRONIC MEASUREMENTS GROUP

Bill Parzybok, General Manager
□ Böblingen Instrument
□ San Diego
□ Colorado Springs
□ Logic Systems
□ Santa Clara
□ YHP Instrument
□ Loveland Instrument
□ Lake Stevens Instrument
□ New Jersey
□ Integrated Circuits
  o Santa Clara
  o Loveland
  o Colorado Springs

MICROWAVE AND COMMUNICATIONS INSTRUMENT GROUP

Dick Anderson, General Manager
□ Colorado Telecom
□ Queensferry Telecom
□ Stanford Park
□ Spokane
□ Signal Analysis
□ Network Measurements
o Santa Rosa Technology Center

INSTRUMENT MARKETING GROUP

Bob Brunner, General Manager
Sales: N. America/Europe/Intercon.
□ Instrument Support

* Chairman, Executive Committee.
† Chairman, Management Council.

Paul Ely,
Executive Vice President

Dean Morton,
Executive Vice President†

HP LABORATORIES

John Doyle
Vice President

Research and
Development

Research Centers

Computer Researc

Physical Research

Technology Research

COMPUTERS

COMPUTER PRODUCTS GROUP

Doug Chance, Vice President
□ Data Systems
□ Computer Systems
  o CSY/Roseville
□ Ft. Collins Systems
□ Engineering Productivity
□ YHP Computer
□ Computer I.C.
  o Cupertino I.C.
  o Systems Technology
  o Corvallis Components
□ Böblingen Computer Products

PERSONAL COMPUTER GROUP

Cyril Yansouni, General Manager
□ Roseville Terminals
□ Portable Terminals
□ Grenoble Personal Computer
□ Personal Office Computer
□ Vancouver
□ Personal Software
  o Puerto Rico
  o Singapore
  o Brazil

INFORMATION PRODUCTS GROUP

Dick Hackborn, Vice President
□ Boise
□ Disc Memory
□ Greeley
o Computer Peripherals Bristol
□ Roseville Networks
□ Information Networks
  o Colorado Networks
  o Grenoble Networks

BUSINESS DEVELOPMENT GROUP

Ed McCracken, General Manager
  Systems Marketing Center
  Business Development Center
  Business Development Europe
o Information Resources
o Systems Re-Marketing
o Guadalajara Computer
□ Manufacturing Productivity
□ Application Marketing
□ Office Productivity

COMPUTER MARKETING GROUP

Jim Arthur, Vice President
Sales: N. America/Europe/Intercon.
□ Computer Support
□ Application Marketing
  o Computer Supplies

MEDICAL

MEDICAL GROUP

Ben Holmes, General Manager
□ Andover
□ Böblingen Medical
□ McMinnville
□ Waltham
  o Bedside Terminals
  o Medical Systems
  o Medical Supplies

ANALYTICAL

ANALYTICAL GROUP
Lew Platt, Vice President
□ Avondale
□ Scientific Instruments
□ Waldbronn

COMPONENTS

COMPONENTS GROUP

John Blokker, General Manager
□ Microwave Semiconductor
□ Optoelectronics
  o Visible Products
  o Interface Products
  o Singapore
  o Malaysia

CORPORATE MANUFACTURING

Hal Edmondson
Vice President

Key:
□ Division
o Operation

CORPORATE DEVELOPMENT

Dave Sanders
Director

INTERNAL AUDIT
George Abbott
Manager

EXHIBIT 11 *(concluded)*

HP's Five Computer Groups after the 1983 Reorganization:

Computer Products Group, with responsibility for the development and manufacture of central processing units, operating software, languages, and very large-scale integrated circuitry (VLSI). General manager is Douglas C. Chance, HP vice president.

Information Products Group, with responsibility for the development and manufacture of system peripherals, data-communications products, data base resources, print centers, and the software to combine these with systems and work stations to form information networks. General manager is Richard A. Hackborn.

Personal Computer Group, with responsibility for the development and manufacture of work stations (terminals), personal computers, and other personal-computation products. General manager is Cyril J. Yansouni.

Business Development Group, with responsibility for market development and merchandising of HP systems, work stations, networks, and applications software as a set of solution systems for each of HP's major markets. General manager is Edward R. McCracken.

Computer Marketing Group, with responsibility for sales, field marketing, maintenance services, and application support for all HP computer products in all markets. General manager is James L. Arthur, HP vice president.

customers wanted information they were often forced to deal with several sales development groups. With the change, the sales centers would serve as the sole interface facilitating the search for information. HP had termed it "one-stop shopping."

Impact of the Reorganization

Reorganizations were not new to HP employees. Growth of 24 percent per year since 1972 and movement into new markets had forced a series of organizational changes. HP's flexibility in adapting to new competitive environments revealed an evolutionary process of change that people had learned to accept. To a large extent this acceptance was based on a faith in the judgment of top management. (Note: All of the remaining quotes were extracted from the casewriter's personal interviews with HP managers.)

> Anytime there is a reorganization at HP, people here know it's the right thing to do. They may be unsure about exactly what will happen, but there is a real belief that management takes actions in the best interests of the organization and the people. Management organizes the company in a way that allows problems to be turned over to someone at lower levels. [A division marketing manager]

*   *   *   *   *

There is tremendous trust and faith in management's actions. We know there are enough bright people around who will say something before a decision is final. People are encouraged to do so. This check-and-balance system works because there is trust and open communication. [An operations manager]

This open communication policy could be seen at all levels in the company.

The top managers of the computer groups [computer strategy council] have been discussing a reorganization of this magnitude for some time. I proposed a structure similar to this one about two years ago to John Young [HP president] and Paul Ely. Although John and Paul agreed such a change was needed, they felt the organization, i.e., the people, was not ready for such a change. We were able to rationally discuss some rather sensitive issues because of a stable environment and mutual trust that exist at HP.

We could have forced the restructuring earlier. Instead we chose to allow the organization to go through its own osmosis in coming to accept that such changes were needed. We may have waited a couple years but I believe it would have taken just as long for people to absorb something forced on them, if ever. People are more committed when they come to the conclusion on their own. This osmosis process is much like Japanese consensus management. [A group vice president]

The Need to Change

HP was very much aware of the changing computer market and what it would take to succeed. And HP believed they were well prepared for the challenge. Their emphasis was on marketing.

Until now HP has tried to manage its computer business much like it has run the instruments business—with decentralized divisions selling stand-alone products based on technological superiority. The computer marketing managers, division managers, and group managers, all knew HP had to become more marketing-oriented. But the organization structure didn't allow for it, at least not executionally.

HP is conservative in its marketing. We tend to understate our strengths by underspecifying product capabilities and not being aggressive enough in promoting products. It's a very tough competitive market. Over the last five years I think we've become more marketing-driven, but we need to expand our market profile. [A marketing manager]

* * * * *

Computer customers today want to buy three things: (1) a relationship with a supplier that is professional, cooperative, and enduring; (2) the ability to integrate different vendors' equipment via communication networks; and (3) solutions to specific problems.

I believe HP's top management team is more end-user oriented than either IBM or DEC top management. What we had to do was reorganize so people at lower levels could participate in this marketing push. [A group general manager]

The need to change was nowhere more evident than in HP's personal computer effort.

With three independent divisions working on personal computers there was no well-defined strategy. Products overlapped and distribution channels were not standardized. This internal competition, while providing benefits up to a point, resulted in an inefficient use of the company's resources.

The high priority placed on this business made the personal computer group reorganization an important driving force behind the subsequent restructuring in February. Nonetheless, the personal computer regrouping was most obvious and could have been done independently of the major restructuring. [A division marketing manager]

Reactions to the Reorganization

While agreeing that a change was needed, not all HP managers and employees were sure how the reorganization would work.

The new structure is a departure from the past. Everyone agrees it is the right thing to do but people are asking how it will work. I believe the change is very important to our success in computers in the 80s. We've had problems with overlapping and incompatible products. For example, several different divisions have been working on their own compiler for the FORTRAN computer language. This work in languages will now be centralized. This will give more freedom to divisions to work on new ideas and to be creative and entrepreneurial. And that leads to a better allocation of resources.

We are investing heavily to build bridges between divisions. A key task will be to define the interface rules. Basically, these rules are the technical standards for integrating the various pieces of a computer. Once these rules are established divisions will be free to develop their piece in the way they choose. HP's MBO management style will help determine the overall division objectives while still allowing them freedom. Often freedom and anarchy are not far apart. I don't think any organization can succeed with absolute freedom. That only exists in academic research. [A division general manager]

*   *   *   *   *

The computer organization that began in the mid-70s to give separate focus to technical and business computers worked well for us until 1980. But that structure no longer works given today's market pressures for integrated applications. Now each division needs its own strategy, or charter, that fits into the overall corporate strategy. This overall strategy will be determined at the group level. Division general managers will develop objectives for their particular product lines within that strategy. And the manufacturing, lab, and marketing people will execute the tasks for achieving the divisions' objectives. This approach fits very well with HP's MBO process.

I think HP now has the best organization structure to effectively compete in the computer business. We have to maintain the divisional structure, but the divisions should each have a charter.

The acid test will be the reactions of our customers to the new organization. Customers must be able to understand the HP structure. In the past they didn't know who in the company did what and what product was best for their needs. [A group vice president]

Most of the managers interviewed argued that providing direction to divisions would actually increase the opportunities for entrepreneurship.

Before the reorganization, there was no definition of charters for divisions. This led to ambiguities, and therefore, waste. With the change, we are in a much better position to clearly define jobs. These cleaner lines of responsibility will help people see how the pieces fit and what their particular role is.

The engineers know it's better to sell integrated systems. Concisely defining product specifications gives them direction. And I believe they want direction. Our divisions have a "can do" attitude. They try to make their products quicker, better, and cheaper than anyone else. If we give them a challenge with direction and support, the result will be innovation. We can do this because HP hires very good people with energy and initiative. They don't need to be instructed how to do a job. They know who to contact in other parts of the company to get the cooperation they need. [A corporate personnel manager]

* * * * *

Even entrepreneurs need boundaries. Nobody can operate in a vacuum. Both small and large entrepreneurial organizations involve a "shared vision." A single entrepreneur has only a few people to communicate this vision to. A large organization must establish and communicate boundaries, set objectives, and let people loose.

There is a big difference between being independent and being entrepreneurial. Independence implies there may not be a cohesive overall fit among the pieces of an organization. Entrepreneurial units, on the other hand, can be managed to fit together if direction is provided. HP's divisions have always had innovation, pride, and openness. The reorganization will get them operating within an overall strategic framework. [A group vice president]

Impact on the Computer Strategy Council

Members of the computer strategy council saw the reorganization as an opportunity for them to concentrate more on what the council had been established for, to discuss longer-term strategic issues.

With these changes the group managers have overall authority to plan and execute programs. They won't have to coordinate every tactical detail with other group managers. What they will coordinate will be the overall strategy for HP's computer business.

As a result, the list of topics on the council's agenda has shrunk as has the length of the meetings. It is now more a matter of managing information exchange than confronting cross-divisional relationships. [A vice president]

*   *   *   *   *

The council had been spending too much time resolving detail issues relating to individual group priorities. We were usually more reactive than proactive. Now we can work on strategies as a team to penetrate new markets. [A group general manager]

*   *   *   *   *

The computer strategy council can now focus on identifying critical issues affecting everyone, and on establishing goals. With the new structure, these issues and goals can be pushed down to increasingly lower levels. [A group vice president]

Potential Problems

HP's management acknowledged there would be some problems. As with any major change, they knew it would take time for the organization to adjust.

Employees' perspective of the changes will determine the success of the new organization. They must expand the way they look at customers, markets, and key issues. The new organization, which emphasizes integrated systems selling, means everyone must know where and how they fit. No one can take a narrow view of the business. [A group general manager]

While undergoing the transition required to fully absorb the new structure, the company suspected that its philosophy of minimizing resource requirements woudl be temporarily jeopardized.

I think we will pay the price of overstaffing during the transition period. We have to make sure the right information and skills get transferred. We can't afford to drop any balls. This is especially true as we consolidate sales development teams from divisions into the centralized sales centers. That critical link to the field just can't be lost. [A division general manager]

The greatest area of concern was definitely the impact the new Business Development Group would have on HP. In particular, it was not clear how the role of the division marketing people would change. An indication that it would change was that the marketing budgets for divisions were to be cut by approximately 40 percent.

The primary task of the business development councils, which will include division marketing managers, will be to generate three-year marketing plans. I see the division marketing people as having three roles: (1) provide technical support to HP's field organization and to our customers, (2) typical marketing responsibilities like market analysis, working with lab in developing new products, and introducing new products, and (3) coming up with strategies for their particular products. Division management can look at strategy on a product basis, whereas BDG will take the systems view of integrating different divisions' product lines. [A group general manager]

The success of the business development councils depended on establishing close relationships between BDG and the divisions. Further, this new marketing group will seek to provide leadership in developing focused marketing programs for key application areas. If BDG was to succeed it had to make some meaningful contributions fairly early on.

I would guess it will take about one or two years for the company to fully accept BDG. We have to establish credibility, and I see at least four ways to do that. First, BDG will primarily consist of people pulled from the divisions. Interestingly, there are a number of marketing managers asking to join BDG. In fact, my move out of the Data Systems Division to manage in BDG was symbolic to show top management's commitment to the new group. Second, we must make some "value added" contribution in three to six months that is visible to the divisions. Only if we can help them will we gain their acceptance. Third, BDG will provide a real career path that will be comparable to a division career path leading up to a general manager. This will help get top people to join BDG. Finally, a fair amount of money is being put into BDG, much of which came from the 40 percent reduction in the divisional marketing budget. This is a very clear signal of top management's commitment.

Nonetheless, some people will not accept their new roles. Division managers, for example, who have a marketing orientation will be most resistant. They'll feel like they're losing something, such as the fun of creative marketing. On the other hand, division managers with an engineering orientation will accept the change immediately. Those managers want help in determining market direction. To them it will make complete sense. [A BDG manager]

One HP group very happy about the creation of BDG was the Personal Computer Group.

HP absolutely has to become more marketing-driven. But HP won't be, nor ever should be, more market-driven than technology-driven. Technology is our business. Computer customers today are buying solutions to their problems. They have broader and more complicated needs. We are very happy about BDG. They will provide an overall perspective. Their experts in our target markets, like office automation, will be a tremendous resource and service. But I'm not sure the other divisions are as happy. [A group general manager]

*   *   *   *   *

The personal computer business separates into two categories: stand-alone personal computers and work stations tied into a network. The former market is intensely competitive. But because of its stand-alone nature I think we can do more in marketing these products by ourselves. In contrast, BDG can and must help us market networked work stations as an HP solution. BDG can pull together the several divisions involved in this huge market. We are motivated to join in this effort because our division gets credit for any personal computers sold, whether they're sold alone or not.

I think strategic marketing has to be done at the group level, but the normal marketing of product lines should continue in the divisions. [A division marketing manager]

PART V

THE GENERAL MANAGER AND CORPORATE RESPONSIBILITY

CASE 29

Environmental Pressures (A)

A prominent politician commented in 1970, "Ecology has become the political substitute for the word 'mother.' "[1] Since the publication of Rachel Carson's *Silent Spring* in 1962, ecology had become a political issue of increasing salience. As early as 1968, it had surpassed law and order in total linage in the *Congressional Record*. By 1970, when the first Earth Day was celebrated, environmental protection had carved out a niche in the federal bureaucracy with 26 quasi-governmental bodies, 14 interagency committees, and 90 separate federal programs dealing with the environment. Federal spending on maintaining or improving the quality of the environment had risen from less than $5 million in the mid-1950s to several hundred million dollars by 1970.

More significant than the federal spending were the new regulations and standards legislated for industry. It had been estimated that business would have to spend approximately $22 billion to meet the air and water pollution standards in effect as of January 1, 1973.[2] Industries that would have to spend the most were:

	($ billions)
Electric utilities	$3.9
Petroleum	2.7
Chemicals	2.3
Iron and steel	1.7
Total spending, manufacturing	16.1
Total spending, business	22.3

When spending for pollution standards was considered as a percentage

---

[1] Jesse Unruh, as quoted in *Newsweek*, January 26, 1970, p. 31.

[2] *Business Week*, May 19, 1973, p. 78.

of estimated total capital spending in 1972 and 1976, industries hardest hit would be:

	Percent	
	1972	1976
Paper.	23.3	19.5
Nonferrous metals	15.3	15.9
Iron and steel	12.3	18.8
Petroleum	10.7	17.6
All manufacturing.	8.2	10.9
All business	5.1	5.9

This case focuses on the effects of government pollution regulations and their enforcement on one alleged industrial polluter, Reserve Mining Company. [A second case, "Environmental Pressures (B)," focuses on the financial implications of various proposed solutions.] This company's situation was chosen because of the importance of the issues to the parties involved and the accessibility of relevant information. The two cases are not intended to illustrate right or wrong, wise or unwise actions by any of the parties involved. That is for the reader to consider, bearing in mind that the information presented was drawn from a variety of published material as well as from almost 20,000 pages of public court records. A great deal of material was of necessity omitted, and these cases represent the casewriter's attempt to present fairly, in a highly condensed form, some of the major issues involved in a long and complex controversy.

Because the issues were still in litigation at the time of the writing of the cases, neither the plaintiffs nor the defendants were given the opportunity to modify the selection of material presented, all of which was drawn from publicly available sources.

RESERVE MINING COMPANY

The Situation in April 1974

On April 20, 1974, Judge Miles Lord of the federal district court in Minneapolis handed down a decision ordering the Reserve Mining Company to halt the discharge of taconite tailings (or wastes) into Lake Superior. The company's plant, the largest in the world, was ordered to close down for an indefinite period of time.

This order climaxed the biggest pollution case ever, "The Classic Pollution Case," according to *Time* magazine. The trial had lasted eight and a half months and had generated almost 20,000 pages of testimony and more than 800 exhibits. The stakes involved dwarfed all previous environmental cases. The Reserve plant produced about 10 million tons of iron ore annually (15 percent of total United States ore production), valued at close to $150 million. The plant supplied between one-half and three-quarters of the ore needs of its parent companies, Republic and Armco Steel, which were two of the country's five largest steel companies. Directly at stake were 3,000 jobs and an estimated 8,000 more were indirectly involved. It was alleged that Reserve's daily discharge of 67,000 tons of taconite tailings threatened the ecological balance of the world's largest fresh-water body, and in addition created a significant health hazard to the communities that drew their drinking water from the lake.

Two days after Judge Lord's decision, an appeals court granted a 70-day stay on the order. The plant was allowed to reopen, but Reserve and its parent firms were given 25 days in which to present plans for abatement of the discharges into the lake.

Reserve's Early History

Reserve Mining Company was organized on March 24, 1939, with ownership divided among Armco Steel, Wheeling Steel, Montreal Mining Co., and Cleveland Cliffs Iron Co. Later that year, the company obtained leases on land near Babbitt, Minnesota, in the Mesabi Range. The land contained a deposit of magnetic taconite nine miles long, an average of 2,800 feet wide, and as thick as 175 feet, with an estimated two million tons of ore.

Although about 95 percent of the Mesabi Range iron formation was taconite, it was not commercially mined until the 1950s. High-grade ores (those up to 70 percent iron oxides, compared to taconite with 30 percent or less) were more economical to mine, as they could be shipped directly to steel mills without processing.

The owners considered the Babbitt property a long-term investment, to be mined if and when taconite became competitive with direct shipment ores. Steel production expanded greatly during World War II, and by the late 1940s the high-grade ores in the Mesabi Range were largely gone. The economy of northern Minnesota declined sharply, unemployment soared, and the Mesabi Range appeared to be becoming another Appalachia.

In 1942, however, Reserve personnel and Dr. E. W. Davis, director of the Mines Experiment Station at the University of Minnesota, began research into processes for transforming taconite into usable form. By 1947 their work had yielded a method of refining and concentrating taconite into small pellets of iron ore, usable as blast furnace feed. The decision was made to build a beneficiation plant for extracting usable ore from taconite mined at Babbitt. The estimated reserves when processed would yield up to 650 million tons of ore, sufficient to keep the plant in operation for 75 years. Because the beneficiation process required large amounts

EXHIBIT 1: Map of the Mesabi Range and Reserve Mining Company Operations

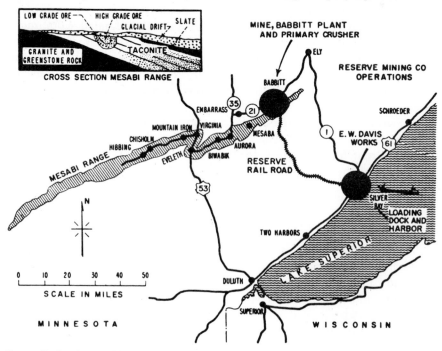

Source: *Engineering and Mining Journal,* December 1956, p. 76. Reprinted by permission.

of water, the owners selected a plant site at Silver Bay, on the north shore of Lake Superior (see Exhibit 1).

In 1950 Republic Steel purchased 42.5 percent ownership of Reserve, and the following year, Republic and Armco made acquisitions of the remaining interest that brought their shares up to 50 percent each.

In late 1955, five years after construction began, the Reserve Mining Company plant at Silver Bay was completed, and by the middle of 1956, it had produced a million tons of iron ore.

The new plant played a key role in revitalizing the economy of northeastern Minnesota. Congressman John Blatnik, who represented the area, said:

> Reserve Mining was not just another industry in Silver Bay, Minnesota. It was the forerunner of a dramatic revolution in the entire economy of northeastern Minnesota and a pacesetter for the iron ore industry. Reserve Mining Company initiated the taconite industry with an investment that eventually totalled $350 million.[3]

---

[3] *National Journal Reports,* March 2, 1974, p. 310.

By 1972, total investment in taconite plants and facilities in the Mesabi Range had amounted to well over a billion dollars.

The Silver Bay plant was hailed as a technological breakthrough of major importance to the American economy. Estimates of future sources of iron ore showed taconite filling the gap caused by depletion of available direct-shipping iron ore (see Exhibit 2). A writer in a 1956 *Engineering and Mining Journal* article commented:

> The Reserve taconite project is one of the most impressive in mining history, not only because of its size, but also because of the numerous technical headaches involved in large-scale mining, concentrating, and pelletizing concentrates from one of the hardest, toughest, abrasive ores known to man.[4]

The Reserve plant employed the world's largest crusher and the world's strongest conveyor belt. The plant required construction of a 47-mile railroad (to haul the ore from Babbit to Silver Bay) with specially constructed railroad cars, which allowed rotation of 180° without uncoupling, to facilitate unloading, and included numerous other innovations in material handling and processing.

Processing Taconite

The process used by Reserve was essentially the same as that developed by Dr. Davis in the forties. First, at the mine in Babbitt, rocks and earth were stripped away to expose the taconite. Jet piercers, invented for this purpose, used a 4,250°F flame to drill 40-foot deep holes in the hard rock. Explosives were loaded into the holes and detonated to break the taconite into pieces. The rocks were hauled by truck to crushing plants where the taconite was reduced to pieces four inches or less in diameter and then loaded on railcars to be carried the 47 miles to Silver Bay.

At Silver Bay another crushing plant further reduced the taconite to less than ¾-inch size. The taconite was then conveyed to the concentrator plant where beneficiation, or separation of the mineral, was performed in three stages of grinding and five steps of separation. In this process, the taconite was reduced to a powder finer than flour. Large magnets were used to separate particles rich in iron oxide from those that were lean or barren. The latter were called "tailings." Hydraulic separation, a process in which heavier iron-rich particles were permitted to sink in a pool of water while lighter, low-iron content particles overflowed as tail-

---

[4] "Reserve's New Taconite Project," *Engineering and Mining Journal,* December 1956, p. 75. Reprinted by permission.

EXHIBIT 2: 1956 Projection of Future Sources of Iron Ore for Steel Plants

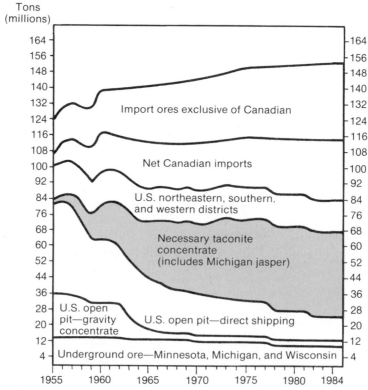

Source: *Engineering and Mining Journal,* December 1956, p. 75. Reprinted by permission.

ings, was also employed. The grinding and separation steps were performed with the solid material suspended in water. Finally, the tailings from each step of separation were joined together and transported down a system of troughs and discharged into Lake Superior. When the discharge entered the lake, it was a slurry (mixture of water and suspended solids) of approximately 1.5 percent solids. In the lake, the slurry formed a heavy density current (the solid material suspended in water made it heavier than the surrounding water), which flowed to the bottom of the lake. Over the years, the coarser tailings discharged from the troughs had settled offshore and formed a delta (see Exhibit 3).

The iron ore concentrate from which the tailings had been separated was conveyed to a pelletizing plant where it was rolled into ⅜-inch pellets and hardened by heating to 2,350°F. Approximately three tons of taconite were required to produce one ton of pellets (see Exhibit 4, a schematic flow diagram of this process).

EXHIBIT 3: Reserve Mining Company Plant at Silver Bay

Source: Reprinted by permission of the *Minneapolis Tribune*.

Importance of Water

Water was vital in taconite processing. Edward Furness, the president of Reserve, explained the importance of water to the company's operations as follows:

> A substantial part of the success of Reserve's taconite operations is the availability of large quantities of water. The grinding and the following magnetic separation stages—where the magnetic iron ore is recovered from the waste sand—is done with the material suspended in water. It requires 50 tons of water to make one ton of finished iron ore concentrate—about 12,000 gallons! We use about 350,000 gallons of water a minute.
>
> On the subject of water used in taconite processing, let me point out one thing—water is used, but it is not lost. The separation process uses no heat; therefore, there is no evaporation except what would occur naturally. Thus, after the water is used and the tailings settle out, the water again becomes part of the existing water supply.
>
> Reserve's earliest studies showed that it wasn't possible to conduct its concentration process at Babbitt, the site of our mine. . . . There simply was no water available in Babbitt in the quantities required by a large-scale operation such as ours. Also, because of its location near the Superior National Forest and near the boundary waters, there was no area available

EXHIBIT 4: Schematic Flow Diagram

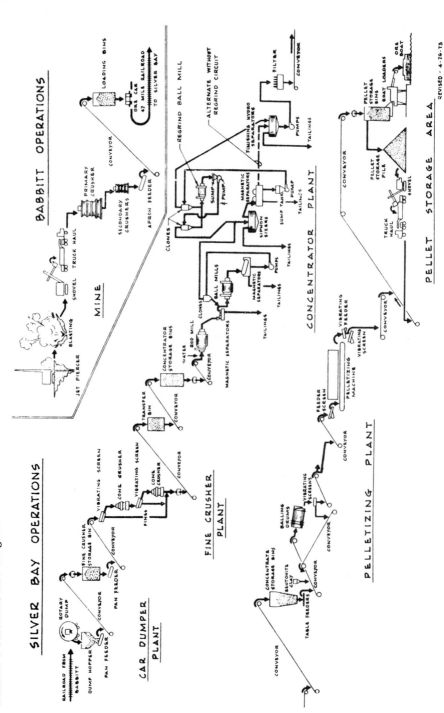

Source: U.S.A. et al. v. Reserve Mining Company et al., Defendant's Exhibit 85A.

to Reserve for tailings disposal. The only solution, engineering studies made clear, was to locate the processing plant at Silver Bay and bring the crude taconite there by rail from Babbitt.

It's very expensive to haul that crude rock down to Silver Bay. We had to build a 47-mile, double-tracked railroad through muskeg and rock—the worst kind of terrain. And, since we mine three tons of taconite for every ton of pellets we make, two-thirds of all the material we haul is unusable.

Of course, we would have located the processing plant near the mine if that had been possible. Other taconite companies do it because there is available sufficient water for processing and large tailings disposal areas. But, Reserve had no choice. Reserve is at the source of the rivers flowing down to Lake Superior, not far enough down them—as are the other taconite companies—to rely on them for a water supply.

After thorough study, then, engineers agreed that the only possible site for our processing plant was on the north shore of Lake Superior at what is now Silver Bay. The site was suitable both because of the existence of nearby islands to which breakwaters could be built forming a harbor and, directly off-shore from the plant, there is a very deep area of Lake Superior.

This deep area—a great depression extending for many miles parallel to the shore—is 600 to 900 feet deep. Its proportions are immense; up to eight miles wide, 59 miles long, big enough to hold our entire Babbitt ore body without raising the bottom more than a few feet. It is here our tailings settle. From a conservation standpoint, Reserve's use of Lake Superior is sound. There is no waste water and no injury to water. Reserve's method of disposal of the sand left over from processing taconite incorporates harmless, permanent deep-water deposition of an inert material—tailings.[5]

Permits for the Plant

Certain federal and state permits were required to either withdraw water from or discharge into a public body of water. In 1947 Reserve applied to the Minnesota Department of Conservation and the Water Pollution Control Commission for permits to use Lake Superior water and discharge taconite tailings into the lake. As required by law, hearings were held, and in December 1947 Reserve received the desired permits. The permits would be revoked if any of the following conditions existed: the tailings included oil; had a material adverse effect on fish or public water supplies; included any material quantities of matter soluble in water; caused any unlawful pollution of Lake Superior; resulted in any nuisance outside the approximately 9-square-mile zone; or were discharged so as to result in any material clouding or discoloration of the water outside that zone.

---

[5] Digest of Statements presented by Reserve Mining Co. to Conference on Pollution of the Interstate Waters of the Lake Superior Basin, May 13, 14, 15, 1969, pp. 2–3.

In 1956 the permit was amended, increasing allowable water usage from 130,000 gallons per minute (GPM) to 260,000 GPM. In 1960, it was further increased to 502,000 GPM.

In 1947 Reserve also applied to the Army Corps of Engineers for a permit to discharge. The Corps routinely issued thousands of permits a year applying the sole criterion of whether the discharge would obstruct navigation. This permit was granted and periodically revised and renewed until 1960, when Reserve was given an indefinite extension.

The Corps of Engineers permit became a problem to Reserve in 1966, however, when President Johnson issued an executive order providing that the secretary of the interior give assistance to other departments in carrying out their responsibilities under the Federal Water Pollution Control Act. The next year,, this policy became operational. The regulations of the Corps were altered so that in granting permits the Corps would consider the "effects of permitted activities on the public interest, including effects upon water quality, recreation, fish and wildlife, pollution, our natural resources, as well as effects on navigation."[6] The Corps was periodically to reexamine indefinitely extended permits such as Reserve's and apply the new criteria.

Stoddard Report

Thus, in November 1967 revalidation proceedings were begun for Reserve's permit, and Charles Stoddard, the Interior Department's regional coordinator, was assigned the task of compiling and consolidating the various reports that could pertain to Reserve's impact on the environment. Studies and reports from the Bureau of Commercial Fisheries, the Bureau of Mines, the Bureau of Sport Fisheries and Wildlife, the Federal Water Pollution Control Administration, the Minnesota Department of Conservation, the Minnesota Pollution Control Agency (PCA), and the Reserve Mining Company were among those considered.

In December 1968, after about a year of preparation, the Stoddard report was completed but not officially released. Its conclusions (see Exhibit 5) and the recommendation that Reserve be required to dispose of its tailings on land after three years posed a serious problem to Reserve. The report, written for Interior Department officials and the Corps of Engineers, was leaked to the press, and its contents soon created controversy. Reserve attacked the report, claiming that it contained serious errors and jeopardized thousands of jobs. Some alleged that pressure was applied on the Johnson administration and that the Interior Department reacted by claiming the report was only preliminary, classifying it as "unofficial" (thus keeping it out of circulation), and rewriting the conclusions and

---

[6] Stanley Ulrich et al., *Superior Polluter* (Duluth: Save Lake Superior Association and Northern Environmental Council, 1972), p. 30.

The following conclusions are derived from the investigations and analysis of findings of the Interior Taconite Study Group on the effects of taconite waste disposal in Lake Superior:

1. Total discharge of solids by the Reserve Mining Company plant in twelve days equals the sediment contribution to the lake by all United States tributaries for one year.

2. Slightly less than half of the tailings waste discharged between 1956 and 1967 was deposited on the delta above the deep trough in Lake Superior; evidence indicates that some of the remainder moves downshore with lake currents.

3. Turbidity is commonly three to five times greater in the area near and southwest of the plant than northeast of the plant and directly offshore from the discharge where offshore water moves toward the delta due to the density current. Turbidity values in bottom water over the tailings deposit are ten to sixty times greater than at the surface.

4. Tailings suspended in the water cause "green water" for distances at least 18 miles southwest from the point of discharge.

5. Tailings are dispersed on the lake bottom at least 10 miles off shore and 18 miles southwest of the plant.

6. Net lake current velocities are sufficient to keep micron-size particles in suspension for long periods and carry them long distances and to carry such particles across State boundaries.

7. Federal–State water quality standards for iron, lead, and copper are violated as a result of tailings discharge.

8. One requirement of the Minnesota Pollution Control Agency permit to discharge tailings into Lake Superior is violated in that there is "material clouding or discoloration of the water at the surface" outside the prescribed permit area.

9. The water quality criteria recommended by the National Technical Advisory Committee for zinc and cadmium for aquatic life production are exceeded.

10. The widely accepted criteria of 0.01 mg/1 of phosphorus to limit algal growth is exceeded.

11. Bottom fauna, especially one species important as a fish food, show progressive reduction in numbers southwest of the plant. Beyond the limits of bottom fauna collection (15.5 miles southwest of the plant), there are no data to establish how much farther such effects continue before recovery begins.

12. In laboratory tests, tailings less than 0.45 microns stimulated additional algal growth in Lake Superior waters.

13. Taconite tailings discharged from the effluent launders diluted to one-fourth and one-tenth of the original concentration were found to be lethal to rainbow trout sac fry in a few days.

14. Even moderate changes in commercial fish catch due to tailings discharge would be masked by much larger changes due to lamprey and overfishing.

15. Alternate disposal methods are available.

Source: An alleged copy of the original (but unofficial and unreleased) Stoddard report provided to the casewriter by Northern Environmental Council. The above conclusions are reproduced here because of their impact at the time of their circulation. Some of the above conclusions still remain unsubstantiated and have been dropped from subsequent actions against Reserve, and thus their validity is open to question.

recommendations.[7] An "official" report, issued later, recommended continuing surveillance of Reserve, but little action to halt the discharge.

Enforcement Conference

On January 16, 1969, Secretary of the Interior Stewart Udall called
for an Enforcement Conference on the pollution of Lake Superior. Under
the terms of the Federal Water Pollution Control Act, the secretary of
the interior could initiate enforcement proceedings if it was believed that
the health and welfare of persons in one state were endangered by pollution originating in another state. The first step in this process was an
Enforcement Conference, to be followed by public hearings and court
action if the pollution persisted.

The first session of the Enforcement Conference began in mid-1969
and lasted for several months. It provided a forum for politicians, company
officials, and environmentalists. Technical consultants for Reserve and
the environmentalists gave conflicting testimony, and the final recommendation called for:

> further engineering and economic studies relating to possible ways and
> means of reducing to the maximum practicable extent the discharge of
> tailings to Lake Superior and . . . a report on progress to the Minnesota
> PCA and the conference within six months of the date of release of these
> recommendations.[8]

In December 1969, Reserve filed a suit against the Minnesota PCA
seeking exemption from a state water pollution regulation (WPC–15) as
it related to Reserve's disposition of tailings. Two months later, the state
filed a countersuit to force compliance with the regulation. The effect
of these suits was to force a delay in hearings scheduled to consider
alleged permit violations by Reserve. The hearings, requested by the Sierra
Club (a nationwide nonprofit environmental protection and educational
organization with more than 140,000 members), could have led to immediate revocation of Reserve's dumping permit.

The trial was held at the Lake County District Court, only 20 miles
from Silver Bay. As in the past, contradictory evidence was presented
by each side. In December 1970, the district court found that WPC–15
was not applicable to Reserve, but Reserve was ordered to alter its method
of disposition so that the tailings would be confined to a small section
of the lake. The PCA appealed the district court ruling to the state supreme
court. In August 1972, a decision was handed down ordering Reserve
to apply to the PCA for a variance from WPC–15, reestablishing the
legal position that had existed three years earlier.

---

[7] David Zwick et al., *Water Wasteland,* Ralph Nader's study group report on water
pollution (New York: Grossman, 1971), pp. 144–149; Ulrich, *Superior Polluter,* pp. 40–43.

[8] Ulrich, *Superior Polluter,* p. 87.

Meanwhile, the focus had shifted back to the federal government. A second session of the Enforcement Conference was convened during 1970. Most notable of its findings was that there was interstate pollution, thereby conferring jurisdiction on the conference. In April 1971, a third session was held. A Reserve proposal to pipe tailings to the bottom of the lake was rejected, and the EPA served notice on Reserve that it was in violation of established federal water quality standards. The company was given 180 days to submit an acceptable plan for tailings disposal. This notice laid the foundation for future court action.

"THE CLASSIC POLLUTION CASE"

In January 1972, EPA chief William Ruckelshaus asked the Justice Department to take Reserve to court to force abatement of its discharge. The government suit, filed a month later, claimed Reserve violated Minnesota water quality standards and the Refuse Act of 1899, created a public nuisance, had an invalid permit to discharge, and polluted the waters of other states.

The trial promised to be important, complex, and lengthy. Intervenors entered the case on both sides, and the final lineup pitted the Justice Department; the states of Minnesota, Wisconsin, and Michigan; the Minnesota PCA; the cities of Duluth, Minnesota, and Superior, Wisconsin; and five environmentalist groups against Reserve, Armco, Republic Steel, and 11 towns, counties, and civic associations in northeastern Minnesota. Highly technical determinations had to be made, especially regarding the taconite tailings and their ecological impact. The two sides were at odds over basic questions, such as the quantity of tailings being discharged, their movement in the lake, the amount of tailings that remained suspended, and their size. The plaintiffs charged that the Reserve discharge adversely affected the lake by:

1. Increasing turbidity and reducing water clarity by 25 percent or more over an area of more than 600 square miles;
2. Causing a "green water" phenomenon, in which sections of the lake reflected a muddy green color;
3. Assisting algae growth and accelerating a process that has severely damaged the other Great Lakes (eutrophication); and
4. Being ingested by fish, altering their feeding habits, and killing trout sac fry.

The most significant controversy centered on the movement of the tailings once they entered the lake. Reserve contended that the slurry, which flowed off the delta in front of the plant, formed a "heavy density current" that flowed down to the lake bottom, where the tailings were deposited. The environmentalists did not dispute the existence of this current, but claimed that a variety of phenomena caused a significant portion of the tailings to become suspended and dispersed over more than 2,000 square miles of the lake. To support their position, Reserve presented an inventory allegedly accounting for 99.6 percent of their tailings within a small area directly offshore from the plant. Environmentalists then pointed out that even if the Reserve inventory were accepted, over one million tons of tailings were still unaccounted for.

Consequences of a Shutdown

To some observers it appeared tht the aesthetic benefits of keeping Lake Superior pure would have to be weighed against the economic hardship that closing it or forcing on-land disposal would create. But Verna Mize, a former Michigan resident who lobbied for seven years in Washington against Reserve (as a Maryland housewife and secretary) and became a leading opponent of the company, pointed to the economic impact of the company's discharge:

> You can't put a price tag on one of the world's largest and cleanest bodies of fresh water, the one lake responsible for flushing the other already polluted Great Lakes. If you want to argue dollars, Lake Superior was conservatively estimated to be worth $1.3 trillion for pure drinking water alone. We may soon know whether that value has been reduced to zero.[9]

On the other hand, if Reserve were to shut down, it appeared the consequences would be far more tangible and immediate.

There would clearly be an economic effect on the economy of northeastern Minnesota. Reserve had 3,000 employees on its payroll, and assuming each had a family of four, 12,000 people depended directly on the company. In 1973 Reserve had purchased $44 million of supplies from 530 Minnesota businesses, and these firms would undoubtedly be forced to cut back. It had been estimated that indirectly each Minnesota mining job supported about nine people, thus 27,000 people could be affected.

Through taxes on taconite operations, real estate, and the company railroads, Reserve contributed a significant portion of the revenues for six taxing districts. A total of $6,500,000 in state and local taxes was paid in 1973. Hardest hit by the loss of revenues would be the towns of Babbitt (80 percent of revenues from Reserve), Silver Bay (64 percent), and Lake County (57 percent). Babbitt and Silver Bay had issued bonds secured by revenues from Reserve, and these probably would go into default. The threat of a Reserve shutdown had already made financing

---

[9] Verna Mize, as quoted in *National Journal Reports,* March 2, 1974, p. 312.

difficult for Silver Bay; the town had recently withdrawn a bond issue when there were no bidders to underwrite it.

The towns of Babbitt, Silver Bay, Ely, and Two Harbors were those most dependent on Reserve. More than 70 percent of the company's employees resided in these towns. Their relative dependence on Reserve is shown in Exhibit 6.

EXHIBIT 6: Four Towns' Dependence on Reserve

	Number of Reserve Employees (8/73)	Estimated Population Directly Dependent on Reserve (at 4 per employee)	Estimated Total Population
Silver Bay	930	3,720	3,800
Babbitt	665	2,660	3,076
Ely	500	2,000	4,904
Two Harbors	249	996	4,437

Silver Bay and Babbitt had been carved out of the wilderness and built entirely by Reserve in the early fifties. In 1974, they remained company towns.

Silver Bay's dependence on Reserve was stated with obvious pride in a Chamber of Commerce brochure:

> The area's industry is Reserve Mining Company. Due to its tremendous tonnage of taconite pellets, Reserve has earned for the village the slogan "Taconite Capital of the World." To produce this tonnage, the village affords a population of 3,800 people.

In the center of town, a 7-foot figure of a taconite man stood on a pedestal of taconite ore. Most local merchants provided visitors with free sample packets of taconite ore and pellets, and the Chamber of Commerce actively distributed bumper stickers proclaiming "Silver Bay— Taconite Capital of the World." Even the altar and baptismal font of the Catholic church were made of taconite. Few would disagree with the mayor, who said the loss of Reserve "would effectively terminate the village."[10]

The people who lived in Silver Bay had come in two migrations, one associated with the opening of the plant in the mid-fifties and the other with its later expansion. Their homes were built by Reserve and sold to them with little or no down payment. Carrying charges on many were below $100 a month. Their children attended one of three schools built by Reserve at a cost of over $6 million, and they played in recreational facilities also built by the company. It appeared that once families had

---

[10] *U.S.A. et al.* v. *Reserve Mining Co. et al..*, U.S. District Court, District of Minnesota, Fifth District Civil Action, No. 5–72, Civ. 19 Offer of Proof, pp. 12–13.

settled into the comfortable security of Silver Bay, few left. The threat of a Reserve shutdown, however, had shaken the community. A *Minneapolis Star* writer noted:

> The problem of their homes is the thorn that keeps awakening in the workers the dimensions of their possible fate. If the company goes, the town goes. No one believes there will be any buyers for the wood frame residences that line the streets of Silver Bay.[11]

Babbitt was haunted by a similar episode in its past. In the early 1920s, the Mesabi Iron Company had attempted a pioneering venture in mining taconite. A town was constructed at Babbitt and 300 workers were employed there until 1924. Unable to compete with direct-shipping ore, Mesabi abandoned the mine and the town. In 1954, when Reserve arrived, there was only one family remaining. Four miles from the abandoned town, in a huge potato farm, Reserve built the new Babbitt: the streets, the houses, water and sewer lines, three schools, and a medical clinic. The company at first rented the houses to employees, but later sold them on what were believed to be excellent terms for the employees. By all accounts, Reserve had been a good benefactor, and Babbitt residents were grateful. The *Minneapolis Tribune* noted the good feeling among the employees:

> They like the company. They don't think of it as patronizing; they think it's just good to its workers. When the men talk of Iron Range jobs, they say Reserve is the best employer of the bunch. The key reason is few layoffs—and perhaps more important, they like Babbitt and its environment of lakes and forest. Talk with a Babbitt resident for all of three minutes, and he'll start the pitch about Babbitt being a great place to raise kids and to hunt and fish.[12]

The effects of a Reserve shutdown would extend beyond Minnesota. There were reports that parent firms Republic and Armco could be forced to shut down some of their operations at least temporarily. Senior officials of the United Steelworkers Union (USW) estimated that as many as 50,000 jobs could be affected. Reserve's stockpile of three million tons of taconite would be sufficient to keep the furnaces operating for only four months. Republic obtained 55 percent of its ore supply from Reserve, and four of its six domestic mills relied primarily on Reserve ore. Armco would likely be hit harder, as 75 percent of its ore came from Reserve. Alternate sources of that magnitude were not believed to be presently available. The University of Minnesota's School of Mineral and Metallurgical Engineering, in 1970, saw the following consequences of a Reserve shutdown:

> A loss of such tonnage would have severe impact on the abilities of the steel producers (particularly Armco and Republic) to meet their de-

---

[11] *Minneapolis Star,* April 22, 1974, p. 4A.

[12] *Minneapolis Tribune,* May 5, 1974, p. 13B.

mands. It would force the reopening of abandoned miles that are incapable of providing the high-grade pellet feed so essential to the economic operation of blast furnaces today. More likely the companies would attempt to purchase on the world market where the supply is already short, tending to increase prices and causing a further deterioration in our balance of payments. A compounding factor is the real and present possibility of long strikes or expropriation of foreign producing mines, causing further disruptions. The loss of some 10 million tons of Canadian production in 1969 due to strikes is a case in point.[13]

The Outlook in Early 1973

In early 1973, despite the magnitude of the stakes involved, the upcoming trial appeared to some observers to be just another step in the long history of unsuccessful attempts to halt Reserve's alleged pollution. Previous suits and hearings had bogged down in contradictory and inconclusive testimony and had resulted in weak court orders and calls for further study. A chronology of the major events relevant to the controversy is shown in Exhibit 7. The case against Reserve did not appear to warrant immediate action, and the economic consequences of a shutdown all but ruled out that path. In 1973, one environmentalist commented:

> How much more time will Reserve Mining gain to continue its dumping? Five years have gone by since Charles Stoddard organized Interior's study, and nearly four years have passed since that first Enforcement Conference in Duluth. If the Federal Court finds against the firm, there are always appeals.[14]

Another predicted that "the case could drag on for years in the courts."[15]

The Asbestos Issue

On June 15, 1973, a totally new factor was introduced into the controversy. The EPA released a report revealing that high concentrations of asbestos fibers, which were alleged to be from Reserve's discharge, were present in the drinking water of four Minnesota communities that depended on Lake Superior for their supply. Asbestos was believed to be a cancer-producing agent (carcinogen) when inhaled. Ingestion of asbestos had not been studied extensively, but it also was believed to cause cancer (see the Appendix).

The EPA warning recommended that "while there is no conclusive evidence to show the present drinking water supply is unfit for human consumption, prudence dictates an alternate source of drinking water

---

[13] *U.S.A. et al.* v. *Reserve Mining Co. et al.*, Defendant Reserve Mining Co.'s Opening Statement, p. 12.

[14] *Audubon* magazine, March 1973, p. 121.

[15] *Minneapolis Tribune*, June 16, 1973, p. 1A.

EXHIBIT 7: Reserve Mining Company (RMC) Chronology, 1939 to 1974

1939	March 24	RMC organized
1942		Research begins on beneficiating taconite
1947	December	Minnesota Dept. of Conservation and Water Pollution Control Commission grants RMC permits
1948	April 22	Army Corps of Engineers grants permit to RMC
1951		Republic and Armco each acquire 50 percent shares of RMC
		Construction begins on Silver Bay plant
1955		Plant opens
1968	December	Stoddard report completed
1969	January 16	Secretary of Interior Udall calls for Enforcement Conference
	May 13	First federal Enforcement Conference meets in Duluth
	December 24	RMC files appeal from state water quality standards in Lake County court
1970	February 13	State of Minnesota files counterclaims against RMC in Lake County court
	April 29	Second session of federal Enforcement Conference convenes in Duluth
	December 15	Lake County court hands down a compromise ruling
1971	January 14	Third session of federal Enforcement Conference meets in Duluth
	April 19	MPCA appeals Lake County court decision to state supreme court
	April 22	Third session of Enforcement Conference reconvenes and rejects RMC abatement plan
	April 28	EPA chief Ruckelshaus issues 180-day notice to Reserve
1972	January	Ruckelshaus asks Justice Dept. to take RMC to court
	August	State supreme court orders RMC to apply to MPCA for a variance, reestablishing the legal position that existed three years earlier
1973	June 15	EPA releases report alleging asbestos fibers in the drinking water of several communities
	August 1	Trial begins in federal district court under Judge Miles Lord
1974	April 20	Armco President Verity offers Palisades Plan
		Judge Lord orders plant closed
	April 22	Appeals court grants stay reopening plant

Source: Compiled by casewriter.

be found for young children."[16] The rationale for suggesting the alternate source for only young people was that even if the water were dangerous, the damage had already been done to those people who had drunk the contaminated water for years.

The asbestos fibers were believed to have originated in Reserve's ore body at Babbitt. It was claimed that at least 25 percent of the ore consisted of minerals closely related to asbestos, and an undetermined portion of those were identical to amosite asbestos, that which was believed to cause cancer. (Most of the other ore in the Mesabi Range was believed to be free of asbestos.) It was also alleged that in processing the ore at Silver Bay, Reserve emitted asbestos fibers into the air as well as discharged them into the lake in the tailings.

Although the EPA warning dealt only with the contamination of drinking water, it also served to focus attention on the potential hazards from emission of asbestos into the air.

Reaction to the EPA Warning

Reserve reacted immediately to the EPA warning. Edward Schmid, assistant to the president, stated:

> We know of no indications to support the charge that there is any present or future hazard to drinking water supplies due to tailings. It is unfortunate that this unfounded charge has been made public without testing its validity. . . . [There is no] more substance to this charge than there was to similar claims involving arsenic and mercury in Reserve's tailings which created mild sensations before they were disproved and abandoned.[17]

In Duluth, the largest city affected, residents were scared by the EPA warning. Bottled water sales took off. In the words of one merchant, it was "selling to beat hell and people don't care about price."[18] State and local officials, working with the EPA, attempted to locate available alternate water supplies. Thirty EPA staff members were brought in from other states to set up water monitoring operations with the PCA. Meanwhile, well water from the Superior, Wisconsin, municipal system was trucked into Duluth, bottled, and sold through food stores.

Political leaders looked to the federal government and Reserve to bear the costs. Within a month:

- The Army Corps of Engineers brought in portable filtration units to test their effectiveness in removing the tiny asbestos fibers.
- Duluth received a $100,000 federal grant to purchase bottled water for low-income families.

---

[16] *Minneapolis Tribune*, June 16, 1973, p. 1A.

[17] Ibid.

[18] Ibid.

- The mayor of Duluth proposed a city water filtration system to be paid for mainly with federal funds.
- A state senator urged that Reserve either be forced to close, or to provide pure drinking water to the affected communities for at least 18 months.

In Silver Bay, where asbestos allegedly contaminated both the air and the water, there was little visible reaction. Most of the bottled water sold continued to go into car batteries and irons, as the average person dismissed the EPA warning. One woman commented, "We've lived here for 16 years. Our children are perfectly healthy. If I worried about this with all these kids, I wouldn't be here today. . . . I just don't believe there's any danger."[19] An accountant for Reserve complained, "Since 1965, everybody has been gunning for us. Let's get these people off our backs . . . they're just trying to take our jobs away."[20]

Asbestos soon became the subject of local jokes. Dr. Selikoff, the asbestos expert who had expressed strong concern for the health hazard, became "Dr. Silly Cough." Asbestos was adopted as a synonym for water. People spoke of a Silver Bay man who died recently, and when they tried to cremate him, his body wouldn't burn. Clearly, in this town where Reserve's plants and offices were located, people felt there were more serious things to be concerned about than a little asbestos in the air and water.

The Trial

On August 1, 1973, the trial began in the federal district court in Minneapolis. The dominant issue had now become the potential health hazard created by Reserve's discharge. During the course of the trial, evidence was taken from nearly all of the world's experts on asbestos. Judge Miles Lord, who presided, commented that "the scope and depth of the review of the literature and scientific knowledge in this area which was presented to this court has not been approached either in the field of science, or in law."[21] Weeks of testimony by experts representing both sides was often contradictory. Judge Lord relentlessly cross-examined the experts and finally reached the following conclusions:

1. There probably would be a consensus of opinion that there is a level of exposure below which there is no detectable increase in asbestos-related diseases—a so-called threshold. Unfortunately, no one can state with any authority what this level of exposure is.

---

[19] *Minneapolis Star,* June 19, 1973, p. 1A.

[20] Ibid., p. 4A.

[21] *U.S.A. et al.* v. *Reserve Mining Co. et al.,* Supplemental Memorandum, p. 53.

2. The state of the art at present is so limited, as indicated by the various studies in this case, that man's abilities to quantify the amount of particles in the air and water are subject to substantial error. Hence, we are faced with a situation where too much exposure to these particles results in fatal disease, and yet nobody knows how much is too much.

3. The asbestosis and various cancers associated with asbestos exposure are generally irreversible and often fatal.

4. There is a significant burden of amphibole (asbestos) fibers from Reserve's discharge in the air of Silver Bay, a burden that is commensurate with the burden that was found in areas in which there had been a proven health hazard.

5. The evidence in this case clearly indicates that the ingestion of amphibole, or asbestos fibers, creates a hazard to human health. . . . When asbestos workers inhale asbestos, approximately 50 percent of what they inhale is coughed up or brought by ciliary action into the back of the throat and then travels to the stomach. Furthermore, once fibers are ingested, they have the ability to pass through membranes and find their way to various parts of the body.

6. It is virtually uncontradicted that there is an extensive latency period before asbestos-related diseases are manifested. Generally, it is not until 20 or 30 years have elapsed from the initial date of exposure to a population that there is a detectable increase in disease. The Reserve plant has been in operation for only 17 years, and it was only in 1960, after a major plant expansion, that present levels of taconite discharge were achieved. Because of these factors, it would be highly unlikely that the public health effects from the discharge would be noticed for some years to come. . . . It should be pointed out that Duluth residents do not at this time enjoy a fortunate position with respect to the cancer experience for the entire state of Minnesota. There is at this time a statistically significant excess of rectal cancer with an increasing trend. . . . Consistent with past experience of populations exposed to asbestos, the actual health effects of Reserve's discharge on the people in Duluth will not be known for many years.[22]

In ordering the plant closed, Judge Lord concluded:

> The court has no other alternative but to order an immediate halt to the discharge which threatens the lives of thousands. In that defendants have no plan to make the necessary modifications, there is no reason to delay any further the issuance of the injunction.[23]

---

[22] *U.S.A. et al.* v. *Reserve Mining Co. et al.,* Supplemental Memorandum, pp. 53–74.

[23] *U.S.A. et al.* v. *Reserve Mining Co. et al.,* Memorandum and Order, p. 12.

ALTERNATE METHODS OF DISPOSALS

During the course of the controversy over Reserve's pollution, the company and its opponents had proposed numerous alternatives to reduce or eliminate the environmental damage resulting from the tailings discharge.

Reserve's Deep-Pipe Plan

In 1971 Reserve had proposed extending a pipe from the Silver Bay plant to the bottom of Lake Superior. The taconite tailings would thus be discharged directly into the lower depths of the lake. It was claimed that this "deep pipe" would ensure that the tailings would fall harmlessly to the bottom. Originally, capital costs were estimated to be $14 million, with $2.4 million added to annual operating costs. By 1972, the estimates had nearly doubled to $27 million of capital costs and $4.7 million in annual operating costs, or about 3 percent of the value of ore shipped.

Numerous disadvantages to the deep-pipe concept were raised. It increased operating costs but produced no improvement in plant efficiency or product quality. There was little chance that the method would eliminate pressure from the environmentalists, because the tailings were still entering the lake, and future legislation could make this "solution" obsolete.

EPA Proposals

The EPA, recognizing the need for alternatives other than simply closing the plant down, commissioned independent studies of Reserve's options.

The most important of these was an International Engineering Company analysis (IECO Plan) of the costs and feasibility of constructing a new concentrator, tailings disposal pond, and related facilities at Babbitt. This alternative would involve moving beneficiating operations from Silver Bay to Babbitt, but leaving the pelletizing plant in Silver Bay.

This plan was strongly endorsed by the state and by the environmentalists, who saw several advantages in this setup. The health hazard would be removed far from Lake Superior, minimizing the chance of further action against the company. The area had a favorable topography, dam construction materials were close by, and there was ample room for expansion of the tailings disposal pond. In addition, savings would probably be realized in transportation costs, as the tonnage hauled to Silver Bay would be reduced by two-thirds because concentrated ore rather than taconite would be carried. There was also the possibility of improvements in pellet quality, which could not be achieved if tailings were pumped into the lake. By decreasing silica content of the pellets, the parent companies could recognize savings in coke costs and blast furnace lining wear. The silica reduction would increase the iron content of the pellets, resulting in further savings by increasing the amount of iron obtained from one operation of the blast furnace. Total capital costs were estimated at $188 to $211 million.

Reserve's Palisades Plan

In April 1974 Reserve advanced a new proposal that provided for total on-land disposal in the Palisades Creek area near Silver Bay. Reserve Chairman William Verity made the following offer:

> Reserve and its shareholders are prepared to authorize commencement of engineering on April 22, 1974, and to recommend to the respective Boards of Directors the construction of facilities which would eliminate the discharge of taconite tailings to Lake Superior and place those tailings in a total on-land system in the Palisades Creek area as modified near Silver Bay. . . . The new facilities will be so designed as to provide for some improvement in the finished pellets in an effort to make the pellets competitive and improve Reserve's posture among similar producers.
>
> The Palisades Creek total tailings plan is estimated to cost approximately $172,000,000. . . . The expenditure of such sums would substantially reduce the rate of return on the Reserve investment to the shareholders far below that of Reserve's competitors.
>
> This additional large investment would not result in any economic benefit to the shareholders, even taking into consideration product improvement. Integral parts of this offer are the following would-be conditions:
>
> 1. Continued operation during construction is required so as to be in a position to generate the coarse tailings essential for dam building in connection with the on-land plan.
> 2. Appropriate permits to be issued by all affected regulatory agencies insuring that the operation of Reserve will be permitted to continue for the anticipated mine life.
> 3. A satisfactory court resolution of the alleged health hazard issues, thus permitting a reasonable operating lifetime for the properties and helping make possible the financing of the project.
> 4. Inasmuch as the existing facilities were constructed and operated in accordance with state and federal permits, it is believed that any change now required constitutes a violation of Reserve's rights to so operate for the life of the permits. Under these circumstances, we believe it appropriate that government financial assistance be extended as may be legally available, including assistance with industrial revenue bonds and a satisfactory mechanism be established for assistance in pledges for repayment of bonds. Consistent with the foregoing, it is the intent that the new facilities would be financed and paid for by Reserve with,

however, assistance in bonding requirements so as to secure a lower interest rate on the substantial indebtedness.[24]

Reaction to Palisades Plan

The state rejected Verity's offer and continued to reject modification of the Palisades concept, for the following reasons:

1. The site of the tailings basin was only a few miles from Lake Superior. It was possible that asbestos particles could flow from there into the lake.

2. The dams would be visible from North Shore scenic and recreational areas. One dam would be 7,000 feet long and 450 feet high or more than twice as long and only 100 feet lower than the Grand Coulee Dam.

3. The dam, constructed from earthen materials, would present a potential hazard to the people and area below it.

4. Any plan must provide for use of asbestos-free ore during the switchover to land disposal.

Judge Lord also found the plan unacceptable. He stated:

> The chief executive officers of both Armco and Republic have proposed a plan for an on-land disposal site in the Palisades Creek area adjacent to the Silver Bay plant. Although this particular plan was in existence for several years, it was not brought forward until the latest stages of this proceeding. The plan, which has been rejected by the plaintiffs because it is not environmentally sound, is totally unacceptable to the court because of the conditions imposed with it. In the first place implementation of the proposal fails to effectively deal with the problem caused by the discharge of amphibole fibers into the air. Secondly, the plan contemplates that the discharge into the water will continue for five more years. In light of the very real threat to public health caused by the existing discharge, this time period for abatement is totally unacceptable. Third, it is suggested that the court order all appropriate state and federal agencies to grant permits that would immunize Reserve's operations from ever complying with future environmental regulations as they might be promulgated. The court seriously doubts that it has the power for such an order and states flatly that if it had the power it would not grant such an order. Reserve in this case has argued that certain state and federal permits granted years ago sanction their noncompliance with existing regulations and should preclude the court from abating the discharge of human carcinogens into the air and water. Such a claim is preposterous and the court will have no part in perpetuating such claims. The proposal is further conditioned on obtaining compensation from the federal and state governments. The court has previously discussed the lack of necessity for such a subsidy and finds the suggestion absurd.

---

[24] *U.S.A. et al.* v. *Reserve Mining Co. et al.,* Transcript, pp. 19,075–78.

Finally, the proposal was conditioned upon favorable findings by the court as to the public health issues. The court finds this condition to be shocking and unbecoming in a court of law. To suggest that this or any other court would make a finding of fact without regard to the weight of the evidence is to ask that judge to violate the oath of his office and to disregard the responsibility that he has not only to the people but also to himself.

Defendants have the economic and engineering capability to carry out an on-land disposal system that satisfies the health and environmental considerations raised. For reasons unknown to this court, they have chosen not to implement such a plan.[25]

RESERVE STRATEGY

Both the plaintiffs and the court were interested in Reserve's strategy for dealing with the pollution issue. Midway through the trial, the court subpoenaed internal company documents relating to the pollution problem. Boxes of reports and correspondence, including confidential memoranda and handwritten notes, were all brought into court and made available to the judge and plaintiffs. Some of these were put under protective order of the court, but others entered into the public domain by being quoted or offered as exhibits in the trial. The documents available to the public and accounts by various observers can be used to sketch a tentative picture of Reserve's responses at various times. Because the issues were still in litigation as of the writing of the case, the casewriter did not discuss Reserve's strategy with company officials.

Political

The Stoddard report, completed in December 1968, appeared to have posed the first serious threat to Reserve.[26] It was alleged that when company officials heard about the report and its recommendation that Reserve be forced to switch to on-land disposal within three years, their response was to contact Congressman John Blatnik, whose district included Reserve's operations.

It was claimed that Blatnik was a good friend of Reserve President Edward Furness, and that he had worked closely with company officials

---

[25] *U.S.A. et al.* v. *Reserve Mining Co. et al.*, Memorandum and Order, pp. 10–11.

[26] This account of the events that transpired was drawn primarily from two sources: *Superior Polluter*, a book by two environmentalist groups, and *Water Wasteland*, written by a Ralph Nader task force. No information was available on the authors of *Superior Polluter*. David Zwick, the editor of *Water Wasteland*, was a third-year law student and graduate student in public policy at Harvard University. The members of the task force were mainly graduate students.

It should be noted that other Nader reports had drawn both praise and criticism and had been quite controversial.

to obtain passage of a 1964 amendment to the Minnesota Constitution, which provided for favorable tax treatment of the taconite industry. An aide to Blatnik had commented that the congressman and Reserve people "have a real rapport." The report prepared by Ralph Nader's task force described their view of Reserve's actions in response to the Stoddard report:

> It was only natural when the Stoddard Report came out on December 31, 1968 with its recommendation that Reserve's dumping permit be terminated in three years, that Ed Schmid, assistant to the president of Reserve Mining for Public Relations, should telephone Blatnik's Washington office immediately to express his outrage at the findings. Schmid's call signaled the beginning of an all-out attempt by Reserve to quash or at least discredit Stoddard's work. . . . Another government official contacted by Reserve was Max Edwards, the Assistant Secretary of Interior for Water Research and Pollution Control. . . . Edwards was leaving government to become an industrial pollution control consultant and presumably wouldn't have minded lining up a future customer—Reserve Mining.
>
> Edwards went right to work. He ordered all Interior copies of the Stoddard Report held in his office for "review" and refused to release the study or its findings to inquiring newsmen . . . when asked by newsmen about the Stoddard study, Edwards described it as not an official document and full of inaccuracies. . . . Congressman Blatnik, who had been in touch with Assistant Secretary Edwards [for fact finding] as well as Udall, echoed for the press what Edwards was saying about the report. The study, according to Blatnik, had no official status, was only a preliminary report . . . [and] was completely false.[27]

The federal Enforcement Conference on the Pollution of Lake Superior became the next hurdle for Reserve. In April 1969, a month before the conference began, Harry Holiday, executive vice president of Armco, wrote a memorandum that appears to have laid out an organizational structure to deal with Reserve's pollution problems. Seven committees were set up "to insure proper coordination and decisive action in the various areas of concern regarding the Reserve tailing disposal problem." One of the seven, the Public Affairs Committee, was instructed to

> meet immediately to determine (1) the identity of those individuals in federal, state, or local governments who should be contacted, (2) the identity of those individuals who should make the contacts, and (3) the type of information that should be supplied. . . . Preparation for and carrying out of the presentation for the May 13 conference has priority in the activities of all committees, but it should be clearly understood that the tailings disposal problem will be a continuing one. Such being the case, all committees will be prepared to continue their efforts in the indefinite future.[28]

---

[27] Zwick, *Water Wasteland*, pp. 144–149.

[28] *U.S.A. et al.* v. *Reserve Mining Co. et al.*, Exhibit, Memorandum from Harry Holiday, April 24, 1969.

According to the Nader report, by the time the Enforcement Conference opened in May 1969, Max Edwards, the first public official to criticize the report, was out of government and on retainer as a consultant to Reserve Mining. The Nader report continues:

> The government was still walking a shaky tightrope between Congressmen Blatnik and Lake Superior. The political sensitivity of the proceedings was underscored by Secretary Hickel's unusual choice for conference chairman. Assistant Secretary of Interior Carl Klein headed the gathering, the first time in 46 federal enforcement actions that FWQA's Murray Stein had not been in charge. If Klein's performance at the conference is any indication, he had been brought there for one reason: to repudiate the Stoddard Report. The Assistant Secretary stayed only one day, just long enough to run through what appeared to be a well-rehearsed routine with Congressman Blatnik.

Blatnik: I ask you for a brief comment at this point, Mr. Secretary. Do you or any of your administrators or officials under your jurisdiction to your knowledge know of any federal report that has been suppressed?

Klein: Congressman Blatnik, you give me a chance to lay the ghost to rest. . . . The official report and the only official report of the Department of the Interior . . . was issued about a week ago. There has been no attempt at suppression by any congressman or any other federal official. There is in existence a report put out by an individual who used to be employed by the Department of the Interior shortly before he left and that is his report, despite the fact it bears the words "Department of Interior." *The Department of the Interior did not authorize it* and is not bound by the report. The only report that was put out officially by the Department of the Interior is this one put out a week ago.[29]

In October 1969, after the first session of the Enforcement Conference had been completed, Armco's manager of Air and Water Pollution Control, in a memo to Harry Holiday, laid out the action alternatives to be considered:

> With a limited amount of time to evaluate this problem, it appears there are several alternatives that must be weighed and considered. Some of these are:
>
> a. The recommendations made at the conference are not "official" until they have been approved and issued by the Secretary of the Interior.
>
>   By vigorous political activity, primarily in Washington, D.C., it may be possible to amend or modify the "conclusions" and "recommendations."
>
> b. While I do not claim to have a detailed knowledge of the legal aspects involved, it appears to me that the federal case of "Interstate Pollution" is very weak. The facts presented both in May and September 1969 have not demonstrated a significant danger to the "health and welfare."
>
>   I would assume that if we [Reserve–Armco–Republic] were to

---

[29] Zwick, *Water Wasteland,* pp. 144–149.

fight this issue in the courts that the "public image" would suffer somewhat from the "robber baron" concept. Nevertheless, I believe this approach must be carefully studied.

c. A careful study should be made of the present processing techniques
    to determine if the production of "super-fine tailings" can be reduced
    by changes in processing—even perhaps if it involves a decrease in
    product quality. This may be a way to satisfy, at least temporarily,
    the recommendations of the conference.

d. The engineering committee can prepare a "broad-brush" type concept
    of several alternate ideas to present at the next meeting of the conference,
    which will probably be in April or May 1970. I would suggest that if
    this is the desired approach that we present several schemes that have
    been studied but without indicating that we have sufficient detailed
    knowledge to recommend any given scheme or that we are prepared
    to designate a timetable for completion. We should indicate to the con-
    ference members the magnitude of the problem, the complexities in-
    volved, and the tremendous impact on the economy of the region.
        I suggest that we should also offer some "pilot" schemes that
    we believe may have merit in reducing the problem. By this technique
    we may be able to gain a few years' time.

e. Another obvious alternative that is available to management is to close
    down the existing facilities, which eliminates the reported water pollu-
    tion problem. If the Federal Government will assume a major part of
    the cost (equity) involved in this decision it may have some merit for
    consideration. After all, they were involved in the original hearings
    that granted the permits which led to the establishment of this particular
    process.[30]

Lobbying efforts in Washington were conducted by Reserve, Armco,
and Republic in late 1971. In April, the federal Enforcement Conference
had rejected the deep-pipe plan and federal action against Reserve appeared likely. Top officers from Armco and Republic went to Washington
to sell key congressmen on the deep-pipe plan, although it had been
claimed that this plan had already been found impractical. In court testimony, William Verity, Armco president, explained:

> We felt it would be very advisable to inform various people as to
> the problem at Reserve Mining, and so a presentation was prepared to
> take this information to various people who might have an interest in the
> Reserve Mining situation. So that this was a joint effort by Republic and
> Armco to do as good a job as we could in describing the underwater system
> and why we felt this system of deposition was the best . . . there was
> Senator Muskie, Senator Humphrey, various congressmen like Mr. Blatnik
> and others who were very interested in this problem. There was a great
> number of people which we felt were entitled to know our view on the
> situation . . . they were mostly in charge of the various committees of
> the Senate. We did meet with Republicans. We showed this to Mr. Taft,

---

[30] *U.S.A. et al.* v. *Reserve Mining Co. et al.,* State of Minnesota, Exhibit 74.

Jennings, Randolph . . . I can't recall the whole list, but we presented this to quite a few different people.[31]

The plaintiffs and the court were also interested in the political activities and relationships of the companies and their executives with the Nixon administration. During several days of intense questioning, no evidence of illegal activity emerged.

Charges of Delay

Reserve was accused by the plaintiffs and Judge Lord of attempting to delay as long as possible resolution of its pollution problems and the associated expenditures. One alleged tactic was to continue to offer variations of the deep-pipe plan after an internal engineering task force had advised against it. In June 1972, this internal task force had reported:

> Information recently obtained from the Colorado School of Mines study indicates that the required pipe flow velocity and related line pressure loss and pipe wear will be far greater than assumed initially. This may make it impossible to move the tailings the distance required underwater from a delta pumping station. A second question is raised by the extreme difficulty anticipated in replacing and extending pipe under all weather conditions in the open and unprotected reaches of Lake Superior. . . . For these reasons, the Engineering Task Force does not recommend pursuing this concept any further.[32]

Although environmentalists, state officials, and the EPA had opposed the deep-pipe concept from the start, and the task force had found it unfeasible, Reserve repeatedly revised and resubmitted it until February 1974, when it was finally abandoned.

The value of the numerous exhibits and data supplied by Reserve was openly questioned by Judge Lord. At a point near the end of the trial, he asked Reserve for cost estimates that were "not padded" and then added:

> I might suggest to you that the reason that I make this statement that I just made about padding figures, and so forth, is based on the nine months of experience in looking at Reserve's exhibits, which have, by and large, not been worth the paper they're written on. And I determine that, well, the profits are at the rate of sixty thousand dollars a day. Every time they can keep the judge looking at an exhibit all day, it's worth sixty thousand dollars. Even though the exhibit is useless in its final analysis.[33]

In April 1974, as the trial was drawing to a conclusion, Judge Lord recounted Reserve's alleged tactics of delay:

---

[31] *U.S.A. et al.* v. *Reserve Mining Co. et al.,* Transcript, pp. 18,879–82.

[32] *U.S.A. et al.* v. *Reserve Mining Co. et al.,* U.S. Exhibit 430.

[33] *U.S.A. et al.* v. *Reserve Mining Co. et al.,* Transcript, p. 19,387.

When the case was started, Mr. Sheran asked me if I could help to negotiate a settlement of this case. I started to negotiate toward a settlement of this case. And my first utterances were "Is there any plan? Can you bring any sort of skeleton plan forward which would provide for on-land disposal?"

Mr. Fride [a lawyer for Reserve] said, "No, Judge, that's not fair to me. You have prejudged the matter by even asking the question. We have an underwater disposal plan which we—the so-called 'Deep Pipe,'—we want you to consider that."

All discussions—I withdrew from discussions then, waiting anxiously to hear about the underwater pipe. About six months later, the underwater pipe was brought forward. That's six months later and ten million dollars' profit later and fifty billion fibers later down the throats of the children in Duluth, after I applied every bit of judiciousness and dedication and study and patience that I could to the problems created here, I found that the six months that I had spent—not the total six months, but a good portion of it—the six months I had spent waiting to hear about Deep Pipe, and the week or two that we spent hearing about it were just another presentation by Armco and Republic to delay that which I now found you then knew to be the inevitable day when that discharge would be taken out of the lake.

We've now gone on about four months past that time. We had a judge named Eckman who about three years ago in a state trial, who heard all the ecology said, "This must come out of the lake. We must change the charge." They were then talking to him. They were feeding him the Deep Pipe.

All of this delay—now you're talking—when we talk about the time from Judge Eckman's trial forward, the total profits to Reserve are somewhere in the vicinity of fifty to sixty million dollars. The total damage to the people of Duluth I cannot equate.

Now, as soon as I saw that Deep Pipe was no longer an alternative method of disposal, when I myself decided it was a joke, I then ordered you into negotiations. The negotiations have gone on.

What you're arguing about is a question of some twenty or thirty million dollars. No matter what I write here, if I appeal—you appeal it, you can have your cake and eat it, too. You can have the time within which to make another twenty million dollars and pay in your profits the cost that you will here argue about.

The cost to the people of Duluth I cannot calculate. I don't wish to alarm anybody. All I can say is I don't know. Dr. Brown, who I retained as a court witness at the suggestion of Reserve, says it should come out. He can't calculate it.

Now, what I want to ask you is there any prospect that you—and I know what the pressures are here and you know what they are. The court here is faced with the prospect of a stranded population, hostages of the Reserve Mining Company, with a whole economic segment standing almost in arms ready to march on the State Capitol or the Federal Government in Washington. They're doing it because Armco and Republic have seen fit to hold out for the last dollar of profit and to the last point of time.

If I indicate to you that you have turn-around time, you will immediately take the indication to the Court of Appeals and say the judge found there was no health hazard. He gave us turn-around time. We want the time for the Court of Appeals to minutely examine this record of some eighteen thousand pages, several thousand exhibits, with all the briefing that goes with it, the people of Duluth for another year will have that unwelcomed addition to their diet. Your own internal documents indicate the game you have been playing with the court.[34]

APPEALS COURT DECISION

After Judge Lord's order closing the plant, Reserve immediately appealed to the U.S. Court of Appeals for a stay of the ruling. Two days later, on April 22, 1974, a 70-day stay was granted and the Reserve plant reopened. The appeals court, in its limited review, stated:

We have reviewed the testimony on the health issue. . . . While not called upon at this stage to reach any final conclusion, our review suggests that this evidence does not support a finding of substantial danger and that, indeed, the testimony indicates that such a finding should not be made. . . . We believe that Judge Lord carried his analysis one step beyond the evidence. Since testimony clearly established that an assessment of the risk was made impossible by the absence of medical knowledge, Judge Lord apparently took the position that all uncertainties should be resolved in favor of health and safety.[35]

The court also instructed Reserve and the plaintiffs to attempt to reach a settlement within the 70-day period. Otherwise, the appeals court would review the status of the stay order based on plans, comments, and recommendations of Reserve, the plaintiffs, and Judge Lord, and decide to either continue it, or let the plant close down.

APPENDIX

Asbestos

The following is quoted from a June 1973 address by Dr. Irving Selikoff. It was reprinted in the March 1974, *American Society of Safety Engineers* and is used here with permission.

The first cases of asbestos disease in our country were reported in 1930, and soon after a very good Public Health Service study under Dr. Dreesen and his colleagues was undertaken. But from that point on, from

---

[34] *U.S.A. et al.* v. *Reserve Mining Co. et al.*, Transcript, pp. 19,069–72.

[35] *Reserve Mining Co. et al.* v. *U.S.A. et al.*, U.S. Court of Appeals, Eighth Circuit, No. 74–1291, pp. 9, 24.

the early 30s to the early 60s, there was virtually a total absence of scientific research into this problem. Therefore when in 1969, '70, and '71, decisions were to be made, we didn't have a great deal on which to rely.

Secondly, data that had been collected during the 1960s suggested that this was a very complex problem. We should not have been surprised at this, because this complexity had, as we reviewed the situation, existed almost from its inception.

The first case of asbestosis, i.e., lung scarring as a result of inhalation of asbestos dust, was reported in 1924 by Dr. Cooke of Leeds, after he had done a post-mortem on a young woman who had very extensive scarring throughout her lungs. He very astutely noted that she had worked in an asbestos textile factory. However, what he did not know and could not answer was how her exposure in that factory had resulted in the disease. What he could not answer was how much of the dust that she had inhaled in the 20 years of her employment was necessary to cause the fibrosis.

She had worked 20 years and had inhaled a great deal of dust, but how much of that dust was "wasted" in terms of production of disease, was not known. He did not know nor do we today, whether one day, one week, one month, one year, or three years of that dust was required for her to have the scarring she suffered, and to subsequently die.

In the years after Dr. Cooke's report we learned a good deal. The most important thing we learned was that whatever asbestos does takes a long time to become clinically evident. For example, 1,000 asbestos insulation workers were examined by us in the New York metropolitan area; of the 725 with less than 20 years from onset of exposure, most had normal X-rays. Only a minority had abnormal X-rays. When they were abnormal they tended to be only minimally so. On the other hand, once the 20-year point had passed, most had abnormal X-rays; and when they were abnormal they frequently were extensively so.

The next lesson we learned was that "years of exposure" was not necessarily synonymous with "years from onset of exposure." In other words, there was an important variable rarely included in the usual analysis of dose–disease response relationships—the variable of residence time of the dust in the lungs.

Cases have been seen of two, four, six weeks of exposure—probably intensive exposure—30 years ago, with extensive current fibrosis. The explanation is that the individual had six weeks of exposure.

The lungs which contained the dust inhaled in those six weeks had since had 30 years of exposure. Thus, residence time had to be added to the complex biological equation we were to formulate.

We also found in these 30 years that, in addition to the lung itself being involved, not infrequently the covering of the lung, the pleura, also was frequently involved, that more than one tissue could be affected. This also followed the 20-year rule. For example, of the 725 with less than 20 years from onset of exposure, most had a normal pleura on X-ray. On the other hand, once the 20-year point had passed, fibrosis and/ or calcification were common.

This has special significance in that whatever we have seen to this point is the result of exposure from 1920, 1930, 1940, or 1950. In 1930, the United States used around 120,000 tons of asbestos, so what we are seeing now is the result of such levels of use. We are now using about 700,000 tons of asbestos each year. Disease associated with current use of asbestos will not be seen until the year 2000.

*   *   *   *   *

In 1954 . . . a second disease, mesothelioma, a cancer of the lining of the chest (the pleura) was reported by Dr. Weiss in Germany in a man who also had asbestosis. This was a very unhappy finding. First of all, to that point mesothelioma was very rare. How rare, we don't know. It was so rare that it was not separately coded in the International Classification of Causes of Death.

Therefore, no valid statistics are available. The best evidence we have is that it was something around one out of every 10,000 deaths.

Among people with asbestos exposure, it soon after 1954 began to be reported frequently. When it was, it was disheartening since it was invariably fatal.

*   *   *   *   *

We didn't know in the 1950s how much of a problem these cancers would turn out to be. The matter was of some importance because until this point, the question was only whether our task was to prevent asbestosis (lung scarring). Now it was whether it was to include something more, cancer. There was, and therefore our precautions would have to be related to all.

In the last several years, a number of studies have been done to bring together data on this aspect of the question. In one, 632 members of the Asbestos Workers Union in 1943 in the New York metropolitan area were studied. Age, year and sex, specific rates indicated that by the end of 1962 there should have been 203 deaths among them. There were 255. Fifty men died in this one union who were not expected to die.

Looking at the death by cause, six or seven deaths of cancer of the lung and pleura were expected. There actually were 45. This obviously was where the major portion of the excess deaths were. . . . Interestingly, there should have been nine or ten deaths of cancer of the stomach, colon, rectum and esophagus. There were 29. Individuals who inhale dust also ingest it. There were, as expected, 12 deaths of scarred lungs. Observation has been maintained of the survivors in this group, to the end of 1971 and the resulting data may be of interest. Where there should have been, from 1963 to 1971, another 85 deaths, 168 occurred. There should have been five deaths or so of lung cancer. There were 42. There should have been no deaths of mesothelioma. There were 25. There were increases in cancer of the stomach, colon, and rectum and excess deaths of asbestosis.

Altogether, from 1943 through 1971, 430 of the 632 men died, giving us a good idea of what happened to asbestos workers. One out of every five deaths was due to lung cancer, one out of every 15 due to mesothelioma, one out of every 10 or so due to gastro-intestinal cancer, and almost one of 15 due to scarred lungs.

Additional Difficulties

In recent years additional difficulties have been placed upon us. To return to mesothelioma, you will remember how rare it has been in the past, about one in 10,000 deaths. One can imagine the consternation, then, when in 1960 J. C. Wagner reported 47 cases of mesothelioma, all in one part of South Africa, in five years, 1956 to 1960. Most were in a part of South Africa in which there were many asbestos mines and mills. Dr. Wagner visited the relatives of these people and inquired about possible asbestos exposure. He found that in most cases there had been 25, 30 years before opportunity for asbestos contact, often not by working with the material but by limited contact in environmental or family circumstances.

With this knowledge, Muriel L. Newhouse, a very capable epidemiologist at the London School of Hygiene, studied the 76 cases of mesothelioma in the files of the London Hospital. She found that of the 76 cases, 31 had worked with asbestos. More important, of the 45 who had not worked with asbestos, nine had simply lived in the household of an asbestos worker and 11 had lived within a half mile of one of the asbestos plants in London.

*   *   *   *   *

These studies raised for the first time the question whether intimate and immediate occupational exposure to asbestos was required for the production of asbestos disease or whether others, as those with indirect occupational exposure, might also have this risk. This new question, not unimportant, has now been placed before us. Incidentally, it is not considered in the asbestos standards that have been set by the Department of Labor.

*   *   *   *   *

In conclusion may I express the hope that we will not long remain in the difficult situation in which we now find ourselves. The Department of Labor has recently announced that it will reopen the question of the asbestos standards. This is all to the good. Surely the problem is a solvable one. Industry is much too competent, labor is much too concerned, science has too much reliable and pertinent data and government is far too responsible for us to admit defeat.

CASE 30

Questionable Payments Abroad: Gulf in Italy

In the aftermath of Watergate, a number of political contributions by large corporations came to light, prompting extensive enquiries by a number of government agencies including the Justice Department, Internal Revenue Service, and the Securities and Exchange Commission. In examining the extent, source, and nature of these contributions, investigators also found in several companies evidence of "questionable payments" abroad.

In this environment, the boards of many corporations began their own internal investigations, and during 1976 and 1977 over 400 "voluntary reports" relating to questionable payments abroad had been filed with the SEC.

One such report by the Special Review Committee of the board of directors of Gulf Oil Corporation received widespread publicity, not only for its revelation of numerous clearly illegal payments, but also because it gave some insight to some of the more common pressures and demands facing managers that are not so clearly defined.

The following incident is only one of scores documented by the special committee, but may serve to illustrate the complexity of the issues involved.

GULF IN ITALY

Background

Gulf first entered the Italian scene in the late 1940s. Drilling concessions were obtained in the Ragusa field in Sicily, and in due course Gulf found oil practically under the nose of ENI/AGIP, the Italian National Oil Company. In due course Gulf's expansion in Italy included installation or acquisition of a chain of filling stations, port and storage facilities, distribution centers, and refining capacity. Other foreign oil companies were then operating in Italy and Gulf was faced with very active competition in its effort to establish itself in the Italian market.

In these activities Gulf utilized, as its Italian representative and eventually head of operations, Nicolo Pignatelli, an Italian national, who had been associated with Gulf's activities in Italy from the very start. He helped guide Gulf through numerous vicissitudes in the Italian venture including the divestment of a number of relatively unsuccessful operations as well as the successful consummation of the exchange of the Ragusa concession for a long-term Kuwait crude oil supply contract with ENI/AGIP.

Although Pignatelli enjoyed a substantial degree of independence he maintained close association with Gulf centers of authority in London and Pittsburgh during the period of his Italian operations. In fact, he was in the habit of making rather frequent trips to Pittsburgh to acquaint the management with the progress of activities in Italy.

The audit committee's investigation acknowledged that Italy was an area where, by custom and law, political contributions by corporations were well-recognized phenomena. Prior to May 1974, corporate political contributions were, generally speaking, lawful in Italy provided the corporation's stockholders were informed.

After its investigation of Gulf's operations in Italy, the audit committee reported that there was no doubt that corporate funds of Gulf were expended in Italy by its Italian subsidiary from time to time for the purpose of inducing minor local functionaries to do or to expedite the performance of their normal duties or to reward them for extra services. Apparently, the giving of "omaggi" or gifts to lubricate the sluggish machinery of petty bureauracy was and is an accepted way of life in Italy.[1] The practice was characterized as tipping rather than bribery and was not considered unlawful. A special "off-the-books fund" (known as the "Fondo Nero" or Black Fund) was used for this purpose, among others. However, there were other practices and events in which Gulf's manage-

---

[1] An example of this was the company's practice of using gas coupons as gratuities or "omaggi." Over $7,000 worth of gas coupons were distributed by the company in Italy during the first quarter of 1975 to various governmental functionaries and others.

ment behavior was less clearly understood. One such example was provided by the events surrounding the so-called "Plum Project."

Expansion of the Milan Refinery (the "Plum Project")

On January 22, 1967, Gulf obtained a license to install a refinery at Zelo Buon Persico near Milan, despite great public opposition. Numerous extremely hostile, if not vitriolic, press reports and editorials denounced Gulf and opposed its plans to construct the refinery. The opposition was expressed to be largely on ecological grounds, but there was an undercurrent of antiforeign sentiment as well. The campaign in the press against the refinery continued into 1968 and 1969, and a change in zoning requirements ultimately blocked construction at the Zelo Buon Persico site which Gulf had already purchased.

By decree dated August 2, 1969, Gulf was granted permission to move the location of the proposed refinery to Bertonico in the Terranova Commune, also near Milan. It appears that Gulf overcame the public opposition, to some extent at least, and the refinery was constructed and went on-stream in June 1972.[2] A formal opening was attended by local officials and citizens, which featured the ceremonial drinking of effluent water from the refinery by Mr. Nicolo Pignatelli, Gulf's head of Italian operations, Dr. M. R. J. Wyllie, head of Gulf's Eastern Hemisphere organization, and various public officials, in an effort to dramatize its freedom from pollution. However, while the actual processing capacity was 5,800,000 tons per annum, an operating permit for only 3,900,000 tons was issued.

In November 1972, Gulf commenced negotiations with Mobil looking to a transaction (ultimately referred to as the "Plum Project") under which Mobil would purchase an interest in the refinery at a price substantially higher than Gulf's cost of construction. The Mobil transaction depended upon Gulf's obtaining a license to utilize fully the actual, installed refining capacity of 5.8 million tons per annum.

Concerned with the sort of extreme opposition from the press, local communities, and various citizens and environmental groups which had plagued its efforts to build the refinery in 1968–69, Gulf felt it needed local assistance to guide it through the bureaucratic maze and to improve the public relations aspect of the application.

The decree authorizing the utilization of the full capacity of the Bertonico refinery would have to be issued jointly by the Ministry of Industry and Commerce and the Ministry of Finance after obtaining favorable opinions of an Interministerial Commission for the Testing of Plant

---

[2] Of the $425,000 distributed through the "off-the-books" Fondo Nero, 11 separate payments totaling $10,800 had been made to journalists and editors for the purpose of influencing press coverage of the Milan refinery controversy.

and Equipment, composed of representatives of three ministries; an Interministerial Commission for Petroleum Affairs composed of representatives of 12 ministries; two bureaus in Milan; the regional government of Lombardy and three of its departments; and the communes of Bertonico, Terranova de' Passerini, and Turano.

Accordingly, Pignatelli enlisted the help of Mr. G. Del Bo, president of a company known as Andergip, S.A., described as a public relations and financial consulting firm, with addresses in Eschen, Liechtenstein, and Lugano, Switzerland (Del Bo was also the president and principal stockholder of a company known as Carbonafta, a large petroleum jobber in Italy with which Gulf had substantial dealings, and president of the Italian Petroleum Jobbers Association). He was described by Pignatelli as "highly knowledgeable in the industry and a man of considerable influence."

On February 21, 1973, Pignatelli received a letter from Andergip, S.A., which set forth the basis on which the organization would assist Gulf in obtaining the authorization. The letter stated in full as follows (translation):

> In relation to the results of the final tests of the Bertonico Refinery, which have ascertained that it has an installed capacity of 5.8 million tons of crude per year, I wish to confirm to you on behalf of our company that we are prepared to put at the disposal of your company our organization in Italy for public relations consulting at a regional, provincial, and local level as well as our necessary technical services in the sector of urban planning and ecology, relative to the application which Gulf Italiana will submit in order to obtain the official acknowledgement of the aforementioned processing capacity of the Bertonico Refinery.
>
> The acknowledgement of said capacity is for us of relevant interest, inasmuch as the development programs of the Italian commercial activities associated with us base themselves on the availability of larger quantities of finished products in the Po Valley.
>
> For our assistance you will credit us an amount of U.S. $870,000 payable at the Bank Institute of the Swiss Confederation, after the aforementioned processing capacity will become operational.[3]

Pignatelli described the contract as a contingency agreement and indicated that there was a "side" oral agreement that the license had to be obtained by September 30 or Andergip would bear all its expenditures. Apparently, the September 30 deadline was established because Gulf had to sign the related deal with Mobil by year-end.

In early February 1973, Pignatelli appeared in Pittsburgh before the Executive Council and made a presentation of the proposed transaction with Mobil ("Plum Project"). The minutes of the March 15, 1973 meeting

---

[3] Report of the Special Review Committee of the Board of Directors of Gulf Oil Corporation, U.S. District Court for the District of Columbia, Civil Action No. 75–0324, December 30, 1975, p. 151.

of the Executive Council record approval "to proceed with arrangements to obtain a government permit to increase the licensed throughput the Milan Refinery to 120,000 B/D."

In the bureaucratic proceedings relating to the Milan Refinery, all applications and formal contacts with governmental agencies were handled, according to Pignatelli, by Gulf officials. However, there was a mass of detail and "promotional" work which had to be undertaken to support the application and this, Pignatelli stated, was handled by Andergip.

In its formal application to the government for full utilization of the installed capacity, Gulf pointed out that the relocation from Zelo Buon Persico to Bertonico, due to denial of zoning authorization, had cost the company some additional $16 million over the original budgeted cost of the refinery project. Gulf also argued that expansion of production to 5,800,000 tons per year would not have adverse ecological consequences or entail any local dislocation due to construction since the refinery already had that capacity. Moreover, the increased production would benefit the public as well as result in substantial economies for Gulf.

On July 4, 1973, the decree authorizing the processing of up to 5,800,000 tons per year at Bertonico was issued by the appropriate ministries. Implementation of the conditions set forth in the decree concerning the installation of additional tankage involved four ministries, the regional government of Lombardy and two of its departments, the three communes referred to above, and a consortium for the Navigation Canal Milano–Cremona–Po. The necessity of obtaining the acquiescence of all of these dispersed governmental agencies would appear to make the implementation task a formidable one.

On July 16, 1973, an interim authority for expenditure (AFE) in the sum of $1 million was prepared and signed by Dr. Wyllie and Mr. J. J. Earnest, president and comptroller, respectively, of Gulf–Eastern Hemisphere, covering the obligation to Andergip. Under "description," the interim AFE stated:

> Preliminary Expenditures
> Note: This AFE will be incorporated into the final AFE for total product cost of about $28 million when finally issued.[4]

The interim AFE was delivered for countersignature to Zane Q. Johnson, executive vice president of Gulf Oil in Pittsburgh, who returned it with a handwritten buckslip initialed by Johnson stating: "I discussed with J. Lee [president of Gulf Oil] and then advised Wyllie that he was to handle some other way." An undated memorandum for file by Mr. J. M. Turnbull, comptroller in London, stated in part:

> While Mr. Johnson did not sign AFE there were discussions between

---

[4] Ibid., p. 152.

Messrs. Wyllie and Johnson on this subject and the Executives were aware that a "special" payment had to be made in order to obtain the permit.

. . . in any event Mr. W. H. Meador, the Corporate Director Internal Auditing, was in London at the time the payment was being arranged and he was made fully aware of the transaction.[5]

In the board's enquiry, neither Lee nor Johnson had any recollection of the transaction. However, Lee stated that his reaction would be not to sign the interim AFE because it was not a usual or normal AFE. Lee distinguished between a "preliminary" AFE, which this was, and a "final" AFE, noting that preliminary AFEs were generally based upon concrete engineering estimates of costs, which the interim AFE in question was not, nor was it for a specific sum for a particular purpose.

On July 26, 1973, Gulf paid $868,853 to Mr. G. Del Bo, president of Andergip, and received a receipt from him. Payment was effected in the following manner. Morgan Guaranty Trust Company, London, was instructed to transfer $868,853 to Swiss Credit Bank, Chiasso, for retention pending instructions from Mr. Giartosio (administrative manager, Gulf Italy) who was to be identified by his passport. On July 26, 1973, Giartosio caused funds to be transferred to Del Bo at Swiss Credit Bank in Chiasso in exchange for appropriate receipts. These receipts were forwarded by Giartosio to Turnbull, the comptroller in London, with a buckslip stating *"Not* for Circulation in Italy." The receipt, said to have been signed by Del Bo with the left hand, stated as follows:

> This is to certify that the remittance of U.S. dollars $868,853 equivalent to Italian lire 530,000,000 attested by the attached bank receipt no. Sirenetta of 26/7/73 represents the agreed full and final settlement of all sums due in reimbursement of any expenses incurred for carrying out preliminary technical, urbanistic and ecological studies and surveys, as well as in payment of consultancy fees for public relations and administrative services rendered at national, regional and provincial levels in preparation of the application and development of information and data in support of the obtainment of the authorization, by means of debottlenecking, to process up to 5.6 million tons per year of crude oil in Gulf's Milan Refinery.[6]

The accounting for this payment on the Gulf books was as follows: Gulf–Eastern Hemisphere charged the payment to a suspense account in July 1973. In December 1973, the charge was transferred to a fixed asset account: Milan Refinery, Italy. In May 1974, the charge was transferred back to Gulf–Eastern Hemisphere, where it was again held in a suspense account. In July 1974, the charge was transferred to Gulf Europe, a Liechtenstein corporation, where it was expensed in 1974. The records of this entry are maintained in Zurich.

---

[5] Ibid., pp. 152–53.

[6] Ibid., pp. 153–54.

Mobil ultimately paid Gulf 36.5 percent ($317,134) of this payment upon the sale to Mobil of an interest in the Milan Refinery.

The committee's investigation was unable to determine what disposition was made of the $868,853. However, Pignatelli claimed that neither he nor to his knowledge any other Gulf official had any intention, understanding, or knowledge that any portion of the payment would be, or was, used for payments to political parties or government officials or in an otherwise improper manner to obtain the authorization. Nor was any part of it to be returned to Gulf for any purpose.

The board committee requested Del Bo to state in writing the general use to which the fee had been put. In response, on July 30, 1975, he wrote a letter to the chairman of the committee which stated as follows (translation):

> As you courteously requested, I am hereby reconfirming in writing what Mr. Del Bo has already declared to you verbally in the course of the meetings in London and in Rome: That is to say that it is certain that no part of the sum turned over by GOC was directly or indirectly destined for political parties or political personalities or to governmental functionaries; as it is also certain that no part of that said sum was returned to dependents or organs of the Gulf Oil Company. . . .
>
> To the extent that this will interest you, we inform you that said sums were destined approximately as follows: 50 to 55 percent to the newspaper and publication agencies specializing in the sector (Petroleum), about 35 percent to consultants and experts, and the remaining to Andergip.
>
> We remain at your disposal for any further information and we welcome the opportunity to give you our best wishes.[7]

Mr. Del Bo did not furnish the committee with copies of any documents constituting the "work product" of the Andergip organization or a detailed description of the work performed or the expenses incurred in obtaining the authorization. However, the committee did not feel it was in any position to demand an accounting, a lump-sum payment having been provided for with no obligation to account for its use.

---

[7] Ibid., pp. 155–56.

CASE 31

Nestlé and the Infant Food Controversy (A) (revised)

In October 1978, Dr. Fürer, managing director of Nestlé S.A., head-quartered in Vevey, Switzerland, was pondering the continuing problems his company faced. Public interest groups, media, health organizations, and other groups had been pressuring Nestlé to change its marketing practices for infant formula products, particularly in developing countries. Those groups had used a variety of pressure tactics, including a consumer boycott in the United States over the past eight years. Critics of Nestlé charged that the company's promotional practices were not only abusive but also harmful, resulting in malnutrition and death in some circumstances. They demanded Nestlé put a stop to all promotion of its infant formula products both to consumers and health personnel.

Nestlé management had always prided itself on its high quality standards, its efforts to serve the best interests of Nestlé customers, and its contribution to the health and prosperity of people in developing countries. Nestlé management was convinced their infant formula products were useful and wanted; they had not taken the first signs of adverse publicity in the early 1970s very seriously. By 1978, massive adverse publicity appeared to be endangering the reputation of the company, particularly in Europe and North America. Despite support from some health officials and organizations throughout the world, Nestlé management in Vevey and White Plains, New York (U.S.A. headquarters), were seriously concerned. Dr. Fürer had been consulting with Mr. Guerrant, president of Nestlé U.S.A., in an effort to formulate a strategy. Of immediate concern to Nestlé management was the scheduled meeting of the National Council of Churches (U.S.A.) in November 1978. On the agenda was a resolution to support the critics of Nestlé who were leading the consumer boycott against Nestlé products in the United States. The fact that the National Council of Churches was an important, prestigious organization caused Nestlé management to fear that NCC support of the boycott might further endanger Nestlé.

Also of concern was the meeting of the World Health Organization (WHO) scheduled in the fall of 1979 to bring together the infant food manufacturers, public interest groups, and the world health community in an attempt to formulate a code of marketing conduct for the industry. Nestlé management, instrumental in establishing this conference, hoped that a clear set of standards would emerge, thus moderating or eliminating the attacks of the public pressure groups.

Dr. Fürer was anxious to clear up what he thought were misunderstandings about the industry. As he reviewed the history of the formula problem, he wondered in general what a company could do when subjected to pressure tactics by activist groups, and in particular, what Nestlé management should do next.

NESTLÉ ALIMENTANA S.A.

The Swiss-based Nestlé Alimentana S.A. was one of the largest food products companies in the world. Nestlé had 80,000 shareholders in Switzerland. Nestlé's importance to Switzerland was comparable to the combined importance of General Motors and Exxon to the United States. In 1977, Nestlé's worldwide sales approximated 20 billion Swiss francs. Of this total, 7.3 percent were infant and dietetic products; more specifically, 2.5 percent of sales were accounted for by infant formula sales in developing countries.

Traditionally a transnational seller of food products, Nestlé's basic goal had always been to be a fully integrated food processor in every country in which it operated. It aimed at maintaining an important market presence in almost every nation of the world. In each country, Nestlé typically established local plants, supported private farms and dairy herds, and sold a wide range of products to cover all age groups. By the end of 1977, Nestlé had 87 factories in the developing countries and provided 35,610 direct jobs. Nestlé management were proud of this business approach and published a 228-page book in 1975 entitled *Nestlé in Developing Countries*. The cover of this book carried the following statement:

> While Nestlé is not a philanthropic society, facts and figures clearly prove that the nature of its activities in developing countries is self-evident as a

factor that contributes to economic development. The company's constant need for local raw materials, processing and staff, and the particular contribution it brings to local industry, support the fact that Nestlé's presence in the Third World is based on common interests in which the progress of one is always to the benefit of the other.

Although it neither produced nor marketed infant formula in the United States, the Nestlé Company Inc. (White Plains) sold a variety of products such as Nescafé, Nestea, Crunch, Quik, Taster's Choice, and Libby, McNeil & Libby products throughout the United States.

With over 95 percent of Nestlé's sales outside of Switzerland, the company had developed an operating policy characterized by strong central financial control along with substantial freedom in marketing strategy by local managers. Each country manager was held responsible for profitability. Through periodic planning meetings, Nestlé management in Vevey ("the Centre") reviewed the broad strategy proposals of local companies. One area of responsibility clearly reserved to Vevey was the maintenance of the overall company image, although no formal public relations department existed. Marketing plans were reviewed in part by Vevey to see if they preserved the company's reputation for quality and service throughout the world.

NESTLÉ AND THE INFANT FORMULA INDUSTRY

The international infant formula industry was composed of two types of firms, pharmaceutically oriented ones and food processing ones. The major companies competing in the developing countries were as follows:

Company	Brands
a. Pharmaceutical	
(U.S.) Wyeth Lab (American Home Products)	SMA, S26, Nursoy
(U.S.) Ross Lab (Abbott Laboratories)	Similac, Isomil
(U.S.) Mead Johnson (Bristol-Myers)	Enfamil, Olac, Prosobee
b. Food processing	
(U.S.) Borden	Klim, New Biolac
(Switzerland) Nestlé	Nestogen, Eledon, Pelargon Nan, Lactogen
(U.K.) Unigate	None

In addition to these six firms, there were about another dozen formula producers chartered in 1978 throughout the world.

The basic distinction between pharmaceutically oriented formula producers and food processing-oriented producers lay in their entry point into the formula business. In the early 1900s, medical research laboratories of major pharmaceutical firms developed "humanized formulas," leading their parents into marketing such products. Essentially, a humanized formula was a modification of normal cow's milk to approximate more closely human milk. Generally speaking, the food processing companies had begun offering infant food as an extension of their full milk powdered products and canned milk.

As early as the 1800s, Nestlé had been engaged in research in the field of child nutrition. In 1867, Henri Nestlé, the founder of the company and the great-grandfather of infant formula, introduced the first specifically designed, commercially marketed infant weaning formula. An infant weaning formula is basically a cereal and milk mixture designed to introduce solids to a child of five to six months of age.

As of the 1860s, both Nestlé and Borden had been producing sweetened and evaporated milk. Nestlé very quickly recognized the need for better artificial infant food and steadily developed a full line of formula products in the early 1900s (for example, Lactogen in 1921, Eledon in 1927, Nestogen in 1930). Although it was a food processing company, Nestlé's product development and marketing were supervised by physicians.

In the U.S. in the early 1900s, the infant formula products developed by the medical laboratories were being used primarily in hospitals. Over time, the industry developed the distinction of formula products for "well babies" versus "sick babies." In the latter category would be included special nutritional and dietary problems, such as allergies to milk requiring babies to have totally artificial formulas made from soybeans. Approximately 2 percent of industry volume was formula designed for "sick babies."

In the late 19th century and early years of the 20th century, Nestlé has developed a commanding position in the sweetened and evaporated milk market in the developing countries (also referred to as the "Third World"). Demand for these products was initially established among European colonials and gradually spread throughout the world and into the rising middle classes in many nations. Nestlé's early marketing efforts focused on switching infant feeding from the previously common sweetened and condensed milk to a more appropriate product, humanized infant formula.

By promoting through doctors (medical detailing) a full product line, Nestlé achieved an overwhelmingly dominant market position in the European colonies, countries which later became independent Third World countries. Meanwhile, most of the competition developed quickly in the industrialized countries, so much so that Nestlé stayed out of the U.S. formula market entirely. Only late in the 1950s did significant intense competition, mainly from American multinationals, develop in Nestlé's markets in developing countries. These markets with their high birth rates and rising affluence became increasingly attractive to all formula producers. After the entry of American competitors, Nestlé's share of markets began to erode.

As of 1978, Nestlé accounted for about half of infant formula sales in the developing countries while American companies held about one fifth. The total world market for infant formula was estimated at about $1.5 billion (U.S.), of that half of the sales were to developing countries in Africa, Asia, the Middle East, and Latin America.

TRADITIONAL METHODS OF PROMOTION

Several methods had been used over the years to promote infant products in developing countries. Five major methods predominated:

a. Media advertising—All media types were employed including posters in clinics and hospitals, outdoor billboards, newspapers, magazines, radio, television, and loudspeakers on vans. Native languages and English were used.

b. Samples—Free sample distribution either direct to new mothers or via doctors was relatively limited until competition increased in the 1960s. Mothers were given either formula or feeding bottles or both, often in a "new mother's kit." Doctors in clinics and hospitals received large packages of product for use while mother and baby were present. The formula producers believed this practice helped educate new mothers on the use of formula products, and hopefully, initiated brand preference. In some instances, doctors actually resold samples to provide an extra source of income for themselves or their institutions.

c. Booklets—Most formula marketers provided new mothers with booklets on baby care which were given free to them when they left the hospitals and clinics with their newborn infants. These booklets, such as Nestlé's *A Life Begins,* offered a variety of advice and advertised the formula products and other infant foods, both Nestlé and home made.

d. Milk nurses—Milk nurses (also known as mothercraft nurses) were formula producer employees who talked with new mothers in the hospitals and clinics or at home. Originally, they were all fully trained nurses, instructed in product knowledge, then sent out to educate new mothers on the correct use of the new formula products. This instruction included the importance of proper personal hygiene, boiling the water, and mixing formula and water in correct quantities. Milk nurses became a major part of many firms' efforts; for example, at one time Nestlé had about 200 mothercraft employees worldwide. The majority of milk nurses were paid a straight salary plus a travel allowance, but over time, some were hired on a sales-related bonus basis. Some companies, other than Nestlé, began to relax standards in the 1960s and hired nonnursing personnel who dressed in nurses' uniforms and acted more in a selling capacity and less in an educational capacity.

e. Milk banks—"Milk bank" was the term used to describe special distribution outlets affiliated with and administered by those hospitals and clinics which served very low-income people. Formula products were provided to low-income families at much reduced prices for mothers who could not afford the commercial product. The producers sold products to these outlets at lower prices to enable this service to occur.

PAG 23

Nestlé management believed the controversy surrounding the sale of infant formula in developing countries began in the early 1970s. Many international organizations were concerned about the problem of malnourishment of infants in the developing countries of South Asia, Africa, and Latin America. In Bogota (1970) and Paris (1972), representatives of the Food and Agricultural Organization (FAO), the World Health Organization (WHO), UNICEF, the International Pediatric Association, and the infant formula industry, including Nestlé, all met to discuss nutrition problems and guidelines. The result was a request that the United Nations Protein-Calorie Advisory Group (PAG), an organization formed in 1955, set guidelines for nutrition for infants. On July 18, 1972, PAG issued Statement 23 on the "Promotion of special foods for vulnerable groups." This statement emphasized the importance of breast-feeding, the danger of overpromotion, the need to take local conditions into account, the problem of misuse of formula products, and the desirability of reducing promotion but increasing education.

Statement 23 included the following statements:

> Breast milk is an optimal food for infants and, if available in sufficient quantities it is adequate as the sole source of food during the first four to six months of age.

> Poor health and adverse social circumstances may decrease the output of milk by the mother . . . in such circumstances supplementation of breast milk with nutritionally adequate foods must start earlier than four to six months if growth failure is to be avoided.

> It is clearly important to avoid any action which would accelerate the trend away from breast-feeding.

> It is essential to make available to the mother, the foods, formulas, and instructions which will meet the need for good nutrition of those infants who are breast-fed.

Nestlé management regarded PAG 23 as an "advisory statement," so management's stance was to see what happened. None of the developing countries took any action on the statement. Nestlé officials consulted with ministers of health in many developing countries to ask what role their governments wished Nestlé to play in bringing nutrition education to local mothers. No major changes were requested.

At the same time, Nestlé Vevey ordered an audit of marketing practices employed by its companies in the developing nations. Based on reports from the field, Nestlé management in Vevey concluded that only a few changes in marketing were required which they ordered be done. In Nigeria, the Nigerian Society of Health and Nutrition asked Nestlé to change its ads for formula to stress breast-feeding. Nestlé complied with this request, and its ads in all developing countries prominently carried the phrase "when breast milk fails, use . . ."

THE BRITISH CONTRIBUTION

In its August 1973 issue, the *New Internationalist,* an English journal devoted to problems in developing countries, published an article entitled "The Baby Food Tragedy." This was an interview with two doctors: Dr. R. G. Hendrikse, director of the tropical child health course, Liverpool University, and medical researcher in Rhodesia, Nigeria, and South Africa and Dr. David Morley, reader in tropical child health, University of London. Both doctors expressed concern with the widespread use of formula among impoverished, less-literate families. They claimed that in such cases, low family incomes prevented mothers from buying the necessary amount of formula for their children. Instead, they used smaller quantities of formula powder, diluting it with more water than recommended. Further, the water used was frequently contaminated. The infant thus received less than adequate nutrition, indeed often was exposed to contaminated formula. The malnourished child became increasingly susceptible to infections, leading to diarrheal diseases. Diarrhea meant the child could assimilate even less of the nutrients given to him because neither his stomach nor intestines were working properly. This vicious cycle could lead to death. The two doctors believed that local conditions made the use of commercial infant formula not only unnecessary, but difficult and dangerous. Breast-feeding was safer, healthier, and certainly less expensive.

The article, in the opinion of many, was relatively restrained and balanced. However, it was accompanied by dramatic photographs of malnourished black babies and of a baby's grave with a tin of milk powder placed on it. The article had a strong emotional impact on readers and reached many people who were not regular readers of the journal. It was widely reprinted and quoted by other groups. The journal sent copies of the article to more than 3,000 hospitals in the developing nations.

The two doctors interviewed for the article had mentioned Nestlé and its promotional practices. Accordingly, the editors of the *New Internationalist* contacted Nestlé S.A. for its position. The company response was published in the October issue of the *New Internationalist* along with an editorial entitled "Milk and Murder."

Nestlé S.A. responded in part as follows:

> We have carefully studied both the editorial and the interviews which Dr. Hendrikse and Dr. Morley published in the August edition of the *New Internationalist*. Although fleeting references are made to factors other than manufacturers' activities which are said to be responsible for the misuse of infant foods in developing countries, their readers would certainly not be in a position to judge from the report the immense socio-economic complexities of the situation. . . .
>
> It would be impossible to demonstrate in the space of a letter the enormous efforts made by the Nestlé organization to ensure the correct usage of their infant food products, and the way in which the PAG guidelines have been applied by the Nestlé subsidiaries. However, if the Editor of the *New Internationalist* (or the author of the article in question) wishes to establish the complete facts as far as we are concerned, then we should be happy to receive him in Vevey on a mutually agreeable date in the near future. We should certainly welcome the opportunity to reply to some of the sweeping allegations made against Nestlé either by implication or by specific references.

The editor of the *New Internationalist* refused the invitation to visit Nestlé's Vevey headquarters. Further, they maintained that PAG 23 guidelines were not being observed and did not have any provisions for enforcement.

In March 1974, War on Want published a pamphlet entitled *The Baby Killer*. War on Want was a private British group established to give aid to Third World nations. In particular, they were devoted "to make world poverty an urgent social and political issue." War on Want issued a set of recommendations to industry, governments, the medical profession, and others to deal with the baby formula problem as they saw it (see Exhibit 1).

The Baby Killer was written by Mike Muller as an attempt to publicize the infant formula issue. Mr. Muller expanded on the *New Internationalist* articles, and in the view of many observers, gave reasonable treatment to the complexity of the circumstances surrounding the use of formula products in the developing countries. On the whole, it was an attack against bottle-feeding rather than an attack against any particular company.

Part of *The Baby Killer* was based on interviews the author had with three Nestlé employees: Dr. H. R. Muller, G. A. Fookes, and J. Mermoud, all of Nestlé S.A. Infant and Dietetics Division. These Nestlé officials argued that Nestlé was acting as responsibly as it could. Further, they said that abuses, if they existed, could not be controlled by single companies. Only a drastic change in the competitive system could check abuses

EXHIBIT 1: War on Want's Recommendations

Industry:

1. The serious problems caused by early weaning onto breast milk substitutes demands a serious response. Companies should follow the Swedish example and refrain from all consumer promotion of breast milk substitutes in high risk communities.

2. The companies should cooperate constructively with the international organisations working on the problems of infant and child nutrition in the developing countries.

3. Companies should abandon promotions to the medical profession which may perform the miseducational function of suggesting that particular brands of milk can overcome the problems of misuse.

Government of developing countries:

1. Governments should take note of the recommendations of the Protein Advisory Group for national nutrition strategies.

2. Where social and economic conditions are such that proprietary infant foods can make little useful contribution, serious consideration should be given to the curtailment of their importation, distribution and/or promotion.

3. Governments should ensure that supplies are made available first to those in need—babies whose mothers cannot breast feed, twins, orphans, etc.— rather than to an economic elite, a danger noted by the PAG.

British Government:

1. The British Government should exercise a constructive influence in the current debate.

2. The Government should insist that British companies such as Unigate and Glaxo set a high standard of behaviour and it should be prepared to enforce a similar standard on multi-nationals like Wyeth who export to developing country markets from Britain.

3. The British representative on the Codex Alimentarius Commission should urge the Commission to consider all aspects of the promotion of infant foods. If necessary, structural alterations should be proposed to set up a sub-committee to consider broader aspects of promotion to enable the Commission to fulfil its stated aims of protecting the consumer interests.

Medical profession:

There is a need in the medical profession for a greater awareness of the problems caused by artificial feeding of infants and of the role of the medical profession in encouraging the trend away from breast feeding.

Other channels:

Practicing health workers in the Third World have achieved startling, if limited, response by writing to local medical journals and the press about any promotional malpractices they see and sending copies of their complaints to the companies involved. This could be done by volunteers and others not in the medical profession but in contact with the problem in the field.

In Britain, student unions at a number of universities and polytechnics decided to ban the use of all Nestlés products where they had control of catering following the initial exposé by the *New Internationalist* magazine. Without any clear objective, or coordination, this kind of action is unlikely to have much effect.

However, if the companies involved continue to be intransigent in the face of the dangerous situation developing in the Third World, a more broadly based campaign involving many national organisations may be the result. At the very least, trade unions, women's organisations, consumer groups and other interested parties need to be made aware of the present dangers.

There is also a clear need to examine on a community scale, how infant feeding practices are determined in Britain today. There is a long history of commercial persuasion, and artificial feeding is now well entrenched.

As has been shown, there are still risks inherent in bottle feeding even in Britain. The available evidence suggests that both mother and child may do better physically and emotionally by breast feeding. An examination of our own irrational social practices can help the Third World to throw a light on theirs.

---

effectively. Mr. Muller apparently was not impressed by this argument, nor did he mention Nestlé management's stated willingness to establish enforceable international guidelines for marketing conduct. In *The Baby Killer,* Mr. Muller revealed he was convinced that Nestlé was exploiting the high birth rates in developing countries by encouraging mothers to replace, not supplement, breast-feeding by formula products. Mr. Muller offered as support for his stance a quotation from Nestlé's 1973 Annual Report:

> . . . the continual decline in birth rates, particularly in countries with a high standard of living, retarded growth of the market. . . . In the developing countries our own products continue to sell well thanks to the growth of population and improved living standards.

Dr. Fürer's reaction to *The Baby Killer* was that Mr. Muller had given too much weight on the negative aspects of the situation. Mr. Muller failed to mention, for example, that infant mortality rates had shown very dramatic declines in the developing countries. Some part of these declines was the result of improved nutrition, Dr. Fürer believed, and improved nutrition was partly the result of the use of formula products. Despite his strong belief that Nestlé's product was highly beneficial rather than harmful, Dr. Fürer ordered a second audit of Nestlé's advertising and promotional methods in developing countries. Again, changes were made. These changes included revision of advertising copy to emphasize further the superiority of breast-feeding, elimination of radio advertising in the developing world, and cessation of the use of white uniforms on the mothercraft nurses.

At the same time, on May 23, 1974, the WHO adopted a resolution that misleading promotion had contributed to the decline in breast-feeding in the developing countries and urged individual countries to take legal action to curb such abuses.

THE THIRD WORLD ACTION GROUP

In June 1974, the infant formula issue moved into Switzerland. A small, poorly financed group called the Third World Action Group located in Bern, the capital of Switzerland, published in German a booklet entitled *Nestlé Kills Babies (Nestlé Totet Kinder)*. This was a partial translation of the War on Want publication *The Baby Killer*. Some of the qualifying facts found in Mr. Muller's booklet were omitted in *Nestlé Kills Babies*, while the focus was changed from a general attack on bottle-feeding to a direct attack on Nestlé and its promotional practices.

Nestlé top management was extremely upset by this publication. Dr. Fürer immediately ordered a follow-up audit of Nestlé's marketing practices to ensure stated corporate ethical standards were being observed. Nestlé management also believed that the infant formula issue was being used as a vehicle by leftist, Marxist groups intent on attacking the free market system, multinational companies in general, and Nestlé in particular. Internal Nestlé memoranda of the time reveal the material available to management that supported their belief that the issue went beyond infant formula promotion. For example, Third World Action Group (AG3W) *Der Zürichbieter*, August 15, 1973:

> Having a closer look at the allies of the AG3W in their actions, we realize that they happen to have the same aim. There are common actions with the Leninist progressive organizations (POCH), who are also considered to be pro-Soviet, with the Swiss communist party (PdA) and the communist youth organization (KJV), as well as with the revolutionary Marxist alliance (RML). Since the AG3W has tried to coordinate the support of (only pro-communist) liberation movements with representatives of the communist bloc, it is not surprising that they also participate at the youth festival in Eastern Berlin.

Believing the issue to be clearly legal, Nestlé management brought suit in July 1974 against 13 members of the Third World Action Group and against two newspapers who carried articles about *Nestlé Kills Babies*. Nestlé charged criminal libel, claiming that the company had been defamed because "the whole report charges Nestlé S.A. with using incorrect sales promotion in the third world and with pulling mothers away from breast-feeding their babies and turning them to its products." More specifically, Nestlé management claimed the following were defamatory:

• The title "Nestlé Kills Babies."

- The charge that the practices of Nestlé and other companies are unethical and immoral (written in the introduction and in the report itself).

- The accusation of being responsible for the death or the permanent physical and mental damage of babies by its sales promotion policy (in the introduction).

- The accusation that in LDC's, the sales representatives for baby foods are dressed like nurses to give the sales promotion a scientific appearance.

The trial in Bern provided the Third World Action Group with a great deal of publicity, giving them a forum to present their views. Swiss television in particular devoted much time to coverage of the trial and the issues involved. The trial ended in fall 1976. Nestlé management won a judgment on the first of the libel charges (because of lack of specific evidence for the Third World Action Group), and the activists were fined 300 Swiss francs each. Nestlé management dropped the remaining charges. In his judgment, the presiding judge added an opinion that became well-publicized:

> . . . the need ensues for the Nestlé company to fundamentally rethink its advertising practices in developing countries as concerns bottle feeding, for its advertising practice up to now can transform a life-saving product into one that is dangerous and life-destroying. If Nestlé S.A. in the future wants to be spared the accusations of immoral and unethical conduct, it will have to change its advertising practices. . . .

THE CONTROVERSY SPREADS

While the trial was in progress, various interest groups from all over the world became interested and involved in the infant formula controversy. In London, England, Mr. Mike Muller founded the Baby Foods Action Group. Late in 1974, the World Food Conference adopted a resolution recommending that developing nation governments actively support breast-feeding. PAG had been organizing a number of international regional seminars to discuss all aspects of the controversy. For example, in November 1974, during the PAG regional seminar in Singapore, PAG recommended that the infant formula industry increase its efforts to implement Statement 23 and cooperate to regulate their promotion and advertising practices through a code of ethics.

The world health organizations kept up the pressure. In March 1975, PAG again met:

> . . . to discuss together the problem of deteriorating infant feeding practices in developing countries and to make recommendations for remedying the situation. The early discontinuance of breast-feeding by mothers in low-

income groups in urban areas, leading to malnutrition, illness and death among infants has been a serious concern to all.

In May 1975 WHO, at its 14th plenary meeting, again called for a critical review of promotion of infant formula products.

In response, representatives of the major formula producers met in Zürich, Switzerland, in May 1975 to discuss the possibility and desirability of establishing an international code of ethics for the industry. Eight of the manufacturers, with the notable exceptions of Borden, Bristol-Myers, and Abbott, created an organization called the International Council of Infant Food Industries (ICIFI) and a code of marketing conduct. This code went into effect November 1, 1975. Some firms also adopted individual codes, including Nestlé, with standards higher than the ICIFI code.

The ICIFI code required that ICIFI members assume responsibility to encourage breast-feeding, that milk nurses be paid on a strict salary basis and wear company uniforms, and that product labels indicate breast milk as the best infant food. At this time, Nestlé began to phase out use of mass media for infant formula in developing countries, but continued to distribute educational materials and product information in the hospitals and clinics. Nestlé management believed such advertising and promotion was of educational value: to ensure proper use of formula and to decrease usage of sweetened and condensed milk for infant feeding.

ICIFI submitted its code of ethics to PAG who submitted it to a number of third parties. On the basis of their opinions, PAG refused to endorse the code, saying it did not go far enough, that substantial amendments were required. ICIFI rejected these suggestions because of difficult anti-trust considerations, so PAG withheld its approval of the code.

An important exception to ICIFI membership was Abbott Laboratories. While Abbott representatives had attended the meeting that led to the establishment of ICIFI, they decided not to join. Abbott, having recently had difficulties with the U.S. Food and Drug Administration regarding the marketing of cyclamates and artificial sweeteners, felt ICIFI was not an adequate response to the public pressure:

> . . . the most important area is to reduce the impact of advertising on the low-income, poorly educated populations where the risk is the greatest. The ICIFI code does not address this very important issue.
>
> Our company decided not to join ICIFI because the organization is not prepared to go far enough in answering this legitimate criticism of our industry. We feel that for Abbott/Ross to identify with this organization and its code would limit our ability to speak on the important issues.

Abbott acted largely independently of the other producers. Later, in 1977, Abbott management announced its intention to commit about $100,000 to a breast-feeding campaign in developing nations and about $175,000 to a task force on breast-feeding, infant formula, and Third World countries.

DEVELOPMENTS IN THE UNITED STATES

Although Nestlé U.S. neither manufactured nor marketed formula, management found itself increasingly embroiled in the controversy during the mid-1970s. The first major group to bring this matter to the public was the Interfaith Center on Corporate Responsibility (ICCR). The ICCR, a union of 14 Protestant denominations and approximately 150 Catholic orders and dioceses, was a group concerned about the social responsibility behavior of corporations. The ICCR advised its members on this topic to guide decisions for the members' combined investment portfolio of several billion dollars. Formerly known as the Center of Corporate Responsibility, the ICCR was established under the tax-exempt umbrella of the American National Council of Churches when the U.S. Internal Revenue Service revoked the CCR tax exemption.

The ICCR urged its members to investigate the marketing practices of the leading American formula producers, American Home Products, Abbott Laboratories, and Bristol-Myers. Stockholder groups demanded from these companies, as they were entitled to do by American law, detailed information regarding market shares, promotion and advertising practices, and general company policies concerning the infant formula business.

Nestlé management believed that the ICCR was interested in ideology more than in baby formula. As support, they pointed to a statement made in a January edition of ICCR's *The Corporate Examiner:*

> . . . the motivations, ethos, and operations of transnational corporations are inimical to the establishment of a new economic order. Both justice and stability are undermined in the fulfillment of their global vision.

Perhaps the major vehicle used by ICCR to get attention was a half-hour film entitled *Bottle Babies.* Well-known German filmmaker Peter Krieg began this film shortly after the Bern trial began. Nestlé Vevey management believed that the film was partially sponsored by the World Council of Churches to provide a public defense for the Third World Action Group position. Most of the filming was done in Kenya, Africa, in 1975 in a "documentary" style, although Nestlé management pointed out that the film was scripted and, in their opinion, highly emotional and misleading. A letter (Exhibit 2) that Nestlé management later received written by Professor Bwibo of the University of Nairobi supported management's views about the *Bottle Babies* film.

ICCR distributed copies of the *Bottle Babies* film to church groups throughout the United States. Typically, the film was shown to a gathering of church members followed by an impassioned plea to write letters of protest and a request for funds to further the campaign. Since the film singled out Nestlé for attack in its last ten minutes, Nestlé became symbolic of all that was wrong in the infant formula controversy in the

EXHIBIT 2

14th April, 1978

Miss June Noronah
644 Summit Avenue
St. Paul
Minnesota 55105

Dear Miss Noronah:

Following your visit to Kenya and my office I write to inform you, your group, your colleagues and any other person interested that the film Peter Krieg filmed in this department and the associated teaching areas, did not represent the right aspects of what we participated in during the filming.

The film which was intended to be a scientific and educational film turned out to be an emotional, biased and exaggerated film—and failed to be a teaching film. It arouses emotions in people who have little chance to check these facts. No wonder it has heated the emotions of the Activists groups in America and I understand now spreading to Europe. I wish I was in an opportunity to be with your groups and we view the film together and I comment.

As a pediatrician, I would like to put on record that I have not seen the Commercial baby food companies pressurise anybody to use their brands of milk. As for Nestlé, we have discussed with their Managing Directors, starting much earlier than the time of the film in 1971, as to the best way of approaching baby feeding and discussed extensively advertisement especially the material to be included. The directors have followed our advice and we are happy with their working conditions.

We are interested in the well being of our children and we are Medical Scientists. So anything of scientific value we will promote but we will avoid imagined exaggerated and distorted views.

I am taking the liberty to copy this letter to Mr. Jones Managing Director of Food Specialty in Nairobi who produce and makes Nestlé's products here for his information.

Yours sincerely,

NIMROD O. BWIBO
Professor & Chairman

minds of these religious groups. Nestlé management, however, were seldom asked for or given an opportunity to present their position on the issues.

While Nestlé felt the growing pressure of *Bottle Babies,* the major American formula producers faced a variety of ICCR–shareholder initiatives. ICCR requested detailed information from American Home Products, Abbott Laboratories, and Bristol-Myers. Each company responded differently.

A. American Home Products—After refusing to release all the information ICCR requested, AHP faced a resolution to be included in its proxy statement. ICCR dropped the resolution the day before printing, when AHP management agreed:

- To provide the requested information.
- To send a report to its shareholders saying that many authorities believe misuse of infant formula in developing countries could be dangerous, that the company promotes breast-feeding while making available formula for mothers who cannot or do not choose to breast-feed, that the company would promote to medical professionals only and that AHP was a member of ICIFI which was developing a voluntary code of promotional practices.

B. Abbott Laboratories—After a year and a half of meetings with ICCR, Abbott released most of the information ICCR wanted. Still, to obtain the rest of the data, ICCR shareholders filed a shareholder resolution. This proposal received less than the 3 percent of the vote required by the Securities and Exchange Commission (SEC) in order to resubmit the proposal at a later time. It was not resubmitted.

C. Bristol-Myers—Bristol-Myers would not cooperate with ICCR, so one church shareholder with 500 shares, Sisters of the Precious Blood, filed a shareholder resolution in 1975 asking that the information be released. After receiving 5.4 percent of the vote and having aroused the concern of The Ford Foundation and the Rockefeller Foundation, it appeared the resolution would be launched again the next year. In August 1975 Bristol-Myers management published a report, "The Infant Formula Marketing Practices of Bristol-Myers Co. in Countries Outside the United States." The 1976 proxy included the Sisters' resolution and a statement entitled "Management's Position." The Sisters maintained the statement was false and misleading and filed suit against management; statements appearing in a proxy statement are required by law to be accurate.

In May 1977 a U.S. district court judge dismissed the case, saying the Sisters had failed to show irreparable harm to themselves as the law requires. The judge would not comment on the accuracy of the company's proxy report. The nuns appealed with the support of the SEC. In early 1978, the management of Bristol-Myers agreed to send a report outlining the dispute to all shareholders and the restrictions on company marketing practices including a ban on all consumer-directed promotion in clinics, hospitals, and other public places and a stop to using milk nurses in Jamaica.

Church groups also managed to get Borden to agree in February 1977 to stop the promotion of its KLIM formula. Also in 1977, Abbott management agreed to revise their code of marketing conduct and to eliminate the use of nurses' uniforms by company salespeople despite the fact some were registered nurses.

ICCR and its supporters also persuaded Representative Michael Harrington (D.-Mass) to co-sponsor a federal resolution requiring an investigation of U.S. infant formula producers.

The campaign against the formula producers took on a new dimension in mid-1977. A group called the Third World Institute, led by Doug Johnson, at the University of Minnesota formed the Infant Formula Action Coalition "INFACT" in June 1977. INFACT members were encouraged by ICCR and the Sisters, but felt that significant progress would not be made until Nestlé was pressured to change. INFACT realized that legal and shareholder action against a foreign-based company would be futile, so on July 4, 1977, INFACT announced a consumer boycott against those infant formula companies whose marketing practices INFACT found abusive. Despite the boycott's original target of several companies, Nestlé was the main focal point, especially after the other major companies made concessions to ICCR. INFACT began the boycott in front of Nestlé's Minneapolis offices with a demonstration of about 100 people. INFACT urged consumers to boycott over 40 Nestlé products.

Nestlé management in White Plains was not sure what response to take. Nestlé U.S. was not at all involved with infant formula, but was genuinely concerned about the publicity INFACT was getting. Nestlé S.A. management on the other hand originally did not think the boycott campaign would amount to anything, that it was a project of some college kids in the United States based on misinformation about events in other parts of the world.

In September and October 1977 Nestlé senior managers from Vevey and White Plains met with members of INFACT, ICCR, The Ford Foundation, and other interested groups. Nestlé management had hoped to resolve what they thought was a problem of poor communication by explaining the facts. Nestlé management argued the company could not meet competition if it stopped all promotion, which would mean less sales and less jobs in the developing nations. Further, management claimed: "We have an instructional and educational responsibility as marketers of these products and, if we failed in that responsibility, we could be justly criticized." INFACT members stated they found the talks useful in clarifying positions, but concluded Nestle was unwilling to abandon all promotion of its formula products.

In November 1977, INFACT decided not only to continue the boycott, but also to increase it to a national scale. INFACT held a conference in Minneapolis on November 2–4, for more than 45 organizers from 24 cities. These organizers represented women's groups, college hunger-action coalitions, health professionals, church agencies, and social justice groups. A clearinghouse was established to coordinate boycott efforts and information collection. The group also agreed to assist ICCR in its shareholder pressure campaign and to press for congressional action. Later, INFACT petitioned all U.S. government officials, state and federal, for support of the boycott. On November 21, the Interfaith Hunger Coalition, a group affiliated with INFACT, demonstrated in front of Nestlé's Los Angeles sales office with about 150 people chanting "Nestlé kills babies." This demonstration received prominent media coverage as did other boycott activities. The combination of INFACT's boycott, ICCR's shareholder efforts, the exhibition of *Bottle Babies,* and the strong support of other U.S. activists (including Ralph Nader, Cesar Chavez, Gloria Steinem, Dr. Benjamin Spock) resulted in an increasingly high profile for the infant formula controversy, even though Nestlé management believed there had been as yet no adverse effect on sales.

In early 1978, an unofficial WHO working group published the following statement:

> The advertising of food for nursing infants or older babies and young children is of particular importance and should be prohibited on radio and television. Advertising for mother's milk substitutes should never be aimed directly at the public or families, and advertising for ready-made infant food preparations should show clearly that they are not meant for less than three-month-old infants. Publicity for public consumption, which should in any case never be distributed without previous recommendation by the competent medical authority, should indicate that breast milk should always constitute the sole or chief constituent of food for those under three months. Finally, the distribution of free samples and other sales promotion practices for baby foods should be generally prohibited.

Nestlé management met again with INFACT representatives in February 1978. No progress was made in reconciling the two sides. Nestlé management could not accept statements from INFACT such as:

> The corporations provide the product and motivate the people to buy it, and set into motion a process that may cause the death of the baby. The corporations are responsible for that death. When the outcome is death, the charge against the corporation is murder.

Nonetheless, management learned what INFACT wanted:

- Stop all direct consumer promotion and publicity for infant formula.
- Stop employing "milk nurses" as sales staff.

- Stop distributing free samples to clinics, hospitals, and maternity hospitals.
- Stop promoting infant formula among the medical and public health professions.

To further publicize their campaign, INFACT representatives and their allies persuaded Senator Edward Kennedy (D-Mass), to hold Senate hearings on the infant formula issue in May 1978. CBS decided to make a TV report of the entire affair. To prepare for the hearings, INFACT organized a number of demonstrations across the United States. At one meeting on April 15, 1978, Doug Johnson said:

> The goal of the Nestlé's Boycott Campaign and of the entire infant formula coalition is to get the multinationals to stop promotion of infant formula. We're not asking them to stop marketing; we're not asking them to pull out of—out of the countries; we're simply asking them to stop the promotion, and in that I think we're—we're in agreement with a number of prestigious organizations. The World Health Organization recently asked the corporations to stop consumer advertising and to stop the use of free samples, and the International Pediatric Association did that several years ago. So, I think we're asking a very reasonable thing: to stop promoting something which is inappropriate and dangerous.

CBS filmed these demonstrations, but did not air them until after the Kennedy hearings.

THE KENNEDY HEARINGS AND THE CBS REPORT

Senator Kennedy was chairman of the Subcommittee on Health and Scientific Research on Infant Nutrition. Both critics and members of the infant formula industry appeared before the Kennedy Committtee in May 1978. Nestlé S.A. management decided not to send headquarters management or management from Nestlé U.S. Instead, they asked R. Oswaldo Ballarin, president and chairman of Nestlé Brazil, to represent Nestlé at the hearings. Dr. Ballarin began with a statement prepared by Nestlé U.S., but Senator Kennedy soon interrupted him as the following excerpt from the testimony indicates:

Dr. Ballarin: United States Nestlé's Company has advised me that their research indicates this is actually an indirect attack on the free world's economic system: a worldwide church organization with its stated purpose of undermining the free enterprise system is at the forefront of this activity.

Senator Kennedy: Now you can't seriously expect . . . [Noise in background: gavel banging]. We'll be in order . . . we'll be in order now please. You don't seriously expect us to accept that on face value, after we've heard as you must've, Doctor, . . . the testimony of probably nine different witnesses. It seemed to me that they were expressing a very deep compassion and concern about the well-being of infants, the most vulnerable in this face of the world. Would you agree with me that your product should not be used where there is impure water? Yes or no?

Dr. Ballarin: Uh, we give all the instructions . . .

Senator Kennedy: Just answer. What is your position?

Dr. Ballarin: Of course not. But we cannot cope with that.

Senator Kennedy: Well, as I understand what you say, is where there's impure water, it should not be used.

Dr. Ballarin: Yes.

Senator Kennedy: Where the people are so poor that they're not going to realistically be able to continue to purchase it, . . . that they're going to dilute it to a point, which is going to endanger the health, that it should not be used.

Dr. Ballarin: Yes, I believe . . .

Senator Kennedy: All right, now . . . then my final question is . . . what do you feel is your corporate responsibility to find out the extent of the use of your product in those circumstances in the developing part of the world? Do you feel that you have any responsibility?

Dr. Ballarin: We can't have that responsibility, sir. May I make a reference to . . .

Senator Kennedy: You can't have that responsibility?

Dr. Ballarin: No.

Dr. Ballarin's testimony continued (for example of excerpts, see Exhibit 3), but Nestlé management believed little attention was paid to it. Mr. Guerrant, president of Nestlé U.S., was very angry and wrote a letter to Senator Kennedy on May 26, 1978, protesting the way he had treated Dr. Ballarin (Exhibit 4).

CBS aired its program on July 5, 1978. Again, Nestlé management was upset. In their view CBS had selected portions of the testimonies to make Nestlé management look inept and confused. Mr. Guerrant wrote a letter of protest to CBS President Richard Salant (Exhibit 5).

Following the Kennedy hearings, representatives of Nestlé S.A., Abbott, Bristol-Myers, and American Home Products met privately with Senator Kennedy to explore a suggestion for a further hearing. Meanwhile, the president of ICIFI wrote Kennedy, pointing out that this was an international and not a U.S. domestic issue—and should therefore be discussed at a forum sponsored by WHO. Kennedy accepted ICIFI's suggestion

EXHIBIT 3: Further Excerpts from Dr. Ballarin's Testimony

Nestlé recognized that even the best products will not give the desired results if used incorrectly. We, therefore, placed great weight on educational efforts aimed at explaining the correct use of our product. Our work in this field has received the public recognition and approval of the official pediatric associations in many countries. Such educational efforts never attempt to infer that our product is superior to breast milk. Indeed, we have devoted much attention to the promotion of breast-feeding, and educational material has always insisted that breast-feeding is best for the baby.

Nevertheless, many factors militate against exclusive breast-feeding in the rapidly growing cities of Brazil as well as other developing countries, and our products are seen today as filling a valid need, just as they did when they were first introduced over 50 years ago. In recognition of this, all such products are subject to strict price control, while in many countries which do not have a local dairy industry, they are classified as essential goods and imported free of duty. In many cases, official agencies establish what they consider to be a fair margin for the manufacturers.

It must be stressed that many problems remain to be solved. Our production is far from reaching the total needs of the population. Hence, many mothers in the poorer population groups continue to supplement breast-feeding with foods of doubtful quality. Owing to the lack of adequate medical services, especially in the rural areas, misuse of any supplement can occur and we are very conscious of the need to improve our efforts. These efforts depend on continued cooperation between the infant food industry and health professionals. We have to be more and more conscious of our responsibility to encourage breast-feeding while re-searching new foods and safer methods for feeding babies who cannot be exclusively breast-fed. The dilemma facing industry and the health service alike, is how to teach these methods without discouraging breast-feeding.

---

and requested the director general of WHO to sponsor a conference at which the question of an international code could be discussed.

A consensus emerged that a uniform code for the industry was required and that Kennedy and ICIFI would suggest that WHO sponsor a conference with that aim in mind. The conference would be comprised of WHO officials, ICIFI members, and other companies, health and government officials from the developing countries, and all appropriate concerned public groups. WHO accepted the idea and announced the conference date in the fall of 1979. Shortly after Nestlé management met with Kennedy, the National Council of Churches, comprised of about 30 major religious groups in the United States, announced that the question of supporting INFACT and ICCR would be discussed and decided at the NCC national conference in November 1978.

EXHIBIT 4: Excerpts from Mr. Guerrant's Letter to Senator Kennedy

I am angry but more important deeply concerned about the example of our governmental processes exhibited this week by the Human Resources Subcommittee on Health and Scientific Research.

It was the general consensus of several people in the audience that your position toward the manufacturers was, "you are guilty until you prove your innocence." Objectivity would have been more becoming, Senator.

Secondly, it seemed equally probable that prior to the hearing the prepared statements were reviewed and you were quite prepared to rebuff Dr. Ballarin on his statement "undermining the free enterprise system." Unaccustomed to television and this type of inquisition, Dr. Ballarin, who appeared voluntarily, was flustered and embarrassed.

Probably, for this gathering, the statement was too strong (though nothing to compare with their theme "Nestle kills babies") and should have been more subtle. But the point is well made, and your apparent denial of this possibility concerns me.

As you may know, this whole issue gained its greatest momentum a few years ago in Europe fostered by clearly identified radical leftist groups. Their stated purpose is opposition to capitalism and the free enterprise system. I submit that they are not really concerned with infants in the third world but are intelligent enough to know that babies, especially sick and dying, create maximum emotional response. Further, they are clever enough to know that the people most easy to "use" for their campaign, to front for them, are in churches and universities. These are good people, ready to rise against oppression and wrong-doing without, regrettably, truthful facts for objective research. I know, as my father is a retired Presbyterian minister, and I have a very warm feeling toward members of the church, Protestant and Catholic.

People with far left philosophies are not confined to Europe and are certainly represented in many accepted organizations here and abroad. (Please take the time to read the enclosed report of the 1977 Geneva Consultation of the World Council of Churches.) Associated with the World Council is the National Council of Churches, and one of their units is the Interfaith Centre for Corporate Responsibility. One of their major spokespersons appears to be Leah Margulies, who was present in your hearing.

Now, just briefly to the very complex infant food issue. As the U.S. Nestlé Company does not manufacture or sell any infant food products, we are unhappy with the attempted boycott of our products—at least 95% of these manufactured in the U.S. The jobs and security of about 12,000 good U.S. employees are being threatened.

From our associates in Switzerland, and Nestlé companies in the third world, we have gathered hundreds of factual documents. Neither Nestlé nor the U.S. companies in this business claim perfection. Companies are comprised of human beings. However, virtually every charge against Nestlé has proved to be erroneous. Distorted "facts" and just pure propaganda have been answered by people with undeniable integrity and technical credentials. Quite some time ago, because of the accusations, Nestlé world headquarters in Switzerland studied every facet of their total infant food business, made immediate changes where warranted and

EXHIBIT 4 *(concluded)*

established new and very clear policies and procedures regarding the conduct of this business.

I might add that Nestlé infant foods have undoubtedly saved hundreds of thousands of lives. There is not even one instance where proof exists that Nestlé infant food was responsible for a single death. The products are as essential in the third world as in the industrialized world. Though the accusers use some statements by apparently qualified people, there is an overwhelming amount of data and number of statements from qualified medical, technical and government representatives in the third world confirming Nestlé's position.

At your hearing this week were the same identical charges made against Nestlé and the others years ago. These people will not recognize the changes made in marketing practices nor the irrefutable facts of the real infant health problems in the third world. They continue to push the U.S. Nestlé boycott and continue to distribute the fraudulent film "Bottle Babies." (Please read Dr. Bwibo's letter enclosed.) Sincere, well-meaning church people continue to be used, as they have not had all the real facts available for analysis.

The above situation made me believe that the organizers must have some motivation for this campaign other than what appears on the surface. If it could possibly be what I think, then our representatives in government should proceed with caution, thorough study and great objectivity, as your ultimate position can be of critical consequence. I am not a crusader, but I do feel the free enterprise system is best.

EXHIBIT 5: Excerpts from Mr. Guerrant's Letter to CBS President Salant

In the first minute of the program the infant formula industry has been tried and convicted of causing infant malnutrition. The remainder of the program is devoted to reinforcing Mr. Myers's conclusion. Tools of persuasion include the emotionality of a needle sticking in a child's head and the uneasy answers of cross-examined industry witnesses who are asked not for the facts but to admit and apologize for their "guilt."

* * * * *

But "CBS Reports" chose to concentrate on the "rhetoric of concern" and the claims which permeate the rhetoric. Industry's response to the rhetoric is not glamorous but hits into the root causes of infant malnutrition—the poverty, disease and ignorance existing in the areas of developing and developed countries. Those conditions are not easy for anthropologists, economists, scientists or medical people to trace or explain. And certainly the reasons for them are not as identifiable as a major corporation. But in thirty minutes Mr. Myers and Ms. Roche identified four companies as a major reason for infant malnutrition.

* * * * *

One way Nestlé has attempted to meet the responsibility is by making capital investments in and transferring technology to the developing countries. Nestlé began this effort in 1921 in Brazil and now has almost 40,000 local employees working in 81 manufacturing facilities in 25 developing countries. Not only does Nestlé have a beneficial impact on those directly employed, the company also encourages and assists the development of other local supporting industries, such as the dairy industry and packaging plants.

Another way Nestlé meets its responsibility is to work with local governments and health authorities in educating consumers. Clinics, pamphlets, posters, books and product labels emphasize the superiority of breast feeding, demonstrate proper sanitation and diet for breast feeding, and show in words and pictures how to correctly use formula products.

Neither of these positive approaches was covered in "CBS Reports" nor was there mention of the fact that infant mortality has declined worldwide over the past thirty years, nor that lack of sufficient breast milk is a major cause of infant malnutrition, nor that tropical diseases cause millions of deaths per year in developing countries. Any one of these facts would have provided some balance to the Myers-Roche report.

THE SITUATION IN OCTOBER 1978

Dr. Fürer knew all senior Nestlé management felt personally attacked by critics of the industry. Not only was this the first major public pressure campaign ever encountered by Nestlé, but also Nestlé management felt its critics were using unfair tactics. For example, again and again they saw in boycott letters and articles a grotesque picture of a wizened child with a formula bottle nearby. Eventually this picture was traced to Dr. Derrick Jeliffe, an outspoken critic of the industry. He admitted to *Newsweek* he had taken the picture in a Caribbean hospital in 1964. Even though it seemed the media and many respected companies were against Nestlé, Dr. Fürer stated publicly:

> No one has the right to accuse us of killing babies. No one has the right to assert that we are guilty of pursuing unethical or immoral sales practices.

Nonetheless, under U.S. law a company is regarded as a public person which meant that the First Amendment applied; that is, Nestlé could not get legal relief against charges made by the critics unless the company could prove those charges were both wrong and malicious.

Further, Dr. Fürer was struck by the fact that all the demands for change were coming from developed countries. In fact, Nestlé had received many letters of support from people in the developing countries (Exhibit 6). Mr. Ernest Saunders, Nestlé vice president for infant nutrition products, summarized his view as follows:

> Government and medical personnel tell us that if we stopped selling infant foods we would be killing a lot of babies.

EXHIBIT 6: Examples of Support for Nestlé

1. I have been associated with the medical representatives of Nestlé in Kenya for the last five years. We have discussed on various occasions the problems of artificial feeding, in particular the use of proprietary milk preparations. We have all been agreed that breast feeding should always come first. As far as I am aware, your representatives have not used any unethical methods when promoting Nestlé products in this country.

   M. L. Oduori, Senior Consultant
   Pediatrician
   Ministry of Health
   Kenyatta National Hospital, Nairobi
   Kenya, Dec. 23, 1974

2. You are not "killing babies," on the contrary your efforts joined with ours contribute to the improvement of the Health Status of our infant population.

   We consider your marketing policies as ethical and as not being opposite to our recommendations. We note with pleasure that you employ a fully qualified nurse and that during discussions with mothers she always encourages breast-feeding, recommending your products when only natural feeding is insufficient or fails.

   Dr. Jerry Lukowski
   Chief Gynecologist, Menelik Hospital
   Ethiopia, Dec. 3, 1974

3. Over several decades I have had direct and indirect dealings with your organisation in South Africa in relation to many aspects of nutrition among the non-white population who fall under our care, as well as the supply of nutriments to the hospital and peripheral clinics.

   I am fairly well aware of the extent of your Company's contributions to medical science and research and that this generosity goes hand in hand with the highest ethical standards of advertising, distribution of products and the nutrition educational services which you provide.

   At no time in the past have my colleagues or I entertained any idea or suspicion that Nestlé have behaved in any way that could be regarded as unethical in their promotions, their products or their educational programmes. On all occasions when discussion of problems or amendments to arrangements have been asked for, full cooperation has been given to this department.

   Your field workers have given and are giving correct priorities in regard to breast feeding, and, where necessary, the bottle feeding of infants.

EXHIBIT 6 *(continued)*

The staff employed to do this work have shown a strong sense of responsibility and duty towards the public whom they serve, no doubt due to the educational instruction they have themselves received in order to fit them for their work.

> S. Wayburne, Chief Pediatrician
> Baragwanath Hospital
> Associate Professor of Pediatrics,
> Acting Head of Department of
> Pediatrics, University of
> Witwatersrand/South Africa
> Dec. 18, 1974

4. I have read about the accusation that "Nestlé Kills Babies" and I strongly refute it, I think it is quite unjustifiable.

On my experience I have never seen any mother being advised to use artificial milk when it was not necessary. Every mother is advised to give breast foods to her baby. It is only when there is failure of this, then artificial foods are advised.

I being a working mother, I have brought up my five children on Nestlé Products and I do not see anything wrong with them. I knew I would have found it difficult to carry on with my profession if I had nothing to rely on like your products.

Your marketing policies are quite in order as I knew them and they are quite ethical. As they stress on breast milk foods first and if this is unobtainable then one can use Nestlé's Products.

> Mrs. M. Lema, Nursing Officer
> Ocean Hospital
> Dar-es-Salaam/TANZANIA
> Dec. 16, 1974

5. On behalf of the Sisters of Nazareth Hospital, I thank you heartily for your generous contribution in giving us the Nestlé products in a way that we can assist and feed many undernourished children freely cured and treated in our hospital.

Trusting in your continuous assistance allow me to express again my sincerest thanks, and may God bless you.

> Nazareth Hospital
> Nairobi, Kenya
> September 9, 1978

6. I am very grateful for this help for our babies in need in the maternity ward.

Another mission has asked me about this milk gift parcels, if there would be any chance for them. It is Butula Mission and they have a health centre with beds and maternity and maternal child health clinics. There is a lot of

EXHIBIT 6 *(concluded)*

malnutrition also in that area, so that mothers often do not produce enough milk for their babies. It would be wonderful if you could help them also.

> Nangina Hospital
> Medical Mission Sisters
> Funyula, Kenya
> June 15, 1976

7. As a doctor who has practiced for eighteen years in a developing country, I was angered by the collection of half-truths, judiciously mixed with falsehoods put out by the Infant Formula Action Coalition as reported in the *Newsweek* article on breast feeding. Whether we like it or not, many mothers cannot or will not resort to breast-feeding. I do not believe that advertising has played any significant part in their decision. It is an inescapable necessity that specific, nutritionally balanced formulas are available. Otherwise, we would witness wholesale feeding with products that are unsuitable.

    I carry no brief for companies like Nestlé, but have always found it to be a company with the highest regard to ethical standards. Infant formulas have saved many thousands of lives. What alternative are their critics proposing?

> D. C. Williams, M.D.
> Kuala Lumpur
> Malaysia

8. Surely, Nestlé is not to blame. There have been similar problems here but through the efforts of the Save the Children Fund and government assistance, feeding bottles can only be purchased through chemists or hospitals by prescription. In this way, the decision of whether to breast-feed or not is decided by qualified personnel.

    I would think that Americans would have better things to do than walk around disrupting commerce with placards.

> Gail L. Hubbard
> Goroka, Papua New Guinea

Dr. Fürer also believed that the scientific facts underlying the breast versus bottle controversy were not being given adequate attention (for example, see Exhibit 7), nor were the changes Nestlé and the other companies had made. Nestlé's policies regarding infant formula products were apparently not well known. Exhibit 8 includes excerpts from the latest edition, dated September 1, 1977.

Many members of management believed the attack against Nestlé was ideologically based. They gathered information about and quotations from many of the activist groups to support their position (for example,

EXHIBIT 7: Examples of Supplementary Information on Breast versus Bottle-Feeding

1. Findings of the Human Lactation Center (HLC)

    The HLC is a scientific research institute, a non-profit organization dedicated to worldwide education and research on lactation. The HLC entered the breast/ bottle controversy between the infant formula industry and the anti-multinational groups in an attempt to clarify certain issues. Eleven anthropologists, all women, studied infant feeding practices in eleven different cultures, ranging from a relatively urbanized Sardinian village to a very impoverished Egyptian agricultural village. Their findings:

*   Poverty is correlated with infant morbidity (disease). Child health is associated with affluence.

*   Infant mortality had decreased in the three decades prior to 1973 when food prices began to escalate.

*   Breast milk is the best infant food but breast-feeding exclusively for most *under-nourished* women in the less developed countries is inadequate beyond the baby's third month. Lack of sufficient food after this time is a major cause of morbidity and mortality whether or not the infant is breast-fed.

*   Mixed feeding is an almost universal pattern in traditional cultures; that is, breast-feeding and supplementary feeding from early on and often into the second year.

*   The preferred additional food for the very young child is milk. Most milk is fresh milk, unprocessed.

*   *Most* women still breast-feed though many do not. The popular assumption that breast-feeding is being reduced has not been verified.

*   Third World women with the least amount of resources, time or access to health care and weaning foods, have no choice but to breast-feed.

*   More than half the infants they bear do not survive due to lack of food for themselves and their children.

*   Women who are separated from close kin, especially the urban poor, lack mothering from a supportive figure. They find themselves unable to lactate adequately or lose their milk entirely. Without suitable substitutes, their infants die.

*   Middle class women in the less-developed countries, market women, the elite and professional women are moving towards bottle feeding with infant formula in much the same way women turned from breast to bottle feeding in the western countries.

*   The current literature on breast-feeding in the developing countries is meager. Information on mortality, the incidence of breast-feeding, the content of infant food, and the amount of breast milk, tend to be impressionistic reports by well-meaning western or western trained persons often unaware of the complexities of feeding practices and insensitive to the real-life situation of the mothers. Judgments for action based on these inconclusive data could be dangerous.

*   Mothers have a sensitive and remarkable grasp of how best to keep their

EXHIBIT 7 *(concluded)*

infants alive. Neither literacy nor what has been called "ignorance" determine which infants live and which die except as they are related directly to social class.

- In seeking solutions to the problems of infant well-being in the developing world, we must listen to the mothers and involve them in the decisions which will affect their lives.

2. *The Feeding of the Very Young: An Approach to Determination of Policies,* report of the International Advisory Group on Infant and Child Feeding to the Nutrition Foundation, October 1978:

> Two basic requirements of successful feeding are: (1) adequate milk during the first four to six months of life, and (2) adequate complementary foods during the transition to adult diets. It is imperative that all societies recognize these requirements as a major component of nutrition policy. The extent to which mothers are able to meet both of these requirements will vary under different cultural and sociological circumstances. In all societies there will be some proportion of mothers who will not be able to meet them without assistance, and policy must be developed to protect those children who are at risk of malnutrition resulting from inadequacy in either one or both of these basic requirements.

Source: Nestlé memoranda.

EXHIBIT 8: Excerpts from Internal Nestlé Directives on Infant and Dietetic Products (PID) Policy

Infant Milks

It is recognized that breast milk is the best food for a baby. Our baby milks are therefore not intended to compete with breast milk, but to supplement breast feeding when the mother's own milk can no longer cover the baby's needs or to replace it when mothers cannot, or elect not to breast feed.

Three to four months after birth, the quantities of breast milk produced by the average mother become insufficient to satisfy the growing needs of the baby. The baby needs a supplement of water and food. From this moment on, in the poor communities of developing countries this baby is in danger because water is sometimes polluted and local foods, like plantain or manioc, are nutritionally inadequate, they are starchy foods with little food value and a young baby cannot digest them. Thus the highest infant mortality occurs precisely in areas where babies receive only mother's milk plus a supplement of unboiled local water and/or starchy decoctions.

This is not a Nestlé theory. This is a fact known by every Third World doctor and recently scientifically demonstrated by British researchers working in Africa.

The alternative to traditional local supplement is a properly formulated breast milk substitute, preferably a humanized formula. It is true that there is a risk of misuse, but these risks exist with a local supplement too, although the baby has a better chance of survival when the starting point is of high quality.

It is precisely to reduce the risks of misuse and thereby increase the chances

EXHIBIT 8 *(concluded)*

of survival that we had developed over the years a comprehensive programme of information and education: contact with doctors, educative advertising, booklets, nurses; all this had the purpose of making the alternative to local supplements known and ensuring a proper and safe use of our products when needed. Nestlé policies are designed to avoid the unnecessary replacement of breast milk.

The real issue is not: Breast milk versus formula, as so often pictured, but: Breast milk + formula + education versus traditional foods like manioc.

Products must be in line with internationally recognized nutritional criteria and offer definite consumer benefits.

Distribution Policy

It is a rule that PID products are never sold to mothers directly by us; distribution aims at making products available to prescribers and users under optimum safety and price conditions.

Within the limits set by the law and by the distribution structure, we practice mixed distribution (pharmacies and general food stores) and use the normal market channels. On the other hand, dietetic specialities and products designed for delicate or sick babies, which are basically sold on medical prescription, are sold only through pharmacies, unless special local conditions warrant mixed distribution.

Communication Policy—Direct Contacts with Mothers

Medical representatives must not enter into direct contact with mothers, unless they are authorized to do so in writing by a medical or health authority and provided that they are properly qualified. Films may be shown with the agreement of the medical or public health authorities concerned.

Visits to mothers in their homes are not allowed unless the responsible medical authority has made a written request for a visit to take place.

Personnel Policy

The main task of the medical promotion personnel consists in contacting the medical and paramedical professions and hospitals. They are not concerned with direct sales to mothers and cannot sell dietetic products other than, exceptionally and exclusively, to the trade or institutions.

Specialized training must be given to such staff, to enable them to render a genuine service to the medical and paramedical professions and give them scientific and unbiased information on product characteristics and utilization.

No sales-related bonus will be paid to any staff engaged in medical promotion or having direct contact with mothers. If a bonus is to be paid, it must depend on elements other than sales, such as, for example, personal qualities, qualifications, etc.

---

see Exhibit 9). Whatever their foundation, the critics seemed to Dr. Fürer to be gaining publicity and momentum. INFACT claimed at least 500 separate action committees in the United States, support in about 75 communities in Canada, as well as support in about 10 other countries.

EXHIBIT 9: Examples of Comments Concerning the Ideology of the Activist Groups

Sue Tafler and Betsy Walker, "Why Boycott Nestlé?" in *Science for the People,* January/February 1978:

> Unfortunately, the power in many developing countries is not held by the people themselves, and local ruling elites often want to encourage corporate investment. . . . What the boycott will not do is overthrow capitalism. . . . The boycott can unite well-meaning groups that see themselves as apolitical with more openly political groups. . . . We can have the effect of politicizing others working in the coalition. If Nestlé does make some concessions to the demands of the boycott, the sense of victory can give encouragement to the organizers of the boycott to continue on to larger struggles.

T. Balasusiya, Centre for Society and Religion, Colombo, Sri Lanka, participant at the World Council of Churches meeting, January 1977:

> The capitalist system is the main cause of the increasing gap and within that system multinationals are a main form. Ideology of wealth is the practical religion of capitalist society. Churches are legitimizers of the system, so their first job is self-purification. There can be no neutrality between money and God.
> Our function is not to judge persons, but we have to judge systems. . . . What alternative solutions do countries propose that have rejected the capitalist system, e.g. U.S.S.R., China, Cuba, Tanzania? Capitalism is inherently contradictory to the Gospel.

M. Ritchie, at a conference Clergy and Laity Concerned, August 1978:

> It's not just babies, it's not just multinational corporations, it's class conflict and class struggle. Broadening the constituency both of people interested in the infant formula issue but also how the infant formula campaign and the people there link up completely in terms of support and action with other types of campaigns. . . .
> I think ultimately what we're trying to do is take an issue-specific focus campaign and move it in conjunction with other issue-specific campaigns into a larger very class-wide very class-conscious campaign and reasserting our power in this country, our power in this world.

Douglas Johnson of INFACT, at an address in Washington, September 1978:

> Our hope is that we can use this [boycott] campaign as the forerunner of legislation for control of multinational corporations.

Source: Nestlé internal memoranda.

"The movement is snowballing," reported Gwen Willens of INFACT. "We're getting over 300 letters of support every day."

As Dr. Fürer consulted with senior management in Nestlé, he wondered what further steps Nestlé might take to deal with the controversy surrounding the marketing of infant formula products in the developing countries.

Notes to Chapters

CHAPTER 2

1. See Kenneth R. Andrews, *The Concept of Corporate Strategy*, rev. ed. (Homewood Ill: Richard D. Irwin, 1980).

CHAPTER 3

1. Michael E. Porter, *Competitive Strategy* (New York: Free Press, 1980).
2. Sidney Schoeffler, Robert D. Buzzell, and Donald F. Heany, "Impact of Strategic Planning on Profit Performance," *Harvard Business Review,* March-April 1974; and Robert D. Buzzell, Bradley T. Gale, and Ralph R. M. Sultan, "Market Share— A Key to Profitability," *Harvard Business Review*, January-February 1975.
3. Note on the "Use of Experience Curves in Competitive Decision Making," Harvard Case Services No. 9-175-174; William K. Abernathy and Kenneth Wayne, "Limits of the Learning Curve," *Harvard Business Review*, September-October 1974; and Bruce D. Henderson, "The Application and Misapplication of the Experience Curve," *Journal of Business Strategy*, 4, no. 3 (Winter 1984).

CHAPTER 4

1. Erich Helfert, *Techniques of Financial Analysis* (Homewood, Ill.: Richard D. Irwin, 1982).

CHAPTER 5

1. Thomas Peters and Robert Waterman, Jr., *In Search of Excellence* (New York: Harper & Row, 1982).
2. *Wall Street Journal*, October 2, 1978.
3. Chester Barnard, *The Functions of the Executive* (Cambridge, Mass.: Harvard University Press, 1960), p. 224. Reprinted by permission.

CHAPTER 6

1. Milton Friedman, "The Social Responsibility of Business Is to Increase Its Profits," *New York Times Magazine*, September 13, 1970.

2. Carl Kaysen, "The Corporation: How Much Power? What Scope?" in *The Corporation in Modern Society*, Edward Mason ed. (Cambridge, Mass.: Harvard University Press, 1960).

CHAPTER 8

1. Bruce R. Scott, "The Industrial State: Old Myths and New Realities," *Harvard Business Review*, March-April 1973. Reprint #73212.

2. Ibid.

3. Alfred D. Chandler, Jr., *Strategy and Structure* (Cambridge, Mass.: MIT Press, 1962).

4. Malcolm S. Salter and Wolf A. Weinhold, *Diversification Through Acquisition* (New York: Free Press, 1979).

5. Norman Berg, "Strategic Planning in Conglomerate Companies," *Harvard Business Review*, May-June 1965.

CHAPTER 9

1. See J. Frederick Weston and Eugene F. Brigham, *Managerial Finance*, 6th ed. (Hinsdale, Ill.: Dryden Press, 1978), especially chap. 22, for some discussion of accounting policies in mergers.

2. See, for example, The Sybron Corporation, Harvard Case Services.

3. Richard P. Rumelt, *Strategy, Structure, and Economic Performance*, (Boston: Division of Research, Harvard Business School, 1974).

4. Richard P. Rumelt, "Diversification Strategy and Profitability," *Strategic Management Journal*, 3, (1982), p. 361.

5. See, for example, Burton Malkiel, *A Random Walk Down Wall Street* (New York: W. W. Norton, 1975); and David Dremen, *Contrarian Investment Strategy* (New York: Random House, 1979).

6. Anthony Sampson, *The Sovereign State: The Secret History of ITT*, (London: Hodder and Stoughton, 1973).

7. For a more detailed explanation of portfolio planning models, see Malcolm S. Salter and Wolf A. Weinhold, *Diversification Through Acquisition* (New York: Free Press, 1979), chap. 4; or Gerald B. Allan, "A Note on the BCG Concept of Competitive Analysis and Corporate Strategy" (Boston: Harvard Case Services, No. 9-175-175).

8. See, for example, William K. Hall, "SBUs: Hot, New Topic in the Management of Diversification," *Business Horizons*, February 1978.

9. Philippe Haspeslagh, "Portfolio Planning: Uses and Limits," *Harvard Business Review*, January-February 1982.

CHAPTER 10

1. Norman Berg, "The Corporate Role in Diversified Companies," Working Paper (Cambridge, Mass.: Harvard Business School, 1970); and Allan Conway, "The Evolution of the Role of the Corporate Office in the Diversified Firm" (Ph.D. diss., Harvard Business School, 1983).

2. Stuart Watson, *Forbes*, November 1, 1968, p. 51.

Index of Cases

This book has been set VideoComp in 10 and 9 point Compano, leaded 2 points. Part numbers are 24 point Compano. Part titles, section letters, and chapter and case numbers are 18 point Compano. Section, chapter, and case titles are 16 point Compano Semibold. The size of the type page is 27 by 46½ picas.